A

HAND-BOOK OF POLITICS

FOR 1872:

BEING A RECORD OF

IMPORTANT POLITICAL ACTION,

NATIONAL AND STATE,

FROM JULY 15, 1870, TO JULY 15, 1872.

BY

HON. EDWARD McPHERSON, LL. D.,

CLERK OF THE HOUSE OF REPRESENTATIVES OF THE UNITED STATES.

FIFTH EDITION.

WASHINGTON CITY:

PHILP & SOLOMONS.

1872.

PREFACE.

The purpose of this Volume is to present, in distinct and classified form, the chief political facts of the last two years, and thereby to trace the direction and progress of political thought throughout the country during that period. Prepared on the same plan as my previous volumes on the Rebellion and on Reconstruction, and constituting with them a continuous series, the three will be found to exhibit with clearness the astounding changes in Constitution and laws which have marked the last twelve years, and the shifting relations of men and parties to them.

This Volume begins the record at the date at which that on Reconstruction closed—July 15, 1870—and includes the two years which have since elapsed. Among its contents will be found the Messages, Annual and Special, of President GRANT touching all the topics which have engaged the attention and energies of his Administration; the votes in both Houses of Congress on all controverted political issues, such as Amnesty, "Ku Klux" legislation, (which involved the old question of a suspension of the *Habeas Corpus.*) and the various phases of the "Civil Rights" agitation; the *status* of Female Suffrage as a constitutional claim; the various steps and votes taken in the direction of Civil Service Reform; the wrestling with the Labor Question, the Education Question, and the Land Grant Question; and the late decision of the Supreme Court of the United States on the constitutionality of "legal-tender" notes, in reversal of the previous decision of 1869; which, with the usual lists of Cabinet and Congress, and an extended variety of miscellaneous matter, will, it is hoped, stamp the work with other value than belongs to a political compendium merely convenient for temporary use.

The chapters containing the actual changes recently made in State Constitutions, and those proposed in the last Congress and the present to the National Constitution by those most familiar with its practical operation, will engage attention. The former indicates the new necessities of State life; the latter is a curious illustration of the variety of view which able men entertain of the need of further amendment of our common charter.

The Tabular Statements are very complete. Chief among them may be remarked those which give an analyzed statement of the Revenues and Expenditures of the Government from 1860 to 1871, inclusive, and the copious explanatory pages which follow them, affording the means for exhaustive comparisons in every direction. The interesting tables showing the amount of the National Debt from 1857 to 1872, the Population, the Manufactures, the Agricultural Products, the Wealth, and the amounts of Debt and Taxation, by States, are a mine of information, and give pleasing contrasts with the same classes of facts developed by the census of 1860. The startling and reliable figures respecting the grants of Public Land, for whatever purpose made, go far to vindicate the increasing sensitiveness shown by the public and by Congress on this subject, while the elaborate statement of the rate of duty levied upon every article by the respective Tariffs of 1870 and 1872 will be found to be the only authentic publication yet made of the important changes about to affect every industrial interest of the Nation. All which are additional to full tables of the returns of the last Presidential and late State elections, of the representation of each State in Congress as fixed by the census of 1870, contrasted with that of 1860, and of the strength of each State and of the various sections of the country in the Electoral College.

A chapter is given to the relations of Great Britain to the United States, which contains the Johnson-Clarendon Convention concluded under President JOHNSON, but not ratified by the Senate, as well as the Treaty of Washington, with the proposed supplemental article as originally proposed by Great Britain and as amended by the Senate, together with the names of the Arbitrators now sitting at Geneva for the settlement of all the differences between the two Governments.

An unusual space is devoted to the Political Platforms adopted in 1871 and 1872 by State Conventions, that the various shades of current sentiment might be fairly reflected. The national declarations of the great parties of the country, with the letters of acceptance of their candidates, are, of course, fully given.

It is hoped that the Volume will, on examination, satisfy, both by its scope and its detail, the expectations formed of it, and prove permanently useful in elucidating the remarkable political phenomena of this period.

In the votes given the names of Republicans are printed in Roman letters; of all others in *italics*.

EDWARD McPHERSON.

WASHINGTON, D. C., *July* 15, 1872.

TABLE OF CONTENTS.

HAND-BOOK OF POLITICS

FOR 1872.

I.

MEMBERS OF FORTY-FIRST CONGRESS.

Third Session, December 5, 1870—March 3, 1871.

Senate.

SCHUYLER COLFAX, of Indiana, *Vice President of the United States, and President of the Senate.*

George C. Gorham, of California, *Secretary.*

Maine—Lot M. Morrill, Hannibal Hamlin.

New Hampshire—Aaron H. Cragin, James W. Patterson.

Vermont—Justin S. Morrill, George F. Edmunds.

Massachusetts—Henry Wilson, Charles Sumner.

Rhode Island—Henry B. Anthony, William Sprague.

Connecticut—Orris S. Ferry, William A. Buckingham.

New York—Roscoe Conkling, Reuben E. Fenton.

New Jersey—Alexander G. Cattell, John P. Stockton.

Pennsylvania—Simon Cameron, John Scott.

Delaware—Willard Saulsbury, Thomas F. Bayard.

Maryland—George Vickers, William T. Hamilton.

Virginia—John W. Johnston, John F. Lewis.

North Carolina—Joseph C. Abbott, John Pool.

South Carolina—Thomas J. Robertson, Frederick A. Sawyer.

*Georgia**—H. V. M. Miller, Joshua Hill.

Alabama—Willard Warner, George E. Spencer.

Mississippi — Hiram R. Revels, Adelbert Ames.

*Mr. Miller qualified February 24, 1871; Mr. Hill, February 1, 1871.

Louisiana—John S. Harris, William P. Kellogg.

Ohio—John Sherman, Allen G. Thurman.

Kentucky—Thomas C. McCreery, Garrett Davis.

Tennessee—Joseph S. Fowler, William G. Brownlow.

Indiana—Oliver P. Morton, Daniel D. Pratt.

Illinois—Richard Yates, Lyman Trumbull.

Missouri—Francis P. Blair, jr.,* Carl Schurz.

Arkansas—Alexander McDonald, Benjamin F. Rice.

Michigan — Jacob M. Howard, Zachariah Chandler.

Florida—Thomas W. Osborn, Abijah Gilbert.

Texas—Morgan C. Hamilton, James W. Flanagan.

Iowa—James B. Howell, James Harlan.

Wisconsin—Timothy O. Howe, Matthew H. Carpenter.

California—Cornelius Cole, Eugene Casserly.

Minnesota—Ozora P. Stearns,† Alexander Ramsey.

Oregon—George H. Williams, Henry W. Corbett.

Kansas—Edmund G. Ross, Samuel C. Pomeroy.

West Virginia—Waitman T. Willey, Arthur I. Boreman.

Nevada—James W. Nye, William M. Stewart.

* Qualified January 25, 1871. in place of Daniel T Jewett, who qualified December 22, 1870, under executive appointment, to fill the vacancy caused December 19, 1870, by the resignation of Charles D. Drake.

† Qualified January 23, 1871, in place of William Windom, who qualified December 5, 1870, under executive appointment, to fill the vacancy caused by the death of Daniel S. Norton, July 13, 1870.

Nebraska—John M. Thayer, Thomas W. Tipton.

House of Representatives.

James G. Blaine, of Maine, *Speaker*.
Edward McPherson, of Pennsylvania, *Clerk*.

Maine—John Lynch, Samuel P. Morrill, James G. Blaine, John A. Peters, Eugene Hale.

New Hampshire—Jacob H. Ela, Aaron F. Stevens, Jacob Benton.

Vermont—Charles W. Willard, Luke P. Poland, Worthington C. Smith.

Massachusetts—James Buffinton, Oakes Ames, Ginery Twichell, Samuel Hooper, Benjamin F. Butler, Nathaniel P. Banks, George M. Brooks, George F. Hoar, William B. Washburn, Henry L. Dawes.

Rhode Island—Thomas A. Jenckes, Nathan F. Dixon.

Connecticut—Julius L. Strong, Stephen W. Kellogg, Henry H. Starkweather, William H. Barnum.

New York—Henry A. Reeves, John G. Schumaker, Henry W. Slocum, John Fox, John Morrissey, Samuel S. Cox, Hervey C. Calkin, James Brooks, Fernando Wood, Clarkson N. Potter, Charles H. Van Wyck, John H. Ketcham, John A. Griswold, Stephen L. Mayham, Adolphus H. Tanner, Orange Ferriss, William A. Wheeler, Stephen Sanford, Charles Knapp, Addison H. Laflin, Alexander H. Bailey, John C. Churchill, Dennis McCarthy, George W. Cowles, William H. Kelsey, Giles W. Hotchkiss, Hamilton Ward, Charles H. Holmes, John Fisher, David S. Bennett, Porter Sheldon.

New Jersey—William Moore, Charles Haight, John T. Bird, John Hill, Orestes Cleveland.

Pennsylvania—Samuel J. Randall, Charles O'Neill, Leonard Myers, William D. Kelley, Caleb N. Taylor, John D. Stiles, Washington Townsend, J. Lawrence Getz, Oliver J. Dickey, Henry L. Cake, Daniel M. Van Auken, George W. Woodward, Ulysses Mercur, John B. Packer, Richard J. Haldeman, John Cessna, Daniel J. Morrell, William H. Armstrong, Glenni W. Scofield, Calvin W. Gilfillan, John Covode,* James S. Negley, Darwin Phelps, Joseph B. Donley.

Delaware—Benjamin T. Biggs.

Maryland—Samuel Hambleton, Stevenson Archer, Thomas Swann, Patrick Hamill, Frederick Stone.

Virginia—Richard S. Ayer, James H. Platt, jr., Charles H. Porter, George W. Booker, Richard T. W. Duke,† William Milnes, jr., Lewis McKenzie, James K. Gibson.

North Carolina—Clinton L. Cobb, Joseph Dixon, Oliver H. Dockery, John Manning, jr., Israel G. Lash, Francis E. Shober, Alexander H. Jones.

South Carolina—Joseph H. Rainey, Christopher C. Bowen, Solomon L. Hoge, Alexander S. Wallace.

*Died January 11, 1871.
†To fill the vacancy caused by the death of Robert Ridgway.

*Georgia**—William W. Paine, Richard H. Whiteley, Marion Bethune, James F. Long, Stephen A. Corker, William P. Price, Pierce M. B. Young.

Alabama—Alfred E. Buck, Charles W. Buckley, Robert S. Heflin, Charles Hays, Peter M. Dox, William C. Sherrod.

Mississippi—George E. Harris, Jos. L. Morphis, Henry W. Barry, George C. McKee, Legrand W. Perce.

Louisiana—J. Hale Sypher, Lionel A. Sheldon, Chester B. Darrall, James P. Newsham, Frank Morey.

Ohio—Peter W. Strader, Job E. Stevenson, Robert C. Schenck,† William Lawrence, William Munger, John A. Smith, James J. Winans, John Beatty, Edward F. Dickinson, Erasmus D. Peck, John T. Wilson, Philadelph Van Trump, George W. Morgan, Martin Welker, Eliakim H. Moore, John A. Bingham, Jacob A. Ambler, William H. Upson, James A. Garfield.

Kentucky—Lawrence S. Trimble, William N. Sweeney, Joseph H. Lewis, J. Proctor Knott, Boyd Winchester, Thomas L. Jones, James B. Beck, George M. Adams, John M. Rice.

Tennessee—Roderick R. Butler, Horace Maynard, William B. Stokes, Lewis Tillman, William F. Prosser, Samuel M. Arnell, Isaac R. Hawkins, William J. Smith.

Indiana—William E. Niblack, Michael C. Kerr, William S. Holman, George W. Julian, John Coburn, Daniel W. Voorhees, Godlove S. Orth, James N. Tyner, John P. C. Shanks, William Williams, Jasper Packard.

Illinois—Norman B. Judd, John F. Farnsworth, Horatio C. Burchard, John B. Hawley, Ebon C. Ingersoll, Burton C. Cook, Jesse H. Moore, Shelby M. Cullom, Thompson W. McNeely, Albert G. Burr, Samuel S. Marshall, John B. Hay, John M. Crebs, John A. Logan.

Missouri—Erastus Wells, Gustavus A. Finkelnburg, James R. McCormick, Sempronius H. Boyd, Samuel S. Burdett, Robert T. Van Horn, Joel F. Asper, John F. Benjamin, David P. Dyer.

Arkansas—Logan H. Roots, Anthony A. C. Rogers, Thomas Boles.

Michigan—Fernando C. Beaman, William L. Stoughton, Austin Blair, Thomas W. Ferry, Omar D. Conger, Randolph Strickland.

Florida—Charles M. Hamilton.

Texas—George W. Whitmore, John C. Conner, William T. Clark, Edward Degener.

Iowa—George W. McCrary, William P. Wolf, William B. Allison, William Loughridge, Frank W. Palmer, Charles Pomeroy.

Wisconsin—Halbert E. Paine; David Atwood, Amasa Cobb, Charles A. Eldredge, Philetus Sawyer, Cadwalader C. Washburn.

California—Samuel B. Axtell, Aaron A. Sargent, James A. Johnson.

*Messrs. Price, Young, Bethune, and Long qualified January 16, 1871; Mr. Paine, January 23; Mr. Corker, January 24, and Mr. Whiteley, February 9.
† Resigned, January 5, 1871.

Minnesota—Morton S. Wilkinson, Eugene M. Wilson.
Oregon—Joseph S. Smith.
Kansas—Sidney Clarke.
West Virginia—Isaac H. Duval, James C. McGrew, John S. Witcher.
Nevada—Thomas Fitch.
Nebraska—John Taffe.

II.

ENFORCEMENT LEGISLATION OF THE FORTY-FIRST CONGRESS.

An Act to Enforce the Right to Vote.

AN ACT to amend an act approved May 31, 1870, entitled "An act to enforce the rights of citizens of the United States to vote in the several States of this Union, and for other purposes."

Be it enacted, &c., That section twenty of the "Act to enforce the rights of citizens of the United States to vote in the several States of this Union, and for other purposes," approved May 31, 1870,* shall be, and hereby is, amended so as to read as follows:

"SEC. 20. That if any registration of voters for an election for Representative or Delegate in the Congress of the United States, any person shall knowingly personate and register, or attempt to register in the name of any other person, whether living, dead, or fictitious, or fraudulently register, or fraudulently attempt to register, not having a lawful right so to do; or do any unlawful act to secure registration for himself or any other person; or by force, threat, menace, intimidation, bribery, reward, or offer, or promise thereof, or other unlawful means, prevent or hinder any person having a lawful right to register from duly exercising such right; or compel or induce by any of such means, or other unlawful means, any officer of registration to admit to registration any person not legally entitled thereto, or interfere in any manner with any officer of registration in the discharge of his duties, or by any such means, or other unlawful means, induce any officer of registration to violate or refuse to comply with his duty or any law regulating the same; or if any such officer shall knowingly and willfully register as a voter any person not entitled to be registered, or refuse to so register any person entitled to be registered; or if any such officer or other person whose duty it is to perform any duty in relation to such registration or election, or to ascertain, announce, or declare the result thereof, or give or make any certificate, document, or evidence in relation thereto, shall knowingly neglect or refuse to perform any duty required by law, or violate any duty imposed by law, or do any act unauthorized by law relating to or affecting such registration or election, or the result thereof, or any certificate, document, or evidence in relation thereto, or if any person shall aid, counsel, procure, or advise any such voter, person, or officer to do any act hereby made a crime, or to omit any act, the omission of which is hereby made a crime, every such person shall be deemed guilty of a crime, and shall be liable to prosecution and punishment therefor as provided in section nineteen of said act of May 31, 1870, for persons guilty of any of the crimes therein specified: *Provided*, That every registration made under the laws of any State or Territory for any State or other election at which such Representative or Delegate in Congress shall be chosen, shall be deemed to be a registration within the meaning of this act, notwithstanding the same shall also be made for the purposes of any State, territorial, or municipal election."

SEC. 2. That whenever in any city or town having upward of twenty thousand inhabitants, there shall be two citizens thereof who, prior to any registration of voters for an election for Representative or Delegate in the Congress of the United States, or prior to any election at which a Representative or Delegate in Congress is to be voted for, shall make known in writing, to the judge of the circuit court of the United States for the circuit wherein such city or town shall be, their desire to have said registration, or said election, or both, guarded and scrutinized, it shall be the duty of the said judge of the circuit court, within not less than ten days prior to said registration, if one there be, or, if no registration be required, within not less than ten days prior to said election, to open the said circuit court at the most convenient point in said circuit. And the said court, when so opened by said judge, shall proceed to appoint and commission, from day to day and from time to time, and under the hand of the said circuit judge, and under the seal of said court, for each election district or voting precinct in each and every such city or town as shall, in the manner herein prescribed, have applied therefor, and to revoke, change, or renew said appointment from time to time, two citizens, residents of said city or town, who shall be of different political parties, and able to read and write the English language, and who shall be known and designated as supervisors of election. And the said circuit court, when opened by the said circuit judge as required herein, shall therefrom and thereafter, and up to and including the day following the day of election, be al-

* For copy of this act, see McPherson's History of Reconstruction, pp. 546-550.

ways open for the transaction of business under this act, and the powers and jurisdiction hereby granted and conferred shall be exercised as well in vacation as in term time; and a judge sitting at chambers shall have the same powers and jurisdiction, including the power of keeping order and of punishing any contempt of his authority, as when sitting in court.

SEC. 3. That whenever, from sickness, injury, or otherwise, the judge of the circuit court of the United States in any judicial circuit shall be unable to perform and discharge the duties by this act imposed, it shall be his duty, and he is hereby required, to select and to direct and assign to the performance thereof in his place and stead, such one of the judges of the district courts of the United States within his circuit as he shall deem best; and upon such selection and assignment being made, it shall be lawful for, and shall be the duty of, the district judge so designated to perform and discharge, in the place and stead of the said circuit judge, all the duties, powers, and obligations imposed and conferred upon the said circuit judge by the provisions of this act.

SEC. 4. That it shall be the duty of the supervisors of election, appointed under this act, and they and each of them are hereby authorized and required, to attend at all times and places fixed for the registration of voters, who, being registered, would be entitled to vote for a Representative or Delegate in Congress, and to challenge any person offering to register; to attend at all times and places when the names of registered voters may be marked for challenge, and to cause such names registered as they shall deem proper to be so marked; to make, when required, the lists, or either of hem, provided for in section thirteen of this act, and verify the same; and upon any occasion, and at any time when in attendance under the provisions of this act, to personally inspect and scrutinize such registry, and for purposes of identification to affix their or his signature to each and every page of the original list, and of each and every copy of any such list of registered voters, at such times, upon each day when any name may or shall be received, entered, or registered, and in such manner as will, in their or his judgment, detect and expose the improper or wrongful removal therefrom, or addition thereto, in any way, of any name or names.

SEC. 5. That it shall also be the duty of the said supervisors of election, and they, and each of them, are hereby authorized and required, to attend at all times and places for holding elections of Representatives or Delegates in Congress, and for counting the votes cast at said elections; to challenge any vote offered by any person whose legal qualifications the supervisors, or either of them, shall doubt; to be and remain where the ballot-boxes are kept at all times after the polls are open until each and every vote cast at said time and place shall be counted, the canvass of all votes polled be wholly completed, and the proper and requisite certificates or returns made, whether said certificates or returns be required under any law of the United States, or any State, territorial, or municipal law, and to personally inspect and scrutinize, from time to time, and at all times, on the day of election, the manner in which the voting is done, and the way and method in which the poll-books, registry-lists, and tallies or check-books, whether the same are required by any law of the United States, or any State, territorial, or municipal law, are kept; and to the end that each candidate for the office of Representative or Delegate in Congress shall obtain the benefit of every vote for him cast, the said supervisors of election are, and each of them is, hereby required, in their or his respective election districts or voting precincts, to personally scrutinize, count, and canvass each and every ballot in their or his election district or voting precinct cast, whatever may be the indorsement on said ballot, or in whatever box it may have been placed or be found; to make and forward to the officer who, in accordance with the provisions of section thirteen of this act, shall have been designated as the chief supervisor of the judicial district in which the city or town wherein they or he shall serve shall be, such certificates and returns of all such ballots as said officer may direct and require, and to attach to the registry-list, and any and all copies thereof, and to any certificate, statement, or return, whether the same, or any part or portion thereof, be required by any law of the United States, or of any State, territorial, or municipal law, any statement touching the truth or accuracy of the registry, or the truth or fairness of the election and canvass, which the said supervisors of election, or either of them, may desire to make or attach, or which should properly and honestly be made or attached, in order that the facts may become known, any law of any State or Territory to the contrary notwithstanding.

SEC. 6. That the better to enable the said supervisors of election to discharge their duties, they are, and each of them is, hereby authorized and directed, in their or his respective election districts or voting precincts, on the day or days of registration, on the day or days when registered voters may be marked to be challenged, and on the day or days of election, to take, occupy, and remain in such position or positions, from time to time, whether before or behind the ballot-boxes, as will, in their judgment, best enable them or him to see each person offering himself for registration or offering to vote, and as will best conduce to their or his scrutinizing the manner in which the registration or voting is being conducted; and at the closing of the polls for the reception of votes, they are, and each of them is, hereby required to place themselves or himself in such position in relation to the ballot-boxes for the purpose of engaging in the work of canvassing the ballots in said boxes contained as will enable them or him to fully perform the duties in respect to such canvass provided in this act, and shall there remain until every duty in respect to such canvass, certificates, returns, and statements shall have been wholly completed, any law of any State or Territory to the contrary notwithstanding.

SEC. 7. That if in any election district or voting precinct in any city, town, or village, for which there shall have been appointed supervisors of election for any election at which a Representative or Delegate in Congress shall be voted for, the said supervisors of election, or either of them, shall not be allowed to exercise and discharge, fully and freely, and without bribery, solicitation, interference, hinderance, molestation, violence, or threats thereof, on the part of or from any person or persons, each and every of the duties, obligations, and powers conferred upon them by this act and the act hereby amended, it shall be the duty of the supervisors of election, and each of them, to make prompt report, under oath, within ten days after the day of election, to the officer who, in accordance with the provisions of section thirteen of this act, shall have been designated as the chief supervisor of the judicial district in which the city or town wherein they, or he served shall be, of the manner and means by which they were or he was not so allowed to fully and freely exercise and discharge the duties and obligations required and imposed by this act. And upon receiving any such report it shall be the duty of the said chief supervisor, acting both in such capacity and officially as a commissioner of the circuit court, to forthwith examine into all the facts thereof; to subpena and compel the attendance before him of any witnesses; administer oaths and take testimony in respect to the charges made; and prior to the assembling of the Congress for which any such Representative or Delegate was voted for, to have filed with the Clerk of the House of Representatives of the Congress of the United States all the evidence by him taken, all information by him obtained, and all reports to him made.

SEC. 8. That whenever an election at which Representatives or Delegates in Congress are to be chosen shall be held in any city or town of twenty thousand inhabitants or upward, the marshal of the United States for the district in which said city or town is situated shall have power, and it shall be his duty, on the application, in writing, of at least two citizens residing in any such city or town, to appoint special deputy marshals, whose duty it shall be, when required as provided in this act, to aid and assist the supervisors of election in the verification of any list of persons made under the provisions of this act, who may have registered, or voted, or either; to attend in each election district or voting precinct at the times and places fixed for the registration of voters, and at all times and places when and where said registration may by law be scrutinized, and the names of registered voters be marked for challenge; and also to attend, at all times for holding such elections, the polls of the election in such district or precinct. And the marshal and his general deputies, and such special deputies, shall have power, and it shall be the duty of such special deputies, to keep the peace, and support and protect the supervisors of elections in the discharge of their duties, preserve order at such places of registration and at such polls, prevent fraudulent registration and fraudulent voting thereat, or fraudulent conduct on the part of any officer of election, and immediately, either at said place of registration, or polling-place, or elsewhere, and either before or after registering or voting, to arrest and take into custody, with or without process, any person who shall commit, or attempt or offer to commit, any of the acts or offenses prohibited by this act, or the act hereby amended, or, who shall commit any offense against the laws of the United States: *Provided*, That no person shall be arrested without process for any offense not committed in the presence of the marshal or his general or special deputies, or either of them, or of the supervisors of election, or either of them, and, for the purposes of arrest or the preservation of the peace, the supervisors of election, and each of them, shall, in the absence of the marshal's deputies, or if required to assist said deputies, have the same duties and powers as deputy marshals: *And provided further*, That no person shall, on the day or days of any such election, be arrested without process for any offense committed on the day or days of registration.

SEC. 9. That whenever any arrest is made under any provision of this act, the person so arrested shall forthwith be brought before a commissioner, judge, or court of the United States for examination of the offenses alleged against him; and such commissioner, judge, or court shall proceed in respect thereto as authorized by law in case of crimes against the United States.

SEC. 10. That whoever, with or without any authority, power, or process, or pretended authority, power, or process, of any State, territorial, or municipal authority, shall obstruct, hinder, assault, or by bribery, solicitation, or otherwise, interfere with or prevent the supervisors of election, or either of them, or the marshal or his general or special deputies, or either of them, in the performance of any duty required of them, or either of them, or which he or they, or either of them, may be authorized to perform by any law of the United States, whether in the execution of process or otherwise, or shall by any of the means before mentioned, hinder or prevent the free attendance and presence at such places of registration or at such polls of election, or full and free access and egress to and from any such place of registration or poll of election, or in going to and from any such place of registration or poll of election, or to and from any room where any such registration or election, or canvass of votes, or of making any returns or certificates thereof, may be had, or shall molest, interfere with, remove, or eject from any such place of registration or poll of election, or of canvassing votes cast thereat, or of making returns or certificates thereof, any supervisor of election, the marshal, or his general or special deputies, or either of them, or shall threaten, or attempt, or offer so to do, or shall refuse or neglect to aid and assist any supervisor of election, or the marshal or his general or special deputies, or either of them, in the performance of his or their duties when required by him or them, or either of them, to give such aid and assistance, he shall be guilty of a misdemeanor, and liable to instant arrest without process, and on conviction thereof shall be punished by imprisonment not more than two years, or by fine not more than three thousand dollars, or by both such fine and imprisonment, and shall pay the costs of the prosecution. Whoever shall, during the progress of any verification of any list of the persons who may have registered or voted, and which shall be had or made under any of the provisions of this act, refuse to answer, or refrain from answering, or answering shall knowingly give false information in respect to any inquiry lawfully made, such person shall be liable to arrest and imprisonment as for a misdemeanor, and on conviction thereof shall be punished by imprisonment not to exceed thirty days, or by fine not to exceed one hundred dollars, or by both such fine and imprisonment, and shall pay the costs of the prosecution.

SEC. 11. That whoever shall be appointed a supervisor of election or a special deputy marshal under the provisions of this act and shall take the oath of office as such supervisor of election or such special deputy marshal, who shall thereafter neglect or refuse, without good and lawful excuse, to perform and discharge fully the duties, obligations, and requirements of such office until the expiration of the term for which he was appointed, shall not only be subject to removal from office with loss of all pay or emoluments, but shall be guilty of a misdemeanor, and on conviction shall be punished by imprisonment for not less than six months nor more than one year, or by fine not less than two hundred dollars and not exceeding five hundred dollars, or by both fine and imprisonment, and shall pay the costs of prosecution.

SEC. 12. That the marshal, or his general deputies, or such special deputies as shall be thereto specially empowered by him in writing and under his hand and seal, whenever he or his said general deputies or his special deputies, or either or any of them, shall be forcibly resisted in executing their duties under this act or the act hereby amended, or shall, by violence, threats, or menaces, be prevented from executing such duties, or from arresting any person or persons who shall commit any offense for which said marshal or his general or his special deputies are authorized to make such arrest, are, and each of them is hereby, empowered to summon and call to his or their aid the bystanders or *posse comitatus* of his district.

SEC. 13. That it shall be the duty of each of the circuit courts of the United States in and for each judicial circuit, upon the recommendation in writing of the judge thereof, to name and appoint, on or before the 1st day of May, in the year 1871, and thereafter as vacancies may from any cause arise, from among the circuit court commissioners in and for each judicial district in each of said judicial circuits, one of such officers, who shall be known for the duties required of him under this act as the chief supervisor of elections of the judicial district in and for which he shall be a commissioner, and shall, so long as faithful and capable, discharge the duties in this act imposed, and whose duty it shall be to prepare and furnish all necessary books, forms, blanks, and instructions for the use and direction of the supervisors of election in the several cities and towns in their respective districts; to receive the applications of all parties for appointment to such positions; and upon the opening, as contemplated in this act, of the circuit court for the judicial circuit in which the commissioner so designated shall act, to present such applications to the judge thereof, and furnish information to said judge in respect to the appointment by the said court of such supervisors of election; to require of the supervisors of election, where necessary, lists of the persons who may register and vote, or either, in their respective election districts or voting precincts, and to cause the names of those upon any such list whose right to register or vote shall be honestly doubted to be verified by proper inquiry and examination at the respective places by them assigned as their residences; and to receive, preserve, and file all oaths of office of said supervisors of election, and of all special deputy marshals appointed under the provisions of this act, and all certificates, returns, reports, and records of every kind and nature contemplated or made requisite under and by the provisions of this act, save where otherwise herein specially directed. And it is hereby made the duty of all United States marshals and commissioners who shall in any judicial district perform any duties under the provisions of this act, or the act hereby amended, relating to, concerning, or affecting the election of Representatives or Delegates in the Congress of the United States, to, from time to time, and with all due diligence, forward to the chief supervisor in and for their judicial district all complaints, examinations, and records pertaining thereto, and all oaths of office by them administered to any supervisor of election or special deputy marshal, in order that the same may be properly preserved and filed.

SEC. 14. That there shall be allowed and paid to each chief supervisor, for his services as such officer, the following compensation, apart from and in excess of all fees allowed by law for the performance of any duty as circuit court commissioner: for filing and caring for every return, report, record, document, or other paper required to be filed by him under any of the provisions of this act, ten cents; for affixing a seal to any paper, record, report, or instrument, twenty cents; for entering and indexing the records of his office, fifteen cents per folio; and for arranging and transmitting to Congress, as provided for in section seven of this act, any report, statement, record, return, or examination, for each folio, fifteen cents; and for any copy thereof, or of any paper on file, a like sum. And there shall be allowed and paid to each and every supervisor of election, and each and every special deputy marshal who shall be appointed and shall perform his duty under the provisions of this act, compensation at the rate of five dollars per day for each and every day he shall have actually been on duty, not exceeding ten days. And the fees of the said chief supervisors shall be paid at the Treasury of the United States, such accounts to be made out, verified, examined, and certified as in the case of accounts of commissioners, save that the examination or certificate required may be made by either the circuit or district judge.

SEC. 15. That the jurisdiction of the circuit court of the United States shall extend to all cases in law or equity arising under the provisions of this act or the act hereby amended; and if any person shall receive any injury to his person or property for or on account of any act by him done under any of the provisions of this act or the act hereby amended, he shall be entitled to maintain suit for damages therefor in the circuit court of the United States in the district wherein the party doing the injury may reside or shall be found.

SEC. 16. That in any case where suit or prosecution, civil or criminal, shall be commenced in a court of any State against any officer of the United States, or other person, for or on account of any act done under the provisions of this act, or under color thereof, or for or on account of any right, authority, or title set up or claimed by such officer or other person under any of said provisions, it shall be lawful for the defendant in such suit or prosecution, at any time before trial, upon a petition to the circuit court of the United States in and for the district in which the defendant shall have been served with process, setting forth the nature of said suit or prosecution, and verifying the said petition by affidavit, together with a certificate signed by an attorney or counselor at law of some court of record of the State in which such suit shall have been commenced, or of the United States, setting forth that as counsel for the petition he has examined the proceedings against him, and has carefully inquired into all the matters set forth in the petition, and that he believes the same to be true, which petition, affidavit, and certificate shall be presented to the said circuit court, if in session, and, if not, to the clerk thereof at his office, and shall be filed in said office, and the cause shall thereupon be entered on the docket of said court, and shall be thereafter proceeded in as a cause originally commenced in that court; and it shall be the duty of the clerk of said court, if the suit was commenced in the court below by summons, to issue a writ of *certiorari* to the State court, requiring said court to send to the said circuit court the record and proceedings in said cause; or if it was commenced by *capias*, he shall issue a writ of *habeas corpus cum causa*, a duplicate of which said writ shall be delivered to the clerk of the State court, or left at his office by the marshal of the district, or his deputy, or some person duly authorized thereto; and thereupon it shall be the duty of the said State court to stay all further proceedings in such cause, and the said suit or prosecution, upon delivery of such process, or leaving the same as aforesaid, shall be deemed and taken to be moved to the said circuit court, and any further proceedings, trial, or judgment therein in the State court shall be wholly null and void; and any person, whether an attorney or officer of any State court, or otherwise, who shall thereafter take any steps, or in any manner proceed in the State court in any action so removed, shall be guilty of a misdemeanor, and liable to trial and punishment in the court to which the action shall have been removed, and upon conviction thereof shall be punished by imprisonment for not less than six months nor more than one year, or by fine not less than five hundred nor more than one thousand dollars, or by both such fine and imprisonment, and shall, in addition thereto, be amenable to the said court to which said action shall have been removed as for a contempt; and if the defendant in any such suit be in actual custody on *mesne* process therein, it shall be the duty of the marshal, by virtue of the writ of *habeas corpus cum causa*, to take the body of the defendant into his custody, to be dealt with in the said cause according to the rules of law and the order of the circuit court, or of any judge thereof in vacation. And all attachments made and all bail or other security given upon such suit or prosecution shall be and continue in like force and effect as if the same suit or prosecution had proceeded to final judgment and execution in the State court. And if upon the removal of any such suit or prosecution it shall be made to appear to the said circuit court that no copy of the record and proceedings therein in the State court can be obtained, it shall be lawful for said circuit court to allow and require the plaintiff to proceed *de novo*, and to file a declaration of his cause of action, and the parties may thereupon proceed as in actions originally brought in said circuit court; and on failure of so proceeding judgment of *non prosequitur* may be rendered against the plaintiff, with costs for the defendant.

SEC. 17. That in any case in which any party is or may be by law entitled to copies of the record and proceedings in any suit or prosecution in any State court, to be used in any court of the United States, if the clerk of said State court shall, upon demand and the payment or tender of the legal fees, refuse or neglect to deliver to such party certified copies of such record and proceedings, the court of the United States in which such record and proceedings may be needed, on proof by affidavit that the clerk of such State court has refused or neglected to deliver copies thereof on demand as aforesaid, may direct and allow such record to be supplied by affidavit or otherwise, as the circumstances of the case may require and allow; and thereupon such proceeding, trial, and judgment may be had in the said court of the United States, and all such processes awarded, as if certified copies of such records and proceedings had been regularly before the said court; and hereafter in all civil actions in the courts of the

United States either party thereto may notice the same for trial.

SEC. 18. That sections five and six of the act of the Congress of the United States, approved July 14, 1870, and entitled "An act to amend the naturalization laws, and to punish crimes against the same," be, and the same are hereby, repealed; but this repeal shall not affect any proceeding or prosecution now pending for any offense under the said sections or either of them, or any question which may arise therein respecting the appointment of the persons in said sections, or either of them, provided for, or the powers, duties, or obligations of such persons.

SEC. 19. That all votes for Representatives in Congress shall hereafter be by written or printed ballot, any law of any State to the contrary notwithstanding; and all votes received or recorded contrary to the provisions of this section shall be of none effect.

Approved February 28, 1871.

IN HOUSE.

1871, February 15—The bill, as above, passed—yeas 144, nays 64, (not voting 32,) as follow:

YEAS—Messrs. Ambler, Ames, Armstrong, Asper, Atwood, Ayer, Bailey, Barry, Beaman, Beatty, Benjamin, Bennett, Bethune, Bingham, Blair, Boles, George M. Brooks, Buck, Buckley, Buffinton, Burdett, Benjamin F. Butler, Roderick R. Butler, Cessna, Churchill, William T. Clark, Sidney Clarke, Amasa Cobb, Clinton L. Cobb, Coburn, Conger, Cook, Cowles, Cullom, Darrall, Degener, Dixon, Dockery, Donley, Duval, Dyer, Ela, Ferriss, Ferry, Finkelnburg, Fisher, Garfield, Gilfillan, Hale, Hamilton, Harris, Hawley, Hays, Hill, Hoar, Holmes, Hooper, Hotchkiss, Jenckes, Judd, Julian, Kelley, Kellogg, Kelsey, Laflin, Lash, Lawrence, Logan, Long, Loughridge, Lynch, Maynard, McCarty, McCrary, McGrew, McKee, McKenzie, Mercur, Eliakim H. Moore, Jesse H. Moore, William Moore, Morey, Morphis, Daniel J. Morrell, Samuel P. Morrill, Myers, Negley, Newsham, O'Neill, Orth, Packard, Halbert E. Paine, Palmer, Peck, Perce, Peters, Phelps, Platt, Poland, Pomeroy, Porter, Prosser, Rainey, Roots, Sanford, Sargent, Sawyer, Scofield, Shanks, Porter Sheldon, John A. Smith, William J. Smith, Worthington C. Smith, Starkweather, Stevens, Stevenson, Stokes, Stoughton, Strickland, Strong, Sypher, Tanner, Taylor, Tillman, Townsend, Twichell, Tyner, Upson, Van Horn, Van Wyck, Wallace, Ward, C. C. Washburn, William B. Washburn, Welker, Wheeler, Whiteley, Whitmore, Wilkinson, Willard, Williams, John T. Wilson, Witcher, Wolf—144.

NAYS—Messrs. *Archer, Axtell, Beck, Biggs, Bird, Booker, James Brooks, Burr, Calkin, Conner, Cox, Crebs*, Dickey, *Dickinson, Duke, Eldredge, Fox, Getz, Gibson, Griswold, Haight, Haldeman, Hambleton, Hamill*, Hawkins, Hay, *Holman, Johnson, Jones, Kerr, Lewis, Manning, Marshall, Mayham, McCormick, McNeely, Morgan, Morrissey, Niblack, William W. Paine, Potter, Price, Randall, Reeves, Rice, Rogers, Schumaker, Sherrod, Shober, Slocum, Joseph S. Smith, Stiles, Stone, Strader, Swann, Trimble, Van Auken, Van Trump, Voorhees, Wells, Eugene M. Wilson, Wood, Woodward, Young*—64.

IN SENATE.

1871, February 25—The bill passed finally, yeas 39, nays 10, as follow:

YEAS—Messrs. Abbott, Ames, Anthony, Boreman, Buckingham, Carpenter, Chandler, Cole, Conkling, Corbett, Cragin, Edmunds, Gilbert, Hamilton of Texas, Hamlin, Harlan, Howard, Howe, Howell, McDonald, Morrill of Vermont, Nye, Osborn, Pomeroy, Pool, Pratt, Ramsey, Revels, Robertson, Ross, Sawyer, Scott, Sherman, Spencer, Stearns, Stewart, Warner, Williams, Wilson—39.

NAYS—Messrs. *Bayard, Blair, Casserly*, Fowler, *Hamilton* of Maryland, *Johnston, McCreery, Miller, Thurman, Vickers*—10.

While the bill was pending, several motions were made to amend, but all were defeated.

Mr. JOHNSTON moved to strike out the tenth section, which was lost—yeas 13, nays 39; as follow:

YEAS—Messrs. *Bayard, Blair, Casserly, Hamilton* of Maryland, *Johnston, McCreery, Miller*, Ross, *Saulsbury, Thurman*, Tipton, Trumbull, *Vickers*—13.

NAYS—Messrs. Abbott, Ames, Anthony, Boreman, Buckingham, Carpenter, Chandler, Cole, Conkling, Corbett, Cragin, Edmunds, Gilbert, Hamilton of Texas, Harlan, Harris, Howard, Howe, Howell, McDonald, Morrill of Vermont, Nye, Osborn, Pomeroy, Pool, Pratt, Ramsey, Revels, Rice, Robertson, Sawyer, Sherman, Spencer, Stearns, Stewart, Thayer, Warner, Wilson, Yates—39.

Mr. JOHNSTON moved to amend by striking from that section the words "or the marshal, or his general, or special deputies, or either of them, in the performance of his or their duties when required by him or them, or either of them;" which was disagreed to—yeas 11, nays 34, as follow:

YEAS—Messrs. *Bayard, Casserly*, Fowler, *Hamilton* of Maryland, *Johnston, McCreery, Miller, Saulsbury, Thurman*, Trumbull, *Vickers*—11.

NAYS—Messrs. Abbott, Ames, Boreman, Buckingham, Carpenter, Chandler, Cole, Conkling, Corbett, Cragin, Edmunds, Gilbert, Hamilton of Texas, Harlan, Harris, Howard, Lewis, McDonald, Morrill of Vermont, Osborn, Pomeroy, Pool, Pratt, Ramsey, Revels, Robertson, Sawyer, Sherman, Spencer, Stearns, Willey, Williams, Wilson, Yates—34.

Mr. CASSERLY moved to insert the word "lawful" before the word "performance" in the clause above recited; which was disagreed to—yeas 12, nays 33, as follow:

YEAS—Messrs. *Casserly*, Fowler, *Hamilton* of Maryland, Hill, *Johnston, McCreery, Miller*, Ross, *Thurman*, Tipton, Trumbull, *Vickers*—12.

NAYS—Messrs. Ames, Boreman, Buckingham, Carpenter, Chandler, Cole, Conkling, Corbett, Gilbert, Hamilton of Texas, Hamlin, Harlan, Harris, Howard, Howe, Howell, Kellogg, McDonald, Morrill of Vermont, Pomeroy, Pool, Pratt, Ramsey, Revels, Robertson, Sawyer, Sherman, Stearns, Stewart, Warner, Williams, Wilson, Yates—33.

Other motions to strike out, or modify, were made, and lost by substantially the same vote.

III.

PROCLAMATIONS OF PRESIDENT GRANT.

Enjoining neutrality in the present war between France and the North German Confederation and its Allies, August 22, 1870.

Whereas a state of war unhappily exists between France on the one side, and the North German Confederation and its allies on the other side;

And whereas the United States are on terms of friendship and amity with all the contending Powers, and with the persons inhabiting their several dominions;

And whereas great numbers of the citizens of the United States reside within the territories or dominions of each of the said belligerents and carry on commerce, trade, or other business or pursuits therein, protected by the faith of treaties;

And whereas great numbers of the subjects or citizens of each of the said belligerents reside within the territory or jurisdiction of the United States, and carry on commerce, trade, or other business or pursuits therein;

And whereas the laws of the United States, without interfering with the free expression of opinion and sympathy, or with the open manufacture or sale of arms or munitions of war, nevertheless impose upon all persons who may be within their territory and jurisdiction the duty of an impartial neutrality during the existence of the contest:

Now, therefore, I, ULYSSES S. GRANT, President of the United States, in order to preserve the neutrality of the United States and of their citizens and of persons within their territory and jurisdiction, and to enforce their laws, and in order that all persons being warned of the general tenor of the laws and treaties of the United States in this behalf, and of the law of nations, may thus be prevented from an unintentional violation of the same, do hereby declare and proclaim that by the act passed on the 20th day of April, A. D. 1818, commonly known as the "neutrality law," the following acts are forbidden to be done, under severe penalties, within the territory and jurisdiction of the United States, to wit:

1. Accepting and exercising a commission to serve either of the said belligerents by land or by sea against the other belligerent.

2. Enlisting or entering into the service of either of the said belligerents as a soldier, or as a marine, or seaman on board of any vessel of war, letter of marque, or privateer.

3. Hiring or retaining another person to enlist or enter himself in the service of either of the said belligerents as a soldier, or as a marine, or seaman on board of any vessel of war, letter of marque, or privateer.

4. Hiring another person to go beyond the limits or jurisdiction of the United States with intent to be enlisted as aforesaid.

5. Hiring another person to go beyond the limits of the United States with the intent to be entered into service as aforesaid.

6. Retaining another person to go beyond the limits of the United States with intent to be enlisted as aforesaid.

7. Retaining another person to go beyond the limits of the United States with intent to be entered into service as aforesaid. (But the said act is not to be construed to extend to a citizen or subject of either belligerent who, being transiently within the United States, shall, on board of any vessel of war, which, at the time of its arrival within the United States, was fitted and equipped as such vessel of war, enlist or enter himself or hire or retain another subject or citizen of the same belligerent, who is transiently within the United States, to enlist or enter himself to serve such belligerent on board such vessel of war, if the United States shall then be at peace with such belligerent.)

8. Fitting out and arming, or attempting to fit out and arm, or procuring to be fitted out and armed, or knowingly being concerned in the furnishing, fitting out, or arming of any ship or vessel with intent that such ship or vessel shall be employed in the service of either of the said belligerents.

9. Issuing or delivering a commission within the territory or jurisdiction of the United States for any ship or vessel to the intent that she may be employed as aforesaid.

10. Increasing or augmenting, or procuring to be increased or augmented, or knowingly being concerned in increasing or augmenting the force of any ship of war, cruiser, or other armed vessel, which at the time of her arrival within the United States was a ship of war, cruiser, or armed vessel in the service of either of the said belligerents, or belonging to the subjects or citizens of either, by adding to the number of guns of such vessels, or by changing those on board of her for guns of a larger caliber, or by the addition thereto of any equipment solely applicable to war.

11. Beginning or setting on foot or providing or preparing the means for any military expedition or enterprise to be carried on from the territory or jurisdiction of the United States against the territories or dominions of either of the said belligerents.

And I do further declare and proclaim that by the nineteenth article of the treaty of amity and commerce, which was concluded between his Majesty the King of Prussia and the United States of America, on the 11th day of July, A. D. 1799, which article was revived by the treaty of May 1, A. D. 1828, between the same parties, and is still in force, it was agreed that "the vessels of war, public and private, of both parties, shall carry freely, wheresoever they please, the vessels and effects taken from their enemies without being obliged to pay any duties, charges, or fees, to officers of admiralty, of the customs, or any others; nor shall such prizes be arrested, searched, or put under any legal process when they come to and enter the ports of the other party, but may freely be carried out again at any time by their captors to the places expressed in their commissions, which the commanding officer of such vessel shall be obliged to show."

And I do further declare and proclaim that it has been officially communicated to the Government of the United States by the envoy extraordinary and minister plenipotentiary of the North German Confederation at Washington, that private property on the high seas will be exempted from seizure by the ships of his Majesty the King of Prussia, without regard to reciprocity.

And I do further declare and proclaim that it has been officially communicated to the Government of the United States by the envoy extraordinary and minister plenipotentiary of his Majesty the Emperor of the French, at Washington, that orders have been given that in the conduct of the war the commanders of the French forces on land and on the seas shall scrupulously observe toward neutral Powers the rules of international law, and that they shall strictly adhere to the principles set forth in the declaration of the Congress of Paris of the 16th of April, 1856, that is to say, first, that privateering is and remains abolished; second, that the neutral flag covers enemy's goods with the exception of contraband of war; third, that neutral goods, with the exception of contraband of war, are not liable to capture under the enemy's flag; fourth, that blockades in order to be binding, must be effective, that is to say, maintained by a force sufficient really to prevent access to the coast of the enemy; and that, although the United States have not adhered to the declaration of 1856, the vessels of his Majesty will not seize enemy's property found on board of a vessel of the United States, provided that property is not contraband of war.

And I do further declare and proclaim that the statutes of the United States and the law of nations alike require that no person within the territory and jurisdiction of the United States shall take part, directly or indirectly, in the said war, but shall remain at peace with each of the said belligerents, and shall maintain a strict and impartial neutrality, and that whatever privileges shall be accorded to one belligerent within the ports of the United States shall be in like manner accorded to the other.

And I do hereby enjoin all the good citizens of the United States, and all persons residing or being within the territory or jurisdiction of the United States, to observe the laws thereof, and to commit no act contrary to the provisions of the said statutes, or in violation of the law of nations in that behalf.

And I do hereby warn all citizens of the United States, and all persons residing or being within their territory or jurisdiction, that, while the free and full expression of sympathies in public and private is not restricted by the laws of the United States, military forces in aid of either belligerent cannot lawfully be originated or organized within their jurisdiction; and that while all persons may lawfully, and without restriction by reason of the aforesaid state of war, manufacture and sell within the United States arms and munitions of war, and other articles, ordinarily known as "contraband of war," yet they cannot carry such articles upon the high seas for the use or service of either belligerent, nor can they transport soldiers and officers of either, or attempt to break any blockade which may be lawfully established and maintained during the war, without incurring the risk of hostile capture, and the penalties denounced by the law of nations in that behalf.

And I do hereby give notice that all citizens of the United States, and others who may claim the protection of this Government, who may misconduct themselves in the premises, will do so at their peril, and that they can in no wise obtain any protection from the Government of the United States against the consequences of their misconduct.

In witness whereof I have hereunto set my hand, and caused the seal of the United States to be affixed.

Done at the city of Washington, this 22d day of August, in the year of our Lord 1870, and of the Independence of the United States of America the ninety-fifth.

[SEAL.]

U. S. GRANT.

By the President:

HAMILTON FISH,
Secretary of State.

Declaring the Neutrality of American Waters and the Rules to govern belligerent Vessels, October 8, 1870.

Whereas on the 22d day of August, 1870, my proclamation was issued, enjoining neutrality in the present war between France and the North German Confederation and its allies, and declaring, so far as then seemed to be necessary, the respective rights and obligations of the belligerent parties and of the citizens of the United States;

And whereas subsequent information gives reason to apprehend that armed cruisers of the belligerents may be tempted to abuse the hospitality accorded to them in the ports, harbors, roadsteads, and other waters of the United States, by making such waters subservient to the purposes of war:

Now, therefore, I, ULYSSES S. GRANT, President of the United States of America, do hereby proclaim and declare that any frequenting and use of the waters within the territorial jurisdiction of the United States by the armed vessels of either belligerent, whether public ships or privateers, for the purpose of preparing for hostile operations, or as posts of observation upon the ships of war or privateers or merchant vessels of the other belligerent lying within or being about to enter the jurisdiction of the United States, must be regarded as unfriendly and offensive, and in violation of that neutrality which it is the determination of this Government to observe; and to the end that the hazard and inconvenience of such apprehended practices may be avoided, I further proclaim and declare that from and after the 12th day of October instant, and during the continuance of the present hostilities between France and the North German Confederation and its allies, no ship of war or privateer of either belligerent shall be permitted to make use of any port, harbor, roadstead, or other waters within the jurisdiction of the United States as a station or place of resort for any warlike purpose, or for the purpose of obtaining any facilities of warlike equipment; and no ship of war or privateer of either belligerent shall be permitted to sail out of or leave any port, harbor, roadstead, or waters subject to the jurisdiction of the United States from which a vessel of the other belligerent (whether the same shall be a ship of war, a privateer, or a merchant ship) shall have previously departed, until after the expiration of at least twenty-four hours from the departure of such last-mentioned vessel beyond the jurisdiction of the United States. If any ship of war or privateer of either belligerent shall, after the time this notification takes effect, enter any port, harbor, roadstead, or waters of the United States, such vessel shall be required to depart and to put to sea within twenty-four hours after her entrance into such port, harbor, roadstead, or waters, except in case of stress of weather or of her requiring provisions or things necessary for the subsistence of her crew, or for repairs; in either of which cases the authorities of the port or of the nearest port (as the case may be) shall require her to put to sea as soon as possible after the expiration of such period of twenty-four hours without permitting her to take in supplies beyond what may be necessary for her immediate use; and no such vessel which may have been permitted to remain within the waters of the United States for the purpose of repair shall continue within such port, harbor, roadstead, or waters for a longer period than twenty-four hours after her necessary repairs shall have been completed, unless within such twenty-four hours a vessel, whether ship of war, privateer, or merchant ship of the other belligerent, shall have departed therefrom, in which case the time limited for the departure of such ship of war or privateer shall be extended so far as may be necessary to secure an interval of not less than twenty-four hours between such departure and that of any ship of war, privateer, or merchant ship of the other belligerent which may have previously quit the same port, harbor, roadstead, or waters. No ship of war or privateer of either belligerent shall be detained in any port, harbor, roadstead, or waters of the United States more than twenty-four hours by reason of the successive departure from such port, harbor, roadstead, or waters of more than one vessel of the other belligerent. But if there be several vessels of each or either of the two belligerents in the same port, harbor, roadstead, or waters, the order of their departure therefrom shall be so arranged as to afford the opportunity of leaving alternately to the vessels of the respective belligerents, and to cause the least detention consistent with the objects of this proclamation. No ship of war or privateer of either belligerent shall be permitted, while in any port, harbor, roadstead, or waters within the jurisdiction of the United States, to take in any supplies except provisions and such other things as may be requisite for the subsistence of her crew, and except so much coal only as may be sufficient to carry such vessel, if without sail-power, to the nearest European port of her own country; or in case the vessel is rigged to go under sail, and may also be propelled by steam-power, then with half the quantity of coal which she would be entitled to receive, if dependent upon steam alone, and no coal shall be again supplied to any such ship of war or privateer in the same or any other port, harbor, roadstead, or waters of the United States, without special permission, until after the expiration of three months from the time when such coal may have been last supplied to her within the waters of the United States, unless such ship of war or privateer shall, since last thus supplied, have entered a European port of the Government to which she belongs.

In testimony whereof, I have hereunto set my hand and caused the seal of the United States to be affixed.

Done at the city of Washington, this 8th day of October, in the year of our Lord 1870, and of the Independence of the United States of America the ninety-fifth.

[SEAL.] U. S. GRANT.

By the President:

HAMILTON FISH,
Secretary of State.

Warning Against Illegal Military Enterprises, October 12, 1870.

Whereas divers evil disposed persons have, at sundry times within the territory or jurisdiction of the United States, begun, or set on foot, or provided, or prepared the means for military expeditions or enterprises to be carried on thence against the territories or dominions of Powers with whom the United States are at peace, by organizing bodies pretending to have powers of government over portions of the territories or dominions of Powers with whom the United States are at peace, or by being or assuming to be members of such bodies, by levying or collecting money for the purpose, or for the alleged purpose of using the same in carrying on military enterprises against such territories or dominions, by enlisting and organizing armed forces to be used against such Powers, and by fitting out, equipping, and arming vessels to transport such organized armed forces to be employed in hostilities against such Powers;

And whereas it is alleged, and there is reason to apprehend, that such evil-disposed persons have also, at sundry times, within the territory and jurisdiction of the United States, violated the laws thereof by accepting and exercising commissions to serve by land or by sea against Powers with whom the United States are at peace, by enlisting themselves or other persons to carry on war against such Powers, by fitting out and arming vessels with intent that the same shall be employed to cruise or commit hostilities against such Powers, or by delivering commissions within the territory or jurisdiction of the United States for such vessels to the intent that they might be employed as aforesaid;

And whereas such acts are in violation of the laws of the United States in such case made and provided, and are done in disregard of the duties and obligations which all persons residing or being within the territory or jurisdiction of the United States owe thereto, and are condemned by all right-minded and law-abiding citizens:

Now, therefore, I, ULYSSES S. GRANT, President of the United States of America, do hereby declare and proclaim that all persons hereafter found within the territory or jurisdiction of the United States committing any of the afore-recited violations of law, or any similar violations of the sovereignty of the

United States for which punishment is provided by law, will be rigorously prosecuted therefor, and, upon conviction and sentence to punishment, will not be entitled to expect or receive the clemency of the Executive to save them from the consequences of their guilt; and I enjoin upon every officer of this Government, civil or military or naval, to use all efforts in his power to arrest for trial and punishment every such offender against the laws providing for the performance of our sacred obligations to friendly Powers.

In testimony whereof, I have hereunto set my hand and caused the seal of the United States to be affixed.

Done at the city of Washington, this 12th day of October, in the year of our Lord 1870, and of the Independnce of the United States of America the ninety-fifth.

[SEAL.]

U. S. GRANT.

By the President:

HAMILTON FISH,

Secretary of State.

Commanding dispersion of Armed Men in South Carolina, March 24, 1871.

Whereas, it is provided in the Constitution of the United States that the United States shall protect every State in this Union, on application of the Legislature or of the Executive, (when the Legislature cannot be convened,) against domestic violence; and

Whereas it is provided in the laws of the United States that in all cases of insurrection in any State, or of obstruction to the laws thereof, it shall be lawful for the President of the United States, on application of the Legislature of such State, or of the Executive, (when the Legislature cannot be convened,) to call forth the militia of any other State or States, or to employ such part of the land and naval force as shall be judged necessary for the purpose of suppressing such insurrection, or of causing the laws to be duly executed; and

Whereas I have received information that combinations of armed men, unauthorized by law, are now disturbing the peace and safety of the citizens of the State of South Carolina, and committing acts of violence in said State of a character and to an extent which render the power of the State and its officers unequal to the task of protecting life and property, and securing public order therein; and

Whereas the Legislature of said State is not now in session and cannot be convened in time to meet the present emergency, and the Executive of said State has therefore made application to me for such part of the military force of the United States as may be necessary and adequate to protect said State and the citizens thereof against the domestic violence hereinbefore mentioned, and to enforce the due execution of the laws; and

Whereas the laws of the United States require that, whenever it may be necessary, in the judgment of the President, to use the military force for the purpose aforesaid, he shall forthwith, by proclamation, command such insurgents to disperse and retire peaceably to their respective abodes within a limited time:

Now, therefore, I, ULYSSES S. GRANT, President of the United States, do hereby command the persons composing the unlawful combinations aforesaid to disperse and retire peaceably to their respective abodes within twenty days from this date.

In witness whereof I have hereunto set my hand, and caused the seal of the United States to be affixed.

Done at the city of Washington, this 24th day of March, in the year of our Lord 1871, and of the Independence of the United States the ninety-fifth.

[SEAL.]

U. S. GRANT.

By the President:

HAMILTON FISH,

Secretary of State.

Calling attention to the Act commonly known as the Ku Klux Law, and enjoining obedience thereto, May 3, 1871.

The act of Congress, entitled "An act to enforce the provisions of the fourteenth amendment to the Constitution of the United States, and for other purposes," approved April 20, A. D. 1871, being a law of extraordinary public importance, I consider it my duty to issue this my proclamation calling the attention of the people of the United States thereto; enjoining upon all good citizens, and especially upon all public officers, to be zealous in the enforcement thereof, and warning all persons to abstain from committing any of the acts thereby prohibited.

This law of Congress applies to all parts of the United States, and will be enforced everywhere, to the extent of the powers vested in the Executive. But inasmuch as the necessity therefor is well known to have been caused chiefly by persistent violations of the rights of citizens of the United States by combinations of lawless and disaffected persons in certain localities lately the theater of insurrection and military conflict, I do particularly exhort the people of those parts of the country to suppress all such combinations by their own voluntary efforts through the agency of local laws, and to maintain the rights of all citizens of the United States, and to secure to all such citizens the equal protection of the laws.

Fully sensible of the responsibility imposed upon the Executive by the act of Congress to which public attention is now called, and reluctant to call into exercise any of the extraordinary powers thereby conferred upon me, except in cases of imperative necessity, I do, nevertheless, deem it my duty to make known that I will not hesitate to exhaust the powers thus vested in the Executive, whenever and wherever it shall become necessary to do so for the purpose of securing to all citizens of the United States the peaceful enjoyment of the rights guarantied to them by the Constitution and laws.

It is my earnest wish that peace and cheerful obedience to law may prevail throughout the land, and that all traces of our late unhappy civil strife may be speedily removed. These ends can be easily reached by acquiescence in the results of the conflict, now written in our Constitution, and by the due and proper enforcement of equal, just, and impartial laws in every part of our country.

The failure of local communities to furnish such means for the attainment of results so earnestly desired imposes upon the national Government the duty of putting forth all its energies for the protection of its citizens of every race and color, and for the restoration of peace and order throughout the entire country.

In testimony whereof I have hereunto set my hand, and caused the seal of the United States to be affixed.

Done at the city of Washington, this 3d day of May, in the year of our Lord 1871, [SEAL.] and of the Independence of the United States the ninety-fifth.

U. S. GRANT.

By the President:
HAMILTON FISH,
Secretary of State.

Commanding the Dispersion of Persons Composing unlawful Combinations and Conspiracies in certain Counties in the State of South Carolina, October 12, 1871.

Whereas unlawful combinations and conspiracies have long existed and do still exist in the State of South Carolina, for the purpose of depriving certain portions and classes of the people of that State of the rights, privileges, immunities, and protection named in the Constitution of the United States, and secured by the act of Congress approved April 20, 1871, entitled "An act to enforce the provisions of the fourteenth amendment to the Constitution of the United States;"

And whereas in certain parts of said State, to wit, in the counties of Spartansburg, York, Marion, Chester, Laurens, Newberry, Fairfield, Lancaster, and Chesterfield, such combinations and conspiracies do so obstruct and hinder the execution of the laws of said State and of the United States as to deprive the people aforesaid of the rights, privileges, immunities, and protection aforesaid, and do oppose and obstruct the laws of the United States and their due execution, and impede and obstruct the due course of justice under the same;

And whereas the constituted authorities of said State are unable to protect the people aforesaid in such rights within the said counties;

And whereas the combinations and conspiracies aforesaid, within the counties aforesaid, are organized and armed, and are so numerous and powerful as to be able to defy the constituted authorities of said State and of the United States within the said State, and by reason of said causes the conviction of such offenders and the preservation of the public peace and safety have become impracticable in said counties:

Now, therefore, I, ULYSSES S. GRANT, President of the United States of America, do hereby command all persons composing the unlawful combinations and conspiracies aforesaid to disperse and to retire peaceably to their homes within five days of the date hereof, and to deliver, either to the marshal of the United States for the district of South Carolina, or to any of his deputies, or to any military officer of the United States within said counties, all arms, ammunition, uniforms, disguises, and other means and implements, used, kept, possessed, or controlled by them, for carrying out the unlawful purposes for which the combinations and conspiracies are organized.

In witness whereof I have hereunto set my hand, and caused the seal of the United States to be affixed.

Done at the city of Washington, this 12th day of October, in the year of our [SEAL.] Lord 1871, and of the Independence of the United States of America the ninety-sixth.

U. S. GRANT.

By the President:
HAMILTON FISH,
Secretary of State.

Suspending the writ of Habeas Corpus in certain Counties in the State of South Carolina, October 17, 1871.

Whereas by an act of Congress entitled "An act to enforce the provisions of the fourteenth amendment to the Constitution of the United States, and for other purposes," approved the 20th day of April, anno Domini 1871, power is given to the President of the United States, when, in his judgment, the public safety shall require it, to suspend the privileges of the writ of *habeas corpus* in any State or part of a State whenever combinations and conspiracies exist in such State or part of a State, for the purpose of depriving any portion or class of the people of such State of the rights, privileges, immunities, and protection named in the Constitution of the United States, and secured by the act of Congress aforesaid; and whenever such combinations and conspiracies do so obstruct and hinder the execution of the laws of any such State, and of the United States, as to deprive the people aforesaid of the rights, privileges, immunities, and protection aforesaid, and do oppose and obstruct the laws of the United States in their due execution, and impede and obstruct the due course of justice under the same; and whenever such combinations shall be organized and armed, and so numerous and powerful as to be able by violence either to overthrow or set at defiance the constituted authorities of said State and of the United States within such State; and whenever, by reason of said causes, the conviction of such offenders, and the preservation of the public peace shall become in such State or part of a State impracticable;

And whereas such unlawful combinations and conspiracies for the purposes aforesaid are declared by the act of Congress aforesaid to be rebellion against the Government of the United States;

And whereas by said act of Congress it is provided that before the President shall suspend the privileges of the writ of *habeas corpus* he shall first have made proclamation commanding such insurgents to disperse;

And whereas on the 12th day of the present month of October, the President of the United States did issue his proclamation, reciting therein, among other things, that such combinations and conspiracies did then exist in the counties of Spartansburg, York, Marion, Chester, Laurens, Newberry, Fairfield, Lancaster, and Chesterfield, in the State of South Carolina, and commanding thereby all persons composing such unlawful combinations and conspiracies to disperse and retire peaceably to their homes within five days from the date thereof, and to deliver either to the marshal of the United States for the district of South Carolina, or to any of his deputies, or to any military officer of the United States within said counties, all arms, ammunition, uniforms, disguises, and other means and implements, used, kept, possessed, or controlled by them for carrying out the unlawful purposes for which the said combinations and conspiracies are organized;

And whereas the insurgents engaged in such unlawful combinations and conspiracies within the counties aforesaid have not dispersed and retired peaceably to their respective homes, and have not delivered to the marshal of the United States, or to any of his deputies, or to any military officer of the United States within said counties, all arms, ammunition, uniforms, disguises, and other means and implements used, kept, possessed, or controlled by them, for carrying out the unlawful purposes for which the combinations and conspiracies are organized, as commanded by said proclamation, but do still persist in the unlawful combinations and conspiracies aforesaid:

Now, therefore, I, Ulysses S. Grant, President of the United States of America, by virtue of the authority vested in me by the Constitution of the United States and the act of Congress aforesaid, do hereby declare that, in my judgment, the public safety especially requires that the privileges of the writ of *habeas corpus* be suspended, to the end that such rebellion may be overthrown, and do hereby suspend the privileges of the writ of *habeas corpus* within the counties of Spartansburg, York, Marion, Chester, Laurens, Newberry, Fairfield, Lancaster, and Chesterfield, in said State of South Carolina, in respect to all persons arrested by the marshal of the United States for the said district of South Carolina, or by any of his deputies, or by any military officer of the United States, or by any soldier or citizen acting under the orders of said marshal, deputy, or such military officer within any one of said counties, charged with any violation of the act of Congress aforesaid during the continuance of such rebellion.

In witness whereof I have hereunto set my hand, and caused the seal of the United States to be affixed.

Done at the city of Washington, this 17th day of October, in the year of our Lord. 1871, and of the Independence of the United States of America the ninety-sixth.

[SEAL.]

U. S. Grant.

By the President:

J. C. Bancroft Davis,
Acting Secretary of State.

Revoking the Suspension of Habeas Corpus as to Marion County, State of South Carolina, November 3, 1871.

Whereas, in my proclamation of the 12th day of October, in the year 1871, it was recited that certain unlawful combinations and conspiracies existed in certain counties in the State of South Carolina for the purpose of depriving certain portions and classes of the people of that State of the rights, privileges, and immunities and protection named in the Constitution of the United States, and secured by the act of Congress, approved April the 20th, 1871, entitled "An act to enforce the provisions of the fourteenth amendment to the Constitution of the United States," and the persons composing such combinations and conspiracies were commanded to disperse and to retire peaceably to their homes within five days from said date;

And whereas by my proclamation of the 17th day of October, in the year 1871, the privileges of the writ of *habeas corpus* were suspended in the counties named in said proclamation;

And whereas the county of Marion was named in said proclamations as one of the counties in which said unlawful combinations and conspiracies for the purposes aforesaid existed, and in which the privileges of the writ of habeas corpus were suspended;

And whereas it has been ascertained that in said county of Marion said combinations and conspiracies do not exist to the extent recited in said proclamations;

And whereas it has been ascertained that unlawful combinations and conspiracies of the character and to the extent and for the purposes described in said proclamations do exist in the county of Union in said State:

Now, therefore, I, Ulysses S. Grant, President of the United States of America, do hereby revoke, as to the said county of Marion, the suspension of the privileges of the writ of *habeas corpus* directed in my said proclamation of the 17th day of October, 1871.

And I do hereby command all persons in the said county of Union, composing the unlawful combinations and conspiracies aforesaid, to disperse and to retire peaceably to their homes within five days of the date hereof and to deliver either to the marshal of the United States for the district of South Carolina, or to any of his deputies, or to any military officer of the United States within said county, all arms, ammunition, uniforms, disguises, and other means and implements used, kept, possessed, or controlled by them for carrying out the unlawful purposes for which the combinations and conspiracies are organized.

In witness whereof I have hereunto set my hand, and caused the seal of the United States to be affixed.

Done at the city of Washington, this 3d day of November, in the year of our Lord, 1871, and of the Independence [SEAL.] of the United States of America the ninety-sixth.

U. S. GRANT.

By the President:

HAMILTON FISH,
Secretary of State.

Suspending the writ of Habeas Corpus in the county of Union, State of South Carolina, November 10, 1871.

Whereas by an act of Congress, entitled "An act to enforce the provisions of the fourteenth amendment to the Constitution of the United States, and for other purposes," approved the 20th day of April, A. D. 1871, power is given to the President of the United States, when, in his judgment, the public safety shall require it, to suspend the privileges of the writ of *habeas corpus* in any State or part of a State, whenever combinations and conspiracies exist in such State or part of a State for the purpose of depriving any portion or class of the people of such State of the rights, privileges, immunities, and protection named in the Constitution of the United States, and secured by the act of Congress aforesaid; and whenever such combinations and conspiracies do so obstruct and hinder the execution of the laws of any such State, and of the United States, as to deprive the people aforesaid of the rights, privileges, immunities, and protection aforesaid, and do oppose and obstruct the laws of the United States and their due execution, and impede and obstruct the due course of justice under the same; and whenever such combinations shall be organized and armed, and so numerous and powerful as to be able by violence either to overthrow or to set at defiance the constituted authorities of said State and of the United States within such State; and whenever, by reason of said causes, the conviction of such offenders and the preservation of the public peace shall become in such State or part of a State impracticable;

And whereas such unlawful combinations and conspiracies for the purposes aforesaid are declared by the act of Congress aforesaid to be rebellion against the Government of the United States;

And whereas, by said act of Congress, it is provided that, before the President shall suspend the privileges of the writ of *habeas corpus*, he shall first have made proclamation commanding such insurgents to disperse;

And whereas on the 3d day of the present month of November the President of the United States did issue his proclamation, reciting therein, among other things, that such combinations and conspiracies did then exist in the county of Union, in the State of South Carolina, and commanding thereby all persons composing such unlawful combinations and conspiracies to disperse and retire peaceably to their homes within five days from the date thereof, and to deliver either to the marshal of the United States for the district of South Carolina, or to any of his deputies, or to any military officer of the United States within said county, all arms, ammunition, uniforms, disguises, and other means and implements used, kept, possessed, or controlled by them for carrying out the unlawful purposes for which the said combinations and conspiracies are organized;

And whereas the insurgents engaged in such unlawful combinations and conspiracies within the county aforesaid have not dispersed and retired peaceably to their respective homes, and have not delivered to the marshal of the United States, or to any of his deputies, or to any military officer of the United States within said county, all arms, ammunition, uniforms, disguises, and other means and implements used, kept, possessed, or controlled by them for carrying out the unlawful purposes for which the combinations and conspiracies are organized, as commanded by said proclamation, but do still persist in the unlawful combinations and conspiracies aforesaid:

Now, therefore, I, ULYSSES S. GRANT, President of the United States of America, by virtue of the authority vested in me by the Constitution of the United States and the act of Congress aforesaid, do hereby declare that, in my judgment, the public safety especially requires that the privileges of the writ of *habeas corpus* be suspended, to the end that such rebellion may be overthrown, and do hereby suspend the privileges of the writ of *habeas corpus* within the county of Union in said State of South Carolina, in respect to all persons arrested by the marshal of the United States for the said district of South Carolina, or by any of his deputies, or by any military officer of the United States, or by any soldier or citizen acting under the orders of said marshal, deputy, or such military officer within said county, charged with any violation of the act of Congress aforesaid, during the continuance of such rebellion.

In witness whereof I have hereunto set my hand, and caused the seal of the United States to be affixed.

Done at the city of Washington, this 10th day of November, in the year of our Lord 1871, and of the Independence [SEAL.] of the United States of America the ninety-sixth.

U. S. GRANT.

By the President:

HAMILTON FISH,
Secretary of State.

Discontinuing Discriminating Duties on Merchandise Imported into the United States in Spanish Vessels, December 19, 1871.

Whereas satisfactory information has been received by me through Don Mauricio Lopez Roberts, envoy extraordinary and minister plenipotentiary of His Majesty the king of Spain, that the Government of that country has abolished discriminating duties heretofore imposed on merchandise imported from all other countries, excepting the islands of Cuba and Porto Rico, into Spain and the adjacent islands, in vessels of the United States, said abolition to take effect from and after the 1st day of January next:

Now, therefore, I, ULYSSES S. GRANT, President of the United States of America, by virtue of the authority vested in me by an act of Congress of the 7th day of January, 1824, and by an act in addition thereto, of the 24th day of May, 1828, do hereby declare and proclaim that on and after the said 1st day of January next, so long as merchandise imported from any other country, excepting the islands of Cuba and Porto Rico, into the ports of Spain and the islands adjacent thereto, in vessels belonging to citizens of the United States shall be exempt from discriminating duties, any such duties on merchandise imported into the United States in Spanish vessels, excepting from the islands of Cuba and Porto Rico, shall be discontinued and abolished.

In testimony whereof I have hereunto set my hand, and caused the seal of the United State to be affixed.

Done at the city of Washington, this 19th day of December, in the year of our [SEAL.] Lord 1871, and of the Independence of the United States of America the ninety-sixth.

U. S. GRANT.

By the President:

HAMILTON FISH,

Secretary of State.

IV.

PRESIDENT GRANT'S SECOND AND THIRD ANNUAL MESSAGES.

[For his First Annual Message, see McPherson's History of Reconstruction, pages 533–540.]

President Grant's Second Annual Message.

December 5, 1870.

To the Senate and House of Representatives :

A year of peace and general prosperity to this nation has passed since the last assembling of Congress. We have, through a kind Providence, been blessed with abundant crops. and have been spared from complications and war with foreign nations. In our midst comparative harmony has been restored. It is to be regretted, however, that a free exercise of the elective franchise has, by violence and intimidation, been denied to citizens in exceptional cases in several of the States lately in rebellion, and the verdict of the people has thereby been reversed. The States of Virginia, Mississippi, and Texas have been restored to representation in our national councils. Georgia, the only State now without representation, may confidently be expected to take her place there also at the beginning of the new year; and then, let us hope, will be completed the work of reconstruction. With an acquiescence on the part of the whole people in the national obligation to pay the public debt, created as the price of our Union; the pensions to our disabled soldiers and sailors, and their widows and orphans; and in the changes to the Constitution which have been made necessary by a great rebellion, there is no reason why we should not advance in material prosperity and happiness, as no other nation ever did, after so protracted and devastating a war. * * * *

It is not understood that the condition of the insurrection in Cuba has materially changed since the close of the last session of Congress. In an early stage of the contest the authorities of Spain inaugurated a system of arbitrary arrests, of close confinement, and of military trial and execution of persons suspected of complicity with the insurgents, and of summary embargo of their properties, and sequestration of their revenues by executive warrant. Such proceedings, so far as they affected the persons or property of citizens of the United States, were in violation of the provisions of the treaty of 1795 between the United States and Spain. Representations of injuries resulting to several persons claiming to be citizens of the United States, by reason of such violations, were made to the Spanish Government. From April 1869 to June last the Spanish minister at Washington had been clothed with a limited power to aid in redressing such wrongs. That power was found to be withdrawn, "in view," as it was said, "of the favorable situation in which the island of Cuba" then "was;" which, however, did not lead to a revocation or suspension of the extraordinary and arbitrary functions exercised by the executive power in Cuba, and we were obliged to make our complaints at Madrid. In the negotiations thus opened, and still pending there, the United States only claimed that, for the future, the rights secured to their citizens by treaty should be respected in Cuba, and that, as to the past, a joint tribunal should be established in the United States, with full jurisdiction over all such claims. Before such an impartial tribunal each claimant would be required to prove his case. On the other hand, Spain would be at liberty to traverse every material fact, and thus complete equity would be done. * * * *

During the last session of Congress a treaty for the annexation of the republic of San Domingo to the United States failed to receive the requisite two-thirds vote of the Senate. I was thoroughly convinced then that the best interests of this country, commercially and materially, demanded its ratification. Time has only confirmed me in this view. I now firmly believe that the moment it is known that the United States have entirely abandoned the project of accepting, as a part of its territory, the island of San Domingo, a free port will be negotiated for by European nations in the Bay of Samana. A large commercial city will spring up, to which we will be tributary without receiving corresponding benefits, and then will be seen the folly of our rejecting so great a prize. The Government of San Domingo has voluntarily sought this annexation. It is a weak Power, numbering probably less than one hundred and twenty thousand souls, and yet possessing one of the richest territories under the sun, capable of supporting a population of ten millions of people in luxury. The people of San Domingo are not capable of maintaining themselves in their present condition, and must look for outside support. They yearn for the protection of our free institutions and laws; our progress and civilization. Shall we refuse them?

The acquisition of San Domingo is desirable because of its geographical position. It commands the entrance to the Caribbean sea and the Isthmus transit of commerce. It possesses the richest soil, best and most capacious harbors, most salubrious climate, and the most valuable products of the forest, mine, and soil of any of the West India islands. Its possession by us will in a few years build up a coastwise commerce of immense magnitude, which will go far toward restoring to us our lost merchant marine. It will give to us those articles which we consume so largely and do not produce, thus equalizing our exports and imports. In case of foreign war it will give us command of all the islands referred to, and thus prevent an enemy from ever again possessing himself of rendezvous upon our very coast. At present our coast trade between the States bordering on the Atlantic and those bordering on the Gulf of Mexico is cut into by the Bahamas and the Antilles. Twice we must, as it were, pass through foreign countries to get, by sea, from Georgia, to the west coast of Florida.

San Domingo, with a stable government, under which her immense resources can be developed, will give remunerative wages to tens of thousands of laborers not now upon the island. This labor will take advantage of every available means of transportation to abandon the adjacent islands and seek the blessings of freedom and its sequence, each inhabitant receiving the reward of his own labor. Porto Rico and Cuba will have to abolish slavery, as a measure of self-preservation, to retain their laborers.

San Domingo will become a large consumer of the products of northern farms and manufactories. The cheap rate at which her citizens can be furnished with food, tools, and machinery will make it necessary that contiguous islands should have the same advantages, in order to compete in the production of sugar, coffee, tobacco, tropical fruits, &c. This will open to us a still wider market for our products. The production of our own supply of these articles will cut off more than one hundred millions of our annual imports, besides largely increasing our exports. With such a picture it is easy to see how our large debt abroad is ultimately to be extinguished. With a balance of trade against us (including interest on bonds held by foreigners and money spent by our citizens traveling in foreign lands) equal to the entire yield of the precious metals in this country it is not so easy to see how this result is to be otherwise accomplished.

The acquisition of San Domingo is an adherence to the "Monroe doctrine;" it is a measure of national protection; it is asserting our just claim to a controlling influence over the great commercial traffic soon to flow from west to east, by way of the Isthmus of Darien; it is to build up our merchant marine; it is to furnish new markets for the products of our farms, shops, and manufactories; it is to make slavery insupportable in Cuba and Porto Rico at once, and ultimately so in Brazil; it is to settle the unhappy condition of Cuba and end an exterminating conflict; it is to provide honest means of paying our honest debts without overtaxing the people; it is to furnish our citizens with the necessaries of every-day life at cheaper rates than ever before; and it is, in fine, a rapid stride toward that greatness which the intelligence, industry, and enterprise of the citizens of the United States entitle this country to assume among nations.

In view of the importance of this question I earnestly urge upon Congress early action, expressive of its views as to the best means of acquiring San Domingo. My suggestion is that, by joint resolution of the two Houses of Congress, the Executive be authorized to appoint a commission to negotiate a treaty with the authorities of San Domingo for the acquisition of that island, and that an appropriation be made to defray the expenses of such commission. The question may then be determined, either by the action of the Senate upon the treaty or the joint action of the two Houses of Congress, upon a resolution of annexation, as in the case of the acquisition of Texas. So convinced am I of the advantages to flow from the acquisition of San Domingo, and of the great disadvantages, I might almost say calamities, to flow from non-acquisition, that I believe the subject has only to be investigated to be approved.

It is to be regretted that our representations in regard to the injurious effects, especially upon the revenue of the United States, of the policy of the Mexican Government, in exempting from impost duties a large tract of its territory on our borders, have not only been fruitless, but that it is even proposed in that country, to extend the limits within which the privilege adverted to has hitherto been enjoyed. The expediency of taking into your serious consideration proper measures for countervailing the policy referred to will, it is presumed, engage your earnest attention.

The massacres of French and Russian residents at Tien-Tsin, under circumstances of great barbarity, were supposed by some to have been premeditated, and to indicate a purpose among the populace to exterminate foreigners in the Chinese empire. The evidence fails to establish such a supposition, but shows a complicity between the local authorities and the mob. The Government at Pekin, however, seems to have been disposed to fulfill its treaty obligations so far as it was able to do so. Unfortunately, the news of the war between the German States and France reached China soon after the massacre. It would appear that the popular mind became possessed with the idea that this contest, extending to Chinese waters, would neutralize the Christian influence and power, and that the time was coming when the superstitious masses might expel all foreigners and restore mandarin influence. Anticipating trouble from this cause I invited France and North Germany to make an authorized suspension of hostilities in the East, (where they were temporarily suspended by act of the commanders,) and to act together for the future protection, in China, of the lives and properties of Americans and Europeans.

Since the adjournment of Congress the ratifications of the treaty with Great Britain for abolishing the mixed courts for the suppression of the slave trade, have been exchanged. It is believed that the slave trade is now confined to the eastern coast of Africa, whence the slaves are taken to Arabian markets.

* * * * *

I regret to say that no conclusion has been reached for the adjustment of the claims against Great Britain growing out of the course adopted by that Government during the rebellion. The cabinet of London, so far as its views have been expressed, does not appear to be willing to concede that her Majesty's Government was guilty of any negligence, or did or permitted any act during the war, by which the United States has just cause of complaint. Our firm and unalterable convictions are directly the reverse. I therefore recommend to Congress to authorize the appointment of a commission to take proof of the amounts, and the ownership of these several claims, on notice to the representative of her Majesty at Washington, and that authority be given for the settlement of these claims by the United States, so that the Government shall have the ownership of the private claims, as well as the responsible control of all the demands against Great Britain. It cannot be necessary to add that, whenever her Majesty's Government shall entertain a desire for a full and friendly adjustment of these claims, the United States will enter upon their consideration with an earnest desire for a conclusion consistent with the honor and dignity of both nations.

The course pursued by the Canadian authorities toward the fishermen of the United States during the past season has not been marked by a friendly feeling. By the first article of the convention of 1818, between Great Britain and the United States, it was agreed that the inhabitants of the United States should have forever, in common with British subjects, the right of taking fish in certain waters therein defined. In the waters not included in the limits named in the convention (within three miles of parts of the British coast) it has been the custom for many years to give to intruding fishermen of the United States a reasonable warning of their violation of the technical rights of Great Britain. The imperial Government is understood to have delegated the whole or a share of its jurisdiction or control of these in-shore fishing grounds to the colonial authority known as the Dominion of Canada, and this semi independent but irresponsible agent has exercised its delegated powers in an unfriendly way. Vessels have been seized without notice or warning, in violation of the custom previously prevailing, and have been taken into the colonial ports, their voyages broken up, and the vessels condemned.

There is reason to believe that this unfriendly and vexatious treatment was designed to bear harshly upon the hardy fishermen of the United States, with a view to political effect upon this Government. The statutes of the Dominion of Canada assume a still broader and more untenable jurisdiction over the vessels of the United States. They authorize officers or persons to bring vessels hovering within three marine miles of any of the coasts, bays, creeks, or harbors of Canada into port, to search the cargo, to examine the master on oath touching the cargo and voyage, and to inflict upon him a heavy pecuniary penalty if true answers are not given; and if such a vessel is found "preparing to fish" within three marine miles of any of such coasts, bays, creeks, or harbors without a license, or after the expiration of the period named in the last license granted to it, they provide that the vessel, with her tackle, &c., shall be forfeited. It is not known that any condemnations have been made under this statute. Should the authorities of Canada attempt to enforce it, it will become my duty to take such steps as may be necessary to protect the rights of the citizens of the United States.

It has been claimed by her Majesty's officers that the fishing-vessels of the United States have no right to enter the open ports of the British possessions in North America, except for the purposes of shelter and repairing damages, of purchasing wood, and obtaining water; that they have no right to enter at the British custom-houses or to trade there except in the purchase of wood and water; and that they must depart within twenty-four hours after notice to leave. It is not known that any seizure of a fishing-vessel carrying the flag of the United States has been made under this claim. So far as the claim is founded on an alleged construction of the convention of 1818 it cannot be acquiesced in by the United States.

It is hoped that it will not be insisted on by her Majesty's Government.

During the conferences which preceded the negotiation of the convention of 1818 the British commissioners proposed to expressly exclude the fishermen of the United States from "the privilege of carrying on trade with any of his Britannic Majesty's subjects residing within the limits assigned for their use;" and also that it should not be "lawful for the vessels of the United States, engaged in said fishery, to have on board any goods, wares, or merchandise whatever, except such as may be necessary for the prosecution of their voyages to and from the said fishing grounds. And any vessel of the United States which shall contravene this regulation may be seized, condemned, and confiscated with her cargo."

This proposition, which is identical with the construction now put upon the language of the convention, was emphatically rejected by the American commissioners, and thereupon was abandoned by the British plenipotentiaries, and article one, as it stands in the convention, was substituted.

If, however, it be said that this claim is founded on provincial or colonial statutes, and not upon the convention, this Government cannot but regard them as unfriendly, and in contravention of the spirit, if not of the letter of, the treaty, for the faithful execution of which the imperial Government is alone responsible.

Anticipating that an attempt may possibly be made by the Canadian authorities in the coming season to repeat their unneighborly acts toward our fishermen, I recommend you to confer upon the Executive the power to suspend, by proclamation, the operation of the laws authorizing the transit of goods, wares, and merchandise in bond across the territory of the United States to Canada; and further, should such an extreme measure become necessary, to suspend the operation of any laws whereby the vessels of the Dominion of Canada are permitted to enter the waters of the United States.

A like unfriendly disposition has been manifested on the part of Canada in the maintenance of a claim of right to exclude the citizens of the United States from the navigation of the St. Lawrence. This river constitutes a natural outlet to the ocean for eight States with an aggregate population of about seventeen million six hundred thousand inhabitants, and with an aggregate tonnage of six hundred and sixty-one thousand three hundred and sixty-seven tons upon the waters which discharge into it. The foreign commerce of our ports on these waters is open to British competition, and the major part of it is done in British bottoms.

If the American seamen be excluded from this natural avenue to the ocean, the monopoly of the direct commerce of the lake ports with the Atlantic would be in foreign hands; their vessels on transatlantic voyages having an access to our lake ports which would be denied to American vessels on similar voyages. To state such a proposition is to refute its justice.

During the administration of Mr. John Quincy Adams, Mr. Clay unanswerably demonstrated the natural right of the citizens of the United States to the navigation of this river, claiming that the act of the congress of Vienna, in opening the Rhine and other rivers to all nations, showed the judgment of European jurists and statesmen that the inhabitants of a country through which a navigable river passes have a natural right to enjoy the navigation of that river to and into the sea, even though passing through the territories of another Power. This right does not exclude the coequal right of the sovereign possessing the territory through which the river debouches into the sea to make such regulations relative to the police of the navigation as may be reasonably necessary; but those regulations should be framed in a liberal spirit of comity, and should not impose needless burdens upon the commerce which has the right of transit. It has been found in practice more advantageous to arrange these regulations by mutual agreement. The United States are ready to make any reasonable arrangement as to the police of the St. Lawrence which may be suggested by Great Britain.

If the claim made by Mr. Clay was just when the population of States bordering on the shores of the lakes was only three million four hundred thousand, it now derives greater force and equity from the increased population, wealth, production, and tonnage of the States on the Canadian frontier. Since Mr. Clay advanced his argument in behalf of our right the principle for which he contended has been frequently, and by various nations, recognized by law or by treaty, and has been extended to several other great rivers. By the treaty concluded at Mayence, in 1831, the Rhine was declared free from the point where it is first navigable into the sea. By the convention between Spain and Portugal, concluded in 1835, the navigation of the Douro, throughout its whole extent, was made free for the subjects of both crowns. In 1853 the Argentine Confederation by treaty threw open the free navigation of the Parana and the Uruguay to the merchant vessels of all nations. In 1856 the Crimean war was closed by a treaty which provided for the free navigation of the Danube. In 1858 Bolivia, by treaty, declared that it regarded the rivers Amazon and La Plata, in accordance with fixed principles of national law, as highways or channels opened by nature for the commerce of all nations. In 1859 the Paraguay was made free by treaty, and in December 1866 the Emperor of Brazil, by imperial decree, declared the Amazon to be open, to the frontier of Brazil, to the merchant ships of all nations.

The greatest living British authority on this subject, while asserting the abstract right of the British claim, says: "It seems difficult to deny that Great Britain may ground her refusal upon strict law, but it is equally difficult to deny, first, that in so doing she exercises harshly an extreme and hard law; secondly, that her conduct with respect to the navigation of the St. Lawrence is in glaring and discreditable inconsistency with her conduct with respect to the navigation of the Mississippi. On the ground that she possessed a small domain, in which the Mississippi took its rise, she insisted on the right to navigate the entire volume of its waters. On the ground that she possesses both banks of the St. Lawrence, where it disembogues itself into the sea, she denies to the United States the right of navigation, though about one half of the waters of Lakes Ontario, Erie, Huron, and Superior, and the whole of Lake Michigan, through which the river flows, are the property of the United States."

The whole nation is interested in securing cheap transportation from the agricultural States of the West to the Atlantic sea-board. To the citizens of those States it secures a greater return for their labor; to the inhabitants of the sea-board it affords cheaper food; to the nation an increase in the annual surplus of wealth. It is hoped that the Government of Great Britain will see the justice of abandoning the narrow and inconsistent claim to which her Canadian provinces have urged her adherence.

Our depressed commerce is a subject to which I called your special attention at the last session, and suggested that we will in the future have to look more to the countries south of us, and to China and Japan, for its revival. Our representatives to all these Governments have exerted their influence to encourage trade between the United States and the countries to which they are accredited. But the fact exists that the carrying is done almost entirely in foreign bottoms, and while this state of affairs exists we cannot control our due share of the commerce of the world. That between the Pacific States and China and Japan is about all the carrying trade now conducted in American vessels. I would recommend a liberal policy toward that line of American steamers, one that will insure its success, and even increased usefulness.

The cost of building iron vessels, the only ones that can compete with foreign ships in the carrying trade, is so much greater in the United States than in foreign countries that, without some assistance from the Government, they cannot be successfully built here. There will be several propositions laid before Congress in the course of the present session looking to a remedy for this evil. Even if it should be at some cost to the national Treasury, I hope such encouragement will be given as will secure American shipping on the high seas and American ship-building at home.

* * * * * * *

The estimates for the expenses of the Government for the next fiscal year are $18,244,346 01 less than for the current one, but exceed the appropriations for the present year, for the same items, $8,972,127 56. In this estimate, however, is included $22,338,278 37 for public works heretofore begun under congressional provision, and of which only so much is asked as Congress may choose to give. The appropriation for the same works for the present fiscal year was $11,984,518 08.

The average value of gold as compared with national currency, for the whole of the year 1869, was about one hundred and thirty-four, and for eleven months of 1870, the same relative value has been about one hundred and fifteen. The approach to a specie basis is very gratifying, but the fact cannot be denied that the instability of the value of our currency is prejudicial to our prosperity, and tends to keep up prices to the detriment of trade. The evils of a depreciated and fluctuating currency are so great that now, when the premium on gold has fallen so much, it would seem that the time has arrived when, by wise and prudent legislation, Congress should look to a policy which would place our currency at par with gold at no distant day.

The tax collected from the people has been reduced more than eighty million of dollars per annum. By steadiness in our present course there is no reason why, in a few short years, the national tax-gatherer may not disappear from the door of the citizen almost entirely. With the revenue stamp dispensed by postmasters in every community, a tax upon liquors of all sorts, and tobacco in all its forms, and by a wise adjustment of the tariff, which will put a duty only upon those articles which we could dispense with, known as luxuries, and on those which we use more of than we produce, revenue enough may be raised, after a few years of peace and consequent reduction of indebtedness, to fulfill all our obligations. A further reduction of expenses, in addition to a reduction of interest account, may be relied on to make this practicable. Revenue reform, if it means this, has my hearty support. If it implies a collection of all the revenue for the support of Government, for the payment of principal and interest of the public debt, pensions, &c., by directly taxing the people, then I am against revenue reform, and confidently believe the people are with me. If it means failure to provide the necessary means to defray all the expenses of Government, and thereby repudiation of the public debt and pensions, then I am still more opposed to such kind of revenue reform. Revenue reform has not been defined by any of its advocates, to my knowledge, but seems to be accepted as something which is to supply every man's wants without any cost or effort on his part.

A true revenue reform cannot be made in a day, but must be the work of national legislation and of time. As soon as the revenue can be dispensed with, all duty should be removed from coffee, tea, and other articles of universal use not produced by ourselves. The necessities of the country compel us to collect revenue from our imports. An army of assessors and collectors is not a pleasant sight to the citizen, but that or a tariff for revenue is necessary. Such a tariff, so far as it acts as an encouragement to home production, affords employment to labor at living wages, in contrast to the pauper labor of the Old World, and also in the development of home resources.

Under the act of Congress of the 15th day

of July, 1870, the Army has gradually been reduced, so that on the 1st day of January, 1871, the number of commissioned officers and men will not exceed the number contemplated by that law. * * * *

The expenses of the Navy for the whole of the last year, *i. e.*, from December 1, 1869, the date of the last report, are less than nineteen million dollars, or about one million dollars less than they were the previous year. The expenses since the commencement of this fiscal year, *i. e.*, since July 1, show for the five months a decrease of over two million four hundred thousand dollars from those of the corresponding months of last year. The estimates for the current year were $28,205,671 37. Those for the next year are $20,683,317, with $955,100 additional for necessary permanent improvements. These estimates are made closely for the mere maintenance of the naval establishment as it now is, without much in the nature of permanent improvement. The appropriations made for the last and current years were evidently intended by Congress, and are sufficient only, to keep the Navy on its present footing by the repairing and refitting of our old ships.

This policy must, of course, gradually but surely destroy the Navy, and it is in itself far from economical, as each year that it is pursued the necessity for mere repairs in ships and navy-yards becomes more imperative and more costly; and our current expenses are annually increased for the mere repair of ships, many of which must soon become unsafe and useless. I hope during the present session of Congress to be able to submit to it a plan by which naval vessels can be built and repairs made with great saving upon the present cost.

It can hardly be wise statesmanship in a Government which represents a country with over five thousand miles of coast line on both oceans, exclusive of Alaska, and containing forty millions of progressive people, with relations of every nature with almost every foreign country, to rest with such inadequate means of enforcing any foreign policy, either of protection or redress. Separated by the ocean from the nations of the eastern continent, our Navy is our only means of direct protection to our citizens abroad, or for the enforcement of any foreign policy.

The accompanying report of the Postmaster General shows a most satisfactory working of that Department. With the adoption of the recommendations contained therein, particularly those relating to a reform in the franking privilege, and the adoption of the "correspondence cards," a self-sustaining postal system may speedily be looked for, and, at no distant day, a further reduction of the rate of postage be attained. * * * *

Always favoring practical reforms, I respectfully call your attention to one abuse of long standing which I would like to see remedied by this Congress. It is a reform in the civil service of the country. I would have it go beyond the mere fixing of the tenure of office of clerks and employés, who do not require "the advice and consent of the Senate" to make their appointments complete. I would have it govern, not the tenure, but the manner of making all appointments. There is no duty which so much embarrasses the Executive and heads of Departments as that of appointments; nor is there any such arduous and thankless labor imposed on Senators and Representatives as that of finding places for constituents. The present system does not secure the best men, and often not even fit men, for public place. The elevation and purification of the civil service of the Government will be hailed with approval by the whole people of the United States.

Reform in the management of Indian affairs has received the special attention of the Administration from its inauguration to the present day. The experiment of making it a missionary work was tried with a few agencies given to the denomination of Friends, and has been found to work most advantageously. All agencies and superintendencies not so disposed of were given to officers of the Army. The act of Congress reducing the Army renders Army officers ineligible for civil positions. Indian agencies being civil offices, I determined to give all the agencies to such religious denominations as had heretofore established missionaries among the Indians, and perhaps to some other denominations who would undertake the work on the same terms; that is, as a missionary work. The societies selected are allowed to name their own agents, subject to the approval of the Executive, and are expected to watch over them and aid them as missionaries, to Christianize and civilize the Indian, and to train him in the arts of peace. The Government watches over the official acts of these agents, and requires of them as strict an accountability as if they were appointed in any other manner. I entertain the confident hope that the policy now pursued will, in a few years, bring all the Indians upon reservations, where they will live in houses, have school-houses and churches, and will be pursuing peaceful and self-sustaining avocations, and where they may be visited by the law-abiding white man with the same impunity that he now visits the civilized white settlements. I call your special attention to the report of the Commissioner of Indian Affairs for full information on this subject.

During the last fiscal year eight million ninety-five thousand four hundred and thirteen acres of public land were disposed of. Of this quantity three million six hundred and ninety-eight thousand nine hundred and ten and five one hundredths acres were taken under the homestead law, and two million one hundred and fifty-nine thousand five hundred and fifteen and eighty-one one hundredths acres sold for cash. The remainder was located with military warrants, college or Indian scrip, or applied in satisfaction of grants to railroads, or for other public uses. The entries under the homestead law during the last year covered nine hundred and sixty-one thousand five hundred and forty-five acres more than those during the preceding year. Surveys have been vigorously prosecuted to the full extent of the means applicable to the purpose. The quantity of land in market will amply supply the present demand. The claim of the settler, under the homestead or the preëmption laws, is not, however, limited to lands subject to sale at private entry. Any unappropriated surveyed public land may, to a limited amount, be acquired under the former laws if the party entitled to enter under them will comply with the requirements they prescribe in regard to the residence and cultivation.

The actual settler's preference right of purchase is even broader, and extends to lands which were unsurveyed at the time of his settlement. His right was formerly confined within much narrower limits, and at one period of our history was conferred only by special statutes. They were enacted from time to time to legalize what was then regarded as an unauthorized intrusion upon the national domain. The opinion that the public lands should be regarded chiefly as a source of revenue is no longer maintained. The rapid settlement and successful cultivation of them are now justly considered of more importance to our well-being than is the fund which the sale of them would produce. The remarkable growth and prosperity of our new States and Territories attest the wisdom of the legislation which invites the tiller of the soil to secure a permanent home on terms within the reach of all. The pioneer who incurs the dangers and privations of a frontier life, and thus aids in laying the foundation of new commonwealths, renders a signal service to his country, and is entitled to its special favor and protection. These laws secure that object and largely promote the general welfare. They should, therefore, be cherished as a permanent feature of our land system.

Good faith requires us to give full effect to existing grants. The time-honored and beneficent policy of setting apart certain sections of public land for educational purposes in the new States should be continued. When ample provision shall have been made for these objects I submit as a question worthy of serious consideration whether the residue of our national domain should not be wholly disposed of under the provisions of the homestead and preëmption laws.

In addition to the swamp and overflowed lands granted to the States in which they are situated, the lands taken under the agricultural college acts, and for internal improvement purposes, under the act of September, 1841, and the acts supplemental thereto, there had been conveyed up to the close of the last fiscal year, by patent or other equivalent title, to States and corporations twenty-seven million eight hundred and thirty-six thousand two hundred and fifty-seven and sixty-three one hundredths acres for railways, canals, and wagon-roads. It is estimated that an additional quantity of one hundred and seventy-four million seven hundred and thirty-five thousand five hundred and twenty-three acres is still due under grants for like uses.

The policy of thus aiding the States in building works of internal improvement was inaugurated more than forty years since in the grants to Indiana and Illinois, to aid those States in opening canals to connect the waters of the Wabash with those of Lake Erie, and the waters of the Illinois with those of Lake Michigan. It was followed, with some modifications, in the grant to Illinois of alternate sections of public lands within certain limits of the Illinois Central railway. Fourteen States and sundry corporations have received similar subsidies in connection with railways completed or in process of construction. As the reserved sections are rated at the double minimum, the sale of them at the enhanced price has thus in many instances indemnified the Treasury for the granted lands. The construction of some of these thoroughfares has undoubtedly given a vigorous impulse to the development of our resources and the settlement of the more distant portions of the country. It may, however, be well insisted that much of our legislation in this regard has been characterized by indiscriminate and profuse liberality. The United States should not loan their credit in aid of any enterprise undertaken by States or corporations, nor grant lands in any instance, unless the projected work is of acknowledged national importance. I am strongly inclined to the opinion that it is inexpedient and unnecessary to bestow subsidies of either description; but should Congress determine otherwise, I earnestly recommend that the rights of settlers and of the public be more effectually secured and protected by appropriate legislation. * * * * * * *

During the last fiscal year the sum paid to pensioners, including the cost of disbursement, was $27,780,811 11, and one thousand seven hundred and fifty-eight bounty-land warrants were issued. At its close one hundred and ninety-eight thousand six hundred and eighty-six names were on the pension-rolls. * * * * * * *

In conclusion, I would sum up the policy of the Administration to be a thorough enforcement of every law; a faithful collection of every tax provided for; economy in the disbursement of the same; a prompt payment of every debt of the nation; a reduction of taxes as rapidly as the requirements of the country will admit; reductions of taxation and tariff, to be so arranged as to afford the greatest relief to the greatest number; honest and fair dealings with all other peoples, to the end that war, with all its blighting consequences, may be avoided, but without surrendering any right or obligation due to us; a reform in the treatment of Indians, and in the whole civil service of the country; and, finally, in securing a pure, untrammeled ballot, where every man entitled to cast a vote may do so, just once, at each election, without fear of molestation or proscription on account of his political faith, nativity, or color.

U. S. GRANT.

President Grant's Third Annual Message.

December 4, 1871.

To the Senate and House of Representatives:

In addressing my third annual message to the law-making branch of the Government, it is gratifying to be able to state that during the past year success has generally attended the effort to execute all laws found upon the statute-books. The policy has been, not to inquire into the wisdom of laws already enacted, but to learn their spirit and intent, and to enforce them accordingly.

The past year has, under a wise Providence, been one of general prosperity to the nation. It has, however, been attended with more than usual chastisements in the loss of life and property by storm and fire. These disasters have served to call forth the best elements of human nature in our country, and to develop a friendship for us on the part of foreign nations which goes far toward alleviating the distresses occasioned by these calamities. The benevolent, who have so generously shared their means with the victims of these misfortunes, will reap their reward in the consciousness of having performed a noble act, and in receiving the grateful thanks of men, women, and children whose sufferings they have relieved.

The relations of the United States with foreign Powers continue to be friendly. The year has been an eventful one in witnessing two great nations, speaking one language and having one lineage, settling, by peaceful arbitration, disputes of long standing, and liable at any time to bring those nations into bloody and costly conflict. An example has thus been set which, if successful in its final issue, may be followed by other civilized nations, and finally be the means of returning to productive industry millions of men now maintained to settle the disputes of nations by the bayonet and the broadside.

I transmit herewith a copy of the treaty alluded to, which has been concluded, since the adjournment of Congress, with her Britannic Majesty, and a copy of the protocols of the conferences of the commissioners by whom it was negotiated. This treaty provides methods for adjusting the questions pending between the two nations.

Various questions are to be adjusted by arbitration. I recommend Congress at an early day to make the necessary provision for the tribunal at Geneva, and for the several commissioners, on the part of the United States, called for by the treaty.

His Majesty the King of Italy, the President of the Swiss Confederation, and his Majesty the Emperor of Brazil have each consented, on the joint request of the two Powers, to name an arbitrator for the tribunal at Geneva. I have caused my thanks to be suitably expressed for the readiness with which the joint request has been complied with, by the appointment of gentlemen of eminence and learning to these important positions.

His Majesty the Emperor of Germany has been pleased to comply with the joint request of the two Governments, and has consented to act as the arbitrator of the disputed water boundary between the United States and Great Britain.

The contracting parties in the treaty have undertaken to regard as between themselves certain principles of public law, for which the United States have contended from the commencement of their history. They have also agreed to bring those principles to the knowledge of the other maritime Powers and to invite them to accede to them. Negotiations are going on as to the form of the note by which the invitation is to be extended to the other Powers.

I recommend the legislation necessary on the part of the United States to bring into operation the articles of the treaty relating to the fisheries, and to the other matters touching the relations of the United States toward the British North American possessions, to become operative so soon as the proper legislation shall be had on the part of Great Britain and its possessions. It is much to be desired that this legislation may become operative before the fishermen of the United States begin to make their arrangements for the coming season.

I have addressed a communication, of which a copy is transmitted herewith, to the Governors of New York, Pennsylvania, Ohio, Indiana, Michigan, Illinois, and Wisconsin, urging upon the governments of those States, respectively, the necessary action on their part to carry into effect the object of the article of the treaty which contemplates the use of the canals, on either side, connected with the navigation of the lakes and rivers forming the boundary, on terms of equality by the inhabitants of both countries. It is hoped that the importance of the object and the benefits to flow therefrom will secure the speedy approval and legislative sanction of the States concerned. * * * * * *

I have been officially informed of the annexation of the States of the Church to the kingdom of Italy, and the removal of the capital of that kingdom to Rome. In conformity with the established policy of the United States, I have recognized this change.

* * * * * * *

The intimate friendly relations which have so long existed between the United States and Russia continue undisturbed. The visit of the third son of the Emperor is a proof that there is no desire on the part of his Government to diminish the cordiality of those relations. The hospitable reception which has been given to the Grand Duke is a proof that on our side we share the wishes of that Government. The inexcusable course of the Russian minister at Washington rendered it necessary to ask his recall, and to decline to longer receive that functionary as a diplomatic representative. It was impossible with self-respect, or with a just regard to the dignity of the country, to permit Mr. Catacazy to continue to hold intercourse with this Government after his personal abuse of Government officials, and during his persistent interference, through various means, with the relations between the United States and other Powers. In accordance with my wishes, this Government has been relieved of further intercourse with Mr. Catacazy, and the management of the affairs of the imperial legation has passed into the hands of a gentleman entirely unobjectionable. * *

The republic of Mexico has not yet repealed the very objectionable laws establishing what is known as the "Free Zone," on the frontier of the United States. It is hoped that this may yet be done, and also that more stringent measures may be taken by that republic for restraining lawless persons on its frontiers. I hope that Mexico, by its own action, will soon relieve this Government of the difficulties experienced from these causes. Our relations with the various republics of Central and South America continue, with one exception, to be cordial and friendly. * * * * *

It is a subject for congratulation that the great empire of Brazil has taken the initiatory step toward the abolition of slavery. Our relations with that empire, always cordial, will naturally be made more so by this act. It is not too much to hope that the Government of Brazil may hereafter find it for its interest as well as intrinsically right to advance toward entire emancipation more rapidly than the present act contemplates.

The true prosperity and greatness of a nation is to be found in the elevation and education of its laborers.

It is a subject for regret that the reforms in this direction, which were voluntarily promised by the statesmen of Spain, have not been carried out in its West India colonies. The laws and regulations for the apparent abolition of slavery in Cuba and Porto Rico leave most of the laborers in bondage, with no hope of release until their lives become a burden to their employers.

I desire to direct your attention to the fact that citizens of the United States, or persons claiming to be citizens of the United States, are large holders, in foreign lands, of this species of property, forbidden by the fundamental law of their alleged country. I recommend to Congress to provide, by stringent legislation, a suitable remedy against the holding, owning, or dealing in slaves, or being interested in slave property in foreign lands. either as owners, hirers, or mortgagers, by citizens of the United States.

It is to be regretted that the disturbed condition of the Island of Cuba continues to be a source of annoyance and of anxiety. The existence of a protracted struggle in such close proximity to our own territory, without apparent prospect of an early termination, cannot be other than an object of concern to a people who, while abstaining from interference in the affairs of other Powers, naturally desire to see every country in the undisturbed enjoyment of peace, liberty, and the blessings of free institutions.

Our naval commanders in Cuban waters have been instructed, in case it should become necessary, to spare no effort to protect the lives and property of *bona fide* American citizens, and to maintain the dignity of the flag.

It is hoped that all pending questions with Spain growing out of the affairs in Cuba may be adjusted in the spirit of peace and conciliation which has hitherto guided the two Powers in their treatment of such questions.

To give importance and to add to the efficiency of our diplomatic relations with Japan and China, and to further aid in retaining the good opinion of those peoples, and to secure to the United States its share of the commerce destined to flow between those nations and the balance of the commercial world, I earnestly recommend that an appropriation be made to support at least four American youths in each of those countries, to serve as a part of the official family of our ministers there. Our representatives would not even then be placed upon an eqnality with the representatives of Great Britain and of some other Powers. As now situated, our representatives in Japan and China have to depend, for interpreters and translators, upon natives of those countries who know our language imperfectly, or procure for the occasion the services of employés in foreign business houses, or the interpreters to other foreign ministers.

I would also recommend liberal measures for the purpose of supporting the American lines of steamers now plying between San Francisco and Japan and China, and the Australian line—almost our only remaining lines of ocean steamers—and of increasing their services.

The national debt has been reduced to the extent of $86,057,126 80 during the year, and by the negotiation of national bonds at a lower rate of interest, the interest on the public debt has been so far diminished that now the sum to be raised for the interest account is nearly seventeen million dollars less than on the 1st of March, 1869. It was highly desirable that this rapid diminution should take place, both to strengthen the credit of the country and to convince its citizens of their entire ability to meet every dollar of liability without bankrupting them. But in view of the accomplishment of these desirable ends; of the rapid development of the resources of the country; its increasing ability to meet large demands, and the amount already paid, it is not desirable that the present resources of the country should continue to be taxed in order to continue this rapid payment. I therefore recommend a modification of both the tariff and internal tax laws. I recommend that all taxes from internal sources be abolished, except those collected from spiritous, vinous, and malt liquors, tobacco in its various forms, and from stamps.

In readjusting the tariff I suggest that a careful estimate be made of the amount of surplus revenue collected under the present laws, after providing for the current expenses of the Government, the interest account, and a sinking fund, and that this surplus be reduced in such a manner as to afford the greatest relief to the greatest number. There are many articles not produced at home, but which enter largely into general consumption through articles which are manufactured at home, such as medicines compounded, &c., from which very little revenue is derived, but which enter into general use. All such articles I recommend to be placed on the "free list." Should a further reduction prove advisable, I would then recommend that it be made upon those articles which can best bear it without disturbing home production or reducing the wages of American labor.

I have not entered into figures, because to do so would be to repeat what will be laid before you in the report of the Secretary of the Treasury. The present laws for collecting revenue pay collectors of customs small salaries, but provide for moieties (shares in all seizures) which, at principal ports of entry particularly, raise the compensation of those officials to a large sum. It has always seemed to me as if this system must, at times, work perniciously. It holds out an inducement to dishonest men, should such get possession of those offices, to be lax in their scrutiny of goods entered to enable them finally to make large seizures. Your attention is respectfully invited to this subject.

Continued fluctuations in the value of gold, as compared with the national currency, has a most damaging effect upon the increase and development of the country in keeping up prices of all articles necessary in every-day life. It fosters a spirit of gambling prejudicial alike to national morals and the national finances. If the question can be met as to how to give a fixed value to our currency, that value constantly and uniformly approaching par with specie, a very desirable object will be gained. * * * * * *

The enlarged receipts of the Post Office Department, as shown by the accompanying report of the Postmaster General, exhibits a gratifying increase in that branch of the public service. It is the index of the growth of education and of the prosperity of the people, two elements highly conducive to the vigor and stability of republics. With a vast territory like ours, much of it sparsely populated, but all requiring the services of the mail, it is not at present to be expected that this Department can be made self-sustaining. But a gradual approach to this end from year to year is confidently relied on, and the day is not far distant when the Post Office Department of the Government will prove a much greater blessing to the whole people than it is now.

The suggestions of the Postmaster General for improvements in the Department presided over by him are earnestly recommended to your special attention. Especially do I recommend favorable consideration of the plan for uniting the telegraphic system of the United States with the postal system. It is believed that by such a course the cost of telegraphing could be much reduced, and the service as well, if not better, rendered. It would secure the further advantage of extending the telegraph through portions of the country where private enterprise will not construct it. Commerce, trade, and, above all, the efforts to bring a people widely separated into a community of interest, are always benefited by a rapid intercommunication. Education, the groundwork of republican institutions, is encouraged by increasing the facilities to gather speedy news from all parts of the country. The desire to reap the benefit of such improvements will stimulate education. I refer you to the report of the Postmaster General for full details of the operations of last year, and for comparative statements of results with former years.

There has been imposed upon the executive branch of the Government the execution of the act of Congress approved April 20, 1871, and commonly known as the Ku Klux law, in a portion of the State of South Carolina. The necessity of the course pursued will be demonstrated by the report of the Committee to Investigate Southern Outrages. Under the provisions of the above act I issued a proclamation calling the attention of the people of the United States to the same, and declaring my reluctance to exercise any of the extraordinary powers thereby conferred upon me, except in case of imperative necessity, but making known my purpose to exercise such powers whenever it should become necessary to do so for the purpose of securing to all citizens of the United States the peaceful enjoyment of the rights guarantied to them by the Constitution and the laws.

After the passage of this law, information was received from time to time that combinations of the character referred to in this law existed, and were powerful in many parts of the southern States, particularly in certain counties in the State of South Carolina.

Careful investigation was made, and it was ascertained that, in nine counties of that State, such combinatons were active and powerful, embracing a sufficient portion of the citizens to control the local authority, and having, among other things, the object of depriving the emancipated class of the substantial benefits of freedom, and of preventing the free political action of those citizens who did not sympathize with their own views. Among their operations were frequent scourgings and occasional assassinations, generally perpetrated at night by disguised persons, the victims in almost all cases being citizens of different political sentiments from their own, or freed persons who had shown a disposition to claim equal rights with other citizens. Thousands of inoffensive and well-disposed citizens were the sufferers by this lawless violence.

Thereupon, on the 12th of October, 1871, a proclamation was issued, in terms of the law, calling upon the members of those combinations to disperse within five days, and to deliver to the marshal or military officers of the United States all arms, ammunition, uniforms, disguises, and other means and implements used by them for carrying out their unlawful purposes.

This warning not having been heeded, on the 17th of October another proclamation was issued, suspending the privileges of the writ of *habeas corpus* in nine counties in that State.

Direction was given that within the counties so designated persons supposed, upon creditable information, to be members of such unlawful combinations should be arrested by the military forces of the United States, and delivered to the marshal, to be dealt with according to law. In two of said counties, York and Spartanburg, many arrests have been made. At the last account, the number of persons thus arrested was one hundred and sixty eight. Several hundred, whose criminality was ascertained to be of an inferior degree, were released for the present. These have generally made confessions of their guilt.

Great caution has been exercised in making these arrests, and, notwithstanding the large number, it is believed that no innocent person is now in custody. The prisoners will be held for regular trial in the judicial tribunals of the United States.

As soon as it appeared that the authorities of the United States were about to take vigorous measures to enforce the law, many persons absconded, and there is good ground for supposing that all of such persons have violated the law. A full report of what has been done under this law will be submitted to Congress by the Attorney General.

In Utah there still remains a remnant of barbarism, repugnant to civilization, to decency, and to the laws of the United States. Territorial officers, however, have been found who are willing to perform their duty in a spirit of equity and with a due sense of the necessity of sustaining the majesty of the law. Neither polygamy nor any other violation of existing statutes will be permitted within the territory of the United States. It is not with the religion of the self-styled Saints that we are now dealing, but with their practices. They will be protected in the worship of God according to the dictates of their consciences, but they will not be permitted to violate the laws under the cloak of religion.

It may be advisable for Congress to consider what, in the execution of the laws against polygamy, is to be the status of plural wives and their offspring. The propriety of Congress passing an enabling act authorizing the territorial Legislature of Utah to legitimize all children born prior to a time fixed in the act might be justified by its humanity to these innocent children. This is a suggestion only, and not a recommendation.

The policy pursued toward the Indians has resulted favorably, so far as can be judged from the limited time during which it has been in operation. Through the exertions of the various societies of Christians to whom has been intrusted the execution of the policy, and the board of commissioners authorized by the law of April 10, 1869, many tribes of Indians have been induced to settle upon reservations, to cultivate the soil, to perform productive labor of various kinds, and to partially accept civilization. They are being cared for in such a way, it is hoped, as to induce those still pursuing their old habits of life to embrace the only opportunity which is left them to avoid extermination.

I recommend liberal appropriations to carry out the Indian peace policy, not only because it is humane, Christian-like, and economical, but because it is right.

I recommend to your favorable consideration also the policy of granting a territorial government to the Indians in the Indian territory west of Arkansas and Missouri and south of Kansas. In doing so, every right guarantied to the Indian by treaty should be secured. Such a course might in time be the means of collecting most of the Indians now between the Missouri and the Pacific and south of the British possessions into one Territory or one State. The Secretary of the Interior has treated upon this subject at length, and I commend to you his suggestions.

I renew my recommendation that the public lands be regarded as a heritage to our children, to be disposed of only as required for occupation and to actual settlers. Those already granted have been in great part disposed of in such a way as to secure access to the balance by the hardy settler who may wish to avail himself of them, but caution should be exercised even in attaining so desirable an object.

Educational interests may well be served by the grant of the proceeds of the sale of public lands to settlers. I do not wish to be understood as recommending, in the least degree, a curtailment of what is being done by the General Government for the encouragement of education. * * * * *

More than six years having elapsed since the last hostile gun was fired between the armies then arrayed against each other—one for the perpetuation, the other for the destruction of the Union—it may well be considered whether it is not now time that the disabilities imposed by the fourteenth amendment should be removed. That amendment does not exclude the ballot, but only imposes the disability to hold offices upon certain classes. When the purity of the ballot is secure, majorities are sure to elect officers reflecting the views of the majority. I do not see the advantage or propriety of excluding men from office merely because they were, before the rebellion, of standing and character sufficient to be elected to positions requiring them to take oaths to support the Constitution, and admitting to eligibility those entertaining precisely the same views, but of less standing in their communities. It may be said that the former violated an oath, while the latter did not. The latter did not have it in their power to do so. If they had taken this oath it cannot be doubted they would have broken it as did the former class. If there are any great criminals, distinguished above all others for the part they took in opposition to the Government, they might, in the judgment of Congress, be excluded from such an amnesty.

This subject is submitted for your careful consideration.

The condition of the southern States is, unhappily, not such as all true patriotic citizens would like to see. Social ostracism for opinion's sake, personal violence or threats toward persons entertaining political views opposed to those entertained by the majority of the old citizens, prevents immigration and the flow of much-needed capital into the States lately in rebellion. It will be a happy condition of the country when the old citizens of these States will take an interest in public affairs, promulgate ideas honestly entertained, vote for men representing their views, and tolerate the same freedom of expression and ballot in those entertaining different political convictions. * * * * *

The number of immigrants ignorant of our laws, habits, &c., coming into our country annually has become so great, and the impositions practiced upon them so numerous and flagrant, that I suggest congressional action for their protection. It seems to me a fair subject of legislation by Congress. I cannot now state as fully as I desire the nature of the complaints made by immigrants of the treatment they receive, but will endeavor to do so during the session of Congress, particularly if the subject should receive your attention.

It has been the aim of the Administration to enforce honesty and efficiency in all public offices. Every public servant who has violated the trust placed in him has been proceeded against with all the rigor of the law. If bad men have secured places it has been the fault of the system established by law and custom for making appointments, or the fault of those who recommend for Government positions persons not sufficiently well known to them personally, or who give letters indorsing the characters of office-seekers without a proper sense of the grave responsibility which such a course devolves upon them. A civil service reform which can correct this abuse is much desired. In mercantile pursuits, the business man who gives a letter of recommendation to a friend, to enable him to obtain credit from a stranger, is regarded as morally responsible for the integrity of his friend, and his ability to meet his obligations. A reformatory law which would enforce this principle against all indorsers of persons for public place would insure great caution in making recommendations. A salutary lesson has been taught the careless and the dishonest public servant in the great number of prosecutions and convictions of the last two years.

It is gratifying to notice the favorable change which is taking place throughout the country in bringing to punishment those who have proven recreant to the trusts confided to them, and in elevating to public office none but those who possess the confidence of the honest and the virtuous, who, it will always be found, comprise the majority of the community in which they live.

In my message to Congress one year ago I urgently recommended a reform in the civil service of the country. In conformity with that recommendation, Congress, in the ninth section of "An act making appropriations for sundry civil expenses of the Government, and for other purposes," approved March 3, 1871, gave the necessary authority to the Executive to inaugurate a civil service reform, and placed upon him the responsibility of doing so. Under the authority of said act I convened a board of gentlemen, eminently qualified for the work, to devise rules and regulations to effect the needed reform. Their labors are not yet complete, but it is believed that they will succeed in devising a plan that can be adopted to the great relief of the Executive, the heads of Departments, and members of Congress, and which will redound to the true interest of the public service. At all events, the experiment shall have a fair trial.

I have thus hastily summed up the operations of the Government during the last year, and made such suggestions as occur to me to be proper for your consideration. I submit them with a confidence that your combined action will be wise, statesmanlike, and in the best interests of the whole country.

U. S. GRANT.

V.

PRESIDENT GRANT'S SPECIAL MESSAGES.

[For President Grant's special messages on increasing American commerce, the ratification of the treaty with San Domingo, and respecting Cuban affairs, and for his proclamation against the Fenian invasion of Canada, see McPherson's History of Reconstruction, page 540 to 544. For his special message on the ratification of the fifteenth amendment, see same volume, page 545. For his order respecting wages and hours of labor, see same volume, page 421.]

Relative to a Territorial Government for the Indians, January 30, 1871.

To the Senate and House of Representatives:

I transmit herewith an official copy of the proceedings of the council of Indian tribes held at Ocmulgee, in December last, which resulted in the adoption of a declaration of rights and a constitution for their government, together with a copy of the report of the Commissioner of Indian Affairs, and the views of the Secretary of the Interior thereon.

It would seem highly desirable that the civilized Indians of the country should be encouraged in establishing for themselves forms of territorial government compatible with the Constitution of the United States and with the previous custom toward communities lying outside of State limits.

I concur in the views expressed by the Secretary of the Interior, that it would not be advisable to receive the new territory with the constitution precisely as it is now framed.

So long as a territorial form of government is preserved, Congress should hold the power of approving or disapproving of all legislative action of the Territory; and the Executive should, with "the advice and consent of the Senate," have the power to appoint the Governor and judicial officers (and possibly some others) of the Territory.

This is the first indication of the aborigines desiring to adopt our form of government, and it is highly desirable that they become self-sustaining, self-relying, christianized, and civilized. If successful in this their first attempt at territorial government, we may hope for a gradual concentration of other Indians in the new Territory. I therefore recommend as close an adherence to their wishes as is consistent with safety.

It might be well to limit the appointment of all territorial officials appointed by the Executive to native citizens of the Territory. If any exception is made to this rule, I would recommend that it should be limited to the judiciary.

It is confidently hoped that the policy now being pursued toward the Indian will fit him for self-government, and make him desire to settle among people of his own race, where he can enjoy the full privileges of civil and enlightened government.

U. S. GRANT.

Relative to the Union of the States of Germany, February 7, 1871.

To the Senate and House of Representatives:

The union of the States of Germany into a form of government similar in many respects to that of the American Union is an event that cannot fail to touch deeply the sympathies of the people of the United States.

This union has been brought about by the long-continued, persistent efforts of the people, with the deliberate approval of the governments and people of twenty-four of the German States, through their regularly-constituted representatives.

In it the American people see an attempt to reproduce in Europe some of the best features of our own Constitution, with such modifications as the history and condition of Germany seem to require. The local governments of the several members of the union are preserved, while the powers conferred upon the chief impart strength for the purposes of self-defense, without authority to enter upon wars of conquest and ambition.

The cherished aspiration for national unity, which for ages has inspired the many millions of people speaking the same language, inhabiting a contiguous and compact territory, but unnaturally separated and divided by dynastic jealousies and the ambition of short-sighted rulers, has been attained; and Germany now contains a population of about thirty-four millions, united, like our own, under one Government for its relations with other Powers, but retaining in its several members the right and power of control of their local interests, habits, and instructions.

The bringing of great masses of thoughtful and free people under a single Government must tend to make Governments what alone they should be, the representatives of the will and the organization of the power of the people.

The adoption in Europe of the American system of union, under the control and direction of a free people, educated to self-restraint, cannot fail to extend popular institutions and to enlarge the peaceful influence of American ideas.

The relations of the United States with Germany are intimate and cordial; the commercial intercourse between the two countries is extensive, and is increasing from year to year; and the large number of citizens and residents in the United States of German extraction, and the continued flow of emigration thence to this country, have produced an intimacy of personal and political intercourse approaching, if not equal, to that with the country from which the founders of our Government derived their origin.

The extent of these interests, and the greatness of the German union, seem to require that in the classification of the representatives of this Government to foreign Powers there should no longer be an apparent undervaluation of the importance of the German mission, such as is made in the difference between the compensation allowed by law to the minister to Germany and those to Great Britain and France. There would seem to be a great propriety in placing the representative of this Government at Berlin on the same footing with that of its representatives at London and Paris. The union of the several States of Germany under one Government, and the increasing commercial and personal intercourse between the two countries, will also add to the labors and the responsibilities of the legation.

I therefore recommend that the salaries of the minister and of the secretary of legation at Berlin be respectively increased to the same amounts as are allowed to those at London and at Paris.

U. S. GRANT.

On the Test-Oath, February 15, 1871.

To the Senate and House of Representatives:

I have this day transmitted to the Senate the announcement that Senate bill No. 218, "An act prescribing an oath of office to be taken by persons who participated in the late rebellion, but who are not disqualified from holding office by the fourteenth amendment to the Constitution of the United States," has become a law in the manner prescribed by the Constitution, without the signature of the President.

If this were a bill for the repeal of the "test oath" required of persons "elected or appointed to offices of honor or trust," it would meet my approval. The effect of the law, however, is to relieve from taking a prescribed oath all those persons whom it was intended to exclude from such offices, and to require it from all others. By this law the soldier who fought and bled for his country is to swear to his loyalty before assuming official functions, while the general who commanded hosts for the overthrow of his Government is admitted to place without it. I cannot affix my name to a law which discriminates against the upholder of his Government.

I believe, however, that it is not wise policy to keep from office by an oath those who are not disqualified by the Constitution and who are the choice of legal voters; but, while relieving them from an oath which they cannot take, I recommend the release also of those to whom the oath has no application.

U. S. GRANT.

On the Condition of the lately Insurrectionary States, March 23, 1871.

To the Senate and House of Representatives:

A condition of affairs now exists in some States of the Union rendering life and property insecure and the carrying of the mails and the collection of the revenue dangerous. The proof that such a condition of affairs exists in some localities is now before the Senate. That the power to correct these evils is beyond the control of the State authorities I do not doubt; that the power of the Executive of the United States, acting within the limits of existing laws, is sufficient for present emergencies, is not clear. Therefore, I urgently recommend such legislation as in the judgment of Congress shall effectually secure life, liberty, and property, and the enforcement of law in all parts of the United States. It may be expedient to provide that such law as shall be passed in pursuance of this recommendation shall expire at the end of the next session of Congress. There is no other subject upon which I would recommend legislation during the present Congress.

U. S. GRANT.

Transmitting the Report of the Commissioners appointed to Visit San Domingo, April 5, 1871.

To the Senate and House of Representatives:

I have the honor to submit herewith to the two Houses of Congress the report of the commissioners appointed in pursuance of joint resolution approved January 12, 1871.

It will be observed that this report more than sustains all that I have heretofore said in regard to the productiveness and healthfulness of the republic of San Domingo, of the unanimity of the people for annexation to the United States, and of their peaceable character.

It is due to the public, as it certainly is to myself, that I should here give all the circumstances which first led to the negotiation of a treaty for the annexation of the republic of San Domingo to the United States.

When I accepted the arduous and responsible position which I now hold, I did not dream of instituting any steps for the acquisition of insular possessions. I believed, however, that our institutions were broad enough to extend over the entire continent as rapidly as other peoples might desire to bring themselves under our protection. I believed further that we should not permit any independent Government within the limits of North America to pass from a condition of independence to one of ownership or protection under a European Power.

Soon after my inauguration as President, I was waited upon by an agent of President Baez with a proposition to annex the republic of San Domingo to the United States. This gentleman represented the capacity of the island, the desire of the people, and their character and habits, about as they have been described by the commissioners, whose report accompanies this message. He stated further that, being weak in numbers and poor in purse, they were not capable of developing their great resources; that the people had no incentive to industry on account of lack of protection for their accumulations; and that, if not accepted by the United States—with institutions which they loved above those of any other nation—they would be compelled to seek protection elsewhere. To these statements I made no reply, and gave no indication of what I thought of the proposition. In the course of time I was waited upon by a second gentleman from San Domingo, who made the same representations, and who was received in like manner.

In view of the facts which had been laid before me, and with an earnest desire to maintain the "Monroe doctrine," I believed that I would be derelict in my duty if I did not take measures to ascertain the exact wish of the Government and inhabitants of the republic of San Domingo in regard to annexation, and communicate the information to the people of the United States. Under the attending circumstances I felt that if I turned a deaf ear to this appeal I might, in the future, be justly charged with a flagrant neglect of the public interests and an utter disregard of the welfare of a downtrodden race praying for the blessings of a free and strong Government, and for protection in the enjoyment of the fruits of their own industry.

Those opponents of annexation who have heretofore professed to be preëminently the friends of the rights of man I believed would be my most violent assailants if I neglected so clear a duty. Accordingly, after having appointed a commissioner to visit the island, who declined on account of sickness, I selected a second gentleman, in whose capacity, judgment, and integrity I had, and have yet, the most unbounded confidence.

He visited San Domingo, not to secure or hasten annexation, but, unprejudiced and unbiased, to learn all the facts about the Government, the people, and the resources of that republic. He went certainly as well prepared to make an unfavorable report as a favorable one, if the facts warranted it. His report fully corroborated the views of previous commissioners, and upon its receipt I felt that a sense of duty and a due regard for our great national interests required me to negotiate a treaty for the acquisition of the republic of San Domingo.

As soon as it became publicly known that such a treaty had been negotiated, the attention of the country was occupied with allegations calculated to prejudice the merits of the case, and with aspersions upon those whose duty had connected them with it. Amid the public excitement thus created the treaty failed to receive the requisite two-thirds vote of the Senate, and was rejected; but whether the action of that body was based wholly upon the merits of the treaty, or might not have been, in some degree, influenced by such unfounded allegations, could not be known by the people, because the debates of the Senate in secret session are not published.

Under these circumstances I deemed it due to the office which I hold, and due to the character of the agents who had been charged with the investigation, that such proceedings should be had as would enable the people to know the truth. A commission was therefore constituted, under authority of Congress, consisting of gentlemen selected with special reference to their high character and capacity for the laborious work intrusted to them, who were instructed to visit the spot and report upon the facts. Other eminent citizens were requested to accompany the commission in order that the people might have the benefit of their views. Students of science and correspondents of the press, without regard to political opinions, were invited to join the expedition, and their numbers were limited only by the capacity of the vessel.

The mere rejection by the Senate of a treaty negotiated by the President only indicates a difference of opinion between two coördinate departments of the Government, without touching the character or wounding the pride of either. But when such rejection takes place simultaneously with charges openly made of corruption on the part of the President, or those employed by him, the case is different. Indeed, in such case the honor of the nation demands investigation. This has been accomplished by the report of the commissioners herewith transmitted, and which fully vindicates the purity of the motives and action of those who represented the United States in the negotiation.

And now my task is finished, and with it ends all personal solicitude upon the subject. My duty being done, yours begins; and I gladly hand over the whole matter to the judgment of the American people, and of their representatives in Congress assembled. The facts will now be spread before the country, and a decision rendered by that tribunal whose convictions so seldom err, and against whose will I have no policy to enforce. My opinion remains unchanged; indeed, it is confirmed by the report that the interests of our country and of San Domingo alike invite the annexation of that republic.

In view of the difference of opinion upon this subject, I suggest that no action be taken at the present session beyond the printing and general dissemination of the report. Before the next session of Congress the people will have considered the subject and formed an intelligent opinion concerning it; to which opinion, deliberately made up, it will be the duty of every department of the Government to give heed, and no one will more cheerfully conform to it than myself. It is not only the theory of our Constitution that the will of the people, constitutionally expressed, is the supreme law, but I have ever believed that "all men are wiser than any one man;" and if the people, upon a full presentation of the facts, shall decide that the annexation of the republic is not desirable, every department of the Government ought to acquiesce in that decision.

In again submitting to Congess a subject upon which public sentiment has been divided, and which has been made the occasion of acrimonious debates in Congress, as well as of unjust aspersions elsewhere, I may, I trust, be indulged in a single remark.

No man could hope to perform duties so delicate and responsible as pertain to the presidential office without sometimes incurring the hostility of those who deem their opinions and wishes treated with insufficient consideration and he who undertakes to conduct the affairs of a great Government as a faithful public servant, if sustained by the approval of his own conscience, may rely with confidence upon the candor and intelligence of a free people, whose best interests he has striven to subserve, and can bear with patience the censure of disappointed men.

U. S. Grant.

Transmitting the Report of the Civil Service Commission, December 19, 1871.

To the Senate and House of Representatives:

In accordance with the act of Congress approved March 4, 1871, I convened a commission of eminent gentlemen to devise rules and regulations for the purpose of reforming the civil service. Their labors are now complete, and I transmit herewith their report, together with the rules which they recommend for my action. These rules have been adopted, and will go into effect on the 1st day of January, 1872.

Under the law referred to, as I interpret it, the authority is already invested in the Executive to enforce these regulations, with full power to abridge, alter, or amend them at his option, when changes may be deemed advisable. These views, together with the report of the commissioners, are submitted for your careful consideration as to whether further legislation may be necessary in order to carry out an effective and beneficial civil service reform.

If left to me, without further congressional action, the rules prescribed by the commission, under the reservation already mentioned, will be faithfully executed; but they are not binding, without further legislation, upon my successors.

Being desirous of bringing this subject to

the attention of Congress before the approaching recess, I have not time to sufficiently examine the accompanying report to enable me to suggest definite legislative action to insure the support which may be necessary in order to give a thorough trial to a policy long needed.

I ask for all the strength which Congress can give me to enable me to carry out the reforms in the civil service recommended by the commissioners, and adopted, to take effect, as before stated, on January 1, 1872.

The law which provides for the convening of a commission to devise rules and regulations for reforming the civil service authorizes, I think, the permanent organization of a primary board, under whose general direction all examinations of applicants for public office shall be conducted. There is no appropriation to continue such a board beyond the termination of its present labors. I therefore recommend that a proper appropriation be made to continue the services of the present board for another year, and in view of the fact that three members of the board hold positions in the public service which precludes them from receiving extra compensation under existing laws, that they be authorized to receive a fair compensation for extra services rendered by them in the performance of this duty.

U. S. GRANT.

On Lawlessness in South Carolina, April 19, 1872.

To the House of Representatives :

In answer to the resolution of the House of Representatives of the 25th of January last, I have the honor to submit the following, accompanied by the report of the Attorney General, to whom the resolution was referred.

Representations having been made to me that in certain portions of South Carolina a condition of lawlessness and terror existed, I requested the then Attorney General Akerman to visit that State and after personal examination to report to me the facts in relation to the subject. On the 16th of October last he addressed me a communication from South Carolina, in which he stated that in the counties of Spartanburg, York, Chester, Union, Laurens, Newberry, Fairfield, Lancaster, and Chesterfield there were combinations for the purpose of preventing the free political action of citizens who were friendly to the Constitution and the Government of the United States, and of depriving the emancipated classes of the equal protection of the laws.

"These combinations embrace at least two thirds of the active white men of those counties, and have the sympathy and countenance of a majority of the other third. They are connected with similar combinations in other counties and States, and no doubt are part of a grand system of criminal associations pervading most of the southern States. The members are bound to obedience and secrecy by oaths which they are taught to regard as of higher obligation than the lawful oaths taken before civil magistrates.

"They are organized and armed. They effect their objects by personal violence, often extending to murder. They terrify witnesses. They control juries in the State courts, and sometimes in the courts of the United States. Systematic perjury is one of the means by which prosecutions of the members are defeated. From information given by officers of the State and of the United States and by credible private citizens, I am justified in affirming that the instances of criminal violence perpetrated by these combinations within the last twelve months in the above-named counties could be reckoned by thousands."

I received information of a similar import from various other sources, among which were the joint select Committee of Congress upon Southern Outrages, the officers of the State, the military officers of the United States on duty in South Carolina, the United States attorney and marshal, and other civil officers of the Government, repentant and abjuring members of those unlawful organizations, persons specially employed by the Department of Justice to detect crimes against the United States, and from other credible persons.

Most, if not all, of this information, except what I derived from the Attorney General, came to me orally, and was to the effect that said counties were under the sway of powerful combinations, properly known as "Ku Klux Klans," the objects of which were, by force and terror, to prevent all political action not in accord with the views of the members, to deprive colored citizens of the right to bear arms, and of the right to a free ballot; to suppress schools in which colored children were taught, and to reduce the colored people to a condition closely akin to that of slavery; that these combinations were organized and armed, and had rendered the local laws ineffectual to protect the classes whom they desired to oppress; that they had perpetrated many murders, and hundreds of crimes of minor degree, all of which were unpunished; and that witnesses could not safely testify against them unless the more active members were placed under restraint.

U. S. GRANT.

On Treatment of Immigrants, May 14, 1872.

To the Senate and House of Representatives of the United States :

In my message to Congress at the beginning of its present session, allusion was made to the hardships and privations inflicted upon poor immigrants on shipboard and upon arrival on our shores; and a suggestion was made favoring national legislation for the purpose of effecting a radical cure of the evil.

Promise was made that a special message on this subject would be presented during the present session should information be received which would warrant it. I now transmit to the two Houses of Congress all that has been officially received since that time bearing upon the subject, and recommend that such legislation be had as will secure, first. such room and accommodations on shipboard as are necessary for health and comfort, and such privacy and protection as not to compel immigrants to be the unwilling witnesses to so much vice and misery; and, second, legislation to protect them upon their arrival at our seaports from the knaves who are ever ready to despoil them of the little all which they are able to bring with them. Such legislation will be in the interests of humanity, and seem to be fully justifiable. The immigrant is not a citizen of any State or Territory upon his arrival, but comes here to become a citizen of a great republic, free to change his residence at will, to enjoy the blessing of a protecting Government, where all are equal before the law, and to add to the national wealth by his industry.

On his arrival he does not know States or corporations, but confides implicitly in the protecting arms of the great, free country of which he has heard so much before leaving his native land. It is a source of serious disappointment and discouragement to those who start with means sufficient to support them comfortably until they can choose a residence and begin employment for a comfortable support to find themselves subject to ill-treatment and every discomfort on their passage here, and at the end of their journey seized upon by professed friends, claiming legal right to take charge of them for their protection, who do not leave them until all their resources are exhausted, when they are abandoned in a strange land, surrounded by strangers, without employment and ignorant of the means of securing it. Under the present system this is the fate of thousands annually, the exposures on shipboard and the treatment on landing driving thousands to lives of vice and shame who, with proper humane treatment, might become useful and respectable members of society.

I do not advise national legislation in affairs that should be regulated by the States, but I see no subject more national in its character than provision for the safety and welfare of the thousands who leave foreign lands to become citizens of this Republic.

When their residence is chosen they may then look to the laws of their locality for protection and guidance.

The mass of immigrants arriving upon our shores, coming as they do on vessels under foreign flags, makes treaties with the nations furnishing these immigrants necessary for their complete protection. For more than two years efforts have been made, on our part, to secure such treaties, and there is now reasonable ground to hope for success.

U. S. Grant.

Veto Message on J. Milton Best's Claim Bill, June 1, 1872.

To the Senate of the United States:

I have examined the bill (S. No. 105) entitled "An act for the relief of J. Milton Best," and being unable to give it my approval, return the same to the Senate, the House in which it originated, without my signature.

The bill appropriates the sum of $25,000 to compensate Dr. J. Milton Best for the destruction of his dwelling house and its contents by order of the commanding officer of the United States military forces at Paducah, Kentucky, on the 26th day of March, 1864. It appears that this house was one of a considerable number destroyed for the purpose of giving open range to the guns of a United States fort. On the day preceding the destruction the houses had been used as a cover for rebel troops attacking the fort, and apprehending a renewal of the attack, the commanding officer caused the destruction of the houses. This, then, is a claim for compensation on account of the ravages of war. It cannot be denied that the payment of this claim would invite the presentation of demands for very large sums of money; and such is the supposed magnitude of the claims that may be made against the Government for necessary and unavoidable destruction of property by the Army that I deem it proper to return this bill for reconsideration.

It is a general principle of both international and municipal law that all property is held subject not only to be taken by the Government for public uses, in which case under the Constitution of the United States the owner is entitled to just compensation, but also subject to be temporarily occupied, or even actually destroyed in times of great public danger, and when the public safety demands it, and in this latter case Governments do not admit a legal obligation on their part to compensate the owner. The temporary occupation of, injuries to, and destruction of property caused by actual and necessary military operations, is generally considered to fall within the last-mentioned principle. If a Government makes compensation under such circumstances, it is a matter of bounty rather than of strict legal right.

If it be deemed proper to make compensation for such losses, I suggest for the consideration of Congress whether it would not be better, by general legislation, to provide some means for the ascertainment of the damage in all similar cases, and thus save to claimants the expense, inconvenience, and delay of attendance upon Congress, and, at the same time, save the Government from the danger of having imposed upon it fictitious or exaggerated claims supported wholly by *ex parte* proof. If the claimant in this case ought to be paid, so ought all others similarly situated, and that there are many such cannot be doubted. Besides, there are strong reasons for believing that the amount of damage in this case has been greatly over-estimated. If this be true, it furnishes an illustration of the danger of trusting entirely to *ex parte* testimony in such matters.

U. S. Grant.

A like bill for the relief of Thomas B. Wallace, of Lexington, Missouri, was also vetoed a day or two later.

VI.

POLITICAL VOTES IN THIRD SESSION OF FORTY-FIRST CONGRESS.

On Appointing Commissioners to San Domingo.

IN SENATE.

1870, December 21—This resolution passed the Senate:

JOINT RESOLUTION authorizing the appointment of commissioners in relation to the Republic of Dominica.

Resolved, &c., That the President of the United States be authorized to appoint three commissioners, and also a secretary, the latter to be versed in the English and Spanish languages, to proceed to the island of San Domingo and to inquire into, ascertain, and report the political state and condition of the republic of Dominica, the desire and disposition of the people of the said republic to become annexed to, and to form part of, the people of the United States; the physical, mental, and moral condition of the said people, and their general condition as to material wealth and industrial capacity; the resources of the country; its mineral and agricultural products; the products of its waters and forests; the general character of the soil; the extent and proportion thereof capable of cultivation; the climate and health of the country; its bays, harbors, and rivers; its general meteorological character, and the existence and frequency of remarkable meteorological phenomena; the debt of the Government and its obligations, whether funded and ascertained and admitted, or unadjusted and under discussion; treaties or engagements with other Powers; extent of boundaries and territory—what proportion is covered by grants or concessions, and generally what concessions or franchises have been granted; the terms and conditions on which the Dominican Government may desire to be annexed to and become part of the United States as one of the Territories thereof; such other information with respect to the said Government, or its territories, as to the said commissioners shall seem desirable or important with reference to the future incorporation of the said Dominican republic into the United States as one of its Territories.

SEC. 2. That the said commissioners shall, as soon as conveniently may be, report to the President of the United States, who shall lay their report before Congress.

SEC. 3. That the said commissioners shall serve without compensation except the payment of expenses, and the compensation of the secretary shall be determined by the Secretary of State, with the approval of the President.

Yeas 32, nays 9:

YEAS—Messrs. Abbott, Ames, Brownlow, Carpenter, Chandler, Cole, Conkling, Corbett, Cragin, Edmunds, Flanagan, Hamilton of Texas, Hamlin, Harlan, Howe, Howell, Morton, Nye, Osborn, Pomeroy, Pool, Ramsey, Revels, Ross, Sawyer, Scott, Sherman, Stewart, Thayer, Warner, Willey, Williams—32.

NAYS—Messrs. *Casserly*, *McCreery*, Morrill of Vermont, Patterson, Schurz, *Stockton*, Sumner, *Thurman*, Tipton—9.

IN HOUSE.

1871, January 10—Mr. AMBLER submitted the following addition:

"*Provided*, That nothing in these resolutions contained shall be held, understood, or construed as committing Congress to the policy of annexing the territory of said republic of Dominica."

Which was agreed to—yeas 108, nays 76:

YEAS—Messrs. *Adams*, Ambler, *Archer*, Asper, *Axtell*, *Barnum*, Beaman, Beatty, *Beck*, *Biggs*, *Bird*, *Booker*, Boyd, G. M. Brooks, *J. Brooks*, Burchard, *Burr*, *Calkin*, Coburn, Conger, *Conner*, Cook, *Cox*, *Crebs*, Dawes, Dickey, *Dickinson*, *Dox*, *Duke*, Ela, *Eldredge*, Farnsworth, Ferriss, Finkelnburg, *Fox*, Garfield, *Getz*, *Gibson*, *Griswold*, *Haight*, *Haldeman*, Hale, *Hamill*, Hawkins, Hawley, Hay, Hoar, *Holman*, Hooper, *Johnson*, Judd, Julian, Kelsey, *Kerr*, *Lewis*, *Manning*, *Marshall*, *Mayham*, *McCormick*, McCrary, *Morgan*, Morrell, *Morrissey*, *Mungen*, *Niblack*, Palmer, Peters, Pomeroy, *Potter*, *Randall*, *Reeves*, *Rice*, *Rogers*, Sargent, *Schumaker*, Shanks, L. A. Sheldon, *Sherrod*, *Shober*, *Slocum*, J. A. Smith, *J. S. Smith*, Starkweather, A. F. Stevens, *Stone*, Strong, *Swann*, *Sweeney*, Tanner, Tillman, W. Townsend, *Trimble*, Tyner, Upson, *Van Auken*, *Van Trump*, *Voorhees*, Washburn, Welker, *Wells*, Wheeler, Willard, Williams, *E. M. Wilson*, J. T. Wilson, *Winchester*, Wolf, *Wood*—108.

NAYS—Messrs. Armstrong, Arnell, Atwood, Ayer, Bailey, Banks, Barry, Benjamin, Bennett, Bingham, Bowen, Buck, Buffinton, Burdett, B. F. Butler, R. R. Butler, Churchill, W. T. Clark, A. Cobb, C. L. Cobb, Degener, Donley, Duval, Fisher, Fitch, Gilfillan, Hamilton, Harris, Heflin, Hoge, Jenckes, A. H. Jones, Kelley, Kellogg, Ketcham, Knapp, Laflin, Lawrence, Loughridge, Maynard, McCarthy, McGrew, McKee, McKenzie, Mercur, J. H. Moore, W. Moore, Morphis, Myers, Negley, O'Neill, Orth, Packard, H. E. Paine, Peck, Perce, Platt, Poland, Porter, Prosser, Rainey, Sawyer, Scofield, P. Sheldon, W. J. Smith, Stevenson, Stokes, Stoughton, Taylor, Twichell, Van Horn, Van Wyck, Wallace, Whitmore, Winans, Witcher—76.

The resolution then passed—yeas 122, nays 63. The negative vote was exclusively Democratic, except Messrs. Beatty, Boyd, Finkelnburg, Hoar, Peters, and Willard. The affirmative vote was exclusively Republican.

IN SENATE.

1871, January 11—Various amendments were proposed and rejected, when the House amendment was agreed to—yeas 57, nays none.

[For President Grant's Message transmitting the report of the commissioners appointed under this act, see chapter V.]

Modification of the Test-Oath.

IN SENATE.

1870, April 22—The following bill passed without a division:

A BILL prescribing an oath of office to be taken by persons who participated in the late rebellion but who were not disqualified from holding office by the fourteenth amendment to the Constitution of the United States.

Be it enacted, &c., That when any person, who is not rendered ineligible to office by the provisions of the fourteenth amendment to the Constitution, shall be elected or appointed to any office of honor or trust under the Government of the United States, and shall not be able on account of his participation in the late rebellion to take the oath prescribed in the act of Congress approved July 2, 1862, said person shall, in lieu of said oath, before entering upon the duties of said office, take and subscribe the oath prescribed in an act of Congress entitled "An act prescribing an oath of office to be taken by persons from whom legal disabilities shall have been removed," approved July 11, 1868.

IN HOUSE.

1871, February 1—The bill passed—yeas 118, nays 90:

YEAS—Messrs. *Adams*, *Archer*, Asper, *Axtell*, Ayer, Bailey, Banks, *Barnum*, *Beck*, Bethune, *Biggs*, Bingham, *Bird*, A. Blair, *Booker*, Buck, Buckley, Burchard, *Burr*, *Calkin*, Churchill, S. Clarke, *Cleveland*, *Conner*, Cook, *Cox*, *Crebs*, Darrall, Degener, *Dickinson*, J. Dixon, Dockery, *Dox*, *Duke*, Dyer, *Eldredge*, Farnsworth, Finkelnburg, Garfield, *Getz*, *Gibson*, *Griswold*, *Haight*, *Haldeman*, Hale, *Hambleton*, *Hamill*, Harris, Hay, Heflin, Hill, *Holman*, Hotchkiss, Jenckes, *Johnson*, *T. L. Jones*, Judd, Kellogg, *Kerr*, Ketcham, Laflin, *Lewis*, Lynch, *Manning*, *Marshall*, *Mayham*, *McCormick*, McKee, McKenzie, *McNeely*, Morey, *Morgan*, Morphis, *Niblack*, H. E. Paine, *W. W. Paine*, Perce, Peters, Platt, Poland, *Potter*, *Price*, *Randall*, *Reeves*, *Rice*, Sanford, Sargent, L. A. Sheldon, *Sherrod*, *Shober*, *Slocum*, John A. Smith, *Joseph S. Smith*, *Stiles*, *Stone*, *Strader*, Strickland, Strong, *Swann*, *Sweeney*, Sypher, Taylor, Tillman, *Trimble*, Upson, *Van Auken*, *Van Trump*, *Voorhees*, Wallace, Washburn, *Wells*, *E. M. Wilson*, Winans, *Winchester*, Witcher, *Wood*, *Woodward*, *Young*—118.

NAYS—Messrs. Allison, Ambler, Arnell, Atwood, Beaman, Beatty, Benjamin, Bennett, Benton, G. M. Brooks, Buffinton, Burdett, B. F. Butler, R. R. Butler, Cessna, W. T. Clark, A. Cobb, C. L. Coburn, Conger, Cowles, Cullom, Dawes, Dickey, N. F. Dixon, Donley, Duval, Ela, Ferriss, Ferry, Fisher, Gilfillan, Hawley, Hoar, Hoge, Holmes, Julian, Kelley, Kelsey, Knapp, Lawrence, Logan, Long, Loughridge, Maynard, McCrary, McGrew, Mercur, E. H. Moore, J. H. Moore, W. Moore, Morrell, Myers, Newsham, O'Neill, Orth, Packard, Packer, Palmer, Peck, Phelps, Pomeroy, Porter, Prosser, Rainey, Roots, Sawyer, Scofield, Shanks, W. J. Smith, Starkweather, Stevens, Stokes, Stoughton, Taffe, Tanner, W. Townsend, Twichell, Tyner, Van Horn, Van Wyck, Ward, W. B. Washburn, Welker, Wheeler, Wilkinson, Willard, Williams, J. T. Wilson, Wolf—90.

[For President Grant's Message on this bill, see chapter V.

Bill to Repeal the Tenure-of-Office Act.

IN HOUSE.

1870, December 12—Mr. BENJAMIN F. BUTLER introduced a bill to repeal the acts relating to the tenure of civil offices, passed March 2, 1867, and April 5, 1869; which passed finally—yeas 159, nays 25:

YEAS—Messrs. Allison, Armstrong, Asper, Atwood, *Axtell*, Ayer, Bailey, Banks, Barry, Beaman, *Beck*, Bingham, *Bird*, A. Blair, Boles, Bowen, Boyd, G. M. Brooks, *J. Brooks*, Buckley, Buffington, Burchard, Burdett, *Burr*, B. F. Butler, R. R. Butler, *Calkin*, Churchill, W. T. Clark, S. Clarke, A. Cobb, C. L. Cobb, Cook, Conger, Cowles, *Cox*, *Crebs*, Cullom, Darrall, Dawes, *Dickinson*, J. Dixon, N. F. Dixon, Dockery, Donley, *Dox*, *Duke*, Duval, *Eldredge*, Ferry, Fisher, Fitch, *Fox*, Garfield, *Getz*, *Gibson*, Gilfillan, *Haldeman*, Hale, *Hamill*, Hamilton, Harris, Hawkins, Hay, Heflin, Hoar, Holmes, Hooper, Ingersoll, *Johnson*, A. H. Jones, *T. L. Jones*, Julian, Kelley, Kellogg, Kelsey, Ketcham, Knapp, *Knott*, Lawrence, Logan, Loughridge, *Manning*, *Mayham*, *McCormick*, McCrary, McGrew, McKee, McKenzie, *McNeely*, J. H. Moore, W. Moore, Morey, *Morgan*, Morphis, Morrell, Morrill, *Morrissey*, *Mungen*, L. Myers, Negley, *Niblack*, O'Neill, Orth, Packard, Packer, H. E. Paine, Palmer, Peck, Peters, Platt, Pomeroy, Porter, *Potter*, Prosser, *Reeves*, *J. M. Rice*, Roots, Sargent, Sawyer, Scofield, L. A. Sheldon, P. Sheldon, *Shober*, *Slocum*, John A. Smith, *Joseph S. Smith*, W. J. Smith, Starkweather, Stevenson, *Stiles*, Stokes, *Stone*, Strickland, Strong, *Swann*, Sypher, Tanner, Taylor, W. Townsend, *Trimble*, Twichell, Tyner, Upson, Van Horn, *Van Trump*, *Voorhees*, Wallace, C. C. Washburn, W. B. Washburn, Welker *Wells*, Williams, *E. M. Wilson*, J. T. Wilson, *Winchester*, Witcher, Wolf, *Wood*—159.

NAYS—Messrs. Ambler, Arnell, Beatty, Benjamin, Benton, Coburn, Degener, Farnsworth, Ferriss, Finkelnburg, Hawley, Jenckes, Laflin, Lynch, Maynard, Mercer, E. H. Moore, Poland, Shanks, W. C. Smith, Stevens, Stoughton, Taffe, Tillman, Willard—25.

IN SENATE.

1871, February 18—The bill was indefinitely postponed, without a division.

[For other votes on this subject, see McPherson's History of Reconstruction, pages 173-178, 397, 413-415.]

Grant of Land to the Texas Pacific Railroad Company.

The following are the principal provisions of this bill, approved March 3, 1871:

The corporation is authorized and empowered to lay out, locate, construct, furnish, maintain, and enjoy a continuous railroad and telegraph line, with the appurtenances, from a point at or near Marshall, county of Harrison, State of Texas; thence by the most direct and eligible route, to be determined by said company, near the thirty-second parallel of north latitude, to a point at or near El Paso; thence by the most direct and eligible route, to be selected by said company, through New Mexico and Arizona, to a point on the Rio Colorado, at or near the southeastern boundary of the State of California; thence by the most direct and eligible route to San Diego, California, to ship's channel, in the bay of San Diego, in the State of California, pursuing in the location thereof, as near as may be, the thirty-second parallel of north latitude, and is vested with all the powers, privileges, and immunities necessary to carry into effect the purposes of this act.

It shall have power to purchase the stock, land grants, franchises, and appurtenances of, and consolidate on such terms as may be agreed upon between the parties, with any railroad company or companies heretofore chartered by congressional, State, or territorial authority, on the route prescribed in the first section of this act; but no such consolidation shall be with any competing through line of railroads to the Pacific ocean.

It shall have power to purchase lands, or to accept donations, or grant of lands, or other property, from States or individuals. The right of way through the public lands is granted to the said company for the construction of the said railroad and telegraph line, and the right is given to take, from the public lands adjacent to the line of said road, earth, stone, timber, and other materials for the construction thereof. Said right of way is granted to said company to the extent of two hundred feet in width on each side of said railroad where it may pass over the public lands; and there is also hereby granted to said company grounds for stations, buildings, workshops, wharves, switches, side-tracks, turn-tables, water-stations, and such other structures as may be necessary for said railroad, not exceeding forty acres of land at any one point.

For the purpose of aiding in the construction of the railroad and telegraph line herein provided for, there is granted to the said Texas Pacific Railroad Company, its successors and assigns, every alternate section of public land, not mineral, designated by odd numbers, to the amount of twenty alternate sections per mile, on each side of said railroad line, as such line may be adopted by said company, through the Territories of the United States, and ten alternate sections of land per mile on each side of said railroad in California, where the same shall not have been sold, reserved, or otherwise disposed of by the United States, and to which a preëmption or homestead claim may not have attached at the time the line of said road is definitely fixed. In case any of said lands shall have been sold, reserved, occupied, or preëmpted, or otherwise disposed of, other lands shall be selected in lieu thereof, by said company, under the direction of the Secretary of the Interior, in alternate sections, and designated by odd numbers, not more than ten miles beyond the limits of said alternate sections first above named, and not including the reserved numbers. If, in the too near approach of the said railroad line to the boundary of Mexico, the number of sections of land to which the company is entitled cannot be selected immediately on the line of said railroad, or in lieu of mineral lands excluded from this grant, a like quantity of unoccupied and unappropriated agricultural lands, in odd-numbered sections nearest the line of said railroad may be selected as above provided; and the word "mineral," where it occurs in this act, shall not be held to include iron or coal; provided, however, that no public lands are hereby granted within the State of California further than twenty miles on each side of said road, except to make up deficiencies as aforesaid, and then not to exceed twenty miles from the lands originally granted. The term "ship's channel," as used in this bill, shall not be construed as conveying any greater right to said company to the water-front of San Diego bay than it may acquire by gift, grant, purchase, or otherwise, except the right of way, as herein granted; and provided further, that all such lands so granted by this section to said company, which shall not be sold, or otherwise disposed of, as provided in this act, within three years after the completion of the entire road, shall be subject to settlement and preëmption like other lands, at a price to be fixed by and paid to said company, not exceeding an average of $2 50 per acre for all the lands herein granted.

The New Orleans, Baton Rouge, and Vicksburg Railroad Company, chartered by the State of Louisiana, shall have the right to connect by the most eligible route to be selected by said company with the said Texas Pacific railroad at its eastern terminus, and shall have the right of way through the public land to the same extent granted hereby to the said Texas Pacific Railroad Company; and in aid of its construction from New Orleans to Baton Rouge, thence by the way of Alexandria, in said State, to connect with the said Texas Pacific Railroad Company at its eastern terminus, there is hereby granted to said company, its successors and assigns, the same number of alternate sections of public lands per mile, in the State of Louisiana, as are by this act granted in the State of California to said Texas Pacific Railroad Company; and said lands shall be withdrawn from market, selected, and patents issued therefor, and opened for settlement and preëmption, upon the same terms and in the same manner and time as is provided for and required from said Texas Pacific Railroad Company within said State of California; provided that said company shall complete the whole of said road within five years from the passage of this act.

That, for the purpose of connecting the Texas Pacific railroad with the city of San Francisco, the Southern Pacific Railroad Company of California is hereby authorized (subject to the laws of California) to construct a line of railroad from a point at or near Tehachapa Pass, by way of Los Angeles, to the Texas Pacific railroad at or near the Colorado river, with the same rights, grants, and privileges, and subject to the same limitations, restrictions, and conditions as were granted to said Southern Pacific Railroad Company of California, by the act of July 27, 1866: *Provided, however*, That this section shall in no way affect or impair the rights, present or prospective, of the Atlantic and Pacific Railroad Company, or any other railroad company.

IN HOUSE.

1871, March 3—The bill passed the House—yeas 125, nays 64:

YEAS—Messrs. Allison, Ames, *Archer*, Atwood, *Axtell*, Ayer, Banks, Beaman, *Beck*, Bennett, Bethune, A. Blair, Boles, *Booker*, Bowen, G. M. Brooks, Buck, Buckley, Burdett, B. F. Butler, R. R. Butler, *Calkin*, Cessna, Churchhill, W. T.

Clark, C. L. Cobb, Conger, *Conner*, *Corker*, Cowles, Darrall, J. Dixon, N. F. Dixon, Dockery, *Dox*, *Duke*, Farnsworth, Ferriss, Fisher, Fitch, Gilfillan, *Griswold*, *Hambleton*, *Hamill*, Hamilton, Harris, Hawkins, Hays, Heflin, Hoar, Hoge, Holmes, Hooper, Hotchkiss, Ingersoll, Jenckes, *J. A. Johnson*, A. H. Jones, *T. L. Jones*, Judd, Kelley, Kelsey, Ketcham, Knapp, Laflin, Lash, Logan, Long, Lynch, *Manning*, *Mayham*, Maynard, McCarthy, McGrew, McKee, McKenzie, J. H. Moore, Morey, Morphis, Morrell, *Morrissey*, *Mungen*, L. Myers, Negley, O'Neill, H. E. Paine, *W. W. Paine*, Palmer, Perce, Platt, Poland, Pomeroy, Porter, *W. P. Price*, Prosser, Rainey, Roots, Sargent, Sawyer, *Schumaker*, Shanks, L. A. Sheldon, *Sherrod*, *Shober*, *J. S. Smith*, W. J. Smith, W. C. Smith, Stokes, Stoughton, *Strader*, Strickland, *Swann*, Sypher, Tillman, W. Townsend, *Trimble*, Twichell, *Van Auken*, Wallace, Wheeler, Whiteley, Whitmore, Williams, *E. M. Wilson*, *Young*—125.

NAYS—Messrs. Ambler, Asper, Beatty, *Biggs*, Bingham, *Bird*, *J. Brooks*, Buffinton, Burchard, S. Clarke, A. Cobb, Coburn, Cook, *Crebs*, Donley, Ela, Finkelnburg, Garfield, *Haight*, *Haldeman*, Hale, Hawley, Hay, Hill, *Holman*, Julian, Lawrence, *Lewis*, *Marshall*, McCrary, *McNeely*, Mercur, E. H. Moore, W. Moore, *Morgan*, Morrill, *Niblack*, Orth, Packer, Peck, Peters, Phelps, *Potter*, *Randall*, *Reeves*, *Rice*, Scofield, J. A. Smith, Starkweather, Stevenson, *Stiles*, Strong, Tanner, Taylor, Upson, *Van Trump*, Van Wyck, Ward, W. B. Washburn, Welker, Willard, J. T. Wilson, Wolf, *Wood*—64.

IN SENATE.

1871, March 3—A motion to lay the bill on the table was disagreed to—yeas 22, nays 33:

YEAS—Messrs. Anthony, Buckingham, *Casserly*, Corbett, Cragin, *Davis*, *Hamilton* of Maryland, Harlan, McDonald, Morrill of Vermont, Patterson, Pool, Pratt, Ramsey, Rice, Schurz, Sherman, Sprague, *Stockton*, Trumbull, *Vickers*, Willey—22.

NAYS—Messrs. Abbott, Ames, *Blair*, Boreman, Brownlow, Cattell, Chandler, Conkling, Edmunds, Fenton, Flanagan, Hamlin, Harris, Hill, Howard, Howell, Kellogg, Lewis, *McCreery*, Nye, Osborn, Pomeroy, Robertson, Sawyer, Scott, Spencer, Stewart, Sumner, Thayer, Tipton, Warner, Wilson, Yates—33.

After further debate, another motion to lay it on the table was lost—yeas 13, nays 40:

YEAS—Messrs. Cragin, Edmunds, Gilbert, Harlan, Howell, McDonald, Pool, Ramsey, Rice, Schurz, Scott, Sprague, Tipton—13.

NAYS—Messrs. Abbott, Ames, *Bayard*, *Blair*, Boreman, Buckingham, Cameron, Chandler, Conkling, Corbett, *Davis*, Fenton, Flanagan, Fowler, *Hamilton* of Maryland, Harris, Hill, Howard, *Johnston*, Kellogg, Lewis, *McCreery*, *Miller*, Nye, Osborn, Pomeroy, Revels, Robertston, Ross, Sawyer, Sherman, Spencer, Stearns, Stewart, *Stockton*, Trumbull, Warner, Williams, Wilson, Yates—40.

The bill then passed without a division.

Right of Secession, and Amnesty.

IN HOUSE.

1870, December 19—Mr. THOMAS L. JONES moved a suspension of the rules that he might offer and the House adopt the following resolution:

Whereas the Government of the United States was established as a confederacy of coequal States, delegating certain powers to a Federal head or common agent, and reserving all others "to the States respectively or to the people;" and whereas the question of secession was from the beginning a debatable one, held by some to be a sovereign right reserved, and denied by others; and whereas the right of revolution is admitted by all and was affirmed in the Declaration of Independence, the great forerunner of the Federal Constitution; and whereas in the course of time, the question of secession being still undecided by any tribunal of the Federal Government, certain States did secede and set up a government of their own in accordance with honest convictions of their reserved rights, and a great civil war ensued in which said States and government were subdued and overthrown, the great experiment having been made and settled by arms; and whereas the leaders and soldiers in said war for secession or revolution and the people of said States have for nearly six years after peace conformed to all the requirements of the Government of the United States, and have been fully reconstructed under the laws and regulations of its Congress: Be it therefore,

Resolved, That it is the bounden duty of the Government and Congress of the United States, if they would revere the common brotherhood, trials, sufferings, and glorious achievements of a noble ancestry, and act in the liberal, magnanimous, and Christian spirit of an enlightened age, to grant free, unqualified, and perfect pardon and amnesty to all political offenders in said war, that the Government of the fathers, with all its privileges and blessings, may be restored for the benefit of the whole people, and that the original, "more perfect union" of the Constitution may be reëstablished, exalted, and secured forever.

Which was disagreed to—yeas 14, nays 143, not voting 78:

YEAS—Messrs. *Beck*, *Bird*, *Duke*, *Gibson*, *Griswold*, *Haldeman*, *Johnson*, *Jones*, *Knott*, *Reeves*, *Rice*, *Sherrod*, *Winchester*, *Woodward*—14.

NAYS—Messrs. Allison, Ambler, Arnell, Asper, Atwood, Ayer, Bailey, Banks, *Barnum*, Barry, Beaman, Beatty, Benjamin, Bennett, Benton, Bingham, A. Blair, Boles, *Booker*, G. M. Brooks, Buckley, Buffinton, Burchard, Burdett, B. F. Butler, Cessna, Churchill, S. Clarke, A. Cobb, C. L. Cobb, Coburn, Cook, Conger, Cowles, *Cox*, *Crebs*, Cullom, Dawes, Degener, Dickey, J. Dixon, N. F. Dixon, Dockery, Duval, Ela, Farnsworth, Ferriss, Ferry, Finkelnburg, Fisher, Fitch, Gilfillan, Hale, Harris, Hawkins, Hawley, Hay, Hill, Hoge, *Holman*, Holmes, Hooper, Hotchkiss, Ingersoll, Jenckes, Jones, Judd, Kelley, Kellogg, Kelsey, Ketcham, Knapp, Laflin, Lawrence, Loughridge, Maynard, McCrary, McGrew, McKee, McKenzie, Mercur, *Milnes*, E. H. Moore, J. H Moore, W. Moore, Morey, Morphis, Morrell, *Morrissey*, *Mungen*, L. Myers, Negley, O'Neill, Orth, Packard, Packer, Paine, Palmer, Peck, Perce, Peters, Phelps, Poland, Pomeroy, Porter, Prosser, Roots, Sargent, Sawyer, *Schumaker*, Scofield, Shanks, L. A. Sheldon, P. Sheldon, *Slocum*, J. A. Smith, W. J. Smith, W. C. Smith, Starkweather, A. F. Stevens, Stevenson, Stokes, Stoughton, Strong, Taffe, Taylor, Tillman, W. Townsend, Twichell, Tyner, Upson, Wallace, C. C. Washburn, W. B. Washburn, Welker, Whitmore, Wilkinson, Willard, Williams, J. T. Wilson, Winans, Witcher, Wolf—143.

NOT VOTING—Messrs. *Adams*, Ames, *Archer*, Armstrong, *Axtell*, *Biggs*, Bowen, Boyd, *J. Brooks*, Buck, *Burr*, R. R. Butler, Cake, *Calkin*, W. T. Clark, *Cleveland*, *Conner*, Covode, Darrall, *Dickinson*, Donley, *Dox*, Dyer, *Eldredge*, *Fox*, Garfield, *Getz*, *Haight*, *Hambleton*, *Hamill*, Hamilton, Hays, Heflin, Hoar, Julian, *Kerr*, Lash, *Lewis*, Logan, Lynch, *Manning*, *Marshall*, *Mayham*, McCarthy, *McCormick*, *McNeely*, *Morgan*, Morrill, Newsham, *Niblack*, Platt, *Potter*, Rainey, *Randall*, *Rogers*, Sanford, Schenck, *Shober*, *J. S. Smith*, *Stiles*, *Stone*, *Strader*, Strickland, *Swann*, *Sweeney*, Sypher, Tanner, *Trimble*, *Van Auken*, Van Horn, *Van Trump*, Van Wyck, *Voorhees*, Ward, *Wells*, Wheeler, *E. M. Wilson*, *Wood*—78.

Tariff and Taxation.

IN HOUSE.

1870, December 12—Mr. KELLEY moved a suspension of the rules that he might offer, and the House adopt this resolution:

Resolved, That the true principle of revenue reform points to the abolition of the internal revenue system which was created as a war measure to provide for extraordinary expenses, and a continuance of which involves the employment, at the cost of millions of dollars annually, of an army of assessors, collectors, supervisors, detectives, and other officers previously unknown; and requires the repeal, at the earliest day consistent with the maintenance of the faith and credit of the Government, of all stamp and other internal taxes; and that properly adjusted rates shall be retained on distilled spirits, tobacco, and malt liquors so long as the legitimate expenses of the Government require the collection of any sum from internal taxes.

Which was agreed to—yeas 168, nays 6:

YEAS—Messrs. Allison, Ambler, Armstrong, Arnell, Atwood, *Axtell*, Barry, Beaman, Beatty, *Beck*, Benton, Bingham, *Bird*, A. Blair, Boles, *Booker*, Bowen, Boyd, G. M. Brooks, *J. Brooks*, Buckley, Buffinton, Burchard, Burdett, *Burr*, R. R. Butler, *Calkin*, Churchill, W. T. Clark, S. Clarke, A. Cobb, C. L. Cobb, Coburn, Cook, Conger, Cowles, *Crebs*, Cullom, Darrall, *Dickinson*, N. F. Dixon, Donley, *Dox*, *Duke*, Duval, *Eldredge*, Farnsworth, Ferriss, Ferry, Fisher, Fitch, *Fox*, Garfield, *Getz*, *Gibson*, Gillfillan, *Griswold*, *Hamill*, Hawkins, Hawley, Hay, Heflin, Holmes, Ingersoll, Jenckes, *Johnson*, A. H. Jones, *T. L. Jones*, Julian, Kelley, Kellogg, Kelsey, Ketcham, Knapp, *Knott*, Laflin, Logan, Lynch, *Manning*, *Mayham*, Maynard, *McCormick*, McCrary, McGrew, McKee, McKenzie, *McNeely*, Mercur, E. H. Moore, J. H. Moore, W. Moore, Morey, *Morgan*, Morphis, Morrell, Morrill, *Morrissey*, *Mungen*, L. Myers, Negley, *Niblack*, O'Neill, Orth, Packard, Packer, Paine, Palmer, Peck, Perce, Peters, Phelps, Platt, Poland, Pomeroy, Porter, Prosser, Rainey, *Reeves*, *J. M. Rice*, Sanford, Sargent, Sawyer, Schenck, *Schumaker*, Scofield, Shanks, L. A. Sheldon, P. Sheldon, *Sherrod*, *Shober*, *Slocum*, J. A. Smith, W. C. Smith, Starkweather, A. F. Stevens, Stevenson, *Stiles*, Stokes, *Stone*, Stoughton, *Strader*, Strickland, Strong, *Swann*, Sypher, Taffe, Tanner, Taylor, Tillman, W. Townsend, *Trimble*, Tyner, Upson, Van Horn, *Van Trump*, *Voorhees*, Wallace, C. C. Washburn, Welker, *Wells*, Wilkinson, Willard, Williams, J. T. Wilson, Witcher, Wolf, *Wood*, *Woodward*—168.

NAYS—Messrs. Asper, Ayer, Benjamin, *Cox*. Finkelnburg, W. J. Smith—6.

First Session Forty-First Congress.

The following resolution was inadvertently omitted from my Hand Book of Politics for 1870:

1869, March 29—Mr. MORGAN submitted the following resolution, namely:

Resolved, That as a means of relief to the people and in some degree to equalize taxation, the Committee of Ways and Means be, and said committee is hereby, instructed to report a bill, first, to exempt salt, tea, coffee, sugar, matches, and tobacco from every species of taxation for Federal purposes; second, to impose a tax of two and a half per cent. in gold on all bonds heretofore issued, or which may hereafter be issued, by the Government of the United States.

Mr. HOOPER moved that it be laid on the table; which was agreed to—yeas 104, nays 40. The affirmative was exclusively Republican; the negative exclusively Democratic, except Mr. Deweese.

The Arlington Estate.

IN SENATE.

1870, December 13—Mr. McCREERY, agreeably to notice, asked leave to bring in this resolution:

Resolved, &c., That a joint committee of five, two from the Senate and three from the House, be appointed, whose duty it shall be to inquire and report what real estate, if any, belonged to the late General Robert E. Lee at the time he entered the confederate service; by what right or title he held the farm and lands known as Arlington Heights, and whether he had any right, title, or claim thereto which rendered Arlington liable to confiscation or forfeiture by reason of his participation in the rebellion. That the committee ascertain and report whether that estate was or was not the property of Mrs. Lee, formerly Miss Custis, and inherited by her from her ancestors, and whether the title was or was not vested by law in herself and her children; and if so, had General Lee any rights subject to forfeiture. If the property was sold for taxes the committee shall report the amount of taxes assessed upon it, the value of the property sold, who paid and who received the money; whether a less quantity than the whole was not sufficient to meet the demands of Government, and whether the sale as made was legal and constitutional. That the committee report what expenditure it would require to put the house and farm in good repair, in order that it may be restored to the owner or owners in as good condition as it was when the United States Government took possession; also, what would be a reasonable and fair compensation in the way of rent since the occupation by the Government, as well as for the waste that has been committed on the premises by felling the trees, destroying the orchards, or otherwise impairing the value of the property. And if grave-yards have been established on the land, then the committee shall ascertain and report the number of interments, on what terms a suitable spot for a cemetery can be purchased in the neighborhood, and the probable cost of removing the bodies to the new place of sepulture. And if improvements have been made upon the land since its occupation by the Government or its agents, the committee shall report upon their character and value, and whether they were necessary and proper, and if of no real value to the owner and only an incumbrance upon her estate, then they shall report the estimated or probable cost of their removal. If the Government hold and occupy any real estate, the title whereof was vested by law in General Robert E. Lee at the time he entered the confederate service, the committee shall report the same. The committee shall also ascertain and report the amount and value of the personal property taken by the Government or its agents from General Lee, or from his family, and whether or not the same can without detriment be restored in kind, and if not, what would be a just and reasonable compensation. If there are in any of the Departments any relics or mementos left by George Washington to the Custis family, and the same were taken from the house or the possession of Mrs. Lee, the committee will report who is the present custodian of such articles, and whether any of them have been lost or damaged while going to or remaining in said Departments. The committee shall take the statements of Mrs. Lee in order to identify her property with greater certainty, to discover the extent of her losses; and they shall report all facts necessary to a settlement upon the principles of substantial justice.

Objection being made by Mr. EDMUNDS, the question arose, shall the leave asked be granted?

Mr. DAVIS moved that the question lie on the table; which was disagreed to—yeas 9, nays 49:

YEAS—Messrs. *Bayard*, *Casserly*, *Davis*, Fowler, *Hamilton* of Maryland, *Johnston*, Lewis, *Saulsbury*, *Vickers*—9.

NAYS—Messrs. Abbott, Ames, Anthony, Boreman, Brownlow, Buckingham, Cameron, Carpenter, Chandler, Cole, Conkling, Corbett, Drake, Edmunds, Fenton, Flanagan, Gilbert, Hamilton of Texas, Hamlin, Harlan, Harris, Howard, Howe, Howell, *McCreery*, Morrill of Vermont, Morton, Nye, Patterson, Pool, Pratt, Ramsey, Revels, Rice, Robertson, Ross, Sawyer, Scott, Sherman, Spencer, Sprague, Stewart, Sumner, Thayer, Tipton, Willey, Williams, Wilson, Windom—49.

Leave to bring in the resolution was then refused—yeas 4, nays 54:

YEAS—Messrs. Fowler, *Hamilton* of Maryland, *McCreery*, *Vickers*—4.

NAYS—Messrs. Abbott, Ames, Anthony, *Bayard*, Boreman, Brownlow, Buckingham, Cameron, Carpenter, *Casserly*, Chandler, Cole, Conkling, Corbett, Drake, Edmunds, Fenton, Flanagan, Gilbert, Hamilton of Texas, Hamlin, Harlan, Harris, Howard, Howe, Howell, Kellogg, Lewis, Morrill of Vermont, Morton, Nye, Patterson, Pomeroy, Pool, Pratt, Ramsey, Revels, Rice, Robertson, Ross, Sawyer, Schurz, Scott, Sherman, Spencer, Sprague, Stewart, Sumner, Thayer, Tipton, Willey, Williams, Wilson, Windom—54.

The petition of Mrs. Mary Ann Lee, widow of General Robert E. Lee, is now pending in the Senate, reciting the circumstances attending the sale of the Arlington estate, and asking that Congress appropriate $300,000 to purchase the estate from her, and proposing in that event to give the Government a clear title.

First Session Forty-Second Congress.

IN HOUSE.

1871, March 18—Mr. BRAXTON offered a bill to quiet the title of the Arlington estate.

[The bill provides that upon a full release and conveyance of all right, title, and interest at law and in equity by the devisees under the last will and testament of George W. P. Custis, deceased, in the tract of land called "Arlington," containing eleven hundred acres, and situate in the county of Alexandria and State of Virginia, the Secretary of the Treasury shall pay, out of any money in the Treasury not otherwise appropriated, to the said devisees, the sum of $300,000, which payment, when made, shall be in full consideration for the said property. The second section provides that this bill shall be in force from and after its passage.]

On motion of Mr. B. F. BUTLER, the bill was laid on the table—yeas 115, nays 74:

YEAS—Messrs. Ambler, Averill, Barber, Beatty, Bigby, Bingham, A. Blair, G. M. Brooks, Buckley, Buffinton, Burchard, Burdett, B. F. Butler, R. R. Butler, F. Clarke, C. L. Cobb, Coburn, Conger, Cook, Cotton, Creely, Dawes, De Large, Dickey, Donnan, Dunnell, Eames, Elliott, Farnsworth, Farwell, Finkelnburg, C. Foster, Frye, Garfield, Goodrich, *Griffith*, Hale, Harmer, G. E. Harris, Havens, Hawley, Hay, G. W. Hazelton, J. W. Hazelton, Hoar, *Holman*, Hooper, Kelley, Ketcham, Lamport, Lansing, Lowe, Lynch, *Manson*, Maynard, McCrary, McGrew, McJunkin, Merriam, Monroe, Moore, Morey, Morphis, L. Myers, Orr, Packard, Packer, Palmer, Parker, Peck, Pendleton, Perce, Peters, Platt, Porter, Prindle, Rainey, *Randall*, E. H. Roberts, Rusk, Sawyer, Scofield, Sessions, Shanks, Sheldon, Shellabarger, Shoemaker, *Slocum*, H. B. Smith, J. A. Smith, W. C. Smith, *R. M. Speer*, T. J. Speer, Sprague, Stevenson, Stoughton, St. John, Sypher, Thomas, W. Townsend, Twichell, Tyner, Upson, *Voorhees*, Wakeman, Walden, Waldron, Wallace, Walls, Wheeler, Whiteley, Willard, Williams of Indiana, J. M. Wilson, J. T. Wilson—115.

NAYS—Messrs. *Acker*, *Adams*, *Archer*, *Arthur*, *Beck*, *Bird*, *J. G. Blair*, *Braxton*, *Bright*, *J. Brooks*, *Caldwell*, *Campbell*, *Carroll*, *Comingo*, *Cox*, *Crebs*, *Critcher*, *Crossland*, *Davis*, *Dox*, *Du Bose*, *Duke*, *Eldredge*, *Ely*, *Forker*, *Garrett*, *Getz*, *Golladay*, *Haldeman*, *Handley*, *Hanks*, *Harper*, *J. T. Harris*, *Hereford*, *Kendall*, *King*, *Kinsella*, *Lamison*, *Leach*, *Lewis*, *McClelland*, *McCormick*, *McHenry*, *McIntyre*, *McKinney*, *Merrick*, *B. F. Meyers*, *Morgan*, *Niblack*, *Perry*, *Price*, *E. Y. Rice*, *J. M. Rice*, *Ritchie*, *W. R. Roberts*, *Roosevelt*, *Shober*, *Slater*, *Sloss*, *Stevens*, *Storm*, *Sutherland*, *Swann*, *Terry*, *Tuthill*, *Van Trump*, *Vaughan*, *Waddell*, *Warren*, *Wells*, *Whitthorne*, *Williams* of New York, *Wood*, *Young*—74.

VII.

PROPOSED AMENDMENTS TO THE CONSTITUTION OF THE UNITED STATES.

The following constitutional amendments were proposed, during the Forty-First and Forty-Second Congresses.

IN SENATE—FORTY-FIRST CONGRESS.

1869, March 18—Mr. ROBERTSON proposed a new article:

The Congress shall have power to establish a tribunal for the purpose of considering and determining all questions which may arise as to the validity of the electoral vote of any State for President and Vice President of the United States; which said tribunal shall exercise its jurisdiction under such regulations as Congress shall make.

1870, January 21—Mr. POMEROY proposed a new article:

The basis of suffrage in the United States

shall be that of citizenship, and all native or naturalized citizens shall enjoy the same rights and privileges of the elective franchise; but each State shall determine by law the age of the citizen and the time of residence required for the exercise of the right of suffrage, which shall apply equally to all citizens, and also shall make all laws concerning the time, places, and manner of holding elections for all State and municipal officers.

1870, April 18—Mr. DRAKE proposed a new article:

SECTION 1. The United States shall protect each State against domestic violence whenever it shall be shown to the President, in such manner as the Congress may by law prescribe, that such violence exists in such State.

SEC. 2. The Congress shall have power to enforce this article by appropriate legislation.

1871, January 17—Mr. YATES proposed a new article:

Every person, whether a native-born or a foreign-born citizen of the United States who shall have attained to the age of thirty-five years, and been fourteen years a resident within the United States, shall be eligible to the office of President.

IN SENATE—FORTY-SECOND CONGRESS.

1871, March 16—Mr. DAVIS, of Kentucky, proposed a new article:

There is hereby established the Constitutional Tribunal, with power to decide all questions of conflict of jurisdiction or power between the United States and the States, or any of them; all questions of the constitutionality of bills passed by Congress, or of acts of every kind done and performed by any department or officer, or other person, under the authority of the Government of the United States; and to open and count the votes of the electors of President and Vice President of the United States. Proceedings may be had before the Constitutional Tribunal by original petition, or by appeal or writ of error from the judgments or decrees of all the courts of the United States and the States, by and in the name of any State or person, natural or artificial, directly interested in the questions involved in the proceedings. The concurrence of a majority of the whole number of the Tribunal, counting one for every State, shall be necessary to enable it to render any judgment or decree; and they shall be executed and enforced by the United States according to law. Each State shall be entitled to and shall choose one member of the Constitutional Tribunal, who at the time of being chosen shall be not less than thirty years of age, and who shall have been for ten years a citizen of the United States, and five years a resident of the State. The members of the Tribunal shall hold their offices during good behavior; shall receive compensation from their respective States; may be removed by them for treason, bribery, corruption in office, or other high crimes and misdemeanors, or mental imbecility. The Tribunal may regulate the times and continuance of its terms for the transaction of business.

1871, December 19—Mr. STEWART proposed a new article:

SECTION 1. There shall be maintained in each State and Territory a system of free common schools; but neither the United States, nor any State, Territory, county, or municipal corporation shall aid in the support of any school wherein the peculiar tenets of any religious denomination are taught.

SEC. 2. Congress shall have power to enforce this article by appropriate legislation.

1871, December 21—Mr. SUMNER proposed a new article, (preamble omitted:)

SECTION 1. No person who has once held the office of President of the United States shall be thereafter eligible to that office.

SEC. 2. This amendment shall not take effect until after the 4th day of March, 1873.

1872, May 30—Mr. SUMNER submitted the following, (preamble omitted:)

Resolved, &c., (two thirds of each House concurring therein,) That the following be proposed as an amendment to the Constitution, which, when ratified by the Legislatures of three fourths of the several States, shall be valid, to all intents and purposes, as part thereof, to wit:

The executive power shall be vested in a President of the United States of America; he shall hold his office during the term of four years, and be elected as follows:

The qualified voters shall meet at the usual places of holding elections in their respective States and Territories on the first Monday in April, in the year one thousand eight hundred and seventy six, and on the first Monday in April every four years thereafter, under such rules and regulations as the Congress may by law prescribe, and vote by ballot for a citizen qualified under the Constitution to be President, and the result of such election in each State and Territory shall be certified, sealed, and forwarded to the seat of Government in such manner as the Congress may by law direct.

The Congress shall be in session on the third Monday in May after such election, and on the Tuesday next succeeding the third Monday in May, if a quorum of each House shall be present, and if not, immediately on the presence of such quorum the Senators and Representatives shall meet in the Representative Chamber in joint convention, and the President of the Senate, in presence of the Senators and Representatives thus assembled, shall open all returns of the election and declare the result. The person having the greatest number of votes cast for President shall be President, if such number be a majority; if no person have such a majority, or if the person having such majority decline the office or die before the counting of the vote, then the President of the Senate shall so proclaim; whereupon the joint convention shall order the proceedings to be officially published, stating particularly the number of votes for each person as President.

Another election shall thereupon take place on the second Tuesday of October next succeeding, at which election the duly qualified voters shall again meet at the usual places of holding elections in their respective States and Territories, and vote for one of the three persons having the highest number of votes, at the preceding election in April, and the result of such election in each State and Territory shall be certified, sealed, and forwarded to the seat of Government as provided by law.

On the third Tuesday in December after such second election, or as soon thereafter as a quorum of each House shall be present, the Senators and Representatives shall again meet in joint convention, and the President of the Senate, in presence of the Senators and Representatives thus assembled, shall open all the returns of the election, and declare the person having the highest number of votes duly elected President for the ensuing term.

No person elected to the office of President shall thereafter be eligible for reëlection.

In case of the removal of the President from office by impeachment, or of his death, resignation, or inability to discharge the powers and duties of the office, the same shall devolve temporarily on the head of an Executive Department senior in years. If there be no head of an Executive Department, then the Senator senior in years shall act as President until a successor is chosen and qualified.

If Congress be in session at the time of the death, resignation, disability, or removal of the President, the Senators and Representatives shall meet in joint convention, under such rules and regulations as the Congress may by law prescribe, and proceed to elect by *viva voce* vote a President to fill such vacancy, each Senator and Representative having one vote. A quorum for this purpose shall consist of a majority in each House of the Senators and Representatives duly elected and qualified, and a majority of all the votes given shall be necessary to the choice of a President. The person thus elected as President shall discharge all the powers and duties of the office until the inauguration of the President elected at the next regular election.

If Congress be not in session at the time a vacancy occurs, then the acting President shall forthwith issue a proclamation convening Congress within thirty days after the occurrence of such vacancy.

On the presence of a quorum in each House, the Senators and Representatives shall meet in joint convention and elect a President, as before provided.

The office of Vice President is abolished.

The Senate shall choose their own Presiding Officer.

In House—Forty-First Congress.

1869, December 22—Mr. Lawrence proposed a new article:

The electors of President and Vice President shall be chosen as follows: two electors of President and Vice President shall be chosen at large from each State by the qualified voters therein. A number of electors in each State equal to the whole number of Representatives to which such State may be entitled in Congress shall be chosen in single districts of contiguous and compact territory, each containing, as nearly as practicable, an equal amount of population. The times, places, and manner of choosing such electors shall be prescribed in each State by the Legislature thereof, but the Congress may at any time by law make or alter such regulations. Congress shall by law provide for the case of absence, death, resignation, or inability of any elector, prescribe the mode of determining the validity of the choice of electors, and of contesting the right to the office of President and Vice President.

1870, February 14—Mr. Ingersoll proposed a new article:

Section 1. The Congress shall have power to issue United States notes and may make them a legal tender in payment of debts.

1870, April 4—Mr. Julian proposed a new article:

Section 1. The right of citizens of the United States to vote shall not be denied or abridged by the United States or by any State on account of sex.

Sec. 2. The Congress shall have the power to enforce this article by appropriate legislation.

1870, April 18—Mr. Burdett proposed a new article:

Section 1. No State or municipal corporation within any State of the United States shall levy or collect any tax for the support or aid of any sectarian, denominational, or religious school, or educational establishment; nor shall the Legislature of any State, or the corporate authorities of any municipality within any State, appropriate any money or make any donation from the public funds or property of such State or municipality for the support or aid of any sectarian, religious, or denominational school, or educational establishment.

Sec. 2. The Congress shall have power to enforce this article by appropriate legislation.

1871, January 4—Mr. Coburn proposed a new article:

Congress may by law vest the election of all officers of the United States whose duties require them to reside in the several States, except judges and officers of the courts of the United States, in the people of the several States, districts, and localities therein in which they are by law required to perform their duties, subject to the directions and regulations of the President of the United States and the heads of Departments, and to arrest, suspension, or removal by the President of the United States.

[This was re-presented by Mr. Coburn in first session of Forty-Second Congress, on 13th of March, 1871.]

In House—Forty-Second Congress.

1871, March 4—Mr. Potter proposed a new article:

Section 1. That the Congress shall make no law impairing the obligations of contracts, nor shall it hereafter charter private corporations to carry on business within the States.

1871, December 5—Mr. POTTER proposed a new article:

SECTION 1. The President and Vice President hereafter elected shall hold office during the term of six years; but no person shall be reëligible to be President who has been once elected to that office.

1871, December 11—Mr. COGHLAN proposed a new article:

SECTION 1. The public land of the United States, except mineral lands, shall not be disposed of except to actual settlers thereon, for homestead purposes only, and in quantities limited by general laws.

Which was—March 8, 1872—disagreed to—yeas 85, nays 87:

YEAS—Messrs. *Acker*, Ambler, *Archer*, *Arthur*, Banks, Beatty, Beveridge, *J. Brooks*, Buffinton, Burchard, Burdett, B. F. Butler, R. R. Butler, Coghlan, *Cox*, *Crebs*, *Crossland*, De Large, Ely, Finkelnburg, *Forker*, C. Foster, *H. D. Foster*, W. D. Foster, Garfield, *Garrett*, *Golladay*, *Griffith*, *Haldeman*, *Hancock*, *Handley*, Harmer, Havens, Hawley, J. W. Hazleton, *Hibbard*, Hill, *Holman*, Houghton, *Kerr*, *King*, Lamport, *Lewis*, Lowe, *Manson*, *McClelland*, McCrary, *McIntyre*, *McNeely*, Merriam, *B. F. Meyers*, Monroe, *Morgan*, Negley, Orr, Packard, *H. W. Parker*, I. C. Parker, Peck, *E. Perry*, *Potter*, *Randall*, *Read*, *E. Y. Rice*, *J. M. Rice*, *Ritchie*, Sargent, Shanks, H. B. Smith, Snapp, Sprague, *Stevens*, Stevenson, *Storm*, Strong, *Swann*, Tyner, Upson, *Van Trump*, *Vaughan*, *Whitthorne*, Willard, Williams of Indiana, *Winchester*, *Wood*—85.

NAYS—Messrs. *Adams*, Ames, Averill, Barber, Barry, *Bell*, Bigby, Bingham, *Bird*, *Braxton*, G. M. Brooks, Buckley, *Caldwell*, Cobb, Coburn, *Comingo*, Conger, *Conner*, Darrall, *Davis*, Dawes, Donnan, *Dox*, *Du Bose*, *Duke*, Dunnell, *Eldredge*, Frye, *Hanks*, *Harper*, G. E. Harris, *J. T. Harris*, Hays, G. W. Hazelton, *Herndon*, Hoar, Hooper, Kelley, *Kendall*, *Lamison*, Lansing, *Leach*, *McCormick*, McGrew, *McHenry*, McJunkin, Mercur, *Merrick*, *Mitchell*, Morey, Morphis, Packer, Palmer, Pendleton, Poland, Porter, Rainey, E. H. Roberts, *J. Rogers*, Rusk, Sawyer, Sessions, Sheldon, *Sherwood*, *Shober*, Shoemaker, *Slater*, J. A. Smith, W. C. Smith, Snyder, T. J. Speer, Starkweather, Stoughton, Stowell, *Sutherland*, Taffe, *Terry*, Thomas, Turner, *Tuthill*, Wakeman, Walden, Waldron, Wallace, *Warren*, Wheeler, *Young*—87.

1871, December 11—Mr. KING proposed a new article, (preamble omitted:)

SEC. 1. It shall not be lawful for the white inhabitants of the United States, either male or female, to contract bonds of matrimony, or enter into the marriage relation, with the African or other colored inhabitants of the United States; and all such marriages are hereby forever prohibited.

SEC. 2. And said fourteenth amendment shall not be understood or construed as prohibiting the States from making and enforcing such laws as may be necessary to provide for the education of the children of the colored inhabitants of the United States in schools and colleges separate and apart from the schools and colleges for the education of the children of the white inhabitants.

1871, December 11—Mr. MCNEELY proposed a new article:

SEC. 1. Congress shall have no power to lay and collect duties on imports or excises.

SEC. 2. That Congress shall raise such revenue as may be required under the Constitution by a direct tax laid annually upon the United States, which shall be apportioned among the several States and Territories and the District of Columbia according to the valuation of property within the same, respectively, so that every person and corporation shall pay a tax in proportion to his, her, or its property, such valuation to be ascertained in such manner as Congress may prescribe: *Provided*, That the property of the United States, of the several States, Territories, the District of Columbia, counties, and other municipal corporations, and such other property as may be used exclusively for agricultural and horticultural societies, for school, religious, cemetery, and charitable purposes, shall be exempt from such taxation.

SEC. 3. That any State or Territory and the District of Columbia may assume, assess, collect, and pay into the Treasury of the United States the direct tax, or its quota thereof, imposed by Congress under this article, in its own way and manner, by and through its own officers, assessors, and collectors; but if any State or Territory or the District of Columbia shall fail to pay into the Treasury of the United States its quota or proportion of such direct tax within ——— months after the same shall have been laid and apportioned, such tax, together with the cost of assessing and collecting the same, shall be assessed and collected within such State or Territory or the District of Columbia so failing to pay the same in such manner as Congress may direct.

1871, December 11—Mr. MORGAN proposed a new article:

SEC. 1. Naturalized citizens of the United States shall be eligible to the offices of President and Vice President. Any provision in the Constitution inconsistent herewith is hereby declared void and of no effect.

1872, January 8—Mr. MORGAN moved to suspend the rules and pass the resolution; which was disagreed to—yeas 81, nays 65:

YEAS—Messrs. *Acker*, *Adams*, *Archer*, *Arthur*, Beatty, *Beck*, *Bird*, *J. G. Blair*, *Braxton*, *Bright*, Buckley, Burchard, B. F. Butler, *Caldwell*, Coghlan, Conger, Cotton, *Cox*, *Crossland*, *Dox*, *DuBose*, *Duke*, Dunnell, *Eldredge*, *Ely*, Farnsworth, Finkelnburg, Frye, *Garrett*, *Getz*, Goodrich, *Hancock*, *Handley*, *Harper*, *J. T. Harris*, Hay, *Hereford*, *Herndon*, *Hibbard*, *Holman*, *Kerr*, *King*, *Leach*, Lynch, *Marshall*, *McClelland*, *McCormick*, *McHenry*, *B. F. Meyers*, *Morgan*, *Niblack*, *H. W. Parker*, I. C. Parker, Porter, *Potter*, *Randall*, *Read*, *E. Y. Rice*, *J. M. Rice*, *W. R. Roberts*, *J. Rogers*, *Roosevelt*, Sheldon, *Sherwood*, *Slater*, *Sloss*, T. J. Speer, Starkweather, *Stevens*, Stevenson, *Swann*, *Terry*, *Van Trump*, *Waddell*, Walden, *Wells*, Whiteley, *Whitthorne*, *Williams* of New York, *Winchester*, *Wood*—81.

NAYS—Messrs. Ambler, Averill, Banks, Barber, Barry, Beveridge, A. Blair, G. M. Brooks, Buffinton, Burdett, R. R. Butler, Coburn, Dawes, Donnan, W. D. Foster, Garfield, Hale, G. E. Harris, G. W. Hazelton, J. W. Hazelton, Hoar, Hooper, Houghton, Kelley, *Lewis*, Lowe, Maynard, McCrary, McKee, Mercur, Merriam, Monroe, Moore, L. Myers, Negley, Orr, Packard, Packer, Palmer, Peck, Peters, Platt, Poland, *Ritchie*, E. H. Roberts, Rusk, Sessions, Shanks, Shellabarger, H. B. Smith, J. A. Smith, Snapp, Sprague, Turner, Twichell, Tyner, Upson, Wakeman, Waldron, Walls, Wheeler, Willard, Williams of Indiana, J. M. Wilson, J. T. Wilson—65.

1872, January 22—Mr. MORGAN moved to suspend the rules and pass the resolution; which was disagreed to—yeas 91, nays 75, (not voting 74:)

YEAS—Messrs. *Acker*, *Archer*, *Arthur*, Beatty,

Beck, *Bell*, *Bird*, *J. G. Blair*, *Braxton*, *Bright*, Burchard, Coghlan, *Comingo*, Conger, *Conner*, Cotton, *Cox*, *Crebs*, *Crossland*, *Dox*, *Du Bose*, Duell, *Duke*, Dunnell, *Eldredge*, Farnsworth, Farwell, Finkelnburg, C. Foster, *Garrett*, *Getz*, *Golladay*, Goodrich, *Griffith*, *Haldeman*, *Hancock*, *Handley*, *Hanks*, *Harper*, *J. T. Harris*, Hay, *Hereford*, *Herndon*, *Hibbard*, *Kerr*, *King*, *Lamison*, *Leach*, *Manson*, *Marshall*, *McClelland*, *McCormick*, McCrary, *McHenry*, *McIntyre*, *McNeely*, *B. F. Meyers*, *Morgan*, Morphis, *Niblack*, *H. W. Parker*, I. C. Parker, *E. Perry*, Porter, *Potter*, *Price*, *Read*, *E. Y. Rice*, *J. M. Rice*, *J. Rogers*, *Sherwood*, *Shober*, Shoemaker, *Slater*, *Sloss*, T. J. Speer, *Stevens*, Stevenson, *Storm*, *Sutherland*, *Swann*, *Terry*, *Vaughan*, *Voorhees*, *Waddell*, *Warren*, *Wells*, Whiteley, *Whitthorne*, *Wood*, *Young*—91.

NAYS—Messrs. Ambler, Averill, Banks, Barber, Barry, Beveridge, Bigby, Bingham, A. Blair, G. M. Brooks, Buffinton, Burdett, R. R. Butler, W. T. Clark, Cobb, Darrall, Dawes, Donnan, Eames, W. D. Foster, Garfield, Hale, Hawley, J. W. Hazelton, Hoar, Houghton, Kelley, Lowe, Maynard, McGrew, McJunkin, Mercur, Merriam, Monroe, Moore, L. Myers, Orr, Packard, Palmer, Peck, Pendleton, Perce, A. F. Perry, Platt, Poland, Rainey, *Ritchie*, E. H. Roberts, Sargent, Sawyer, Seeley, Sessions, Shanks, Shellabarger, J. A. Smith, W. C. Smith, Snapp, Snyder, Sprague, Stoughton, Stowell, Taffe, W. Townsend, Turner, Twichell, Upson, Wakeman, Walden, Waldron, Wallace, Walls, Wheeler, Willard, Williams of Indiana, J. T. Wilson—75.

1871, December 18—Mr. COMINGO proposed a new article:

No Territory or district of country shall hereafter be admitted into the Union as a State that does not contain a representative population that will entitle it to at least one Representative, according to the ratio of representation at the time of its admission.

1872, January 8—Mr. MCCRARY proposed a new article:

All civil officers of the United States, except judges of the supreme and inferior courts, the heads of Departments, and those whose duties are temporary in their character, shall hold office for a term of four years, unless a longer term shall be fixed by law. Congress may by law provide for the election by the people, of postmasters, and other officers whose duties are to be performed within the limits of any State or part of a State; but the President shall have the power of removal of any such officer, whether appointed or elected, for any cause affecting the incumbent's character, habits, or other qualifications, excepting political or religious opinions.

1872, January 8—Mr. SNAPP proposed a new article:

SEC. 1. No person shall be eligible to the office of President of the United States who is, or has been, a judge of the Supreme Court of the United States.

1872, January 15—Mr. MCINTYRE proposed a new article:

First. The Supreme Court of the United States shall have original as well as appellate jurisdiction in cases involving or affecting the constitutionality of any Federal law so far as to determine the question of the constitutionality of the same; and the Supreme Court, upon the application of any State, corporation, or person suggesting the unconstitutionality of any Federal law, or any part thereof, on notice to the Executive of the United States, within six months from the date of said application, shall determine the question. If the law, or any part thereof, shall be adjudged constitutional, such law, or part thereof, so adjudged to be constitutional, shall be operative and shall be enforced. If the law, or any part thereof, shall be adjudged unconstitutional, then such law, or part thereof, so adjudged to be unconstitutional, shall be inoperative, and shall not be enforced.

Second. The Supreme Court shall have appellate jurisdiction in all cases when the writ of *habeas corpus* will lie in the several Federal courts inferior to the Supreme Court. The right of appeal from such inferior tribunal to the Supreme Court shall not be abridged.

1872, January 22—Mr. ISAAC C. PARKER proposed a new article:

SECTION 1. No person shall be eligible to the office of President or Vice President of the United States while such person is a member of the Senate or House of Representatives of the United States, nor for two years after such membership shall cease.

1872, April 8—Mr. HAWLEY proposed a new article:

The Senate of the United States shall be composed of two Senators from each State, chosen by the people thereof for six years, and the electors in each State shall have the qualifications requisite for electors of the most numerous branch of the State Legislature; and if vacancies happen by resignation or otherwise, the executive authority of such State shall issue writs of election to fill such vacancies.

April 29—Mr. GOLLADAY submitted the following as a new article:

The Congress shall have no power to make any grants of the public lands of the United States, except for purposes of homesteads and common-school education of the people of the respective States and Territories. Nor shall Congress make any law impairing the obligation of contracts, nor shall they hereafter charter private corporations to carry on business within the States.

May 6—Mr. POLAND submitted the following new article:

No Senator or Representative shall, during the time for which he was elected, be chosen President or Vice President; nor shall any judge of any court of the United States be chosen President or Vice President within two years after the termination of his judicial office.

1872, March 4—Mr. WILLIAM T. JONES, Delegate from the Territory of Wyoming, proposed a new article:

SECTION 1. The House of Representatives shall be composed of members chosen every second year by the people of the several States and Territories of the United States; and hereafter each of the organized Territories of the United States shall be entitled to one Representative in the House of Representatives, who shall be entitled to all the privileges and powers enjoyed by members from the several States.

SEC. 2. No distinction as to the qualifications of electors in the States or Territories shall hereafter be made on account of sex.

"Religious" Amendment.

The National Association, whose object is to secure a recognition of Almighty God and the Christian religion in the Constitution of the United States, ask for the substance of the following amendment: to insert in the preamble to the Constitution, after the words "We, the people of the United States," the following:

Acknowledging Almighty God as the source of all authority and power in civil government, the Lord Jesus Christ as the Ruler among the nations, and His revealed will as of supreme authority, in order to constitute a Christian government.

VIII.

THIRTEENTH, FOURTEENTH, AND FIFTEENTH AMENDMENTS TO THE CONSTITUTION, AND VOTES ON THE VALIDITY THEREOF.

ARTICLE XIII.*

SEC. 1. Neither slavery nor involuntary servitude, except as a punishment for crime whereof the party shall have been duly convicted, shall exist within the United States, or any place subject to their jurisdiction.

SEC. 2. Congress shall have power to enforce this article by appropriate legislation.

ARTICLE XIV.†

SEC. 1.‡ All persons born or naturalized in the United States, and subject to the jurisdiction thereof, are citizens of the United States, and of the States wherein they reside. No State shall make or enforce any law which shall abridge the privileges or immunities of citizens of the United States; nor shall any State deprive any person of life, liberty, or property without due process of law, nor deny to any person within its jurisdiction the equal protection of the laws.

SEC. 2. Representatives shall be apportioned among the several States according to their respective numbers, counting the whole number of persons in each State, excluding Indians not taxed. But when the right to vote at any election for the choice of electors for President and Vice President of the United States, Representatives in Congress, the executive and judicial officers of a State, or the members of the Legislature thereof, is denied to any of the male inhabitants of such State, being twenty-one years of age, and citizens of the United States, or in any way abridged, except for participation in rebellion or other crime, the basis of representation therein shall be reduced in the proportion which the number of such male citizens shall bear to the whole number of male citizens twenty-one years of age in such State.

SEC. 3. No person shall be a Senator or Representative in Congress, or elector of President and Vice President, or hold any office, civil or military, under the United States, or under any State, who, having previously taken an oath as a member of Congress, or as an officer of the United States, or as a member of any State Legislature, or as an executive or judicial officer of any State, to support the Constitution of the United States, shall have engaged in insurrection or rebellion against the same, or given aid or comfort to the enemies thereof. But Congress may by a vote of two thirds of each House remove such disability.

SEC. 4. The validity of the public debt of the United States, authorized by law, including debts incurred for payment of pensions and bounties for services in suppressing insurrection or rebellion, shall not be questioned. But neither the United States nor any State shall assume or pay any debt or obligation incurred in aid of insurrection or rebellion against the United States, or any claim for the loss or emancipation of any slave; but all such debts, obligations, and claims shall be held illegal and void.

SEC. 5. The Congress shall have power to enforce, by appropriate legislation, the provisions of this article.

ARTICLE XV.*

SEC. 1. The right of citizens of the United States to vote shall not be denied or abridged

---

*Declared ratified by Mr. Secretary Seward, December 18, 1865. For certificate, see McPherson's History of Reconstruction, page 6.

†Declared ratified by Mr. Secretary Seward, July 28, 1868. For certificate, see McPherson's History of Reconstruction, page 379.

‡Respecting the history of this section of the amendment, it is proper to say that the clause defining citizens was not reported from the joint Committee on Reconstruction, but was offered in the Senate by Mr. JACOB M. HOWARD, of Michigan, as an amendment to the section as passed by the House. But the residue of the section was reported from the joint Committee on Reconstruction, in which it was offered in the precise form in which it stands by Mr. JOHN A. BINGHAM, of Ohio, a member of the committee, as stated by him in a speech in the House of Representatives, March 31, 1871, (Congressional Globe, volume 86, page 83,) and as appears from the unpublished journal of said committee, now in the hands of the heirs of the late Senator FESSENDEN, of Maine, its chairman.

*Declared ratified by Mr. Secretary Fish, March 30, 1870. For certificate, see McPherson's History of Reconstruction, page 545.

by the United States, or by any State, on account of race, color, or previous condition of servitude.

SEC. 2. The Congress shall have power to enforce this article by appropriate legislation.

IN HOUSE.

1871, March 13—Mr. JEREMIAH M. WILSON moved to suspend the rules to enable him to introduce, and the House to pass, the following joint resolution:

Whereas the Democratic members of the senate of the State of Indiana voted for and passed through that branch of the Legislature of said State the following joint resolution, to wit:

"Joint resolution of the Legislature of Indiana withdrawing its assent to the ratification of the fifteenth article of amendments to the Constitution.

"*Resolved by the General Assembly of the State of Indiana*, That the pretended ratification of the fifteenth amendment proposed to the Constitution of the United States on the part of the State of Indiana was and is null and void, and of no binding force or effect whatever, and the counting of the vote of the State in favor of the same was done without any lawful warrant or authority, and that, protesting against the same, this General Assembly does now withdraw and rescind all action, perfect or imperfect, on the part of this State, purporting to assent to and ratify said proposed fifteenth amendment.

"*Resolved, further, by the authority aforesaid*, That Congress has no lawful power derived from the Constitution of the United States, nor from any other source whatever, to require any State of the Union to ratify an amendment proposed to the Constitution of the United States as a condition-precedent to representation in Congress; that all such acts of ratification are null and void; and the votes so obtained ought not to be counted to affect the rights of the people and the States of the whole Union; and that the State of Indiana protests and solemnly declares that the so-called fifteenth amendment is not this day, nor ever has been in law, a part of the Constitution of the United States.

"*Resolved, further, by the authority aforesaid*, That the State of Indiana does now propose and ask that the Congress of the United States may and will, as soon as practicable, call a convention of the States and the people, according to the provisions of the fifth article of the Constitution of the United States, for the purpose of proposing amendments to said Constitution for the ratification by the States.

"*Resolved, further, by the authority aforesaid*, That the Governor of Indiana be, and is hereby, directed to transmit an authenticated copy of these resolutions, and the preamble thereto, to each of the Governors of the several States of the Union, and to each of our Senators and Representatives in Congress."

And whereas the validity of the act of Congress approved the 10th day of April, 1869, in relation to the ratification of the fifteenth article of amendments to the Constitution by the States of Virginia, Mississippi, and Texas; and also the validity and binding force of the ratification of said article by either of said States, is called in question by the resolutions aforesaid: Therefore,

Be it resolved by the Senate and House of Representatives, &c., That the Congress of the United States had the lawful power to impose upon the said States the ratification of the fifteenth article of amendments to the Constitution as a condition-precedent to representation in Congress, and that the ratification thereof, pursuant to such act of Congress, by either of said States is valid, to all intents and purposes, and binding upon the States so ratifying, and upon all the States, and that the State having so ratified has no lawful right to rescind the same.

And be it further resolved, That the thirteenth, fourteenth, and fifteenth articles of amendments to the Constitution of the United States have been duly ratified by the Legislatures of three fourths of the several States, and that said amendments are valid to all intents and purposes as a part of the Constitution of the United States, and as such binding and obligatory upon the Executive, the Congress, the several States and Territories, and all the citizens of the United States.

Which (two thirds not having voted in the affirmative) was not agreed to—yeas 109, nays 76, not voting 38:

YEAS—Messrs. Ambler, Averill, Barber, Beatty, Bigby, Bingham, A. Blair, *J. G. Blair*, G. M. Brooks, Buckley, Buffinton, Burchard, Burdett, R. R. Butler, F. Clarke, Cobb, Coburn, Conger, Cook, Cotton, Creely, Dawes, De Large, Dickey, Donnan, Dunnell, Eames, Elliott, Farnsworth, Finkelnburg, C. Foster, Frye, Garfield, Goodrich, Hale, Harmer, G. E. Harris, Havens, Hawley, G. W. Hazelton, J. W. Hazelton, Hoar, Hooper, Kelley, *Kendall*, Ketcham, Killinger, *Kinsella*, Lamport, Lansing, Lynch, Maynard, McCrary, McGrew, McJunkin, Merriam, Monroe, Moore, Morey, Morphis, L. Myers, Orr, Packard, Packer, Palmer, Pendleton, Perce, Peters, Platt, Poland, Porter, Prindle, Rainey, E. H. Roberts, Rusk, Sawyer, Scofield, Seeley, Sessions, Shanks, Sheldon, Shellabarger, Shoemaker, H. B. Smith, J. A. Smith, T. J. Speer, Sprague, Stevenson, Stoughton, Stowell, St. John, *Sutherland*, Sypher, Taffe, Thomas, W. Townsend, Twichell, Tyner, Upson, Wakeman, Walden, Waldron, Wallace, Wheeler, Whiteley, Willard, Williams of Indiana, J. M. Wilson, J. T. Wilson—109.

NAYS—Messrs. *Acker, Adams, Archer, Arthur, Beck, Biggs, Bird, Braxton, Bright, J. Brooks, Caldwell, Campbell, Carroll, Comingo, Cox, Critcher, Crossland, Davis, Dox, Du Bose, Duke, Eldredge, Forker, Garrett, Getz, Golladay, Griffith, Haldeman, Handley, Hanks, Harper, J. T. Harris, Hereford, Holman, King, Lamison, Leach, Lewis, Manson, McClelland, McCormick, McHenry, McIntyre, McKinney, Merrick, B. F. Meyers, Morgan, Niblack, Parker, E. Perry, Potter, Price, Randall, Read, E. Y. Rice, J. M. Rice, Ritchie, Robinson, Shober, Slater, Sloss, R. M. Speer, Storm, Swann, Terry, Tuthill, Van Trump, Vaughan, Voorhees, Waddell, Warren, Wells, Whitthorne, Williams* of New York, *Wood, Young*—76.

NOT VOTING—Messrs. Ames, Banks, Barry, B. F. Butler, *Crebs*, Darrall, Duell, *Ely*, Farwell, *H. D. Foster*, Halsey, *Hambleton*, Hay, Hays, Hill, *Kerr*, Lowe, *Marshall*, McKee, *McNeely*, Mercur, *Mitchell*, Negley, Peck, A. F. Perry, *W. R. Roberts, J. Rogers, Roosevelt, Sherwood, Slocum*, W. C. Smith, Snyder, *Stevens, D. Townsend*, Turner, Walls, Washburn, *Winchester*—38.

1872, February 5—Mr. PETERS offered the

following, and moved to suspend the rules and adopt it:

Resolved, That the thirteenth, fourteenth, and fifteenth amendments to the Constitution of the United States having been ratified by the number of State Legislatures necessary to make their adoption valid and binding, as well as having been sanctioned by the most significant popular approval, the highest patriotism and most enlightened public policy demand of all political parties and all citizens an acquiescence in the validity of such constitutional provisions, and such reasonable legislation of Congress as may be necessary to make them in their letter and spirit most effectual.

Which was agreed to—yeas 124, nays 58, not voting 57:

YEAS—Messrs. Ambler, Averill, Banks, Barber, Beatty, *Bell*, Beveridge, Bigby, Bingham, A. Blair, G. M. Brooks, Buckley, Buffinton, Burchard, Burdett, B. F. Butler, R. R. Butler, W. T. Clark, F. Clarke, Cobb, Coburn, Coghlan, Conger, Cotton, *Cox*, Darrall, Dickey, Donnan, Duell, Dunnell, Eames, Farnsworth, Farwell, Finkelnburg, C. Foster, W. D. Foster, Frye, Garfield, Goodrich, *Griffith*, Hale, Harmer, G. E. Harris, Havens, Hawley, Hay, G. W. Hazelton, J. W. Hazelton, Hoar, Hooper, Houghton, Kelley, Ketcham, Killinger, Lamport, Lansing, Lowe, Lynch, Maynard, *McClelland*, McGrew, McJunkin, McKee, Merriam, Monroe, Moore, Morey, Morphis, L. Myers, Negley, Orr, Packard, Packer, Palmer, *H. W. Parker*, I. C. Parker, Peck, Pendleton, Perce, Peters, Platt, Poland, Porter, Prindle, Rainey, E. H. Roberts, Rusk, Sargent, Sawyer, Seeley, Sessons, Shanks, Sheldon, Shellabarger, *Sherwood*, J. A. Smith, W. C. Smith, Snapp, T. J. Speer, Sprague, Starkweather, Stevenson, Stoughton, Stowell, Strong, *Sutherland*, Sypher, Taffe, Thomas, W. Townsend, Turner, Tyner, Upson, Wakeman, Walden, Waldron, Wallace, Walls, *Wells*, Wheeler, Whiteley, Willard, Williams of Indiana, J. M. Wilson, John T. Wilson—124.

NAYS—Messrs. *Acker, Adams, Arthur, Barnum, Beck, Biggs, Bright, Caldwell, Campbell, Comingo, Conner, Critcher, Crossland, Davis, Dox, Du Bose, Duke, Eldredge, Garrett, Getz, Golladay, Haldeman, Hambleton, Hancock, Handley, Hanks, Harper, Hereford, Herndon, Holman, King, Lamison, Lewis, Manson, Marshall, McHenry, McIntyre, McNeely, Merrick, Niblack, Price, Read, E. Y. Rice, J. M. Rice, Ritchie, Slater, Sloss, Storm, Swann, Terry, Van Trump, Vaughan, Voorhees, Waddell, Warren, Whitthorne, Winchester, Young*—58.

NOT VOTING—Messrs. Ames, *Archer*, Barry, *Bird, J. G. Blair, Braxton, J. Brooks, Carroll, Crebs*, Creely, Dawes, De Large, *Edwards*, Elliott, *Ely, Forker, H. D. Foster*, Halsey, *J. T. Harris*, Hays, *Hibbard*, Hill, Kellogg, *Kendall, Kerr, Kinsella, Leach, McCormick*, McCrary, *McKinney*, Mercur, *B. F. Meyers, Mitchell, Morgan*, A. F. Perry, *E. Perry, Potter, Randall, W. R. Roberts, Robinson, J. Rogers, Roosevelt*, Scofield, *Shober*, Shoemaker, *Slocum*, H. Boardman Smith, Snyder, *R. M. Speer, Stevens*, St. John, *D. Townsend, Tuthill*, Twichell, *Williams* of New York, *Wood*—57.

Same day—Mr. JAMES BROOKS offered the following, and moved to suspend the rules and adopt it:

Resolved, That we recognize the thirteenth, fourteenth, and fifteenth amendments to the Constitution as valid parts thereof; which was agreed to—yeas 166, nays 22:

YEAS.—Messrs. Ambler, Averill, Banks, Barber, *Barnum*, Beatty, *Beck, Bell*, Beveridge, Bigby, Bingham, *Bird, J. G. Blair, Bright*, G. M. Brooks, *J. Brooks*, Buckley, Buffinton, Burchard, Burdett, B. F. Butler, R. R. Butler, *Campbell, Carroll*, W. T. Clark, Cobb, Coburn, *Comingo*, Conger, Cotton, *Cox, Crebs*, Creely, Dickey, Donnan, *Dox*, Duell, *Duke*, Dunnell, Eames, *Edwards, Eldredge, Ely*, Farnsworth, Farwell, Finkelnburg, C. Foster, W. D. Foster, Frye, *Garrett, Getz, Golladay*, Goodrich, *Griffith, Haldeman*, Hale, *Hancock, Handley*, Harmer, *Harper*, G. E. Harris, Havens, Hawley, Hay, Hays, G. W. Hazelton, J. W. Hazelton, *Herndon, Hibbard*, Hoar, *Holman*, Hooper, Houghton, Kelley, *Kerr*, Ketcham, Killinger, *King, Lamison*, Lamport, *Leach*, Lowe, Lynch, *Manson, Marshall*, Maynard, *McClelland, McCormick*, McGrew, *McIntyre*, McJunkin, *McNeely*, Mercur, Merriam, *Merrick*, Monroe, Moore, Morphis, L. Myers, Negley, Packard, Packer, Palmer, *H. W. Parker*, I. C. Parker, Peck, Pendleton, Perce, *E. Perry*, Peters, Platt, Poland, Porter, Prindle, Rainey, *Randall, E. Y. Rice*, E. H. Roberts, *W. R. Roberts, Robinson, Roosevelt*, Sargent, Sawyer, Seeley, Sessions, Shanks, Sheldon, Shellabarger, *Sherwood, Slocum*, J. A. Smith, W. C. Smith, Snapp, T. J. Speer, Starkweather, *Stevens*, Stevenson, *Storm*, Stoughton, Stowell, Strong, *Sutherland, Swann*, Sypher, Thomas, W. Townsend, Turner, Twichell, Tyner, Upson, *Waddell*, Wakeman, Walden, Waldron, Wallace, Walls, *Warren, Wells*, Wheeler, Whiteley, Willard, Williams of Indiana, J. M. Wilson, J. T. Wilson, *Wood*—166.

NAYS—Messrs. *Acker, Adams, Arthur, Biggs, Conner, Critcher, Crossland, Davis, Du Bose, Hambleton, Hanks, Hereford, Lewis, McHenry, Niblack, Read, J. M. Rice, Ritchie, Terry, Voorhees, Winchester, Young*—22.

1872, February 12—The vote was taken on suspending the rules, and passing the following resolution offered on the 5th by Mr. STEVENSON:

Resolved, That we recognize as valid and binding all existing laws passed by Congress for the enforcement of the thirteenth, fourteenth, and fifteenth amendments to the Constitution of the United States, and for the protection of citizens in their rights under the Constitution as amended.

The vote was—yeas 107, nays 65:

YEAS—Messrs. Ambler, Ames, Averill, Banks, Barber, Barry, Beatty, Beveridge, Bigby, Bingham, Boles, G. M. Brooks, Buffinton, Burchard, Burdett, B. F. Butler, W. T. Clark, F. Clarke, Cobb, Coburn, Coghlan, Conger, Cotton, Dawes, Donnan, Duell, Dunnell, Finkelnburg, C. Foster, W. D. Foster, Frye, Garfield, Goodrich, Hale, Halsey, Harmer, Havens, Hawley, Hay, Hays, G. W. Hazelton, J. W. Hazelton, Hill, Hoar, Hooper, Kelley, Ketcham, Killinger, Lamport, Lansing, Lowe, Maynard, McGrew, McJunkin, McKee, Mercur, Merriam, Morphis, L. Myers, Negley, Orr, Packard, Packer, Palmer, I. C. Parker, Peck, Pendleton, Perce, A. F. Perry, Peters, Platt, Poland, Porter, Prindle, Rainey, E. H. Roberts, Rusk, Sargent, Seeley, Shanks, Sheldon, Shellabarger, J. A. Smith, Snapp, Snyder, T. J. Speer, Sprague, Starkweather, Stevenson, Stoughton, Stowell, Sypher, Taffe, W. Townsend, Turner, Twichell, Tyner, Upson, Wakeman, Walden, Waldron, Wallace, Whiteley, Willard, Williams of Indiana, J. M. Wilson, J. T. Wilson—107.

NAYS—Messrs. *Acker, Adams, Arthur, Beck, Bell, Bird, Bright, J. Brooks, Caldwell, Comingo, Conner, Cox, Crossland, Davis, Dox, Du Bose, Duke, Eldredge, Garrett, Getz, Golladay, Griffith, Haldeman, Handley, Hanks, J. T. Harris, Herndon, Hibbard, Holman, King, Kinsella, Lamison, Lewis, McClelland, McCormick, McHenry, McIntyre, McNeely, Merrick, Niblack, H. W. Parker, E. Perry, Potter, Price, Randall, Read, J. M. Rice, W. R. Roberts, Sherwood, Shober, Slater, Slocum, Sloss, Stevens, Storm, Vaughan, Voorhees, Waddell, Warren, Wells, Whitthorne, Williams* of New York, *Winchester, Wood, Young*—65.

Two-thirds being required, the motion failed.

IX.

AMENDMENTS TO STATE CONSTITUTIONS, PROPOSED AND MADE.

STATE CONSTITUTIONS.

—

Illinois.*

* * * * * * *

ARTICLE IV.

SEC. 5. Members of the General Assembly, before they enter upon their official duties, shall take and subscribe the following oath or affirmation:

"I do solemnly swear (or affirm) that I will support the Constitution of the United States and the constitution of the State of Illinois, and will faithfully discharge the duties of Senator (or Representative) according to the best of my ability; and that I have not, knowingly or intentionally, paid or contributed anything, or made any promise in the nature of a bribe, to directly or indirectly influence any vote at the election at which I was chosen to fill the said office, and have not accepted, nor will I accept or receive, directly or indirectly, any money or other valuable thing, from any corporation, company or person, for any vote or influence I may give or withhold on any bill, resolution, or appropriation, or for any other official act." * * * * *

SECS. 7 and 8. The House of Representatives shall consist of three times the number of the members of the Senate, and the term of office shall be two years. Three representatives shall be elected in each senatorial district at the general election in the year of our Lord 1872, and every two years thereafter. In all elections of representatives aforesaid, each qualified voter may cast as many votes for one candidate as there are representatives to be elected, or may distribute the same, or equal parts thereof, among the candidates, as he shall see fit; and the candidates highest in votes shall be declared elected. * * *

SEC. 11. On the final passage of all bills the vote shall be by yeas and nays, upon each bill separately, and shall be entered upon the journal; and no bill shall become a law without the concurrence of a majority of the members elected to each House.

SEC. 13. Every bill shall be read at large on three different days in each House; and the bill and all amendments thereto shall be printed before the vote is taken on its final passage. * * * * No act hereafter passed shall embrace more than one subject, and that shall be expressed in the title. But if any subject shall be embraced in an act which shall not be expressed in the title, such act shall be void only as to so much thereof as shall not be so expressed; and no law shall be revived or amended by reference to its title only, but the law revived, or the section amended, shall be inserted at length in the new act. * * *

ARTICLE VI.

SEC. 31. All judges of courts of record, inferior to the supreme court, shall, on or before the 1st day of June, of each year, report in writing to the judges of the supreme court such defects and omissions in the laws as their experience may suggest; and the judges of the supreme court shall, on or before the 1st day of January, of each year, report in writing to the Governor such defects and omissions in the constitution and laws as they may find to exist, together with appropriate forms of bills to cure such defects and omissions in the law. * * * *

ARTICLE VII.

SEC. 1. Every person having resided in this State one year, in the county ninety days, and in the election district thirty days next preceding any election therein, who was an elector in this State on the 1st day of April, in the year of our Lord 1848, or obtained a certificate of naturalization, before any court of record in this State, prior to the 1st day of January, in the year of our Lord 1870, or who shall be a male citizen of the United States, above the age of twenty-one years, shall be entitled to vote at such election.

SEC. 3. Neither the General Assembly nor any county, city, town, township, school district, or other public corporation, shall ever make any appropriation or pay from any public fund whatever, anything in aid of any church or sectarian purpose, or to help support or sustain any school, academy, seminary, college, university, or other literary or scientific institution, controlled by any church or sectarian denomination whatever; nor shall any grant or donation of land, money, or other personal property ever be made by the State, or any such public corporation, to any church, or for any sectarian purpose.

ARTICLE XI.

SEC. 1. No corporation shall be created by special laws, or its charter extended, changed, or amended, except those for charitable, educational, penal or reformatory purposes, which are to be and remain under the patronage and control of the State, but the General Assembly shall provide, by general laws, for the organization of all corporations hereafter to be created. * * * * *

---

* Owing to its length, only such extracts of the Illinois constitution of 1870 as seem to be novel or especially noteworthy are given; and so with other constitutions following.

VOTES—For new constitution, 134,227; against it, 35,443. For Illinois Central Railroad section, 147,032; against, 21,310. For other railroad sections, 144,750; against, 23,525. For minority representation, 99,022; against, 70,080. For canal section, 142,540; against, 27,017.

SEC. 8. The General Assembly shall provide, by law, that in all elections for directors or managers of incorporated companies every stockholder shall have the right to vote, in person or by proxy, for the number of shares of stock owned by him, for as many persons as there are directors or managers to be elected, or to cumulate said shares, and give one candidate as many votes as the number of directors multiplied by the number of his shares of stock, shall equal, or to distribute them on the same principle among as many candidates as he shall think fit; and such directors or managers shall not be elected in and other manner. * * * *

SEC. 9. Every railroad corporation organized or doing business in this State, under the laws or authority thereof, shall have and maintain a public office or place in this State for the transaction of its business, where transfers of stock shall be made and in which shall be kept, for public inspection, books, in which shall be recorded the amount of capital stock subscribed, and by whom; the names of the owners of its stock, and the amounts owned by them respectively; the amount of stock paid in and by whom; the transfers of said stock; the amount of its assets and liabilities, and the names and place of residence of its officers. The directors of every railroad corporation shall, annually, make a report, under oath, to the auditor of public accounts, or some officer to be designated by law, of all their acts and doings, which report shall include such matters relating to railroads as may be prescribed by law. And the General Assembly shall pass laws enforcing by suitable penalties the provisions of this section.

SEC. 10. The rolling stock and all other movable property belonging to any railroad company or corporation in this State shall be considered personal property, and shall be liable to execution and sale in the same manner as the personal property of individuals, and the General Assembly shall pass no law exempting any such property from execution and sale.

SEC. 11. No railroad corporation shall consolidate its stock, property, or franchises with any other railroad corporation owning a parallel or competing line; and in no case shall any consolidation take place except upon public notice given, of at least sixty days, to all stockholders in such manner as may be provided by law. A majority of the directors of any railroad corporation, now incorporated or hereafter to be incorporated by the laws of this State, shall be citizens and residents of this State.

SEC. 12. Railways heretofore constructed or that may hereafter be constructed in this State, are hereby declared public highways, and shall be free to all persons, for the transportation of their persons and property thereon, under such regulations as may be prescribed by law. And the General Assembly shall, from time to time, pass laws establishing reasonable maximum rates of charges for the transportation of passengers and freight on the different railroads in this State.

SEC. 13. No railroad corporation shall issue any stock of bonds, except for money, labor or property actually received and applied to the purposes for which such corporation was created; and all stock dividends, and other fictitious increase of the capital stock or indebtedness of any such corporation, shall be void. The capital stock of no railroad corporation shall be increased for any purpose, except upon giving sixty days' public notice, in such manner as may be provided by law.

SEC. 14. The exercise of the power and the right of eminent domain shall never be so construed or abridged as to prevent the taking, by the General Assembly, of the property and franchises of incorporated companies already organized, and subjecting them to the public necessity the same as of individuals. The right of jury shall be held inviolate, in all trials of claims for compensation, when, in the exercise of the said right of eminent domain, any incorporated company shall be interested either for or against the exercise of said right.

SEC. 15. The General Assembly shall pass laws to correct abuses and prevent unjust discrimination and extortion in the rates of freight and passenger tariffs on the different railroads in this State, and enforce such laws by adequate penalties, to the extent, if necessary for that purpose, of forfeiture of their property and franchises.

(Separate sections.)

Illinois Central Railroad.

No contract, obligation, or liability whatever of the Illinois Central Railroad Company to pay any money into the State treasury, nor any lien of the State upon or right to tax property of said company, in accordance with the provisions of the charter of said company, approved February 10, in the year of our Lord 1851, shall ever be released, suspended, modified, altered, remitted, or in any manner diminished or impaired by legislative or other authority; and all moneys derived from said company, after the payment of the State debt, shall be appropriated and set apart for the payment of the ordinary expenses of the State government, and for no other purposes whatever.

Municipal subscriptions to railroads or private corporations.

No county, city, town, township, or other municipality, shall ever become subscriber to the capital stock of any railroad or private corporation, or make donation to or loan its credit in aid of such corporation; provided, however, that the adoption of this article shall not be construed as affecting the right of any such municipality to make such subscriptions where the same have been authorized, under existing laws, by a vote of the people of such municipalities prior to such adoptions.

Canal.

The Illinois and Michigan canal shall never be sold or leased until the specific proposition for the sale or lease thereof shall first have been submitted to a vote of the people of the State, at a general election, and have been approved by a majority of all the votes polled at such election. The General Assembly shall never loan the credit of the State, or make appropriations from the Treasury thereof, in aid of railroads or canals; provided, that any surplus earnings of any canal may be appropriated for its enlargement or extension.

Louisiana.

The following amendments to the constitution of 1868 were ratified by popular vote November 7, 1870:

ART. 50. Abrogating and striking out article 50 of the constitution, which renders the Governor ineligible for the succeeding four years after the expiration of his term of office.

For, 64,447; against, 40,928.

ART. 59. No person shall hold any office, or shall be permitted to vote at any election, or to act as a juror, who, in due course of law, shall have been convicted of treason, perjury, forgery, bribery, or other crime punishable by imprisonment in the penitentiary, or who shall be under interdiction.

For, 103,848; against, 263.

ART. —. No person who, at any time, may have been a collector of taxes, whether State, parish, or municipal, or who may have been otherwise intrusted with public money, shall be eligible to the General Assembly or to any office of profit or trust under the State government, until he shall have obtained a discharge for the amount of such collection and for all public moneys with which he may have been intrusted.

For, 102,972; against, 748.

ART. —. Prior to the 1st day of January, 1890, the debt of the State shall not be so increased as to exceed twenty five millions of dollars.

For, 100,170; against, 3,150.

Michigan.

The following proposed amendments to the constitution of the State of Michigan were submitted to popular vote at fall election in 1870:

ART. X. To stand as section nine, limiting county supervisors to $2,000 annual expenditures, unless otherwise authorized by majority of the county voters. Lost: 39,180 yeas; 61,904 nays.

ART. IV. To stand as sections three and four; section one of article seven, and section one of article seventeen.

SEC. 3. The House of Representatives to consist of not less than sixty-four nor more than one hundred members. Representatives to be chosen for two years, and by single districts. The balance of the section relates to equalizing representation, mode and manner of dividing the districts, &c.

Section four provides for a State census every ten years after 1854, and for the rearrangement of the Senate districts at the first session after each such census, and after every United States census, and apportion anew the representatives.

ARTICLE VII.

SEC. 1. In all elections every male citizen, every male inhabitant residing in the State on the 24th day of June 1835; every male inhabitant residing in the State on the 1st day of January, 1850, who has declared his intention to become a citizen of the United States, pursuant to the laws thereof, six months preceding an election, or who has resided in this State two years and six months, and declared his intention as aforesaid, and every civilized male inhabitant of Indian descent, a native of the United States, and not a member of any tribe, shall be an elector and entitled to vote; but no citizen or inhabitant shall be an elector or entitled to vote at any election unless, he shall be above the age of tweny-one years, and has resided in this State three months, and in the township or ward in which he offers to vote, ten days next preceding such election; provided that in time of war, insurrection or rebellion, no qualified elector in the actual military service of the United States, or of this State, in the army or navy thereof, shall be deprived of his vote by reason of his absence from the township, ward, or State in which he resides; and the Legislature shall have the power, and shall provide the manner in which, and the time and place at which such absent electors may vote, and for the canvass and return of their votes to the township or ward election district in which they respectively reside, or otherwise.

ARTICLE IX.

Section one provides annual salaries: to the Governor $2,500; and $2,000 each to the judges of the circuit court, State treasurer, auditor general, superintendent of public instruction, secretary of State, commissioner of the land office, and attorney general, prohibiting any increase of same, and abolishing all fees and perquisites for the performance of their duties. [Rejected—yeas, 36,109; nays, 68,912.]

ARTICLE XVII.

SEC. 1. The militia shall be composed of all able-bodied male citizens between the ages of eighteen and forty-five years, except such as are exempted by the laws of the United States, or of this State; but all such citizens of any religious denomination whatever, who, from scruples of conscience, may be averse to bearing arms, shall be excused therefrom, upon such conditions as shall be prescribed by law.

Which was agreed to—yeas, 54,105; nays, 50,598.

ARTICLE XIX—A. Railroads.

SEC. 1. The Legislature may from time to time pass laws establishing reasonable maximum rates of charges for the transportation of passengers and freight on different railroads in this State, and shall prohibit running contracts between such railroad companies whereby discrimination is made in favor of either of such companies as against other companies owning connecting or intersecting lines of railroads.

SEC. 2. No railroad corporation shall consolidate its stock, property, or franchises with any other railroad corporation owning a parallel or competing line; and in no case shall any consolidation take place except upon public notice given of at least sixty days to all stockholders, in such manner as shall be provided by law.

SEC. 3. The Legislature may provide by law for the payment by the counties, townships, and municipalities of this State of all bonds or other obligations heretofore issued or incurred in pursuance of acts of the Legislature, by such counties, townships, and municipalities severally, for and in aid of any railroad company. Such bonds or obligations shall be paid by the county, township, or municipality issuing or incurring the same; and in no event shall the State pay or become liable for any portion of such bonds or obligations. The Legislature shall submit to the electors of each of said several counties, townships, and municipalities for their decision the question of payment, together with the mode and manner of the same.

Which was voted on separately.

For section 1, the vote was—yeas, 78,602; nays, 51,397.

For section 2, the vote was—yeas, 76,912; nays, 51.194.

For section 3, the vote was—yeas, 50,078; nays, 78,543.

Missouri.

The following amendments to the constitution of Missouri were submitted to popular vote in November, 1870, and adopted:

ARTICLE VIII.

SEC. 6. Dues from private corporations shall be secured by such means as may be prescribed by law, but in no case shall any stockholder be individually liable in any amount over or above the amount of stock owned by him or her.

ARTICLE IX.

SEC. 10. Neither the General Assembly nor any county, city, town, township, school district, or other municipal corporation, shall ever make any appropriation or pay from any public fund whatever anything in aid of any creed, church, or sectarian purpose, or to help support or sustain any school, academy, seminary, college, university, or other institution of learning controlled by any creed, church or sectarian denomination whatever, nor shall any grant or donation of personal property or real estate ever be made by State, county, city, town, or such public corporation for any creed, church, or sectarian purpose whatever.

ARTICLE II.

Section eleven, requiring jurors to take the oath of loyalty prescribed in the sixth section of this article, is hereby stricken out and forever rescinded.

ARTICLE —.

SEC. 1. Every male citizen of the United States and every person of foreign birth, who may have declared his intention to become a citizen of the United States, according to law, not less than one year nor more than five years before he offers to vote, who is over the age of twenty-one years, who has resided in this State one year next preceding his registration as a voter, and during the last sixty days of that period shall have resided in the county, city, or town where he seeks registration as a voter, who is not convicted of bribery, perjury, or other infamous crime, nor directly or indirectly interested in any bet or wager depending upon the result of the election for which said registration is made, nor serving at the time of such registration in the regular Army or Navy of the United States, shall be entitled to vote at such election, for all officers, State, county, or municipal, made elective by the people, or any other election held in pursuance of the laws of this State, but he shall not vote elsewhere than in the election district where his name is registered, except as provided in the twenty-first section of the second article of the constitution. Any person who shall, after the adoption of this amendment, engage in any rebellion against this State, or the United States, shall forever be disqualified from voting at any election.

SEC. 2. Hereafter it shall not be required of any person, before he is registered as a voter or offers to vote, to take the oath of loyalty prescribed in the sixth section of the second article of the constitution; but every person, before he is registered as a qualified voter, shall take an oath to support the Constitution of the United States and of the State of Missouri.

SEC. 3. Sections five, fifteen, sixteen, seventeen, and eighteen of the second article of the constitution, and all provisions thereof, and all laws of this State not consistent with this amendment, shall, upon its adoption, be forever rescinded and of no effect.

ARTICLE —.

SEC. 1. No person shall hereafter be disqualified from holding in this State any office of honor, trust, or profit under its authority, or of being an officer, councilman, director, trustee, or other manager of any corporation, public or private, now existing or hereafter established by its authority, or of acting as a professor or a teacher in any educational institution, or in any common or other school, or of holding any real estate or other property in trust for the use of any church, religious society or congregation, on account of race, or color, or previous condition of servitude, nor on account of any of the provisions of the third section of the second article of the constitution; nor shall hereafter any such person, before he enters upon the discharge of his said duties, be required to take the oath of loyalty prescribed in the sixth section of said article, but every person who may be elected or appointed to any office shall, before entering upon its duties, take and subscribe an oath or affirmation that he will support the Constitution of the United States and of the State of Missouri, and to the best of his skill and ability diligently and faithfully, without partiality or prejudice, discharge the duties of such office according to the constitution and laws of this State.

SEC. 2. Sections seven, eight, nine, ten, thirteen, fourteen, of the second article of the Constitution, and all provisions thereof, and all laws of this State, not consistent with this amendment, shall, upon its adoption, be forever rescinded and of no effect.

Nebraska.

The votes upon the new Nebraska constitution, and upon the several independent propositions submitted therewith, at an election held September 19, 1871, were as below. Constitution: for, 7,986 votes; against it, 8,627. Liabilities of stockholders in banking companies and associations: for, 7,286; against, 8,580. Prohibitory courts, and municipal aid to corporations: for, 6,690; against, 9,549. Compulsory education and reformatory schools: for, 6,289; against, 9,958. Inhibition and license: for, 6,071; against, 10,160. Extension of the right of suffrage: for, 3,502; against, 12,676.

North Carolina.

The following amendments to the constitution of North Carolina were adopted by a two-thirds vote of the last Legislature, and if adopted by a three-fifths vote of the next Legislature will become a part of said constitution:

ARTICLE I.

SEC. 6. Strike out the words "to maintain the honor and good faith of the State untarnished, the public debt, regularly contracted before and since the rebellion, shall be regarded as inviolable and never be questioned; but"

ARTICLE II.

SEC. 2. Strike out "annually" and insert "biennially," so as to provide for biennial sessions of the Legislature.

SEC. 5. Strike out the clause providing for an enumeration of the population every ten years, and the words "as aforesaid, or," which relate to it.

Add a new section (section 30) to Article II, fixing the ordinary compensation and mileage of members of the Legislature at $300 per term, and ten cents per mile each session.

ARTICLE III.

SEC 1. Strike out "four years" and insert "two years," so as to limit the terms of State executive officers to two years.

Strike out "Superintendent of Public Works" throughout the constitution, thus abolishing the office.

SEC. 6. Strike out "annually" and insert "biennially," so that the Governor shall "biennially communicate" with the Legislature.

ARTICLE IV.

Strike out sections two and three, so as to do away with appointment and duties of code commissioners.

SEC. 4. Strike out the establishment of "special courts," and insert "such inferior courts as may be established by law."

SEC. 8. Strike out "four" and insert "two," and add a proviso, so that the justices of the supreme court, after the expiration of their present official terms, shall be limited to one chief and two associates.

Strike out sections twelve and thirteen and insert, so that the former shall read:

"SEC. 12. The State shall be divided into nine judicial districts, for each of which a judge shall be chosen; and in each district a superior court shall be held at least twice in each year, to continue for such time in each county respectively as may be prescribed by law. The General Assembly shall lay off said districts in due time, so that the said nine judges may be chosen and begin their official term at the first general election for members of the General Assembly which shall occur after the ratification of this section." The General Assembly may reduce or increase the number of districts, to take effect at the end of each judicial term.

SEC. 14. Strike out all after the word "office;" so that instead of leaving the matter to the Governor, it will read:

"The General Assembly shall prescribe a proper system of rotation for the judges of the superior courts, so that no judge may ride the same district twice in succession, and the judges may also exchange districts with each other, as may be provided by law."

SEC. 15. Strike out this section and insert:

"The General Assembly shall have no power to deprive the judicial department of any power or jurisdiction which rightfully pertains to it as a coördinate department; but the General Assembly shall allot and distribute that portion of this power and jurisdiction which does not pertain to the supreme court among the other courts prescribed in this constitution, or which may be established by law, in such manner as it may deem best, provide also a proper system of appeals, and regulate by law when necessary the methods of proceeding, in the exercise of their powers, of all the courts below the supreme court, so far as the same may be done without conflict with other provisions of this constitution."

Sections sixteen, seventeen, nineteen, twenty-five, and thirty-three to be stricken out. These relate to appellate jurisdiction of superior courts, jurisdiction of clerks of superior courts, the establishment of special courts, the transfer of causes, the jurisdiction of justices of the peace, and modes of procedure.

SEC. 26. Strike out the word "but" and all the words following it, which prescribe that the judges shall draw lots for four and eight-year terms at the first election, and insert certain other matter relative to the mode of electing judicial officers, the jurisdiction of peace justices, and judicial powers of chief magistrates of cities and incorporated towns.

SEC. 30 so amended as to provide a constable for each "precinct," instead of "township;" and in case of vacancy in the offices of sheriff, coroner, or constable, the power of appointment is taken from the county commissioners and will be "prescribed by law."

ARTICLE V.

SEC. 1 so amended as to empower the "county authorities established and authorized by law," instead of the county "commissioners," to, exempt from capitation tax in special cases.

SEC. 4. Strike out this section, as follows: "The General Assembly shall, by appropriate legislation and by adequate taxation, provide for the prompt and regular payment of the interest on the public debt; and after the year 1880 it shall lay a specific annual tax upon the real and personal property of the State, and the sum thus realized shall be set apart as a sinking fund, to be devoted to the payment of the public debt."

SEC. 6 so amended that the General Assembly may exempt from taxation any personal property not exceeding $300 in value.

ARTICLE VII.

SEC. 1. That portion providing for the biennial election in each county of "five commissioners" stricken out, and this added: "The General Assembly shall provide for a system of county government for the several counties of the State."

SEC. 2 substitutes "county authorities, &c., established, &c., by law," for "commissioners," in prescribing certain duties, and strikes out that portion under which the register of deeds is *ex officio* clerk, &c.

SEC. 3 strikes out this section, relating to the division of each county by the commissioners into districts, and prescribes that the above-named "county authorities" shall make such subdivisions of the county, which are to be known as "precincts" instead of "townships," and have the same boundaries until altered. "They shall have no corporate powers." The township governments are also abolished.

Sections four, five, six, ten, and eleven, relating to this abolished township system, are stricken out, as also are such parts of sections eight and nine as refer to such townships.

ARTICLE IX.

Section three, which provides that "each county of the State shall be divided into a convenient number of districts, in which one or more public schools shall be maintained at least four months in every year; and if the commissioners of any county shall fail to comply with the aforesaid requirements of this section, they shall be liable to indictment," is stricken out, as also are sections thirteen, fourteen, and fifteen, which relate to the mode of election, powers, duties, organization, privileges, &c., of the Board of Trustees of the University of North Carolina, and insert as section three that the General Assembly shall have the power to provide for the election of trustees of the university, in whom shall be vested all the privileges, rights, franchises, and endowments heretofore conferred upon the board of trustees of said university; and the General Assembly may make such regulations as may be expedient, for the management of said university.

ARTICLE XI.

Section ten is amended so that all the deaf mutes, the blind, and the insane of the State shall be cared for by the State, but only such of them as have less property than the homestead and personal property exemption would cover, to be a charge to the State.

ARTICLE XIV.

Section seven strikes out that "no person shall hold more than one lucrative office under the State at one time," &c., and provides that no person holding a Federal or a State office (with certain petty exceptions) shall be eligible to a seat in either house of the Legislature.

Add a section (section 8) providing that occupants of abolished or changed offices shall exercise their functions until the necessary legislation is had.

Rhode Island.

The following amendments were submitted to popular vote in 1871, and rejected, a three-fifths affirmative vote being required:

ARTICLE.

SEC. 1. Instead of sections one and two of Article II of the Constitution, the following is adopted, viz:

Every male citizen of the United States, of the age of twenty-one years, who has had his residence and home in this State two years, and in the town or city in which he may offer to vote six months, next preceding the time of voting, who shall give evidence of his ability to read the constitution, and whose name shall be registered in the town where he resides, on or before the last day of December in the year next preceding, and for at least seven days before he shall offer to vote, (except persons enumerated in section four of said Article II of said constitution,) shall have the right to vote in all questions in all legally organized town or ward meetings; provided that no person shall, at any time, be allowed to vote upon any proposition to impose a tax or for the expenditure of money, in any town or city, or upon the election of the city council for the city of Providence, unless he shall have paid a tax, within a year preceding upon his property, within the town or city where he shall offer to vote, valued at least at $134.*

The ayes were 3,236; nays, 6,960.

ARTICLE.

Instead of section three, of Article II, of the constitution, the following is adopted, viz:

No registry tax shall hereafter be assessed, nor shall the payment of such tax be required as a qualification of an elector.

The ayes were 3,787; nays 6,100.

ARTICLE.

No sectarian or denominational school or institution shall receive any aid or support from the revenues of the State, nor shall any tax be

* The effect of this amendment would have been to abolish the real estate qualification as to naturalized citizens.

imposed upon the people or property of the State in aid of any such school or institution.

The ayes were 5,177; nays 4,574.

West Virginia.

The constitution was amended in 1871 by the adoption of what is commonly known as the "Flick amendment," the effect of which was to enfranchise those citizens of the State who had been disfranchised by reason of their participation in the rebellion, and also by striking out the word "white," enfranchised colored citizens otherwise qualified.

A new constitution has been prepared by a convention elected for the purpose, and is to be voted on on the fourth Thursday in August, 1872. Its leading provisions are:

ARTICLE IV.

Section one entitles "the male citizens of the State" to vote.

Section four declares that "no person, except citizens entitled to vote, shall be elected or appointed to any State, county, or municipal office."

ARTICLE VI.

SEC. 42. Bills making appropriations for the pay of members and officers of the Legislature, and for salaries for the officers of the government, shall contain no provision on any other subject.

Section forty-five declares it to be the duty of the Legislature, at its first session after the adoption of this constitution, to provide by law for the punishment, by imprisonment in the penitentiary, of any person who shall bribe or attempt to bribe any executive or judicial officer or member of the Legislature, and similar punishment for any such officials or member who shall demand or receive bribes; compelling the briber to testify, and exempting him in that case from punishment; and forever disqualifying any person convicted from holding office.

SEC. 47. No charter of incorporation shall be granted to any church or religious denomination. Provision may be made by general laws for securing title to church property, &c.

SEC. 48. Any husband or parent, or the infant children of deceased parents, may hold a homestead of the value of $1,000, and personal property to the value of $200, exempt from forced sale.

SEC. 49. The Legislature shall pass such laws as may be necessary to protect the property of married women from the debts, liabilities, and control of their husbands.

ARTICLE VII.

Section four declares the Governor ineligible for the same office for the four years next succeeding the term for which he was elected.

ARTICLE VIII.

SEC. 35. No citizen of this State who aided or participated in the late war between the Government of the United States and a part of the people thereof, on either side, shall be liable in any proceeding, civil or criminal; nor shall his property be seized or sold under final process issued upon judgments or decrees heretofore rendered, or otherwise, because of any act done according to the usages of civilized warfare in the prosecution of said war, by either of the parties thereto. The Legislature shall provide by general law for giving full force and effect to this section, by due process of law.

ARTICLE X.

Section six prohibits the State from granting its credit, assuming debts, or becoming an owner or stock holder in any corporation.

Section seven prohibits the assessment of more than ninety-three cents county taxes per annum on each $100, except in certain cases.

Section eight limits county, city, school district, and municipal corporation debts to five per cent. on the value of taxable property, and provides for the payment of interest and principal.

ARTICLE XI.

SEC. 2. The stockholders of all corporations and joint stock companies, except banks and banking institutions, created by the laws of this State, shall be liable for the indebtedness of such corporations to the amount of their stock subscribed and unpaid, and no more.

Section four provides that every share of stock in an incorporated company entitles the holder to a vote in person or by proxy in the election of directors, and for cumulative voting thereat.

Section six provides for the creation of banks of issue or circulation, and the personal liability of the stockholders of all banks in the amount of their shares, and an additional amount equal thereto.

ARTICLE XII.

Section five provides for the support of free schools.

SEC. 8. White and colored persons shall not be taught in the same school.

With the Constitution will be submitted a separate proposition, which, if adopted will take the place of section four, Article IV, of the constitution, and which is as follows:

"Any white citizen entitled to vote, and no other, may be elected or appointed to any office; but the Governor and judges must have attained the age of thirty, and the Attorney General and Senators the age of twenty-five years at the beginning of their respective terms of service, and must have been citizens of the State for five years next preceding their election or appointment, or citizens at the time this constitution goes into operation."

Wisconsin.

The eighth section of the first article, being the declaration of rights, of the constitution of Wisconsin was as follows:

SEC. 8. No person shall be held to answer for a criminal offense, [unless on the presentment or indictment of a grand jury, except in cases of impeachment, or in cases cognizable by justices of the peace, or arising in the Army or Navy, or in the militia when in actual service in time of war or public danger;] and no person for the same offense shall be put twice in jeopardy of punishment, nor shall be compelled in any criminal case to be a witness against himself, &c.

The question of striking out the words inclosed above in brackets, and inserting in their place the words "without due process of law," was submitted to a vote of the people of the State in November, 1870, and resulted affirmatively, as follows: against grand jury system, 48,894; for grand jury system, 18,606.

An amendment to add to Article IV the following words:

"SEC. 31. The Legislature is prohibited from enacting any special or private laws in the following cases: first, for changing the names of persons or constituting one person the heir-at-law of another; second, for laying out, opening, or altering highways, except in cases of State roads extending into more than one county, and military roads to aid in the construction of which lands may be granted by Congress; third, for authorizing persons to keep ferries across streams at points wholly within this State; fourth, for authorizing the sale or mortgage of real or personal property of minors or others under disability; fifth, for locating or changing any county seat; sixth, for assessment or collection of taxes, or for extending the time for the collection thereof; seventh, for granting corporate powers or privileges, except to cities; eighth, for authorizing the apportionment of any part of the school fund; ninth, for incorporating any town or village or to amend the charter thereof.

SEC. 32. The Legislature shall provide general laws for the transaction of any business that may be prohibited by section thirty-one of this article, and all such laws shall be uniform in their operation throughout the State"—was submitted to popular vote at the election in 1871, and was adopted—yeas, 54,087; nays, 3,675.

X.

THE "LEGAL-TENDER" DECISION OF 1871.

Supreme Court of the United States.

Nos. 10 and 17.—DECEMBER TERM, 1870.

William B. Knox, plaintiff in error, *vs.* Phœbe G. Lee and Hugh Lee, her husband.	In error to the Circuit Court of the United States for the western district of Texas.
Thomas H. Parker, plaintiff in error, *vs.* George Davis.	In error to the Supreme Judicial Court of the Commonwealth of Massachusetts.

Mr. Justice Strong delivered the opinion of the Court.

The controlling questions in these cases are the following: Are the acts of Congress, known as the legal-tender acts, constitutional when applied to contracts made before their passage; and, secondly, are they valid as applicable to debts contracted since their enactment? These questions have been elaborately argued, and they have received from the court that consideration which their great importance demands. It would be difficult to over estimate the consequences which must follow our decision. They will affect the entire business of the country, and take hold of the possible continued existence of the Government. If it be held by this court that Congress has no constitutional power, under any circumstances, or in any emergency, to make Treasury notes a legal tender for the payment of all debts, (a power confessedly possessed by every independent sovereignty other than the United States,) the Government is without those means of self preservation which, all must admit, may in certain contingencies become indispensable, even if they were not when the acts of Congress now called in question were enacted. It is also clear that if we hold the acts invalid as applicable to debts incurred, or transactions which have taken place since their enactment, our decision mus cause, throughout the country, great business derangement, widespread distress, and the rankest injustice. The debts which have been contracted since February 25, 1862, constitute, doubtless, by far the greatest portion of the existing indebtedness of the country. They have been contracted in view of the acts of Congress declaring Treasury notes a legal tender, and in reliance upon that declaration. Men have bought and sold, borrowed and lent, and assumed every variety of obligations contemplating that payment might be made with such notes. Indeed, legal-tender Treasury notes have become the universal measure of values. If now, by our decision, it be established that these debts and obligations can be discharged only by gold coin; if, contrary to the expectation of all parties to these contracts, legal tender notes are rendered unavailable, the Government has become an instrument of the grossest injustice; all debtors are loaded with an obligation it was never contemplated they should assume; a large percentage is added to every debt, and such must become the demand for gold to satisfy contracts that ruinous sacrifices, general distress, and bankruptcy may be expected. These consequences are too obvious to admit of question. And there is no well-founded distinction to be made between the constitutional validity of an act of Congress declaring Treasury notes a legal tender for the payment of debts contracted after its passage and that of an act making them a legal tender for the discharge of all debts, as well those incurred before as those made after its enactment. There may be a difference in the effects produced by the acts, and in the hardship of their operation, but in both cases the fundamental question, that which tests the validity of the legislation, is, can Congress constitutionally give to Treasury notes the character and qualities of money? Can such notes be constituted a legitimate circulating medium, having a defined legal value? If they can, then such notes must be available to fulfill all contracts (not expressly excepted) solvable in money, without reference to the time when the contracts were made. Hence it is not strange that those who hold the legal-tender acts unconstitutional when applied to contracts made before February, 1862, find themselves compelled also to hold that the acts are invalid as to debts created after that time, and to hold that both classes of debts alike can be discharged only by gold and silver coin.

The consequences of which we have spoken, serious as they are, must be accepted, if there is a clear incompatibility between the Constitution and the legal-tender acts. But we are unwilling to precipitate them upon the country unless such an incompatibility plainly appears. A decent respect for a coördinate branch of the Government demands that the judiciary should presume, until the contrary is clearly shown, that there has been no transgression of power by Congress—all the members of which act under the obligation of an oath of fidelity to the Constitution. Such has always been the rule. In Commonwealth *vs.* Smith, (4 Bin., 123,) the language of the court was: "it must be remembered that for weighty reasons, it has been assumed as a principle, in construing constitutions, by the Supreme Court of the United States, by this court, and by every other court of reputation in the United States, that an act of the Legislature is not to be declared void unless the violation of the Constitution is so manifest as to leave no room for reasonable doubt;" and. in Fletcher *vs.* Peck, (6 Cranch, 87,) Chief Justice Marshall said "it is not on slight implication and vague conjecture that the Legislature is to be pronounced to have transcended its powers and its acts to be considered void. The opposition between the Constitution and the law should be such that the judge feels a clear and strong conviction of their incompatibility with each other." It is incumbent, therefore, upon those who affirm the unconstitutionality of an act of Congress to show clearly that it is in violation of the provisions of the Constitution. It is not sufficient for them that they succeed in raising a doubt.

Nor can it be questioned that when investigating the nature and extent of the powers conferred by the Constitution upon Congress, it is indispensable to keep in view the objects for which those powers were granted. This is an universal rule of construction applied alike to statutes, wills, contracts, and constitutions. If the general purpose of the instrument is ascertained, the language of its provisions must be construed with reference to that purpose and so as to subserve it. In no other way can the intent of the framers of the instrument be discovered. And there are more urgent reasons for looking to the ultimate purpose in examining the powers conferred by a constitution than there are in construing a statute, a will, or a contract. We do not expect to find in a constitution minute details. It is necessarily brief and comprehensive. It prescribes outlines, leaving the filling up to be deduced from the outlines. In Martin *vs.* Hunter, 1 Wheaton, 326, it was said, "the Constitution unavoidably deals in general language. It did not suit the purpose of the people in framing this great charter of our liberties to provide for minute specifications of its powers, or to declare the means by which those powers should be carried into execution." And with singular clearness was it said by Chief Justice Marshall, in McCullough *vs.* The Bank of Maryland, 4 Wheaton, 405: "A constitution, to contain an accurate detail of all the subdivisions of which its great powers will admit, and of all the means by which it may be carried into execution, would partake of the prolixity of a political code, and would scarcely be embraced by the human mind. It would probably never be understood by the public. Its nature, therefore, requires that only its great outlines should be marked, its important objects designated, and the minor ingredients which compose those objects be deduced from the nature of the objects themselves." If these are correct principles, if they are proper views of the manner in which the Constitution is to be understood, the powers conferred upon Congress must be regarded as related to each other, and all means for a common end. Each is but a part of a system, a constituent of one whole. No single power is the ultimate end for which the Constitution was adopted. It may, in a very proper sense, be treated as a means for the accomplishment of a subordinate object, but that object is itself a means designed for an ulterior purpose. Thus the power to levy and collect taxes, to coin money and regulate its value, to raise and support armies, or to provide for and maintain a Navy, are instruments for the paramount object, which was to establish a Government, sovereign within its sphere, with capability of self-preservation, thereby forming an union more perfect than that which existed under the old Confederacy.

The same may be asserted also of all the non-enumerated powers included in the authority expressly given "to make all laws which shall be necessary and proper for carrying into execution the specified powers vested in Congress, and all other powers vested by the Constitution in the Government of the United States, or in any department or officer thereof." It is impossible to know what those non-enumerated powers are, and what is their nature and extent, without considering the purposes they were intended to subserve. Those purposes, it must be noted, reach beyond the mere execution of all powers definitely intrusted to Congress, and mentioned in detail. They embrace the execution of all other powers vested by the Constitution in the Government of the United States, or in any department or officer thereof. It certainly was intended to confer upon the Government the power of self-preservation. Said Chief Justice Marshall, in Cohens *vs.* The Bank of Virginia, (6 Wheat., 414:) "America has chosen to be, in many respects and to many purposes, a nation, and for all these purposes her Government is complete; for all these objects it is supreme. It can then, in effecting these objects, legitimately control all individuals or governments within the American territory." He added, in the same case: "A constitution is framed for ages to come, and is designed to approach immortality as near as mortality can approach it. Its course cannot always be tranquil. It is exposed to storms and tempests, and its framers must be unwise statesmen, indeed, if they have not provided it, as far as its nature will permit, with the means of self-preservation from the perils it is sure to encounter." That would appear, then, to be a most unreasonable construction of the Constitution which denies to the Government created by it the right to employ freely every means, not prohibited, necessary for its preservation, and for the fulfillment of its acknowledged duties. Such a right, we hold, was given by the last clause of the eighth section of its first article. The means or instrumentalities referred to in that clause, and authorized, are not enumerated or defined. In the nature of things enumeration and specification were impossible. But they were left to the discretion of Congress, subject only to the restrictions that they be not prohibited, and be necessary and proper for carrying into execution the enumerated powers given to Congress, and all other powers vested in the Government of the United States, or in any department or officer thereof.

And here it is to be observed it is not indispensable to the existence of any power claimed for the Federal Government that it can be found specified in the words of the Constitution, or clearly and directly traceable to some one of the specified powers. Its existence may be deduced fairly from more than one of the substantive powers expressly defined, or from them all combined. It is allowable to group together any number of them and infer from them all that the power claimed has been conferred. Such a treatment of the Constitution is recognized by its own provisions. This is well illustrated in its language respecting the writ of *habeas corpus*. The power to suspend the privilege of that writ is not expressly given, nor can it be deduced from any one of the particularized grants of power. Yet it is provided that the privileges of the writ shall not be suspended except in certain defined contingencies. This is no express grant of power. It is a restriction. But it shows irresistibly that somewhere in the Constitution power to suspend the privilege of the writ was granted, either by some one or more of the specifications of power, or by them all combined. And that important powers were understood by the people who adopted the Constitution to have been created by it, powers not enumerated, and not included incidentally in any one of those enumerated, is shown by the amendments. The first ten of these were suggested in the conventions of the States, and proposed at the first session of the First Congress, before any complaint was made of a disposition to assume doubtful powers. The preamble to the resolution submitting them for adoption recited that the "conventions of a number of the States had, at the time of their adopting the Constitution, expressed a desire, in order to prevent misconstruction or abuse of its powers, that further declaratory and restrictive clauses should be added." This was the origin of the amendments, and they are significant. They tend plainly to show that, in the judgment of those who adopted the Constitution, there were powers created by it, neither expressly specified nor deducible from any one specified power, or ancillary to it alone, but which grew out of the aggregate of powers conferred upon the Government, or out of the sovereignty instituted. Most of these amendments are denials of power which had not been expressly granted, and which cannot be said to have been necessary and proper for carrying into execution any other powers. Such, for example, is the prohibition of any laws respecting the establishment of religion, prohibiting the free exercise thereof, or abridging the freedom of speech or of the press.

And it is of importance to observe that Congress has often exercised without question powers that are not expressly given or ancillary to any single enumerated power. Powers thus exercised are what are called by Judge Story in his Commentaries on the Constitution, resulting powers, arising from the aggregate powers of the Government. He instances the right to sue and make contracts. Many others might be given. The oath required by law from officers of the Government is one. So is building a capitol or a presidential mansion, and so also is the penal code. This last is worthy of brief notice. Congress is expressly authorized "to provide for the punishment of counterfeiting the securities and current coin of the United States, and to define and punish piracies and felonies committed on the high seas and offenses against the laws of nations." It is also empowered to declare the punishment of treason, and provision is made for impeachments. This is the extent of power to punish crime expressly conferred. It might be argued that the expression of these limited powers implies an exclusion of all other subjects of criminal legislation. Such is the argument in the present cases. It is said because Congress is authorized to coin money and regulate its value it cannot declare anything other than gold and silver to be money or make it a legal tender. Yet Congress, by the act of April 30, 1790, entitled "An act more effectually to provide for the punishment of certain crimes against the United States," and the supplementary act of March 3, 1825, defined and provided for the punishment of a large class of crimes other than those mentioned in the Constitution, and some of the punishments prescribed are manifestly not in aid of any single substantive power. No one doubts that this was rightfully done, and the power thus exercised has been affirmed by this court. (United States *vs.* Marigold, 9 Howard, 560.) This case shows that a power may exist as an aid to the execution of an express power, or an aggregate of such powers, though there is another express power given relating in part to the same subject but less extensive. Another illustration of this may be found in connection with the provisions respecting a census. The Constitution orders an enumeration of free persons in the different States every ten years. The direction extends no further. Yet Congress has repeatedly directed an enumeration not only of free persons in the States, but of free persons in the Territories, and not only an enumeration of persons but the collection of statistics respecting age, sex, and production. Who questions the power to do this?

Indeed, the whole history of the Government and of congressional legislation has exhibited the use of a very wide discretion, even in times of peace and in the absence of any trying emergency, in the selection of the necessary and proper means to carry into effect the great objects for which the Government was framed, and this discretion has generally been unquestioned, or, if questioned, sanctioned by this court. This is true not only when an attempt has been made to execute a single power specifically given, but equally true when the means adopted have been appropriate to the execution, not of a single authority, but of all the powers created by the Constitution. Under the power to establish post offices and post roads Congress has provided for carrying the mails, punishing theft of letters and mail robberies, and even for transporting the mails to foreign countries. Under the power to regulate commerce provision has been made by law for the improvement of harbors, the establishment of observatories, the erection of light houses, breakwaters, and buoys, the registry, enrollment, and construction of ships, and a code has been enacted for the government of seamen. Under the same power and other powers over the revenue and the currency of the country, for the convenience of the Treasury and internal commerce, a corporation known as the United States Bank was early created. To its capital the Government subscribed one fifth of its stock. But the corporation was a private one, doing business for its own profit. Its incorporation was a constitutional exercise of congressional power for no other reason than that it was deemed to be a convenient instrument or means for accomplishing one or more of the ends for which the Government was established, or, in the language of the first article, already quoted, "necessary and proper" for carrying into execution some or all the powers vested in the Government. Clearly this necessity, if any existed, was not a direct and obvious one. Yet this court, in McCullough *vs.* The State of Maryland, 4 Wheat., 416, unanimously ruled that in authorizing the bank Congress had not transcended its powers. So debts due to the United States have been declared by acts of Congress entitled to priority of payment over debts due to other creditors, and this court has held such acts warranted by the Constitution. (Fisher *vs.* Blight, 2 Cranch, 358.)

This is enough to show how, from the earliest period of our existence as a nation, the powers conferred by the Constitution have been construed by Congress and by this court whenever such action by Congress has been called into question. Happily the true meaning of the clause authorizing the enactment of all laws necessary and proper for carrying into execution the express powers conferred upon Congress, and all other powers vested in the Government of the United States, or in any of its departments or officers, has long since been settled. In Fisher *vs.* Blight (above cited) this court, speaking by Chief Justice Marshall, said that in construing it "it would be incorrect and would produce endless difficulties if the opinion should be maintained that no law was authorized which was not indispensably necessary to give effect to a specified power. Where various systems might be adopted for that purpose it might be said with respect to each that it was not necessary because the end might be obtained by other means." Congress, said this court, "must possess the choice of means, and must be empowered to use any means which are in fact conducive to the exercise of a power granted by the Constitution. The Government is to pay the debt of the Union, and must be authorized to use the means which appear to itself most eligible to effect that object. It has, consequently, a right to make remittances by bills or otherwise, and to take those precautions which will render the transaction safe." It was in this case, as we have already remarked, that a law giving priority to debts due to the United States was ruled to be constitutional for the reason that it appeared to Congress to be an eligible means to enable the Government to pay the debts of the Union.

It was, however, in McCullough *vs.* Maryland that the fullest consideration was given to this clause of the Constitution granting auxiliary powers, and a construction adopted that has ever since been accepted as determining its true meaning. We shall not now go over the ground there trodden. It is familiar to the legal profession, and, indeed, to the whole country. Suffice it to say, in that case it was finally settled that in the gift by the Constitution to Congress of authority to enact laws "necessary and proper" for the execution of all the powers created by it, the necessity spoken of is not to be understood as an absolute one. On the contrary, this court then held that the sound construction of the Constitution must allow to the national Legislature that discretion with respect to the means by which the powers it confers are to be carried into execution, which will enable that body to perform the high duties assigned to it in the manner most beneficial to the people. Said Chief Justice Marshall, in delivering the opinion of the court: "Let the end be legitimate, let it be within the scope of the Constitution, and all means which are appropriate, which are plainly adapted to that end, which are not prohibited, but consist with the letter and spirit of the Constitution, are constitutional." The case also marks out with admirable precision the province of this court. It declares that "when the law (enacted by Congress) is not prohibited and is really calculated to effect any of the objects intrusted to the Government, to undertake here to inquire into the degree of its necessity would be to pass the line which circumscribes the judicial department and to tread on legislative ground. This court (it was said) disclaimed all pretensions to such a power." It is hardly necessary to say that these principles are received with universal assent. Even in Hepburn *vs.* Griswold, 8 Wallace, 603, both the majority and minority of the court concurred in accepting the doctrines of McCullough *vs.* Maryland as sound expositions of the Constitution, though disagreeing in their application.

With these rules of constitutional construction before us, settled at an early period in the history of the Government, hitherto universally accepted and not even now doubted, we have a safe guide to a right decision of the questions before us. Before we can hold the legal-tender acts unconstitutional, we must be convinced they were not appropriate means, or means conducive to the execution of any or all of the powers of Congress, or of the Government, not appropriate in any degree, (for we are not judges of the degree of appropriateness,) or we must hold that they were prohibited. This brings us to the inquiry whether they were, when enacted, appropriate instrumentalities for carrying into effect or executing any of the known powers of Congress, or of any department of the Government. Plainly to this inquiry a consideration of the time when they were enacted, and of the circumstances in which the Government then stood, is important. It is not to be denied that acts may be adapted to the exercise of lawful power, and appropriate to it in seasons of exigency which would be inappropriate at other times.

We do not propose to dilate at length upon the circumstances in which the country was placed when Congress attempted to make Treasury notes a legal tender. They are of too recent occurrence to justify enlarged description. Suffice it to say that a civil war was then raging which seriously threatened the overthrow of the Government, and the destruction of the Constitution itself. It demanded the equipment and support of large armies and navies, and the employment of money to an extent beyond the capacity of all ordinary sources of supply. Meanwhile the public Treasury was nearly empty, and the credit of the Government, if not stretched to its utmost tension, had become nearly exhausted. Moneyed institutions had advanced largely of their means, and more could not be expected of them. They had been compelled to suspend specie payments. Taxation was inadequate to pay even the interest on the debt already incurred, and it was impossible to await the income of additional taxes. The necessity was immediate and pressing. The Army was unpaid. There was then due to the soldiers in the field nearly a score of millions of dollars. The requisitions from the War and Navy Departments for supplies exceeded fifty millions, and the current expenditure was over one million per day. The entire amount of coin in the country, including that in private hands, as well as that in banking institutions, was insufficient to supply the need of the Government three months, had it all been poured into the Treasury. Foreign credit we had none. We say nothing of the overhanging paralysis of trade, and of business generally, which threatened loss of confidence in the ability of the Government to maintain its continued existence, and therewith the complete destruction of all remaining national credit.

It was at such a time and in such circumstances that Congress was called upon to devise means for maintaining the Army and Navy, for securing the large supplies of money needed, and, indeed, for the preservation of the Government created by the Constitution. It was at such a time and in such an emergency that the legal-tender acts were passed. Now, if it were certain that nothing else would have supplied the absolute necessities of the Treasury, that nothing else would have enabled the Government to maintain its armies and Navy, that nothing else would have saved the Government and the Constitution from destruction, while the legal-tender acts would, could any one be bold enough to assert that Congress transgressed its powers? Or if these enactments did work these results, can it be maintained now that they were not for a legitimate end, or "appropriate and adapted to that end," in the language of Chief Justice Marshall? That they did work such results is not to be doubted. Something revived the drooping faith of the people; something brought immediately to the Government's aid the resources of the nation, and something enabled the successful prosecution of the war, and the preservation of the national life. What was it if not the legal-tender enactments?

But if it be conceded that some other means might have been chosen for the accomplishment of these legitimate and necessary ends, the concession does not weaken the argument. It is urged now, after the lapse of nine years, and when the emergency has passed, that Treasury notes without the legal-tender clause might have been issued, and that the necessities of the Government might thus have been supplied. Hence it is inferred there was no necessity for giving to the notes issued the capability of paying private debts. At best this is mere conjecture. But admitting it to be true, what does it prove? Nothing more than that Congress had the choice of means for a legitimate end, each appropriate and adapted to that end, though perhaps in different degrees. What then? Can this court say that it ought to have adopted one rather than the other? Is it our province to decide that the means selected were beyond the constitutional power of Congress because we may think that other means to the same ends would have been more appropriate and equally efficient? That would be to assume legislative power, and to disregard the accepted rules for construing the Constitution. The degree of the necessity for any congressional enactment, or the relative degree of its appropriateness, if it have any appropriateness, is for consideration in Congress, not here. Said Chief Justice Marshall, in McCullough *vs.* Maryland, as already stated, "When the law is not prohibited, and is really calculated to effect any of the objects intrusted to the Government, to undertake here to inquire into the degree of its necessity would be to pass the line which circu*mscribes the judicial department*, and to tread on legislative ground."

It is plain to our view, however, that none of those measures which it is now conjectured might have been substituted for the legal-tender acts could have met the exigencies of the case at the time when those acts were passed. We have said that the credit of the Government had been tried to its utmost endurance. Every new issue of notes which had nothing more to rest upon than Government credit must have paralyzed it more and more, and rendered it increasingly difficult to keep the Army in the field, or the Navy afloat. It is an historical fact that many persons and institutions refused to receive and pay those notes that had been issued, and even the head of the Treasury represented to Congress the necessity of making the new issues legal tenders, or rather, declared it impossible to avoid the necessity. The vast body of men in the military service was composed of citizens who had left their farms, their workshops, and their business with families and debts to be provided for. The Government could not pay them with ordinary Treasury notes, nor could they discharge their debts with such a currency. Something more was needed, something that had all the uses of money. And as no one could be compelled to take common Treasury notes in payment of debts, and as the prospect of ultimate redemption was remote and contingent, it is not too much to say that they must have depreciated in the market long before the war closed, as did the currency of the confederate States. Making the notes legal tender gave them a new use, and it needs no argument to show that the value of things is in proportion to the uses to which they may be applied.

It may be conceded that Congress is not authorized to enact laws in furtherance even of a legitimate end merely because they are useful, or because they make the Government stronger. There must be some relation between the means and the end; some adaptedness or appropriateness of the laws to carry into execution the powers created by the Constitution. But when a statute has proved effective in the execution of powers confessedly existing, it is not too much to say that it must have had some appropriateness to the execution of those powers. The rules of construction heretofore adopted do not demand that the relationship between the means and the end shall be direct and immediate. Illustrations of this may be found in several of the cases above cited. The charter of a Bank of the United States, the priority given to the debts due the Government over private debts, and the exemptiou of Federal loans from liability to State taxation, are only a few of the many which might be given. The case of Veazie Bank *vs.* Fenno, (8 Wal., 533,) presents a suggestive illustration. There a tax of ten per cent. on State bank notes in circulation was held constitutional, not merely because it was a means of raising revenue, but as an instrument to put out of existence such a circulation in competition with notes issued by the *Government.* There, this court, speaking through the Chief Justice, avowed that it is the constitutional right of Congress to provide a currency for the whole country; that this might be done by coin, or United States notes, or notes of national banks; and that it cannot be questioned Congress may constitutionally secure the benefits of such a currency to the people by appropriate legislation. It was said there can be no question of the power of this Government to emit bills of credit; to make them receivable in payment of debts to itself; to fit them for use by those who see fit to use them in all the transactions of commerce; to make them a currency uniform in value and description, and convenient and useful for circulation. Here the substantive power to tax was allowed to be employed for improving the currency. It is not easy to see why, if State bank notes can be taxed out of existence for the purpose of indirectly making United States notes more convenient and useful for commercial purposes, the same end may not be secured directly by making them a legal tender.

Concluding, then, that the provision which made Treasury notes a legal tender for the payment of all debts other than those expressly excepted was not an inappropriate means for carrying into execution the legitimate powers of the Government, we proceed to inquire whether it was forbidden by the letter or spirit of the Constitution. It is not claimed that any express prohibition exists, but it is insisted that the spirit of the Constitution was violated by the enactment. Here those who assert the unconstitutionality of the acts mainly rest their argument. They claim that the clause which conferred upon Congress power "to coin money, regulate the value thereof, and of foreign coin," contains an implication that nothing but that which is the subject of coinage, nothing but the precious metals, can ever be declared by law to be money, or to have the uses of money. If by this is meant that because certain powers over the currency are expressly given to Congress all other powers relating to the same subject are impliedly forbidden, we need only remark that such is not the manner in which the Constitution has always been construed. On the contrary it has been ruled that power over a particular subject may be exercised as auxiliary to an express power, though there is another express power relating to the same subject, less comprehensive. (United States *vs.* Marigold, 9 Howard, 560.) There an express power to punish a certain class of crimes (the only direct reference to criminal legislation contained in the Constitution) was not regarded as an objection to deducing authority to punish other crimes from another substantive and defined grant of power. There are other decisions to the same effect. To assert, then, that the clause enabling Congress to coin money and regulate its value tacitly implies a denial of all other power over the currency of the nation, is an attempt to introduce a new rule of construction against the solemn decisions of this court. So far from its containing a lurking prohibition, many have thought it was intended to confer upon Congress that general power over the currency which has always been an acknowledged attribute of sovereignty in every other civilized nation than our own, especially when considered in connection with the other clause which denies to the States the power to coin money, emit bills of credit, or make anything but gold and silver coin a tender in payment of debts. We do not assert this now, but there are some considerations touching these clauses which tend to show that if any implications are tó be deduced from them, they are of an enlarging rather than a restraining character. The Constitution was intended to frame a government as distinguished from a league or compact, a government supreme in some particulars over States and people. It was designed to provide the same currency, having a uniform legal value in all the States. It was for this reason the power to coin money and regulate its value was conferred upon the Federal Government, while the same power as well as the power to emit bills of credit was withdrawn from the States. The States can no longer declare what shall be money, or regulate its value. Whatever power there is over the currency is vested in Congress. If the power to declare what is money is not in Congress, it is annihilated. This may indeed have been intended. Some powers that usually belong to sovereignties were extinguished, but their extinguishment was not left to inference. In most cases, if not in all, when it was intended that governmental powers, commonly acknowledged as such, should cease to exist, both in the States and in the Federal Government, it was expressly denied to both, as well to the United States as to the individual States. And generally, when one of such powers was expressly denied to the States only, it was for the purpose of rendering the Federal power more complete and exclusive. Why, then, it may be asked, if the design was to prohibit to the new government, as well as to the States, that general power over the currency which the States had when the Constitution was framed, was such denial not expressly extended to the new government, as it was to the States? In view of this it might be argued with much force that when it is considered in what brief and comprehensive terms the Constitution speaks, how sensible its framers must have been that emergencies might arise when the precious metals (then more scarce than now) might prove inadequate to the necessities of the Government and the demands of the people—when it is remembered that paper money was almost exclusively in use in the States as the medium of exchange, and when the great evil sought to be remedied was the want of uniformity in the current value of money, it might be argued, we say, that the gift of power to coin money and regulate the value thereof, was understood as conveying general power over the currency, the power which had belonged to the States, and which they surrendered. Such a construction, it might be said, would be in close analogy to the mode of construing other substantive powers granted to Congress. They have never been construed literally, and the Government could not exist if they were. Thus the power to carry on war is conferred by the power to "declare war." The whole system of the transportation of the mails is built upon the power to establish post offices and post roads. The power to regulate commerce has also been extended far beyond the letter of the grant. Even the advocates of a strict literal construction of the phrase, "to coin money and regulate the value thereof," while insisting that it defines the material to be coined as metal, are compelled to concede to Congress large discretion in all other particulars. The Constitution does not ordain what metals may be coined, or prescribe that the legal value of the metals, when coined, shall correspond at all with their intrinsic value in the market. Nor does it even affirm that Congress may declare anything to be a legal tender for the payment of debts. Confessedly the power to regulate the value of money coined, and of foreign coins, is not exhausted by the first regulation. More than once in our history has the regulation been changed without any denial of the power of Congress to change it, and it seems to have been left to Congress to determine alike what metal shall be coined, its purity, and how far its statutory value, as money, shall correspond from time to time with the market value of the same metal as bullion. How then can the grant of a power to coin money and regulate its value, made in terms so liberal and unrestrained, coupled also with a denial to the States of all power over the currency, be regarded as an implied prohibition to Congress against declaring Treasury notes a legal tender, if such declaration is appropriate, and adapted to carrying into execution the admitted powers of the Government?

We do not, however, rest our assertion of the power of Congress to enact legal-tender laws upon this grant. We assert only that the grant can, in no just sense, be regarded as containing an implied prohibition against their enactment, and that, if it raises any implications, they are of complete power over the currency, rather than restraining.

We come next to the argument much used, and, indeed, the main reliance of those who assert the unconstitutionality of the legal-tender acts. It is that they are prohibited by the spirit of the Constitution because they indirectly impair the obligation of contracts. The argument, of course, relates only to those contracts which were made before February,

1862, when the first act was passed, and it has no bearing upon the question whether the acts are valid when applied to contracts made after their passage. The argument assumes two things: first, that the acts do, in effect, impair the obligation of contracts, and, second, that Congress is prohibited from taking any action which may indirectly have that effect. Neither of these assumptions can be accepted. It is true that under the acts a debtor, who became such before they were passed, may discharge his debt with the notes authorized by them, and the creditor is compellable to receive such notes in discharge of his claim. But whether the obligation of the contract is thereby weakened can be determined only after considering what was the contract obligation. It was not a duty to pay gold or silver, or the kind of money recognized by law at the time when the contract was made, nor was it a duty to pay money of equal intrinsic value in the market. (We speak now of contracts to pay money generally, not contracts to pay some specifically defined species of money.) The expectation of the creditor and the anticipation of the debtor may have been that the contract would be discharged by the payment of coined metals, but neither the expectation of one party to the contract respecting its fruits, nor the anticipation of the other constitutes its obligation. There is a well-recognized distinction between the expectation of the parties to a contract, and the duty imposed by it. (Apsden *vs.* Austin, 5 Ad. & Ellis, N. S., 671; Dunn *vs.* Sayles, *Ibid.*, 685; Coffin *vs.* Landis, 10 Wright, 426.) Were it not so the expectation of results would be always equivalent to a binding engagement that they should follow. But the obligation of a contract to pay money is to pay that which the law shall recognize as money when the payment is to be made. If there is anything settled by decision it is this, and we do not understand it to be controverted. (Davies's Reps., 28; Barrington *vs.* Potter, Dyer, 81, b, fol. 67; Faw *vs.* Marsteller, 2 Cranch, 29.) No one ever doubted that a debt of $1,000, contracted before 1834, could be paid by one hundred eagles coined after that year, though they contained no more gold than ninety-four eagles such as were coined when the contract was made, and this not because of the intrinsic value of the coin, but because of its legal value. The eagles coined after 1834 were not money until they were authorized by law, and had they been coined before, without a law fixing their legal value, they could no more have paid a debt than uncoined bullion, or cotton, or wheat. Every contract for the payment of money, simply, is necessarily subject to the constitutional power of the Government over the currency, whatever that power may be, and the obligation of the parties is, therefore, assumed with reference to that power. Nor is this singular. A covenant for quiet enjoyment is not broken nor is its obligation impaired by the Government's taking the land granted in virtue of its right of eminent domain. The expectation of the covenantee may be disappointed. He may not enjoy all he anticipated, but the grant was made and the covenant undertaken in subordination to the paramount right of the Government. (Dobbins *vs.* Brown, 2 Jones, 75; Workman *vs.* Mifflin, 6 Casey, 362.) We have been asked whether Congress can declare that a contract to deliver a quantity of grain may be satisfied by the tender of a less quantity. Undoubtedly not. But this is a false analogy. There is a wide distinction between a tender of quantities, or of specific articles, and a tender of legal values. Contracts for the delivery of specific articles belong exclusively to the domain of State legislation, while contracts for the payment of money are subject to the authority of Congress, at least so far as relates to the means of payment. They are engagements to pay with lawful money of the United States, and Congress is empowered to regulate that money. It cannot, therefore, be maintained that the legal-tender acts impaired the obligation of contracts.

Nor can it be truly asserted that Congress may not, by its action, indirectly impair the obligation of contracts, if by the expression be meant rendering contracts fruitless, or partially fruitless. Directly it may, confessedly, by passing a bankrupt act, embracing past as well as future transactions. This is obliterating contracts entirely. So it may relieve parties from their apparent obligations indirectly in a multitude of ways. It may declare war, or, even in peace, pass non-intercourse acts, or direct an embargo. All such measures may and must operate seriously upon existing contracts, and may not merely hinder but relieve the parties to such contracts entirely from performance. It is, then, clear that the powers of Congress may be exerted, though the effect of such exertion may be in one case to annul and in other cases to impair the obligation of contracts. And it is no sufficient answer to this to say it is true only when the powers exerted were expressly granted. There is no ground for any such distinction. It has no warrant in the Constitution, or in any of the decisions of this court. We are accustomed to speak for mere convenience of the express and implied powers conferred upon Congress. But in fact the auxiliary powers, those necessary and appropriate to the execution of other powers singly described, are as expressly given as is the power to declare war or to establish uniform laws on the subject of bankruptcy. They are not catalogued, no list of them is made, but they are grouped in the last clause of section eight of the first article, and granted in the same words in which all other powers are granted to Congress. And this court has recognized no such distinction as is now attempted. An embargo suspends many contracts and renders performance of others impossible, yet the power to enforce it has been declared constitutional, (Gibbons *vs.* Ogden, 9 Wheat., 1.) The power to enact a law directing an embargo is one of the auxiliary powers, existing only because appropriate in time of peace to regulate commerce, or appropriate to carrying on war. Though not conferred as a substantive power, it has not been thought to be in conflict with the Constitution, because it impairs indirectly the obligation of contracts. That discovery calls for a new reading of the Constitution.

If, then, the legal-tender acts were justly chargeable with impairing contract obligations, they would not, for that reason, be forbidden, unless a different rule is to be applied to them from that which has hitherto prevailed in the construction of other powers granted by the fundamental law. But, as already intimated, the objection misapprehends the nature and extent of the contract obligation spoken of in the Constitution. As in a state of civil society property of a citizen or subject is ownership, subject to the lawful demands of the sovereign, so contracts must be understood as made in reference to the possible exercise of the rightful authority of the Government, and no obligation of a contract can extend to the defeat of legitimate government authority.

Closely allied to the objection we have just been considering is the argument pressed upon us that the legal-tender acts were prohibited by the spirit of the fifth amendment, which forbids taking private property for public use without just compensation or due process of law. That provision has always been understood as referring only to a direct appropriation, and not to consequential injuries resulting from the exercise of lawful power. It has never been supposed to have any bearing upon, or to inhibit laws that indirectly work harm and loss to individuals. A new tariff, an embargo, a draft, or a war may inevitably bring upon individuals great losses; may, indeed, render valuable property almost valueless. They may destroy the worth of contracts. But whoever supposed that because of this a tariff could not be changed, or a non-intercourse act or an embargo be enacted, or a war be declared? By the act of June 28, 1834, a new regulation of the weight and value of gold coin was adopted, and about six per cent. was taken from the weight of each dollar. The effect of this was that all creditors were subjected to a corresponding loss. The debts then due became solvable with six per cent. less gold than was required to pay them before. The result was thus precisely what it is contended the legal-tender acts worked. But was it ever imagined this was taking private property without compensation or without due process of law? Was the idea ever advanced that the new regulation of gold coin was against the spirit of the fifth amendment? And has any one in good faith avowed his belief that even a law debasing the current coin, by increasing the alloy, would be taking private property? It might be impolitic and unjust, but could its constitutionality be doubted? Other statutes have, from time to time, reduced the quantity of silver in silver coin without any question of their constitutionality. It is said, however, now, that the act of 1834 only brought the legal value of gold coin more nearly into correspondence with its actual value in the market, or its relative value to silver. But we do not perceive that this varies the case or diminishes its force as an illustration. The creditor who had a thousand dollars due him on the 31st of July, 1834, (the day before the act took effect,) was entitled to a thousand dollars of coined gold of the weight and fineness of the then existing coinage. The day after he was entitled only to a sum six per cent. less in weight and in market value, or to a smaller number of silver dollars. Yet he would have been a bold man who had asserted that, because of this, the obligation of the contract was impaired, or that private property was taken without compensation or without due process of law. No such assertion, so far as we know, was ever made. Admit it was a hardship, but it is not every hardship that is unjust, much less that is unconstitutional; and certainly it would be an anomaly for us to hold an act of Congress invalid merely because we might think its provisions harsh and unjust.

We are not aware of anything else which has been advanced in support of the proposition that the legal-tender acts were forbidden by either the letter or the spirit of the Constitution. If, therefore, they were, what we have endeavored to show, appropriate means for legitimate ends, they were not transgressive of the authority vested in Congress.

Here we might stop; but we will notice briefly an argument presented in support of the position that the unit of money value must possess intrinsic value. The argument is derived from assimilating the constitutional provision respecting a standard of weights and measures to that conferring the power to coin money and regulate its value. It is said there can be no uniform standard of weights without weight, or of measure without length or space, and we are asked how anything can be made an uniform standard of value which has itself no value? This is a question foreign to the subject before us. The legal-tender acts do not attempt to make paper a standard of value. We do not rest their validity upon the assertion that their emission is coinage, or any regulation of the value of money; nor do we assert that Congress may make anything which has no value money. What we do assert is, that Congress has power to enact that the Government's promises to pay money shall be, for the time being, equivalent in value to the representative of value determined by the coinage acts, or to multiples thereof. It is hardly correct to speak of a standard of value. The Constitution does not speak of it. It contemplates a standard for that which has gravity or extension; but value is an ideal thing. The coinage acts fix its unit as a dollar; but the gold or silver thing we call a dollar is, in no sense, a standard of a dollar. It is a representative of it. There might never have been a piece of money of the denomination of a dollar. There never was a pound sterling coined until 1815, if we except a few coins struck in the reign of Henry VIII, almost immediately debased, yet it has been the unit of British currency for many generations. It is, then, a mistake to regard the legal-tender acts as either fixing a standard of value or regulating money values, or making that money which has no intrinsic value.

But, without extending our remarks further, it will be seen that we hold the acts of Congress constitutional as applied to contracts made either before or after their passage. In so holding we overrule so much of what was decided in Hepburn *vs.* Griswold (8 Wall., 603,) as ruled the acts unwarranted by the Constitution so far as they apply to contracts made before their enactment. That case was decided by a divided court, and by a court having a less number of judges than the law then in existence provided this court shall have. These cases have been heard before a full court, and they have received our most careful consideration. The questions involved are constitutional questions of the most vital importance to the Government and to the public at large. We have been in the habit of treating cases involving a consideration of constitutional power differently from those which concern merely private right. (Briscoe *vs.* Bank of Kentucky, 8 Peters, 118.) We are not accustomed to hear them in the absence of a full court, if it can be avoided. Even in cases involving only private rights, if convinced we had made a mistake, we would hear another argument and correct our error. And it is no unprecedented thing in courts of last resort, both in this country and in England, to overrule decisions previously made. We agree this should not be done inconsiderately, but in a case of such far-reaching consequences as the present, thoroughly convinced as we are that Congress has not transgressed its powers, we regard it as our duty so to decide and to affirm both these judgments.

The other questions raised in the case of William B. Knox against Phœbe Lee and Hugh Lee were substantially decided in Texas *vs.* White, (7 Wallace, 700.)

The judgment in each case is affirmed.

[NOTE.—Mr. Justice BRADLEY concurring, delivered a separate opinion. Chief Justice CHASE delivered a dissenting opinion, representing Justices NELSON, CLIFFORD, and FIELD. The last two also delivered separate opinions. The opinion pronounced December term, 1869, will be found in McPherson's History of Reconstruction, pages 511–523.]

XI.

PRESIDENT GRANT'S CABINET, AND MEMBERS OF THE FORTY-SECOND CONGRESS.

The Cabinet.

Secretary of State—Hamilton Fish, of New York.

Secretary of the Treasury—George S. Boutwell, of Massachusetts.

Secretary of War—William W. Belknap, of Iowa.

Secretary of the Navy—George M. Robeson, of New Jersey.

Secretary of the Interior—Columbus Delano, of Ohio, *vice* Jacob D. Cox, of Ohio, resigned October 30, 1870.

Postmaster General—John A. J. Creswell, of Maryland.

Attorney General—George H. Williams, of Oregon, *vice* Amos T. Akerman, of Georgia, resigned January 9, 1872.

Members of Forty-Second Congress.

First Session, March 4, 1871—April 20, 1871.

Second Session, December 4, 1871—June 10, 1872.

Senate.

SCHUYLER COLFAX, of Indiana, *Vice-President of the United States, and President of the Senate.*

George C. Gorham, of California, *Secretary.*

Maine—Hannibal Hamlin, Lot M. Morrill.

New Hampshire—James W. Patterson, Aaron H. Cragin.

Vermont—George F. Edmunds, Justin S. Morrill.

Massachusetts—Charles Sumner, Henry Wilson.

Rhode Island—William Sprague, Henry B. Anthony.

Connecticut—Orris S. Ferry, William A. Buckingham.

New York—Roscoe Conkling, Reuben E. Fenton.

New Jersey—John P. Stockton, Frederick T. Frelinghuysen.

Pennsylvania—Simon Cameron, John Scott.

Delaware—Thomas F. Bayard, Eli Saulsbury.

Maryland—George Vickers, William T. Hamilton.

Virginia—John F. Lewis, John W. Johnston.*

North Carolina—John Pool, Matthew W. Ransom.†

South Carolina—Frederick A. Sawyer, Thomas J. Robertson.

Georgia—Joshua Hill, Thomas M. Norwood.‡

Alabama—George E. Spencer, George Goldthwaite.‖

Mississippi—Adelbert Ames, James L. Alcorn.§

* Qualified March 17, 1871.
† Qualified April 24, 1872.
‡ Qualified December 19, 1871.
‖ Qualified January 15, 1872.
§ Qualified December 4, 1871.

Louisiana—William Pitt Kellogg, J. Rodman West.
Ohio—John Sherman, Allen G. Thurman.
Kentucky—Garret Davis, John W. Stevenson.
Tennessee—William G. Brownlow, Henry Cooper.
Indiana—Oliver P. Morton, Daniel D. Pratt.
Illinois—Lyman Trumbull, John A. Logan.
Missouri—Francis P. Blair, jr., Carl Schurz.
Arkansas—Benjamin F. Rice, Powell Clayton.
Michigan—Zachariah Chandler, Thomas W. Ferry.
Florida—Thomas W. Osborn, Abijah Gilbert.
Texas—James W. Flanagan, Morgan C. Hamilton.*
Iowa—James Harlan, George G. Wright.
Wisconsin—Timothy O. Howe, Matthew H. Carpenter.
California—Cornelius Cole, Eugene Casserly.
Minnesota—Alex. Ramsey, William Windom.
Oregon—Henry W. Corbett, James K. Kelly.
Kansas—Samuel C. Pomeroy, Alexander Caldwell.
West Virginia—Arthur I. Boreman, Henry G. Davis.
Nevada—James W. Nye, William M. Stewart.
Nebraska—Thomas W. Tipton, Phineas W. Hitchcock.

House of Representatives.

JAMES G. BLAINE, of Maine, *Speaker*.
Edward McPherson, of Pennsylvania, *Clerk*.
Maine—John Lynch, William P. Frye, James G. Blaine, John A. Peters, Eugene Hale.
New Hampshire†—Ellery A. Hibbard, Samuel N. Bell, Hosea W. Parker.
Vermont—Charles W. Willard, Luke P. Poland, Worthington C. Smith.
Massachusetts‡—James Buffinton, Oakes Ames, Ginery Twichell, Samuel Hooper, Benjamin F. Butler, Nathaniel P. Banks, George M. Brooks, George F. Hoar, Alvah Crocker, Henry L. Dawes.
Rhode Island—Benjamin T. Eames, James M. Pendleton.
Connecticut‖—Julius D. Strong, Stephen W. Kellogg, Henry H. Starkweather, William H. Barnum.
New York—Dwight Townsend, Thomas Kinsella, Henry W. Slocum, Robert B. Roosevelt, William R. Roberts, Samuel S. Cox, Smith Ely, jr., James Brooks, Fernando Wood, Clarkson N. Potter, Charles St. John, John H. Ketcham, Joseph H. Tuthill, Eli Perry, Joseph M. Warren, John Rogers, William A. Wheeler, John M. Carroll, Elizur H. Prindle, Clinton L. Merriam, Ellis H. Roberts, William E. Lansing, R. Holland Duell, John E. Seeley, William H. Lamport, Milo Goodrich, Horace Boardman Smith, Freeman Clarke, Seth Wakeman, William Williams, Walter L. Sessions.

* Qualified March 20, 1871.
† Qualified March 22, 1871.
‡ Mr. Brooks resigned May 3, 1872; and Mr. Crocker qualified February 14, 1872, in place of William B. Washburn, resigned, December 4, 1871, to take effect January 1, 1872.
‖ Messrs. Strong and Starkweather qualified April 12, 1871; Mr. Barnum, April 13; Mr. Kellogg, December 4.

New Jersey—John W. Hazelton, Samuel C. Forker, John T. Bird, John Hill, George A. Halsey.
Pennsylvania—Samuel J. Randall, John V. Creely, Leonard Myers, William D. Kelley, Alfred C. Harmer, Ephraim L. Acker, Washington Townsend, J. Lawrence Getz, Oliver J. Dickey, John W. Killinger, John B. Storm, Lazarus D. Shoemaker, Ulysses Mercur, John B. Packer, Richard J. Haldeman, Benjamin F. Meyers, R. Milton Speer, Henry Sherwood, Glenni W. Scofield, Samuel Griffith, Henry D. Foster, James S. Negley, Ebenezer McJunkin, William McClelland.
Delaware—Benjamin T. Biggs.
Maryland—Samuel Hambleton, Stevenson Archer, Thomas Swann, John Ritchie, William M. Merrick.
Virginia—John Critcher, James H. Platt, jr., Charles H. Porter, William H. H. Stowell, Richard T. W. Duke, John T. Harris, Elliott M. Braxton, William Terry.
North Carolina—Clinton L. Cobb, Charles R. Thomas, Alfred M. Waddell, Sion H. Rogers,* James M. Leach, Francis E. Shober, James C. Harper.
South Carolina—Joseph H. Rainey, Robert C. De Large, Robert B. Elliott, Alexander S. Wallace.
Georgia—Archibald T. McIntyre, Richard H. Whiteley, John S. Bigby, Thomas J. Speer, Dudley M. Du Bose, William P. Price, Pierce M. B. Young.
Alabama—Benjamin S. Turner, Charles W. Buckley, William A. Handley, Charles Hays, Peter M. Dox, Joseph H. Sloss.
Mississippi—George E. Harris, Joseph L. Morphis, Henry W. Barry, George C. McKee, Legrand W. Perce.
Louisiana—J. Hale Sypher, Lionel A. Sheldon, Chester B. Darrall, (vacancy,) Frank Morey.
Ohio—Aaron F. Perry, Job E. Stevenson, Lewis D. Campbell, John F. McKinney, Charles N. Lamison, John A. Smith, Samuel Shellabarger, John Beatty, Charles Foster, Erasmus D. Peck, John T. Wilson, Philadelph Van Trump, George W. Morgan, James Monroe, William P. Sprague, John A. Bingham, Jacob A. Ambler, William H. Upson, James A. Garfield.
Kentucky—Edward Crossland, Henry D. McHenry, Joseph H. Lewis, William B. Read, Boyd Winchester, William E. Arthur, James B. Beck, George M. Adams, John M. Rice.
Tennessee—Roderick R. Butler, Horace Maynard, Abraham E. Garrett, John M. Bright, Edward I. Golladay, Washington C. Whitthorne, Robert P. Caldwell, William W. Vaughan.
Indiana—William E. Niblack, Michael C. Kerr, William S. Holman, Jeremiah M. Wilson, John Coburn, Daniel W. Voorhees, Mahlon D. Manson, James N. Tyner, John P. C. Shanks, William Williams, Jasper Packard.

* Qualified May 23, 1872, his disabilities (as member of Thirty-Third Congress) having been removed by the amnesty act approved that day.

Illinois—Charles B. Farwell, John F. Farnsworth, Horatio C. Burchard, John B. Hawley, Bradford N. Stevens, Henry Snapp,* Jesse H. Moore, James C. Robinson, Thompson W. McNeely, Edward Y. Rice, Samuel S. Marshall, John B. Hay, John M. Crebs, John L. Beveridge.†

Missouri—Erastus Wells, Gustavus A. Finkelnburg, James R. McCormick, Harrison E. Havens, Samuel S. Burdett, Abram Comingo, Isaac C. Parker, James G. Blair, Andrew King.

Arkansas—James M. Hanks, Oliver P. Snyder, Thomas Boles.‡

Michigan—Henry Waldron, William L. Stoughton, Austin Blair, Wilder D. Foster,‖ Omar D. Conger, Jabez G. Sutherland.

Florida—Josiah T. Walls.

*Texas**—William S. Herndon, John C. Conner, De Witt C. Giddings, John Hancock.

Iowa—George W. McCrary, Aylett R. Cotton, William G. Donnan, Madison M. Walden, Frank W. Palmer, Jackson Orr.

Wisconsin—Alexander Mitchell, Gerry W. Hazelton, J. Allen Barber, Charles A. Eldredge, Philetus Sawyer, Jeremiah M. Rusk.

California†—Sherman O. Houghton, Aaron A. Sargent, John M. Coghlan.

Minnesota—Mark H. Dunnell, John T. Averill.

Oregon—James H. Slater.

Kansas—David P. Lowe.

West Virginia—John J. Davis, James C. McGrew, Frank Hereford.

Nevada—Charles W. Kendall.

Nebraska—John Taffe.

XII.

THE CIVIL SERVICE.

IN SENATE.

1871, March 3—The sundry civil appropriation bill pending—

Mr. TRUMBULL moved to add the following new section:

That the President of the United States be, and he is hereby, authorized to prescribe such rules and regulations for the admission of persons into the civil service of the United States as will best promote the efficiency thereof, and ascertain the fitness of each candidate in respect to age, health, character, knowledge, and ability for the branch of service into which he seeks to enter; and for this purpose the President is authorized to employ suitable persons to conduct said inquiries, to prescribe their duties, and to establish regulations for the conduct of persons who may receive appointments in the civil service.§

Mr. WILLIAMS moved that it be tabled; which, on a division, was disagreed to—yeas 25, nays 26.

The section was then adopted—yeas 32, nays 24.

The House agreed to this and other amendments added by the Senate, without a yea and nay vote.

IN SENATE.

1872, March 7—Pending the legislative appropriation bill, and the question being on concurring in Senate in an amendment made as in Committee of the Whole, appropriating $50,000 to enable the President of the United States to perfect and put in force such rules as may from time to time be adopted by him—

Mr. CARPENTER moved to substitute for that the following:

That all laws or parts of laws under which the present civil service commission is appointed by the President of the United States be, and the same are hereby, repealed.

Mr. TRUMBULL moved to lay the amendment on the table; which was agreed to—yeas 29, nays 21:

YEAS—Messrs. Ames, Anthony, *Bayard*, Boreman, Buckingham, *Casserly*, Cole, Conkling, Corbett, *Davis* of West Virginia, Edmunds, Flanagan, Frelinghuysen, *Goldthwaite*, Harlan, Hill, *Johnston*, *Kelly*, Morrill of Vermont, Pratt, Schurz, Scott, Sherman, *Stevenson*, *Stockton*, Trumbull, *Vickers*, Wilson, Wright—29.

NAYS—Messrs. Alcorn, *Blair*, Caldwell, Cameron, Carpenter, Chandler, Clayton, *Cooper*, Hamilton of Texas, Hitchcock, Kellogg, Logan, Osborn, Pomeroy, Pool, Ramsey, Rice, *Saulsbury*, Tipton, West, Windom—21.

March 11—The amendment appropriating $50,000, as above, was concurred in—yeas 25, nays 21:

YEAS—Messrs. Ames, Anthony, *Blair*, Cole, *Cooper*, Corbett, *Davis* of West Virginia, Edmunds, Ferry of Michigan, Flanagan, Frelinghuysen, *Hamilton*

* Qualified December 4, 1871, *vice* Burton C. Cook, resigned.

† Qualified December 4, 1871, *vice* John A. Logan, resigned.

‡ Qualified February 9, 1872, *vice* John Edwards, qualified March 22, 1871, and unseated without a division.

‖ Qualified December 4, 1871, *vice* Thomas W. Ferry, resigned.

§ This is a copy of a joint resolution offered in the House, January 30, 1871, by Hon. William H. Armstrong, and referred to the select committee on the reorganization of the civil service, with the exception that his resolution contained the following additional clause:

The President is also authorized to prescribe fees to be paid by all persons applying for appointments, except such classes of honorably discharged soldiers as he may exempt, which fees shall be applied to the payment of the expenses of making such inquiries.

* Messrs. Conner and Hancock qualified December 4, 1871; Mr. Herndon December 12; and Mr. Giddings May 13, 1872, in place of Mr. William T. Clark, unseated on that day, and who had qualified, on a *prima facie* certificate, January 10, 1872.

† Messrs. Houghton and Coghlan qualified December 4, 1871; Mr. Sargent, January 10, 1872.

of Maryland, *Johnston*, Kellogg, Kelly, Morrill of Maine, Morton, *Norwood*, Nye, Pratt, Schurz, Sherman, Trumbull, *Vickers*, Wilson—25.

NAYS—Messrs. Alcorn, Boreman, Caldwell, Chandler, Clayton, Gilbert, *Goldthwaite*, Hamilton of Texas, Harlan, Hill, Hitchcock, Howe, Lewis, Osborn, Pomeroy, Ramsey, Spencer, Sprague, West, Windom, Wright—21.

IN HOUSE.

1872, April 12—The Committee of the Whole reduced this appropriation to $10,000; and the House concurred in the amendment of the committee—yeas 115, nays 58:

YEAS—Messrs. Ames, *Archer*, *Arthur*, Barry, Beatty, *Beck*, *Bell*, Beveridge, Bigby, *Biggs*, *Bird*, Boles, *Braxton*, Buckley, Buffinton, B. F. Butler, F. Clarke, Cobb, Coburn, Coghlan, *Comingo*, *Critcher*, *Crossland*, De Large, Donnan, *Dox*, *Du Bose*, Duell, *Duke*, Dunnell, Farwell, *Forker*, Frye, *Garrett*, *Golladay*, Goodrich, *Haldeman*, *Hambleton*, *Hancock*, *Handley*, *Hanks*, *Harper*, *J. T. Harris*, Havens, Hays, G. W. Hazelton, J. W. Hazelton, *Herndon*, Houghton, *Kerr*, *Lamison*, Lamport, Lansing, *Leach*, *Lewis*, *Manson*, *Marshall*, *McClelland*, McGrew, *McHenry*, *McIntyre*, McJunkin, Mercur, Merriam, *Merrick*, *B. F. Meyers*, Morey, *Morgan*, Morphis, Negley, Orr, Packer, Palmer, Peck, Pendleton, Perce, *E. Perry*, Prindle, Rainey, *Randall*, *Read*, *W. R. Roberts*, Rusk, Sargent, Sawyer, Scofield, Seeley, Shanks, Sheldon, *Sherwood*, *Shober*, *Slater*, J. A. Smith, Snapp, Snyder, T. J. Speer, Stoughton, Stowell, *Sutherland*, Taffe, *Terry*, Thomas, Turner, Tyner, *Van Trump*, *Vaughan*, Walden, Wallace, Wheeler, Whiteley, Williams of Indiana, *Williams* of New York, J. M. Wilson, J. T. Wilson, *Wood*—115.

NAYS—Messrs. Ambler, Banks, Bingham, G. M. Brooks, Burchard, Burdett, R. R. Butler, W. T. Clarke, Conger, Cotton, Dawes, Eames, *Ely*, Finkelnburg, C. Foster, W. D. Foster, *Griffith*, Hale, G. E. Harris, Hay, *Hibbard*, Hill, Hoar, *Holman*, Hooper, Kelley, Kellogg, *Kendall*, *King*, Lowe, Maynard, *McCormick*, McCrary, Monroe, Moore, L. Myers, Packard, A. F. Perry, Peters, Poland, Potter, *E. Y. Rice*, E. H. Roberts, Sessions, H. B. Smith, Sprague, Starkweather, *Stevens*, Stevenson, *Storm*, Strong, W. Townsend, Twichell, Upson, Wakeman, Waldron, *Whitthorne*, Willard—58.

The amendment of the Senate, as amended, was then concurred in.

Subsequently, in conference committee, the sum was fixed at $25,000.

IN HOUSE.

1872, April 19—This bill, reported by Mr. WILLARD, from the Committee on the Civil Service pending:

A Bill to preserve the independence of the several departments of the Government.

Be it enacted, &c., That hereafter it shall be unlawful for any member of either House of Congress, or delegate from a Territory, verbally or in writing, directly or indirectly, or by any agent or third person, to solicit or recommend, or advise the President of the United States, or any head of a Department, or of any bureau thereof, or any official who has by law power to nominate or appoint to positions in the civil service of the United States, to nominate or appoint, or to refuse to nominate or appoint any person to, or to remove any person from, office or employment in the civil service, except as hereinafter provided.

SEC. 2. That whenever the President or the head of a Department shall, in writing, ask the opinion or advice of a member of Congress or a delegate from a Territory, respecting any appointment or removal, such member or delegate may, in writing only, give his advice or opinion respecting such appointment or removal. And such member or delegate may also, without being requested so to do, give, in writing, to the President or head of Department any information which such member or delegate may have of the misconduct or unfaithfulness of any person in the civil service. Any such information, advice, or opinion given to the President or head of a Department by any member or delegate, shall be regarded as official, and shall at all times be open to the inspection of members and delegates; and copies thereof shall be transmitted to either House of Congress whenever called for by them for information or publication. All appointments and removals concerning which communications shall have been received by the President or heads of Departments from members or delegates shall be reported to Congress at the session thereof next after such appointment or removal shall have been made, together with all correspondence with or communications from members or delegates respecting the same.

SEC. 3. That any person who shall violate any of the provisions of this act shall be guilty of a misdemeanor, and on conviction thereof shall be fined not less than $100, and not more than $1,000.

Mr. BUTLER moved that the bill, with the pending amendments, be recommitted to the committee; which was agreed to—yeas 97, nays 79:

YEAS — Messrs. Ames, Averill, Banks, Barber, *Beck*, Bigby, Bingham, *Bird*, *J. G. Blair*, Boles, *Braxton*, *Bright*, Buckley, B. F. Butler, R. R. Butler, W. T. Clark, F. Clarke, Coburn, Coghlan, *Comingo*, Conger, *Critcher*, Crocker, Darrall, De Large, Dickey, Donnan, *Dox*, Duell, Dunnell, Farwell, *Golladay*, Goodrich, Harmer, *Harper*, G. E. Harris, *J. T. Harris*, Havens, Hays, G. W. Hazelton, J. W. Hazelton, *Kendall*, *Kerr*, Ketcham, *King*, *Lamison*, Lamport, Lansing, Maynard, McJunkin, McKee, Mercur, Moore, Morey, *Morgan*, L. Myers, *Niblack*, Packer, Palmer, I. C. Parker, Peck, Perce, Peters, Prindle, Rainey, Rusk, Sargent, Scofield, Seeley, Sessions, Shanks, Sheldon, Shoemaker, *Slater*, *Sloss*, J. A. Smith, Snapp, Snyder, *R. M. Speer*, T. J. Speer, Sprague, Stoughton, Sypher, Taffe, *Terry*, W. Townsend, Turner, Twichell, Tyner, *Van Trump*, *Waddell*, Walden, Wallace, Wheeler, Whiteley, J. M. Wilson, J. T. Wilson—97.

NAYS — Messrs. *Acker*, *Adams*, *Archer*, *Arthur*, Beatty, A. Blair, *J. Brooks*, Buffinton, Burchard, Burdett, Cotton, *Cox*, *Crossland*, *Du Bose*, *Duke*, Eames, *Eldredge*, *Ely*, Farnsworth, Finkelnburg, W. D. Foster, Frye, Garfield, *Garrett*, *Getz*, *Griffith*, *Haldeman*, Hale, Halsey, *Hambleton*, *Hancock*, *Handley*, *Hanks*, Hay, *Hibbard*, Hoar, *Holman*, Kelley, Lowe, Lynch, *Manson*, *Marshall*, *McClelland*, *McCormick*, McCrary, *McIntyre*, Merriam, Monroe, Morphis, Orr, Packard, *H. W. Parker*, A. F. Perry, *E. Perry*, Poland, *Potter*, *Price*, *Read*, *Ritchie*, E. H. Roberts, *W. R. Roberts*, *Rogers*, *Roosevelt*, *Sherwood*, Starkweather, *Stevens*, Stevenson, *Storm*, Strong, *Sutherland*, *Swann*, Upson, *Voorhees*, Wakeman, Waldron, *Wells*, *Whitthorne*, Willard, *Young*—79.

I.

Executive Order.

WASHINGTON, *April* 16, 1872.

The advisory board of the civil service, having completed the grouping contemplated by the rules already adopted, have recommended certain provisions for carrying the rules into effect.

The recommendations, as herewith published, are approved, and the provisions will be enforced as rapidly as the proper arrangements can be made, and the thirteenth of the rules adopted on the 19th day of December last is amended to read as published herewith.

The utmost fidelity and diligence will be expected of all officers in every branch of the public service. Political assessments, as they are called, have been forbidden within the various Departments; and while the right of all persons in official position to take part in politics is acknowledged, and the elective franchise is recognized as a high trust to be discharged by all entitled to its exercise, whether in the employment of the Government or in private life, honesty and efficiency, not political activity, will determine the tenure of office. U. S. GRANT.

By the President:

HAMILTON FISH, *Secretary of State.*

Regulations.

1. No person will be appointed to any position in the civil service who shall not have furnished satisfactory evidence of his fidelity to the Union and the Constitution of the United States.

2 The evidence in regard to character, health, age, and knowledge of the English language, required by the first rule, shall be furnished in writing, and if such evidence shall be satisfactory to the head of the Department in which the appointment is to be made, the applicant shall be notified when and where to appear for examination; but when the applicants are so numerous that the examination of all whose preliminary papers are satisfactory is plainly impracticable, the head of the Department shall select for examination a practicable number of those who are apparently best qualified.

3. Examinations to fill vacancies in any of the Executive Departments in Washington shall be held not only at the city of Washington, but also, when directed by the head of the Department in which the vacancy may exist, in the several States, either at the capital or other convenient place.

4. The appointment of persons to be employed exclusively in the secret service of the Government; also of persons to be employed as translators, stenographers, or private secretaries, or to be designated for secret service, to fill vacancies in clerkships in either of the Executive Departments at Washington, may be excepted from the operation of the rules.

5. When a vacancy occurs in a consular office, of which the lawful annual compensation is three thousand dollars or more, it will be filled at the discretion of the President, either by the transfer of some person already in the service or by a new appointment, which may be excepted from the operation of the rules. But if the vacancy occur in an office of which the lawful annual compensation, by salary or by fees ascertained by the last official returns, is more than one thousand dollars and less than three thousand dollars, and it is not filled by transfer, applications will be addressed to the Secretary of State, inclosing proper certificates of character, responsibility, and capacity, and the Secretary will notify the applicant who, upon investigation, appears to be most suitable and competent to attend for examination; and if he shall be found qualified, he will be nominated for confirmation; but if not found qualified, or if his nomination be not confirmed by the Senate, the Secretary will proceed in like manner with the other applicants who appear to him to be qualified. If, however, no applicants under this regulation shall be found suitable and qualified, the vacancy will be filled at discretion. The appointment of commercial agents and of consuls whose annual compensation is one thousand dollars or less, (if derived from fees, the amount to be ascertained by the last official returns,) of vice consuls, deputy consuls, and of consular agents and other officers who are appointed upon the nomination of the principal officer, and for whom he is responsible upon his official bond, may be, until otherwise ordered, excepted from the operation of the rules.

6. When a vacancy occurs in the office of collector of the customs, naval officer, appraiser, or surveyor of the customs, in the customs districts of New York, Boston and Charlestown, Baltimore, San Francisco, New Orleans, Philadelphia, Vermont, (Burlington.) Oswego, Niagara, Buffalo Creek, Champlain, Portland and Falmouth, Corpus Christi, Oswegatchie, Mobile, Brazos de Santiago, (Brownsville,) Texas, (Galveston, &c.) Savannah, Charleston, Chicago, or Detroit, the Secretary of the Treasury shall ascertain if any of the subordinates in the customs district in which such vacancy occurs are suitable persons qualified to discharge efficiently the duties of the office to be filled, and, if such persons be found, he shall certify to the President the name or names of those subordinates, not exceeding three, who, in his judgment, are best qualified for the position, from which the President will make the nomination to fill the vacancy. But if no such subordinate be found qualified, or if the nomination be not confirmed, the nomination will be made at the discretion of the President. Vacancies occurring in such positions in the customs service in the said districts as are included in the subjoined classification will be filled in accordance with the rules. Appointments to all other positions in the customs service in said districts may be, until otherwise ordered, excepted from the operation of the rules.

7. When a vacancy occurs in the office of collector, appraiser, surveyor, or other chief officer in any customs district not specified in the preceding regulation, applications in writing from any subordinate or subordinates in the customs service of the district, or from other person or persons residing within the said district, may be addressed to the Secretary of the Treasury, inclosing proper certificates of character, responsibility, and

capacity; and if any of the subordinates so applying shall be found suitable and qualified, the name or names, not exceeding three, of the best qualified shall be certified by the board of examiners to the Secretary, and from this list the nomination or appointment will be made. But if no such subordinate be found qualified, the said board shall certify to the Secretary the name or names, not exceeding three, of the best qualified among the other applicants, and from this list the nomination or appointment will be made. If, however, no applicants under this regulation shall be found suitable and qualified, the vacancy will be filled at discretion. Appointments to all other positions in the customs service in said districts may be, until otherwise ordered, excepted from the operation of the rules.

8. When a vacancy occurs in the office of postmaster in cities having, according to the census of 1870, a population of twenty thousand or more, the Postmaster General shall ascertain if any of the subordinates in such office are suitable persons qualified to discharge efficiently the duties of postmaster, and, if such are found, he shall certify to the President the name or names of those subordinates, not exceeding three in number, who, in his judgment, are best qualified for the position, from which list the President will make the nomination to fill the vacancy. But if no such subordinate be found so qualified, or if the nomination be not confirmed by the Senate, the nomination will be made at the discretion of the President. Vacancies occurring in such positions in the said post offices as are included in the subjoined classification will be filled in accordance with the rules. Appointments to all other positions in the said post offices may be, until otherwise ordered, excepted from the operation of the rules.

9. When a vacancy occurs in the office of postmaster, of a class not otherwise provided for, applications for the position from any subordinate or subordinates in the office, or from other persons residing within the delivery of the office, may be addressed to the Postmaster General, inclosing proper certificates of character, responsibility, and capacity; and if any of the subordinates so applying shall be found suitable and qualified, the name or names of the best qualified, not exceeding three, shall be certified by the board of examiners to the Postmaster General, and from them the nomination or appointment shall be made. But if no subordinate be found qualified, the said board shall certify to the Postmaster General the name or names, not exceeding three, of the best qualified among the other applicants, and from them the nomination or appointment shall be made. If, however, no applicants under this regulation shall be found suitable and qualified, the vacancy will be filled at discretion. Appointments to all other positions in the said post offices may be, until otherwise ordered, excepted from the operation of the rules.

10. Special agents of the Post Office Department shall be appointed by the Postmaster General at discretion from persons already in the postal service, and who shall have served therein for a period of not less than one year immediately preceding the appointment. But if no person within the service shall, in the judgment of the Postmaster General, be suitable and qualified, the appointment shall be made from all applicants under the rules.

11. Mail route messengers shall be appointed in the manner provided for the appointment of postmasters whose annual salary is less than two hundred dollars.

12. When a vacancy occurs in the office of register or receiver of the land office, or of pension agent, applications in writing from residents in the district in which the vacancy occurs may be addressed to the Secretary of the Interior, inclosing proper certificates of character, responsibility, and capacity; and if any of the applicants shall be found suitable and qualified, the name or names, not exceeding three, of the best qualified, shall be certified by the board of examiners to the Secretary, and from this list the nomination will be made. If, however, no applicants under this regulation shall be found suitable and qualified, the nomination will be made at discretion.

13. When a vacancy occurs in the office of United States marshal, applications in writing from residents in the district in which the vacancy occurs may be addressed to the Attorney General of the United States, inclosing proper certificates of character, responsibility, and capacity; and if any of the applicants shall be found suitable and qualified, the name or names, not exceeding three, of the best qualfied shall be certified by the board of examiners to the Attorney General, and from this list the nomination will be made. If, however, no applicants under this regulation shall be found suitable and qualified, the nomination will be made at discretion.

14. Appointments to fill vacancies occurring in offices in the several Territories, excepting those of judges of the United States courts, Indian agents and superintendents, will be made from suitable and qualified persons domiciled in the Territory in which the vacancy occurs, if any such are found.

15. It shall be the duty of the examining board in each of the Departments to report to the advisory board such modifications in the rules and regulations as, in the judgment of such examining board, are required for appointments to certain positions, to which, by reason of distance, or of difficult access, or of other sufficient cause, the rules and regulations cannot be applied with advantage; and if the reason for such modifications shall be satisfactory to the advisory board, said board will recommend them for approval.

16. Nothing in these rules and regulations shall prevent the reappointment at discretion of the incumbents of any office the term of which is fixed by law; and when such reappointment is made no vacancy within the meaning of the rules shall be deemed to have occurred.

17. Appointments to all positions in the civil

service not included in the subjoined classifications, nor otherwise specially provided for by the rules and regulations, may, until otherwise ordered, be excepted from the operation of the rules.

[Classification omitted.]

II.

Rules and Regulations for the Civil Service Promulgated by the President 19th December, 1871, as Amended by the Executive Order, 16th April, 1872.

1. No person shall be admitted to any position in the civil service within the appointment of the President or the heads of Departments who is not a citizen of the United States; who shall not have furnished satisfactory evidence in regard to character, health, and age; and who shall not have passed a satisfactory examination in speaking, reading, and writing the English language.

2. An advisory board of suitable persons to be employed by the President under the ninth section of the act of March 3, 1871, entitled "An act making appropriations for sundry civil expenses of the Government for the fiscal year ending June 30, 1872, and for other purposes," shall, so far as practicable, group the positions in each branch of the civil service according to the character of the duties to be performed, and shall grade each group from lowest to highest for the purpose of promotion within the group. Admission to the civil service shall always be to the lowest grade of any group; and to such positions as cannot be grouped or graded, admission shall be determined as provided for the lowest grade.

3. A vacancy occurring in the lowest grade of any group of offices shall be filled, after due public notice, from all applicants who shall present themselves, and who shall have furnished the evidence and satisfied the preliminary examination already mentioned, and who shall have passed a public competitive examination to test knowledge, ability, and special qualifications for the performance of the duties of the office. The board conducting such competitive examination shall prepare, under the supervision of the advisory board, a list of the names of the applicants, in the order of their excellence, as proved by such examination, beginning with the highest; and shall then certify to the nominating or appointing power, as the case may be, the names standing at the head of such list not exceeding three; and from the names thus certified the appointment shall be made.

4. A vacancy occurring in any grade of a group of offices, above the lowest, shall be filled by a competitive examination of applicants from the other grades of that group, and the list of names from which the appointment is to be made shall be prepared and certified as provided in the preceding rule; but if no such applicants are found competent, the appointment shall be made upon an examination of all applicants, conducted in accordance with the provisions for admission to the lowest grade.

5. Applicants certified as otherwise qualified for appointment as cashiers of collectors of customs, cashiers of assistant treasurers, cashiers of postmasters, superintendents of money-order divisions in post offices, and such other custodians of large sums of money as may hereafter be designated by the advisory board, and for whose pecuniary fidelity another officer is responsible, shall, nevertheless, not be appointed, except with the approval of such other officer.

6. Postmasters whose annual salary is less than two hundred dollars may be appointed upon the written request of applicants, with such evidence of character and fitness as shall be satisfactory to the head of the Department.

7. The appointment of all persons entering the civil service in accordance with these regulations, excepting persons appointed by the President, by and with the advice and consent of the Senate, postmasters, and persons appointed to any position in a foreign country, shall be made for a probationary term of six months, during which the conduct and capacity of such persons shall be tested; and if, at the end of said probationary term, satisfactory proofs of their fitness shall have been furnished by the board of examiners to the head of the Department in which they shall have been employed during said term, they shall be reappointed.

8. The President will designate three persons in each Department of the public service to serve as a board of examiners, which, under the supervision of the advisory board, and under regulations to be prescribed by it, and at such times and places as it may determine, shall conduct personally, or by persons approved by the advisory board, all investigations and examinations for admission into said Departments, or for promotion therein.

9. Any person who, after long and faithful service in a Department, shall be incapacitated by mental or bodily infirmity for the efficient discharge of the duties of his position, may be appointed by the head of the Department, at his discretion, to a position of less responsibility in the same Department.

10. Nothing in these rules shall prevent the appointment of aliens to positions in the consular service, which, by reason of small compensation or of other sufficient cause, are, in the judgment of the appointing power, necessarily so filled; nor the appointment of such persons within the United States as are indispensable to a proper discharge of the duties of certain positions, but who may not be familiar with the English language or legally capable of naturalization.

11. No head of a Department, nor any subordinate officer of the Government, shall, as such officer, authorize or permit, or assist in levying, any assessment of money, for political purposes, under the form of voluntary contributions or otherwise, upon any person employed under his control, nor shall any such person pay any money so assessed.

12. The advisory board shall at any time recommend to the President such changes in these rules as it may consider necessary to

secure the greater efficiency of the civil service.

13. From these rules are excepted the heads of Departments, Assistant Secretaries of Departments, Assistant Attorneys General, Assistant Postmasters General, Solicitor General, Solicitor of the Treasury, Naval Solicitor, Solicitor of Internal Revenue, Examiner of Claims in the State Department, Treasurer of the United States, Register of the Treasury, First and Second Comptrollers of the Treasury, other heads of bureaus in the several Departments, judges of the United States courts, district attorneys, private secretary of the President, embassadors and other public ministers, Superintendent of the Coast Survey, Director of the Mint, Governors of Territories, special commissioners, special counsel, visiting and examining boards, persons appointed to positions without compensation for services, dispatch agents, and bearers of dispatches.

XIII.

THE LABOR QUESTION.

The Eight-Hour Law.

FORTIETH CONGRESS—SECOND SESSION.

1868, January 6—The House passed this bill, without a division:

Be it enacted, &c., That eight hours shall constitute a day's work for all laborers, workmen, and mechanics now employed, or who may be hereafter employed, by or on behalf of the Government of the United States; and that all acts and parts of acts inconsistent with this act be, and the same are hereby, repealed.

June 24—The Senate considered it, and Mr. SHERMAN moved to insert after the words "United States," in the fifth line, the following:

"And unless otherwise provided by law, the rate of wages paid by the United States shall be the current rate for the same labor, for the same time, at the place of employment."

Which was disagreed to—yeas 16, nays 21:

YEAS—Messrs. Cattell, Corbett, *Davis*, Edmunds, Ferry, Fessenden, Howard, Morgan, Morrill of Maine, Morrill of Vermont, Patterson of New Hampshire, Ross, Sherman, Sumner, Van Winkle, Williams—16.

NAYS—Messrs. *Buckalew*, Cole, Conkling, Conness, Cragin, *Dixon*, *Doolittle*, Harlan, *Hendricks*, *Johnson*, McDonald, *McCreery*, Morton, Nye, *Patterson* of Tennessee, Pomeroy, Ramsey, Stewart, Tipton, Wade, Wilson—21.

The bill then passed—yeas 26, nays 11:

YEAS—Messrs. *Buckalew*, Chandler, Cole, Conness, Cragin, *Dixon*, *Doolittle*, Fowler, Harlan, *Hendricks*, Howard, *McCreery*, McDonald, Morton, Nye, Patterson of New Hampshire, *Patterson* of Tennessee, Ramsey, Ross, Stewart, Thayer, Tipton, Wade, Williams, Wilson, Yates—26.

NAYS—Messrs. Corbett, *Davis*, Edmunds, Ferry, Fessenden, Morgan, Morrill of Vermont, Pomeroy, Sherman, Sumner, Van Winkle—11.

Opinion of Attorney General Hoar as to its Effect.

ATTORNEY GENERAL'S OFFICE,
WASHINGTON, *April* 21, 1869.

HON. A. E. BORIE, *Secretary of the Navy*.

SIR: I have the honor to acknowledge the receipt of your letter of April 3, 1869, in which you ask my opinion upon the true meaning and effect of the act of Congress approved June 25, 1868, which fixes the number of hours constituting a day's work of laborers, workmen, and mechanics in the employment of the United States, taken in connection with the act of July 16, 1862, which provided "that section eight of an act to further promote the efficiency of the Navy, approved December 21, 1861, be amended so as to read as follows: that the hours of labor and the rate of wages of the employés in the navy-yards shall conform, as nearly as is consistent with the public interest, with those of the private establishments in the immediate vicinity of the respective yards, to be determined by the commandants of the navy-yards, subject to the approval and revision of the Secretary of the Navy."

In reply, I have the honor to say that the whole subject was fully considered in the opinion given by my predecessor in office, Mr. Evarts, to the President, on the 25th of November, 1868, to which I beg leave to refer you, and from the conclusions of which I see no reason to differ.

In my opinion the statute of June 25, 1868, has nothing to do with the compensation to be paid to workmen in the navy-yards, and leaves that to be determined under the provisions of the act of July 16, 1862. The provision that eight hours shall constitute a day's labor has no tendency whatever to show whether the day's labor thus established shall be paid at a lower or higher rate than the day of ten hours' labor or at the same rate. The rate of compensation is still left by law to be determined under the rules prescribed by the statute of July 16, 1862, so as to "conform as nearly as is consistent with the public interest, with those of private establishments in the immediate vicinity of the respective yards, to be determined by the commandants of the navy-yards, subject to the approval and revision of the Secretary of the Navy."

If the private establishments in the neighborhood employed their hands for five hours a day only, there would obviously be no justice in reducing the wages of those employed in the navy-yards to the amount paid by the day in private establishments; and the law intended no such results. On the other hand, I find nothing in the statute which requires you to pay the same price for eight hours' labor which private establishments pay for ten or twelve, unless the amount of service or the quality of the work make the fewer hours in the navy-yards equivalent in value to the longer time hired in private establishments, or for some other reason make it consistent with the public interest.

Very respectfully, your obedient servant,

E. R. HOAR, *Attorney General.*

President Grant's order Respecting Wages of Labor, May 19, 1869.

Whereas the act of Congress, approved June 25, 1868, constituted on and after that date eight hours a day's work for all laborers, workmen, and mechanics employed by or on behalf of the Government of the United States, and repealed all acts and parts of acts inconsistent therewith:

Now, therefore, I, Ulysses S. Grant, President of the United States, do hereby direct that from and after this date no reduction shall be made in the wages paid by the Government by the day to such laborers, workmen, and mechanics, on account of such reduction of the hours of labor.

In testimony whereof I have hereto set my hand and caused the seal of the United States to be affixed.

Done at the city of Washington, this 19th day of May, in the year of our Lord 1869, [SEAL.] and of the independence of the United States the ninety-third.

U. S. GRANT.

By the President:

HAMILTON FISH,
Secretary of State.

Forty-Second Congress, Second Session.

IN HOUSE.

1872, March 7—Pending the deficiency appropriation bill, Mr. DAWES moved this new section:

SEC. 2. That the proper accounting officers be, and hereby are, authorized and required, in the settlement of all accounts for the services of laborers, workmen, and mechanics employed by or on behalf of the Government of the United States, between the 25th day of June, 1868, the date of the act constituting eight hours a day's work for all such laborers, workmen, and mechanics, and the 19th day of May, 1869, the date of the proclamation of the President concerning such pay, to settle and pay for the same, without reduction on account of reduction of hours of labor by said act, and a sufficient sum for said purpose is hereby appropriated out of any money in the Treasury not otherwise appropriated.

Mr. FARNSWORTH moved to add these words:

Provided, That no part of the money hereby appropriated shall be paid to any mechanics or laborers who have already been paid for eight hours' labor four fifths as much as the amount which was paid to like laborers and mechanics for ten hours' labor.

The amendment was agreed to—yeas 88, nays 80:

YEAS—Messrs. *Adams*, Ambler, Averill, Barber, *Barnum*, Barry, Beatty, Biggs, Bingham, *Bird*, A. Blair, *Braxton*, Burchard, *Caldwell*, *Carroll*, Coburn, *Conner*, Cotton, *Critcher*, *Crossland*, *Davis*, Donnan, *Dox*, *Du Bose*, *Duke*, *Eldredge*, Farnsworth, Farwell, Finkelnburg, *Forker*, *Garrett*, *Golladay*, *Hambleton*, *Handley*, *Hanks*, *Harper*, *J. T. Harris*, G. W. Hazelton, *Hereford*, *Kerr*, *King*, *Lamison*, *Lewis*, *Manson*, *McCormick*, McGrew, *McHenry*, *McIntyre*, McJunkin, *McKinney*, *Merrick*, *Mitchell*, Moore, Orr, Palmer, I. C. Parker, Peck, *E. Perry*, Peters, *Potter*, *Price*, *Read*, *E. Y. Rice*, *J. M. Rice*, Shanks, Sheldon, *Slater*, *Slocum*, *Sloss*, J. A. Smith, W. C. Smith, *Stevens*, *Sutherland*, Taffe, *Terry*, *Tuthill*, Tyner, *Van Trump*, *Vaughan*, *Voorhees*, Walden, Waldron, *Warren*, *Wells*, Willard, Williams of Indiana, J. T. Wilson, *Winchester*—88.

NAYS—Messrs. *Acker*, *Archer*, *Arthur*, Banks, Bigby, G. M. Brooks, Buckley, Buffinton, Burdett, R. R. Butler, Coghlan, Conger, Creely, Dawes, Duell, Dunnell, W. D. Foster, Frye, Garfield, *Getz*, *Haldeman*, Halsey, Harmer, Hawley, Hay, Hays, J. W. Hazelton, Hill, Hoar, *Holman*, Hooper, Houghton, Kelley, Kellogg, *Kendall*, Ketcham, Killinger, Lansing, *Marshall*, *McClelland*, McCrary, Mercur, Merriam, *B. F. Meyers*, Monroe, *Morgan*, L. Myers, *Niblack*, Packard, Packer, Pendleton, Perce, Platt, Rainey, *Randall*, E. H. Roberts, Rusk, Sargent, Sawyer, Seeley, Sessions, *Sherwood*, Shoemaker, H. B. Smith, Snapp, Snyder, T. J. Speer, Sprague, Starkweather, Stevenson, Strong, *D. Townsend*, Turner, Upson, *Waddell*, Wakeman, Wallace, Wheeler, Whiteley, J. M. Wilson—80.

The motion, as amended, was then agreed to—yeas 117, nays 42:

YEAS—Messrs. *Acker*, *Archer*, *Arthur*, Banks, *Barnum*, Barry, Bigby, *Bird*, *Braxton*, *Bright*, G. M. Brooks, *J. Brooks*, Buckley, Buffinton, B. F. Butler, R. R. Butler, *Caldwell*, *Carroll*, Cobb, Coghlan, *Comingo*, Conger, Cotton, *Crebs*, *Critcher*, *Davis*, Dawes, *Du Bose*, Duell, *Duke*, *Eldredge*, Finkelnburg, *Forker*, C. Foster, W. D. Foster, Frye, *Garrett*, *Getz*, *Golladay*, *Haldeman*, Halsey, Harmer, *J. T. Harris*, Hawley, Hay, Hays, G. W. Hazelton, J. W. Hazelton, Hill, Hoar, *Holman*, Hooper, Houghton, Kelley, Kellogg, *Kendall*, *Kerr*, Ketcham, Killinger, *King*, *Lamison*, *Lewis*, *Marshall*, *McClelland*, *McCormick*, McCrary, *McHenry*, *McKinney*, Mercur, Merriam, *Merrick*, *B. F. Meyers*, *Mitchell*, Monroe, *Morgan*, L. Meyers, Negley, *Niblack*, Packer, I. C. Parker, Pendleton, Perce, *E. Perry*, Platt, Rainey, *Randall*, E. H. Roberts, *Robinson*, Rusk, Sawyer, Sheldon, *Sherwood*, Shoemaker, *Slater*, *Slocum*, H. B. Smith, Snapp, Snyder, T. J. Speer, Sprague, Starkweather, Stevenson, Stowell, Strong, W. Townsend, *Tuthill*, Twichell, Upson, *Voorhees*, Wakeman, Wallace, *Warren*, Wheeler, Whiteley, *Williams* of New York, J. M. Wilson, *Wood*—117.

NAYS—Messrs. Ambler, Barber, Beatty, A. Blair, *J. G. Blair*, Burchard, Creely, *Crossland*, Donnan, *Dox*, Dunnell, Farnsworth, Garfield, *Hambleton*, *Handley*, *Harper*, *Manson*, McGrew, *McIntyre*, McJunkin, Orr, Palmer, Peck, Peters, Prindle, *Read*, *E. Y. Rice*, *J. M. Rice*, Seeley, Sessions, Shanks, J. A. Smith, W. C. Smith, *Terry*, Tyner, *Waddell*, Walden, Waldron, Willard, Williams of Indiana, J. T. Wilson, *Winchester*—42.

IN SENATE.

April 15—The Senate adopted, in Committee of the Whole, without a division, the following substitute, reported by the Committee on Appropriations, for the above:

That there shall be paid to the policemen, oilers, and shop-tenders who were employed at the Springfield armory, in Massachusetts, or at any other armory or Government establishment, under similar circumstances, on and after the 30th day of July, 1868, the sums respectively by which their wages were reduced by order of the War Department under the eight hour law, so called.

April 27—Mr. MORRILL, of Vermont, moved

to insert the words "and all laws regulating the hours of labor are hereby repealed."

Mr. SPENCER moved that the amendment be laid on the table; which was agreed to—yeas 24, nays 20:

YEAS—Messrs. *Bayard*, Boreman, Carpenter. *Casserly*, Cole, *Cooper*, *Davis* of West Virginia, *Goldthwaite*, Kellogg, *Kelly*, Morton, Pomeroy, Pratt, Ramsey, *Ransom*, Rice, Schurz, Spencer, *Stevenson*, Stewart, *Stockton*, Sumner, West, Wilson—24.

NAYS—Messrs. Alcorn, Ames, Anthony, Buckingham, Caldwell, Chandler, Corbett, Edmunds, Ferry of Connecticut, Ferry of Michigan, *Hamilton* of Maryland, Hamilton of Texas, Hamlin, Morrill of Maine, Morrill of Vermont, Nye, Robertson, Trumbull, Vickers, Wright—20.

The Senate first refused (yeas 22, nays 24) to strike out the proviso to the House section, but afterward struck it out, without a division, after having been reconsidered—yeas 27, nays 23:

YEAS—Messrs. *Bayard*, *Blair*, Boreman, *Casserly*, Conkling, *Cooper*, *Davis* of West Virginia, Hamlin, Hill, *Johnston*, *Kelly*, Logan, Morton, Nye, Pratt, Ramsey, *Ransom*, Rice, Sawyer, Schurz, Spencer, *Stockton*, Sumner, Tipton, Trumbull, West, Wilson—27.

NAYS—Messrs. Alcorn, Ames, Anthony, Buckingham, Caldwell, Chandler, Cole, Corbett, Edmunds, Ferry of Connecticut, Ferry of Michigan, Gilbert, *Goldthwaite*, *Hamilton* of Maryland, Hamilton of Texas, Harlan, Morrill of Maine, Pomeroy, Robertson, *Stevenson*, *Vickers*, Windom, Wright—23.

And then—yeas 24, nays 25—non-concurred in the amendment reported by the Committee on Appropriations, stated above, thus concurring in the House section less the proviso.

IN HOUSE.

May 6—The Senate amendment was concurred in on a division, yeas 78, nays 59, after having voted down an amendment offered by Mr. FARNSWORTH to add the following words:

And shall also pay those who worked ten hours as a day's work twenty per cent. in addition to the sum they have already received.

Proposed Labor Commission.

IN HOUSE.

1871, December 20—The following bill passed:

That there shall be appointed by the President, by and with the advice and consent of the Senate, a commission of three persons, who shall be selected from civil life, solely with reference to their character and capacity for an honest and impartial investigation, and of whom at least one shall be practically identified with the laboring interests of the country, and who shall hold office for the period of one year from the date of their appointment, unless their duties shall have been sooner accomplished, who shall investigate the subject of the wages and hours of labor, and of the division of the joint profits of labor and capital between the laborer and the capitalist, and the social, educational, and sanitary condition of the laboring classes of the United States, and how the same are affected by existing laws regulating commerce, finance, and currency: *Provided*, That said commissioners shall be appointed irrespective of political or partisan considerations, and from civil life.

SEC. 2. That said commissioners shall receive an annual salary of $5,000 each, shall be authorized to employ a clerk, and shall report the result of their investigation to the President, to be by him transmitted to Congress.

Yeas 135, nays 36:

YEAS—Messrs. *Acker*, Ambler, *Archer*, *Arthur*, Banks, Barry, Beatty, *Bell*, Bingham, A. Blair, G. M. Brooks, Buckley, Buffinton, Burdett, Cobb, Coghlan, Conger, Cox, *Crebs*, Creely, Dawes, Donnan, *Dox*, Duell, Eames, Finkelnburg, *Forker*, C. Foster, Frye, Garfield, *Getz*, *Golladay*, Goodrich, *Griffith*, *Haldeman*, *Hancock*, Harmer, G. E. Harris, Havens, Hawley, Hay, Hays, G. W. Hazelton, J. W. Hazelton, *Hereford*, *Herndon*, *Hibbard*, Hill, Hoar, *Holman*, Houghton, Kelley, Ketcham, Killinger, *King*, *Kinsella*, Lamport, Lansing, Lowe, Lynch, *Manson*, *Marshall*, Maynard, *McClelland*, McCrary, McJunkin, McKee, *McKinney*, *McNeely*, Mercur, Merriam, *Merrick*, *B. F. Meyers*, Monroe, Moore, Morphis, Negley, *Niblack*, Packard, Packer, *H. W. Parker*, I. C. Parker, Pendleton, Perce, *E. Perry*, Porter, Prindle, Rainey, E. H. Roberts, *W. R. Roberts*, *Robinson*, *J. Rogers*, Rusk, Scofield, Seeley, Shanks, Sheldon, *Sherwood*, *Shober*, Shoemaker, *Slocum*, H. B. Smith, J. A. Smith, Snyder, *R. M. Speer*, T. J. Speer, Sprague, *Stevens*, Stevenson, *Storm*, Stoughton, Stowell, *Swann*, Sypher, Thomas, W. Townsend, Twichell, Tyner, Upson, *Van Trump*, *Voorhees*, *Waddell*, Wakeman, Walden, Waldron, Wallace, Walls, Washburn, *Wells*, Wheeler, Whiteley, Williams of Indiana, J. M. Wilson, J. T. Wilson, *Wood*—135.

NAYS—Messrs. *Adams*, Barber, *Bird*, *Braxton*, *Bright*, Burchard, *Caldwell*, *Campbell*, F. Clarke, *Comingo*, *Conner*, *Critcher*, *Crossland*, *Davis*, *Du Bose*, *Eldredge*, *Handley*, *J. T. Harris*, *Kerr*, *Lewis*, *McCormick*, *McIntyre*, Palmer, Peck, *Price*, *Read*, *E. Y. Rice*, *J. M. Rice*, *Ritchie*, Sessions, *Slater*, Taffe, *Terry*, *Whitthorne*, *Winchester*, *Young*—36.

IN SENATE.

1872, May 29—As in Committee of the Whole, the tax and tariff bill pending,

Mr. SAWYER moved to amend by inserting after section eleven the above sections, with an addition so that the second section, after the word "clerk" read: "at an annual salary of $1,400, and shall report the result of their investigation to the President, to be by him transmitted to Congress; and there is hereby appropriated, for the payment of said salaries, $16,400, and $1,000 in addition thereto for stationery and postage for the use of said commissioners."

Mr. POMEROY moved to amend the amendment by striking out the words "from civil life," where they first occur in the first section; which was disagreed to.

Mr. POMEROY moved to amend the amendment by striking out the words:

Provided, That said commissioners shall be appointed irrespective of political or partisan consideration, and from civil life,

Which was disagreed to—yeas 18, nays 35:

YEAS—Messrs. Ames, Anthony, Boreman, Caldwell, Carpenter, Chandler, Clayton, Cole, Corbett, Ferry of Michigan, Flanagan, Frelinghuysen, Hitchcock, Logan, Morrill of Maine, Nye, Pomeroy, Ramsey—18.

NAYS—Messrs. Alcorn, *Bayard*, *Blair*, Cameron, *Casserly*, Conkling, *Cooper*, Cragin, *Goldthwaite*, *Hamilton* of Maryland, Hamilton of Texas, Hamlin, Hill, *Johnston*, *Kelly*, Lewis, Morrill of Vermont, Morton, Patterson, Pool, Robertson, *Saulsbury*, Sawyer, Scott, Sherman, Spencer, Sprague, *Stevenson*, *Stockton*, Tipton, Trumbull, *Vickers*, West, Wilson, Wright—35.

Mr. WILSON moved to strike the word

"three" from the amendment and insert "five," so as to make the commission consist of five persons; which was disagreed to.

Mr. WILSON moved to strike out "one year" and insert "two years" as the term of office of the commissioners; which,

May 30, was disagreed to—ayes 9, noes 32.

Mr. WILSON moved to strike out the word "classes" and insert the word "population;" which was agreed to.

Mr. WILSON moved to strike out "$1,400" and insert "$2,500;" which was agreed to.

Mr. CONKLING moved to amend the amendment by striking out all of the first section thereof after the word "persons," and inserting:

To consider and examine the various plans and methods of raising revenue, to report the best tax and tariff system they can devise, having regard to the interests of labor in its relations to capital and otherwise, and having regard also to the interests of commerce and of all classes of the American people; and said persons shall hold office for one year from the date of their appointment.

Which was agreed to—yeas 30, nays 23:

YEAS—Messrs. *Bayard*, Buckingham, Caldwell, Chandler, Clayton, Cole, Conkling, Corbett, Edmunds, Ferry of Connecticut, Ferry of Michigan, Gilbert, *Goldthwaite*, *Hamilton* of Maryland, Hamilton of Texas, Harlan, Hill, *Johnston*, Kellogg, *Kelly*, Nye, Pomeroy, Pratt, Robertson, *Saulsbury*, Schurz, Stewart, Trumbull, *Vickers*, Windom—30.

NAYS—Messrs. Alcorn, *Casserly*, *Cooper*, Cragin, Flanagan, Frelinghuysen, Howe, Morrill of Vermont, Morton, Osborn, Ramsey, *Ransom*, Sawyer, Scott, Sherman, Spencer, Sprague, *Stevenson*, Sumner, *Thurman*, Tipton, Wilson, Wright—23.

Mr. ROBERTSON moved to reconsider the vote by which Mr. CONKLING's amendment to the amendment was adopted; which was disagreed to—yeas 25, nays 32:

YEAS—Messrs. Alcorn, Ames, *Casserly*, Cragin, Flanagan, Frelinghuysen, Hitchcock, Howe, Lewis, Morrill of Vermont, Morton, Osborn, Patterson, Pool, Ramsey, Robertson, Sawyer, Scott, Sherman, Spencer, Sprague, Sumner, *Thurman*, Tipton, Wilson—25.

NAYS—Messrs. *Bayard*, *Blair*, Buckingham, Caldwell, Cameron, Chandler, Clayton, Cole, Conkling, Corbett, Edmunds, Ferry of Connecticut, Ferry of Michigan, Gilbert, *Goldthwaite*, *Hamilton* of Maryland, Hamilton of Texas, *Johnston*, Kellogg, Logan, *Norwood*, Pomeroy, Pratt, *Ransom*, *Saulsbury*, Schurz, *Stevenson*, Stewart, Trumbull, *Vickers*, Windom, Wright—32.

Mr. CASSERLY moved to amend the amendment by inserting after the word "persons" and before Mr. CONKLING's amendment the words:

Who shall be selected from civil life, solely with reference to character and capacity for an intelligent, honest, and impartial investigation, irrespective of partisan considerations, and of whom at least one shall be practically identified with the laboring interests of the country, and shall have had sufficient personal experience and information in respect to the same.

Which was agreed to.

The amendment, as amended, was then disagreed to—yeas 17, nays 37:

YEAS—Messrs. Alcorn, Cameron, Clayton, Conkling, Corbett, Edmunds, Frelinghuysen, Hitchcock, Howe, Nye, Osborn, Pomeroy, Pool, Ramsey, Stewart, Sumner, Wilson—17.

NAYS—Messrs. Ames, *Bayard*, Boreman, Buckingham, Caldwell, *Casserly*, Cole, *Cooper*, Cragin, Ferry of Connecticut, Ferry of Michigan, Flanagan, Gilbert, *Goldthwaite*, Hamilton of Texas, Hill, *Johnston*, *Kelly*, Logan, Morrill of Maine, Morrill of Vermont, Morton, *Norwood*, Patterson, Pratt, *Ransom*, Robertson, Schurz, Scott, Sherman, Sprague, *Stevenson*, *Thurman*, Trumbull, *Vickers*, Windom, Wright—37.

A subsequent attempt to reintroduce the proposition was ruled out on a question of order—the vote being yeas 18 to nays 28 on receiving it.

XIV.

THE AMNESTY ACT AND THE SUPPLEMENTAL CIVIL RIGHTS BILLS.

The Amnesty Act as Passed and Approved.

IN HOUSE.

1872, May 13—Mr. BENJAMIN F. BUTLER, from the Judiciary Committee, reported the following bill, (H. R. No. 2760:)

Be it enacted, &c., (two thirds of each House concurring therein,) That all legal and political disabilities imposed by the third section of the fourteenth article of the amendments of the Constitution of the United States are hereby removed from all persons whomsoever, except Senators and Representatives of the Thirty-Sixth and Thirty Seventh Congress, officers in the judicial, military, and naval service of the United States, heads of Departments, and foreign ministers of the United States.

Which was passed (two thirds voting in favor thereof) on a division.

IN SENATE.

1872, May 21—The final vote was—yeas 38, nays 2:

YEAS—Messrs. Anthony, *Bayard*, *Blair*, Caldwell, Cameron, Carpenter, *Casserly*, Clayton, Cole, Conkling, *Cooper*, Corbett, *Davis* of West Virginia, Ferry of Michigan, Flanagan, *Goldthwaite*, *Hamilton* of Maryland, Hamlin, Hill, *Johnston*, *Kelly*, Logan, Morrill of Maine, Morrill of Vermont, *Norwood*, Patterson, Pool, *Ransom*, Robertson, *Saulsbury*, Sawyer, Scott, Sprague, *Stevenson*, *Thurman*, Tipton, Trumbull, *Vickers*—38.

NAYS—Messrs. Nye, Sumner—2.

The bill was approved May 22, 1872.

Previous Proceedings.

This bill pending,

Mr. SPENCER moved to strike out all after the enacting clause and insert Senate bill No. 5, removing political disabilities from—

First, all persons who, being members of

the Congress of the United States, withdrew from their seats and aided the rebellion; second, all persons who, being officers of the Army or Navy of the United States, and being above the age of twenty-one years, left said Army or Navy, and aided the rebellion; third, all persons who, being members of State conventions which adopted pretended ordinances of secession, voted in favor of the adoption of such ordinances.

Which was disagreed to—yeas 14, nays 32:

YEAS—Messrs. Ames, Anthony, Caldwell, Chandler, Clayton, Frelinghuysen, Morrill of Vermont, Nye, Osborn, Patterson, Pomeroy, Spencer, Wilson, Wright—14.

NAYS—Messrs. *Bayard, Blair*, Cameron, Carpenter, *Casserly*, Cole, Conkling, *Cooper*, Corbett, Cragin, *Davis* of West Virginia, Ferry of Michigan, Flanagan, *Goldthwaite, Hamilton* of Maryland, Hamlin, *Johnston, Kelly*, Logan, Morrill of Maine, *Norwood*, Pool, *Ransom*, Robertson, *Saulsbury*, Sawyer, Scott, Sprague, *Stevenson, Thurman*, Tipton, *Vickers*—32.

Mr. AMES moved to amend the bill by adding the two sections of the civil rights bill passed as a separate measure a few minutes before, (for text of which see page 74;) which was disagreed to—yeas 11, nays 31:

YEAS—Messrs. Ames, Chandler, Clayton, Flanagan, Frelinghuysen, Nye, Osborn, Pomeroy, Spencer, Wilson, Wright—11.

NAYS—Messrs. *Bayard, Blair*, Caldwell, Cameron, Carpenter, *Casserly*, Cole, *Cooper*, Corbett, Cragin, *Davis* of West Virginia, Ferry of Michigan, *Goldthwaite, Hamilton* of Maryland, Hamlin, *Johnston, Kelly*, Logan, Morrill of Maine, *Norwood*, Pool, *Ransom*, Robertson, *Saulsbury*, Sawyer, Scott, Sprague, *Stevenson, Thurman*, Tipton, *Vickers*—31.

Mr. FRELINGHUYSEN moved to amend by adding the following section:

SEC. —. That before any person shall be entitled to the benefit of the preceding section of this act he shall, within the district where he resides, before a clerk of some court of the United States, or a United States commissioner, take and subscribe an oath or affirmation to support the Constitution of the United States, and to bear true faith and allegiance to the same; which oath or affirmation shall be forwarded by said officer to the Secretary of State of the United States, who shall cause a list of all persons complying with the provisions of this act to be laid before Congress at the opening of each session thereof; and the officer before whom such oath or affirmation is made shall give to the person taking it a certificate of the fact, under such forms and regulations as the Secretary of State shall prescribe.

Which was disagreed to.

Mr. FRELINGHUYSEN moved to amend so as to make the bill read: "Officers who were at the commencement of the rebellion in the judicial, military, or naval service of the United States, or the heads of Departments, or foreign ministers of the United States;" which was disagreed to—yeas 18, nays 27:

YEAS—Messrs. Ames, Anthony, Caldwell, Chandler, Clayton, Conkling, Corbett, Ferry of Michigan, Flanagan, Frelinghuysen, Morrill of Vermont, Nye, Osborn, Patterson, Pomeroy, Spencer, Sumner, Wright—18.

NAYS—Messrs. *Bayard, Blair*, Cameron, Carpenter, *Casserly*, Cole, *Cooper*, *Davis* of West Virginia, *Goldthwaite, Hamilton* of Maryland, Hamlin, *Johnston, Kelly*, Logan, Morrill of Maine, *Norwood*, Pool, *Ransom*, Robertson, *Saulsbury*, Sawyer, Scott, Sprague, *Stevenson, Thurman*, Tipton, *Vickers*—27.

The bill was reported to the Senate without amendment.

Mr. SUMNER moved to amend by adding the supplementary civil rights bill (S. No. 1102;) which was disagreed to—yeas 13, nays 27:

YEAS—Messrs. Ames, Anthony, Clayton, Flanagan, Frelinghuysen, Morrill, of Vermont, Nye, Patterson, Pomeroy, Spencer, Sprague, Sumner, Wilson—13.

NAYS—Messrs. *Bayard, Blair*, Caldwell, Cameron, Carpenter, *Casserly*, Cole, *Cooper*, Corbett, *Davis* of West Virginia, Ferry of Michigan, *Goldthwaite, Hamilton* of Maryland, Hamlin, *Johnston, Kelly*, Logan, Morrill of Maine, *Norwood*, Pool, *Ransom*, Robertson, *Saulsbury*, Sawyer, Scott, *Stevenson, Thurman*, Tipton, *Vickers*—27.

The bill was then passed as above—the Ku Klux bill, civil rights bill, and this amnesty having been passed at one sitting of the Senate.

President Grant's Proclamation Enforcing the Amnesty Act, June 1, 1872.

Whereas the act of Congress, approved May 22, 1872, removes all political disabilities imposed by the third section of the fourteenth article of amendments to the Constitution of the United States from all persons whomsoever, except Senators and Representatives of the Thirty-Sixth and Thirty-Seventh Congresses and officers in the judicial, military, and naval service of the United States, heads of Departments, and foreign ministers of the United States;

And whereas it is represented to me that there are now pending in the several circuit and district courts of the United States proceedings by *quo warranto*, under the fourteenth section of the act of Congress approved May 31, 1870, to remove from office certain persons who are alleged to hold said offices in violation of the provisions of said article of amendment to the Constitution of the United States, and also penal prosecutions against such persons under the fifteenth section of the act of Congress aforesaid:

Now, therefore, I, Ulysses S. Grant, President of the United States, do hereby direct all district attorneys having charge of such proceedings and prosecutions to dismiss and discontinue the same, except as to persons who may be embraced in the exceptions named in the act of Congress first above cited.

In testimony whereof I have hereunto set my hand and caused the seal of the United States to be affixed.

Done at the city of Washington, this 1st day of June, in the year of our Lord [SEAL.] 1872, and of the Independence of the United States of America the ninety-sixth.

U. S. GRANT.

By the President:
HAMILTON FISH, *Secretary of State.*

Supplementary Civil Rights Bill as Passed by the Senate.

IN SENATE.

1872, May 21—Mr. CARPENTER moved to proceed to the consideration of Senate bill 99, being the supplementary civil rights bill proposed by Mr. SUMNER, March 9, 1871; which was agreed to, and the Senate, as in Committee of the Whole, resumed consideration thereof.

Mr. CARPENTER moved to amend the bill by striking out all after the enacting clause and inserting the following:

Whoever, being a corporation or natural person, and owner, or in charge of any public inn, or of any place of public amusement or entertainment for which a license from any legal authority is required; or of any line of stage-coaches, railroad, or other means of public carriage of passengers or freight, shall make any distinction as to admission or accommodation therein, of any citizen of the United States, because of race, color, or previous condition of servitude, shall, on conviction thereof, be fined not less than five hundred nor more than five thousand dollars for each offense; and the person or corporation so offending shall be liable to the citizens thereby injured in damages to be recovered in an action of debt.

SEC. —. That the offense under this act, and actions to recover damages, may be prosecuted before any territorial, district, or circuit court of the United States having jurisdiction of crimes at the place where the offense was charged to have been committed.

Mr. THURMAN moved to amend the amendment by striking out the words "or of any place of public amusement or entertainment;" which was disagreed to—yeas 14, nays 29:

YEAS—Messrs. *Bayard, Blair, Casserly, Cooper, Davis* of West Virginia, *Hamilton* of Maryland, *Johnston, Kelly, Norwood, Ransom, Saulsbury, Stevenson, Thurman, Vickers*—14.

NAYS—Messrs. Ames, Caldwell, Cameron, Carpenter, Chandler, Clayton, Cole, Conkling, Corbett, Cragin, Ferry of Michigan, Flanagan, Frelinghuysen, Hamilton of Texas, Hamlin, Logan, Morrill of Vermont, Nye, Osborn, Patterson, Pomeroy, Pool, Robertson, Sawyer, Scott, Spencer, Sprague, Wilson, Wright—29.

Mr. THURMAN moved to amend the amendment by striking out the word "hundred," so as to make the minimum fine five instead of five hundred dollars; which was disagreed to.

The amendment was then agreed to—yeas 22, nays 20:

YEAS—Messrs. *Bayard, Blair*, Caldwell, Carpenter, *Casserly*, Cole, Corbett, *Davis* of West Virginia, *Hamilton* of Maryland, *Johnston, Kelly*, Logan, Morrill of Maine, *Norwood*, Pool, *Ransom, Saulsbury*, Scott, *Stevenson, Thurman, Vickers*, Wright—22.

NAYS—Messrs. Ames, Anthony, Cameron, Chandler, Clayton, Conkling, Cragin, Ferry of Michigan, Flanagan, Frelinghuysen, Hamlin, Morrill of Vermont, Nye, Osborn, Pomeroy, Robertson, Sawyer, Spencer, Sprague, Wilson—20.

Mr. THURMAN moved to lay the bill on the table; which was disagreed to.

In the Senate the amendment made as in Committee of the Whole was concurred in.

Mr. CASSERLY moved to amend by adding to the bill the words "with the right of appeal, or to have a writ of error in any case to the Supreme Court of the United States;" which was agreed to.

The bill was then passed—yeas 28, nays 14:

YEAS—Messrs. Ames, Anthony, Caldwell, Cameron, Carpenter, Chandler, Clayton, Cole, Conkling, Corbett, Cragin, Ferry of Michigan, Flanagan, Frelinghuysen, Hamlin, Logan, Morrill of Vermont, Nye, Osborn, Patterson, Pool, Robertson, Sawyer, Scott, Sprague, Wilson, Wright—28.

NAYS—Messrs *Bayard, Blair, Casserly, Cooper, Davis* of West Virginia, *Hamilton* of Maryland, *Johnston, Kelly, Norwood, Ransom, Saulsbury, Stevenson, Thurman, Vickers*—14.

Mr. CARPENTER moved to amend the title so as to read: "A bill to declare and enforce the civil rights of citizens of the United States;" which was agreed to.

Votes in House.

May 28—Mr. MAYNARD moved to suspend the rules to take from the Speaker's table the above bill; which was disagreed to, two thirds not having voted in favor thereof—yeas 114, nays 83:

YEAS—Messrs. Ambler, Ames, Barber, Beatty, Beveridge, Bigby, Bingham, Buckley, Buffinton, Burchard, Burdett, B. F. Butler, R. R. Butler, Clarke, Cobb, Coburn, Coghlan, Conger, Cotton, Darrall, Dawes, Donnan, Duell, Dunnell, Eames, Elliott, Farnsworth, Finkelnburg, C. Foster, W. D. Foster, Frye, Garfield, Hale, Halsey, Harmer, Havens, Hawley, Hay, Hays, G. W. Hazelton, J. W. Hazelton, Hill, Hoar, Hooper, Houghton, Ketcham, Killinger, Lamport, Lansing, Lowe, Lynch, Maynard, McCrary, McGrew, McJunkin, McKee, Mercur, Merriam, Monroe, Morey, Morphis, L. Myers, Negley, Orr, Packard, Packer, Palmer, I. C. Parker, Pendleton, Perce, A. F. Perry, Peters, Poland, Rainey, E. H. Roberts, Rusk, Sargent, Sawyer, Scofield, Sessions, Shanks, Sheldon, Shellabarger, Shoemaker, H. B. Smith, J. A. Smith, W. C. Smith, Snyder, T. J. Speer, Sprague, Starkweather, Stevenson, Stoughton, Stowell, Strong, St. John, Sypher, Taffe, Thomas, W. Townsned, Turner, Twichell, Tyner, Upson, Wakeman, Waldron, Wallace, Walls, Whiteley, Willard, Williams of Indiana, J. M. Wilson, J. T. Wilson—114.

NAYS—Messrs. *Acker, Adams, Archer, Arthur, Beck, Biggs, Bird, J. G. Blair, Braxton, Bright, Brooks, Caldwell, Campbell, Carroll, Comingo, Conner, Crebs, Critcher, Crossland, Dox, Du Bose, Duke, Eldredge, Forker, H. D. Foster, Garrett, Getz, Giddings, Golladay, Griffith, Haldeman, Hancock, Handley, Hanks, Harper, J. T. Harris, Hereford, Herndon, Hibbard, Holman, Kendall, Kerr, King, Lewis, Manson, Marshall, McClelland, McCormick, McHenry, McIntyre, McNeely, Merrick, Mitchell, Morgan, Niblack, H. W. Parker, Price, Randall, Read, E. Y. Rice, J. M. Rice, Ritchie, W. R. Roberts, Robinson, S. H. Rogers, Roosevelt, Slater, Slocum, Sloss, R. M. Speer, Stevens, Swann, Terry, Tuthill, Van Trump, Waddell, Warren, Wells, Whitthorne, Williams* of New York, *Winchester, Wood, Young*—83.

June 7—Mr. POLAND moved to suspend the rules and pass the bill with an amendment changing the penalty so that it shall not exceed $1,000, and leaving the minimum amount to the discretion of the court. The motion was lost—yeas 86, nays 73, (two thirds being required:)

YEAS—Messrs. Ames, Banks, Barber, Beatty, Beveridge, A. Blair, Buckley, Buffinton, Burchard, B. F. Butler, R. R. Butler, Coburn, Conger, Cotton, Crocker, Darrall, Dawes, Donnan, Duell, Dunnell, Eames, Farnsworth, Finkelnburg, C. Foster, Garfield, Harmer, G. E. Harris, Havens, Hawley, J. W. Hazelton, Hill, Hoar, Hooper, Houghton, Kellogg, Ketcham, Lamport, Lowe, McCrary, McGrew, Mc-

Junkin, Mercur, Merriam, Monroe, Morphis, L. Myers, Orr, Packard, Packer, Palmer, Pendleton, Perce, A. F. Perry, Peters, Poland, Prindle, Rainey, E. H. Roberts, Rusk, Sawyer, Sessions, Shanks, Sheldon, Shellabarger, H. B. Smith, J. A. Smith, T. J. Speer, Sprague, Starkweather, Stevenson, Strong, Sypher, Thomas, W. Townsend, Turner, Twichell, Tyner, Wakeman, Walden, Waldron, Walls, Whiteley, Willard, Williams of Indiana, J. M. Wilson, J. T. Wilson—86.

NAYS—Messrs. *Acker, Adams, Archer, Arthur, Beck, Biggs, Bird, J. G. Blair, Braxton, Brooks, Caldwell, Campbell, Carroll, Comingo, Conner, Critcher, Crossland, Dox, Du Bose, Duke, Eldredge, Forker, H. D. Foster, Garrett, Getz, Giddings, Golladay, Haldeman, Hambleton, Hancock, Handley, Hanks, Harper, J. T. Harris, Hereford, Hibbard, Holman, Kendall, Kerr, King, Lamison, Manson, Marshall, McClelland, McCormick, McHenry, McIntyre, Merrick, Morgan, Niblack, Price, Randall, Read, E. Y. Rice, Ritchie, W. R. Roberts, S. H. Rogers, Sherwood, Shober, Slater, Slocum, Stevens, Storm, Swann, Terry, Tuthill, Van Trump, Vaughan, Waddell, Warren, Wells, Williams* of New York, *Winchester*—73.

Mr. POLAND then modified his amendment so that the penalty shall not exceed $100, with no minimum; which was disagreed to—yeas 83, nays 73, (two thirds being required:)

YEAS—Messrs. Ames, Banks, Barber, Beatty, Beveridge, A. Blair, Buckley, Buffinton, Burchard, R. R. Butler, Coburn, Conger, Cotton, Crocker, Darrall, Dawes, Donnan, Duell, Dunnell, Eames, Farnsworth, Finkelnburg, C. Foster, Garfield, Harmer, G. E. Harris, Havens, Hawley, Hay, J. W. Hazelton, Hill, Hoar, Hooper, Houghton, Kellogg, Ketcham, Lamport, Lowe, McCrary, McGrew, McJunkin, Mercur, Merriam, Monroe, L. Myers, Packard, Packer, Palmer, Pendleton, Perce, A. F. Perry, Peters, Poland, Potter, Prindle, Rainey, E. H. Roberts, Sawyer, Sessions, Shanks, Sheldon, Shellabarger, H. B. Smith, T. J. Speer, Sprague, Starkweather, Stevenson, Strong, Sypher, Taffe, Thomas, W. Townsend, Turner, Twichell, Tyner, Walden, Waldron, Walls, Whiteley, Willard, Williams of Indiana, J. M. Wilson, J. T. Wilson—83.

NAYS—Messrs. *Acker, Adams, Archer, Arthur, Beck, Biggs, Bird, J. G. Blair, Braxton, Brooks, Caldwell, Campbell, Carroll, Comingo, Conner, Critcher, Crossland, Dox, Du Bose, Duke, Eldredge, Forker, H. D. Foster, Garrett, Getz, Giddings, Golladay, Haldeman, Hambleton, Hancock, Handley, Hanks, Harper, J. T. Harris, Hereford, Hibbard, Holman, Kendall, Kerr, King, Lamison, Manson, Marshall, McClelland, McCormick, McHenry, McIntyre, Merrick, Morgan, Niblack, Price, Randall, Read, E. Y. Rice, Ritchie, W. R. Roberts, S. H. Rogers, Sherwood, Shober, Slater, Slocum, Stevens, Storm, Swann, Terry, Tuthill, Van Trump, Vaughan, Waddell, Warren, Wells, Williams* of New York, *Winchester*—73.

Amnesty and Civil Rights Jointly Considered.

IN HOUSE.

1872, January 15—Mr. HALE moved to suspend the rules and pass a bill removing all political disabilities imposed by third article of fourteenth amendment, except from the following classes:

First. Members of the Congress of the Union who withdrew therefrom to aid the rebellion.

Second. Officers of the Army or the Navy of the United States who, being above the age of twenty-one years, left said Army or Navy and aided the rebellion.

Which was agreed to—yeas 171, nays 31:

YEAS—Messrs. *Acker*, Ames, *Archer, Arthur*, Banks, Barber, *Barnum*, Barry, *Beck, Bell*, Beveridge, *Biggs*, Bingham, *Bird*, A. Blair, *J. G. Blair, Braxton, Bright*, G. M. Brooks, *J. Brooks*, Buckley, Burchard, Burdett, *Caldwell, Carroll*, W. T. Clark, Coghlan, *Comingo, Conner*, Cotton, *Crebs, Critcher, Crossland*, Darrall, *Davis*, Dawes, Dickey, Donnan, *Dox, Du Bose*, Duell, *Duke*, Eames, *Edwards, Eldredge, Ely*, Farwell, Finkelnburg, *Forker*, C. Foster, W. D. Foster, Frye, Garfield, *Garrett, Getz, Golladay, Griffith, Haldeman*, Hale, Halsey, *Hambleton, Hancock, Handley, Hanks, Harper*, G. E. Harris, *J. T. Harris*, Hawley, Hay, G. W. Hazelton, J. W. Hazelton, *Hereford, Herndon, Hibbard*, Hill, *Holman*, Hooper, Houghton, Kelley, Kellogg, *Kerr*, Ketcham, *King, Kinsella, Lamison*, Lamport, *Leach, Lewis*, Lynch, *Manson, Marshall, McClelland, McCormick*, McGrew, *McHenry, McIntyre*, McKee, *McNeely*, Merriam, *Merrick, B. F. Meyers, Mitchell*, Monroe, Morey, *Morgan*, L. Myers, *Niblack, H. W. Parker*, I. C. Parker, Peck, Pendleton, A. F. Perry, Poland, *Potter, Price*, Prindle, *Randall, Read, E. Y. Rice, J. M. Rice, Ritchie*, E. H. Roberts, *W. R. Roberts, Roosevelt*, Sawyer, Scofield, Sessions, Sheldon, Shellabarger, *Sherwood*, Shoemaker, *Slater, Slocum, Sloss*, H. B. Smith, J. A. Smith, W. C. Smith, Snapp, Snyder, *R. M. Speer*, T. J. Speer, Starkweather, *Stevens*, Stevenson, *Storm*, Strong, *Sutherland, Swann*, Sypher, *Terry*, Thomas, Turner, *Tuthill*, Twichell, Upson, *Van Trump, Vaughan, Voorhees, Waddell*, Wakeman, Wallace, *Warren, Wells*, Wheeler, Whiteley, *Whitthorne*, Willard, *Williams* of New York, J. T. Wilson, *Winchester, Wood*—171.

NAYS—Messrs. Ambler, Beatty, Buffinton, Coburn, Conger, Dunnell, Goodrich, Hoar, Killinger, Lansing, Lowe, Maynard, McCrary, McJunkin, Mercur, Orr, Packard, Packer, Palmer, Porter, Rainey, Rusk, Seeley, Shanks, Sprague, Taffe, W. Townsend, Tyner, Waldron, Walls, J. M. Wilson—31.

IN SENATE.

1872, May 9—In Committee of the Whole Mr. SUMNER moved to strike out all after the enacting clause, and insert the following civil rights bill:

SEC. 1. That no citizen of the United States shall, by reason of race, color, or previous condition of servitude, be excepted or excluded from the full and equal enjoyment of any accommodation, advantage, facility, or privilege furnished by innkeepers; by common carriers, whether on land or water; by licensed owners, managers, or lessees of theaters or other places of public amusement; by trustees, commissioners, superintendents, teachers, and other officers of common schools and other public institutions of learning, the same being supported by moneys derived from general taxation, or authorized by law; by trustees and officers of cemetery associations and benevolent institutions incorporated by national or State authority. But private schools, cemeteries, and institutions of learning established exclusively for white or colored persons, and maintained respectively by voluntary contributions, shall remain according to the terms of the original establishment.

SEC. 2. That any person violating any of the provisions of the foregoing section, or aiding in their violation, or inciting thereto, shall, for every such offense, forfeit and pay the sum of $500 to the person aggrieved thereby, to be recovered in an action on the case with full costs, and shall also, for every such offense, be deemed guilty of a misdemeanor, and, upon conviction thereof, shall be fined not less than $500 nor more than $1,000, or shall be imprisoned not less than thirty days nor more than one year: *Provided*, That the party aggrieved shall not recover more than one penalty; and when the offense is a refusal of burial, the penalty may be recovered by the heirs-at-law of the person whose body has been refused burial.

SEC. 3. That the same jurisdiction and powers are hereby conferred, and the same duties enjoined upon the courts and officers of the United States in the execution of this act as are conferred and enjoined upon such courts and officers in sections three, four, five, seven, and ten of an act entitled "An act to protect all persons in the United States in their civil rights, and to furnish the means of their vindication," passed April 9, 1866, and these sections are hereby made a part of this act; and any of the aforesaid officers failing to institute and prosecute such proceedings herein required shall, for every such offense, forfeit and pay the sum of $500 to the person aggrieved thereby, to be recovered by an action on the case, with full costs, and shall, on conviction thereof, be deemed guilty of a misdemeanor, and be fined not less than $1,000 nor more than $5,000.

SEC. 4. That no citizen possessing all other qualifications which are or may be prescribed by law shall be disqualified for service as juror in any court, national or State, by reason of race, color, or previous condition of servitude; and any officer or other persons charged with any duty in the selection or summoning of jurors who shall exclude or fail to summon any citizen for the reason above named shall, on conviction thereof, be deemed guilty of a misdemeanor, and be fined not less than $1,000 nor more than $5,000.

SEC. 5. That every discrimination against any citizen on account of color by the use of the word "white" in any law, statute, ordinance, or regulation, is hereby repealed and annulled.

Mr. FERRY, of Connecticut, moved to amend the amendment by striking out, in the first section, the following words:

By trustees, commissioners, superintendents, teachers, and other officers of common schools and other public institutions of learning, the same being supported by moneys derived from general taxation or authorized by law.

Which was lost—yeas 25, nays 26:

YEAS—Messrs. Alcorn, *Bayard*, Boreman, Buckingham, *Casserly*, *Cooper*, *Davis* of West Virginia, Fenton, Ferry of Connecticut, *Goldthwaite*, *Hamilton* of Maryland, Hamilton of Texas, Harlan, Hill, Hitchcock, *Johnston*, *Kelly*, *Norwood*, Pratt, *Saulsbury*, Scott, *Stevenson*, Tipton, Trumbull, *Vickers*—25.

NAYS—Messrs. Ames, Anthony, Cameron, Carpenter, Chandler, Clayton, Cragin, Edmunds, Ferry of Michigan, Flanagan, Gilbert, Hamlin, Howe, Kellogg, Morrill of Vermont, Morton, Osborn, Pomeroy, Ramsey, Rice, Sherman, Spencer, Sumner, Wilson, Windom, Wright—26.

Mr. BLAIR offered the following proviso, to come in at the end of the first section of the amendment:

Provided, however, That the people of every city, county, or State shall decide for themselves, at an election to be held for that purpose, the question of mixed or separate schools for the white or black people.

Which was lost—yeas 23, nays 30:

YEAS—Messrs. Alcorn, *Bayard*, Boreman, *Casserly*, *Cooper*, *Davis* of West Virginia, Fenton, Ferry of Connecticut, *Goldthwaite*, *Hamilton* of Maryland, Hamilton of Texas, Hitchcock, *Johnston*, *Kelly*, *Norwood*, Pratt, *Saulsbury*, Sprague, *Stevenson*, Tipton, Trumbull, *Vickers*, West—23.

NAYS—Messrs. Ames, Anthony, Caldwell, Cameron, Carpenter, Chandler, Clayton, Conkling, Corbett, Cragin, Edmunds, Ferry of Michigan, Flanagan, Gilbert, Hamlin, Howe, Kellogg, Morrill of Vermont, Morton, Osborn, Pomeroy, Ramsey, Rice, Scott, Sherman, Spencer, Sumner, Wilson, Windom, Wright—30.

Mr. FERRY, of Connecticut, offered the following as an additional section to the amendment:

SEC. 6. That all legal and political disabilities imposed by the third section of the fourteenth article of amendments to the Constitution of the United States on persons therein mentioned, because of their having engaged in insurrection or rebellion against the United States, or given aid or comfort to the enemies thereof, be, and the same are hereby, removed: *Provided*, That this act shall not apply to or in any way affect or remove the disability of any person included in either of the following classes, namely: first, members of the Congress of the United States who withdrew therefrom and aided the rebellion; second, officers of the Army or Navy of the United States who, being above the age of twenty-one years, left said Army or Navy and aided the rebellion.

Which was adopted—yeas 38, nays 14:

YEAS—Messrs. Alcorn, Ames, *Bayard*, *Blair*, Boreman, Buckingham, Caldwell, Cameron, Carpenter, *Casserly*, Clayton, *Cooper*, Corbett, *Davis* of West Virginia, Edmunds, Ferry of Connecticut, Ferry of Michigan, Flanagan, *Goldthwaite*, *Hamilton* of Maryland, Hamilton of Texas, Harlan, Hitchcock, *Johnston*, Kellogg, *Kelly*, *Norwood*, Osborn, Pomeroy, Pratt, *Saulsbury*, Sprague, *Stevenson*, Stewart, Tipton, Trumbull, *Vickers*, West—38.

NAYS—Messrs. Cragin, Fenton, Gilbert, Hamlin, Morrill of Vermont, Morton, Pool, Rice, Scott, Sherman, Spencer, Sumner, Wilson, Windom—14.

Mr. BOREMAN offered the following additional section:

SEC. 7. That before any person shall be entitled to the benefit of the preceding section of this act, he shall, within the district where he resides, before a clerk of some court of the United States, or a United States commissioner, take and subscribe an oath or affirmation to support the Constitution of the United States, and to bear true faith and allegiance to the same; which oath or affirmation shall be forwarded by said officer to the Secretary of State of the United States, who shall cause a list of all persons complying with the provisions of this act to be laid before Congress at the opening of each session thereof; and the officer before whom such oath or affirmation is made shall give to the person taking it a certificate of the fact, under such forms and regulations as the Secretary of State shall prescribe.

Which was adopted—yeas 31, nays 24:

YEAS—Messrs. Alcorn, Ames, Anthony, Boreman, Buckingham, Caldwell, Cameron, Clayton, Conkling, Corbett, Cragin, Edmunds, Fenton, Ferry of Michigan, Flanagan, Gilbert, Hamlin, Harlan, Hitchcock, Morton, Osborn, Pomeroy, Pool, Pratt, Scott, Sherman, Spencer, Sumner, West, Wilson, Windom—31.

NAYS—Messrs. *Bayard*, *Blair*, *Casserly*, *Cooper*, *Davis* of West Virginia, Ferry of Connecticut, *Goldthwaite*, *Hamilton* of Maryland, Hamilton of Texas, Hill, *Johnston*, Kellogg, *Kelly*, Logan, Morrill of Vermont, *Norwood*, Rice, *Saulsbury*, Sprague, *Stevenson*, Stewart, Tipton, Trumbull, *Vickers*—24.

Mr. CARPENTER moved to strike out the fourth section of the amendment, (relating to jurors;) which was disagreed to—yeas 16, nays 33:

YEAS—Messrs. Alcorn, *Bayard*, Boreman, Carpenter, *Casserly*, *Davis* of West Virginia, *Goldthwaite*, *Hamilton* of Maryland, Hamilton of Texas, Hitchcock, *Johnston*, *Kelly*, Logan, *Saulsbury*, *Stevenson*, *Vickers*—16.

NAYS—Messrs. Ames, Anthony, Buckingham, Caldwell, Cameron, Chandler, Clayton, Conkling, *Cooper*, Cragin, Edmunds, Fenton, Ferry of Michigan, Flanagan, Gilbert, Harlan, Hill, Kellogg, Morrill of Vermont, Morton, *Norwood*, Osborn, Pomeroy, Pratt, Ramsey, Rice, Sherman, Spencer, Sprague, Sumner, West, Wilson, Windom—33.

Mr. TRUMBULL move to strike out the first, second, third, fourth, and fifth sections (being the civil rights bill) of the amendment as amended; which was lost—yeas 29, nays 29, the Vice President voting in the negative:

YEAS—Messrs. Alcorn, *Bayard*, Boreman, Carpenter, *Casserly*, *Cooper*, Corbett, Cragin, *Davis* of West Virginia, Fenton, Ferry of Connecticut, *Goldthwaite*, *Hamilton* of Maryland, Hamilton of Texas, Hill, Hitchcock, *Johnston*, *Kelly*, Logan, *Norwood*, Pratt, *Saulsbury*, Scott, Sprague, *Stevenson*, Stewart, Tipton, Trumbull, *Vickers*—29.

NAYS—Messrs. Ames, Anthony, Buckingham, Caldwell, Cameron, Chandler, Clayton, Conkling, Edmunds, Ferry of Michigan, Flanagan, Gilbert, Hamlin, Harlan, Howe, Kellogg, Morrill of Vermont, Morton, Osborn, Pomeroy, Pool, Ramsey, Rice, Sherman, Spencer, Sumner, West, Wilson, Windom—29.

Mr. COOPER moved to amend the amendment by inserting after the word "servitude," in section one, the words "or pecuniary condition;" so as to read:

That no citizen of the United States shall, by reason of race, color, or previous condition of servitude or pecuniary condition be excepted or excluded, &c.

Which was lost—yeas 7, nays 35:

YEAS—Messrs. *Cooper*, Cragin, *Davis* of West Virginia, *Hamilton* of Maryland, Hill, *Kelly*, Tipton—7.

NAYS—Messrs. Alcorn, Ames, Anthony, Boreman, Buckingham, Caldwell, Cameron, Carpenter, *Casserly*, Clayton, Conkling, Corbett, Edmunds, Ferry of Connecticut, Ferry of Michigan, Flanagan, Gilbert, Howe, Kellogg, Morrill of Vermont, Morton, Osborn, Pomeroy, Pool, Pratt, Ramsey, Scott, Sherman, Spencer, *Stevenson*, Sumner, *Vickers*, West, Wilson, Windom—35.

Mr. VICKERS moved to amend the same section by striking out the words "or State;" so that it would read:

By trustees and officers of cemetery associations and benevolent institutions incorporated by national authority.

Which was agreed to—yeas 21, nays 21; the Vice President voting in the affirmative:

YEAS—Messrs. Alcorn, Boreman, *Casserly*, *Cooper*, Corbett, *Davis* of West Virginia, Ferry of Connecticut, *Goldthwaite*, *Hamilton* of Maryland, Hamilton of Texas, Hill, Hitchcock, *Johnston*, *Kelly*, *Norwood*, Pool, *Saulsbury*, Sprague, *Stevenson*, Tipton, *Vickers*—21.

NAYS—Messrs. Ames, Anthony, Buckingham, Cameron, Clayton, Conkling, Edmunds, Ferry of Michigan, Flanagan, Gilbert, Harlan, Morton, Osborn, Pomeroy, Pratt, Ramsey, Rice, Spencer, Sumner, Wilson, Wright—21.

Mr. SUMNER moved to strike out of the first section, after the word "institutions," the words "incorporated by national authority," and to transfer the words "the same being supported by moneys derived from general taxation, or authorized by law;" so that it would read:

Other public institutions of learning; by trustees and officers of cemetery associations and benevolent institutions, the same being supported by moneys derived from general taxation, or authorized by law.

Which was agreed to.

Mr. VICKERS moved to add to the third section the following: "And that the right of appeal as in other cases shall be allowed to any party aggrieved;" which was agreed to.

Mr. BOREMAN moved to insert in the first section, after the word "institutions," the words "of a public character;" which was agreed to.

Mr. SUMNER's amendment as amended was then rejected—yeas 27, nays 28:

YEAS—Messrs. Ames, Anthony, Buckingham, Caldwell, Cameron, Clayton, Conkling, Corbett, Edmunds, Ferry of Michigan, Flanagan, Gilbert, Harlan, Howe, Kellogg, Morrill of Vermont, Morton, Osborn, Pomeroy, Pool, Ramsey, Rice, Spencer, Sumner, West, Wilson, Windom—27.

NAYS—Messrs. Alcorn, Boreman, Carpenter, *Casserly*, *Cooper*, Cragin, *Davis* of West Virginia, Fenton, Ferry of Connecticut, *Goldthwaite*, *Hamilton* of Maryland, Hamilton of Texas, Hill, Hitchcock, *Johnston*, *Kelly*, Logan, *Norwood*, Pratt, *Saulsbury*, Scott, Sprague, *Stevenson*, Stewart, Tipton, Trumbull, *Vickers*, Wright—28.

Mr. SUMNER then offered the civil rights bill as amended as an addition to the pending bill; which was agreed to—yeas 28, nays 28; the Vice President voting in the affirmative:

YEAS—Messrs. Ames, Anthony, Buckingham, Caldwell, Cameron, Clayton, Conkling, Corbett, Edmunds, Ferry of Michigan, Flanagan, Gilbert, Harlan, Howe, Kellogg, Morrill of Vermont, Morton, Osborn, Pomeroy, Pool, Ramsey, Rice, Spencer, Sumner, West, Wilson, Windom, Wright—28.

NAYS—Messrs. Alcorn, Boreman, Carpenter, *Casserly*, *Cooper*, Cragin, *Davis* of West Virginia, Fenton, Ferry of Connecticut, *Goldthwaite*, *Hamilton* of Maryland, Hamilton of Texas, Hill, Hitchcock, *Johnston*, *Kelly*, Lewis, Logan, *Norwood*, Pratt, *Saulsbury*, Scott, Sprague, *Stevenson*, Stewart, Tipton, Trumbull, *Vickers*—28.

In the Senate, on concurring in the amendment reported from the Committee of the Whole to the amnesty bill, the vote was—yeas 27, nays 25:

YEAS—Messrs. Ames, Anthony, Buckingham, Caldwell, Clayton, Conkling, Corbett, Edmunds, Ferry of Michigan, Flanagan, Gilbert, Harlan, Howe, Kellogg, Lewis, Morrill of Vermont, Morton, Osborn, Pomeroy, Pool, Ramsey, Rice, Spencer, Sumner, Wilson, Windom, Wright—27.

NAYS—Messrs. Alcorn, Boreman, Carpenter, *Casserly*, *Cooper*, *Davis* of West Virginia, Fenton, Ferry of Connecticut, *Goldthwaite*, *Hamilton* of Maryland, Hill, Hitchcock, *Johnston*, *Kelly*, Logan, *Norwood*, Pratt, *Saulsbury*, Scott, Sprague, *Stevenson*, Stewart, Tipton, Trumbull, *Vickers*—25.

Mr. MORTON moved to amend the second section of the amnesty bill by requiring the party to swear "that he is not, and has not been at any time within two years preceding the passage of this act, a member of either of the organizations commonly known by the names of the 'Invisible Empire of America,' the 'White Brotherhood,' or the 'Constitutional Union Guard,' respectively, nor of any branch of the organization commonly known as the 'Ku Klux Klan;'" which was agreed to—yeas 30, nays 17:

YEAS—Messrs. Alcorn, Ames, Boreman, Buckingham, Caldwell, Clayton, Corbett, Cragin, Edmunds, Ferry of Michigan, Flanagan, Gilbert, Harlan, Hitchcock, Lewis, Logan, Morrill of Vermont, Morton, Osborn, Pomeroy, Pool, Pratt, Ramsey, Rice, Scott, Spencer, Sumner, Wilson, Windom, Wright—30.

NAYS—Messrs. *Bayard*, *Blair*, *Casserly*, *Cooper*, *Davis* of West Virginia, *Goldthwaite*, *Hamilton* of Maryland, Hill, *Johnston*, *Kelly*, *Norwood*, *Saulsbury*, Sprague, *Stevenson*, Tipton, Trumbull, *Vickers*—17.

Mr. EDMUNDS moved to amend the first section by inserting after the word "the," and before the word "Congress," the word "Thirty Sixth," and by striking out the words "withdraw from and;" so that that proviso would read:

First, members of the Thirty-Sixth Congress of the United States who aided the rebellion.

Mr. HILL moved to amend the amendment by striking out the words "Thirty-Sixth;" so as to read:

Members of the Congress of the United States who aided the rebellion.

Which was rejected.

The amendment was then rejected—yeas 23, nays 24:

YEAS—Messrs. Ames, Boreman, Buckingham, Clayton, Corbett, Edmunds, Ferry of Michigan, Flanagan, Gilbert, Harlan, Morrill of Vermont, Morton, Osborn, Pomeroy, Pratt, Ramsey, Rice, Scott, Spencer, Sumner, Wilson, Windom, Wright—23.

NAYS—Messrs. Alcorn, *Bayard*, *Blair*, Caldwell, *Casserly*, *Cooper*, *Davis* of West Virginia, Ferry of Connecticut, *Goldthwaite*, *Hamilton* of Maryland, Hill, Hitchcock, *Johnston*, Kellogg, *Kelly*, Lewis, *Norwood*, *Saulsbury*, Sprague, *Stevenson*, Tipton, Trumbull, *Vickers*, West—24.

Mr. EDMUNDS moved to amend by making it read "members of the Thirty-Sixth and Thirty-Seventh Congress of the United States who aided the rebellion."

Mr. HILL moved to amend the amendment by striking out "Thirty Sixth and Thirty-Seventh;" so as to read, "all members of the Congress of the United States who aided the rebellion;" which was rejected.

The amendment was then adopted—yeas 22, nays 21:

YEAS—Messrs. Ames, Boreman, Buckingham, Caldwell, Clayton, Corbett, Edmunds, Ferry of Michigan, Flanagan, Gilbert, Harlan, Morrill of Vermont, Morton, Pomeroy, Pratt, Ramsey, Scott, Spencer, Sumner, Wilson, Windom, Wright—22.

NAYS—Messrs. Alcorn, *Bayard*, *Blair*, *Casserly*, *Cooper*, *Davis* of West Virginia, Ferry of Connecticut, *Goldthwaite*, *Hamilton* of Maryland, Hill, *Johnston*, Kellogg, *Kelly*, *Norwood*, Rice, *Saulsbury*, Sprague, *Stevenson*, Tipton, *Vickers*, West—21.

Upon the passage of the House amnesty bill as amended by the addition of the amended civil rights bill the vote was—yeas 32, nays 22:

YEAS—Messrs. Ames, Buckingham, Caldwell, Clayton, Conkling, Corbett, Cragin, Edmunds, Fenton, Ferry of Michigan, Flanagan, Gilbert, Harlan, Hitchcock, Howe, Kellogg, Lewis, Morrill of Vermont, Morton, Osborn, Pomeroy, Pool, Pratt, Ramsey, Rice, Spencer, Sprague, Stewart, Sumner, West, Wilson, Windom—32.

NAYS—Messrs. Alcorn, *Bayard*, *Blair*, Boreman, *Casserly*, *Cooper*, *Davis* of West Virginia, Ferry of Connecticut, *Goldthwaite*, *Hamilton* of Maryland, Hamilton of Texas, Hill, *Johnston*, *Kelly*, Logan, *Norwood*, *Saulsbury*, *Stevenson*, Tipton, Trumbull, *Vickers*, Wright—22.

Two thirds not having voted in the affirmative, the bill was rejected.

Proceedings on another Amnesty Bill.

IN HOUSE.

1871, April 10—Mr. HALE moved to suspend the rules and pass a disability bill containing the following exceptions:

First. Members of the Congress of the United States who withdrew therefrom and aided the rebellion.

Second. Officers of the Army or Navy of the United States who, being above the age of twenty-one years, left said Army or Navy and aided the rebellion.

Third. Members of State conventions which adopted pretended ordinances of secession who voted for the adoption of such ordinances.

Which was agreed to—yeas 134, nays 45:

YEAS—Messrs. *Acker*, *Adams*, *Archer*, *Arthur*, Averill, Banks, Barry, *Beck*, *Bell*, *Bird*, A. Blair, *Braxton*, *Bright*, G. M. Brooks, Buckley, Burchard, *Caldwell*, *Campbell*, *Comingo*, Cook, *Cox*, *Crebs*, *Crossland*, *Davis*, Dawes, De Large, Donnan, *Dox*, *Du Bose*, *Duke*, Eames, *Edwards*, *Eldridge*, *Ely*, Farnsworth, Farwell, Finkelnburg, C. Foster, *H. D. Foster*, Frye, Garfield, *Garrett*, *Golladay*, *Griffith*, Hale, *Hambleton*, *Handley*, *Hanks*, *Harper*, G. E. Harris, *J. T. Harris*, Hawley, Hay, Hays, *Hereford*, *Hibbard*, Hill, *Holman*, Hooper, Kelley, *Kendall*, *Kerr*, Ketcham, *King*, *Lamison*, Lamport, *Leach*, *Lewis*, Lynch, *Manson*, *Marshall*, *McClelland*, *McCormick*, McGrew, *McHenry*, *McIntyre*, McKee, *McKinney*, *McNeely*, *Merrick*, *B. F. Meyers*, Moore, Morey, *Niblack*, *H. W. Parker*, I. C. Parker, Peck, Pendleton, Perce, *E. Perry*, Platt, Poland, *Potter*, *Randall*, *E. Y. Rice*, *J. M. Rice*, *W. R. Roberts*, *Robinson*, *Rogers*, *Roosevelt*, Scofield, Sheldon, *Sherwood*, *Shober*, *Slater*, *Slocum*, *Sloss*, Snyder, Sprague, *Stevens*, Stevenson, *Storm*, Stoughton, *Sutherland*, *Swann*, Sypher, *Terry*, Thomas, Turner, Twichell, *Van Trump*, *Vaughan*, *Voorhees*, *Waddell*, Wakeman, Walls, *Wells*, Whiteley, *Whitthorne*, *Williams* of New York, J. T. Wilson, *Winchester*, *Wood*, *Young*—134.

NAYS—Messrs. Ambler, Barber, Beatty, Buffinton, Coburn, Conger, Cotton, Creely, Dunnell, Elliott, Havens, G. W. Hazelton, J. W. Hazelton, Hoar, Lansing, Lowe, Maynard, McCrary, McJunkin, Mercur, Merriam, Monroe, Orr, Packard, Packer, Palmer, Porter, Prindle, E. H. Roberts, Rusk, Sawyer, Seeley, Shanks, Shellabarger, J. A. Smith, St. John, Taffe, W. Townsend, Tyner, Walden, Waldron, Wallace, Wheeler, Williams of Indiana, J. M. Wilson—45.

IN SENATE.

1871, December 11—Reported to the Senate without amendment.

December 20—Mr. MORTON, in Committee of the Whole, moved to add to the bill the following, as finally modified by him:

And provided further, That this act shall not be construed to relate back to or validate the election or appointment of any person to the position of Senator or Representative in Congress, or to any office, civil or military, under the United States.

Same day, Mr. SUMNER moved to add at the end of the bill substantially the same bill as he offered to the preceding bill. The first and last two sections were as follows:

SEC. 1. That no citizen of the United States shall, by reason of race, color, or previous condition of servitude, be excepted or excluded from the full and equal enjoyment of any accommodation, advantage, facility, or privilege furnished by inn-keepers; by common-carriers, whether on land or water; by licensed owners, managers, or lessees of theaters or other places of public amusement; by trustees. commissioners, superintendents, teachers, and other officers of common schools and other public institutions of learning, the same being supported by moneys derived from general taxation or authorized by law; by trustees and officers of church organizations, cemetery associations, and benevolent institutions incorporated by national or State authority. But churches, schools, cemeteries, and institutions of learning established exclusively for white or colored persons, and maintained respectively by the contributions of such persons, shall remain according to the terms of the original establishment.

SEC. 5. That every law, statute, ordinance, regulation, or custom inconsistent with this act, or making any discriminations against any person on account of color, by the use of the word "white," is hereby repealed and annulled.

SEC. 6. That it shall be the duty of the judges of the several courts upon which jurisdiction is hereby conferred to give this act in charge to the grand jury of their respective courts at the commencement of each term thereof.

December 21—Mr. MORTON's amendment was disagreed to—yeas 28, nays 29.

Mr. SUMNER's motion was disagreed to—yeas 29, nays 30:

YEAS—Messrs. Ames, Anthony, Brownlow, Buckingham, Caldwell, Carpenter, Clayton, Conkling, Corbett, Edmunds, Ferry of Michigan, Flanagan, Frelinghuysen, Hamlin, Kellogg, Morrill of Vermont, Morton, Nye, Patterson, Pomeroy, Pratt, Ramsey, Rice, Sherman, Spencer, Sumner, West, Wilson, Windom—29.

NAYS—Messrs. Alcorn, *Bayard*, *Blair*, Boreman, *Casserly*, *Cooper*, *Davis* of Kentucky, *Davis* of West Virginia, Fenton, Ferry of Connecticut, *Hamilton* of Maryland, Hill, Hitchcock, *Johnston*, *Kelly*, Lewis, Logan, Morrill of Maine, *Norwood*, Pool, Robertson, *Saulsbury*, Sawyer, Schurz, Scott, *Stevenson*, Stewart, *Thurman*, Tipton, Trumbull—30.

Mr. EDMUNDS moved to make the first clause of exceptions read as follows:

First. Members of any Congress of the United States after the Thirty-Fifth who aided the rebellion.

Which was disagreed to—yeas 27, nays 31:

YEAS—Messrs. Ames, Anthony, Brownlow, Buckingham, Caldwell, Carpenter, Clayton, Conkling, Corbett, Edmunds, Ferry of Michigan, Flanagan, Frelinghuysen, Hamlin, Howe, Morrill of Vermont, Morton, Nye, Pomeroy, Pool, Pratt, Ramsey, Scott, Spencer, Sumner, Wilson, Windom—27.

NAYS—Messrs. Alcorn, *Bayard*, *Blair*, *Casserly*, *Cooper*, *Davis* of Kentucky, *Davis* of West Virginia, Fenton, Ferry of Connecticut, *Hamilton* of Maryland, Hill, Hitchcock, *Johnston*, Kellogg, *Kelly*, Lewis, Logan, Morrill of Maine, *Norwood*, Robertson, *Saulsbury*, Sawyer, Schurz, Sherman, *Stevenson*, Stewart, *Thurman*, Tipton, Trumbull, *Vickers*, West—31.

Mr. PRATT moved to add the following to the first section:

Provided, That the removal of such disabilities shall not have the effect of giving the persons relieved the status in court or elsewhere of loyal persons in asserting any claim against the United States which they do not now possess, either for money claimed to be due, or for appropriation of or injury to property belonging to them.

Which was disagreed to—yeas 25, nays 34:

YEAS—Messrs. Ames, Anthony, Brownlow, Buckingham, Caldwell, Carpenter, Clayton, Conkling, Edmunds, Ferry of Michigan, Frelinghuysen, Hamlin, Howe, Morrill of Vermont, Morton, Nye, Patterson, Pomeroy, Pool, Pratt, Ramsey, Sherman, Sumner, Wilson, Windom—25.

NAYS—Messrs. Alcorn, *Bayard*, *Blair*, *Casserly*, *Cooper*, Corbett, *Davis* of Kentucky, *Davis* of West Virginia, Fenton, Ferry of Connecticut, Flanagan, *Hamilton* of Maryland, Hill, Hitchcock, *Johnston*, Kellogg, *Kelly*, Lewis, Logan, Morrill of Maine, *Norwood*, Rice, Robertson, *Saulsbury*, Sawyer, Schurz, Scott, *Stevenson*, Stewart, *Thurman*, Tipton, Trumbull, *Vickers*, West—34.

Mr. WILSON moved to make the exceptions read as follows:

First. All persons who, being members of the Thirty Sixth and Thirty-Seventh Congresses of the United States, withdrew from their seats and aided the rebellion.

Second All persons who having held the office of judge of the Supreme Court of the United States or head of one of the Executive Departments of the Government of the United States in the year 1860 or 1861, shall have engaged in rebellion against the same.

Which was disagreed to—yeas 4, (Messrs. Brownlow, Edmunds, Flanagan, and Wilson,) nays 55.

Mr. MORTON moved to add the following proviso:

Provided, That this act shall not be construed to relate back to or validate the election or appointment of any person to the position of Senator or Representative in Congress, or to any office, civil or military, under the United States, which person was at the date of such election or appointment ineligible to the office or position to which he may have been so elected or appointed.

Which was agreed to—yeas 29, nays 26:

YEAS—Messrs. Ames, Anthony, Brownlow, Buckingham, Caldwell, Carpenter, Clayton, Conkling, Corbett, Edmunds, Ferry of Michigan, Flanagan, Frelinghuysen, Howe, Morrill of Maine, Morrill of Vermont, Morton, Nye, Patterson, Pomeroy, Pool, Pratt, Ramsey, Rice, Scott, Spencer, Sumner, Wilson, Windom—29.

NAYS—Messrs. Alcorn, *Bayard*, *Blair*, *Casserly*, *Cooper*, *Davis* of Kentucky, *Davis* of West Virginia, Fenton, Ferry of Connecticut, *Hamilton* of Maryland, Hill, Hitchcock, *Johnston*, *Kelly*, Lewis, Logan, *Norwood*, Robertson, *Saulsbury*, Schurz, Sherman, *Stevenson*, Stewart, Tipton, Trumbull, West—26.

Mr. MORTON moved to add the following to the clause prescribing the oath to be taken:

And that he is not, and has not been within twelve months from the date of the passage of this act, a member of any association commonly known as the Ku Klux Klan.

Which was disagreed to—yeas 27, nays 28:

YEAS—Messrs. Ames, Anthony, Brownlow, Buckingham, Caldwell, Carpenter, Clayton, Conkling, Corbett, Edmunds, Ferry of Michigan, Flanagan, Frelinghuysen, Howe, Morrill of Vermont, Morton, Nye, Pomeroy, Pool, Pratt, Rice, Scott, Sherman, Spencer, Sumner, Wilson, Windom—27.

NAYS—Messrs. Alcorn, *Bayard*, *Blair*, *Casserly*, *Cooper*, *Davis* of Kentucky, *Davis* of West Virginia, Fenton, *Hamilton* of Maryland, Hill, Hitchcock, *Johnston*, Kellogg, *Kelly*, Lewis, Logan, *Norwood*, Robertson, *Saulsbury*, Sawyer, Schurz, *Stevenson*, Stewart, *Thurman*, Tipton, Trumbull, *Vickers*, West—28.

Mr. CONKLING offered a proviso to the first section, slightly modifying that of Mr. PRATT, above; which was disagreed to—yeas 21, nays 32.

Mr. PRATT moved to add to the oath section the following:

Take and subscribe an oath or affirmation to support the Constitution of the United States, and to bear true faith and allegiance to the same, and that he has never been engaged or concerned in person or as aider and abettor in inflicting any outrage upon person, life, or property in what is commonly called a Ku Klux raid.

Which was disagreed to—yeas 27, nays 29:

YEAS—Messrs. Ames, Anthony, Brownlow, Buckingham, Caldwell, Carpenter, Clayton, Conkling, Corbett, Edmunds, Ferry of Michigan, Flanagan, Frelinghuysen, Howe, Morrill of Vermont, Morton, Nye, Patterson, Pomeroy, Pool, Pratt, Scott, Sherman, Spencer, Sumner, Wilson, Windom—27.

NAYS—Messrs. Alcorn, *Bayard*, *Blair*, *Casserly*, *Cooper*, *Davis* of Kentucky, *Davis* of West Virginia, Fenton, *Hamilton* of Maryland, Hill, Hitchcock, *Johnston*, Kellogg, *Kelly*, Lewis, Logan, Morrill of Maine, *Norwood*, Robertson, *Saulsbury*, Sawyer, Schurz, *Stevenson*, Stewart, *Thurman*, Tipton, Trumbull, *Vickers*, West—29.

The bill was reported to the Senate with the amendment adopted above, on motion of Mr. MORTON.

And it was concurred in—yeas 29, nays 26.

Mr. SUMNER then renewed in the Senate his amendment rejected in Committee of the Whole, as above.

1872, February 6—Pending the House bill No. 380 and Mr. SUMNER's amendment,

Mr. ROBERTSON moved to lay it on the table with a view to take up House bill No. 1050, which excepted only the two following classes:

First. Members of the Congress of the United States who withdrew therefrom and aided the rebellion. Second. Officers of the Army or Navy of the United States who, being above the age of twenty-one years, left said Army or Navy and aided the rebellion.

Which was disagreed to—yeas 20, nays 33:

YEAS—Messrs. *Blair*, *Davis* of West Virginia, Fenton, Ferry of Connecticut, *Goldthwaite*, Hill, Hitchcock, *Johnston*, *Kelly*, Logan, *Norwood*, Robertson, Schurz, Scott, *Stevenson*, *Stockton*, *Thurman*, Tipton, Trumbull, *Vickers*—20.

NAYS—Messrs. Ames, Anthony, Boreman, Brownlow, Caldwell, Cameron, Carpenter, Chandler, Clayton, Cole, Corbett, Cragin, Edmunds, Ferry of Michigan, Flanagan, Frelinghuysen, Gilbert, Hamilton of Texas, Hamlin, Harlan, Morrill of Vermont, Morton, Nye, Osborn, Pomeroy, Pool, Sherman, Spencer, Sumner, West, Wilson, Windom, Wright—33.

February 7—Mr. CARPENTER moved to amend the amendment by substituting for it the following:

Whoever, being a corporation or natural person, and owner, or in charge of any public inn, or of any place of public amusement or entertainment for which a license from any legal authority is required; or of any line of stage-coaches, railroad, or other means of public carriage of passengers or freight; or of any cemetery or other benevolent institutions; or any public school supported, in whole or in part, at public expense or by endowment for public use, shall make any distinction as to admission or accommodation therein of any citizen of the United States, because of race, color, or previous condition of servitude, shall, on conviction thereof, be fined not less than $500 nor more than $5,000 for each offense; and the person or corporation so offending shall be liable to the citizens thereby injured in damages to be recovered in an action of debt.

SEC. —. That the offenses under this act, and actions to recover damages, may be prosecuted before any territorial, district, or circuit court of the United States having jurisdiction of crimes at the place where the offense was charged to have been committed.

Which was disagreed to—yeas 17, nays 34:

YEAS—Messrs. Anthony, Carpenter, Chandler, Cole, Conkling, Corbett, Fenton, Ferry of Michigan, Frelinghuysen, Hamilton of Texas, Hamlin, Hitchcock, Morrill of Maine, Pool, Ramsey, Scott, Wright—17.

NAYS—Messrs. Ames, *Blair*, Boreman, Brownlow, Cameron, Clayton, *Davis* of West Virginia, Edmunds, Ferry of Connecticut, *Goldthwaite*, Harlan, Hill, *Johnston*, *Kelly*, Logan, Morrill of Vermont, Morton, *Norwood*, Osborn, Pomeroy, Rice, Robertson, *Saulsbury*, Sawyer, Sherman, Spencer, Sprague, *Stevenson*, *Stockton*, Sumner, Trumbull, *Vickers*, West, Wilson—34.

February 8—Mr. CARPENTER moved to strike out the fifth section and substitute the following for it; which was agreed to without a division:

That every discrimination against any person on account of color, by the use of the word "white" in any law, statute, ordinance, or regulation, is hereby repealed and annulled.

Mr. SHERMAN moved to strike out the section as amended above; which was disagreed to—yeas 25, nays 34:

YEAS—Messrs. *Blair*, Boreman, Brownlow, Cole, Corbett, *Davis* of West Virginia, Flanagan, Frelinghuysen, *Goldthwaite*, Hill, Hitchcock, *Johnston*, *Kelly*, *Norwood*, Nye, Pool, *Saulsbury*, Sawyer, Scott, Sherman, *Stevenson*, *Stockton*, *Thurman*, Tipton, *Vickers*—25.

NAYS—Messrs. Ames, Anthony, Caldwell, Cameron, Carpenter, Chandler, Clayton, Conkling, Cragin, Fenton, Ferry of Connecticut, Ferry of Michigan, Gilbert, Hamilton of Texas, Hamlin, Harlan, Kellogg, Logan, Morrill of Maine, Morrill of Vermont, Morton, Patterson, Pomeroy, Ramsey, Rice, Robertson, Schurz, Spencer, Sumner, Trumbull, West, Wilson, Windom, Wright—34.

Mr. FRELINGHUYSEN moved to strike from the first section the words "of church organizations" and the word "churches;" which was agreed to—yeas 29, nays 24:

YEAS—Messrs. Anthony, Boreman, Caldwell, Cameron, Carpenter, Cole, Conkling, Corbett, Cragin, Fenton, Ferry of Michigan, Flanagan, Frelinghuysen, *Goldthwaite*, Hamilton of Texas, Hamlin, Morrill of Maine, Morrill of Vermont, Morton, Patterson, Pool, Scott, Sherman, Sprague, Tipton, *Vickers*, Wilson, Windom, Wright—29.

NAYS—Messrs. Ames, *Blair*, Clayton, *Davis* of West Virginia, Gilbert, Hill, Hitchcock, *Johnston*, *Kelly*, Logan, *Norwood*, Osborn, Pomeroy, Ramsey, Rice, Robertson, Schurz, Spencer, *Stevenson*, *Stockton*, Sumner, *Thurman*, Trumbull, West—24.

February 9—Mr. COLE moved to amend the amendment by striking out the fifth section and inserting the following words:

That every discrimination against *citizens of the United States* on account of color, by the use of the word "white" in any law, statute, ordinance, or regulation, is hereby repealed and annulled.

[The only change was to strike the word "person" from the section and substitute the words "citizens of the United States."

The intention stated was to exclude Asiatics from the operation of the naturalization laws.]

The vote was—yeas 15, nays 34:

YEAS—Messrs. Boreman, Caldwell, Cole, Corbett, Cragin, Flanagan, Frelinghuysen, Gilbert, Morton, Nye, Scott, Sherman, Spencer, West, Wilson—15.

NAYS—Messrs. Ames, Anthony, *Blair*, Brownlow, Carpenter, Clayton, *Davis* of West Virginia, Fenton, Ferry of Connecticut, *Goldthwaite*, Hamlin, Hill, Hitchcock, *Johnston*, *Kelly*, Logan, Morrill of Vermont, *Norwood*, Osborn, Patterson, Ramsey, Rice, Robertson, *Saulsbury*, Sawyer, Schurz, *Stevenson*, *Stockton*, Sumner, *Thurman*, Tipton, Trumbull, *Vickers*, Wright—34.

Mr. COLE offered a proviso to that section, as follows:

Provided, That this section shall not be construed to alter or affect the laws of the United States concerning naturalization.

Which was disagreed to—yeas 15, nays 34:

YEAS—Messrs. Boreman, Brownlow, Cole, Corbett, Flanagan, Frelinghuysen, Gilbert, Nye, Osborn, Pool, Scott, Sherman, Spencer, *Vickers*, West—15.

NAYS—Messrs. Ames, Anthony, *Blair*, Carpenter, *Davis* of West Virginia, Fenton, Ferry of Connecticut, Ferry of Michigan, *Goldthwaite*, Hamilton of Texas, Hamlin, Harlan, Hill, Hitchcock, *Johnston*, *Kelly*, Logan, Morrill of Maine, Morrill of Vermont, *Norwood*, Ramsey, Rice, Robertson, *Saulsbury*, Sawyer, Schurz, *Stevenson*, *Stockton*, Sumner, *Thurman*, Tipton, Trumbull, Windom, Wright—34.

Mr. CORBETT moved to add this proviso to the fifth section:

Provided, That this section shall not be held to authorize the naturalization of Chinese.

Which was disagreed to—yeas 13, nays 32:

YEAS—Messrs. Boreman, Caldwell, Clayton, Cole, Corbett, Flanagan, Gilbert, Nye, Osborn, Pool, Scott, *Vickers*, West—13.

NAYS—Messrs. Ames, Anthony, *Blair*, Brownlow, Carpenter, *Davis* of West Virginia, Fenton, Ferry of Connecticut, Ferry of Michigan, *Goldthwaite*, Hamilton of Texas, Hamlin, Harlan, Hill, Hitchcock, *Johnston*, Logan, Morrill of Vermont, Morton, *Norwood*, Ramsey, Rice, Robertson, *Saulsbury*, Sawyer, Schurz, *Stevenson*, *Stockton*, Sumner, *Thurman*, Trumbull, Wilson—32.

The amendment of Mr. SUMNER was then agreed to—yeas 29, nays 28:

YEAS—Messrs. Ames, Anthony, Brownlow, Cameron, Chandler, Clayton, Conkling, Cragin, Fenton, Ferry of Michigan, Frelinghuysen, Gilbert, Hamlin, Harlan, Morrill of Vermont, Morton, Osborn, Patterson, Pomeroy, Ramsey, Rice, Sherman, Spencer, Sumner, West, Wilson, Windom, Wright, and the Vice President—29.

NAYS—Messrs. *Blair*, Boreman, Carpenter, Cole, Corbett, *Davis* of West Virginia, Ferry of Connecticut, *Goldthwaite*, Hamilton of Texas, Hill, Hitchcock, *Johnston*, *Kelly*, Logan, Morrill of Maine, *Norwood*, Pool, Robertson, *Saulsbury*, Sawyer, Schurz, Scott, *Stevenson*, *Stockton*, *Thurman*, Tipton, Trumbull, *Vickers*—28.

Mr. MORTON moved to add the following to the classes excepted from amnesty:

Fourth. All persons who have been or shall be members of what is known as the Ku Klux Klan, or any organization existing or which may exist for like objects and purposes.

Which was agreed to—yeas 34, nays 16:

YEAS—Messrs. Ames, Anthony, Boreman, Brownlow, Caldwell, Cameron, Carpenter, Chandler, Clayton, Cole, Conkling, Corbett, Ferry of Michigan, Flanagan, Frelinghuysen, Gilbert, Hamilton of Texas, Hamlin, Harlan, Morrill of Vermont, Morton, Osborn, Patterson, Pomeroy, Pool, Ramsey, Robertson, Sawyer, Spencer, Sumner, West, Wilson, Windom, Wright—34.

NAYS—Messrs. *Blair*, *Davis* of West Virginia, *Goldthwaite*, Hill, *Johnston*, *Kelly*, Morrill of Maine, *Norwood*, *Saulsbury*, Schurz, *Stevenson*, *Stockton*, *Thurman*, Tipton, Trumbull, *Vickers*—16.

The bill, as amended, was then rejected—yeas 33, nays 19; (two thirds being required to pass it:)

YEAS—Messrs. Ames, Anthony, Brownlow, Caldwell, Cameron, Clayton, Conkling, Cragin, Fenton, Ferry of Michigan, Flanagan, Frelinghuysen, Gilbert, Hamilton of Texas, Hamlin, Harlan, Kellogg, Morrill of Vermont, Morton, Osborn, Patterson, Pomeroy, Pool, Ramsey, Rice, Robertson, Sawyer, Sherman, Spencer, Sumner, West, Wilson, Windom—33.

NAYS—Messrs. *Blair*, Boreman, *Davis* of West Virginia, *Goldthwaite*, Hill, *Johnston*, *Kelly*, Logan, Morrill of Maine, *Norwood*, *Saulsbury*, Scott, *Stevenson*, *Stockton*, *Thurman*, Tipton, Trumbull, *Vickers*, Wright—19.

Other Amnesty Bills.

IN HOUSE.

1871, March 14—Pending a bill for the removal of all legal and political disabilities imposed by the third section of the fourteenth amendment,

Mr. POLAND moved to add the following:

Provided, That this act shall not apply to or in any way affect or remove the disability of any person included in either of the following classes:

First. Members of the Congress of the United States who withdrew therefrom and aided the rebellion.

Second. Officers of the Army or Navy of the United States, above the age of twenty-one years, who left said Army or Navy and aided the rebellion.

Third. Members of State conventions which adopted pretended ordinances of secession who voted for the adoption of such ordinances.

Which was agreed to—yeas 123, nays 59.

The negative vote consisted of the following members: *Adams*, *Arthur*, Averill, *Biggs*, B. F. Butler, Coburn, Creely, *Crossland*, *Davis*, Dawes, De Large, Dickey, Duell, *Eldredge*, Elliott, Farwell, C. Foster, *Getz*, *Golladay*, *Handley*, *Hanks*, Harmer, Havens, Hawley, J. W. Hazelton, *Hereford*, Hoar, Kelley, *Kendall*, Lansing, McGrew, McJunkin, Merriam, *Merrick*, Morphis, Orr, I. C. Parker, Perce, Porter, *Price*, Rainey, *Read*, *J. M. Rice*, *Ritchie*, E. H. Roberts, *Robinson*, Sessions, Shanks, Shellabarger, *Sloss*, Stevenson, Stoughton, *Swann*, Taffe, *Van Trump*, *Voorhees*, Wallace, Walls, Wheeler.

On passing the bill, as amended, the vote was—yeas 120, nays 82; and it was lost, two thirds not having voted in the affirmative:

YEAS—Messrs. *Acker*, *Adams*, *Archer*, *Arthur*, *Beck*, Bigby, *Biggs*, Bingham, *Bird*, *J. G. Blair*, *Braxton*, *Bright*, *J. Brooks*, Buckley, Burchard, *Caldwell*, *Campbell*, *Carroll*, *Comingo*, Cook, *Cox*, *Crebs*, *Critcher*, *Crossland*, *Davis*, De Large, *Dox*, *Du Bose*, *Duke*, *Eldredge*, *Ely*, Farnsworth, Farwell, Finkelnburg, *Forker*, *H. D. Foster*, Frye, *Garrett*, *Getz*, *Golladay*, *Griffith*, *Haldeman*, Hale, Halsey, *Hambleton*, *Handley*, *Hanks*, *Harper*, G. E. Harris, *J. T. Harris*, Hay, *Hereford*, Hill, *Holman*, *Kendall*, *Kerr*, *King*, *Kinsella*, *Lamison*, *Leach*, *Lewis*, *Manson*, *Marshall*, *McClelland*, *McCormick*, McGrew, *McHenry*, *McIntyre*, *McKinney*, *Merrick*, *B. F. Meyers*, *Mitchell*, Moore, Morey, *Morgan*, Morphis, *Niblack*, Perce, *E. Perry*, Platt, Poland, *Potter*, *Price*, *Randall*, *Read*, *E. Y. Rice*, *J. M. Rice*, *Ritchie*, *W. R. Roberts*, *Robinson*, *J. Rogers*, *Roosevelt*, Sheldon, *Shober*, Shoemaker, *Slater*, *Slocum*, *Sloss*, W. C. Smith, *R. M. Speer*, T. J. Speer, *Stevens*, *Storm*, *Sutherland*,

Swann, Sypher, *Terry*, Thomas, *Tuthill*, *Vaughan*, *Voorhees*, *Waddell*, Wakeman, *Warren*, *Wells*, Whiteley, *Whitthorne*, *Williams* of New York, *Wood*, *Young*—120.

NAYS—Messrs. Ambler, Averill, Barber, Beatty, A. Blair, G. M. Brooks, Buffinton, Burdett, B. F. Butler, R. R. Butler, Coburn, Conger, Cotton, Creely, Dawes, Dickey, Donnan, Duell, Dunnell, Eames, Elliott, C. Foster, Garfield, Harmer, Havens, Hawley, G. W. Hazelton, J. W. Hazelton, Hoar, Hooper, Kelley, Ketcham, Killinger, Lansing, Lowe, Lynch, Maynard, McCrary, McJunkin, Merriam, Monroe, L. Myers, Orr, Packard, Packer, Palmer, I. C. Parker, Peck, Pendleton, Peters, Porter, Prindle, Rainey, E. H. Roberts, Rusk, Sawyer, Scofield, Seeley, Sessions, Shanks, Shellabarger, H. B. Smith, J. A. Smith, Sprague, Stevenson, Stoughton, Stowell, St. John, Taffe, W. Townsend, Twichell, Tyner, Upson, Walden, Waldron, Wallace, Walls, Wheeler, Willard, Williams of Indiana, J. M. Wilson, J. T. Wilson—82.

1872, January 15—Mr. ACKER moved to suspend the rules and pass the following bill:

Whereas the President of the United States in his late annual message thinks "it may well be considered whether it is not now time that the disabilities imposed by the fourteenth amendment should be removed;" and whereas in a republic of freemen perfect equality of rights ought to exist between the citizens thereof, to the end that peace and good will may prevail throughout its borders: Therefore,

Be it enacted, &c., (two thirds of each House concurring therein,) That from and after the passage of this act all legal and political disabilities imposed by any article or section of the Constitution of the United States, or its laws, the same be, and are hereby, removed, and a general amnesty is hereby granted to any and all political offenders in any section of the United States who shall obey the Constitution of the United States, and the laws passed in pursuance therewith.

Which was not agreed to—yeas 106, nays 93, (two thirds being required:)

YEAS—Messrs. *Acker*, *Adams*, *Archer*, *Arthur*, *Barnum*, Barry, *Beck*, *Bell*, *Biggs*, *Bird*, A. Blair, *Braxton*, *Bright*, *J. Brooks*, Buckley, *Caldwell*, *Carroll*, *Comingo*, *Conner*, *Cox*, *Crebs*, *Critcher*, *Crossland*, *Davis*, Donnan, *Dox*, *Du Bose*, *Duke*, *Eldredge*, *Ely*, Farnsworth, Farwell, Finkelnburg, *Forker*, W. D. Foster, *Garrett*, *Getz*, *Golladay*, *Griffith*, *Haldeman*, *Hambleton*, *Hancock*, *Handley*, *Hanks*, *Harper*, G. E. Harris, *J. T. Harris*, Hay, *Hereford*, *Herndon*, *Hibbard*, *Holman*, *Kerr*, *King*, *Kinsella*, *Lamison*, *Leach*, *Lewis*, *Manson*, *Marshall*, *McClelland*, *McCormick*, *McHenry*, *McIntyre*, McKee, *McNeely*, *Merrick*, *B. F. Meyers*, *Mitchell*, Morey, *Morgan*, *Niblack*, *H. W. Parker*, *Potter*, *Price*, *Randall*, *Read*, *E. Y. Rice*, *J. M. Rice*, *Ritchie*, *W. R. Roberts*, *Roosevelt*, Sheldon, *Sherwood*, *Slater*, *Slocum*, *Sloss*, *R. M. Speer*, T. J. Speer, *Stevens*, *Storm*, *Sutherland*, *Swann*, *Terry*, Turner, *Tuthill*, *Van Trump*, *Vaughan*, *Voorhees*, *Waddell*, *Warren*, *Wells*, *Whitthorne*, *Williams*, of New York, *Winchester*, *Wood*—106.

NAYS—Messrs. Ambler, Ames, Averill, Barber, Beatty, Bingham, G. M. Brooks, Buffinton, Burchard, Burdett, R. R. Butler, W. T. Clark, Coburn, Conger, Cotton, Dawes, Dickey, Duell, Dunnell, Eames, C. Foster, Frye, Garfield, Hale, Halsey, Havens, Hawley, G. W. Hazelton, J. W. Hazelton, Hill, Hoar, Hooper, Houghton, Kelley, Ketcham, Killinger, Lamport, Lansing, Lowe, Lynch, Maynard, McCrary, McGrew, McJunkin, Mercur, Merriam, Monroe, L. Myers, Negley, Orr, Packard, Packer, Palmer, I. C. Parker, Peck, Pendleton, Peters, Poland, Porter, Rainey, E. H. Roberts, Rusk, Sawyer, Scofield, Seeley, Sessions, Shanks, Shellabarger, Shoemaker, H. B. Smith, J. A. Smith, Snyder, Sprague, Starkweather, Stevenson, Stoughton, Strong, Taffe, Thomas, W. Townsend, Twichell, Tyner, Upson, Wakeman, Walden, Waldron, Wallace, Walls, Wheeler, Willard, Williams of Indiana, J. M. Wilson, and J. T. Wilson—93.

Mr. DAWES moved to suspend the rules, and pass this bill:

A bill to remove political disabilities.

Be it enacted, &c., That from and after the passage of this act, all political disabilities incurred under and by virtue of the third section of the fourteenth amendment of the Constitution be, and the same time are hereby, removed.

Which was not agreed to—yeas 132, nays 70:

YEAS—Messrs. *Acker*, *Adams*, *Archer*, *Arthur*, Banks, Barry, *Beck*, *Bell*, Beveridge, *Biggs*, *Bird*, A. Blair, *Braxton*, *Bright*, G. M. Brooks, *J. Brooks*, Buckley, Burdett, *Caldwell*, *Carroll*, W. T. Clark, Coghlan, *Comingo*, *Conner*, *Cox*, *Crebs*, *Critcher*, *Crossland*, Darrall, *Davis*, Dawes, Donnan, *Dox*, *Du Bose*, *Duke*, *Edwards*, *Eldredge*, *Ely*, Farnsworth, Farwell, Finkelnburg, *Forker*, C. Foster, W. D. Foster, Garfield, *Garrett*, *Getz*, *Golladay*, *Haldeman*, Hale, Halsey, *Hambleton*, *Hancock*, *Handley*, *Hanks*, *Harper*, G. E. Harris, *J. T. Harris*, Hay, *Hereford*, *Herndon*, *Hibbard*, Hill, *Holman*, Houghton, Kellogg, *Kerr*, *Ketcham*, *King*, *Kinsella*, *Lamison*, *Leach*, *Lewis*, *Manson*, *Marshall*, *McClelland*, *McCormick*, *McHenry*, *McIntyre*, McKee, *McNeely*, *Merrick*, *B. F. Meyers*, *Mitchell*, Morey, *Morgan*, Negley, *Niblack*, *H. W. Parker*, A. F. Perry, *E. Perry*, Peters, *Potter*, *Price*, *Randall*, *Read*, *E. Y. Rice*, *J. M. Rice*, *Ritchie*, *W. R. Roberts*, *J. Rogers*, *Roosevelt*, Sheldon, *Sherwood*, Shoemaker, *Slater*, *Slocum*, *Sloss*, W. C. Smith, *R. M. Speer*, T. J. Speer, *Stevens*, Stevenson, *Storm*, *Sutherland*, *Swann*, *Terry*, Thomas, Turner, *Tuthill*, Twichell, *Van Trump*, *Vaughan*, *Voorhees*, *Waddell*, Wakeman, *Warren*, *Wells*, *Whitthorne*, *Williams* of New York, *Winchester*, *Wood*—132.

NAYS—Messrs. Ambler, Barber, Beatty, Bingham, Buffinton, Burchard, B. F. Butler, R. R. Butler, Coburn, Conger, Cotton, Duell, Dunnell, Eames, Frye, Goodrich, Hawley, G. W. Hazelton, J. W. Hazelton, Hooper, Kelley, Killinger, Lamport, Lowe, Lynch, Maynard, McCrary, McGrew, McJunkin, Mercur, Merriam, Monroe, L. Myers, Orr, Packard, Packer, Palmer, Peck, Pendleton, Porter, Prindle, Rainey, E. H. Roberts, Rusk, Sawyer, Seeley, Sessions, Shanks, Shellabarger, H. B. Smith, J. A. Smith, Snapp, Snyder, Sprague, Starkweather, Stoughton, Strong, Taffe, W. Townsend, Tyner, Upson, Walden, Waldron, Wallace, Walls, Wheeler, Willard, Williams of Indiana, J. M. Wilson, J. T. Wilson—70.

February 5—Mr. RANDALL moved to suspend the rules and pass the following bill; which was agreed to on a division—yeas 93, nays 38; the yeas and nays not having been ordered:

Be it enacted, &c., (two thirds of each House concurring therein,) That the political disabilities imposed by the third section of the fourteenth article of the amendments to the Constitution of the United States are hereby removed from all persons included in the following designated classes to whom disabilities attach by reason of participation and implication in the late rebellion, after having taken an oath to support the Constitution of the United States in connection with, and as part of their oaths of office, to wit: all persons who took such oath as postmasters or clerks of postmasters, as United States marshals and deputy or assistant United States marshals, as judges of probate and judges of other courts of inferior jurisdiction in any State, and the clerks and other officers of such courts, clerks and registers of equity courts, and masters and examiners in chancery, sheriffs and deputy sheriffs, justices of the peace, all municipal officers, including the mayor, aldermen, and other officers of any city, town, or village, commissioners of roads and revenue, constables, and all other executive and administrative officers who were by law elected to office prior to the rebellion by the people of any city, county, town, village, or parish, the general duties of whose offices were restricted in their performance to such city, county, town, village, or parish: *Provided, however*, That the benefits of this act shall not extend to any persons, although included by the above specified classes, who resigned their seats as members of Congress, or who resigned as officers of the Army or Navy, and afterward joined the rebellion; nor to persons who voted for an ordinance of secession while members of a convention of any State which adopted such ordinance: *Provided further*, That all persons relieved by this act shall take and subscribe an oath of allegiance to the United States before any officer authorized to administer oaths, which said oath shall be filed in the United States district court for the district in which said persons reside.

Supplementary Civil Rights Bill.

IN HOUSE.

1872, February 12—Mr. HOOPER, of Massachusetts, introduced a supplement to an act to protect all citizens of the United States in their civil rights, and to furnish the means for their vindication, passed April 9, 1866; which was referred to the Committee on the Judiciary.

February 19—Mr. FRYE, at the request of Mr. HOOPER, introduced this bill during the morning hour under the call for resolutions:

A bill supplemental to an act entitled "An act to protect all citizens of the United States in their civil rights, and to furnish the means for their vindication," passed April 9, 1866.

Be it enacted, &c., That no citizen of the United States shall, by reason of race, color, or previous condition of servitude, be excepted or excluded from the full and equal enjoyment of any accommodation, advantage, facility, or privilege furnished by inn-keepers; by common-carriers, whether on land or water; by licensed owners, managers, or lessees of theaters or other places of public amusement; by trustees, commissioners, superintendents, teachers, and other officers of common schools and other public institutions of learning, the same being supported by moneys derived from general taxation, or authorized by law; by trustees and officers of cemetery associations and benevolent institutions incorporated by national or State authority. But private schools, cemeteries, and institutions of learning established exclusively for white or colored persons, and maintained respectively by voluntary contributions, shall remain according to the terms of the original establishment.

SEC. 2. That any person violating any of the provisions of the foregoing section, or aiding in their violation, or inciting thereto, shall, for every such offense, forfeit and pay the sum of $500 to the person aggrieved thereby, to be recovered in an action on the case, with full costs, and shall also, for every such offense, be deemed guilty of a misdemeanor, and, upon conviction thereof, shall be fined not less than $500 nor more than $1,000, or shall be imprisoned not less than thirty days nor more than one year: *Provided*, That the party aggrieved shall not recover more than one penalty; and when the offense is a refusal of burial, the penalty may be recovered by the heirs at law of the person whose body has been refused burial.

SEC. 3. That the same jurisdiction and powers are hereby conferred and the same duties enjoined upon the courts and officers of the United States in the execution of this act as are conferred and enjoined upon such courts and officers in sections three, four, five, seven, and ten of an act entitled "An act to protect all persons in the United States in their civil rights, and to furnish the means of their vindication," passed April 9, 1866, and these sections are hereby made a part of this act; and any of the aforesaid officers failing to institute and prosecute such proceedings herein required shall, for every such offense, forfeit and pay the sum of $500 to the person aggrieved thereby, to be recovered by an action on the case, with full costs, and shall, on conviction thereof, be deemed guilty of a misdemeanor, and be fined not less than $1,000 nor more than $5,000.

SEC. 4. That no citizen possessing all other qualifications which are or may be prescribed by law shall be disqualified for service as juror in any court, national or State, by reason of race, color, or previous condition of servitude; and any officer or other persons charged with any duty in the selection or summoning of jurors who shall exclude or fail to summon any citizen for the reason above named shall, on conviction thereof, be deemed guilty of a misdemeanor and be fined not less than $1,000 nor more than $5,000.

SEC. 5. That every discrimination against any citizen on account of color by the use of the word "white" in any law, statute, ordinance, or regulation is hereby repealed and annulled.

Mr. ELDREDGE moved to reject the bill; which was disagreed to—yeas 89, nays 116:

YEAS—Messrs. *Acker, Adams, Arthur, Barnum, Beck, Biggs, Bird, J. G. Blair, Braxton, Bright, J. Brooks, Caldwell, Campbell, Carroll,* Coghlan, *Comingo, Cox, Crebs, Critcher, Crossland, Davis, Dox, Du Bose, Duke, Eldredge, Forker, Garrett, Getz, Golladay, Griffith, Haldeman, Hambleton, Hancock, Handley, Hanks, Harper, J. T. Harris, Hereford, Herndon, Hibbard, Holman,* Houghton, *Kendall, Kerr, King, Leach, Lewis, Manson, Marshall, McClelland, McCormick, McHenry, McIntyre, McKinney, McNeely, Merrick, B. F. Meyers, Morgan, Niblack, H. W. Parker, E. Perry, Potter, Price, Read, E. Y. Rice, W. R. Roberts, Robinson, Rogers, Sherwood, Shober, Slater, Slocum, Sloss, R. M. Speer, Stevens, Storm, Swann, Terry, Tuthill, Van Trump, Vaughan, Voorhees, Waddell, Wells, Whitthorne, Williams* of New York, *Winchester, Wood, Young*—89.

NAYS—Messrs. Ambler, Averill, Banks, Barber, Barry, Beatty, Bell, Beveridge, Bigby, Bingham, Boles, G. M. Brooks, Buckley, Buffinton, Burchard, Burdett, B. F. Butler, W. T. Clark, Cobb, Coburn, Conger, Cotton, Creely, Crocker, Darrall, Dawes, Dickey, Donnan, Duell, Dunnell, Eames, Finkelnburg, C. Foster, W. D. Foster, Frye, Garfield, Harmer, G. E. Harris, Havens, Hawley, Hay, Hays, G. W. Hazelton, J. W. Hazelton, Hill, Hoar, Hooper, Kelley, Ketcham, Killinger, Lamport, Lowe, Lynch, Maynard, McCrary, McGrew, McJunkin, McKee, Mercur, Merriam, Monroe, Moore, Morphis, L. Myers, Negley, Orr, Packard, Packer, Palmer, I. C. Parker, Peck, Perce, A. F. Perry, Platt, Poland, Porter, Prindle, Rainey, E. H. Roberts, Rusk, Sargent, Sawyer, Scofield, Seeley, Sessions, Shanks, Sheldon, Shellabarger, Shoemaker, H. B. Smith, J. A. Smith, Snapp, T. J. Speer, Sprague, Starkweather, Stevenson, Stoughton, Stowell, Strong, Sypher, Taffe, Thomas, W. Townsend, Turner, Twichell, Tyner, Upson, Walden, Waldron, Wallace, Wheeler, Whiteley, Willard, Williams of Indiana, J. M. Wilson, J. T. Wilson—116.

February 26—The bill came up in order, but no vote was reached, dilatory motions having been interposed by Democratic members. So on March 11 and 18, and other days

March 25—Mr. ELLIOTT offered this resolution:

Resolved, That the rules be so suspended as to bring House bill No. 1647 before the House for consideration, to the exclusion of other orders, on Wednesday, April 10, at two o'clock p. m.

Which was not agreed to, (two thirds being required)—yeas 98, nays 80:

YEAS—Messrs. Ames, Averill, Barber, Barry, Beatty, Beveridge, Bigby, Bingham, A. Blair, G. M. Brooks, Buckley, Buffinton, Burchard, Burdett, Coghlan, Conger, Cotton, Dawes, Dickey, Donnan, Dunnell, Eames, Elliott, Finkelnburg, C. Foster, W. D. Foster, Frye, Garfield, Goodrich, Harmer, G. E. Harris, Havens, Hawley, G. W. Hazelton, J. W. Hazelton, Hill, Hoar, Hooper, Houghton, Kelley, Ketcham, Killinger, Lamport, Lansing, Lowe, Maynard, McCrary, McJunkin, Mercur, Merriam, Monroe, Moore, Morey, L. Myers, Negley, Orr, Packard, Palmer, I. C. Parker, Peck, Pendleton, Perce, A. F. Perry, Poland, Prindle, E. H. Roberts, Rusk, Sargent, Sawyer, Scofield, Shanks, Sheldon, Shellabarger, Shoemaker, H. B. Smith, J. A. Smith, T. J. Speer, Sprague, Starkweather, Stevenson, Stoughton, Stowell, Sypher, Taffe, Thomas, W. Townsend, Turner, Tyner, Upson, Wakeman, Walden, Waldron, Wallace, Wheeler, Whiteley, Willard, Williams of Indiana, J. M. Wilson—98.

NAYS—Messrs. *Acker, Adams, Archer, Arthur, Biggs, Bird, J. G. Blair, Braxton, Bright, Caldwell, Campbell, Carroll, Conner, Cox, Critcher, Crossland, Davis, Dox, Du Bose, Duke, Eldredge, H. D. Foster, Getz, Golladay, Griffith, Haldeman, Hambleton, Hancock, Handley, Hanks, Harper, J. T. Harris*, Hays, *Herndon, Hibbard, Kendall, Kerr, King, Lamison, Leach, Lewis, Manson, Marshall, McClelland, McCormick*, McGrew, *McIntyre, McNeely, Merrick, B. F. Meyers, Mitchell, Niblack, H. W. Parker, E. Perry, Potter, Price, Randall, Read, E. Y. Rice, J. M. Rice, Ritchie, Rogers, Roosevelt, Sherwood, Shober, Slater, Sloss, Storm, Swann, Terry, Van Trump, Vaughan, Voorhees, Waddell, Warren, Wells, Whitthorne, Williams* of New York, *Winchester, Wood*—80.

April 1—This bill being before the House, Mr. NIBLACK moved to lay it on the table; which was not agreed to—yeas 73; nays 99:

YEAS—Messrs. *Acker, Archer, Arthur, Beck, Biggs, Braxton, Bright, Caldwell, Campbell, Carroll*, Coghlan, *Conner, Cox, Crebs, Critcher, Crossland, Dox, Du Bose, Duke, Eldredge, H. D. Foster, Garrett, Golladay, Griffith, Haldeman, Hancock, Handley, Hanks, Harper, J. T. Harris, Hereford, Herndon, Hibbard, Holman*, Houghton, *Kendall, Kerr, King, Lamison, Lewis, Manson, Marshall, McCormick, McHenry, McIntyre, McKinney, McNeely, B. F. Meyers, Niblack, H. W. Parker, E. Perry, Randall, Read, E. Y. Rice, J. M. Rice, Ritchie, W. R. Roberts, Rogers, Sherwood, Shober, Slater, R. M. Speer, Swann, Terry, D. Townsend, Tuthill, Van Trump, Vaughan, Warren, Wells, Whitthorne, Winchester, Wood*—73.

NAYS—Messrs. Ambler, Averill, Banks, Barber, Barry, Beatty, Beveridge, Bigby, Buckley, Buffinton, Burchard, Burdett, B. F. Butler, Cobb, Coburn, Conger, Cotton, Creely, Crocker, Darrall, De Large, Donnan, Dunnell, Eames, Elliott, Farnsworth, Finkelnburg, C. Foster, W. D. Foster, Frye, Hale, Halsey, Harmer, G. E. Harris, Havens, Hawley, Hay, Hays, G. W. Hazelton, J. W. Hazelton, Hill, Hooper, Kelley, Lamport, Lansing, Lowe, Maynard, McCrary, McGrew, McJunkin, Mercur, Merriam, Monroe, Moore, Morey, Morphis, L. Myers, Negley, Orr, Packard, Palmer, I. C. Parker, Peck, Pendleton, Platt, Poland, Porter, Prindle, Rainey, E. H. Roberts, Rusk, Sargent, Sawyer, Sessions, Shanks, Sheldon, H. B. Smith, J. A. Smith, W. C. Smith, Snyder, Sprague, Starkweather, Stevenson, Stoughton, Stowell, Thomas, Turner, Twichell, Tyner, Upson, Wakeman, Walden, Waldron, Wallace, Wheeler, Whiteley, Willard, Williams of Indiana, J. T. Wilson—99.

April 8—The bill was ordered to be engrossed and read a third time—yeas 100, nays 78:

YEAS—Messrs. Ambler, Ames, Averill, Banks, Barber, Barry, Beatty, Beveridge, Bigby, Bingham, G. M. Brooks, Buckley, Buffinton, Burchard, Burdett, B. F. Butler, Cobb, Coburn, Conger, Cotton, Darrall, Dawes, De Large, Donnan, Dunnell, Eames, Finkelnburg, C. Foster, Frye, Garfield, Harmer, G. E. Harris, Havens, Hawley, Hays, G. W. Hazelton, J. W. Hazelton, Hill, Hoar, Hooper, Kelley, Lamport, Lansing, Lowe, Maynard, McCrary, McJunkin, Mercur, Merriam, Monroe, Morey, Morphis, L. Myers, Negley, Packard, Packer, Palmer, I. C. Parker, Peck, Pendleton, A. F. Perry, Poland, Porter, Prindle, Rainey, E. H. Roberts, Rusk, Sargent, Sawyer, Sessions, Shanks, Sheldon, Shoemaker, H. B. Smith, J. A. Smith, W. C. Smith, Snapp, Snyder, Sprague, Starkweather, Stevenson, Stoughton, Stowell, Strong, Sypher, Taffe, Thomas, W. Townsend, Turner, Twichell, Tyner, Upson, Wakeman, Walden, Waldron, Wallace, Wheeler, Whiteley, Willard, Williams of Indiana—100.

NAYS—Messrs. *Acker, Adams, Archer, Arthur, Beck, Bell, Biggs, Bird, Braxton, Bright, J. Brooks*, R. R. Butler, *Caldwell, Carroll, Comingo, Conner, Cox, Crebs, Critcher, Crossland, Davis, Dox, Du Bose, Duke, Eldredge, Forker, H. D. Foster, Garrett, Golladay, Haldeman, Hancock, Handley, Hanks, Harper, J. T. Harris, Herndon, Hibbard, Holman, Kendall, Kerr, King, Lamison, Leach, Lewis, Manson, McClelland, McCormick, McHenry, McIntyre, McNeely, Merrick, B. F. Meyers, Mitchell, Morgan, H. W. Parker, Randall, Read, E. Y. Rice, J. M. Rice, Ritchie, Robinson, Rogers, Sherwood, Shober, Slater, Storm, Swann, Terry, Tuthill, Van Trump, Vaughan, Voorhees, Warren, Wells, Whitthorne, Winchester, Wood, Young*—78.

May 13—Mr. ELLIOTT moved to suspend the rules and pass this resolution:

Resolved, That the Committee on the Judiciary be, and it is hereby, directed to report, upon the next call of their committee, a bill supplemental to the act to protect all citizens of the United States in their civil rights and to furnish means for their vindication, commonly known as the "civil rights bill."

Which (two thirds not voting in the affirmative) was lost—yeas 112, nays 76:

YEAS—Messrs. Ambler, Ames, Averill, Banks, Barber, Barry, Beatty, Beveridge, Bigby, Bingham, Boles, Buckley, Buffinton, Burchard, Burdett, B. F. Butler, W. T. Clark, F. Clarke, Cobb, Coburn, Conger, Cotton, Darrall, Dawes, Dickey, Donnan, Duell, Dunnell, Eames, Elliott, Finkelnburg, C. Foster, W. D. Foster, Frye, Garfield, Goodrich, Hale, Harmer, G. E. Harris, Havens, Hawley, Hays, G. W. Hazelton, J. W. Hazelton, Hill, Hoar, Hooper, Kelley, Ketcham, Killinger, Lamport, Lansing, Lowe, McCrary, McJunkin, McKee, Merriam, Monroe, Moore, Morey, Morphis, L. Myers, Negley, Orr, Packard, Packer, Palmer, I. C. Parker, Peck, Pendleton, Perce, A. F. Perry, Poland, Rainey, E. H. Roberts, Rusk, Sargent, Sawyer, Scofield, Seeley, Sessions, Shanks, Sheldon, Shoemaker, H. B. Smith, J. A. Smith, W. C. Smith, Snapp, Snyder, T. J. Speer, Sprague, Starkweather, Stoughton, Strong, St. John, Sutherland, Taffe, Turner, Twichell, Tyner, Upson, Wakeman, Walden, Waldron, Wallace, Walls, Wheeler, Whiteley, Willard, Williams of Indiana, J. M. Wilson, J. T. Wilson—112.

NAYS—Messrs. *Acker, Adams, Archer, Beck, Bell, Bird, J. G. Blair, Braxton, J. Brooks, Caldwell, Campbell, Comingo, Conner, Cox, Crebs, Critcher,*

Crossland, Davis, Dox, Du Bose, Eldredge, H. D. Foster, Getz, Golladay, Griffith, Hambleton, Hancock, Handley, Hanks, Harper, J. T. Harris, Hereford, Herndon, Hibbard, Holman, Houghton, *Kendall, Kerr, Lamison, Leach, Lewis, Manson, McClelland, McCormick, McIntyre, McKinney, McNeely, Merrick, B. F. Meyers, Niblack, H. W. Parker, Price, Randall, Read, E. Y. Rice, J. M. Rice, Robinson, Roosevelt, Sherwood, Shober, Slater, Sloss, R. M. Speer, Stevens, Storm, Swann, Terry, Vaughan, Voorhees, Waddell, Warren, Wells, Whitthorne, Williams* of New York, *Winchester, Young*—76.

XV.

THE "KU KLUX" ACT AND THE PROPOSED EXTENSION OF IT, AND THE AMENDATORY ENFORCEMENT ACT.

The Ku Klux Act.

AN ACT to enforce the provisions of the fourteenth amendment to the Constitution of the United States, and for other purposes.

Be it enacted, &c., That any person who, under color of any law, statute, ordinance, regulation, custom, or usage of any State, shall subject, or cause to be subjected, any person within the jurisdiction of the United States to the deprivation of any rights, privileges, or immunities secured by the Constitution of the United States, shall, any such law, statute, ordinance, regulation, custom, or usage of the State to the contrary notwithstanding, be liable to the party injured in any action at law, suit in equity, or other proper proceeding for redress; such proceeding to be prosecuted in the several district or circuit courts of the United States, with and subject to the same rights of appeal, review upon error, and other remedies provided in like cases in such courts, under the provisions of the act of the 9th of April, 1866, entitled "An act to protect all persons in the United States in their civil rights, and to furnish the means of their vindication;" and the other remedial laws of the United States which are in their nature applicable in such cases.

SEC. 2. That if two or more persons within any State or Territory of the United States shall conspire together to overthrow, or to put down, or to destroy by force the Government of the United States, or to levy war against the United States, or to oppose by force the authority of the Government of the United States, or by force, intimidation, or threat to prevent, hinder, or delay the execution of any law of the United States, or by force to seize, take, or possess any property of the United States contrary to the authority thereof, or by force, intimidation, or threat to prevent any person from accepting or holding any office or trust or place of confidence under the United States, or from discharging the duties thereof, or by force, intimidation, or threat to induce any officer of the United States to leave any State, district, or place where his duties as such officer might lawfully be performed, or to injure him in his person or property on account of his lawful discharge of the duties of his office, or to injure his person while engaged in the lawful discharge of the duties of his office, or to injure his property so as to molest, interrupt, hinder, or impede him in the discharge of his official duty, or by force, intimidation, or threat, to deter any party or witness in any court of the United States from attending such court, or from testifying in any matter pending in such court fully, freely, and truthfully, or to injure any such party or witness in his person or property on account of his having so attended or testified, or by force, intimidation, or threat to influence the verdict, presentment, or indictment of any juror or grand juror in any court of the United States, or to injure such juror in his person or property on account of any verdict, presentment, or indictment lawfully assented to by him, or on account of his being or having been such juror, or shall conspire together, or go in disguise upon the public highway, or upon the premises of another for the purpose, either directly or indirectly, of depriving any person or any class of persons of the equal protection of the laws, or of equal privileges or immunities under the laws, or for the purpose of preventing or hindering the constituted authorities of any State from giving or securing to all persons within such State the equal protection of the laws, or shall conspire together for the purpose of in any manner impeding, hindering, obstructing, or defeating the due course of justice in any State or Territory, with intent to deny to any citizen of the United States the due and equal protection of the laws, or to injure any person in his person or his property for lawfully enforcing the right of any person or class of persons to the equal protection of the laws, or by force, intimidation, or threat to prevent any citizen of the United States lawfully entitled to vote from giving his support or advocacy in a lawful manner towards or in favor of the election of any lawfully qualified person as an elector of President or Vice President of the United States, or as a member of the Congress of the United States, or to injure any such citizen in his person or property on account of such support or advocacy, each and every person so offending shall be deemed guilty of a high crime, and, upon conviction thereof in any district or circuit court of the United States or district or supreme court of any Territory of the United States having jurisdiction of similar offenses, shall be punished by a fine not less than $500 nor more than $5,000, or by imprisonment, with or without hard labor, as the court may determine, for a period of not less than six months nor more than six years, as the court may determine, or by both such fine and imprisonment as the court shall determine. And if any one or more persons engaged in any such conspiracy shall do, or cause to be done, any act in furtherance of the object of such conspiracy, whereby any person shall be injured in his person or property, or deprived of having and exercising any right or privilege of a citizen of the United States, the person so injured or deprived of such rights and privileges may have and maintain an action for the recovery of damages occasioned by such injury or deprivation of rights and privileges against any one or more of the persons engaged in such conspiracy, such action to be prosecuted in the proper district or circuit court of the United States, with and subject to the same rights of appeal, review upon error, and other remedies provided in like cases in such courts under the provisions of the act of April 9, 1866, entitled "An act to protect all persons in the United States in their civil rights, and to furnish the means of their vindication."

Sec. 3. That in all cases where insurrection, domestic violence, unlawful combinations, or conspiracies in any State shall so obstruct or hinder the execution of the laws thereof, and of the United States, as to deprive any portion or class of the people of such State of any of the rights, privileges, or immunities, or protection named in the Constitution and secured by this act, and the constituted authorities of such State shall either be unable to protect, or shall, from any cause, fail in or refuse protection of the people in such rights, such facts shall be deemed a denial by such State of equal protection of the laws to which they are entitled under the Constitution of the United States; and in all such cases, or whenever any such insurrection, violence, unlawful combination, or conspiracy shall oppose or obstruct the laws of the United States or the due execution thereof, or impede or obstruct the due course of justice under the same, it shall be lawful for the President, and it shall be his duty to take such measures, by the employment of the militia or the land and naval forces of the United States, or of either, or by other means as he may deem necessary for the suppression of such insurrection, domestic violence, or combinations; and any person who shall be arrested under the provisions of this and the preceding section shall be delivered to the marshal of the proper district to be dealt with according to law.

Sec. 4. That whenever in any State or part of a State the unlawful combinations named in the preceding section of this act shall be organized and armed, and so numerous and powerful as to be able by violence to either overthrow or set at defiance the constituted authorities of such State, and of the United States within such State, or when the constituted authorities are in complicity with or shall connive at the unlawful purposes of such powerful and armed combinations; and whenever, by reason of either or all of the causes aforesaid, the conviction of such offenders and the preservation of the public safety shall become in such district impracticable, in every such case such combinations shall be deemed a rebellion against the Government of the United States, and during the continuance of such rebellion, and within the limits of the district which shall be so under the sway thereof, such limits to be prescribed by proclamation, it shall be lawful for the President of the United States, when in his judgment the public safety shall require it, to suspend the privileges of the writ of *habeas corpus*, to the end that such rebellion may be overthrown: *Provided*, That all the provisions of the second section of an act entitled "An act relating to *habeas corpus*, and regulating judicial proceedings in certain cases," approved March 3, 1863, which relate to the discharge of prisoners other than prisoners of war, and to the penalty for refusing to obey the order of the court, shall be in full force so far as the same are applicable to the provisions of this section: *Provided further*, That the President shall first have made proclamation, as now provided by law, commanding such insurgents to disperse: *And provided also*, That the provisions of this section shall not be in force after the end of the next regular session of Congress.

Sec. 5. That no person shall be a grand or petit juror in any court of the United States upon any inquiry, hearing, or trial of any suit, proceeding, or prosecution based upon or arising under the provisions of this act who shall, in the judgment of the court, be in complicity with any such combination or conspiracy; and every such juror shall, before entering upon any such inquiry, hearing, or trial, take and subscribe an oath in open court that he has never, directly or indirectly, counseled, advised, or voluntarily aided any such combination or conspiracy; and each and every person who shall take this oath, and shall therein swear falsely, shall be guilty of perjury, and shall be subject to the pains and penalties declared against that crime, and the first section of the act entitled "An act defining additional causes of challenge and prescribing an additional oath for grand and petit jurors in the United States courts," approved June 17, 1862, be, and the same is hereby, repealed.

Sec. 6. That any person or persons, having knowledge that any of the wrongs conspired to be done and mentioned in the second section of this act are about to be committed, and having power to prevent or aid in preventing the same, shall neglect or refuse so to do, and such wrongful act shall be committed, such person or persons shall be liable to the person injured, or his legal representatives, for all damages caused by any such wrongful act which such first-named person or persons by reasonable diligence could have prevented; and such damages may be recovered in an action on the case in the proper circuit court of the United States, and any number of persons guilty of such wrongful neglect or refusal may be joined as defendants in such action: *Provided,* That such action shall be commenced within one year after such cause of action shall have accrued; and if the death of any person shall be caused by any such wrongful act and neglect, the legal representatives of such deceased person shall have such action therefor, and may recover not exceeding $5,000 damages therein for the benefit of the widow of such deceased person, if any there be, or if there be no widow, for the benefit of the next of kin of such deceased person.

SEC. 7. That nothing herein contained shall be construed to supersede or repeal any former act or law except so far as the same may be repugnant thereto; and any offenses heretofore committed against the tenor of any former act shall be prosecuted, and any proceeding already commenced for the prosecution thereof shall be continued and completed the same as if this act had not been passed, except so far as the provisions of this act may go to sustain and validate such proceedings.

Approved, April 20, 1871.

The final votes were as follows:

IN HOUSE, *April* 19, 1871.

YEAS—Messrs. Averill, Barber, Barry, Beatty, Bigby, Bingham, A. Blair, G. M. Brooks, Buckley, Buffinton, Burchard, B. F. Butler, Coburn, Conger, Cook, Cotton, Creely, Dawes, Donnan, Dunnell, Eames, Elliott, Farwell, C. Foster, Garfield, Hale, Halsey, Harmer, G. E. Harris, Havens, Hawley, J. W. Hazelton, Hill, Hoar, Hooper, Kelley, Ketcham, Killinger, Lamport, Lansing, Lowe, Maynard, McJunkin, Mercur, Merriam, Monroe, Morey, L. Myers, Negley, Orr, Packard, Packer, Palmer, Peck, Pendleton, Perce, A. F. Perry, Platt, Poland, Porter, Rainey, E. H. Roberts, Rusk, Sawyer, Scofield, Seeley, Sessions, Shanks, Sheldon, Shellabarger, Shoemaker, H. B. Smith, J. A. Smith, Sprague, Starkweather, Stevenson, Stoughton, St. John, Taffe, W. Townsend, Turner, Twichell, Tyner, Wakeman, Walden, Waldron, Wallace, Walls, Wheeler, Whiteley, Willard, J. M. Wilson, J. T. Wilson—93.

NAYS—Messrs. *Acker, Adams, Archer, Arthur, Beck, Bell, Biggs, Bird, Braxton, Bright, J. Brooks, Caldwell, Cox, Crossland, Davis, Dox, Du Bose, Duke, Edwards, Eldredge, Ely, Forker, H. D. Foster, Getz, Golladay, Griffith, Handley, Hanks, Harper, J. T. Harris, Hereford, Hibbard, Holman, Kendall, Kerr, King, Kinsella, Lamison, Leach, Lewis, Manson, Marshall, McClelland, McCormick, McHenry, McIntyre, McKinney, McNeely, Merrick, B. F. Meyers, Morgan, Niblack, E. Perry, Potter, Randall, Read, E. Y. Rice, J. M. Rice, Ritchie, W. R. Roberts, Shober, Slater, Slocum, Sloss, Stevens, Storm, Sutherland, Swann, Terry, Waddell, Warren, Whitthorne, Williams* of New York, *Young*—74.

IN SENATE, *April* 20, 1871.

YEAS—Messrs. Ames, Anthony, Boreman, Caldwell, Carpenter, Clayton, Cole, Conkling, Cragin, Edmunds, Fenton, Ferry of Michigan, Frelinghuysen, Gilbert, Hamilton of Texas, Harlan, Hitchcock, Howe, Lewis, Logan, Morrill of Maine, Morrill of Vermont, Nye, Osborn, Patterson, Pomeroy, Ramsey, Rice, Sawyer, Scott, Sherman, Spencer, Stewart, West, Wilson, Wright—36.

NAYS—Messrs. *Bayard, Blair, Casserly, Cooper, Davis* of Kentucky, *Davis* of West Virginia, Hill, *Johnston, Kelly,* Robertson, *Saulsbury, Stockton, Vickers*—13.

IN HOUSE.

1871, April 6—Pending a motion of Mr. SHELLABARGER to strike from his bill the second and third sections and substitute other sections,

Mr. FARNSWORTH moved to strike from the proposed third section the following words:

Provided, That the President of the United States be, and he is hereby, authorized, if, in his judgment, it should be deemed expedient, to direct voluntary enlistments of any of the militia of the United States in lieu of all or any part of the force herein authorized to be employed for the purposes aforesaid, for a term of service not exceeding thirty days after the final adjournment of the next session of Congress.

Which was agreed to—yeas 116, nays 86:

YEAS—Messrs. *Acker, Adams,* Ambler, *Archer, Arthur, Beck, Bell, Biggs,* Bingham, *Bird,* A. Blair, *Braxton, Bright, J. Brooks,* Burchard, *Caldwell, Campbell, Carroll, Comingo,* Conger, *Cox, Crebs, Critcher, Crossland, Davis,* Dawes, Donnan, *Dox, Du Bose, Duke, Edwards, Eldredge, Ely,* Farnsworth, Finkelnburg, *Forker, H. D. Foster,* Frye, Garfield, *Garrett, Getz, Golladay, Griffith,* Hale, Halsey, *Handley, Hanks, Harper,* G. E. Harris, *J. T. Harris,* Hay, *Hereford, Hibbard,* Hill, *Holman, Kendall, Kerr,* Ketcham, *King, Kinsella, Lamison, Leach, Lewis, Manson, Marshall, McClelland, McCormick, McHenry, McIntyre, McKinney, McNeely, Merrick, B. F. Meyers, Mitchell,* Moore, *Morgan, Niblack, H. W. Parker, E. Perry,* Poland, *Potter, E. Y. Rice, J. M. Rice, Ritchie, W. R. Roberts, Robinson, J. Rogers, Roosevelt,* Sheldon, *Sherwood, Shober, Slater, Slocum, Sloss,* J. A. Smith, W. C. Smith, *R. M. Speer, Stevens, Storm,* Stoughton, *Sutherland, Swann,* Sypher, *Terry, Van Trump, Vaughan, Voorhees, Waddell, Warren, Wells,* Whiteley, *Whitthorne, Williams* of New York, *Winchester, Wood, Young*—116.

NAYS—Messrs. Averill, Banks, Barber, Barry, Beatty, Bigby, G. M. Brooks, Buckley, Buffinton, B. F. Butler, Clarke, Coburn, Cook, Cotton, Creely, De Large, Dickey, Eames, Elliott, C. Foster, Goodrich, Harmer, Havens, Hawley, G. W. Hazelton, J. W. Hazelton, Hoar, Kelley, Killinger, Lamport, Lansing, Lowe, Maynard, McCrary, McGrew, McJunkin, McKee, Mercur, Merriam, Monroe, L. Myers, Negley, Orr, Packard, Packer, Palmer, I. C. Parker, Peck, Pendleton, Perce, A. F. Perry, Platt, Porter, Prindle, Rainey, E. H. Roberts, Rusk, Sawyer, Scofield, Seeley, Sessions, Shanks, Shellabarger, Shoemaker, H. B. Smith, Snyder, Sprague, Stevenson, Stowell, St. John, Taffe, Thomas, Turner, Twichell, Tyner, Upson, Wakeman, Walden, Waldron, Wallace, Walls, Washburn, Wheeler, Willard, Williams of Indiana, J. M. Wilson—86.

Mr. AMBLER moved to strike from section four the following words:

And during the continuance of such rebellion, and within the limits of the district which shall be so under the sway thereof, such limits to be prescribed by proclamation, it shall be lawful for the President of the United States, when in his judgment the public safety shall require it, to suspend the privileges of the writ of *habeas corpus,* to the end that such rebellion may be overthrown: *Provided,* That the President shall first have made proclamation, as now provided by law, commanding such insurgents to disperse: *And provided also,* That the provisions of this section shall not be in force after the 1st day of June, A. D. 1872.

Which was disagreed to—yeas 100, nays 105:

YEAS—Messrs. *Acker, Adams,* Ambler, *Archer, Arthur, Beck, Bell, Biggs,* Bingham, *Bird, Braxton, Bright, J. Brooks,* Burchard, *Caldwell, Campbell, Carroll, Comingo, Cox, Crebs, Critcher, Crossland, Davis, Dox, Du Bose, Duke, Edwards, Eldredge, Ely,* Farnsworth, Finkelnburg, *Forker, H. D. Foster, Garrett, Getz, Golladay, Griffith,* Hale, *Handley, Hanks, Harper,* G. E. Harris, *J. T. Harris,* Hay, *Hereford, Hibbard, Kendall, Kerr, King, Kinsella,*

Lamison. Leach, Lewis, Manson, Marshall. McClelland, McCormick, McHenry, McIntyre, McKinney, McNeely, Merrick, B. F. Meyers, Mitchell, Moore, Morgan, Niblack, H. W. Parker, E. Perry, Potter, E. Y. Rice, J. M. Rice. Ritchie, W. R. Roberts, Robinson, J. Rogers, Roosevelt, Sheldon, Sherwood, Shober, Slater, Slocum, Sloss, R. M. Speer, Stevens, Storm, Sutherland, Swann, Terry, Van Trump. Vaughan, Voorhees, Waddell, Warren, Wells, Whitthorne, Williams of New York, *Winchester, Wood, Young*—100,

NAYS—Messrs. Averill, Banks, Barber, Barry, Beatty, Bigby, A. Blair, G. M. Brooks, Buckley, Buffinton, Burdett, B. F. Butler, Clarke, Coburn, Conger, Cook, Cotton, Dawes, De Large, Dickey, Donnan, Eames, Elliott, Farwell, C. Foster, Frye, Garfield, Goodrich, Halsey, Harmer, Havens, Hawley, G. W. Hazelton, J. W. Hazelton, Hill, Hoar, *Holman**, Hooper, Kelley, Ketcham, Killinger, Lamport, Lansing, Lowe, Maynard, McCrary, McGrew, McJunkin, McKee, Mercur, Merriam, Monroe, Morey, L. Myers, Negley, Orr, Packard, Packer, Palmer, I. C. Parker, Peck, Pendleton, Perce, A. F. Perry, Platt, Poland, Porter, Prindle, Rainey, E. H. Roberts, Rusk, Sawyer, Scofield, Seeley, Sessions, Shanks, Shellabarger, Shoemaker, H. B. Smith, J. A. Smith, W. C. Smith, Snyder, Sprague, Stevenson, Stoughton, Stowell, St. John, Taffe, Thomas, Turner, Twichell, Tyner, Upson, Wakeman, Walden, Waldron, Wallace, Walls, Washburn, Wheeler, Whiteley, Willard, Williams of Indiana, J. M. Wilson, J. T. Wilson—105.

Mr. DAWES moved to reconsider this vote, and to lay the motion to reconsider on the table; which latter motion was agreed to—yeas 113, nays 94:

Mr. HOLMAN moved to strike out the remainder of section three; which was disagreed to—yeas 91, nays 115.

The bill finally passed—yeas 118, nays 91.

IN SENATE.

The bill was reported from the Judiciary Committee of the Senate with sundry amendments.

1871, April 14—Pending the amendment to the fourth section, to limit the provisions of the section "to the end of the next regular session of Congress,"

Mr. MORTON moved to amend so as to make them operative during the "Forty-Second Congress;" which was disagreed to—yeas 23, nays 42:

YEAS—Messrs. Ames, Brownlow, Caldwell, Chandler, Clayton, Cole, Corbett, Cragin, Gilbert, Hamilton of Texas, Hamlin, Lewis, Morton, Nye, Osborn, Pomeroy, Pratt, Rice, Sherman, Spencer, Stewart, West, Wright—23.

NAYS—Messrs. Anthony, *Bayard, Blair*, Boreman, Buckingham, Cameron, Carpenter, *Casserly*, Conkling, *Cooper, Davis* of Kentucky, *Davis* of West Virginia, Edmunds, Ferry of Michigan, Frelinghuysen, *Hamilton* of Maryland, Harlan, Hill, Hitchcock, Howe, *Johnston, Kelly*, Logan, Morrill of Maine, Morrill of Vermont, Patterson, Pool, Ramsey, Robertson, *Saulsbury*, Sawyer, Schurz, Scott, *Stevenson, Stockton*, Sumner, *Thurman*, Tipton, Trumbull, *Vickers*, Wilson, Windom—42.

The amendment was then agreed to—yeas 44, nays 17.

Mr. SHERMAN moved the following additional section:

SEC. —. That if any house, tenement, cabin, shop, building, barn, or granary shall be unlawfully or feloniously demolished, pulled down, burned, or destroyed, wholly or in part, by any persons riotously and tumultuously assembled together; or if any person shall unlawfully and with force and violence be whipped, scourged, wounded, or killed by any persons riotously and tumultuously assembled together; and if such offense was committed to deprive any person of any right conferred upon him by the Constitution and laws of the United States, or to deter him or punish him for exercising any such right, or by reason of his race, color, or previous condition of servitude, in every such case the inhabitants of the county, city, or parish in which any of the said offenses shall be committed shall be liable to pay full compensation to the person or persons damnified by such offense if living, or to his legal representative if dead; and such compensation may be recovered by such person or his representative by a suit in any court of the United States of competent jurisdiction in the district in which the offense was committed, to be in the name of the person injured, or his legal representative, and against said county, city, or parish; and execution may be issued on a judgment rendered in such suit, and may be levied upon any property, real or personal, of any person in said county, city, or parish; and the said county, city, or parish may recover the full amount of said judgment, cost, and interest from any person or persons engaged as principal or accessory in such riot, in an action in any court of competent jurisdiction.

Which was agreed to—yeas 39, nays 25:

YEAS—Messrs. Ames, Anthony, Boreman, Brownlow, Caldwell, Cameron, Carpenter, Chandler, Clayton, Cole, Conkling, Corbett, Cragin, Edmunds, Ferry of Michigan, Gilbert, Hamilton, of Texas, Hamlin, Harlan, Howe, Lewis, Logan, Morton, Nye, Osborn, Patterson, Pomeroy, Pool, Pratt, Ramsey, Rice, Sawyer, Sherman, Stewart, Sumner, West, Wilson, Windom, Wright—39.

NAYS—Messrs. *Bayard, Blair*, Buckingham, *Casserly, Cooper, Davis* of Kentucky, *Davis* of West Virginia, Frelinghuysen, *Hamilton* of Maryland, Hill, Hitchcock, *Johnston, Kelly*, Morrill of Maine, Robertson, *Saulsbury*, Schurz, Scott, Spencer, *Stevenson, Stockton, Thurman*, Tipton, Trumbull, *Vickers*—25.

Mr. TRUMBULL moved to strike out the fourth section, (relating to *habeas corpus*.)

Which was disagreed to—yeas 21, nays 42:

YEAS—Messrs. *Bayard, Blair, Casserly, Cooper, Davis* of Kentucky, *Davis* of West Virginia, *Hamilton* of Maryland, Hill, *Johnston, Kelly*, Morrill of Maine, Robertson, *Saulsbury*, Schurz, *Stevenson, Stockton, Thurman*, Tipton, Trumbull, *Vickers*, Wright—21.

NAYS—Messrs. Ames, Anthony, Boreman, Brownlow, Buckingham, Caldwell, Cameron, Carpenter, Chandler, Clayton, Cole, Conkling, Cragin, Edmunds, Ferry of Michigan, Frelinghuysen, Gilbert, Hamilton of Texas, Hamlin, Harlan, Hitchcock, Howe, Lewis, Morrill of Vermont, Morton, Nye, Osborn, Patterson, Pomeroy, Pool, Pratt, Ramsey, Rice, Sawyer, Scott, Sherman, Spencer, Stewart, Sumner, West, Wilson, Windom—42.

IN HOUSE.

April 15—The House accepted some and rejected others of the Senate amendments. The House disagreed—yeas 86, nays 93—to the amendment of the Senate substituting "the end of the next regular session of Congress" as the period at which the law shall cease, instead of the 1st day of June, 1872.

The new section, added by the Senate on

* Mr. HOLMAN stated that he voted in the negative, so as to be able to move a reconsideration.

motion of Mr. SHERMAN, was disagreed to—yeas 45, nays 132:

YEAS—Messrs. Barber, Barry, Buckley, Buffinton, Burdett, B. F. Butler, Cobb, Creely, Duell, Dunnell, Elliott, Havens, G. W. Hazelton, Kelley, Lansing, Lowe, Maynard, McJunkin, Merriam, Monroe, L. Myers, Orr, Palmer, Peck, Pendleton, Porter, Prindle, Rainey, E. H. Roberts, Rusk, Sawyer, Seeley, Shanks, H. B. Smith, Sprague, Stevenson, Stoughton, Stowell, St. John, Taffe, Turner, Walden, Wallace, Walls, Wheeler—45.

NAYS—Messrs. *Acker*, *Adams*, Ambler, *Archer*, *Arthur*, Averill, Beatty, *Beck*, *Bell*, Bigby, Bingham, *Bird*, A. Blair, *Braxton*, *Bright*, G. M. Brooks, *J. Brooks*, Burchard, *Caldwell*, *Carroll*, Conger, Cook, Cotton, *Cox*, *Crossland*, *Davis*, Dawes, De Large, *Dox*, *Du Bose*, *Duke*, Eames, *Edwards*, *Eldredge*, Farnsworth, Farwell, Finkelnburg, *Forker*, C. Foster, *H. D. Foster*, Frye, Garfield, *Garrett*, *Getz*, *Golladay*, *Griffith*, Halsey, *Handley*, *Hanks*, *Harper*, G. E. Harris, *J. T. Harris*, Hawley, Hay, J. W. Hazelton, *Hereford*, *Hibbard*, Hill, *Holman*, Hooper, *Kendall*, *Kerr*, *King*, *Kinsella*, *Lamison*, Lamport, *Leach*, *Lewis*, Lynch, *Manson*, *Marshall*, *McClelland*, *McCormick*, McCrary, *McHenry*, *McIntyre*, *McKinney*, *McNeely*, Mercur, *Merrick*, *B. F. Meyers*, Moore, *Morgan*, *Niblack*, Packard, Packer, A. F. Perry, *E. Perry*, Platt, Poland, *Potter*, *Randall*, *Read*, *E. Y. Rice*, *J. M. Rice*, *W. R. Roberts*, *Roosevelt*, Scofield, Shellabarger, *Sherwood*, *Shober*, Shoemaker, *Slater*, *Slocum*, *Sloss*, J. A. Smith, T. J. Speer, Starkweather, *Storm*, Strong, *Sutherland*, *Swann*, *Terry*, *D. Townsend*, W. Townsend, Twichell, Tyner, *Van Trump*, *Vaughan*, *Waddell*, Wakeman, Waldron, *Warren*, *Wells*, Whiteley, *Whitthorne*, Willard, *Williams* of New York, J. M. Wilson, *Winchester*, *Wood*, *Young*—132.

April 18—A committee of conference made a report, signed by Messrs. EDMUNDS and SHERMAN, of Senate, and Messrs. SHELLABARGER and SCOFIELD, of the House, recommending certain modifications of the action of each House. The Senate agreed to the report—yeas 32, nays 16; but the House rejected it—yeas 74, nays 106. The section of Mr. SHERMAN was modified by the committee to read as follows:

That if any house, tenement, cabin, shop, building, barn, or granary shall be unlawfully or feloniously demolished, pulled down, burned, or destroyed, wholly or in part, by any persons riotously and tumultuously assembled together; or if any person shall unlawfully and with force and violence be whipped, scourged, wounded, or killed by any persons riotously and tumultuously assembled together, with intent to deprive any person of any right conferred upon him by the Constitution and laws of the United States, or to deter him or punish him for exercising such right, or by reason of his race, color, or previous condition of servitude, in every such case the county, city, or parish in which any of the said offenses shall be committed shall be liable to pay full compensation to the person or persons damnified by such offense if living, or to his widow or legal representative if dead; and such compensation may be recovered in an action on the case by such person or his representative in any court of the United States of competent jurisdiction in the district in which the offense was committed, such action to be in the name of the person injured, or his legal representative, and against said county, city, or parish; and in which action any of the parties committing such acts may be joined as defendants. And any payment of any judgment, or part thereof, unsatisfied, recovered by the plaintiff in such action, may, if not satisfied by the individual defendant therein within two months next after the recovery of such judgment upon execution duly issued against such individual defendant in such judgment, and returned unsatisfied, in whole or in part, be enforced against such county, city, or parish by execution, attachment, mandamus, garnishment, or any other proceeding in aid of execution or applicable to the enforcement of judgments against municipal corporations; and such judgment shall be a lien as well upon all moneys in the treasury of such county, city, or parish, as upon the other property thereof. And the court in any such action may, on motion, cause additional parties to be made therein prior to issue joined, to the end that justice may be done. And the said county, city, or parish may recover the full amount of such judgment, by it paid, with costs and interest, from any person or persons engaged as principal or accessory in such riot, in an action in any court of competent jurisdiction. And such county, city, or parish, so paying shall also be subrogated to all the plaintiff's rights under such judgment.

April 19—A further conference, consisting of Senators EDMUNDS, CARPENTER, and THURMAN, and Representatives SHELLABARGER, POLAND, and WHITTHORNE, a majority of whom agreed upon a report which left the bill as finally passed by the vote given at the beginning of this chapter.

Proposed Extension of "Ku-Klux" Act.

IN SENATE.

1872, May 21—As in Committee of the Whole, the following bill pending:

Be it enacted, &c., That the provisions of the fourth section of the act approved April 20, 1871, entitled "An act to enforce the provisions of the fourteenth amendment to the Constitution of the United States, and for other purposes," shall continue in force until the end of the next regular session of Congress.

Mr. FENTON moved to lay the bill upon the table; which was disagreed to—yeas 18, nays 27:

YEAS—Messrs. Alcorn, *Bayard*, *Blair*, *Casserly*, *Cooper*, *Davis* of West Virginia, Fenton, *Hamilton* of Maryland, *Johnston*, *Kelly*, *Ransom*, *Saulsbury*, Sprague, *Stevenson*, *Thurman*, Trumbull, *Vickers*, West—18.

NAYS—Messrs. Ames, Anthony, Boreman, Caldwell, Carpenter, Chandler, Clayton, Cole, Conkling, Corbett, Edmunds, Ferry of Michigan, Flanagan, Frelinghuysen, Logan, Morrill of Maine, Nye, Osborn, Patterson, Pomeroy, Pool, Pratt, Ramsey, Robertson, Scott, Spencer, Windom—27.

Mr. VICKERS moved to amend by inserting at the end of the bill the following:

Provided, That before the President shall suspend the writ of *habeas corpus* in any State he shall be satisfied by the affidavits of at least ten respectable residents of the county or district where such unlawful combinations and disorders are alleged to exist, that insurrection, domestic violence, unlawful combinations, or conspiracies to obstruct or hinder the execution of the laws of such State or of the United States exist to deprive a portion or class of the people of such State of some of the rights, privileges, immunities, or protections named in the Constitution and secured by law, and that such combinations are so organized, armed, numerous, and powerful as to be able by violence to overthrow or set at defiance the constituted authorities of such State and of the United States within such State, or that the constituted authorities are in complicity with or connive at the unlawful purposes of such armed and powerful combinations.

Which was disagreeed to—yeas 12, nays 26.

YEAS—Messrs. *Bayard, Blair, Cooper, Davis* of West Virginia, *Hamilton* of Maryland, *Johnston, Kelly, Ransom, Saulsbury,* Sprague, *Stevenson, Thurman.*—12.

NAYS—Messrs. Ames, Anthony, Boreman, Caldwell, Carpenter, Chandler, Clayton, Cole, Conkling, Corbett, Edmunds, Ferry of Michigan, Flanagan, Frelinghuysen, Logan, Morrill of Maine, Nye, Osborn, Patterson, Pomeroy, Pool, Pratt, Robertson, Sawyer, Scott, Spencer—26.

In the Senate the bill was reported without amendment, and passed—yeas 28, nays 15:

YEAS—Messrs. Ames, Anthony, Boreman, Caldwell, Carpenter, Chandler, Clayton, Cole, Conkling, Corbett, Edmunds, Ferry of Michigan, Flanagan, Frelinghuysen, Hamlin, Logan, Morrill of Maine, Morrill of Vermont, Nye, Osborn, Patterson, Pomeroy, Pool, Pratt, Robertson, Sawyer, Scott, Spencer—28.

NAYS—Messrs. Alcorn, *Bayard, Blair, Casserly, Cooper, Davis* of West Virginia, *Hamilton* of Maryland, *Johnston, Kelly, Ransom, Saulsbury,* Sprague, *Stevenson, Thurman, Vickers*—15.

IN HOUSE.

May 28—Mr. POLAND moved to suspend the rules and pass the above bill; which was disagreed to—yeas 94, nays 108:

YEAS—Messrs. Ames, Averill, Banks, Barber, Beatty, Beveridge, Bigby, Bingham, Buckley, Buffinton, Burdett, B. F. Butler, R. R. Butler, Coburn, Coghlan, Conger, Darrall, Dawes, Dickey, Duell, Dunnell, Eames, Elliott, C. Foster, W. D. Foster, Frye, Halsey, Harmer, G. E. Harris, Hawley, Hays, G. W. Hazelton, J. W. Hazelton, Hill, Hoar, Hooper, Houghton, Kelley, Killinger, Lamport, Lansing, Lynch, Maynard, McGrew, McJunkin, McKee, Mercur, Merriam, Monroe, Moore, L. Myers, Negley, Orr, Packard, Packer, Palmer, I. C. Parker, Pendleton, Perce, A. F. Perry, Poland, Prindle, Rainey, E. H. Roberts, Rusk, Sargent, Sawyer, Scofield, Sessions, Shanks, Shellabarger, H. B. Smith, J. A. Smith, Snyder, T. J. Speer, Sprague, Starkweather, Stevenson, Stowell, St. John, Taffe, Thomas, W. Townsend, Twichell, Tyner, Upson, Wakeman, Walden, Waldron, Wallace, Walls, Williams of Indiana, J. M. Wilson, J. T. Wilson—94.

NAYS—Messrs. *Acker,* Ambler, *Archer, Arthur, Beck, Bell, Biggs, Bird,* A. Blair, *J. G. Blair, Braxton, Bright, Brooks,* Burchard, *Caldwell, Campbell, Carroll, Comingo, Conner,* Cotton, *Crebs, Critcher, Crossland,* Dounan, *Dox, Du Bose, Duke, Eldredge, Ely,* Farnsworth, Finkelnburg, *Forker, H. D. Foster,* Garfield, *Garrett, Getz, Giddings, Golladay,* Goodrich, *Griffith, Haldeman,* Hale, *Hambleton, Hancock, Handley, Hanks, Harper, J. T. Harris,* Hay, *Hereford, Herndon, Hibbard, Holman,* Kellogg, *Kendall, Kerr, King, Lewis,* Lowe, *Manson, Marshall, McClelland, McCormick,* McCrary, *McHenry, McIntyre, McNeely, Merrick, Mitchell, Morgan,* Morphis, *Niblack,* Peters, *Potter, Price, Randall, Read, E. Y. Rice, J. M. Rice, Ritchie, W. R. Roberts, J. Rogers, S. H. Rogers, Roosevelt,* Sheldon, *Slater, Slocum, Sloss,* W. C. Smith, *R. M. Speer, Stevens,* Stoughton, Strong, *Sutherland, Swann,* Sypher, *Terry, Tuthill, Van Trump, Waddell, Warren, Wells,* Whiteley, *Whitthorne,* Willard, *Winchester, Wood, Young*—108.

1872, June 6—Another vote was taken on the passage of this bill; which was disagreed to—yeas 56, nays 89:

YEAS—Messrs. Beatty, Buckley, Buffinton, R. R. Butler, Coburn, Conger, Crocker, Dawes, Duell, Dunnell, C. Foster, Harmer, G. E. Harris, Havens, Hawley, J. W. Hazelton, Hill, Hoar, Houghton, Lamport, McGrew, McJunkin, Mercur, Merriam, Monroe, L. Myers, Orr, Packard, Packer, Palmer, Pendleton, Perce, A. F. Perry, Poland, Prindle, Rainey, E. H. Roberts, Sawyer, Sessions, Shanks, Shellabarger, H. B. Smith, J. A. Smith, Sprague, Starkweather, Stevenson, W. Townsend, Turner, Twichell, Tyner, Wakeman, Walden, Waldron, Williams of Indiana, J. M. Wilson, J. T. Wilson—56

NAYS—Messrs. *Acker, Adams, Archer, Arthur, Beck, Bell, Biggs, Bird,* A. Blair, *J. G. Blair, Braxton, Brooks,* Burchard, *Caldwell, Campbell, Carroll, Comingo, Conner,* Cotton, *Critcher, Crossland,* Donnan, *Dox, Du Bose, Duke, Eldredge,* Farnsworth, Finkelnburg, *Forker, H. D. Foster,* Garfield, *Garrett, Getz, Giddings, Golladay, Haldeman, Hambleton, Hancock, Handley, Hanks, Harper, J. T. Harris,* Hay, *Hereford, Hibbard, Holman,* Kellogg, *Kendall, Kerr, King, Lamison, Manson, Marshall, McClelland, McCormick,* McCrary, *McHenry, McIntyre, Merrick, Morgan,* Morphis, *Niblack,* Peters, *Potter, Price, Randall, Read, E. Y. Rice, Ritchie, S. H. Rogers, Sherwood, Shober, Slocum, Stevens, Storm,* Strong, *Swann, Terry, Tuthill, Van Trump, Vaughan, Waddell, Warren, Wells,* Whiteley, *Whitthorne,* Willard, *Williams* of New York, *Winchester*—89.

Amendatory Enforcement Act.

The Act of February 28, 1871, (for which see pages 3-8,) has been supplemented and amended so as to further provide as follows:

That whenever, in any county or parish, in any congressional district, there shall be ten citizens thereof of good standing who, prior to any registration of voters for an election for Representative in Congress, or prior to any election at which a Representative in Congress is to be voted for, shall make known in writing, to the judge of the circuit court of the United States for the district wherein such county or parish is situate, their desire to have said registration or election both guarded and scrutinized, it shall be the duty of the said judge of the circuit court, within not less than ten days prior to said registration or election, as the case may be, to open the said court at the most convenient point in said district; and the said court, when so opened by said judge, shall proceed to appoint and commission, from day to day, and from time to time, and under the hand of the said judge, and under the seal of said court, for such election district or voting precinct in said congressional district, as shall, in the manner herein prescribed, have been applied for, and to revoke, change, or renew said appointment from time to time, two citizens, residents of said election district or voting precinct in said county or parish, who shall be of different political parties, and able to read and write the English language, and who shall be known and designated as supervisors of election; and the said court, when opened by the said judge as required herein, shall, therefrom and thereafter, and up to and including the day following the day of the election, be always open for the transaction of business under this act; and the powers and jurisdiction hereby granted and conferred shall be exercised, as well in vacation as in term time; and a judge, sitting at chambers, shall have the same powers and jurisdiction, including the power of keeping order and of punishing any contempt of his authority, as when sitting in the court: *Provided*, That no compensation shall be allowed to the supervisors herein authorized to be appointed, except those appointed in cities or towns of twenty thousand or more inhabitants. And no person shall be appointed under this act as supervisor of election who is not at the time of his appointment a qualified voter of the county, parish, election district, or voting precinct for which he is appointed. And no person shall be appointed deputy marshal under the act of which this is amendatory who is not a qualified voter, at the time of his appointment, in the county, parish, district, or precinct in which his duties are to be performed. And section thirteen of the act of which this is an amendment shall be construed to authorize and require the circuit courts of the United States in said section mentioned to name and appoint, as soon as may be after the passage of this act, the commissioners provided for in said section, in all cases in which such appointments have not already been made in conformity therewith. And the third section of the act to which this is an amendment shall be taken and construed to authorize each of the judges of the circuit courts of the United States to designate one or more of the judges of the district courts within his circuit to discharge the duties arising under this act or the act to which this is an amendment. And the words "any person," in section four of the act of May 31, 1870, shall be held to include any officer or other person having powers or duties of an official character under this act or the act to which this is an amendment: *Provided*, That nothing in this section shall be so construed as to authorize the appointment of any marshals or deputy marshals in addition to those heretofore authorized by law: *And provided further*, That the supervisors herein provided for shall have no power or authority to make arrests or to perform other duties than to be in the immediate presence of the officers holding the election and to witness all their proceedings, including the counting of the votes and the making of a return thereof. And so much of said sum herein appropriated as may be necessary for said supplemental and amendatory provisions is hereby appropriated from and after the passage of this act.

These provisions were inserted in the sundry civil bill, approved June 10, 1872, and were adopted in each House by the following votes:

In Senate, *June* 10, 1872.

Yeas—Messrs. Alcorn, Ames, Anthony, Boreman, Buckingham, Caldwell, Carpenter, Chandler, Clayton, Cole, Conkling, Corbett, Cragin, Edmunds, Ferry of Michigan, Flanagan, Frelinghuysen, Harlan, Howe, Kellogg, Logan, Morrill of Maine, Morrill of Vermont, Morton, Nye, Osborn, Pomeroy, Pool, Pratt, Ramsey, Robertson, Sawyer, Scott, Sherman, Spencer, Stewart, Sumner, West, Windom—39.

Nays—Messrs. *Bayard*, *Blair*, *Casserly*, *Cooper*, Fenton, Hamilton of Texas, *Kelly*, *Norwood*, *Ransom*, *Saulsbury*, Sprague, *Stevenson*, *Stockton*, *Thurman*, Tipton, Trumbull, *Vickers*—17.

In House, *June* 10, 1872.

Yeas—Messrs. Ames, Averill, Banks, Barber, Beatty, Beveridge, Bigby, Bingham, Buckley, Buffinton, Burchard, Burdett, B. F. Butler, R. R. Butler, Cobb, Coburn, Coghlan, Conger, Cotton, Crocker, Darrall, Dawes, De Large, Donnan, Duell, Dunnell, Eames, Elliott, Finkelnburg, C. Foster, W. D. Foster, Frye, Garfield, Goodrich, Halsey, Harmer, G. E. Harris, Havens, Hawley, Hay, Hays, G. W. Hazelton, J. W. Hazelton, Hill, Hoar, Houghton, Kelley, Kellogg, Ketcham, Killinger, Lansing, Lowe, Maynard, McGrew, McJunkin, McKee, Mercer, Merriam, Monroe, L. Myers, Packard, Packer, Palmer, Peck, Pendleton, Perce, A. F. Perry, Peters, Platt, Poland, Prindle, Rainey, E. H. Roberts, Rusk, Sawyer, Sessions, Shanks, Sheldon, Shellabarger, H. B. Smith, J. A. Smith, Snyder, Sprague, Starkweather, Stevenson, Strong, Sypher, Taffe, Thomas, W. Townsend, Turner, Twichell, Tyner, Wakeman, Walden, Wallace, Walls, Whiteley, Willard, Williams of Indiana, J. M. Wilson, J. T. Wilson—102.

Nays—Messrs. *Acker*, *Archer*, *Arthur*, *Beck*, *Bell*, *Biggs*, *Bird*, *J. G. Blair*, *Braxton*, *Bright*, *J. Brooks*, *Caldwell*, *Campbell*, *Carroll*, *Comingo*, *Conner*, *Critcher*, *Crossland*, *Dox*, *Du Bose*, *Duke*, *Eldredge*, Farnsworth, *Forker*, *H. D. Foster*, *Garrett*, *Getz*, *Giddings*, *Golladay*, *Haldeman*, *Hambleton*, *Hancock*, *Handley*, *Hanks*, *Harper*, *J. T. Harris*, *Hereford*, *Hibbard*, *Holman*, *Kendall*, *Kerr*, *King*, *Lamison*, *Lewis*, *Manson*, *Marshall*, *McClelland*, *McCormick*, *McHenry*, *McIntyre*, *McNeely*, *Merrick*, *Morgan*, *Niblack*, *Potter*, *Price*, *Randall*, *Read*, *E. Y. Rice*, *J. M. Rice*, *Ritchie*, *W. R. Roberts*, *S. H. Rogers*, *Sherwood*, *Shober*, *Slater*, *Slocum*, *Sloss*, *Stevens*, *Storm*, *Swann*, *Terry*, *Waddell*, *Warren*, *Wells*, *Whitthorne*, *Williams* of New York, *Winchester*, *Young*—79.

The Senate, May 10, 1872, passed a substantially similar bill—yeas 36, nays 17. May 28, and again May 31, votes were taken in the House on suspending the rules and passing it, but in each case it failed—the former vote being, yeas 115, nays 87; the latter, yeas 101, nays 96. Mr. B. F. Butler, May 29, reported, from the Committee on Condition of Affairs in the Insurrectionary States, a similar bill, on which he proposed to call the previous question, a majority vote being sufficient to pass it, but the Democrats resorted to dilatory motions, and a vote was not reached.

XVI.

TARIFF AND TAXATION.

Duties on Tea and Coffee.

In House.

1871, March 13—Mr. Randall moved to suspend the rules and put upon its passage a bill (H. R. No. 174) that from and after the passage of this act tea and coffee shall be placed on the free list, and no further import duties shall be collected on the same; which was agreed to—yeas 140, nays 48:

Yeas—Messrs. *Acker*, *Adams*, Ambler, *Archer*, *Arthur*, Beatty, Bigby, *Biggs*, Bingham, A. Blair, *Braxton*, *Bright*, Buckley, Buffinton, Burdett, B. F. Butler, R. R. Butler, *Caldwell*, *Campbell*, *Carroll*, Cobb,

Comingo, Conger, *Crebs*, Creely, *Critcher*, *Crossland*, *Davis*, De Large, Dickey, *Dox*, *Duke*, Dunnell, *Eldredge*, Elliott, Finkelnburg, *Forker*, *H. D. Foster*, *Garrett*, *Getz*, *Golladay*, *Griffith*, *Haldeman*, Hale, *Handley*, *Hanks*, Harmer, *Harper*, *J. T. Harris*, Havens, Hay, J. W. Hazelton, *Hereford*, *Holman*, Kelley, *Kendall*, Killinger, *King*, *Lamison*, Lamport, *Leach*, *Lewis*, *Manson*, *Marshall*, Maynard, *McClelland*, *McCormick*, McGrew, *McHenry*, *McIntyre*, McJunkin, *McKinney*, *Merrick*, *B. F. Meyers*, Moore, Morey, *Morgan*, Morphis, L. Myers, *Niblack*, Packard, Packer, I. C. Parker, Perce, *E. Perry*, Platt, Porter, *Price*, Rainey, *Randall*, *Read*, *J. M. Rice*, *Ritchie*, E. H. Roberts, *W. R. Roberts*, *Robinson*, *J. Rogers*, Sawyer, Scofield, Seeley, Shanks, Sheldon, *Shober*, Shoemaker, *Slater*, *Slocum*, *Sloss*, J. A. Smith, W. C. Smith, *R. M. Speer*, T. J. Speer, *Stevens*, Stevenson, *Storm*, Stowell, St. John, *Sutherland*, *Swann*, Sypher, Terry, W. Townsend, *Tuthill*, Twichell, Tyner, Upson, *Van Trump*, *Vaughan*, *Voorhees*, *Waddell*, Waldron, Wallace, Walls, Whiteley, *Whitthorne*, Williams of Indiana, *Williams* of New York, J. M. Wilson, J. T. Wilson, *Wood*, *Young*—140.

NAYS—Messrs. Averill, Barber, *Bird*, *J. G. Blair*, G. M. Brooks, *J. Brooks*, Burchard, F. Clarke, Coburn, Cook, Cotton, *Cox*, Donnan, Eames, C. Foster, Frye, Garfield, Goodrich, Hawley, G. W. Hazelton, Hoar, *Kerr*, *Kinsella*, Lansing, Lynch, McCrary, Merriam, Monroe, Orr, Palmer, Peck, Pendleton, Peters, Poland, *Potter*, Prindle, *Roosevelt*, Rusk, Shellabarger, H. B. Smith, Stoughton, Taffe, Thomas, Wakeman, Walden, *Warren*, Wheeler, Willard—48.

IN SENATE.

1872, April 30—Mr. SCOTT moved to amend so as to make the bill read as follows:

That on and after the 1st day of July next tea and coffee shall be placed on the free list, and no further import duties shall be collected upon the same. And all tea and coffee which may be in the public stores or bonded warehouses on said first day of July shall be subject to no duty upon the entry thereof for consumption, and all tea and coffee remaining in bonded warehouses on said first day of July, upon which the duties shall have been paid, shall be entitled to a refund of the duties paid.

Which was agreed to, without a division, in Committee of the Whole.

Mr. MORRILL, of Vermont, moved two additional sections, one being the free list as previously adopted by the Senate, and the other making the same provision in relation to it as has been made in respect to tea and coffee. The amendment was disagreed to—yeas 17, nays 32:

YEAS—Messrs. Alcorn, *Bayard*, *Casserly*, Cole, *Goldthwaite*, Harlan, *Johnston*, Logan, Morrill of Maine, Morrill of Vermont, *Norwood*, Sherman, Spencer, Sprague, *Stevenson*, Trumbull, Wright—17.

NAYS—Messrs. Boreman, Buckingham, Caldwell, Cameron, Chandler, Clayton, Conkling, Corbett, Cragin, *Davis* of West Virginia, Ferry of Michigan, Flanagan, Frelinghuysen, Gilbert, *Hamilton* of Maryland, Hill, Howe, Lewis, Osborn, Patterson, Pomeroy, Pratt, Ramsey, Rice, Scott, Stewart, *Stockton*, Sumner, *Vickers*, West, Wilson, Windom—32.

Mr. TRUMBULL moved to insert the words "salt and coal" in the bill; which was disagreed to—yeas 14, nays 33:

YEAS—Messrs. Alcorn, *Bayard*, *Casserly*, Cole, Hamlin, Harlan, *Johnston*, Logan, *Norwood*, *Saulsbury*, Spencer, *Stevenson*, Trumbull, Windom—14.

NAYS—Messrs. Boreman, Buckingham, Caldwell, Cameron, Chandler, Clayton, Conkling, Corbett, Cragin, *Davis* of West Virginia, Ferry of Michigan, Flanagan, Frelinghuysen, Gilbert, *Goldthwaite*, *Hamilton* of Maryland, Hill, Hitchcock, Howe, Lewis, Osborn, Pomeroy, Pratt, Ramsey, Rice, Scott, Sherman, Sprague, Stewart, *Stockton*, *Vickers*, West, Wilson—33.

The amendment made in Committee of the Whole, fixing the 1st of July as the time at which it shall take effect, was concurred in—yeas 41, nays 7.

The negatives were Messrs. *Bayard*, *Casserly*, *Goldthwaite*, *Hamilton* of Maryland, *Saulsbury*, *Stockton*, and *Vickers*.

The bill then passed—yeas 39, nays 10:

YEAS—Messrs. Alcorn, Anthony, Boreman, Buckingham, Caldwell, Cameron, Chandler, Clayton, Cole, Conkling, Corbett, Cragin, *Davis* of West Virginia, Ferry of Michigan, Flanagan, Frelinghuysen, Gilbert, *Goldthwaite*, Harlan, Hill, Hitchcock, Howe, Lewis, Logan, *Norwood*, Osborn, Patterson, Pomeroy, Pratt, Ramsey, Rice, *Saulsbury*, Scott, Spencer, Stewart, *Stockton*, *Vickers*, West, Wilson—39.

NAYS—Messrs. *Bayard*, *Casserly*, *Hamilton* of Maryland, Hamlin, Morrill of Vermont, Sherman, Sprague, *Stevenson*, Trumbull, Windom—10.

IN HOUSE.

May 1—The amendments of the Senate were concurred in.

The bill was approved by the President May 1.

Previous Votes.

1872, February 12—Mr. MERCUR moved to suspend the rules, and pass the following:

Resolved, That the Committee of Ways and Means be, and hereby is, instructed to report a bill repealing all import duties upon tea and coffee.

Which was agreed to—yeas 139, nays 37, (not voting 63;) as follow:

YEAS—Messrs. *Acker*, *Adams*, Ambler, Ames, *Arthur*, Averill, Banks, Barber, Beatty, *Bell*, Bigby, Bingham, A. Blair, *J. G. Blair*, *Bright*, G. M. Brooks, Buffinton, Burdett, B. F. Butler, *Caldwell*, W. T. Clark, Cobb, Coghlan, Conger, *Conner*, *Crebs*, *Crossland*, *Davis*, Donnan, Duell, *Duke*, Dunnell, *Eldredge*, C. Foster, W. D. Foster, Frye, *Garrett*, *Getz*, *Golladay*, Goodrich, *Griffith*, *Haldeman*, Halsey, *Handley*, *Hanks*, Harmer, *J. T. Harris*, Havens, G. W. Hazelton, J. W. Hazelton, *Herndon*, Hill, Hoar, *Holman*, Houghton, Kelley, Kellogg, *Kendall*, Ketcham, Killinger, *King*, *Lamison*, Lamport, Lansing, *Leach*, Lowe, *Manson*, Maynard, *McClelland*, *McCormick*, McGrew, *McIntyre*, McJunkin, McKee, *McKinney*, *McNeely*, Mercur, Merriam, Monroe, *Morgan*, Morphis, L. Myers, Negley, *Niblack*, Packard, Packer, I. C. Parker, Peck, Pendleton, Perce, *E. Perry*, Platt, Porter, *Price*, Prindle, Rainey, *Randall*, *Read*, *J. M. Rice*, E. H. Roberts, *W. R. Roberts*, Sargent, Sawyer, Seeley, Shanks, Sheldon, Shellabarger, *Sherwood*, *Shober*, W. C. Smith, Snapp, Snyder, T. J. Speer, Sprague, Starkweather, *Storm*, *Sutherland*, Sypher, Taffe, W. Townsend, Turner, Tyner, Upson, *Vaughan*, *Voorhees*, *Waddell*, Walden, Waldron, Wallace, *Wells*, Wheeler, Whiteley, *Whitthorne*, Williams of Indiana, J. M. Wilson, J. T. Wilson, *Winchester*, *Wood*, *Young*—139.

NAYS—Messrs. *Beck*, Beveridge, *Bird*, *J. Brooks*, Burchard, F. Clarke, Coburn, *Comingo*, Cotton, Dawes, Farnsworth, Finkelnburg, Garfield, Hale, Hawley, *Hibbard*, Hooper, *Kerr*, *Kinsella*, *Lewis*, *Merrick*, Moore, Orr, Palmer, *H. W. Parker*, A. F. Perry, Poland, *Potter*, *Slater*, J. A. Smith, *Stevens*, Stoughton, Stowell, Twichell, Wakeman, *Warren*, Willard—37.

February 19—The bill was reported from the committee, and referred to the Committee of the Whole on the state of the Union.

February 19—Mr. MERCUR moved to suspend the rules, discharge the committee, and pass the bill, (H. R. No. 1537;) which was agreed to—yeas 155, nays 38:

YEAS—Messrs. *Acker*, *Adams*, Ambler, *Arthur*, Banks, Barber, *Barnum*, Barry, Beatty, *Bell*, Beveridge, Bigby, *Biggs*, Bingham, A. Blair, Boles, *Braxton*, G. M. Brooks, Buckley, Buffinton, B. F. Butler, *Caldwell*, *Campbell*, *Carroll*, W. T. Clark, Cobb, Coghlan, Conger, *Crebs*, Creely, Crocker, *Crossland*, Darrall, *Davis*, Dickey, Donnan, *Dox*, *Du Bose*, Duell, *Duke*, Eames, *Eldredge*, Farwell, *Forker*, C. Foster, W. D. Foster, Frye, *Garrett*, *Getz*, *Golladay*, *Griffith*, *Haldeman*, *Hambleton*, *Hancock*, *Handley*, *Hanks*, Harmer, *Harper*, *J. T. Harris*, Hays, G. W. Hazelton, J. W. Hazelton, *Hereford*, *Herndon*, Hill, Hoar, *Holman*, Kelley, Kellogg, *Kendall*, Killinger, *King*, *Lamison*, Lamport, *Leach*, Lowe, Lynch, *Manson*, Maynard, *McClelland*, *McCormick*, McGrew, *McHenry*, *McIntyre*, McJunkin, *McKinney*, *McNeely*, Mercur, Merriam, *B. F. Meyers*, Monroe, *Morgan*, Morphis, L. Myers, Negley, *Niblack*, Packard, Packer, I. C. Parker, Peck, *E. Perry*, Platt, Porter, *Price*, Prindle, Rainey, *Read*, E. H. Roberts, *W. R. Roberts*, *Robinson*, *J. Rogers*, Rusk, Sargent, Sawyer, Scofield, Sessions, Shanks, Sheldon, Shellabarger, *Sherwood*, *Shober*, Shoemaker, *Sloss*, *R. M. Speer*, T. J. Speer, Starkweather, *Storm*, Strong, *Sutherland*, *Swann*, Sypher, Taffe, *Terry*, Thomas, W. Townsend, Turner, *Tuthill*, Twichell, Tyner, Upson, *Van Trump*, *Vaughan*, *Voorhees*, *Waddell*, Walden, *Wells*, Wheeler, Whiteley, *Whitthorne*, Williams of Indiana, J. M. Wilson, J. T. Wilson, *Winchester*, *Wood*, *Young*—155.

NAYS—Messrs. *Beck*, *Bird*, *J. G. Blair*, *J. Brooks*, Burchard, Coburn, *Comingo*, Cotton, *Cox*, Dawes, Farnsworth, Finkelnburg, Garfield, Hale, Hawley, Hay, *Hibbard*, Hooper, *Kerr*, *Lewis*, McCrary, *Merrick*, Moore, Orr, Palmer, A. F. Perry, Peters, Poland, *Potter*, *E. Y. Rice*, *Slocum*, H. B. Smith, J. A. Smith, *Stevens*, Stevenson, Stoughton, Stowell, Willard—38.

IN SENATE.

Pending the consideration of the substitute reported by the Committee on Finance for House bill to repeal the duties on salt, (H. R. 173.)

Mr. SCOTT moved an amendment to the substitute offered by the committee, so as to place tea and coffee on the free list, striking out the proposed tax of ten cents on the former, and two cents per pound on the latter; which was agreed to—

1872, March 22—yeas 35, nays 13:

YEAS—Messrs. Alcorn, Anthony, Boreman, Caldwell, Cameron, Chandler, Clayton, *Cooper*, Corbett, *Davis* of West Virginia, Edmunds, Ferry of Michigan, Frelinghuysen, Gilbert, *Goldthwaite*, Hill, Hitchcock, Howe, Kellogg, *Kelly*, Morton, *Norwood*, Nye, Osborn, Pomeroy, Pratt, Ramsey, Rice, Robertson, Sawyer, Scott, Stewart, *Vickers*, West, Windom—35.

NAYS—Messrs. Ames, *Blair*, Conkling, Fenton, *Hamilton* of Maryland, Hamlin, *Johnston*, Morrill of Vermont, Schurz, Sherman, Sumner, Trumbull, Wright—13.

The Tariff Act.

IN HOUSE.

May 8—Pending the bill (No. 2322) reported by the majority of the Committee of Ways and Means, in Committee of the Whole,

Mr. KELLEY moved to strike out the enacting clause; which was agreed to—ayes 95, noes 75. Whereupon the committee rose and reported the fact to the House.

Mr. KELLEY moved that the House concur in this action, and that the bill reported by the minority of the Ways and Means—Mr. MAYNARD and himself—(No. 2348) be referred to the Committee of Ways and Means, with instructions to report the same to-morrow, as a substitute.

Mr. DAWES moved, as a substitute for the above instructions, the following:

Substitute for so much of said bill as is contained between lines twenty-two, page 2, and lines three hundred and seventy-two, page 16, inclusive, the following:

SEC. —. That on and after the day and year when this act shall take effect, in lieu of the duties imposed by law on the articles in this section enumerated, there shall be levied, collected, and paid on the goods, wares, and merchandise in this section enumerated and provided for, imported from foreign countries, ninety per cent. of the several duties and rates of duty now imposed by law upon said articles severally, it being the intent of this section to reduce existing duties on said articles ten per cent. of such duties; that is to say:

On all manufactures of cotton, or of which cotton is the component part of chief value;

On all wools, hair of the alpaca goat, and other animals, and all manufactures wholly or in part of wool or hair of the alpaca, and other animals;

On all iron and manufactures of iron, or manufactures of which iron is the component material of chief value, excepting on all metals not herein otherwise provided for, and on all manufactures of metals, of which either of them is the component part of chief value;

On all manufactures of India rubber, gutta-percha, or straw, and on oil-cloths of all descriptions: *Provided*, That the rate of duty upon umbrellas, parasols, and sunshades shall in no case be less than is imposed upon goods of the same material and quality as the coverings thereof.

Mr. FINKELNBURG moved to make the duties "eighty" per cent. on existing rates instead of "ninety;" which was disagreed to—yeas 80, nays 110:

YEAS—Messrs. *Adams*, *Archer*, *Arthur*, Averill, Beatty, *Beck*, Beveridge, *Bird*, *J. G. Blair*, *Braxton*, *Bright*, *J. Brooks*, Burchard, *Caldwell*, *Comingo*, *Conner*, Cotton, *Cox*, *Crebs*, *Critcher*, *Crossland*, Donnan, *Dox*, *Duke*, Dunnell, *Eldredge*, *Ely*, Farnsworth, Finkelnburg, *Golladay*, *Handley*, *Hanks*, Hawley, Hay, *Hereford*, *Herndon*, *Hibbard*, *Kendall*, *Kerr*, *King*, *Lamison*, Lowe, *Marshall*, *McCormick*, McCrary, *McHenry*, *McIntyre*, *McKinney*, *McNeely*, *Merrick*, *Morgan*, Orr, *H. W. Parker*, *E. Perry*, *Potter*, *Price*, *Read*, *E. Y. Rice*, *J. M. Rice*, *Ritchie*, *W. R. Roberts*, *Robinson*, *Roosevelt*, Shanks, *Slater*, *Slocum*, Stevenson, *Terry*, *D. Townsend*, Turner, *Tuthill*, Tyner, *Vaughan*, *Voorhees*, *Waddell*, *Whitthorne*, *Williams* of New York, J. M. Wilson, *Winchester*, *Wood*—80.

NAYS—Messrs. *Acker*, Ambler, Ames, Banks, Barber, *Barnum*, *Bell*, Bigby, Bingham, Boles, G. M. Brooks, Buffinton, Burdett, B. F. Butler, R. R. Butler, Cobb, Coburn, Coghlan, Conger, Creely, Crocker, Darrall, Dawes, Duell, Eames, Elliott, Farwell, C. Foster, *H. D. Foster*, W. D. Foster, Frye, Garfield, *Getz*, Goodrich, *Griffith*, *Haldeman*, Hale, Halsey, Harmer, *Harper*, G. W. Hazelton, Hill, Hoar, Houghton, Kelley, Kellogg, Ketcham, Killinger, Lamport, Lansing, Maynard, *McClelland*, McGrew, Mercur, Merriam, *B. F. Meyers*, Monroe, Morey, L. Meyers, Packard, Packer, Palmer, I. C. Parker, Peck, Pendleton, Perce, Peters, Poland, Prindle, Rainey, *Randall*, E. H. Roberts, *Rogers*, Rusk, Sargent, Sawyer, Scofield, Seeley, Sessions, Sheldon, *Sherwood*, Shoemaker, H. B. Smith, J. A. Smith, W. C. Smith, Snapp, Snyder, *R. M. Speer*, T. J. Speer, Sprague, *Storm*, Stoughton, Strong, St. John, *Sutherland*, Sypher, Taffe, W. Townsend, Twichell, Upson, Wakeman, Walden, Wallace, Walls, *Warren*, Wheeler, Whiteley, Willard, Williams of Indiana, J. T. Wilson—110.

Mr. DAWES's substitute was then agreed to—yeas 111, nays 77:

YEAS—Messrs. *Adams*, *Archer*, *Arthur*, Averill,

Barnum, Beatty, *Beck*, Beveridge, Bigby, *Bird*, *Braxton*, *Bright*, *J. Brooks*, Buffinton, Burchard, *Caldwell*, Coburn, Coghlan, *Comingo*, *Conner*, Cotton, *Cox*, *Crebs*, *Critcher*, *Crossland*, Dawes, Donnan, *Dox*, *Duke*, Dunnell, *Eldredge*, *Ely*, Farnsworth, Finkelnburg, Frye, Garfield, *Getz*, *Golladay*, Goodrich, *Haldeman*, Hale, *Handley*, *Hanks*, Havens, Hawley, Hay, G. W. Hazelton, *Hereford*, *Herndon*, *Hibbard*, *Kendall*, *Kerr*, Ketcham, *King*, *Lamison*, Lowe, *Marshall*, *McCormick*, McCrary, *McHenry*, *McIntyre*, *McKinney*, *McNeely*, *Merrick*, *B. F. Meyers*, *Morgan*, Orr, Packard, Palmer, *H. W. Parker*, Perce, *E. Perry*, Peters, *Potter*, *Price*, *Read*, *E. Y. Rice*, *J. M. Rice*, *Ritchie*, E. H. Roberts, *W. R. Roberts*, *Roosevelt*, Rusk, Shanks, *Slater*, *Slocum*, W. C. Smith, Snyder, T. J. Speer, Stevenson, *Storm*, Stoughton, Strong, *Terry*, *D. Townsend*, Turner, *Tuthill*, Twichell, Tyner, *Vaughan*, *Voorhees*, Walden, *Warren*, Wheeler, Whiteley, *Whitthorne*, Williams of Indiana, *Williams* of New York, J. M. Wilson, *Winchester*, *Wood*—111.

NAYS—Messrs. *Acker*, Ames, Banks, Barber, *Bell*, Bingham, Boles, G. M. Brooks, Burdett, R. R. Butler, Conger, Creely, Crocker, Darrall, Duell, Eames, Elliott, Farwell, C. Foster, *H. D. Foster*, W. D. Foster, *Griffith*, Halsey, Harmer, *Harper*, Hill, Hoar, Houghton, Kelley, Kellogg, Killinger, Lamport, Lansing, *Leach*, Maynard, *McClelland*, McGrew, Mercur, Merriam, Monroe, Morey, L. Myers, Packer, I. C. Parker, Peck, Pendleton, Platt, Poland, Prindle, Rainey, *Randall*, *Rogers*, Sargent, Sawyer, Scofield, Seeley, Sessions, Sheldon, *Sherwood*, Shoemaker, H. B. Smith, J. A. Smith, Snapp, *R. M. Speer*, Sprague, Stowell, St. John, Sypher, Taffe, W. Townsend, Upson, *Waddell*, Wakeman, Wallace, Walls, Willard, J. T. Wilson—77.

The motion to refer the bill, as amended, was then agreed to—yeas 117, nays 75:

YEAS—Messrs. *Adams*, *Archer*, *Arthur*, Averill, *Barnum*, Beatty, *Beck*, Beveridge, Bigby, *Bird*, *J. G. Blair*, *Braxton*, *Bright*, *J. Brooks*, Buffinton, Burchard, B. F. Butler, *Caldwell*, Coburn, Coghlan, *Comingo*, Cotton, *Cox*, *Crebs*, *Critcher*, *Crossland*, Dawes, Donnan, *Dox*, *Duke*, Dunnell, *Eldredge*, *Ely*, Farnsworth, Finkelnburg, Frye, Garfield, *Golladay*, Goodrich, *Haldeman*, Hale, *Handley*, *J. T. Harris*, Havens, Hawley, Hay, G. W. Hazelton, *Hereford*, *Herndon*, *Hibbard*, Hoar, Kellogg, *Kendall*, *Kerr*, *King*, *Lamison*, Lowe, *Marshall*, *McCormick*, McCrary, *McHenry*, *McIntyre*, *McNeely*, *Merrick*, *B. F. Meyers*, *Morgan*, Orr, Packard, Palmer, *H. W. Parker*, Perce, *E. Perry*, Peters, Platt, *Potter*, *Price*, Prindle, *Read*, *E. Y. Rice*, *J. M. Rice*, *Ritchie*, E. H. Roberts, *W. R. Roberts*, *Robinson*, Rusk, Sargent, Sawyer, Shanks, Sheldon, *Slater*, *Slocum*, W. C. Smith, T. J. Speer, *Stevens*, Stevenson, *Storm*, Stoughton, Strong, Sypher, Taffe, *Terry*, *D. Townsend*, Turner, *Tuthill*, Twichell, Tyner, *Vaughan*, Walden, *Warren*, Wheeler, Whiteley, *Whitthorne*, Williams of Indiana, *Williams* of New York, J. M. Wilson, *Winchester*, *Wood*—117.

NAYS—Messrs. *Acker*, Ambler, Ames, Banks, Barber, *Bell*, Bingham, A. Blair, Boles, G. M. Brooks, Burdett, R. R. Butler, Cobb, Conger, *Conner*, Creely, Crocker, Darrall, Duell, Eames, Elliott, Farwell, *H. D. Foster*, W. D. Foster, *Getz*, *Griffith*, Halsey, Harmer, *Harper*, Hill, Houghton, Kelley, Killinger, Lamport, Lansing, *Leach*, Maynard, *McClelland*, McGrew, McJunkin, Mercur, Merriam, Monroe, Morey, L. Myers, Packer, I. C. Parker, Peck, Pendleton, Poland, Rainey, *Randall*, *Rogers*, Scofield, Seeley, Sessions, *Sherwood*, Shoemaker, H. B. Smith, J. A. Smith, Snapp, Snyder, *R. M. Speer*, Sprague, Starkweather, Stowell, St. John, W. Townsend, Upson, *Waddell*, Wakeman, Wallace, Walls, Willard, J. T. Wilson—75.

The bill was subsequently reported by the committee, considered and amended in several respects by the House, sitting in Committee of the Whole; when—

May 20—Mr. DAWES offered this resolution:

Resolved, That the rules be so suspended that the Committee of the Whole be discharged from the further consideration of the substitute for the House bill No. 2322, being a bill to reduce duties on imports, and to reduce internal taxes, and for other purposes, and that the same, as it has been amended in Committee of the Whole, do pass.

Which was agreed to—yeas 149, nays 61:

YEAS—Messrs. Ames, *Archer*, Banks, *Barnum*, *Beck*, *Bell*, Bigby, *Biggs*, *Bird*, *J. G. Blair*, *Braxton*, *Bright*, Buckley, Buffinton, Burchard, Burdett, B. F. Butler, R. R. Butler, *Caldwell*, Clarke, Cobb, Coburn, *Comingo*, *Conner*, Cotton, *Cox*, *Crebs*, *Critcher*, *Crossland*, Darrall, *Davis*, Dawes, Donnan, *Duke*, Dunnell, *Ely*, Farnsworth, Farwell, Finkelnburg, *Forker*, C. Foster, Frye, Garfield, *Garrett*, *Giddings*, *Golladay*, *Haldeman*, Hale, *Hancock*, *Handley*, *Harper*, G. E. Harris, *J. T. Harris*, Havens, Hawley, Hay, Hays, G. W. Hazelton, *Hereford*, *Herndon*, *Hibbard*, Hoar, *Holman*, Houghton, Kellogg, *Kendall*, *Kerr*, Ketcham, *King*, Lamport, Lansing, *Leach*, *Lewis*, Lowe, Lynch, *Manson*, *Marshall*, *McCormick*, McCrary, McGrew, *McHenry*, *McIntyre*, *McNeely*, Merriam, *Merrick*, *Mitchell*, Moore, *Morgan*, Morphis, *Niblack*, Orr, Packard, Palmer, *H. W. Parker*, I. C. Parker, Peters, *Potter*, *Price*, Rainey, *Read*, *E. Y. Rice*, E. H. Roberts, *W. R. Roberts*, *Robinson*, Rusk, Sawyer, Seeley, Sessions, Shanks, Sheldon, Shellabarger, *Sherwood*, *Slater*, *Sloss*, Snapp, T. J. Speer, Sprague, *Stevens*, *Storm*, Stoughton, Stowell, Strong, *Swann*, Taffe, *Terry*, Thomas, Turner, *Tuthill*, Twichell, Tyner, *Vaughan*, *Voorhees*, *Waddell*, Wakeman, Walden, Waldron, Wallace, Walls, *Warren*, *Wells*, Wheeler, Whiteley, *Whitthorne*, Williams of Indiana, *Williams* of New York, J. M. Wilson, *Winchester*, *Wood*, *Young*—149.

NAYS—Messrs. *Acker*, *Adams*, Ambler, *Arthur*, Averill, Barber, Barry, Beatty, Bingham, A. Blair, *Campbell*, *Carroll*, Coghlan, Conger, Dickey, Duell, Eames, *Eldredge*, Elliott, *H. D. Foster*, W. D. Foster, *Getz*, *Griffith*, Halsey, Harmer, J. W. Hazelton, Hill, Hooper, Kelley, Killinger, *Lamison*, Maynard, *McClelland*, McJunkin, McKee, Mercur, *B. F. Meyers*, L. Myers, Negley, Packer, Peck, Pendleton, Perce, A. F. Perry, Poland, *Randall*, *J. M. Rice*, *Rogers*, Scofield, Shoemaker, *Slocum*, H. B. Smith, J. A. Smith, *R. M. Speer*, Starkweather, Stevenson, *Sutherland* W. Townsend, Upson, Willard, J. T. Wilson—61.

IN SENATE.

The bill was considered, amended in many respects, and passed May 31—yeas 49, nays 3, (Messrs. Chandler, Scott, and Sprague.)

It finally went to a committee of conference, whose report was adopted by both Houses without a division.

The duties, as fixed in it and contrasted with the previous rates, will be found stated in table H, chapter XXIII.

Duty on Salt.

IN HOUSE.

1871, March 14—Mr. EUGENE HALE moved to suspend the rules and pass a bill which provides that from and after the passage of this act salt shall be placed on the free list, and no further import duties shall be collected on the same; which was agreed to—yeas 147, nays 46, as follow:

YEAS—Messrs. *Acker*, *Adams*, *Archer*, *Arthur*, Averill, Barber, Beatty, *Beck*, Bigby, Bingham, *Bird*, *J. G. Blair*, *Braxton*, *Bright*, G. M. Brooks, *J. Brooks*, Buckley, Buffinton, Burchard, Burdett, R. R. Butler, *Caldwell*, *Campbell*, Cobb, Coburn, *Comingo*, Cook, Cotton, *Crebs*, *Critcher*, *Crossland*, *Davis*, Dawes, De Large, Donnan, *Dox*, *Du Bose*, *Duke*, Dunnell, Eames, *Eldredge*, Elliott, *Ely*, Farnsworth, Finkelnburg, *Forker*, C. Foster, Frye, Garfield, *Garrett*, *Getz*, *Golladay*, *Haldeman*, Hale, *Handley*, *Hanks*, *Harper*, G. E. Harris, *J. T. Harris*, Hawley, Hay, G. W. Hazelton, *Hereford*, Hoar, *Holman*, *Kendall*, *Kerr*, Ketcham, *King*, *Kinsella*, *Lamison*, Lamport, *Leach*, *Lewis*, Lynch, *Manson*, *Marshall*, *McCormick*, McCrary, *McHenry*, *McIntyre*, *McKinney*, *Merrick*, *B. F. Meyers*, Monroe, Moore, Morey, *Morgan*, Morphis, *Niblack*, Orr, Packard, Pendleton, Perce, *E. Perry*, Peters, *Potter*, *Price*, *Read*,

E. Y. Rice, *J. M. Rice*, *Ritchie*, *W. R. Roberts*, *Robinson*, *Roosevelt*, Rusk, Shanks, Sheldon, Shellabarger, *Shober*, *Slater*, *Slocum*, *Sloss*, H. B. Smith, J. A. Smith, W. C. Smith, T. J. Speer, *Stevens*, Stevenson, *Storm*, Stoughton, *Swann*, Sypher, Taffe, *Terry*, *Tuthill*, Twichell, Tyner, Upson, *Van Trump*, *Vaughan*, *Voorhees*, *Waddell*, Wakeman, Walden, Waldron, Wallace, *Warren*, Wheeler, Whiteley, *Whitthorne*, Williams of Indiana, *Williams* of New York, J. M. Wilson, J. T. Wilson, *Wood*, *Young*—147.

NAYS—Messrs. Ambler, A. Blair, Conger, Creely, Dickey, *H. D. Foster*, Goodrich, *Griffith*, Harmer, Havens, J. W. Hazelton, Hooper, Kelley, Killinger, Lansing, Lowe, Maynard, *McClelland*, McGrew, McJunkin, Merriam, L. Myers, Packer, I. C. Parker, Peck, Platt, Porter, Prindle, Rainey, *Randall*, E. H. Roberts, *J. Rogers*, Sawyer, Scofield, Seeley, Sessions, Shoemaker, *R. M. Speer*, Sprague, Stowell, St. John, *Sutherland*, Thomas, W. Townsend, Walls, Willard—46.

The Senate took no action upon the bill.

Duty on Coal.

IN HOUSE.

1871, March 13—Mr. FARNSWORTH moved to suspend the rules and pass a bill that from and after the passage of this joint resolution no tax or duty shall be levied or collected upon foreign coal; which was agreed to—yeas 130, nays 57:

YEAS—Messrs. *Acker*, *Adams*, *Arthur*, Averill, Barber, Beatty, *Beck*, Bingham, *Bird*, *J. G. Blair*, *Braxton*, *Bright*, G. M. Brooks, *J. Brooks*, Buckley, Buffinton, Burchard, *Caldwell*, *Campbell*, *Carroll*, F. Clarke, Coburn, *Comingo*, Cook, Cotton, *Cox*, *Crebs*, *Critcher*, *Crossland*, Dawes, Donnan, *Du Bose*, *Duke*, Dunnell, Eames, *Eldredge*, *Ely*, Farnsworth, Finkelnburg, *Forker*, C. Foster, Frye, Garfield, *Garrett*, *Golladay*, *Haldeman*, Hale, *Handley*, *Hanks*, *Harper*, *J. T. Harris*, Hawley, Hay, G. W. Hazelton, *Holman*, *Kendall*, *Kerr*, Ketcham, *King*, *Kinsella*, *Lamison*, *Leach*, *Lewis*, Lynch, *Manson*, *Marshall*, *McCormick*, McCrary, *McHenry*, *McIntyre*, *McKinney*, Merriam, *B. F. Meyers*, Monroe, Moore, Morey, *Morgan*, *Niblack*, Orr, Packard, Palmer, Pendleton, *E. Perry*, Peters, *Potter*, *Price*, *Read*, *E. Y. Rice*, *J. M. Rice*, E. H. Roberts, *W. R. Roberts*, *Robinson*, *Roosevelt*, Seeley, Shanks, Shellabarger, *Shober*, *Slater*, *Slocum*, *Sloss*, J. A. Smith, W. C. Smith, *Stevens*, Stevenson, *Storm*, Stoughton, Sypher, Taffe, *Terry*, *Tuthill*, Twichell, Tyner, Upson, *Van Trump*, *Vaughan*, *Voorhees*, *Waddell*, Wakeman, Walden, Waldron, *Warren*, Wheeler, Whiteley, *Whitthorne*, Williams of Indiana, *Williams* of New York, J. M. Wilson, J. T. Wilson, *Wood*, *Young*—130.

NAYS—Messrs. Ambler, *Archer*, Bigby, A. Blair, Burdett, B. F. Butler, R. R. Butler, Cobb, Conger, Creely, *Davis*, De Large, Dickey, *Dox*, Elliott, *H. D. Foster*, *Getz*, Goodrich, *Griffith*, Harmer, Havens, J. W. Hazelton, *Hereford*, Kelley, Killinger, Lamport, Maynard, *McClelland*, McGrew, McJunkin, *Merrick*, Morphis, L. Myers, Packer, I. C. Parker, Platt, Poland, Porter, Prindle, Rainey, *Randall*, *Ritchie*, Sawyer, Scofield, Shoemaker, H. B. Smith, *R. M. Speer*, T. J. Speer, Sprague, Stowell, St. John, *Swann*, Thomas, W. Townsend, Wallace, Walls, Willard—57.

The Senate took no action on the bill.

Resolutions on Tariff and Taxation.

IN HOUSE.

1871, March 27—Mr. HIBBARD offered the following; which were referred to the Committee of Ways and Means:

Resolved, First, that the financial policy which aims merely at a rapid extinguishment of the public debt by perpetuating the burdens of taxation is inexpedient and impolitic, and that the faith and credit of the Government depend on the development of the resources of the country and their relief from inordinate taxation.

Second, that economy requires that the annual taxation should not exceed $250,000,000, including interest, and $25,000,000 principal of the public debt.

Third, that the tariff should be so reformed as to be a tax for revenue only, and not for the protection of class interests at the general expense.

A motion to table them was lost—yeas 2, (Messrs. G. M. BROOKS and MAYNARD,) nays 153.

Same day—Mr. HOSEA W. PARKER offered the following; which was also referred to the Committee of Ways and Means:

Resolved, That the tariff should be so reformed as to be a tax for revenue only, and not for the protection of class interests at the general expense.

April 10—The vote on referring was—yeas 98, nays 78:

YEAS—Messrs. *Acker*, Ambler, Averill, Barber, Barry, Bigby, A. Blair, G. M. Brooks, Buckley, Buffinton, Burdett, Cobb, Coburn, Conger, Cook, Cotton, Creely, De Large, Donnan, Dunnell, Eames, Elliott, C. Foster, *H. D. Foster*, Frye, Garfield, *Griffith*, Hale, G. E. Harris, Havens, Hawley, J. W. Hazelton, Hill, Hoar, Hooper, Kelley, *Kendall*, Ketcham, Lamport, Lansing, Lowe, Lynch, Maynard, *McClelland*, McCrary, McGrew, McJunkin, McKee, Mercur, Merriam, Monroe, Moore, Morey, Orr, Packard, Palmer, I. C. Parker, Peck, Pendleton, Perce, A. F. Perry, Platt, Poland, Porter, Prindle, *Randall*, E. H. Roberts, *J. Rogers*, Rusk, Sawyer, Scofield, Seeley, Shanks, Sheldon, Shellabarger, Shoemaker, J. A. Smith, Snyder, Sprague, Stoughton, Stowell, St. John, Taffe, Thomas, W. Townsend, Turner, Twichell, Tyner, Wakeman, Walden, Waldron, Wallace, Walls, Wheeler, Whiteley, Williams of Indiana, J. M. Wilson, J. T. Wilson—98.

NAYS—Messrs. *Adams*, *Archer*, *Arthur*, Beatty, *Beck*, *Bell*, *Bird*, *Braxton*, *Bright*, Burchard, *Caldwell*, *Campbell*, *Comingo*, *Cox*, *Crebs*, *Crossland*, *Davis*, *Dox*, *Du Bose*, *Duke*, *Edwards*, *Eldredge*, *Ely*, Farnsworth, Finkelnburg, *Garrett*, *Golladay*, *Hambleton*, *Handley*, *Hanks*, *Harper*, *J. T. Harris*, Hay, *Hereford*, *Hibbard*, *Holman*, *Kerr*, *King*, *Lamison*, *Leach*, *Lewis*, *Manson* *Marshall*, *McCormick*, *McHenry*, *McIntyre*, *McKinney*, *McNeely*, *B. F. Meyers*, *Niblack*, *H. W. Parker*, *E. Perry*, *Potter*, *E. Y. Rice*, *J. M. Rice*, *W. R. Roberts*, *Robinson*, *Roosevelt*, *Sherwood*, *Shober*, *Slater*, *Slocum*, *Sloss*, *Stevens*, Stevenson, *Storm*, *Swann*, *Terry*, *Van Trump*, *Vaughan*, *Voorhees*, *Waddell*, *Wells*, *Whitthorne*, *Williams* of New York, *Winchester*, *Wood*, *Young*—78.

April 10—Mr. BELL submitted the following:

Whereas the Government of the United States was established by the people for their own protection and benefit, and should be administered on the strictest principles of frugality and economy in its expenditures, and that no money should be taken from the people by taxation except to supply the necessary wants of the Government administered upon such principles; and whereas the money annually raised by taxation upon the people should not exceed the sum of $250,000,000, said sum being amply sufficient to provide for the ordinary expenditures of the Government, the payment of the interest of the public debt, and in part liquidating the interest of said debt: Therefore,

Resolved, That this House disapproves the inordinate taxation to pay off immense sums of the public debt, as heretofore practiced by the Secretary of the Treasury, and would limit the sum for the principal of said debt to $25,000,000.

No vote was taken upon it.

1871, April 10—Mr. KELLEY moved that the rules be suspended that he may offer, and the House pass, this resolution:

Resolved, That this House reaffirms the resolution adopted on the 12th of December, 1870, by the House of Representatives of the Fortieth* Congress, declaring that the true principle of revenue reform points to the abolition of the internal revenue system, which was created as a war measure to provide for extraordinary expenses, and the continuance of which involves the employment, at a cost of millions of dollars annually, of an army of assessors, collectors, supervisors, detectives, and other officers previously unknown, and requires the repeal at the earliest day consistent with the maintenance of the faith and credit of the Government of all stamp and other internal taxes; and that properly adjusted rates shall be retained on distilled spirits, tobacco, and malt liquors so long as the legitimate expenses of the Government require the collection of any sum from internal taxes.

Which was agreed to—yeas 130, nays 21:

YEAS—Messrs. *Acker*, *Adams*, Ambler, *Archer*, *Arthur*, Averill, Barber, Barry, Beatty, Blair, *Braxton*, G. M. Brooks, Buffinton, Burdett, *Carroll*, Coburn, *Comingo*, Conger, Creely, *Crossland*, *Davis*, Dawes, De Large, Dickey, *Du Bose*, *Duke*, Eames, *Edwards*, Elliott, *Ely*, Farwell, C. Foster, Garfield, *Golladay*, *Griffith*, *Handley*, *Hanks*, *Harper*, Havens, Hawley, G. W. Hazelton, J. W. Hazelton, *Hereford*, *Hibbard*, Hill, Hoar, *Holman*, Hooper, Kelley, *Kendall*, Ketcham, *King*, *Lamison*, Lamport, Lansing, *Leach*, *Lewis*, Lowe, Lynch, *Manson*, Maynard, *McClelland*, *McCormick*, *McHenry*, *McIntyre*, McJunkin, McKee, *McKinney*, Mercur, Merriam, *Merrick*, *B. F. Meyers*, Monroe, Moore, Morey, *Niblack*, Orr, Packard, Packer, Palmer, *H. W. Parker*, I. C. Parker, Peck, Pendleton, *E. Perry*, Platt, Poland, Porter, *Randall*, E. H. Roberts, *W. R. Roberts*, *J. Rogers*, Rusk, Sawyer, Scofield, Seeley, Sheldon, Shellabarger, *Sherwood*, *Shober*, *Slater*, *Slocum*, *Sloss*, J. A. Smith, Snyder, T. J. Speer, Sprague, *Stevens*, *Storm*, Stoughton, St. John, Thomas, W. Townsend, Turner, Twichell, Tyner, *Waddell*, Wakeman, Walden, Waldron, Wallace, Walls, *Wells*, Wheeler, Whiteley, Williams of Indiana, *Williams* of New York, J. T. Wilson, *Wood*, *Young*—130.

NAYS—Messrs. *Bell*, *Bird*, *Bright*, Buckley, Burchard, *Caldwell*, *Campbell*, Cotton, *Cox*, Donnan, Dunnell, Finkelnburg, *Garrett*, G. E. Harris, *Kerr*, *E. Y. Rice*, *Roosevelt*, Shanks, Taffe, *Terry*, *Vaughan*—21.

Duty on Salt and Coal.

1872, February 19—Mr. HALE moved to suspend the rules and pass this resolution:

Resolved, That the Committee of Ways and Means be, and the same is hereby, instructed, whenever it shall report a bill changing any import duties, to place salt and coal upon the free list.

Which was disagreed to—yeas 102, nays 86, (two-thirds not having voted in the affirmative:)

YEAS—Messrs. *Acker*, *Adams*, *Arthur*, Barber, *Barnum*, Beatty, *Bell*, *Biggs*, *Bird*, *Braxton*, G. M. Brooks, Buckley, *Caldwell*, *Campbell*, Coburn, Coghlan, Cotton, *Cox*, *Crebs*, *Critcher*, *Crossland*, Donnan, *Dox*, *Du Bose*, *Duke*, Dunnell, Eames, *Eldredge*, Farnsworth, *Forker*, *Garrett*, *Getz*, *Golladay*, *Haldeman*, Hale, *Handley*, *Hanks*, G. E. Harris, *J. T. Harris*, Hawley, Hay, Hays, G. W. Hazelton, *Herndon*, *Hibbard*, *Holman*, Kellogg, *Kendall*, *King*, *Lamison*, Lowe, Lynch, *Marshall*, *McCormick*, *McHenry*, McKee, *McKinney*, *McNeely*, *B. F. Meyers*, Monroe, Moore, *Morgan*, *Niblack*, Orr, Packard, Palmer, *H. W. Parker*, I. C. Parker, *E. Perry*, *Price*, *Read*, *E. Y. Rice*, *W. R. Roberts*, *Robinson*, Sargent, Shanks, Sheldon, *Shober*, *Slater*, *Sloss*, *Stevens*, Stevenson, *Storm*, Stougaton, Strong, *Terry*, *Tuthill*, Twichell, Tyner, *Van Trump*, *Vaughan*, *Voorhees*, *Waddell*, Walden, Wheeler, *Whitthorne*, Williams of Indiana, *Williams* of New York, J. M. Wilson, *Winchester*, *Wood*, *Young*—102.

NAYS—Messrs. Ambler, Averill, Barry, *Beck*, Beveridge, Bigby, Bingham, A. Blair, *J. G. Blair*, Boles, *J. Brooks*, Buffinton, Burchard, Burdett, W. T. Clark, Cobb, Conger, Creely, Crocker, Darrall, *Davis*, Dawes, Dickey, Duell, Finkelnburg, C. Foster, W. D. Foster, Frye, *Griffith*, *Hancock*, Harmer, *Harper*, J. W. Hazelton, Hill, Hoar, Houghton, Kelley, Ketcham, Killinger, Lamport, *Lewis*, Maynard, *McClelland*, McCrary, McGrew, McJunkin, Mercur, *Merrick*, Morphis, L. Myers, Negley, Packer, Peck, Perce, Platt, Poland, Porter, *Potter*, Prindle, Rainey, E. H. Roberts, *J. Rogers*, Sawyer, Scofield, Seeley, Sessions, Shellabarger, *Sherwood*, Shoemaker, H. B. Smith, J. A. Smith, *R. M. Speer*, T. J. Speer, Sprague, Starkweather, Stowell, *Sutherland*, *Swann*, Sypher, Taffe, Thomas, W. Townsend, Turner, Upson, Whiteley, Willard, J. T. Wilson—86.

Duty on Pig Iron.

1872, February 26—Mr. COX moved to suspend the rules and pass this resolution:

Whereas it appears by the report of the Secretary of the Treasury, page 4, that during the first six months of the calendar year 1871 there was an increase of one hundred and twenty per cent in the quantity of pig iron, which result, as well as the increase of revenue therefrom, was produced by the reduction of the tariff on that article under the act of the 14th July, 1870; and whereas iron is an article of general use and consumption: Therefore,

Resolved, That in the judgment of this House a bill should be passed reducing the tariff on pig iron to five dollars per ton or less, and that the Committee of Ways and Means be instructed to bring in a bill for that purpose.

Which was disagreed to—yeas 74, nays 99:

YEAS—Messrs. *Adams*, *Archer*, *Arthur*, Beatty, *Beck*, *Bell*, Beveridge, *Biggs*, *Bird*, *J. G. Blair*, *Braxton*, *Bright*, *Caldwell*, *Campbell*, *Comingo*, *Conner*, Cotton, *Cox*, *Crebs*, *Critcher*, *Crossland*, Darrall, *Du Bose*, *Duke*, Dunnell, *Eldredge*, *Ely*, *Golladay*, Hale, *Hambleton*, *Hancock*, *Handley*, G. E. Harris, *J. T. Harris*, Hay, Hays, *Hereford*, *Herndon*, *Hibbard*, *Holman*, Houghton, *Kendall*, *Kerr*, *King*, *Lamison*, *Lewis*, *Manson*, *Marshall*, *McCormick*, *McHenry*, *McIntyre*, *McNeely*, *Merrick*, *Morgan*, *H. W. Parker*, *Potter*, *Read*, *E. Y. Rice*, *W. R. Roberts*, *Roosevelt*, *Slater*, *Slocum*, *Sloss*, *Stevens*, Stevenson, *Terry*, *Tuthill*, *Van Trump*, *Vaughan*, Walden, *Warren*, *Whitthorne*, *Winchester*, *Wood*, *Young*—74.

NAYS—Messrs. *Acker*, Ames, Banks, Barber, Bigby, Bingham, A. Blair, Boles, G. M. Brooks, Buckley, Buffinton, Burchard, R. R. Butler, Cobb, Coburn, Coghlan, Conger, Crocker, Dawes, Dickey, Donnan, Duell, Eames, Finkelnburg, *H. D. Foster*, W. D. Foster, Garfield, *Garrett*, *Getz*, *Griffith*, *Haldeman*, Halsey, Hawley, G. W. Hazelton, J. W. Hazelton, Hill, Hoar, Kelley, Ketcham, Killinger, Lamport, Lowe, Lynch, Maynard, *McClelland*, McGrew, McJunkin, Mercur, Merriam, *B. F. Meyers*, Monroe, Morphis, L. Myers, Negley, Packard, Packer, I. C. Parker, Peck, Pendleton, Perce, A. F. Perry, Platt, Porter, Prindle, Sargent, Sawyer, Scofield, Seeley, Sessions, Shanks, Shellabarger, *Sherwood*, Shoemaker, H. B. Smith, Snapp, Snyder, *R. M. Speer*, T. J. Speer, Sprague, Starkweather, Stoughton, *Sutherland*, Taffe, Thomas, W. Townsend, Turner, Twichell, Tyner, Upson, Wakeman, Waldron, Wallace, Wheeler, Whiteley, Willard, Williams of Indiana, J. M. Wilson, J. T. Wilson—99.

* Forty-First.

XVII.

RELATIONS OF THE UNITED STATES AND GREAT BRITAIN.

Treaty between the United States and Great Britain—Claims, Fisheries, Navigation of the St. Lawrence, &c., American Lumber on the River St. John, Boundary—Concluded May 8, 1871; ratifications exchanged June 17, 1871; proclaimed July 4, 1871.

By the President of the United States of America.

A Proclamation.

Whereas a treaty, between the United States of America and her Majesty the Queen of the United Kingdom of Great Britain and Ireland, concerning the settlement of all causes of difference between the two countries, was concluded and signed at Washington by the high commissioners and plenipotentiaries of the respective Governments on the 8th day of May last; which treaty is, word for word, as follows:

The United States of America and her Britannic Majesty, being desirous to provide for an amicable settlement of all causes of difference between the two countries, have for that purpose appointed their respective plenipotentiaries, that is to say: the President of the United States has appointed, on the part of the United States, as commissioners in a joint high commission and plenipotentiaries, Hamilton Fish, Secretary of State; Robert Cumming Schenck, envoy extraordinary and minister plenipotentiary to Great Britain; Samuel Nelson, an associate justice of the Supreme Court of the United States; Ebenezer Rockwood Hoar, of Massachusetts; and George Henry Williams, of Oregon; and her Britannic Majesty, on her part, has appointed as her high commissioners and plenipotentiaries the right honorable George Frederick Samuel, Earl de Grey and Earl of Ripon, Viscount Goderich, Baron Grantham, a baronet, a peer of the United Kingdom, lord president of her Majesty's most honorable Privy Council, knight of the most noble order of the Garter, &c.; the right honorable Sir Stafford Henry Northcote, baronet, one of her Majesty's most honorable Privy Council, a member of Parliament, a companion of the most honorable order of the Bath, &c.; Sir Edward Thornton, knight commander of the most honorable order of the Bath, her Majesty's envoy extraordinary and minister plenipotentiary to the United States of America; Sir John Alexander Macdonald, knight commander of the most honorable order of the Bath, a member of her Majesty's Privy Council for Canada, and minister of justice and attorney general of her Majesty's Dominion of Canada; and Montague Bernard, esq., Chichele professor of international law in the University of Oxford.

And the said plenipotentiaries, after having exchanged their full powers, which were found to be in due and proper form, have agreed to and concluded the following articles:

ARTICLE I.

Whereas differences have arisen between the Government of the United States and the Government of her Britannic Majesty, and still exist, growing out of the acts committed by the several vessels which have given rise to the claims generically known as the "Alabama claims;"

And whereas her Britannic Majesty has authorized her high commissioners and plenipotentiaries to express, in a friendly spirit, the regret felt by her Majesty's Government for the escape, under whatever circumstances, of the Alabama and other vessels from British ports, and for the depredations committed by those vessels:

Now, in order to remove and adjust all complaints and claims on the part of the United States, and to provide for the speedy settlement of such claims, which are not admitted by her Britannic Majesty's Government, the high contracting parties agree that all the said claims, growing out of acts committed by the aforesaid vessels and generically known as the "Alabama claims," shall be referred to a tribunal of arbitration to be composed of five arbitrators, to be appointed in the following manner, that is to say: one shall be named by the President of the United States; one shall be named by her Britannic Majesty; his Majesty the King of Italy shall be requested to name one; the President of the Swiss Confederation shall be requested to name one; and his Majesty the Emperor of Brazil shall be requested to name one.

In case of the death, absence, or incapacity to serve of any or either of the said arbitrators, or, in the event of either of the said arbitrators omitting or declining or ceasing to act as such, the President of the United States, or her Britannic Majesty, or his Majesty the King of Italy, or the President of the Swiss Confederation, or his Majesty the Emperor of Brazil, as the case may be, may forthwith name another person to act as arbitrator in the place and stead of the arbitrator originally named by such head of a State.

And in the event of the refusal or omission for two months after receipt of the request from either of the high contracting parties of his Majesty the King of Italy, or the President of the Swiss Confederation, or his Majesty the Emperor of Brazil, to name an arbitrator either to fill the original appointment or in the place of one who may have died, be absent, or incapacitated, or who may omit, decline, or from any cause cease to act as such arbitrator, his

Majesty the King of Sweden and Norway shall be requested to name one or more persons, as the case may be, to act as such arbitrator or arbitrators.

ARTICLE II.

The arbitrators shall meet at Geneva, in Switzerland, at the earliest convenient day after they shall have been named, and shall proceed impartially and carefully to examine and decide all questions that shall be laid before them on the part of the Governments of the United States and her Britannic Majesty respectively. All questions considered by the tribunal, including the final award, shall be decided by a majority of all the arbitrators.

Each of the high contracting parties shall also name one person to attend the tribunal as its agent to represent it generally in all matters connected with the arbitration.

ARTICLE III.

The written or printed case of each of the two parties, accompanied by the documents, the official correspondence, and other evidence on which each relies, shall be delivered in duplicate to each of the arbitrators and to the agent of the other party as soon as may be after the organization of the tribunal, but within a period not exceeding six months from the date of the exchange of the ratifications of this treaty.

ARTICLE IV.

Within four months after the delivery on both sides of the written or printed case, either party may, in like manner, deliver in duplicate to each of the said arbitrators, and to the agent of the other party, a counter case and additional documents, correspondence, and evidence, in reply to the case, documents, correspondence, and evidence so presented by the other party.

The arbitrators may, however, extend the time for delivering such counter case, documents, correspondence, and evidence, when, in their judgment, it becomes necessary, in consequence of the distance of the place from which the evidence to be presented is to be procured.

If in the case submitted to the arbitrators either party shall have specified or alluded to any report or document in its own exclusive possession without annexing a copy, such party shall be bound, if the other party thinks proper to apply for it, to furnish that party with a copy thereof; and either party may call upon the other, through the arbitrators, to produce the originals or certified copies of any papers adduced as evidence, giving in each instance such reasonable notice as the arbitrators may require.

ARTICLE V.

It shall be the duty of the agent of each party, within two months after the expiration of the time limited for the delivery of the counter case on both sides, to deliver in duplicate to each of the said arbitrators and to the agent of the other party a written or printed argument showing the points and referring to the evidence upon which his Government relies; and the arbitrators may, if they desire further elucidation with regard to any point, require a written or printed statement or argument, or oral argument by counsel upon it; but in such case the other party shall be entitled to reply either orally or in writing, as the case may be.

ARTICLE VI.

In deciding the matters submitted to the arbitrators, they shall be governed by the following three rules, which are agreed upon by the high contracting parties as rules to be taken as applicable to the case, and by such principles of international law not inconsistent therewith as the arbitrators shall determine to have been applicable to the case:

Rules.

A neutral Government is bound—

First, to use due diligence to prevent the fitting out, arming, or equipping, within its jurisdiction, of any vessel which it has reasonable ground to believe is intended to cruise or to carry on war against a Power with which it is at peace; and also to use like diligence to prevent the departure from its jurisdiction of any vessel intended to cruise or carry on war as above, such vessel having been specially adapted, in whole or in part, within such jurisdiction, to warlike use.

Secondly, not to permit or suffer either belligerent to make use of its ports or waters as the base of naval operations against the other, or for the purpose of the renewal or augmentation of military supplies or arms, or the recruitment of men.

Thirdly, to exercise due diligence in its own ports and waters, and, as to all persons within its jurisdiction, to prevent any violation of the foregoing obligations and duties.

Her Britannic Majesty has commanded her high commissioners and plenipotentiaries to declare that her Majesty's Government cannot assent to the foregoing rules as a statement of principles of international law which were in force at the time when the claims mentioned in Article I arose, but that her Majesty's Government, in order to evince its desire of strengthening the friendly relations between the two countries, and of making satisfactory provision for the future, agrees that in deciding the questions between the two countries arising out of those claims the arbitrators should assume that her Majesty's Government had undertaken to act upon the principles set forth in these rules.

And the high contracting parties agree to observe these rules as between themselves in future, and to bring them to the knowledge of other maritime Powers, and to invite them to accede to them.

ARTICLE VII.

The decision of the tribunal shall, if possible, be made within three months from the close of the argument on both sides.

It shall be made in writing and dated, and shall be signed by the arbitrators who may assent to it.

The said tribunal shall first determine as to each vessel separately whether Great Britain has, by any act or omission, failed to fulfill any of the duties set forth in the foregoing three rules, or recognized by the principles of international law not inconsistent with such rules, and shall certify such fact as to each of the said vessels. In case the tribunal find that Great Britain has failed to fulfill any duty or duties as aforesaid, it may, if it think proper, proceed to award a sum in gross to be paid by Great Britain to the United States for all the claims referred to it; and in such case the gross sum so awarded shall be paid in coin by the Government of Great Britain to the Government of the United States, at Washington, within twelve months after the date of the award.

The award shall be in duplicate, one copy whereof shall be delivered to the agent of the United States for his Government, and the other copy shall be delivered to the agent of Great Britain for his Government.

ARTICLE VIII.

Each Government shall pay its own agent and provide for the proper remuneration of the counsel employed by it and of the arbitrator appointed by it, and for the expense of preparing and submitting its case to the tribunal. All other expenses connected with the arbitration shall be defrayed by the two Governments in equal moieties.

ARTICLE IX.

The arbitrators shall keep an accurate record of their proceedings, and may appoint and employ the necessary officers to assist them.

ARTICLE X.

In case the tribunal finds that Great Britain has failed to fulfil any duty or duties as aforesaid, and does not award a sum in gross, the high contracting parties agree that a board of assessors shall be appointed to ascertain and determine what claims are valid, and what amount or amounts shall be paid by Great Britain to the United States on account of the liability arising from such failure, as to each vessel, according to the extent of such liability as decided by the arbitrators.

The board of assessors shall be constituted as follows: one member thereof shall be named by the President of the United States, one member thereof shall be named by her Britannic Majesty, and one member thereof shall be named by the representative at Washington of his Majesty the King of Italy; and in case of a vacancy happening from any cause, it shall be filled in the same manner in which the original appointment was made.

As soon as possible after such nominations the board of assessors shall be organized in Washington, with power to hold their sittings there, or in New York, or in Boston. The members thereof shall severally subscribe a solemn declaration that they will impartially and carefully examine and decide, to the best of their judgment and according to justice and equity, all matters submitted to them, and shall forthwith proceed, under such rules and regulations as they may prescribe, to the investigation of the claims which shall be presented to them by the Government of the United States, and shall examine and decide upon them in such order and manner as they may think proper, but upon such evidence or information only as shall be furnished by or on behalf of the Governments of the United States and of Great Britain, respectively. They shall be bound to hear on each separate claim, if required, one person on behalf of each Government, as counsel or agent. A majority of the assessors in each case shall be sufficient for a decision.

The decision of the assessors shall be given upon each claim in writing, and shall be signed by them respectively and dated.

Every claim shall be presented to the assessors within six months from the day of their first meeting, but they may, for good cause shown, extend the time for the presentation of any claim to a further period not exceeding three months.

The assessors shall report to each Government at or before the expiration of one year from the date of their first meeting the amount of claims decided by them up to the date of such report. If further claims then remain undecided, they shall make a further report at or before the expiration of two years from the date of such first meeting, and in case any claims remain undetermined at that time they shall make a final report within a further period of six months.

The report or reports shall be made in duplicate, and one copy thereof shall be delivered to the Secretary of State of the United States, and one copy thereof to the representative of her Britannic Majesty at Washington.

All sums of money which may be awarded under this article shall be payable at Washington, in coin, within twelve months after the delivery of each report.

The board of assessors may employ such clerks as they shall think necessary.

The expenses of the board of assessors shall be borne equally by the two Governments, and paid from time to time, as may be found expedient, on the production of accounts certified by the board. The remuneration of the assessors shall also be paid by the two Governments in equal moieties in a similar manner.

ARTICLE XI.

The high contracting parties engage to consider the result of the proceedings of the tribunal of arbitration and of the board of assessors, should such board be appointed, as a full, perfect, and final settlement of all the claims hereinbefore referred to; and further engage that every such claim, whether the same may or may not have been presented to the notice of, made, preferred, or laid before the tribunal or board, shall, from and after the conclusion of the proceedings of the tribunal or board, be considered and treated as finally settled, barred, and thenceforth inadmissible.

ARTICLE XII.

The high contracting parties agree that all

claims on the part of corporations, companies, or private individuals, citizens of the United States, upon the Government of her Britannic Majesty, arising out of acts committed against the persons or property of citizens of the United States during the period between the 13th of April, 1861, and the 9th of April, 1865, inclusive, not being claims growing out of the acts of the vessels referred to in Article I of this treaty; and all claims, with the like exception, on the part of corporations, companies, or private individuals, subjects of her Britannic Majesty, upon the Government of the United States, arising out of acts com mitted against the persons or property of subjects of her Britannic Majesty during the same period, which may have been presented to either Government for its interposition with the other, and which yet remain unsettled, as well as any other such claims which may be presented within the time specified in Article XIV of this treaty, shall be referred to three commissioners, to be appointed in the following manner, that is to say: one commissioner shall be named by the President of the United States, one by her Britannic Majesty, and a third by the President of the United States and her Britannic Majesty conjointly; and in case the third commissioner shall not have been so named within a period of three months from the date of the exchange of the ratifications of this treaty, then the third commissioner shall be named by the representative at Washington of his Majesty the King of Spain. In case of the death, absence, or incapacity of any commissioner, or in the event of any commissioner omitting or ceasing to act, the vacancy shall be filled in the manner hereinbefore provided for making the original appointment; the period of three months in case of such substitution being calculated from the date of the happening of the vacancy.

The commissioners so named shall meet at Washington at the earliest convenient period after they have been respectively named; and shall, before proceeding to any business, make and subscribe a solemn declaration that they will impartially and carefully examine and decide, to the best of their judgment, and according to justice and equity, all such claims as shall be laid before them on the part of the Governments of the United States and of her Britannic Majesty, respectively; and such declaration shall be entered on the record of their proceedings.

ARTICLE XIII.

The commissioners shall then forthwith proceed to the investigation of the claims which shall be presented to them. They shall investigate and decide such claims in such order and such manner as they may think proper, but upon such evidence or information only as shall be furnished by or on behalf of the respective Governments. They shall be bound to receive and consider all written documents or statements which may be presented to them by or on behalf of the respective Governments in support of or in answer to any claim, and to hear, if required, one person on each side, on behalf of each Government, as counsel or agent for such Government, on each and every separate claim. A majority of the commissioners shall be sufficient for an award in each case. The award shall be given upon each claim in writing, and shall be signed by the commissioners assenting to it. It shall be competent for each Government to name one person to attend the commissioners as its agent, to present and support claims on its behalf, and to answer claims made upon it, and to represent it generally in all matters connected with the investigation and decision thereof.

The high contracting parties hereby engage to consider the decision of the commissioners as absolutely final and conclusive upon each claim decided upon by them, and to give full effect to such decisions without any objection, evasion, or delay whatsoever.

ARTICLE XIV.

Every claim shall be presented to the commissioners within six months from the day of their first meeting, unless in any case where reasons for delay shall be established to the satisfaction of the commissioners, and then, and in any such case, the period for presenting the claim may be extended by them to any time not exceeding three months longer.

The commissioners shall be bound to examine and decide upon every claim within two years from the day of their first meeting. It shall be competent for the commissioners to decide in each case whether any claim has or has not been duly made, preferred, and laid before them, either wholly or to any and what extent, according to the true intent and meaning of this treaty.

ARTICLE XV.

All sums of money which may be awarded by the commissioners on account of any claim shall be paid by the one Government to the other, as the case may be, within twelve months after the date of the final award, without interest, and without any deduction save as specified in Article XVI of this treaty.

ARTICLE XVI.

The commissioners shall keep an accurate record, and correct minutes or notes of all their proceedings, with the dates thereof, and may appoint and employ a secretary, and any other necessary officer or officers to assist them in the transaction of the business which may come before them.

Each Government shall pay its own commissioner and agent or counsel. All other expenses shall be defrayed by the two Governments in equal moieties.

The whole expenses of the commission, including contingent expenses, shall be defrayed by a ratable deduction on the amount of the sums awarded by the commissioners, provided always that such deduction shall not exceed the rate of five per cent. on the sums so awarded.

ARTICLE XVII.

The high contracting parties engage to con

sider the result of the proceedings of this commission as a full, perfect, and final settlement of all such claims as are mentioned in Article XII of this treaty upon either Government; and further engage that every such claim, whether or not the same may have been presented to the notice of, made, preferred, or laid before the said commission, shall, from and after the conclusion of the proceedings of the said commission, be considered and treated as finally settled, barred, and thenceforth inadmissible.

ARTICLE XVIII.

It is agreed by the high contracting parties that in addition to the liberty secured to the United States fishermen by the convention between the United States and Great Britain, signed at London on the 20th day of October, 1818, of taking, curing, and drying fish on certain coasts of the British North American colonies therein defined, the inhabitants of the United States shall have, in common with the subjects of her Britannic Majesty, the liberty, for the term of years mentioned in Article XXXIII of this treaty, to take fish of every kind, except shell fish, on the sea-coasts and shores, and in the bays, harbors, and creeks of the provinces of Quebec, Nova Scotia, and New Brunswick, and the colony of Prince Edward's Island, and of the several islands thereunto adjacent, without being restricted to any distance from the shore, with permission to land upon the said coasts and shores and islands, and also upon the Magdalen Islands, for the purpose of drying their nets and curing their fish; provided that in so doing they do not interfere with the rights of private property, or with British fishermen in the peaceable use of any part of the said coasts in their occupancy for the same purpose.

It is understood that the above-mentioned liberty applies solely to the sea fishery, and that the salmon and shad fisheries, and all other fisheries in rivers and the mouths of rivers, are hereby reserved exclusively for British fishermen.

ARTICLE XIX.

It is agreed by the high contracting parties that British subjects shall have, in common with the citizens of the United States, the liberty, for the term of years mentioned in Article XXXIII of this treaty, to take fish of every kind, except shell-fish, on the eastern sea-coasts and shores of the United States north of the thirty-ninth parallel of north latitude, and on the shores of the several islands thereunto adjacent, and in the bays, harbors, and creeks of the said sea-coasts and shores of the United States and of the said islands, without being restricted to any distance from the shore, with permission to land upon the said coasts of the United States and of the islands aforesaid, for the purpose of drying their nets and curing their fish; provided that, in so doing, they do not interfere with the rights of private property, or with the fishermen of the United States in the peaceable use of any part of the said coasts in their occupancy for the same purpose.

It is understood that the above-mentioned liberty applies solely to the sea fishery, and that salmon and shad fisheries, and all other fisheries in rivers and mouths of rivers, are hereby reserved exclusively for fishermen of the United States.

ARTICLE XX.

It is agreed that the places designated by the commissioners appointed under the first article of the treaty between the United States and Great Britain, concluded at Washington on the 5th of June, 1854, upon the coasts of her Britannic Majesty's dominions and the United States, as places reserved from the common right of fishing under that treaty, shall be regarded as in like manner reserved from the common right of fishing under the preceding articles. In case any question should arise between the Governments of the United States and of her Britannic Majesty as to the common right of fishing in places not thus designated as reserved, it is agreed that a commission shall be appointed to designate such places, and shall be constituted in the same manner and have the same powers, duties, and authority as the commission appointed under the said first article of the treaty of the 5th of June, 1854.

ARTICLE XXI.

It is agreed that, for the term of years mentioned in Article XXXIII of this treaty, fish oil and fish of all kinds, (except fish of the inland lakes, and of the rivers falling into them, and except fish preserved in oil,) being the produce of the fisheries of the United States, or of the Dominion of Canada, or of Prince Edward's Island, shall be admitted into each country, respectively, free of duty.

ARTICLE XXII.

Inasmuch as it is asserted by the Government of her Britannic Majesty that the privileges accorded to the citizens of the United States under Article XVIII of this treaty are of greater value than those accorded by Articles XIX and XXI of this treaty to the subjects of her Britannic Majesty, and this assertion is not admitted by the Government of the United States, it is further agreed that commissioners shall be appointed to determine, having regard to the privileges accorded by the United States to the subjects of her Britannic Majesty, as stated in Articles XIX and XXI of this treaty, the amount of any compensation which, in their opinion, ought to be paid by the Government of the United States to the Government of her Britannic Majesty in return for the privileges accorded to the citizens of the United States under Article XVIII of this treaty; and that any sum of money which the said commissioners may so award shall be paid by the United States Government, in a gross sum, within twelve months after such award shall have been given.

ARTICLE XXIII.

The commissioners referred to in the preceding article shall be appointed in the following manner, that is to say: one commissioner shall be named by the President of the

United States, one by her Britannic Majesty and a third by the President of the United States and her Britannic Majesty conjointly, and in case the third commissioner shall not have been so named within a period of three months from the date when this article shall take effect, then the third commissioner shall be named by the representative at London of his Majesty the Emperor of Austria and King of Hungary. In case of the death, absence, or incapacity of any commissioner, or in the event of any commissioner omitting or ceasing to act, the vacancy shall be filled in the manner hereinbefore provided for making the original appointment, the period of three months in case of such substitution being calculated from the date of the happening of the vacancy.

The commissioners so named shall meet in the city of Halifax, in the province of Nova Scotia, at the earliest convenient period after they have been respectively named, and shall, before proceeding to any business, make and subscribe a solemn declaration that they will impartially and carefully examine and decide the matters referred to them to the best of their judgment, and according to justice and equity; and such declaration shall be entered on the record of their proceedings.

Each of the high contracting parties shall also name one person to attend the commission as its agent, to represent it generally in all matters connected with the commission.

Article XXIV.

The proceedings shall be conducted in such order as the commissioners appointed under Articles XXII and XXIII of this treaty shall determine. They shall be bound to receive such oral or written testimony as either Government may present. If either party shall offer oral testimony, the other party shall have the right of cross examination, under such rules as the commissioners shall prescribe.

If in the case submitted to the commissioners either party shall have specified or alluded to any report or document in its own exclusive possession, without annexing a copy, such party shall be bound, if the other party thinks proper to apply for it, to furnish that party with a copy thereof; and either party may call upon the other, through the commissioners, to produce the originals or certified copies of any papers adduced as evidence, giving in each instance such reasonable notice as the commissioners may require.

The case on either side shall be closed within a period of six months from the date of the organization of the commission, and the commissioners shall be requested to give their award as soon as possible thereafter. The aforesaid period of six months may be extended for three months in case of a vacancy occurring among the commissioners under the circumstances contemplated in Article XXIII of this treaty.

Article XXV.

The commissioners shall keep an accurate record and correct minutes or notes of all their proceedings, with the dates thereof, and may appoint and employ a secretary and any other necessary officer or officers to assist them in the transaction of the business which may come before them.

Each of the high contracting parties shall pay its own commissioner and agent or counsel; all other expenses shall be defrayed by the two Governments in equal moieties.

Article XXVI.

The navigation of the river St. Lawrence, ascending and descending, from the forty fifth parallel of north latitude, where it ceases to form the boundary between the two countries, from, to, and into the sea, shall forever remain free and open for the purposes of commerce to the citizens of the United States, subject to any laws and regulations of Great Britain, or of the Dominion of Canada, not inconsistent with such privilege of free navigation.

The navigation of the rivers Yukon, Porcupine, and Stikine, ascending and descending, from, to, and into the sea, shall forever remain free and open for the purposes of commerce to the subjects of her Britannic Majesty and to the citizens of the United States, subject to any laws and regulations of either country within its own territory, not inconsistent with such privilege of free navigation.

Article XXVII.

The Government of her Britannic Majesty engages to urge upon the Government of the Dominion of Canada to secure to the citizens of the United States the use of the Welland, St. Lawrence, and other canals in the Dominion on terms of equality with the inhabitants of the Dominion; and the Government of the United States engages that the subjects of her Britannic Majesty shall enjoy the use of the St. Clair Flats canal on terms of equality with the inhabitants of the United States, and further engages to urge upon the State governments to secure to the subjects of her Britannic Majesty the use of the several State canals connected with the navigation of the lakes or rivers traversed by or contiguous to the boundary line between the possessions of the high contracting parties, on terms of equality with the inhabitants of the United States.

Article XXVIII.

The navigation of Lake Michigan shall also, for the term of years mentioned in Article XXXIII of this treaty, be free and open for the purposes of commerce to the subjects of her Britannic Majesty, subject to any laws and regulations of the United States or of the States bordering thereon not inconsistent with such privilege of free navigation.

Article XXIX.

It is agreed that, for the term of years mentioned in Article XXXIII of this treaty, goods, wares, or merchandise arriving at the ports of New York, Boston, and Portland, and any other ports in the United States which have been or may, from time to time, be specially designated by the President of the United

States, and destined for her Britannic Majesty's possessions in North America, may be entered at the proper custom-house and conveyed in transit, without the payment of duties, through the territory of the United States, under such rules, regulations, and conditions for the protection of the revenue as the Government of the United States may from time to time prescribe; and under like rules, regulations, and conditions, goods, wares, or merchandise may be conveyed in transit, without the payment of duties, from such possessions through the territory of the United States for export from the said ports of the United States.

It is further agreed that, for the like period, goods, wares, or merchandise arriving at any of the ports of her Britannic Majesty's possessions in North America, and destined for the United States, may be entered at the proper custom-house and conveyed in transit, without the payment of duties, through the said possessions, under such rules and regulations and conditions for the protection of the revenue as the Governments of the said possessions may from time to time prescribe; and, under like rules, regulations, and conditions, goods, wares, or merchandise may be conveyed in transit, without payment of duties, from the United States through the said possessions to other places in the United States, or for export from ports in the said possessions.

ARTICLE XXX.

It is agreed that for the term of years mentioned in Article XXXIII of this treaty, subjects of her Britannic Majesty may carry in British vessels, without payment of duty, goods, wares, or merchandise from one port or place within the territory of the United States upon the St. Lawrence, the great lakes, and the rivers connecting the same, to another port or place within the territory of the United States as aforesaid; provided, that a portion of such transportation is made through the Dominion of Canada by land carriage and in bond, under such rules and regulations as may be agreed upon between the Government of her Britannic Majesty and the Government of the United States.

Citizens of the United States may for the like period carry in United States vessels, without payment of duty, goods, wares, or merchandise from one port or place within the possessions of her Britannic Majesty in North America to another port or place within the said possessions; provided, that a portion of such transportation is made through the territory of the United States by land carriage and in bond, under such rules and regulations as may be agreed upon between the Government of the United States and the Government of her Britannic Majesty.

The Government of the United States further engages not to impose any export duties on goods, wares, or merchandise carried under this article through the territory of the United States; and her Majesty's Government engages to urge the Parliament of the Dominion of Canada and the Legislatures of the other colonies not to impose any export duties on goods, wares, or merchandise carried under this article; and the Government of the United States may, in case such export duties are imposed by the Dominion of Canada, suspend, during the period that such duties are imposed, the right of carrying granted under this article in favor of the subjects of her Britannic Majesty.

The Government of the United States may suspend the right of carrying granted in favor of the subjects of her Britannic Majesty, under this article, in case the Dominion of Canada should at any time deprive the citizens of the United States of the use of the canals in the said Dominion on terms of equality with the inhabitants of the Dominion, as provided in Article XXVII.

ARTICLE XXXI.

The Government of her Britannic Majesty further engages to urge upon the Parliament of the Dominion of Canada and the Legislature of New Brunswick that no export duty, or other duty, shall be levied on lumber or timber of any kind cut on that portion of the American territory in the State of Maine watered by the river St. John and its tributaries, and floated down that river to the sea, when the same is shipped to the United States from the province of New Brunswick. And in case any such export or other duty continues to be levied after the expiration of one year from the date of the exchange of the ratifications of this treaty, it is agreed that the Government of the United States may suspend the right of carrying hereinbefore granted under Article XXX of this treaty for such period as such export or other duty may be levied.

ARTICLE XXXII.

It is further agreed that the provisions and stipulations of Articles XVIII to XXV of this treaty, inclusive, shall extend to the colony of Newfoundland, so far as they are applicable. But if the Imperial Parliament, the Legislature of Newfoundland, or the Congress of the United States, shall not embrace the colony of Newfoundland in their laws enacted for carrying the foregoing articles into effect, then this article shall be of no effect; but the omission to make provision by law to give it effect, by either of the legislative bodies aforesaid, shall not in any way impair any other articles of this treaty.

ARTICLE XXXIII.

The foregoing Articles XVIII to XXV inclusive, and Article XXX of this treaty, shall take effect as soon as the laws required to carry them into operation shall have been passed by the Imperial Parliament of Great Britain, by the Parliament of Canada, and by the Legislature of Prince Edward's Island on the one hand, and by the Congress of the United States on the other. Such assent having been given, the said articles shall remain in force for the period of ten years from the date at which they may come into operation; and further, until the expiration of two years after either of the high contracting parties shall have given notice to the other of its wish to terminate the same, each of the high contracting parties being at liberty to give such notice to the other at the end of the said period of ten years, or at any time afterward.

ARTICLE XXXIV.

Whereas it was stipulated by Article I of the treaty concluded at Washington on the 15th of June, 1846, between the United States and her Britannic Majesty, that the line of boundary between the territories of the United States and those of her Britannic Majesty, from the point on the forty ninth parallel of north latitude up to which it had already been ascertained, should be continued westward along the said parallel of north latitude "to the middle of the channel which separates the continent from Vancouver's Island, and thence southerly, through the middle of the said channel and of Fuca straits, to the Pacific ocean;" and whereas the commissioners appointed by the two high contracting parties to determine that portion of the boundary which runs southerly through the middle of the channel aforesaid were unable to agree upon the same; and whereas the Government of her Britannic Majesty claims that such boundary line should, under the terms of the treaty above recited, be run through the Rosario straits, and the Government of the United States claims that it should be run through the Canal de Haro, it is agreed that the respective claims of the Government of the United States and of the Government of her Britannic Majesty shall be submitted to the arbitration and award of his Majesty the Emperor of Germany, who, having regard to the above-mentioned article of the said treaty, shall decide thereupon, finally and without appeal, which of those claims is most in accordance with the true interpretation of the treaty of June 15, 1846.

ARTICLE XXXV.

The award of his Majesty the Emperor of Germany shall be considered as absolutely final and conclusive; and full effect shall be given to such award without any objection, evasion, or delay whatsoever. Such decision shall be given in writing and dated; it shall be in whatsoever form his Majesty may choose to adopt; it shall be delivered to the representatives or other public agents of the United States and of Great Britain, respectively, who may be actually at Berlin, and shall be considered as operative from the day of the date of the delivery thereof.

ARTICLE XXXVI.

The written or printed case of each of the two parties, accompanied by the evidence offered in support of the same, shall be laid before his Majesty the Emperor of Germany within six months from the date of the exchange of the ratifications of this treaty, and a copy of such case and evidence shall be communicated by each party to the other, through their respective representatives at Berlin.

The high contracting parties may include in the evidence to be considered by the arbitrator such documents, official correspondence, and other official or public statements bearing on the subject of the reference as they may consider necessary to the support of their respective cases.

After the written or printed case shall have been communicated by each party to the other, each party shall have the power of drawing up and laying before the arbitrator a second and definitive statement, if it think fit to do so, in reply to the case of the other party so communicated, which definitive statement shall be so laid before the arbitrator, and also be mutually communicated in the same manner as aforesaid, by each party to the other, within six months from the date of laying the first statement of the case before the arbitrator.

ARTICLE XXXVII.

If, in the case submitted to the arbitrator, either party shall specify or allude to any report or document in its own exclusive possession without annexing a copy, such party shall be bound, if the other party thinks proper to apply for it, to furnish that party with a copy thereof, and either party may call upon the other, through the arbitrator, to produce the originals or certified copies of any papers adduced as evidence, giving in each instance such reasonable notice as the arbitrator may require. And if the arbitrator should desire further elucidation or evidence with regard to any point contained in the statements laid before him, he shall be at liberty to require it from either party, and he shall be at liberty to hear one counsel or agent for each party, in relation to any matter, and at such time and in such manner as he may think fit.

ARTICLE XXXVIII.

The representatives or other public agents of the United States and of Great Britain at Berlin, respectively, shall be considered as the agents of their respective Governments to conduct their cases before the arbitrator, who shall be requested to address all his communications and give all his notices to such representatives or other public agents who shall represent their respective Governments, generally, in all matters connected with the arbitration.

ARTICLE XXXIX.

It shall be competent to the arbitrator to proceed in the said arbitration, and all matters relating thereto, as and when he shall see fit, either in person, or by a person or persons named by him for that purpose, either in the presence or absence of either or both agents, and either orally or by written discussion or otherwise.

ARTICLE XL.

The arbitrator may, if he think fit, appoin. a secretary, or clerk, for the purposes of the proposed arbitration, at such rate of remuneration as he shall think proper. This, and all other expenses of and connected with the said arbitration, shall be provided for as hereinafter stipulated.

ARTICLE XLI.

The arbitrator shall be requested to deliver,

together with his award, an account of all the costs and expenses which he may have been put to in relation to this matter, which shall forthwith be repaid by the two Governments in equal moieties.

ARTICLE XLII.

The arbitrator shall be requested to give his award in writing as early as convenient after the whole case on each side shall have been laid before him, and to deliver one copy thereof to each of the said agents.

ARTICLE XLIII.

The present treaty shall be duly ratified by the President of the United States of America, by and with the advice and consent of the Senate thereof, and by her Britannic Majesty; and the ratifications shall be exchanged either at Washington or at London within six months from the date hereof, or earlier if possible.

In faith whereof, we, the respective plenipotentiaries, have signed this treaty and have hereunto affixed our seals.

Done in duplicate at Washington the 8th day of May, in the year of our Lord 1871.

[L. S.] HAMILTON FISH.
[L. S.] ROBERT C. SCHENCK.
[L. S.] SAMUEL NELSON.
[L. S.] EBENEZER ROCKWOOD HOAR.
[L. S.] GEORGE H. WILLIAMS.
[L. S.] DE GREY & RIPON.
[L. S.] STAFFORD H. NORTHCOTE.
[L. S.] EDWARD THORNTON.
[L. S.] JOHN A. MACDONALD.
[L. S] MOUNTAGUE BERNARD.

And whereas the said treaty has been duly ratified on both parts, and the respective ratifications of the same were exchanged in the city of London, on the 17th day of June, 1871, by Robert C. Schenck, envoy extraordinary and minister plenipotentiary of the United States, and Earl Granville, her Majesty's principal Secretary of State for Foreign Affairs, on the part of their respective Governments:

Now, therefore, be it known that I, Ulysses S. Grant, President of the United States of America, have caused the said treaty to be made public, to the end that the same, and every clause and article thereof, may be observed and fulfilled with good faith by the United States and the citizens thereof.

In witness whereof, I have hereunto set my hand and caused the seal of the United States to be affixed.

Done at the city of Washington this 4th day of July, in the year of our Lord 1871, and of the Independence of the United States the ninety-sixth. [SEAL.]

U. S. GRANT.

By the President:
HAMILTON FISH,
Secretary of State.

President's Special Message to the Senate.

The following, unofficial, purports to be a copy of the President's message to the Senate, dated May 14, 1872, transmitting a proposed additional article submitted by the British Government:

To the Senate of the United States:

I transmit herewith the correspondence which has recently taken place respecting the differences of opinion which have arisen between this Government and Great Britain with regard to the power of the tribunal of arbitration created under the treaty signed at Washington May 8, 1871.

I respectfully invite the attention of the Senate to the proposed article submitted by the British Government with the object of removing differences which seem to threaten the prosecution of the arbitration, and request an expression by the Senate of their disposition in regard to advising and consenting to the formal adoption of an article such as is proposed by the British Government.

The Senate is aware that consultation with that body in advance of entering into agreements with foreign States has many precedents. In the early days of the Republic General Washington asked their advice upon pending questions with such Powers. The most important recent precedent is that of the Oregon boundary treaty of 1846. The importance of the results hanging upon the present state of the treaty with Great Britain leads me to follow these precedents, and to desire the counsel of the Senate in advance of agreeing to the proposals of Great Britain.

U. S. GRANT.

Proposed New Article.

Whereas the Government of her Britannic Majesty has contended in the recent correspondence with the Government of the United States, as follows, namely, that such indirect claims as those for the national losses stated in the case presented on the part of the Government of the United States to the Tribunal of Arbitration at Geneva, to have been sustained by the loss in the transfer of the American commercial marine to the British flag, the enhanced payment of insurance, the prolongation of the war, and the addition of a large sum to the cost of the war and the suppression of the rebellion, firstly, were not included in the treaty of Washington, and, further, and secondly, should not be admitted in principle as growing out of the acts committed by particular vessels alleged to have been enabled to commit depredations upon the shipping of a belligerent by reason of such want of due diligence in the performance of the neutral obligations as that which is imputed by the United States to Great Britain; and whereas the President of the United States, while adhering to his contention that the said claims were included in the Treaty, adopts for the future the principle contained in the second of the said contentions, as far as to declare that it will hereafter guide the conduct of the Government of the United States; and that the two countries are, therefore, agreed in this respect:

In consideration thereof, the President of the United States, by and with the advice and consent of the Senate thereof, consents that he will make no claim on the part of the United States in respect of indirect losses, as aforesaid, before the Tribunal of Arbitration at Geneva.

[The Senate, sitting in executive session, is understood to have assented (yeas 43, nays 18) to the new article, modified by striking out all after the word "whereas" (in the twenty second line of the above) and inserting in lieu thereof the following:

"Both Governments adopt for the future the principle that claims for remote or indirect losses should not be admitted as the result of failure to observe neutral obligations, so far as to declare that it will hereafter guide the conduct of both Governments in their relations with each other.

"Now, therefore, in consideration thereof, the President of the United States, by and with the advice and consent of the Senate thereof, consents that he will make no claim on the part of the United States in respect of indirect losses as aforesaid before the Tribunal of Arbitration at Geneva."

It is understood, also, that such modification was not acceptable to the British Government; that upon the assembling of the Tribunal of Arbitration at Geneva, June 15, it adjourned from time to time so as to enable some understanding to be reached between the High Contending Powers, the agent of Great Britain refusing to present his "case" and demanding a protracted adjournment, while the agent of the United States insisted on the presentation of such "case" and opposed such adjournment; that June 27 a solution was reached, and the British "case" was lodged with the Tribunal; that June 28 the Tribunal again met and put upon record their decision, to the effect that the "indirect claims," upon preliminary consideration by the Tribunal—such as comported with the dignity of the court and was satisfactory to both parties—have been disposed of and set aside by a qualified dictum, that if the Tribunal has jurisdiction in the matter of the indirect claims it rejects them, and that the court is in full possession of the whole matter of controversy except what has been put away; and at the same time the Tribunal refused the demand of Great Britain for a protracted adjournment, and took a recess until July 15, in order to give time for the printing of the British case. As the seal of secrecy has not been removed from these latter proceedings, the message, draft of article, and statements touching the action of the Tribunal are given subject to the risk of possible error.]

Tribunal of Arbitration between the United States and Great Britain, at Geneva.

Arbitrator on the part of the United States—CHARLES FRANCIS ADAMS.

Arbitrator on the part of Great Britain—The Right Honorable Sir ALEXANDER COCKBURN, Baronet, Lord Chief Justice of England.

Arbitrator on the part of Italy—His Excellency Senator Count SCLOPIS.

Arbitrator on the part of Switzerland—Mr. JACOB STAMPFLI.

Arbitrator on the part of Brazil—Baron D'ITAJUBÁ.

Agent on the part of the United States—J. C. BANCROFT DAVIS.

Agent on the part of Great Britain—Right Honorable Lord TENTERDEN.

Counsel for the United States—CALEB CUSHING, WILLIAM M EVARTS, MORRISON R WAITE.

Counsel for Great Britain—SIR ROUNDELL PALMER.

Solicitor for the United States—CHARLES C. BEAMAN, jr.

The Johnson-Clarendon Convention.

Convention between Great Britain and the United States of America for the settlement of all outstanding claims; signed at London, January 14, 1869.

Whereas claims have, at various times since the exchange of the ratifications of the convention between the United States of America and Great Britain, signed at London on the 8th of February, 1853, been made upon the United States on the part of subjects of her Britannic Majesty, and upon the Government of her Britannic Majesty on the part of citizens of the United States; and whereas some of such claims are still pending and remain unsettled, the President of the United States of America, and her Majesty the Queen of the United Kingdom of Great Britain and Ireland, being of opinion that a speedy and equitable settlement of all such claims will contribute much to the maintenance of the friendly feelings which subsist between the countries, have resolved to make arrangements for that purpose by means of a convention, and have named as their plenipotentiaries to confer and agree thereupon, that is to say:

The President of the United States of America, Reverdy Johnson, esq., envoy extraordinary and minister plenipotentiary from the United States to her Britannic Majesty;

And her Majesty, the Queen of the United Kingdom of Great Britain and Ireland, the Right Honorable George William Frederick, Earl of Clarendon, Baron Hyde of Hindon, a peer of the United Kingdom, a member of her Britannic Majesty's most honorable Privy Council, knight of the most noble order of the Garter, knight grand cross of the most honorable order of the Bath, her Britannic Majesty's principal Secretary of State for Foreign Affairs;

Who, after having communicated to each other their respective full powers, found in good and due form, have agreed as follows:

ARTICLE I.

The high contracting parties agree that all claims on the part of citizens of the United States upon the Government of her Britannic Majesty,, including the so-called Alabama claims, and all claims on the part of subjects of her Britannic Majesty upon the Government of the United States, which may have been presented to either Government for its interposition with the other since the 26th of

July, 1853, the day of the exchange of the ratifications of the convention concluded between the United States of America and Great Britain, at London, on the 8th of February, 1853, and which yet remain unsettled, as well as any other such claims which may be presented within the time specified in Article III of this convention, whether or not arising out of the late civil war in the United States, shall be referred to four commissioners, to be appointed in the following manner, that is to say: two commissioners shall be named by the President of the United States, by and with the advice and consent of the Senate, and two by her Britannic Majesty. In case of the death, absence, or incapacity of any commissioner, or in the event of any commissioner omitting or declining or ceasing to act as such, the President of the United States, or her Britannic Majesty, as the case may be, shall forthwith name another person to act as commissioner in the place or stead of the commissioner originally named.

The commissioners so named shall meet at Washington at the earliest convenient period after they shall have been respectively named, and shall, before proceeding to any business, make and subscribe a solemn declaration that they will impartially and carefully examine and decide, to the best of their judgment, and according to justice and equity, without fear, favor, or affection to their own country, upon all such claims as shall be laid before them on the part of the Governments of the United States and of her Britannic Majesty, respectively, and such declaration shall be entered on the record of their proceedings.

The commissioners shall then, and before proceeding to any other business, name some person to act as an arbitrator or umpire, to whose final decision shall be referred any claim upon which they may not be able to come to a decision. If they should not be able to agree upon an arbitrator or umpire, the commissioners on either side shall name a person as arbitrator or umpire, and in each and every case in which the commissioners may not be able to come to a decision, the commissioners shall determine by lot which of the two persons so named shall be the arbitrator or umpire in that particular case. The person or persons so to be chosen as arbitrator or umpire shall, before proceeding to act as such in any case, make and subscribe a solemn declaration in a form similar to that made and subscribed by the commissioners, which shall be entered on the record of their proceedings. In the event of the death, absence, or incapacity of such person or persons, or of his or their omitting, or declining, or ceasing to act as such arbitrator or umpire, another person shall be named, in the same manner as the person originally named, to act as arbitrator or umpire in his place and stead, and shall make and subscribe such declaration as aforesaid.

ARTICLE II.

The commissioners shall then forthwith proceed to the investigation of the claims which shall be presented to their notice. They shall investigate and decide upon such claims in such order and in such manner as they may think proper, but upon such evidence or information only as shall be furnished by or on behalf of their respective Governments. The official correspondence which has taken place between the two Governments respecting any claims shall be laid before the commissioners, and they shall, moreover, be bound to receive and peruse all other written documents or statements which may be presented to them by or on behalf of the respective Governments, in support of or in answer to any claim, and to hear, if required, one person on each side on behalf of each Government, as counsel or agent for such Government, on each and every separate claim. Should they fail to decide by a majority upon any individual claim, they shall call to their assistance the arbitrator or umpire whom they may have agreed upon, or who may be determined by lot, as the case may be; and such arbitrator or umpire, after having examined the official correspondence which has taken place between the two Governments, and the evidence adduced for and against the claim, and after having heard, if required, one person on each side as aforesaid, and consulted with the commissioners, shall decide thereupon finally and without appeal.

Nevertheless, if the commissioners, or any two of them, shall think it desirable that a sovereign or head of a friendly State should be arbitrator or umpire in case of any claim, the commissioners shall report to that effect to their respective Governments, who shall thereupon, within six months, agree upon some sovereign or head of a friendly State, who shall be invited to decide upon such claim, and before whom shall be laid the official correspondence which has taken place between the two Governments, and the other written documents or statements which may have been presented to the commissioners in respect of such claims.

The decision of the commissioners, and of the arbitrator or umpire, shall be given upon each claim in writing, and shall be signed by them respectively, and dated.

In the event of a decision involving a question of compensation to be paid being arrived at by a special arbitrator or umpire, the amount of such compensation shall be referred back to the commissioners for adjudication; and in the event of their not being able to come to a decision, it shall then be decided by the arbitrator or umpire appointed by them, or who shall have been determined by lot.

It shall be competent for each Government to name one person to attend the commissioners as agent on its behalf, to present and support claims on its behalf, and to answer claims made upon it, and to represent it generally in all matters connected with the investigation and decision thereof.

The President of the United States of America, and her Majesty the Queen of the United Kingdom of Great Britain and Ireland, hereby solemnly and sincerely engage to consider the decision of the commissioners, or of the arbitrator or umpire, as the case may be, as absolutely final and conclusive upon each of such claims, decided upon by him or them respectively, and to give full effect to such decision without any objection or delay whatsoever.

It is agreed that no claim arising out of any transaction of a date prior to the 26th of July, 1853, the day of the exchange of the ratifications of the convention of the 8th of February, 1853, shall be admissible under this convention.

ARTICLE III.

Every claim shall be presented to the commissioners within six months from the day of their first meeting, unless in any case where reasons for delay shall be established to the satisfaction of the commissioners, or of the arbitrator or umpire in the event of the commissioners differing in opinion thereupon; and then, and in any such case, the period for presenting the claim may be extended to any time not exceeding three months longer.

The commissioners shall be bound to examine and decide upon every claim within two years from the day of their first meeting. It shall be competent for the commissioners, or for the arbitrator or umpire if they differ, to decide in each case whether any claim has or has not been duly made, preferred, or laid before them, either wholly, or to any and what extent, according to the true intent and meaning of this convention.

ARTICLE IV.

All sums of money which may be awarded by the commissioners, or by the arbitrator or umpire, on account of any claim, shall be paid in coin or its equivalent by the one Government to the other, as the case may be, within eighteen months after the date of the decision, without interest.

ARTICLE V.

The high contracting parties engage to consider the result of the proceedings of this commission as a full and final settlement of every claim upon either Government arising out of any transaction of a date prior to the exchange of the ratifications of the present convention; and further engage that every such claim, whether or not the same may have been presented to the notice of, made, preferred, or laid before the said commission, shall, from and after the conclusion of the proceedings of the said commission, be considered and treated as finally settled and barred, and thenceforth inadmissible.

ARTICLE VI.

The commissioners and the arbitrator or umpire appointed by them shall keep an accurate record and correct minutes or notes of all their proceedings, with the dates thereof, and shall appoint and employ clerks or other persons to assist them in the transaction of the business which may come before them.

The secretary shall be appointed by the Secretary of State of the United States and by her Britannic Majesty's representative at Washington jointly.

Each Government shall pay the salaries of its own commissioners. All other expenses, and the contingent expenses of the commission, including the salary of the secretary, shall be defrayed in moieties by the two parties.

ARTICLE VII.

The present convention shall be ratified by the President of the United States, by and with the advice and consent of the Senate thereof, and by her Britannic Majesty; and the ratifications shall be exchanged at London as soon as may be within twelve months from the date hereof.

In witness whereof the respective plenipotentiaries have signed the same, and have affixed thereto their respective seals.

Done at London, the fourteenth day of January, in the year of our Lord one thousand eight hundred and sixty-nine.

[SEAL.] REVERDY JOHNSON.
[SEAL.] CLARENDON.

[NOTE.—Although the seal of secrecy has not been removed from the proceedings of the Senate upon this treaty, it is understood that but one vote—that of Mr. Thomas C. McCreery, of Kentucky—was given in favor of its ratification.—E. McP.]

XVIII.

FEMALE SUFFRAGE.

Report of the Committee on the Judiciary of the House of Representatives.

1871, January 30—Mr. BINGHAM, from the Committee on the Judiciary, to which was referred the memorial of Victoria C. Woodhull, made the following report; which was recommitted and ordered printed:

The memorialist asks the enactment of a law by Congress which shall secure to citizens of the United States in the several States the right to vote "without regard to sex." Since the adoption of the fourteenth amendment of the Constitution there is no longer any reason to doubt that all persons born or naturalized in the United States, and subject to the jurisdiction thereof, are citizens of the United States and of the State wherein they reside; for that is the express declaration of the amendment.

The clause of the fourteenth amendment, "no State shall make or enforce any law which shall abridge the privileges or immunities of citizens of the United States," does not, in the opinion of the committee, refer to privileges and immunities of citizens of the United States other than those privileges and immunities embraced in the original text of the Constitution, article four, section two. The fourteenth amendment, it is believed, did not add to the privileges or immunities before mentioned, but was deemed necessary for their enforcement as an express limitation upon the powers of the States. It had been judicially determined that the first eight articles of amendment of the Constitution were not limitations on the power of the States, and it was apprehended that the same might be held of the provision of the second section, fourth article.

To remedy this defect of the Constitution, the express limitations upon the States contained in the first section of the fourteenth amendment, together with the grant of power in Congress to enforce them by legislation, were incorporated in the Constitution. The words "citizens of the United States," and "citizens of the States," as employed in the fourteenth amendment, did not change or modify the relations of citizens of the State and nation as they existed under the original Constitution.

Attorney General Bates gave the opinion that the Constitution uses the word "citizen" only to express the political quality of the individual in his relation to the nation; to declare that he is a member of the body-politic, and bound to it by the reciprocal obligation of allegiance on the one side and protection on the other. "The phrase 'a citizen of the United States,' without addition or qualification, means neither more nor less than a member of the nation." (Opinion of Attorney General Bates on citizenship.)

The Supreme Court of the Unites States has ruled that, according to the express words and clear meaning of the second section, fourth article of the Constitution, no privileges are secured by it except those which belong to citizenship. (Conner *et al. vs.* Elliott *et al.*, 18 Howard, 593.)

In Corfield *vs.* Coryell, (4 Washington Circuit Court Reports, 380,) the court say:

"The inquiry is, what are the privileges and immunities of citizens in the several States? We feel no hesitation in confining these expressions to those privileges and immunities which are in their nature fundamental; which belong of right to the citizens of all free Governments, and which have at all times been enjoyed by the citizens of the several States which compose this Union, from the time of their becoming free, independent, and sovereign. What these fundamental principles are would perhaps be more tedious than difficult to enumerate. They may, however, be all comprehended under the following general heads: protection by the Government; the enjoyment of life and liberty, with the right to acquire and possess property of every kind, and to pursue and obtain happiness and safety, subject, nevertheless, to such restraints as the Government may justly prescribe for the general good of the whole; the right of a citizen of one State to pass through or to reside in any other State for the purposes of trade, agriculture, professional pursuits, or otherwise; to claim the benefit of the writ of *habeas corpus;* to institute and maintain actions of any kind in the courts of the State; to take, hold, and dispose of property either real or personal; and an exemption from higher taxes or impositions than are paid by the other citizens of the State may be mentioned as some of the particular privileges and immunities of citizens which are clearly embraced by the general description of privileges deemed to be fundamental; to which may be added the elective franchise as regulated and established by the laws or constitution of the State in which it is to be exercised." * * * *

"But we cannot accede to the proposition which was insisted on by the counsel, that under this provision of the Constitution (section two, article four) the citizens of the several States are permitted to participate in all the rights which belong exclusively to the citizens of any other particular State."

The learned Justice Story declared that the intention of the clause ("the citizens of each State shall be entitled to all the privileges and immunities of citizens in the several States") was to confer on the citizens of each State a general citizenship, and communicated all the privileges and immunities which a citizen of the same State would be entitled to under the same circumstances. (Story on the Constitution, volume two, page 605.)

In the case of the Bank of the United States *vs.* Primrose, in the Supreme Court of the United States, Mr. Webster said:

"That this article in the Constitution (article four, section two) does not confer on the citizens of each State political rights in every other State, is admitted. A citizen of Pennsylvania cannot go into Virginia and vote at any election in that State, though when he has acquired a residence in Virginia, and is otherwise qualified as is required by the constitution (of Virginia) he becomes, without formal adoption as a citizen of Virginia, a citizen of that State politically. (Webster's Works, volume six, page 112.)

It must be obvious that Mr. Webster was of opinion that the privileges and immunities of citizens, guarantied to them in the several States, did not include the privilege of the elective franchise otherwise than as secured by the State constitution. For, after making the statement above quoted, that a citizen of Pennsylvania cannot go into Virginia and vote, Mr. Webster adds, "but for the purposes of trade, commerce, buying and selling, it is evidently not in the power of any State to impose any hinderance or embarrassment, &c., upon citizens of other States, or to place them, going there, upon a different footing from her own citizens." (*Ibid.*)

The proposition is clear that no citizen of the United States can rightfully vote in any State of this Union who has not the qualifications required by the constitution of the State in which the right is claimed to be exercised, except as to such conditions in the constitution of such States as deny the right to vote to citizens resident therein "on account of race, color, or previous condition of servitude."

The adoption of the fifteenth amendment of the Constitution, imposing these three limitations upon the power of the several States, was, by necessary implication, a declaration that the States had the power to regulate by a uniform rule the conditions upon which the elective franchise should be exercised by citizens of the United States resident therein. The limitations specified in the fifteenth amendment exclude the conclusion that a State of this Union, having a government republican in form, may not prescribe conditions upon which alone citizens may vote other than those prohibited. It can hardly be said that a State law which excludes from voting women citizens, minor citizens, and non-resident citizens of the United States, on account of sex, minority, or domicile, is a denial of the right to vote on account of race, color, or previous condition of servitude.

It may be further added that the second section of the fourteenth amendment, by the provision that "when the right to vote at any election for the choice of electors of President and Vice President of the United States, Representatives in Congress, or executive and judicial officers of the State, or the members of the Legislature thereof, is denied to any of the male inhabitants of such State, being twenty-one years of age, a citizen of the United States, or in any way abridged, except for participation in rebellion or other crime, the basis of representation therein shall be reduced in the proportion which the number of such male citizens shall bear to the whole number of male citizens twenty-one years of age in such State," implies that the several States may restrict the elective franchise as to other than male citizens. In disposing of this question effect must be given, if possible, to every provision of the Constitution. Article one, section two, of the Constitution provides:

"That the House of Representatives shall be composed of members chosen every second year by the people of the several States, and the electors in each State shall have the qualifications requisite for electors of the most numerous branch of the State Legislature."

This provision has always been construed to vest in the several States the exclusive right to prescribe the qualifications of electors for the most numerous branch of the State Legislature, and therefore for members of Congress. And this interpretation is supported by section four, article one, of the Constitution, which provides—

"That the time, places, and manner of holding elections for Senators and Representatives shall be prescribed in each State by the Legislature thereof; but the Congress may at any time by law make or alter such regulations except as to the place of choosing Senators."

Now, it is submitted, if it had been intended that Congress should prescribe the qualification of electors, that the grant would have read: the Congress may at any time by law make or alter such regulations, and also prescribe the qualification of electors, &c. The power, on the contrary, is limited exclusively to the time, place, and manner, and does not extend to the qualification of the electors. This power to prescribe the qualification of electors in the several States has always been exercised, and is to-day, by the several States of the Union; and we apprehend, until the Constitution shall be changed, will continue to be so exercised, subject only to the express limitations imposed by the Constitution upon the several States, before noticed. We are of opinion, therefore, that it is not competent for the Congress of the United States to establish by law the right to vote without regard to sex in the several States of this Union without the consent of the people of such States and against their constitutions and laws; and that such legislation would be, in our judgment, a violation of the Constitution of the United States, and of the rights reserved to the States respectively by the Constitution. It is undoubtedly the right of the people of the several States so to reform their constitutions and laws as to secure the equal exercise of the right of suffrage at all elections held therein, under the Constitution of the United States, to all citizens, without regard to sex; and as public opinion creates constitutions and governments in the several States, it is not to be doubted that whenever, in any State, the people are of opinion that such a reform is advisable, it will be made.

If, however, as is claimed in the memorial referred to, the right to vote "is vested by the Constitution in the citizens of the United States without regard to sex," that right can be established in the courts without further legislation.

The suggestion is made that Congress by a mere declaratory act shall say that the construction claimed in the memorial is the true construction of the Constitution, or, in other words, that by the Constitution of the United States the right to vote is vested in citizens of the United States "without regard to sex," anything in the constitution and laws of any State to the contrary notwithstanding. In the opinion of the committee such declaratory act is not authorized by the Constitution nor within the legislative power of Congress. We therefore recommend the adoption of the following resolution:

Resolved, That the prayer of the petitioner be not granted; that the memorial be laid on the table, and that the Committee on the Judiciary be discharged from the further consideration of the subject.

February 1—Mr. LOUGHRIDGE, from the same committee, submitted the following minority report, (which, from its extreme length, it becomes necessary to condense,) signed by himself and Mr. B. F. BUTLER:

* * * * * * * *

The question presented is one of exceeding interest and importance, involving as it does the constitutional rights not only of the memorialist but of more than one half of the citizens of the United States—a question of constitutional law in which the civil and the natural rights of the citizen are involved. Questions of propriety or of expediency have nothing to do with it. The question is not "Would it be expedient to extend the right of suffrage to women?" but "Have women citizens that right by the Constitution as it is?" * * * * The question is to be decided by the Constitution and the fundamental principles of our Government, and not by the usage and dogmas of the past. * * * * * *

The people of the United States determined this question by the fourteenth amendment to the Constitution, which declares that—

"All persons born or naturalized in the United States, and subject to the jurisdiction thereof, are citizens of the United States, and of the State wherein they reside. No State shall make or enforce any law which shall abridge the privileges or immunities of citizens of the United States; nor shall any State deprive any person of life, liberty, or property, without due process of law; nor deny to any person within its jurisdiction the equal protection of the law."

This amendment, after declaring who are citizens of the United States, and thus fixing but one grade of citizenship, which insures to all citizens alike all the privileges, immunities, and rights which accrue to that condition, goes on in the same section and prohibits these privileges and immunities from abridgment by the States.

Whatever these "privileges and immunities" are, they attach to the female citizen equally with the male. It is implied by this amendment that they are inherent, that they belong to citizenship as such, for they are not therein specified or enumerated.

The majority of the committee hold that the privileges guarantied by the fourteenth amendment do not refer to any other than the privileges embraced in section two of article four of the original text. * * *

Section two of article four provides for the privileges of "citizens of the States," while the first section of the fourteenth amendment protects the privileges of "citizens of the United States." The terms "citizens of the States" and "citizens of the United States" are by no means convertible.

A circuit court of the United States seems to hold a different view of this question from that stated by the committee.

In the case of the Live Stock Association *vs.* Crescent City, (1 Abbott, 396.) Justice Bradley, of the Supreme Court of the United States, delivering the opinion, uses the following language in relation to the first clause of the fourteenth amendment:

"The new prohibition that 'no State shall make or enforce any law which shall abridge the privileges or immunities of citizens of the United States' is not identical with the clause in the Constitution which declared that 'the citizens of each State shall be entitled to all the privileges and immunities of citizens in the several States.' It embraces much more.

"It is possible that those who framed the article were not themselves aware of the far-reaching character of its terms, yet if the amendment does in fact bear a broader meaning, and does extend its protecting shield over those who were never thought of when it was conceived and put in form, and does reach social evils which were never before prohibited by constitutional enactment, it is to be presumed that the American people in giving it their *imprimatur* understood what they were doing, and meant to decree what in fact they have decreed.

"The 'privileges and immunities' secured by the original Constitution were only such as each State gave to its own citizens," * * * * "but the fourteenth amendment prohibits any State from abridging the privileges or immunities of citizens of the United States, whether its own citizens or any others. It not merely requires equality of privileges, but it demands that the privileges and immunities of all citizens shall be absolutely unabridged and unimpaired."

In the same opinion, after enumerating some of the "privileges" of the citizens, such as were pertinent to the case on trial, but declining to enumerate all, the court further says:

"These privileges cannot be invaded without sapping the very foundation of republican government. A republican government is not merely a government of the people, but it is a free government." * * * *

"It was very ably contended on the part of the defendants that the fourteenth amendment was intended only to secure to all citizens equal capacities before the law. That was at first our view of it. But it does not so read. The language is, 'No State shall abridge the privileges or immunities of citizens of the United States.' What are the privileges and immunities of citizens of the United States? Are they capacities merely? Are they not also rights?"

The court in this case seems to intimate very strongly that the amendment was intended to secure the natural rights of citizens, as well as their equal capacities before the law.

In a case in the supreme court of Georgia, in 1869, the question was before the court whether a negro was competent to hold office in the State of Georgia. The case was ably argued on both sides, Mr. Akerman, the present Attorney General of the United States, being of counsel for the petitioner. Although the point was made and argued fully that the right to vote and hold office were both included in the privileges and immunities of citizens, and were thus guarantied by the fourteenth amendment, yet that point was not directly passed upon by the court, the court holding that under the laws and constitution of Georgia the negro citizen had the right claimed. In delivering the opinion, Chief Justice Brown said:

"It is not necessary to the decision of this case to inquire what are the 'privileges and immunities' of a citizen which are guarantied by the fourteenth amendment to the Constitution of the United States. Whatever they may be, they are protected against all abridgment by legislation." * * * * *

"Whether the 'privileges and immunities' of the citizen embrace political rights, including the right to hold office, I need not now inquire. If they do, that right is guarantied alike by the Constitution of the United States and of Georgia, and is beyond the control of the Legislature."

In the opinion of Justice McKay, among other propositions he lays down the following:

"2. The rights of the people of this State, white and black, are not granted to them by the constitution thereof; the object and effect of that instrument is not to give, but to restrain, deny, regulate, and guarantee rights, and all persons recognized by that constitution as citizens of the State have equal legal and political rights, except as otherwise expressly declared.

"3. It is the settled and uniform sense of the word 'citizen,' when used in reference to the citizens of the separate States of the United States, and to their rights as such citizens, that it describes a person entitled to every right, legal and political, enjoyed by any person in that State, unless there be some express exception made by positive law covering the particular person or class of persons whose rights are in question."

In the course of the argument of this case Mr. Akerman used the following language upon the point as to whether citizenship carried with it the right to hold office:

"It may be profitable to inquire how the term (citizen) has been understood in Georgia." * * * * "It will be seen that men whom Georgians have been accustomed to revere believed that citizenship in Georgia carried with it the right to hold office in the absence of positive restrictions."

The majority of the committee having started out with the erroneous hypothesis that the term "privileges of citizens of the United States," as used in the fourteenth amendment, means no more than the term "privileges of citizens" as used in section two of article four, discuss the question thus:

"The right of suffrage was not included in the privileges of citizens as used in section two, article four, therefore that right is not included in the privileges of citizens of the United States as used in the fourteenth amendment."

Their premise being erroneous, their whole argument fails. But if they were correct in their premise, we yet claim that their second position is not sustained by the authorities, and is shown to be fallacious by a consideration of the principles of free government.

We claim that from the very nature of our Government the right of suffrage is a fundamental right of citizenship, not only included in the term "privileges of citizens of the United States" as used in the fourteenth amendment, but also included in the term as used in section two of article four, and in this we claim we are sustained both by the authorities and by reason.

In Abbott *vs.* Bayley, (6 Pick., 92,) the supreme court of Massachusetts say:

"'The privileges and immunities' secured to the people of each State in every other State can be applied only to the case of a removal from one State into another. By such removal they become citizens of the adopted State without naturalization, and have a right to sue and be sued as citizens; and yet this privilege is qualified and not absolute, for they cannot enjoy the right of suffrage or eligibility to office without such term of residence as shall be prescribed by the constitution and laws of the State into which they shall remove."

This case fully recognizes the right of suffrage as one of the "privileges of the citizen," subject to the right of the State to regulate as to the term of residence. The same principle was laid down in Corfield *vs.* Coryell.

In the case of Corfield *vs.* Coryell, in the Supreme Court of the United States, Justice Washington, in delivering the opinion of the court, used the following language:

"'The privileges and immunities conceded by the Constitution of the United States to citizens in the several States,' are to be confined to those which are in their nature fundamental, and belong of right to the citizens of all free Governments. Such are the rights of protection of life and liberty, and to acquire and enjoy property, and to pay no higher impositions than other citizens, and to pass through and reside in the State at pleasure, and to enjoy the elective franchise as regulated and established by the laws or constitution of the State in which it is to be exercised."

And this is cited approvingly by Chancellor Kent, (2 Kent, section 72.)

This case is cited by the majority of the committee as sustaining their view of the law, but we are unable so to understand it. It is for them an exceedingly unfortunate citation.

In that case the court enumerated some of the "privileges of citizens," such as are "in their nature fundamental and belong of right to the citizens of all free Governments," (mark the language,) and among those rights place the "right of the elective franchise" in the same category with those great rights of life, liberty, and property. And yet the committee cite this case to show that this right is not a fundamental right of the citizen!

But it is added by the court that the right of the elective franchise "is to be enjoyed as regulated and established by the State in which it is to be exercised."

These words are supposed to qualify the right, or rather take it out of the list of fundamental rights, where the court had just placed it. The court is made to say by this attempt in the same sentence, "The elective franchise is a fundamental right of the citizen, and it is not a fundamental right." It is a "fundamental right," provided the State sees fit to grant the right. It is a "fundamental right of the citizen," but it does not exist unless the laws of the State give it. A singular species of "fundamental rights!" Is there not a clear distinction between the regulation of a right and its destruction? The State may regulate the right, but it may not destroy it.

What is the meaning of "regulate" and "establish?" Webster says: "Regulate—to put in good order." "Establish—to make stable or firm."

This decision, then, is that "the elective franchise is a fundamental right of the citizen of all free Governments, to be enjoyed by the citizen, under such laws as the State may enact to regulate the right and make it stable or firm." Chancellor Kent, in the section referred to, in giving the *substance* of this opinion, leaves out the word "establish," regarding the word "regulate" as sufficiently giving the meaning of the court.

This case is, in our opinion, a very strong one against the theory of the majority of the committee.

The committee cite the language of Mr. Webster, as counsel in United States *vs.* Primrose.

We indorse every word in that extract. We do not claim that a citizen of Pennsylvania can go into Virginia and vote in Virginia, being a citizen of Pennsylvania. No person has ever contended for such an absurdity. We claim that when the citizen of the United States becomes a citizen of Virginia, that the State of Virginia has neither right nor power to abridge the privileges of such citizen by denying him entirely the right of suffrage, and thus all political rights. The authorities cited by the majority of the committee do not seem to meet the case, certainly do not sustain their theory.

The case of Cooper *vs.* The Mayor of Savannah (4 Geo., 72) involved the question whether a free negro was a citizen of the United States. The court, in the opinion, says:

"Free persons of color have never been recognized as citizens of Georgia; they are not entitled to bear arms, vote for members of the Legislature, or hold any civil office; they have no political rights, but have personal rights, one of which is personal liberty."

That they could not vote, hold office, &c., was held evidence that they were not regarded as citizens.

In the Supreme Court of the United States, in the case of Scott *vs.* Sanford, (19 Howard, page 476,) Mr. Justice Daniel, in delivering his opinion, used the following language as to the rights and qualities of citizenship:

"For who it may be asked is a citizen? What do the character and status of citizens import? Without fear of contradiction, it does not import the condition of being private property, the subject of individual power and ownership. Upon a principle of etymology alone, the term "citizen," as derived from *civitas*, conveys the idea of connection or identification with the State or Government, and a participation in its functions. But beyond this there is not, it is believed, to be found, in the theories of writers on government, or in any actual experiment heretofore tried, an exposition of the term "citizen" which has not been understood as conferring the actual possession and enjoyment, or the perfect right of acquisition and enjoyment, of an entire equality of privileges, civil and political."

And in the same case Chief Justice Taney said: "The words 'people of the United States' and 'citizens' are synonymous terms, and mean the same thing; they both describe the political body, who, according to our republican institutions, form the sovereignty, and who hold the power, and conduct the Government through their representatives. They are what we familiarly call the sovereign people, and every citizen is one of this people, and a constituent member of this sovereignty." (19 Howard, 404.)

In an important case in the Supreme Court of the United States, Chief Justice Jay, in delivering the opinion of the court, said: "At the Revolution the sovereignty devolved on the people, and they are truly the sovereigns of the country, but they are sovereigns without subjects, (unless the African slaves may be so called,) and have none to govern but themselves. The citizens of America are equal as fellow-citizens, and joint tenants of the sovereignty." (Chishol *vs.* Georgia. 2 Dallas, 470.)

In Conner *vs.* Elliott, (18 Howard,) Justice Curtis, in declining to give an enumeration of all the "privileges" of the citizen, said: "According to the express words and clear meaning of the clause no privileges are secured except those that belong to citizenship."

The Supreme Court said, in Corfield *vs.* Coryell, that the elective franchise is such privilege; therefore, according to Justice Curtis, it belongs to citizenship. In a case in the supreme court of Kentucky, (1 Littell's Kentucky Reports, page 333,) the court say:

"No one can, therefore, in the correct sense of the term, be a citizen of a State who is not entitled upon the terms prescribed by the institutions of the State to all the rights and privileges conferred by these institutions upon the highest class of society."

Mr. Wirt, when Attorney General of the United States, in an official opinion to be found on page 508, first volume Opinions of Attorneys General, came to the conclusion that the negroes were not citizens of the United States, for the reason that they had very few of the "privileges" of citizens, and among the "privileges of citizens" of which they were deprived, that they could not vote at any election.

Webster defines a citizen to be a person, native or naturalized, who has the privilege of voting for public officers, and who is qualified to fill offices in the gift of the people.

Worcester defines the word thus: "An inhabitant of a republic who enjoys the rights of a citizen or freeman, and who has a right to vote for public officers as a citizen of the United States."

Bouvier, in his Law Dictionary, defines the term "citizen" thus: "One who, under the Constitution and laws of the United States, has a right to vote for Representatives in Congress and other public officers, and who is qualified to fill offices in the gift of the people."

Aristotle defines a citizen to be one who is a partner in the legislative and judicial power, and who shares in the honors of the State. (Aristotle de Repub., lib. 3, cap. 5, D.)

The essential properties of Athenian citizenship consisted in the share possessed by every citizen in the Legislature, in the election of magistrates, and in the courts of justice. (See Smith's Dictionary of Greek Antiquities, page 289.)

The possession of the *jus suffragii*, at least, if not also of the *jus honorum*, is the principle which governs at this day in defining citizenship in the countries deriving their jurisprudence from the civil law. (Wheaton's International Law, page 892.)

The Dutch publicist, Thorbecke, says:

"What constitutes the distinctive character of our epoch is the development of the right of citizenship. In its most extended as well as its most restricted sense it includes a great many properties.

"The right of citizenship is the right of voting in the government of the local, provincial, or national community of which one is a member. In this last sense the right of citizenship signifies a participation in the right of voting, in the general government as member of the State." (Rev. & Fr. Etr., tom. v., page 383.)

In a recent work of some research, written in opposition to female suffrage, the author takes the ground that women are not citizens, and urges that as a reason why they can properly be denied the elective franchise, his theory being that if full citizens they would be entitled to the ballot. He uses the following language:

"It is a question about which there may be some diversity of opinion, what constitutes citizenship, or who are citizens. In a loose and improper sense the word 'citizen' is sometimes used to denote any inhabitant of the country, but this is not a correct use of the word. Those, and no others, are properly citizens who were parties to the original compact by which the Government was formed, or their successors who are qualified to take part in the affairs of government by their votes in the election of public officers.

"Women and children are represented by their domestic directors or heads, in whose wills theirs is supposed to be included. They, as well as others not entitled to vote, are not properly citizens, but are members of the State, fully entitled to the protection of its laws. A citizen, then, is a person entitled to vote in the elections. He is one of those in whom the sovereign power of the State resides." (Jones on Suffrage, page 48.)

But all such fallacious theories as this are swept away by the fourteenth amendment, which abolishes the theory of different grades of citizenship, or different grades of rights and privileges, and declares all persons born in the country or naturalized in it to be citizens, in the broadest and fullest sense of the term, leaving no room for cavil, and guaranteeing to all citizens the rights and privileges of citizens of the Republic.

We think we are justified in saying that the weight of authority sustains us in the view we take of this question. But considering the nature of it, it is a question depending much for its solution upon a consideration of the Government under which citizenship is claimed. Citizenship in Turkey or Russia is essentially different in its rights and privileges from citizenship in the United States. In the former, citizenship means no more than the right to the protection of his absolute rights, and the "citizen" is a subject; nothing more. Here, in the language of Chief Justice Jay, there are no subjects. All, native-born and naturalized, are citizens of the highest class; here all citizens are sovereigns, each citizen bearing a portion of the supreme sovereignty, and therefore it must necessarily be that the right to a voice in the Government is the right and privilege of a citizen as such, and that which is undefined in the Constitution is undefined because it is self-evident.

Could a State disfranchise and deprive of the right to a vote all citizens who have red hair; or all citizens under six feet in height? All will consent that the States could not make such arbitrary distinctions the ground for denial of political privileges; that it would be a violation of the first article of the fourteenth amendment; that it would be abridging the privileges of citizens. And yet the denial of the elective franchise to citizens on account of sex is equally as arbitrary as the distinction on account of stature, or color of hair, or any other physical distinction * * *

But it is said in opposition to the "citizen's right" of suffrage that at the time of the establishment of the Constitution women were in all the States denied the right of voting, and that no one claimed at the time that the Constitution of the United States would change their status; that if such a change was intended it would have been explicitly declared in the Constitution, or at least carried into practice by those who framed the Constitution, and, therefore, such a construction of it is against what must have been the intention of the framers.

This is a very unsafe rule of construction. As has been said, the Constitution necessarily deals in general principles; these principles are to be carried out to their legitimate conclusion and result by legislation, and we are to judge of the intention of those who established the Constitution by what they say, guided by what they declare on the face of the instrument to be their object.

It is said by Judge Story, in Story on Constitution, "Contemporary construction is properly resorted to to illustrate and confirm the text." * * * * "It can never abrogate the text; it can never fritter away its obvious sense; it can never narrow down its true limitations."

It is a well-settled rule that in the construction of the Constitution the objects for which it was established, being expressed in the instrument, should have great influence; and when words and phrases are used which are capable of different constructions, that construction should be given which is the most consonant with the declared objects of the instrument.

We go to the preamble to ascertain the objects and purpose of the instrument. Webster defines "preamble" thus: "the introductory part of a statute, which states the reason and intent of the law."

In the preamble, then, more certainly than in any other way, aside from the language of the instrument, we find the intent.

Judge Story says:

"The importance of examining the preamble for the purpose of expounding the language of a statute has been long felt and universally conceded in all juridicial discussion. It is an admitted maxim" * * * * "that the preamble is a key to open the mind of the matters as to the mischiefs to be remedied and the objects to be accomplished by the statute." * * * * "It is properly resorted to where doubts or ambiguities arise upon the words of the enacting part, for if they are clear and unambiguous there seems little room for interpretation, except in cases leading to an obvious absurdity or to a direct overthrow of the intention expressed in the preamble." (Story on the Constitution, sec. 457.)

Try this question by a consideration of the objects for which the Constitution was established, as set forth in the preamble, "to establish justice." Does it establish justice to deprive of all representation or voice in the Government one half of its adult citizens and compel them to pay taxes to and support a Government in which they have no representation? Is "taxation without representation" justice established?

"To insure domestic tranquillity." Does it insure domestic tranquillity to give all the political power to one class of citizens, and deprive another class of any participation in the Government? No. The sure means of tranquillity is to give "equal political rights to all," that all may stand "equal before the law."

"To provide for the common defense." We have seen that the only defense the citizen has against oppression and wrong is by his voice and vote in the selection of the rulers and law-makers. Does it, then, "provide for the common defense," to deny to one half the adult citizens of the Republic that voice and vote?

"To secure the blessings of liberty to ourselves and our posterity." As has been already said, there can be no political liberty to any citizen deprived of a voice in the Government. This is self evident; it needs no demonstration. Does it, then, "secure the blessings of liberty to ourselves and our posterity," to deprive one half the citizens of adult age of this right and privilege?

Tried by the expressed objects for which the Constitution was established, as declared by the people themselves, this denial to the women citizens of the country of the right and privilege of voting is directly in contravention of these objects, and must, therefore, be contrary to the spirit and letter of the entire instrument.

And according to the rule of construction referred to no "contemporaneous construction, however universal it may be, can be allowed to set aside the expressed objects of the makers as declared in the instrument." The construction which we claim for the first section of the fourteenth amendment is in perfect accord with those expressed objects; and even if there were anything in the original text of the Constitution at variance with the true construction of that section, the amendment must control. Yet we believe that there is nothing in the original text at variance with what we claim to be the true construction of the amendment.

It is claimed by the majority of the committee that the adoption of the fifteenth amendment was by necessary implication a declaration that the States had the power to deny the right of suffrage to citizens for any other reasons than those of race, color, or previous condition of servitude.

We deny that the fundamental rights of the American citizen can be taken away by "implication."

There is no such law for the construction of the Constitution of our country. The law is the reverse—that the fundamental rights of citizens are not to be taken away by implication, and a constitutional provision for the protection of one class can certainly not be used to destroy or impair the same rights in another class.

It is too violent a construction of an amendment which prohibits States from or the United States from abridging the right of a citizen to vote, by reason of race, color, or previous condition of servitude, to say that by implication it conceded to the States the power to deny that right for any other reason. On that theory the States could confine the right of suffrage to a small minority, and make the State government aristocratic, overthrowing their republican form.

The fifteenth article of amendment to the Constitution clearly recognizes the right to vote as one of the rights of a citizen of the United States. This is the language:

"The right of citizens of the United States to vote shall not be denied or abridged by the United States, or by any State, on account of race, color, or previous condition of servitude."

Here is stated, first, the existence of a right; second, its nature. Whose right is it? The right of citizens of the United States. What is the right? The right to vote. And this right of citizens of the United States, States are forbidden to abridge. Can there be a more direct recognition of a right? Can that be abridged which does not exist? The denial of the power to abridge the right recognizes the existence of the right. Is it said that this right exists by virtue of State citizenship, and State laws and constitutions? Mark the language: "the right of citizens of the United States to vote;" not citizens of States. The right is recognized as existing independent of State citizenship.

But, it may be said, if the States had no power to abridge the right of suffrage, why the necessity of prohibiting them?

There may not have been a necessity; it

may have been done through caution, and because the peculiar condition of the colored citizens at that time rendered it necessary to place their rights beyond doubt or cavil.

It is laid down as a rule of construction by Judge Story that the natural import of a single clause is not to be narrowed so as to exclude implied powers resulting from its character simply because there is another clause which enumerates certain powers which might otherwise be deemed implied powers within its scope, for in such cases we are not to assume that the affirmative specification excludes all other implications. (2 Story on Constitution, section 449.)

There are numerous instances in the Constitution where a general power is given to Congress, and afterward a particular power given, which was included in the former; yet the general power is not to be narrowed because the particular power is given. On this same principle the fact that by the fifteenth amendment the States are specifically forbidden to deny the right of suffrage on account of race, color, or previous condition of servitude does not narrow the general provision in the fourteenth amendment which guaranties the privileges of all the citizens against abridgment by the States on any account.

The rule of interpretation relied upon by the committee in their construction of the fifteenth amendment is "that the expression of one thing is the exclusion of another," or the specification of particulars is the exclusion of generals.

Of these maxims Judge Story says:

"They are susceptible of being applied, and often are ingeniously applied, to the subversion of the text and the objects of the instrument. The truth is, in order to ascertain how far an affirmative or negative provision excludes or implies others, we must look to the nature of the provision, the subject-matter, the objects, and the scope of the instrument; these, and these only, can properly determine the rule of construction." (2 Story, 448.)

It is claimed by the committee that the second section of the fourteenth amendment implies that the several States may restrict the right of suffrage as to other than male citizens. We may say of this, as we have said of the theory of the committee upon the effect of the fifteenth amendment, it is a proposal to take away from the citizens guarantees of fundamental rights, by implication, which have been previously given in absolute terms.

The first section includes all citizens in its guarantees, and includes all the "privileges and immunities" of citizenship and guards them against abridgment, and under no recognized or reasonable rule of construction can it be claimed that by implication from the provisions of the second section the States may not only abridge but entirely destroy one of the highest privileges of the citizen to one half of the citizens of the country. What we have said in relation to the committee's construction of the effect of the fifteenth amendment applies equally to this.

The object of the first section of this amendment was to secure all the rights, privileges, and immunities of all the citizens against invasion by the States. The object of the second section was to fix a rule or system of apportionment for Representatives and taxation; and the provision referred to, in relation to the exclusion of males from the right of suffrage, might be regarded as in the nature of a penalty in case of denial of that right to that class. While it, to a certain extent, protected that class of citizens, it left the others where the previous provisions of the Constitution placed them. To protect the colored man more fully than was done by that penalty was the object of the fifteenth amendment.

In no event can it be said to be more than the recognition of an existing fact that only the male citizens were by the State laws allowed to vote, and that existing order of things was recognized in the rule of representation just as the institution of slavery was recognized in the original Constitution, in the article fixing the basis of representation, by the provision that only three fifths of all the slaves ("other persons") should be counted. There slavery was recognized as an existing fact, and yet the Constitution never sanctioned slavery, but, on the contrary, had it been carried out according to its true construction, slavery could not have existed under it; so that the recognition of facts in the Constitution must not be held to be a sanction of what is so recognized.

The majority of the committee say that this section implies that the States may deny suffrage to others than male citizens. If it implies anything it implies that the States may deny the franchise to all the citizens. It does not provide that they shall not deny the right to male citizens, but only provides that if they do so deny they shall not have representation for them.

So, according to that argument, by the second section of the fourteenth amendment the power of the States is conceded to entirely take away the right of suffrage even from that privileged class, the male citizens. And thus this rule of "implication" goes too far, and fritters away all the guarantees of the Constitution of the right of suffrage, the highest of the privileges of the citizen; and herein is demonstrated the reason and safety of the rule that fundamental rights are not to be taken away by implication, but only by express provision.

When the advocates of a privileged class of citizens under the Constitution are driven to implication to sustain the theory of taxation without representation, and American citizenship without political liberty, the cause must be weak indeed.

It is claimed by the majority that by section two, article one, the Constitution recognizes the power in States to declare who shall and who shall not exercise the elective franchise. That section reads as follows:

"The House of Representatives shall be composed of members chosen every second year by the people of the several States, and the electors in each State shall have the qualifications requisite for electors of the most numerous branch of the State Legislature."

The first clause of this section declares who shall choose the Representatives—mark the language: "Representatives shall be chosen by the people of the States," not by the male people, not by certain classes of the people, but by the people; so that the construction sought to be given this section, by which it would recognize the power of the State to disfranchise one half the citizens, is in direct contravention of the first clause of the section, and of its whole spirit, as well as of the objects of the instrument. The States clearly have no power to nullify the express provisions that the election shall be by the people, by any laws limiting the election to a moiety of the people.

It is true the section recognizes the power in the State to regulate the qualification of the electors; but, as we have already said, the power to regulate is a very different thing from the power to destroy.

The two clauses must be taken together, and both considered in connection with the declared purpose and objects of the Constitution.

The Constitution is necessarily confined to the statement of general principles. There are regulations necessary to be made as to the qualifications of voters, as to their proper age, their domicile, the length of residence necessary to entitle the citizen to vote in a given State or place. These particulars could not be provided in the Constitution but are necessarily left to the States, and this section is thus construed as to be in harmony with itself, and with the expressed objects of the framers of the Constitution and the principles of free government.

When the majority of the committee can demonstrate that "the people of the States" and "one half the people of the States" are equivalent terms, or that when the Constitution provides that the Representatives shall be elected by the people its requirements are met by an election in which less than one half the adult people are allowed to vote, then it will be admitted that this section to some extent sustains them.

The committee say that if it had been intended that Congress should prescribe the qualifications of electors the grant would have given Congress that power specifically. We do not claim that Congress has that power; on the contrary, admit that the States have it, but the section of the Constitution does prescribe who the electors shall be. That is what we claim—nothing more. They shall be "the people;" their qualifications may be regulated by the States; but to the claim of the majority of the committee that they may be "qualified" out of existence we cannot assent.

We are told that the acquiescence by the people, since the adoption of the Constitution, in the denial of political rights to women citizens, and the general understanding that such denial was in conformity with the Constitution, should be taken to settle the construction of that instrument.

Any force this argument may have it can only apply to the original text, and not to the fourteenth amendment, which is of but recene date.

But, as a general principle, this theory is fallacious. It would stop all political progress; it would put an end to all original thought, and put the people under that tyranny with which the friends of liberty have always had to contend—the tyranny of precedent.

From the beginning, our Government has been right in theory but wrong in practice. The Constitution, had it been carried out in its true spirit, and its principles enforced, would have stricken the chains from every slave in the Republic long since. Yet, for all this, it was but a few years since declared, by the highest judicial tribunal of the Republic, that, according to the "general understanding," the black man in this country had no rights the white man was bound to respect. General understanding and acquiescence is a very unsafe rule by which to try questions of constitutional law, and precedents are not infallible guides toward liberty and the rights of man. * * * * * * *

It is said by the majority of the committee that "if the right of female citizens to suffrage is vested by the Constitution, that right can be established in the courts."

We respectfully submit that with regard to the competency and qualification of electors for members of this House the courts have no jurisdiction.

This House is the sole judge of the election return and qualification of its own members, (article one, section five, of Constitution:) and it is for the House alone to decide upon a contest who are and who are not competent and qualified to vote. The judicial department cannot thus invade the prerogatives of the political department.

And it is therefore perfectly proper, in our opinion, for the House to pass a declaratory resolution, which would be an index to the action of the House, should the question be brought before it by a contest for a seat.

We therefore recommend to the House the adoption of the following resolution:

Resolved by the House of Representatives, That the right of suffrage is one of the inalienable rights of citizens of the United States, subject to regulation by the States, through equal and just laws; that this right is included in the "privileges of citizens of the United States" which are guaranteed by section one of article fourteen of amendments to the Constitution of the United States; and that women citizens, who are otherwise qualified by the laws of the State where they reside, are competent voters for Representatives in Congress.

Report of the Judiciary Committee of the Senate.

1872, January 25—Mr. CARPENTER, from the Committee on Judiciary, to whom was referred the memorial of Elizabeth Cady Stanton, Isabella Beecher Hooker, Elizabeth S. Bladen, Olympia Brown, Susan B. Anthony, and Josephine J. Griffing, citizens of the United States, praying for the enactment of a law, during the present session of Congress, to assist and protect them in the exercise of their right, and the right of all women, to participate in the elective franchise, which the memorialists claim they are entitled to under the Constitution of the United States, together with various other petitions and memorials to the same effect, and various protests in opposition thereto, reported as follows:

By the Constitution of the United States, prior to the fourteenth and fifteenth amendments, the power to regulate suffrage, even in the election of President and Vice President, Senators and Representatives in Congress, was possessed by the States composing the Union, so that Congress could make no affirmative provision concerning the same; nor could Congress alter or amend regulations made upon this subject by the respective States. Article one, section two provides as follows:

"The House of Representatives shall be composed of members chosen every second year by the people of the several States; and the electors in each State shall have the qualifications requisite for electors of the most numerous branch of the State Legislature."

Section three of the same article provides:

"The Senate of the United States shall be composed of two Senators from each State, chosen by the Legislature thereof for six years; and each Senator shall have one vote."

Article three, section one, provides:

"Each State shall appoint, in such manner as the Legislature thereof may direct, a number of electors equal to the whole number of Senators and Representatives to which the State may be entitled in the Congress."

From these provisions of the Constitution it is apparent that the States possessed the sole power of determining the qualifications of electors therein. And, so far as these provisions are concerned, it is manifest that each State had the power to make such discrimination as it pleased between its own citizens in regard to their participation in the elective franchise. Each State might admit all citizens, male and female, over a prescribed age, or only some classes of them, or might require a property qualification, which would, in effect, exclude all citizens not possessing the required amount of property. Each State might discriminate in this particular between its citizens on account of race, color, servitude, or upon any other ground. And under this Constitution the several States established various and incongruous regulations upon this subject. In Massachusetts no distinction on account of color was recognized, while in other States all persons having even admixture of African blood, however slight, were excluded; and some States required a property qualification, while others did not.

There is, however, another provision of the Constitution which merits consideration in this connection. Article four, section four, provides:

"The United States shall guarantee to every State in this Union a republican form of government."

Under this provision it is insisted, with some plausibility, that a State government which denies the elective franchise to a majority of the citizens of such State is not "a republican form of government." But your committee are not satisfied that this proposition can be maintained. In construing the Constitution we are compelled to give it such interpretation as will secure the result which was intended to be accomplished by those who framed it and the people who adopted it. The Constitution, like a contract between private parties, must be read in the light of the circumstances which surrounded those who made it. The history of the Colonies, the history of the Confederation, and the circumstances under which the Constitution itself was framed and adopted, must all be taken into account; and then we must ascertain by reading the whole instrument together the sense in which particular provisions and phrases were employed. If any State government which to-day excludes from suffrage a majority of its citizens is not in form a republican government, then a State government which did the same thing at the time the Constitution was adopted was not in form a republican government. The exclusion of all female citizens from the suffrage cannot impair the republican form of an existing State government unless the same thing worked the same result upon the State governments in existence when the Constitution of the United States was adopted.

It was assumed on all hands that the governments of the thirteen States which framed and adopted the constitution were in form republican; and this provision was intended to keep them so and make it impossible for any State to change its government into a monarchy. The construction of this provision now contended for would have made it the duty of the government of the Union during the first year of its existence to enter upon the reconstruction or remodeling the governments of the States by which the Union itself had been spoken into existence. In view of the history of those times, it cannot be maintained that the States or the people intended to confer such a power upon the Government of the Union; and no one can doubt that such an attempt on the part of the Union, in regard to the thirteen States, would have been condemned by the unanimous voice and resisted by the united force of the people. If such a power did not then exist under the Constitution of the United States, it does not now exist under this provision of the Constitution, which has not been amended. A construction which should give the phrase a "republican form of government" a meaning differing from the sense in which it was understood and employed by the people when they adopted the Constitution would be as unconstitutional as a departure from the plain and express language of the Constitution in any other particular. This is the rule of interpretation adopted by all commentators on the Constitution and in all judicial expositions of that instrument; and your committee are satisfied of the entire soundness of this principle. A change in the popular use of any word employed in the Constitution cannot retroact upon the Constitution, either to enlarge or limit its provisions.

There is another provision of the Constitution which is generally referred to in this connection, but which, in the opinion of your committee, has no application to the subject. Article four, section two, provides:

"The citizens of each State shall be entitled to all privileges and immunities of citizens in the several States."

It has been much discussed whether the right to vote and hold office in a State was within the privileges and immunities protected by the provision above quoted. But it is unnecessary to consider that question here, because, even if the right to vote and hold office be considered as embraced within this provision, still it was in the power of the State to which a citizen might remove to determine what class of citizens should or should not vote or hold office in such State, and the citizen removing to such State was only entitled to the privileges and immunities possessed by the class of citizens to which such removing citizen belonged under the constitution and laws of the State to which he had removed.

We come now to consider the fourteenth and fifteenth amendments to the Constitution, under which, also, the right of female suffrage is claimed. The fourteenth amendment, so far as applicable to this subject, is as follows:

"All persons born and naturalized in the United States, &c., are citizens of the United States and of the State wherein they reside. No State shall make or enforce any law which shall abridge the privileges or immunities of citizens of the United States, nor shall any State deprive any person of life, liberty, or property without due process of law, nor deny to any person within its jurisdiction the equal protection of the laws."

The second section of this amendment provides that—

"Representatives shall be apportioned among the several States according to their respective numbers, counting the whole number of persons in each State, excluding Indians not taxed. But when the right to vote at any election, &c., is denied to any of the male inhabitants being twenty-one years of age, &c., the basis of representation therein shall be reduced in the proportion which the number of such male citizens shall bear to the whole number of male citizens twenty-one years of age in such State."

It is evident from the second section of this amendment above quoted that the States are considered to possess the power of excluding a portion of their male citizens from the right to vote upon grounds or reasons to be determined by themselves; because this section determines that, in case the State shall exercise this right so as to exclude citizens of the United States, except for commission of crime, the basis of representation for such State shall be correspondingly reduced.

It was argued before your committee by the memorialists, who, by a departure from the usual practice of the committee, were admitted to a public discussion of the principles involved in the memorial, that the right of every citizen, male or female, to vote was secured by that clause of the first section of the fourteenth amendment which provides, "No State shall make or enforce any law which shall abridge the privileges or immunities of citizens of the United States;" and that the second section was designed to fix a penalty upon the State for a violation of the former provision.

But such a construction is at war with all the theories of constitutional government. An unconstitutional act is void. In other words, an unconstitutional act is no act. The Legislature of a State may attempt to pass a law impairing the obligation of contracts; but, as the Legislature cannot pass such an act, the attempt is void, and the obligation of the contract is not impaired. It would, therefore, be absurd to punish a State for the vain, ineffectual attempt to impair the obligation of a contract—a thing it could not do, and therefore had not done. So, if by the first section of the fourteenth amendment no State could make or enforce any law to deny the right of suffrage to any portion of its male citizens over twenty-one years of age not guilty of crime, then an attempt to do so would be merely void, wholly inoperative, and it would be absurd to punish such State for doing what it could not do, and therefore had not done.

The remedy under the Constitution against any attempted but unconstitutional legislation of a State is by application to the judicial courts of the Union, which have jurisdiction in all causes arising under the Constitution and laws of the United States, and a supervisory control by writ of error over State courts in regard to causes in which either party asserts a right or privilege under the Constitution or laws of the Union which is denied or overruled by the State court.

The positions maintained, first, that no State can deny to a citizen the right to vote; and second, that in case the State shall do what it cannot do certain consequences shall follow, would degrade the fourteenth amendment to the level of compounding or granting indulgence for the commission of unconstitutional acts. It would make the amendment say, first, no State shall do a certain thing; but, second, if a State shall do what it cannot do, it shall forfeit certain rights. It is hardly to be supposed that the fourteenth amendment intended to say that a State was forbidden by the Constitution to do a certain thing, but might do so by submitting to a reduction of its basis of representation in Congress.

But there is another reason, equally conclusive, against the construction contended for. By the fourteenth amendment Congress is empowered to enforce all the provisions of that amendment by appropriate legislation. Therefore, if a State should attempt to exclude from the right of suffrage any persons entitled under the fourteenth amendment to participate therein, it would be the undoubted duty of Congress to defeat such attempt by appropriate legislation. So that to regard the second section of this amendment as imposing upon the State a penalty for denying this right includes the absurdity of imposing such penalty for an attempt of the State to do what it is the duty of Congress to prevent.

Again, the right of female suffrage is inferentially denied by the second section of the fourteenth amendment, which provides that in case a State, in the exercise of a right conceded to exist, shall exclude a portion of the male inhabitants specified, "the basis of representation therein shall be reduced in the proportion which the number of such (excluded) male citizens shall bear to the whole number of male citizens twenty-one years of age in such State." The basis is not to be reduced in the proportion which the number of the excluded male citizens shall bear to the whole population of the State, male or female, but only in the proportion which they bear to the number of male citizens twenty-one years of age in such State. It is evident from this provision that females are not regarded as belonging to the voting population of a State.

The fifteenth amendment is equally decisive. It provides:

"The right of citizens of the United States to vote shall not be abridged or denied by the United States or by any State on account of race, color, or previous condition of servitude."

This amendment would have been wholly unnecessary if the fourteenth amendment had secured to all citizens the right to vote. It must be regarded as recognizing the right of every State, under the Constitution as it previously stood, to deny or abridge the right of a citizen to vote on any account, in the pleasure of such State; and by the fifteenth amendment the right of States in this respect is only so far restricted that no State can base such exclusion upon "race, color, or previous condition of servitude." With this single exception—race, color, and previous condition of servitude—the power of a State to make such exclusion is left untouched, and, indeed, is actually recognized by the fifteenth amendment as existing.

Your committee have confined themselves to the precise question involved in the memorial, namely, the present constitutional right of female citizens to vote, as to which your committee are unanimous, and have not considered the broader question, whether the Constitution ought to be so amended as to permit female suffrage, a report upon which might develop a difference of opinion among the members of your committee.

State Action.

Iowa.

A joint resolution to strike the word "male" from section one of article two, and from section four of article three of the constitution of the State was proposed in the Legislature of 1870, and voted on as follows:

IN HOUSE. *March* 29, 1870.

YEAS—Messrs. Delos Arnold, James W. Beatty, P. G. Bonewitz, Aaron Brown, William Butler, William H. Campbell, T. B. Carpenter, John H. Carver, *Theophilus Crawford*, Harwood G. Day, D. Dickerson, Charles Dudley, D. T. Durham, William C. Evans, Amos S. Faville, John W. Green, William Harper, O. C. Harrington, B. A. Haycock, *James M. Hood*, John F. Hopkins, William Hopkirk, *John P. Irish*, George W. Jones, John A. Kasson, John F. Lacey, Daniel S. Lee, George H. McGarven, Wesley W. Merritt, Joseph D. Miles, Lewis Miles, jr., John L. Millard, Claudius B. Miller, *William Mills*, J.D. Miracle, John Morrison, jr., Samuel Murdock, Joshua G. Newbold, Cole Noel, Timothy O. Norris, Galusha Parsons, Samuel H. Rogers, Neal W. Rowell, John Russell, Cummings Sanborn, Joshua W. Satterthwait, A. H. Slutsman, Alexander H. Swan, John H. Tait, Gilium S. Toliver, John M. Traer, J. Q. Tufts, James Wilson, Aylett R. Cotton, (Speaker)—54.

NAYS—Messrs. Carlos C. Applegate, Joseph Ball, *David S. Bell*, John Berasheim, Joel Brown, Geo. W. Butterfield, *John Christoph*, M. E Cutts, *Emory De Groat*, *James Dunne*, *Patrick Gibbons*, Geo. D. Harrison, *John H. Hartenbower*, B. F. Hartshorn, *Christian Hirschler*, Joseph Hobson, Henry L. Huff, John D. Hunter, Benj. F. Keables, James P. Ketcham, Anders O. Lommen, John Mahin, Constant R. Marks, *Fred. O'Donnell*, Henry O. Pratt, Matthias J. Rohlfs, Geo. N. Rasser, Erastus Snow, David Stewart, John Y. Stone, Hamilton B. Taylor, Edgar A. Warner, William K. Wood, Pierce G. Wright, Geo. H. Wright—35.

IN SENATE, *March* 30, 1870.

YEAS—Messrs. Benj. F. Allen, Chas. Beardsley, G. G. Bennett, Frank T. Campbell, *J. P. Casady*, John M. Cathcart, James Chapin, Geo. W. Couch, William G. Donnan, *Lewis B. Dunham*. Joseph Dysart, Geo. E. Griffith, A. H. Hamilton, Joseph W. Havens, Alexander B. Ireland, Isaac W. Keller, Matthew Long, Robert Lowry, John McKean, Samuel McNutt, Napoleon B. Moore, Benj. F. Murray, Homer E. Newell, Abial R. Pierce, Robt. Smyth, Henry C. Traverse, Marcus Tuttle, Jacob G. Vale, W. F. Vermillion, John P. West, Wm. P. Wolf, J. D. Wright—32.

NAYS—Messrs. Chas. Atkins, Edward M. Bill, Henry C. Bulis, Hans R. Claussen, John N. Dixon, *Liberty E. Fellows*, Joseph Grimes, *F. M. Knoll* William Larrabee, *E. S. McCulloch*, John G. Patterson—11.

The House voted, February 21, 1872, on the ratification of this resolution, passed by the thirteenth General Assembly, as follows:

YEAS—Messrs. Amos R. Appleton, *Webster Ballinger*, James W. Beatty, John P. Beatty, Wm. W. Blackman, Fletcher A. Blake, *Isaac Blakely*. Lewis O. Bliss, Peter G. Bonewitz, Caleb Booth, Phineas Cadwell, Leander E. Cardell, John H. Carver, John C. Clarke, Frank M. Davis, David D. Davisson, *Elmus Day*, Ira E. Draper, Samuel B. Dumont, David T. Durham, Charles J. A. Ericson, William C. Evans, John H. Gear, Marshall Goodspeed, John M. Hanson, Sumner B. Hewett, jr., William Hopkirk, Joseph M. Hovey, *John P. Irish*, Andrew Johnston, John A. Kasson, Michael A. Leahy, Wm. D. Litzenberg, William Maxwell, David J. McCoy, Oliver Mills, Claudius B. Miller, John Morrison, jr., Joshua G. Newbold, Cornelius T. Peet, Henry O. Pratt, Geo. Rule, David Secor, Eli M. Stedman, Robert Struthers. John Tasker, J. Q. Tufts. *James M. Tuttle*, Geo. B. Van Sauer, Samuel Whitten, James L. Williams, John F. Wilson, Henry B. Wood, Appler R. Wright, James Wilson, (Speaker)—39.

NAYS—Messrs. John Beresheim, Knut E. Bergh, William Butler, Samuel T. Caldwell, *Edward Campbell*, jr., *John Christoph*, Frank C. Clark, Cicero Close, James H. Crawford, Warren Danforth, *Henry Dayton*, Francis A. Duncan, Lauren F. Ellsworth, Robert B. Flenniken, Joseph H. Freeman, George C. Heberling, *James Hilton*, Benj. F. Keables, John M. Lee, Joseph McClurn, Nathaniel A. Merrell, *Fred. O'Donnell*, *George Paul*, Charles G. Perkins, *William H. Reed*, Lewis Reuther, James Rice, M. J. Rohlfs, *Andrew Sandry*, Conrad Schweer, *James A. Skillen*, *E. M. Stewart*, *Washburn A. Stow*, Fred. Teale, James Van De Venter, Hugo G. Van Meter, Charles H. Wilson, John R. Wright, and James Wilson, (Speaker)—39.

In the senate, March 29, 1872, the vote was as follows:

YEAS—Messrs. Charles Beardsley, George W. Bemis, John E. Burke, Frank T. Campbell, John C. Chambers, Alonzo Converse, Robert Dague, Mark A. Dashiell, Joseph Dysart, E. A. Howland, James S. Hurley, E. B. Kephart, George M. Maxwell, M. A. McCoid, John McKean, Samuel McNutt, Martin Read, John Shane, Elish T. Smith, Jacob G. Vale, John P. West, James A. Young—22.

NAYS—Messrs. Benjamin F. Allen, Albert Boomer, Hans R. Claussen, Oliver W. Crary, *Samuel H. Fairall*, William H. Fitch, *Edward J. Gault*, Joseph W. Havens, Alex. B. Ireland, James P. Ketcham, *Samuel H. Kirine*, William Larrabee, John H. Leavitt, Robert Lowry, *E. S. McCulloch*, Joseph H. Merrill, Joseph D. Miles, Benjamin F. Murray, John J. Russell, John Y. Stone, *L. W. Stuart*, R. Howe Taylor, George R. Willett, *Horatio A. Wonn*—24.

So the proposed amendments were defeated.

Maine.

Following is the text of a bill, acted upon by the Legislature of Maine, "abolishing all law discriminating between female and male suffrage in the election of President and Vice President of the United States:"

SECTION 1. Every female citizen of the United States of the age of twenty-one years and upwards, with the same exception as is applied to male citizens in section one of article second of the constitution of this State, having her residence established in this State for the term of three months next preceding any election for President and Vice President of the United States, shall be an elector for President and Vice President of the United States, in the city, town, or plantation where her residence is so established, in the same manner as now provided by law for male citizens in such elections.

IN SENATE.

1872, February 28.—The bill passed by a vote of 15 yeas to 8 nays, as follows:

YEAS—Messrs. C. A. Chaplin, C. L. Dunning, *C. S. Fletcher*, R. Foster, W. E. Hadlock, S. F. Hinks, C. Humphrey, W. Irish, A. Kennedy, J. May, *W. H. McLellan*, J. B. Nickels, A. G. O'Brion, W. Philbrick, F. R. Webber—15.

NAYS—Messrs. I. Cole, J. Dingley, jr., C. H. Hobbs, J. Kimball, J. Davis, J. B. Foster, F. M. Howes, H. Pennell—8.

IN HOUSE.

February 29—The bill failed to pass—yeas 41, nays 53; as follows:

YEAS—Messrs. R. T. Allen, O. D. Bailey, D. Barker, H. Bliss, jr., W. W. Bragdon, C. P. Brown, J. M. Carleton, *G. B. Carll*, A. B. Erskine, M. M. Folsome, C. K. Foss, R. H. Goding, E. Gray, *A. D. Griffin*, E. Hahn, *F. Haines*, *S. K. Hamilton*, C. Holden, N. Howard, E. Jepson, G. B. Kenniston, A. G. Lebroke, L. Lord, H. McAllister, J. Nash, J. C. Pierce, O. D. Potter, J. W. Porter, J. W. Perkins, J. J. Perry, G. H. Snow, I. W. Springer, *I. B. Thompson*, *A. J. Tibbetts*, S. Titcomb, W. Tufts, A. B. Wells, J. F. Whitcomb, W. Wilson, E. Woodbury, M. M. Evans—41.

NAYS—Messrs. *B. M. Baker*, J. F. Brackett, J. H. Burleigh, *J. Bennett, jr.*, D. A. Campbell, *G. W. Clark*, *I. Coombs*, *W. O. Counce*, J. H. Crandon, *C. Deering*, C. A. Erskine, D. Farrar, J. D. Fessenden, E. Fields, *J. Fog*, A. Gary, *I. C. Glidden*, J. Harrison, R. Harding, *J. O. A. Harmon*, H. Harmon, E. Hayes, J. Holbrook, C. C. Humphreys, *P. C. Kegan*, E. Knight, T. N. Lord, E. J. Millay, A. Mitchell, *A. Moore*, J. W. Palmer, W. Paul, W. F. Perry, J. W. Phillips, F. A. Pike, *W. A. Potter*, *W. H. Preble*, R. Prince, F. M. Ray, *A. R. Reed*, F. Robie, B. A. Sautelle, W. Silsby, M. Smith, *S. Stuart*, S. W. Tibbetts, O. D. Turner, *I. A. Walker*, *B. T. Wentworth*, A. H. Whitmore, *E. Wilson*, A. T. Winslow, J. P. Wyman—53.

Massachusetts.

March 16, 1872, the committee on female suffrage, consisting of three members of the senate and eight members of the house, a majority favoring and a minority dissenting, reported a concurrent resolution to amend the constitution of the Commonwealth by adding to it the following article:

ARTICLE OF AMENDMENT.

The word male is hereby stricken from the third article of the amendments of the constitution. Hereafter women of this Commonwealth shall have the right of voting at all elections, and of holding all offices, upon the same terms, conditions, and qualifications, and subject to the same restrictions and disabilities, as male citizens of this Commonwealth are, and no others.

The resolution required the affirmative vote of a majority of the senators and two thirds of the members of the house present and voting thereon; if thus adopted, to be referred to the general court next to be chosen; and if then agreed to, to be submitted to the people for ratification.

During the first of these three stages the resolution of amendment failed.

Territorial Action.

February 12, 1870, the following became a law of the Territory of Utah: that every woman of the age of twenty-one years who has resided in this Territory six months next preceding any general or special election, born or naturalized in the United States, or who is the wife, widow, or the daughter of a native born or naturalized citizen of the United States, shall be entitled to vote at any election in this Territory.

This law still remains in force.

In Wyoming the Legislature of 1871 passed the bill to repeal the act authorizing woman suffrage, but the Governor of the Territory, John A. Campbell, vetoed the bill, and the veto was sustained. The act giving the right passed in 1870, and about six hundred voted at the election of that year.

XIX.

COMMON-SCHOOL BILL.

Common-School Fund.

1872, February 8—The following bill passed the House:

Section first provides that the net proceeds of the public lands be forever consecrated and set apart for the education of the people.

The second section requires the Secretary of the Interior to ascertain the total receipts from the sale of public lands, and to certify to the Secretary of the Treasury the amount of the net cash proceeds.

The third section requires the Secretary of the Treasury to invest one half the amount in United States five per cent. bonds, to constitute a perpetual fund to be known as the national education fund, and to certify each year to the Secretary of the Interior the amount so paid into the Treasury.

Section four provides that the Commissioner of Education shall apportion one half of the net proceeds for the previous year, with the whole amount of the income of the educational fund, to the several States and Territories and to the District of Columbia, upon the basis of population of said States and Territories between the ages of four and twenty-one years: *Provided, however*, That for the first ten years the distribution of the said fund to and among the several States and Territories, including the District of Columbia, shall be made according to the ratio of the illiteracy of their respective populations, as shown, from time to time, by the last preceding published census of the United States.

Section five provides that each of the States and Territories and the District of Columbia that shall, before January 1, 1873, provide by law for the free education of all its children between the ages of six and sixteen years, shall be entitled to its share of the first distribution.

Section six provides that fifty per cent. of the amount received by any State or Territory or by the District of Columbia for the first year, and ten per cent. in any year thereafter, may be applied to the maintenance of schools, for the instruction of teachers of common schools, said sum after the first year to be applied wholly to the payment of teachers.

Section seven prescribes the conditions upon which each of the States and Territories and the District of Columbia shall be entitled to receive its share of every apportionment after the first.

Section eight requires the Commissioner of Education to certify each year to the Secretary of the Treasury whether each State, Territory, and District is entitled to its share, and the amount of such share. If he withhold a certificate from either, its share to be kept separate in the Treasury until the close of the next session of Congress, and then, if Congress shall not, at its next session, direct such share to be paid, it shall be added to the general educational fund: *Provided*, That no moneys belonging to any State or Territory under this act shall be withheld from any State or Territory, for the reason that the laws thereof provide for separate schools for white children and black children, or refuse to organize a system of mixed schools.

Section nine requires the superintendent of public instruction of each State and Territory and the District of Columbia to apportion the amount certified to his State, Territory, or District to the several school districts therein which shall have maintained free public schools for three months during the preceding year, upon such basis of population, number of children of school age, or attendance upon the schools during the preceding year, as may be by law determined by such State, Territory, or District; the amount to be applied in payment of teachers.

Section ten provides that the amount apportioned to the school districts shall be paid upon the warrant of the Commissioner of Education, countersigned by the Secretary of the Interior, to the State, territorial, or District treasury, or to such officer as shall be designated by the laws of such State, Territory, or District; and requires the treasurer or officer to report each year to the Commissioner of Education a detailed statement of the payments made and the balance on hand; and defines "school district."

Section eleven provides that in case any State or Territory shall misapply the funds received, or fail to comply with the prescribed conditions, or to report the disposition thereof, such State or Territory to forfeit its right to any subsequent appropriation until the full amount misapplied, lost, or misappropriated shall have been replaced by such State or Territory; that all forfeited apportionments be added to the educational fund; and making the misapplying, misappropriating, squandering or embezzling the funds a felony, punishable by fine or imprisonment, or by both.

Section twelve gives the circuit courts of the United States exclusive jurisdiction of all offenses committed against the provisions of this act.

Section thirteen provides that the existing laws and regulations regarding the payment to States upon their admission into the Union of five per cent. of the net proceeds of the sales of the public lands within their respective limits, shall not be affected by this act.

The vote on passing was—yeas 117, nays 98:

YEAS—Messrs. *Acker*, Ames, Banks, Barber, Barry, *Bell*, Beveridge, Bigby, A. Blair, G. M. Brooks, Buckley, Buffinton, Burchard, Burdett, W. T. Clark, Cobb,

Coburn, Coghlan, Conger, Darrall, Dawes, Donnan, Duell, Dunnell, Eames, *Edwards*, *Ely*, Farnsworth, Farwell, Finkelnburg, C. Foster, W. D. Foster, Frye, Garfield, *Garrett*, *Golladay*, Goodrich, Hale, Halsey, Harmer, *Harper*, G. E. Harris, Havens, Hawley, Hay, Hays, G. W. Hazelton, J. W. Hazelton, Hill, Hoar, Hooper, Kelley, Kellogg, *Kerr*, Ketcham, Lamport, Lansing, *Leach*, Lowe, Lynch, Maynard, McGrew, McKee, Merriam, Monroe, Moore, Morphis, Packard, Palmer, I. C. Parker, Pendleton, Perce, A. F. Perry, Platt, Poland, Porter, *Potter*, Prindle, Rainey, E. H. Roberts, Sawyer, Seeley, Sessions, Shanks, Sheldon, Shellabarger, *Slocum*, J. A. Smith, W. C. Smith, Snapp, Snyder, T. J. Speer, Sprague, Starkweather, Stevenson, *Storm*, Stowell, Strong, *Sutherland*, Sypher, Taffe, Thomas, *D. Townsend*, W. Townsend, Turner, Twichell, Tyner, Upson, Wakeman, Walden, Wallace, Walls, Wheeler, Whiteley, Willard, Williams of Indiana, J. M. Wilson—117.

NAYS—Messrs. *Adams*, Ambler, *Arthur*, Averill, *Barnum*, Beatty, *Beck*, *Biggs*, Bingham, *Bird*, *Braxton*, *Bright*, *J. Brooks*, *Caldwell*, *Campbell*, *Carroll*, F. Clarke, *Comingo*, *Conner*, Cotton, *Cox*, *Crebs*, *Critcher*, *Crossland*, *Davis*, Dickey, *Dox*, *Du Bose*, *Duke*, *Eldredge*, *Forker*, *H. D. Foster*, *Getz*, *Griffith*, *Haldeman*, *Hancock*, *Handley*, *Hanks*, *J. T. Harris*, *Hereford*, *Herndon*, *Hibbard*, *Holman*, Houghton, *Kendall*, Killinger, *King*, *Lamison*, *Lewis*, *Manson*, *Marshall*, *McClelland*, *McCormick*, *McHenry*, *McIntyre*, McJunkin, *McKinney*, *McNeely*, Mercur, *Merrick*, *Morgan*, L. Myers, Negley, *Niblack*, Orr, Packer, *H. W. Parker*, Peck, *E. Perry*, *Price*, *Read*, *E. Y. Rice*, *J. M. Rice*, *Ritchie*, *Roosevelt*, Sargent, *Sherwood*, *Shober*, *Slater*, *Sloss*, *Stevens*, Stoughton, *Swann*, *Terry*, *Tuthill*, *Van Trump*, *Vaughan*, *Voorhees*, *Waddell*, Waldron, *Warren*, *Wells*, *Whitthorne*, *Williams* of New York, J. T. Wilson, *Winchester*, *Wood*, *Young*—98.

There were many votes upon details, the pending bill being that reported from the Committee on Education and Labor. The most important were these:

February 7—Mr. HOLMAN moved to add the following proviso to section two:

Provided, however, That after the passage of this act no public lands of the United States shall be sold except mineral land and town sites, and all the public lands of the United States adapted to agriculture shall be reserved for actual settlers under the provisions of the homestead laws, subject, however, to land warrants and college scrip issued by authority of Congress, and the grants which Congress shall hereafter make in the Territories and new States for the purposes of education.

Which was disagreed to—yeas 103, nays 107:

YEAS—Messrs. *Acker*, *Adams*, Ambler, *Arthur*, *Barnum*, Beatty, *Beck*, Beveridge, *Biggs*, Bingham, *Bird*, *J. G. Blair*, *Braxton*, *Bright*, *J. Brooks*, *Caldwell*, *Campbell*, *Carroll*, Coghlan, *Comingo*, *Conner*, Cotton, *Cox*, *Crebs*, *Critcher*, *Crossland*, *Davis*, *Dox*, *Du Bose*, *Duke*, *Eldredge*, *Ely*, Farnsworth, Finkelnburg, *Forker*, *Garrett*, *Getz*, *Golladay*, *Griffith*, *Haldeman*, *Hancock*, *Handley*, *Hanks*, *Harper*, *J. T. Harris*, Hawley, Hay, *Hereford*, *Herndon*, *Hibbard*, *Holman*, Houghton, *Kerr*, *King*, *Lamison*, *Leach*, *Lewis*, *Manson*, *Marshall*, *McClelland*, *McCormick*, *McHenry*, *McIntyre*, *McKinney*, *McNeely*, *Merrick*, Moore, *Morgan*, *Niblack*, Orr, *H. W. Parker*, *E. Perry*, *Potter*, *Price*, *Randall*, *Read*, *E. Y. Rice*, *J. M. Rice*, *Ritchie*, *W. R. Roberts*, *Robinson*, *Roosevelt*, *Sherwood*, *Shober*, *Slater*, *Sloss*, *Stevens*, *Storm*, *Swann*, *Terry*, *D. Townsend*, *Tuthill*, *Van Trump*, *Vaughan*, *Voorhees*, *Waddell*, *Walden*, *Warren*, *Wells*, *Whitthorne*, *Winchester*, *Wood*, *Young*—103.

NAYS—Messrs. Averill, Banks, Barber, Barry, Bigby, A. Blair, G. M. Brooks, Buckley, Buffinton, Burchard, Burdett, B. F. Butler, R. R. Butler, F. Clarke, W. T. Clark, Cobb, Coburn, Conger, Creely, Darrall, Dickey, Donnan, Duell, Dunnell, Eames, Farwell, C. Foster, W. D. Foster, Frye, Garfield, Goodrich, Hale, Halsey, Harmer, G. E. Harris, Havens, Hays, G. W. Hazelton, J. W. Hazelton, Hill, Hoar, Kelley, Kellogg, Ketcham, Killinger, Lamport, Lansing, Lowe, Lynch, Maynard, McGrew, McJunkin, McKee, Mercur, Merriam, Monroe, Morey, Morphis, L. Myers, Negley, Packard, Packer, I. C. Parker, Peck, Pendleton, Perce, A. F. Perry, Peters, Platt, Poland, Porter, Rainey, E. H. Roberts, Rusk, Sawyer, Seeley, Sessions, Shanks, Sheldon, Shellabarger, J. A. Smith, W. C. Smith, Snapp, T. J. Speer, Sprague, Starkweather, Stevenson, Stoughton, Stowell, Strong, *Sutherland*, Taffe, Thomas, W. Townsend, Turner, Tyner, Upson, Wakeman, Waldron, Wallace, Walls, Wheeler, Whiteley, Willard, Williams of Indiana, J. M. Wilson, J. T. Wilson—107.

Mr. GOODRICH moved to add to section four the following:

Provided, however, That for the first ten years the distribution of the said fund to and among the several States and Territories, including the District of Columbia, shall be made according to the ratio of the illiteracy of their respective populations, as shown, from time to time, by the last preceding published census of the United States.

Which was agreed to—yeas 125, nays 83:

YEAS—Messrs. *Acker*, *Barnum*, Barry, *Beck*, Beveridge, Bigby, *Biggs*, A. Blair, *J. G. Blair*, *Braxton*, *Bright*, *J. Brooks*, Buckley, Burdett, R. R. Butler, *Caldwell*, *Campbell*, *Carroll*, Cobb, Coburn, *Comingo*, *Conner*, *Crebs*, *Critcher*, *Crossland*, *Davis*, Donnan, *Dox*, *Du Bose*, Duell, *Duke*, *Edwards*, *Ely*, Farnsworth, Farwell, *Forker*, *Garrett*, *Getz*, *Golladay*, Goodrich, *Griffith*, *Haldeman*, *Hancock*, *Handley*, *Hanks*, *J. T. Harris*, Hawley, Hay, Hays, G. W. Hazelton, *Hereford*, *Herndon*, *Hibbard*, *Kerr*, *King*, *Lamison*, Lamport, Lansing, *Leach*, *Lewis*, *Manson*, *Marshall*, Maynard, *McClelland*, *McCormick*, *McHenry*, *McIntyre*, McKee, *McKinney*, *McNeely*, Merriam, *Merrick*, Moore, Morey, *Morgan*, Morphis, *Niblack*, Packard, *H. W. Parker*, I. C. Parker, Perce, *E. Perry*, Platt, Porter, *Potter*, *Price*, Prindle, Rainey, *Read*, *E. Y. Rice*, *J. M. Rice*, *Ritchie*, E. H. Roberts, *W. R. Roberts*, *Robinson*, *Roosevelt*, Sheldon, *Sherwood*, *Shober*, *Slater*, *Slocum*, *Sloss*, Snapp, Snyder, T. J. Speer, *Stevens*, *Storm*, Stowell, *Swann*, Taffe, *Terry*, Thomas, *D. Townsend*, Turner, *Tuthill*, *Vaughan*, *Waddell*, Wallace, *Warren*, *Wells*, Whiteley, *Whitthorne*, *Winchester*, *Wood*, *Young*—125.

NAYS—Messrs. *Adams*, Ambler, *Arthur*, Averill, Banks, Barber, Beatty, Bingham, *Bird*, G. M. Brooks, Buffinton, Burchard, B. F. Butler, W. T. Clark, F. Clarke, Conger, Cotton, *Cox*, Creely, Dawes, Dickey, Dunnell, Eames, *Eldredge*, Finkelnburg, C. Foster, W. D. Foster, Frye, Garfield, Hale, Harmer, G. E. Harris, J. W. Hazelton, Hill, Hoar, *Holman*, Hooper, Houghton, Kelley, Kellogg, Ketcham, Killinger, Lowe, McJunkin, Mercur, Monroe, L. Myers, Negley, Orr, Packer, Palmer, Peck, Pendleton, A. F. Perry, Peters, Poland, *Randall*, Sawyer, Seeley, Sessions, Shanks, Shellabarger, J. A. Smith, W. C. Smith, Sprague, Starkweather, Stoughton, Strong, *Sutherland*, W. Townsend, Twichell, Tyner, Upson, *Van Trump*, *Voorhees*, Wakeman, Walden, Waldron, Wheeler, Willard, Williams of Indiana, J. M. Wilson, J. T. Wilson—83.

Mr. HEREFORD moved to add to section eight the following:

Provided, That no moneys belonging to any State or Territory under this act shall be withheld from any State or Territory for the reason that the laws thereof provide for separate schools for white children and black children, or refuse to organize a system of mixed schools.

Which was agreed to—yeas 115, nays 81:

YEAS.—Messrs. *Acker*, *Adams*, *Arthur*, *Beck*, *Biggs*, *Bird*, *J. G. Blair*, *Braxton*, *Bright*, *J. Brooks*, Burchard, R. R. Butler, *Caldwell*, *Campbell*, Coburn, Coghlan, *Comingo*, *Conner*, *Cox*, *Crebs*, *Critcher*, *Crossland*, *Davis*, *Dox*, *Du Bose*, *Duke*, *Edwards*, *Eldredge*, *Ely*, Farnsworth, Farwell, *Forker*, *H. D. Foster*, *Garrett*, *Getz*, *Golladay*, *Griffith*, *Haldeman*, Hale, Halsey, *Hancock*, *Handley*, *Hanks*, *Harper*, *J. T. Harris*, Hawley, Hay, Hays, *Hereford*, *Hern*-

don, *Hibbard*, *Holman*, *Kerr*, Killinger, *King*, *Lamison*, *Leach*, *Lewis*, *Manson*, *Marshall*, *McClelland*, *McCormick*, McGrew, *McHenry*, *McIntyre*, *McKinney*, *McNeely*, *Merrick*, Moore, *Morgan*, L. Myers, *Niblack*, Orr, Packard, Packer, *H. W. Parker*, I. C. Parker, *E. Perry*, *Potter*, *Price*, *Randall*, *Read*, *E. Y. Rice*, *J. M. Rice*, *Ritchie*, *W. R. Roberts*, *Robinson*, *Roosevelt*, Shanks, *Sherwood*, *Shober*, *Slater*, *Sloss*, T. J. Speer, *Stevens*, *Storm*, *Sutherland*, *Swann*, *Terry*, *D. Townsend*, *Tuthill*, Tyner, *Van Trump*, *Vaughan*, *Voorhees*, *Waddell*, *Warren*, *Wells*, Whiteley, *Whitthorne*, Williams of Indiana, J. M. Wilson, *Winchester*, *Wood*, *Young*—115.

NAYS.—Messrs. Ambler, Averill, Banks, Barber, Barry, Beatty, Beveridge, Bingham, A. Blair, G. M. Brooks, Buckley, Buffinton, Burdett, B. F. Butler, Cobb, Conger, Cotton, Creeley, Darrall, Dawes, Dickey, Donnan, Duell, Dunnell, Eames, Finkelnburg, C. Foster, W. D. Foster, Frye, Garfield, Goodrich, Harmer, G. W. Hazelton, J. W. Hazelton, Hoar, Hooper, Kelley, Kellogg, Lamport, Lansing, Lynch, Maynard, McJunkin, McKee, Mercur, Merriam, Monroe, Negley, Palmer, Peck, Pendleton, Perce, A. F. Perry, Platt, Porter, Prindle, Rainey, E. H. Roberts, Sawyer, Seeley, Sessions, Shellabarger, J. A. Smith, W. C. Smith, Sprague, Starkweather, Stevenson, Stoughton, Stowell, Strong, Thomas, W. Townsend, Turner, Twichell, Upson, Wakeman, Walden, Wallace, Walls, Wheeler, Willard—81

Mixed Schools.

1872, March 11—Mr. HEREFORD moved to suspend the rules and pass this resolution:

Whereas it is one of the fundamental principles of our form of government that Governments derive their just powers from the consent of the governed: Therefore,

Be it resolved, That it would be contrary to the Constitution and a tyrannical usurpation of power for Congress to force mixed schools upon the States, and equally unconstitutional and tyrannical for Congress to pass any law interfering with churches, public carriers, or innkeepers, such subjects of legislation belonging of right to the States respectively.

Which was disagreed to—yeas 60, nays 86:

YEAS—Messrs. *Acker*, *Arthur*, *Beck*, *Biggs*, *Bird*, *Braxton*, *J. Brooks*, *Caldwell*, *Comingo*, *Conner*, *Crebs*, *Critcher*, *Crossland*, *Davis*, *Dox*, *Du Bose*, *Eldredge*, *Garrett*, *Getz*, *Golladay*, *Hambleton*, *Hancock*, *Handley*, *Harper*, *J. T. Harris*, *Hereford*, Hill, *Kerr*, *King*, *Leach*, *Lewis*, *Manson*, *Marshall*, *McClelland*, *McCormick*, *McHenry*, *Merrick*, *B. F. Meyers*, *Morgan*, *Niblack*, *E. Perry*, *Potter*, *Price*, *Read*, *E. Y. Rice*, *J. M. Rice*, *W. R. Roberts*, *Roosevelt*, *Shober*, *Slater*, *Sloss*, *Storm*, *Swann*, *Terry*, *Van Trump*, *Voorhees*, *Warren*, *Wells*, *Winchester*, *Wood*—60.

NAYS—Messrs. *Adams*, Beatty, Beveridge, Bingham, A. Blair, Buckley, Buffinton, Burchard, Burdett, B. F. Butler, R. R. Butler, Cobb, Coburn, Conger, Darrall, Dawes, Donnan, Dunnell, Finkelnburg, C. Foster, W. D. Foster, Frye, Garfield, Goodrich, Harmer, Hawley, G. W. Hazelton, J. W. Hazelton, Hoar, Hooper, Houghton, Kelley, Lamport, Lansing, Lynch, McGrew, McJunkin, McKee, Mercur, Merriam, Monroe, Morey, L. Myers, Negley, Orr, Packard, Palmer, I. C. Parker, Peck, Pendleton, Perce, A. F. Perry, Platt, Poland, Prindle, E. H. Roberts, Rusk, Sawyer, Seeley, Shanks, Sheldon, Shoemaker, H. B. Smith, J. A. Smith, W. C. Smith, Snapp, Snyder, T. J. Speer, Sprague, Starkweather, Stoughton, Strong, Sypher, Taffe, W. Townsend, Turner, Tyner, Upson, Waddell, Wakeman, Walden, Wheeler, *Whitthorne*, Willard, J. M. Wilson, J. T. Wilson—86.

The bill was not considered in the Senate.

XX.

ST. CROIX AND BAYFIELD RAILROAD BILL.

IN SENATE.

1872, February 16—This bill passed:

Be it enacted, &c., That in case there shall be completed within one year from the passage of this act forty miles of the road from the St. Croix river or lake to Lake Superior, as authorized by act of Congress approved June 3, 1856, and act of Congress approved May 5, 1864, and the Secretary of the Interior shall be satisfied of such completion, the time for completing the construction of said road as authorized by said acts shall be extended to the State of Wisconsin five years from the passage of this act, and all the grants, rights, and privileges contained in said original acts shall be continued in full force and virtue for said time of five years: *Provided*, That the word mineral, when used in the acts hereinbefore referred to, shall not be held to include coal, and subject to the further condition that the lands granted by the acts hereby extended, excepting only such as are necessary for the company to which the benefits of this act may inure, reserve for depots, stations, side tracks, wood-yards, standing-grounds, and other needful uses in operating the road, and pine and coal lands shall be sold to actual settlers only, and in quantities not exceeding one hundred and sixty acres to any one person, under such rules and restrictions as may be prescribed by the Secretary of the Interior, at such prices as will secure to said company, its successors or assigns, an average price of not more than $2 50 per acre, and subject to the further condition that the right of way is hereby granted to said company to the extent of one hundred feet in width on each side of said road through the public lands: *Provided*, That the grant hereby extended shall inure only to the benefit of such company or companies as the State of Wisconsin may hereafter designate.

Yeas 31, nays 7:

YEAS—Messrs. Boreman, Cameron, Carpenter, Chandler, Conkling, Fenton, Ferry of Connecticut, Ferry of Michigan, Flanagan, Frelinghuysen, Hamilton of Texas, Hamlin, Harlan, Hitchcock, Kellogg, Lewis, Logan, Morton, Nye, Osborn, Pomeroy, Pratt, Ramsey, Rice, Sawyer, Scott, Spencer, Sumner, Tipton, *Vickers*, Windom—31.

NAYS—Messrs. Anthony, *Casserly*, Edmunds, *Hamilton* of Maryland, Morrill of Vermont, Patterson, Robertson—7.

IN HOUSE.

1872, February 28—This bill coming up in order on the Speaker's table—

Mr. HOLMAN moved to lay it on the table; which was not agreed to—yeas 78, nays 99:

YEAS—Messrs. *Acker*, *Adams*, Ambler, *Archer*, *Arthur*, *Barnum*, Beatty, *Bell*, *Biggs*, Bingham, *Bird*, *Braxton*, Buffinton, R. R. Butler, *Campbell*,

Coburn, *Conner*, *Cox*, *Crebs*, *Critcher*, *Crossland*, Dickey, Finkelnburg, *Forker*, *H. D. Foster*, *Garrett*, *Getz*, *Griffith*, *Haldeman*, *Hancock*, *Handley*, Harmer, Hawley, Hay, Hays, *Hereford*, *Hibbard*, *Holman*, Kelley, *Kerr*, Ketcham, Killinger, *King*, *Lamison*, *Manson*, *McClelland*, *McNeely*, Mercur, Monroe, *Niblack*, Packard, Packer, Prindle, *Read*, *J. M. Rice*, E. H. Roberts, Shanks, *Sherwood*, Shoemaker, *Slocum*, H. B. Smith, J. A. Smith, *R. M. Speer*, T. J. Speer, *Stevens*, Stevenson, Strong, *Terry*, Turner, Tyner, Upson, *Van Trump*, *Voorhees*, Whiteley, Williams of Indiana, J. M. Wilson, J. T. Wilson, *Winchester*—78.

NAYS—Messrs. Ames, Averill, Banks, Barber, Barry, *Beck*, Beveridge, Bigby, A. Blair, Boles, *Bright*, G. M. Brooks, *J. Brooks*, Buckley, *Caldwell*, F. Clarke, *Comingo*, Conger, Cotton, Crocker, Darrall, Dawes, Donnan, *Du Bose*, Duell, *Duke*, Dunnell, Eames, *Eldredge*, Farnsworth, Farwell, C. Foster, Frye, *Golladay*, Goodrich, Hale, Halsey, *Hanks*, *Harper*, G. E. Harris, *J. T. Harris*, Havens, G. W. Hazelton, *Herndon*, Hill, Hoar, Hooper, Houghton, *Kendall*, Lamport, *Leach*, Lowe, Lynch, *Marshall*, Maynard, *McCormick*, *McHenry*, McJunkin, Merriam, *Mitchell*, Orr, Palmer, I. C. Parker, Peck, A. F. Perry, *E. Perry*, Peters, Platt, *Price*, Rainey, Rusk, Sargent, Sawyer, Scofield, Seeley, Sheldon, *Slater*, *Sloss*, Snapp, Snyder, Stoughton, *Sutherland*, Taffe, Thomas, *D. Townsend*, W. Townsend, *Tuthill*, Twichell, *Vaughan*, *Waddell*, Wakeman, Walden, Waldron, Wallace, *Warren*, Wheeler, *Whitthorne*, *Williams* of New York, *Young*—99.

Mr. HOLMAN asked unanimous consent to propose this amendment:

Provided, however, That this grant shall be construed to apply to such lands only as would inure to the benefit of the Northern Pacific Railroad Company if this act had not been passed.

Which was refused, when he moved again to table the bill; which was lost—yeas 80, nays 94.

February 29—Mr. HOLMAN moved to recommit the bill to the Committee on Public Lands, with these instructions:

To so amend the bill as that it shall grant to the State of Wisconsin all the lands specified in the bill which would inure to the North Pacific Railroad Company under existing laws, by any location of said North Pacific road authorized by existing laws, if this grant or extension was not made to said State of Wisconsin; and to limit the grant to the lands which, in the absence of such legislation, would, by fair interpretation of existing laws, inure to the benefit of the North Pacific road.

And to further amend the bill so that it shall not be construed to enlarge the grant of land to the Northern Pacific Railroad Company, or to authorize the Northern Pacific Railroad Company to select lands elsewhere in lieu of any lands specified in the pending bill.

Mr. DONNAN, by unanimous consent, offered the following additional instruction:

Provided further, That all lands hereby granted, which may remain unsold at the expiration of five years after the completion of said road, shall be subject to settlement and preëmption like other public lands, at a price to be paid to such railroad company not exceeding $2 50 per acre.

The whole being treated as one amendment, was agreed to—yeas 101, nays 78:

YEAS—Messrs. *Acker*, *Adams*, Ambler, *Archer*, *Arthur*, *Barnum*, Beatty, *Bell*, *Biggs*, Bingham, *Bird*, *Bright*, Buffinton, Burchard, Burdett, B. F. Butler, *Carroll*, Coburn, Coghlan, *Conner*, *Cox*, *Crebs*, *Critcher*, *Crossland*, Dickey, *Duke*, Dunnell, *Ely*, Finkelnburg, *Forker*, C. Foster, *H. D. Foster*, *Getz*, *Golladay*, *Haldeman*, *Handley*, *Hanks*, Harmer, G. E. Harris, *J. T. Harris*, Hawley, Hay, Hays, *Hereford*, *Hibbard*, Hill, *Holman*, Kelley, Kellogg, *Kerr*, Ketcham, Killinger, *King*, *Lamison*, Lamport, *Lewis*, Lowe, *Manson*, *Marshall*, *McClelland*, McGrew, *McKinney*, *McNeely*, Mercur, Monroe, *Niblack*, Packard, Packer, Prindle, *Read*, *J. M. Rice*, E. H. Roberts, *W. R. Roberts*, *Robinson*, Sessions, Shanks, Shoemaker, *Slocum*, H. B. Smith, J. A. Smith, *R. M. Speer*, Sprague, Starkweather, *Stevens*, Stevenson, Strong, *Terry*, *D. Townsend*, Turner, Tyner, Upson, *Van Trump*, *Vaughan*, *Voorhees*, Walden, Whiteley, Williams of Indiana, J. M. Wilson, J. T. Wilson, *Winchester*, *Wood*—101.

NAYS—Messrs. Ames, Averill, Banks, Barber, *Beck*, Beveridge, A. Blair, *J. G. Blair*, Boles, G. M. Brooks, Buckley, *Caldwell*, *Comingo*, Conger, Cotton, Crocker, Dawes, Donnan, *Du Bose*, Duell, Eames, *Eldredge*, Farnsworth, Farwell, Frye, Garfield, Goodrich, *Hancock*, *Harper*, Havens, G. W. Hazelton, Hoar, Hooper, Houghton, Lynch, Maynard, *McCormick*, *Mitchell*, L. Myers, Negley, Orr, Palmer, I. C. Parker, Peck, Pendleton, *E. Perry*, Peters, Platt, *Price*, Rainey, Rusk, Sargent, Sawyer, Scofield, Seeley, Sheldon, *Sherwood*, *Shober*, *Slater*, *Sloss*, Snapp, Snyder, T. J. Speer, Stoughton, *Sutherland*, Taffe, W. Townsend, *Tuthill*, Twichell, *Waddell*, Wakeman, Waldron, Wallace, *Warren*, Wheeler, Willard, *Williams* of New York, *Young*—78.

March 1—The bill, with various propositions submitted, was recommitted to the Committee on Public Lands, with the right to report it back at any time the next week after Monday.

March 7—The committee reported back the bill with these amendments:

Amend the first section so as to exclude all "coal" lands from the grant; and add the following sections:

SEC. 2. That this act shall be so construed as to grant to the State of Wisconsin all the lands heretofore reserved and embraced in its provisions, which would inure to the Northern Pacific Railroad Company, under existing laws, by any location of said Northern Pacific Railroad Company authorized by existing laws, if this grant or extension had not been made to said State of Wisconsin, and as limiting the grant to the lands which, in the absence of further legislation, would, by fair interpretation of existing laws, inure to the benefit of or might be taken by the Northern Pacific Railroad Company: *Provided*, That this act shall not be construed to enlarge the grant of land to the Northern Pacific Railroad Company, or to authorize said Northern Pacific Railroad Company to select lands elsewhere in lieu of any lands embraced in this act, or as granting to said State any lands in lieu of which other lands might be selected by said Northern Pacific Railroad Company, or as granting any coal lands.

SEC. 3. That the extent of the grant to said State under this act shall be determined by the Secretary of the Interior and the Attorney General, subject to the approval of the President of the United States, and shall be reported to Congress by the Secretary of the Interior as soon as such determination is made.

March 15—An amendment was offered by Mr. ELDREDGE to strike out of section two the words:

"Or as granting to said State any lands in lieu of which other lands might be selected by said Northern Pacific Railroad Company;" which was adopted—yeas 84, nays 83:

YEAS—Messrs. Averill, Barber, *Beck*, Beveridge, Bigby, A. Blair, G. M. Brooks, Buckley, Burchard, *Caldwell*, W. T. Clark, *Comingo*, Conger, *Conner*, Cotton, Crocker, Darrall, Dawes, Donnan, *Dox*, *Du Bose*, Duell, *Duke*, Dunnell, Eames, *Eldredge*, Farnsworth, W. D. Foster, Frye, Garfield, *Garrett*, Goodrich, Hale, *Handley*, *Harper*, G. W. Hazelton, J. W. Hazelton, Hooper, Houghton, Lansing, *Leach*, *McCormick*, McJunkin, Merriam, *Mitchell*, Moore, Morey, Orr, Palmer, I. C. Parker, Pendleton, *E. Perry*, Peters, Platt, Poland, *Price*, *Ritchie*, *Rogers*, Rusk, Sargent, Sawyer, Scofield, Seeley, Sheldon, *Sherwood*, *Slater*, *Slocum*, *Sloss*, J. A. Smith, W. C. Smith, Snapp, Snyder, T. J. Speer, Stoughton, *Sutherland*, Taffe, Thomas, W. Townsend, Twichell, *Waddell*, Waldron, *Warren*, *Wells*, *Young*—84.

NAYS—Messrs. *Adams*, Ambler, *Archer*, *Arthur*, Beatty, *Biggs*, Bingham, *Braxton*, Buffinton, Coburn, Coghlan, *Crebs*, *Critcher*, *Crossland*, *Davis*, Dickey, Finkelnburg, *Forker*, *Getz*, *Golladay*, *Griffith*, *Haldeman*, *Hancock*, *Hanks*, Harmer, *J. T. Harris*, Havens, Hawley, Hay, Hays, *Herndon*, *Holman*, Kelley, *Kendall*, *Kerr*, Ketcham, Killinger, *King*, *Lewis*, Lowe, *Manson*, *Marshall*, *McClelland*, McCrary, McGrew, *McKinney*, Mercur, *Merrick*, *Morgan*, *Niblack*, Packard, Packer, A. F. Perry, Porter, Prindle, *Randall*, *Read*, *J. M. Rice*, E. H. Roberts, *W. R. Roberts*, *Robinson*, Shanks, Shoemaker, *R. M. Speer*, Sprague, *Stevens*, Stevenson, *Storm*, Strong, *Terry*, Turner, Tyner, Upson, *Van Trump*, *Voorhees*, Wakeman, Walden, Whiteley, *Whitthorne*, Williams of Indiana, J. M. Wilson, J. T. Wilson, *Winchester*—83.

An amendment was offered by Mr. KILLINGER to add to the first section the following:

Provided, That in the construction of the said railroad there shall be used none other than rails manufactured from American iron.

Which was rejected—yeas 52, nays 112:

YEAS—Messrs. Ambler, *Archer*, Bigby, Bingham, W. T. Clark, Cobb, Coghlan, Crocker, Darrall, Dickey, Duell, W. D. Foster, *Getz*, Goodrich, *Griffith*, Harmer, Hays, J. W. Hazelton, Hooper, Ketcham, Killinger, Lowe, *McClelland*, McGrew, McJunkin, Mercur, Merriam, Morey, L. Myers, Negley, Packer, *E. Perry*, *Randall*, Sawyer, Scofield, Sheldon, Shoemaker, W. C. Smith, Snyder, *R. M. Speer*, T. J. Speer, Sprague, Stoughton, Stowell, Strong, *Swann*, W. Townsend, Turner, Upson, Whiteley, Williams of Indiana, J. T. Wilson—52.

NAYS—Messrs. *Adams*, *Arthur*, Averill, Beatty, *Beck*, Beveridge, A. Blair, *J. G. Blair*, *Braxton*, G. M. Brooks, Buffinton, Burchard, *Caldwell*, F. Clarke, Coburn, *Comingo*, Conger, *Conner*, Cotton, *Cox*, *Critcher*, *Crossland*, *Davis*, Dawes, Donnan, *Dox*, *Du Bose*, *Duke*, Dunnell, Eames, *Eldredge*, Farnsworth, Finkelnburg, *Forker*, Frye, Garfield, *Garrett*, *Golladay*, *Haldeman*, *Hambleton*, *Hancock*, *Handley*, *Hanks*, *Harper*, *J. T. Harris*, Hawley, Hay, G. W. Hazelton, *Herndon*, Hoar, *Holman*, *Kerr*, *King*, Lansing, *Leach*, *Lewis*, *Manson*, *Marshall*, *McCormick*, McCrary, *McIntyre*, *McKinney*, *Merrick*, Moore, *Morgan*, Orr, Packard, Palmer, Pendleton, Perce, A. F. Perry, Peters, Porter, *Price*, Prindle, *Read*, *E. Y. Rice*, *J. M. Rice*, *Ritchie*, E. H. Roberts, *W. R. Roberts*, *Robinson*, Rusk, Sargent, Seeley, Shanks, *Sherwood*, *Shober*, *Slater*, *Slocum*, *Sloss*, Snapp, *Stevens*, Stevenson, *Storm*, Taffe, Thomas, Tyner, *Van Trump*, *Voorhees*, *Waddell*, Wakeman, Walden, Waldron, *Warren*, *Wells*, Wheeler, *Whitthorne*, J. M. Wilson, *Winchester*, *Wood*, *Young*—112.

Mr. KETCHAM moved to strike out all after the enacting clause and insert:

That all the lands which were granted by Congress in the year 1856 and the year 1864 to the State of Wisconsin to aid in the construction of a railroad from St. Croix river or lake to Lake Superior, with a branch road to Bayfield, the said grant having expired by limitation, be, and hereby are, forfeited to the United States, and shall henceforward be subject to homestead entry and settlement under the act of Congress approved May 20, 1862, "to secure homesteads to actual settlers on the public domain," and shall be disposed of according to the provisions of said act. But no part of said lands shall be selected by or inure to the benefit of any railroad company under any assumed grant from the United States; and said lands are expressly reserved for the benefit of actual settlers under the provisions of the said homestead act.

Mr. BANKS moved to add to the substitute:

Provided, That no land embraced in the grant to the St. Croix railroad shall in any case revert to the Northern Pacific Railroad Company; and all acts or parts of acts inconsistent with this provision are hereby repealed.

Which, on a division, was adopted—yeas 66, nays 64.

The substitute, as amended, was then agreed to—yeas 94, nays 85:

YEAS—Messrs. *Adams*, Ambler, *Archer*, *Arthur*, Beatty, *Biggs*, Bingham, *Braxton*, Buffinton, Burchard, Burdett, *Carroll*, F. Clarke, Coburn, Coghlan, *Crebs*, *Critcher*, *Crossland*, Darrall, *Davis*, Dickey, Finkelnburg, *Forker*, Garfield, *Getz*, *Golladay*, *Griffith*, *Haldeman*, *Hanks*, Harmer, *J. T. Harris*, Havens, Hawley, Hay, Hays, *Herndon*, *Holman*, Kelley, *Kendall*, *Kerr*, Ketcham, Killinger, *King*, *Lewis*, Lowe, *Manson*, *Marshall*, *McClelland*, McGrew, *McIntyre*, *McKinney*, Mercur, Merriam, *Merrick*, Monroe, *Morgan*, *Niblack*, Packard, Packer, A. F. Perry, Porter, Prindle, *Randall*, *Read*, *J. M. Rice*, E. H. Roberts, *W. R. Roberts*, *Robinson*, Rusk, Shanks, Shoemaker, J. A. Smith, Snyder, *R. M. Speer*, Sprague, *Stevens*, Stevenson, *Storm*, Stowell, Strong, Sypher, Turner, Tyner, Upson, *Van Trump*, *Voorhees*, Wakeman, Whiteley, *Whitthorne*, Williams of Indiana, J. M. Wilson, J. T. Wilson, *Winchester*, *Wood*—94.

NAYS—Messrs. Averill, Banks, Barber, *Beck*, Beveridge, Bigby, A. Blair, *J. G. Blair*, G. M. Brooks, Buckley, *Caldwell*, W. T. Clark, *Comingo*, Conger, *Conner*, Cotton, Crocker, Dawes, Donnan, *Dox*, *Du Bose*, Duell, *Duke*, Dunnell, *Eldredge*, Farnsworth, W. D. Foster, Frye, *Garrett*, Goodrich, Hale, *Hancock*, *Handley*, *Harper*, G. W. Hazelton, J. W. Hazelton, Hoar, Hooper, Houghton, Lamport, Lansing, *Leach*, Lynch, *McCormick*, McCrary, *Mitchell*, Moore, Negley, Orr, Palmer, I. C. Parker, Peck, Pendleton, *E. Perry*, Peters, Platt, Poland, *Price*, *E. Y. Rice*, *Rogers*, Sargent, Sawyer, Scofield, Seeley, *Sherwood*, *Shober*, *Slater*, *Slocum*, *Sloss*, W. C. Smith, Snapp, T. J. Speer, Stoughton, *Sutherland*, Taffe, Thomas, *D. Townsend*, W. Townsend, Twichell, *Waddell*, Walden, Waldron, *Warren*, Wheeler, *Young*—85.

The bill was then passed.

IN SENATE,

March 28—The Senate disagreed to the amendment of the House.

IN HOUSE.

April 16—Report was made that the committees of conference had failed to agree.

Mr. SCOFIELD moved that the House recede from its amendment; which was disagreed to—yeas 56, nays 115:

YEAS—Messrs. Ames, Averill, Barber, *Beck*, A. Blair, Boles, G. M. Brooks, Buckley, Conger, Dawes, De Large, Donnan, *Du Bose*, Dunnell, *Eldredge*, Goodrich, Hale, *Hancock*, *Harper*, G. W. Hazelton, J. W. Hazelton, Hoar, Hooper, Houghton, Lansing, Maynard, *McCormick*, Orr, Palmer, Peck, Perce, *E. Perry*, Peters, Poland, *Roosevelt*, Rusk, Sargent, Sawyer, Scofield, Seeley, Sheldon, *Sherwood*, *Slater*, *Sloss*, Snapp, Snyder, Stoughton, Taffe, *D. Townsend*, W. Townsend, Twichell, *Waddell*, Walden, Waldron, Wheeler, *Williams* of New York—56.

NAYS—Messrs. *Acker*, *Adams*, Ambler, *Archer*, *Arthur*, Barry, Beatty, *Bell*, Beveridge, *Biggs*, Bingham, *Bird*, *Braxton*, Buffinton, Burchard, Burdett, *Carroll*, W. T. Clark, Coburn, Coghlan, *Conner*, *Cox*, *Critcher*, *Crossland*, Darrall, *Davis*, Dickey, Duell, Eames, *Ely*, Farnsworth, Finkelnburg, *Forker*, Garfield, *Garrett*, *Golladay*, *Griffith*, *Haldeman*, Halsey, *Hambleton*, *Handley*, *Hanks*, Harmer, G. E. Harris, *J. T. Harris*, Havens, Hay, Hays, *Hereford*, *Herndon*, *Hibbard*, *Holman*, Kelley, Kellogg, *Kendall*, Ketcham, Killinger, *King*, *Lewis*, Lowe, *Manson*, *Marshall*, *McClelland*, McCrary, *McHenry*, *McIntyre*, McJunkin, *McKinney*, *McNeely*, Mercur, Merriam, *Merrick*, Moore, *Morgan*, Morphis, Negley, *Niblack*, Packard, Packer, I. C. Parker, A. F. Perry, *Potter*, Prindle, Rainey, *Randall*, *Read*, *E. Y. Rice*, *J. M. Rice*, E. H. Roberts, *W. R. Roberts*, Sessions, Shanks, Shoemaker, J. A. Smith, *R. M. Speer*, Sprague, *Stevens*, Stevenson, *Storm*, Strong, Sypher, *Terry*, Turner, Tyner, Upson, *Van Trump*, *Wells*, Whiteley, *Whitthorne*, Williams of Indiana, J. M. Wilson, J. T. Wilson, *Winchester*, *Wood*, *Young*—115.

Mr. HOLMAN moved that the House adhere to its amendment; which was agreed to—yeas 110, nays 54.

[The differences in this vote from the last were these: to the yeas on this motion (being the nays on the last) add Messrs. *Bright*, R. R. Butler, *Dox*, J. W. Hazelton, *Lamison*, Seeley, and T. J. Speer, and subtract Messrs. Beveridge, Bingham, *Davis*, Eames, *Ely*, Farnsworth, Garfield, *Hanks*, Lowe, *Marshall*, Moore, and *Niblack*. To the nays on this motion (being the yeas on the last) add Messrs. Beveridge, *Comingo*, Cotton, *Duke*, Farnsworth, W. D. Foster, Frye, Moore, and Wallace, and substract Messrs. Buckley, Hale, J. W. Hazelton, Hoar, Peck, Peters, *Roosevelt*, Seeley, Snyder, *D. Townsend*, and Wheeler.]

Thus the bill fell.

XXI.

MISCELLANEOUS.

"Test-Oath."

IN HOUSE.

1872, May 15—Mr. PETERS, from the Judiciary Committee, reported the following bill; which passed without a division:

Be it enacted, &c., That the act entitled "An act to prescribe an oath of office, and for other purposes," approved July 2, 1862, and the act entitled "An act prescribing an oath of office to be taken by persons from whom legal disabilities shall have been removed," approved July 11, 1868, be, and the same are hereby, repealed.

To Repeal Several Acts Relating to the Tenure of Civil Offices.

IN HOUSE.

1872, May 14—Mr. B. F. BUTLER reported from the Judiciary Committee the following bill; which passed without a division:

Be it enacted, &c., That the act entitled "An act regulating the tenure of certain civil offices," passed March 2, 1867, and an act entitled "An act to amend an act regulating the tenure of certain civil offices," approved April 5, 1869, be, and the same are hereby, repealed: *Provided*, That the repeal of said acts shall not affect the suspension or designation of any civil officer heretofore made by the President, except so far as to prevent the restoration to office or pay, by virtue of said acts, of any person suspended under their provisions.

"Legal-Tender" Notes in One-Third Payment of Customs.

1872, March 11—Mr. B. F. BUTLER moved to suspend the rules and pass a bill that from and after April 1, 1872, the Secretary of the Treasury be authorized and directed to collect and receive one third of the amount of customs duties assessed upon imports in legal-tender notes of the United States; which was disagreed to—yeas 89, nays 68, (two thirds being required:)

YEAS—Messrs. *Acker*, *Arthur*, Averill, *Beck*, Beveridge, Bigby, *Bird*, *J. G. Blair*, G. M. Brooks, Buffinton, B. F. Butler, R. R. Butler, *Caldwell*, W. T. Clark, Cobb, Coburn, Coghlan, Conger, *Conner*, *Critcher*, *Crossland*, Darrall, *Davis*, *Dox*, Dunnell, *Eldredge*, Finkelnburg, *Getz*, *Golladay*, *Haldeman*, *Hambleton*, *Handley*, *Harper*, *J. T. Harris*, Havens, Hay, Hays, G. W. Hazelton, J. W. Hazelton, *Holman*, Houghton, *King*, Lansing, *Leach*, *Lewis*, Lowe, *Manson*, *Marshall*, *McClelland*, McCrary, *McHenry*, *McKinney*, *Merrick*, *B. F. Meyers*, *Mitchell*, Morey, *Morgan*, I. C. Parker, Pendleton, Perce, A. F. Perry, Peters, Platt, *Price*, Prindle, *Read*, *E. Y. Rice*, *J. M. Rice*, Sargent, Shanks, Sheldon, *Shober*, *Slater*, *Sloss*, H. B. Smith, Snapp, Snyder, T. J. Speer, *Stevens*, Sypher, Taffe, Twichell, *Warren*, *Wells*, Willard, Williams of Indiana, *Williams* of New York, J. M. Wilson, *Wood*—89.

NAYS—Messrs. Ambler, Banks, Barber, Beatty, Bingham, A. Blair, *Braxton*, *Bright*, Burchard, F. Clarke, *Comingo*, *Crebs*, Dawes, Donnan, Duell, Farwell, C. Foster, W. D. Foster, Frye, *Garrett*, Goodrich, Halsey, Harmer, Hawley, Hill, Hooper, Kelley, *Kerr*, Ketcham, Killinger, Lynch, *McCormick*, McGrew, McJunkin, Mercur, Merriam, Monroe, L. Myers, Negley, *Niblack*, Orr, Packard, Palmer, Peck, *E. Perry*, *Randall*, E. H. Roberts, *W. R. Roberts*, Sawyer, *Sherwood*, Shoemaker, J. A. Smith, W. C. Smith, Sprague, *Storm*, Stoughton, Strong, *Sutherland*, Terry, W. Townsend, *Van Trump*, *Waddell*, Wakeman, Walden, Waldron, Wheeler, J. T. Wilson, *Winchester*—68.

House Resolution on Treatment of Prisoners of War.

IN HOUSE.

1872, February 19—Mr. SHANKS moved to suspend the rules and pass the subjoined joint resolution; which was agreed to without a division:

Joint resolution authorizing the President to open negotiations with all civilized nations in reference to captives in war.

Resolved by the Senate and House of Representatives of the United States of America in Congress assembled, That the President be, and he is hereby, authorized and requested to open friendly correspondence and negotiations with any or all civilized nations, with the view to procure the adoption in the laws of nations of a provision that captives in war shall not be personally retained as prisoners, but shall, under flags of truce, be returned at the earliest possible time to their own lines or vessels, and paroled until properly exchanged, so that the books of the commissioners of exchange of the respective belligerents shall determine the relative advantages in captives, and thus the horrors and sacrifices of prison life be prevented.

On Disposition of Public Lands.

1872, March 11—Mr. KILLINGER offered the following; which was agreed to without a division:

Resolved, That in the judgment of this House the policy of granting subsidies in public lands to railroad and other corporations ought to be discontinued, and that every consideration of public policy and equal justice to the whole people requires that the public lands should be held for the purposes of securing homesteads to actual settlers, and for educational purposes, as may be provided by law.

On the Action of the Secretary of the Treasury.

IN HOUSE.

1872, February 1—The House considered the following resolution, reported by the Committee of Ways and Means:

Resolved, That in the opinion of this House the Secretary of the Treasury, in negotiating the loan authorized by the act of July 14, 1870, has neither increased the bonded debt nor incurred an expenditure contrary to law.

Which was agreed to—yeas 110, nays 86:

YEAS—Messrs. Averill, Banks, Barber, Barry, Beatty, Beveridge, Bigby, Bingham, A. Blair, G. M. Brooks, Buckley, Buffinton, Burchard, Burdett, B. F. Butler, W. T. Clark, Cobb, Coburn, Coghlan, Conger, Cotton, Creely, Dawes, Dickey, Donnan, Duell, Dunnell, Eames, Farwell, Finkelnburg, C. Foster, W. D. Foster, Frye, Hale, Halsey, Harmer, G. E. Harris, Havens, Hay, G. W. Hazelton, J. W. Hazelton, Hill, Hoar, Houghton, Kelley, Kellogg, Ketcham, Killinger, Lamport, Lansing, Lowe, Lynch, Maynard, McGrew, McJunkin, McKee, Mercur, Merriam, Monroe, Moore, Morey, Morphis, L. Myers, Negley, Orr, Packard, Packer, Palmer, I. C. Parker, Peck, Pendleton, Perce, A. F. Perry, Peters, Poland, Rainey, E. H. Roberts, Rusk, Sargent, Sawyer, Seeley, Sessions, Shanks, Sheldon, Shellabarger, Shoemaker, J. A. Smith, Snapp, T. J. Speer, Sprague, Starkweather, Stevenson, Stoughton, Stowell, Strong, Sypher, W. Townsend, Turner, Twichell, Tyner, Upson, Wakeman, Walden, Waldron, Wallace, Wheeler, Whiteley, Williams of Indiana, J. M. Wilson, J. T. Wilson—110.

NAYS—Messrs. *Acker, Arthur, Barnum, Beck, Bell, Biggs, Bird, J. G. Blair, Braxton, Bright, J. Brooks, Caldwell, Campbell, Carroll, Comingo, Conner, Cox, Crebs, Critcher, Crossland, Davis, Dox, Du Bose, Duke, Eldredge, Ely, H. D. Foster, Garrett, Getz, Golladay, Griffith, Haldeman, Hambleton, Hancock, Handley, Hanks, Harper, J. T. Harris, Hereford, Herndon, Hibbard, Holman, Kerr, King, Kinsella, Lamison, Leach, Lewis, Manson, Marshall, McClelland, McCormick, McHenry, McIntyre, McKinney, McNeely, Merrick, B. F. Meyers, Mitchell, Morgan, Niblack, H. W. Parker, E. Perry, Potter, Randall, Read, E. Y. Rice, Ritchie, Roosevelt, Shober, Slater, Sloss, Storm, Sutherland, Swann, Terry, Van Trump, Vaughan, Voorhees, Waddell, Warren, Wells, Whitthorne, Winchester, Wood, Young*—86.

On the Privileges of the House.

IN HOUSE.

1871, April 20—Mr. BECK moved that the rules be suspended, and the House pass the following resolution; which was agreed to without a division:

Resolved, That it being declared by the second section of the second article of the Constitution "that the President shall have power, by and with the advice and consent of the Senate, to make treaties, provided two thirds of the Senators present concur," the House of Representatives do not claim any agency in making treaties; but that when a treaty stipulates regulations on any of the subjects submitted by the Constitution to the power of Congress, it must depend for its execution as to such stipulations on the law or laws to be passed by Congress; and it is the constitutional right and duty of the House of Representatives in all such cases to deliberate on the expediency or inexpediency of carrying such treaty into effect, and to determine and act thereon as in their judgment may be most conducive to the public good.*

1872, April 2—Mr. DAWES, from the Committee of Ways and Means, submitted the following resolutions:

Resolved, That the substitution by the Senate, under the form of an amendment, for the bill of the House (H. R. No. 1537) entitled "An act to repeal existing duties on tea and coffee," of a bill entitled "An act to reduce existing taxes," containing a general revision, reduction, and repeal of laws imposing import duties and internal taxes, is in conflict with the true intent and purposes of that clause of the Constitution which requires that "all bills for raising revenue shall originate in the House of Representatives;" and that therefore said

---

*This resolution is a copy of a resolution adopted by the House of Representatives of the Fourth Congress, (in Washington's administration,) when, after a protracted debate, it passed, April 7, 1795—yeas 57, nays 35; as follows:

YEAS—Messrs. Theodorus Bailey, Abraham Baldwin, David Bard, Lemuel Benton, Thomas Blount, Nathan Bryan, Dempsey Burges, Samuel J. Cabell, Gabriel Christie, John Clopton, Isaac Coles, Jeremiah Crabb, Henry Dearborn, George Dent, Samuel Earle, William Findley, Jesse Franklin, Albert Gallatin, William B. Giles, Nicholas Gilman, Andrew Gregg, William B. Grove, Wade Hampton, George Hancock, Carter B. Harrison, John Hathorn, Jonathan N. Havens, John Heath, Daniel Hiester, George Jackson, Edward Livingston, Matthew Locke, William Lyman, Samuel Maclay, Nathaniel Macon, James Madison, John Milledge, Andrew Moore, Frederick A. Muhlenberg, John Nicholas, Alexander D. Orr, John Page, Josiah Parker, John Patten, Francis Preston, John Richards, Robert Rutherford, John S. Sherburne, Israel Smith, Samuel Smith, Thomas Sprigg, John Swanwick, Absalom Tatom, Philip Van Cortlandt, Joseph B. Varnum, Abraham Venable, Richard Winn—57.

NAYS—Messrs. Fisher Ames, Benjamin Bourne, Theophilus Bradbury, Daniel Buck, Joshua Coit, William Cooper, Abiel Foster, Dwight Foster, Ezekiel Gilbert, Henry Glen, Benjamin Goodhue, Chauncey Goodrich, Roger Griswold, Robert Goodloe Harper, Thomas Hartley, Thomas Henderson, James Hillhouse, William Hindman, John Wilkes Kittera, Samuel Lyman, Francis Malbone, William Vans Murray, John Reed, Theodore Sedgwick, Jeremiah Smith, Nathaniel Smith, William Smith, Zephaniah Swift, George Thatcher, Richard Thomas, Mark Thompson, Uriah Tracey, John E. Van Allen, Peleg Wadsworth, John Williams—35.

substitute for House bill No. 1537 do lie upon the table.

And be it further resolved, That the Clerk of the House be, and is hereby, directed to notify the Senate of the passage of the foregoing resolution.

Which were adopted—yeas 153, nays 9:

YEAS—Messrs. *Acker*, Ambler, Ames, *Arthur*, Averill, Barber, Barry, Beatty, *Beck*, Beveridge, Bigby, A. Blair, *Braxton*, G. M. Brooks, *J. Brooks*, Buckley, Buffinton, Burchard, Burdett, B. F. Butler, R. R. Butler, *Caldwell*, *Campbell*, *Carroll*, Coghlan, Conger, *Cox*, *Critcher*, Crocker, *Crossland*, *Davis*, Dawes, Donnan, *Dox*, *Du Bose*, *Duke*, Dunnell, Eames, *Ela*, Farnsworth, Farwell, Finkelnburg, C. Foster, W. D. Foster, Frye, Garfield, *Garrett*, *Getz*, *Golladay*, *Griffith*, *Haldeman*, Hale, Halsey, *Handley*, *Harper*, G. E. Harris, *J. T. Harris*, Hawley, Hay, G. W. Hazelton, J. W. Hazelton, *Hereford*, *Herndon*, *Hibbard*, Hill, Hoar, *Holman*, Hooper, Houghton, Kelley, *Kerr*, Ketcham, *Lamison*, Lansing, *Manson*, *Marshall*, Maynard, McCrary, McGrew, *McHenry*, *McIntyre*, *McNeely*, Mercur, Merriam, *Merrick*, B. F. Meyers, Monroe, Moore, Morey, Morphis, L. Myers, Negley, *Niblack*, Orr, Packard, Packer, Palmer, *H. W. Parker*, I. C. Parker, Peck, Pendleton, A. F. Perry, *E. Perry*, Platt, Porter, *Potter*, Rainey, *E. Y. Rice*, *J. M. Rice*, E. H. Roberts, *W. R. Roberts*, *Robinson*, *Rogers*, Rusk, Sargent, Sawyer, Sessions, Shanks, *Sherwood*, *Shober*, *Slater*, *Slocum*, H. B. Smith, J. A. Smith, W. C. Smith, T. J. Speer, Starkweather, *Stevens*, *Storm*, Stoughton, *Swann*, Taffe, *Terry*, *D. Townsend*, Turner, *Tuthill*, Twichell, Tyner, Upson, *Van Trump*, *Vaughan*, Wakeman, Walden, Wallace, *Warren*, *Wells*, Wheeler, Whiteley, *Whitthorne*, Willard, *Winchester*, *Wood*, *Young*—153.

NAYS—Messrs. *Archer*, *Conner*, *Hanks*, *Kendall*, *Lewis*, *McCormick*, *Read*, *Ritchie*, *R. M. Speer*—9.

Vote in the Legislature of New York, rescinding a resolution of 1870, purporting to withdraw a previous ratification of the Fifteenth Amendment.

IN SENATE, *January*, 3, 1872.

Whereas the Legislature of the State of New York, at its annual session in 1870, adopted a preamble and resolution in the words and figures following, to wit:

"Whereas at the last session of the Legislature of this State a preamble and concurrent resolution were adopted in the words and figures following, to wit:

"'Whereas at the session of the Fortieth Congress it was resolved by the Senate and House of Representatives of the United States of America in Congress assembled (two thirds of both Houses concurring) that the following article shall be proposed to the Legislatures of the several States as an amendment to the Constitution of the United States, which amendment, when it shall have beeu ratified by three fourths of the said Legislatures, shall be valid, to all intents and purposes, as a part of the said Constitution, namely:

"'ARTICLE FIFTEEN.

"'SECTION. 1. The right of citizens of the United States to vote shall not be denied or abridged by the United States, or by any State. on account of race, color, or previous condition of servitude.

"'SEC. 2. The Congress shall have power to enforce this article by appropriate legislation,'

"*Therefore resolved*, (if the Assembly concur,) That the said proposed amendment to the Constitution be, and the same is hereby, ratified by the Legislature of the State of New York.

"And whereas, the proposed fifteenth amendment, above recited, has not been ratified by the Legislatures of three fourths of the several States, and has not become a part of the Constitution of the United States; and whereas the State of New York, represented in the Legislature here now assembled, desire to withdraw the consent expressed in the above recited concurrent resolutions: Now, therefore,

"*Be it resolved*, (if the Assembly concur,) That the above recited concurrent resolution be, and it is hereby, repealed, rescinded, and amended.

"*And be it further resolved*, (if the Assembly concur.) That the Legislature of the State of New York refuse to ratify the above recited proposed fifteenth amendment to the Constitution of the United States, and withdraw absolutely any expression of consent heretofore given thereto or ratification thereof.

"*Be it further resolved*, (if the Assembly concur,) That the Governor be requested to transmit a copy of these resolutions and preamble to the Secretary of State of the United States, at Washington, and to every member of the Senate and House of Representatives of the United States, and the Governors of the several States." *

And whereas the said preamble and resolution were transmitted to and are now on file in the Department of State at Washington, purporting to withdraw the assent of the people of the State of New York to the fifteenth amendment to the Federal Constitution, previously given by the Legislature of this State, to which said amendment had been regularly proposed; and whereas the action of the Legislature of 1870, in entertaining and adopting the said preamble and resolution, is deemed an unwarranted assumption of authority over a subject-matter not within its prerogatives; and whereas it is desirable that the record of the State of New York shall be clear and unequivocal in favor of the said fifteenth amendment: Therefore,

Resolved, (if the Assembly concur,) That the preamble and resolutions adopted by the Legislature of this State in 1870, purporting to withdraw the assent of the people of this State previously given to the fifteenth amendment of the Federal Constitution, be, and the same are hereby, rescinded.

Resolved, (if the Assembly concur,) That the Secretary of the Department of State at Washington be, and he is hereby, requested (if not inconsistent with the rules and regulations of his Department) to return to the Governor of this State the preamble and resolutions of the Legislature of this State, passed in 1870, and now on file in his office, which purport to withdraw the assent of the people of this State to the adoption of the fifteenth amendment of the Federal Constitution.

*For the vote on these resolutions see McPherson's History of Reconstruction, page 562. For vote on original ratification, *ibid.*, page 495.

Resolved, (if the Assembly concur,) That the Governor be, and he is hereby, requested to transmit a copy of this preamble and the resolutions accompanying the same to the Secretary of State of the United States.

YEAS—Messrs. Charles H. Adams, Norman M. Allen, Samuel Ames. Isaac V. Baker, jr., Erastus C. Benedict, George Bowen, Thomas I. Chatfield, *Townsend D. Cock*, Wells S. Dickinson, William Foster, James H. Graham, *William Johnson*, Loren L. Lewis, Samuel S. Lowery, Archibald C. McGowen, Edward M. Madden, JAMES O'BRIEN,* Abiah W. Palmer, John C. Perry, William H. Robertson, DANIEL F. TIEMAN,* Webster Wagner, Augustus Weismann, Norris Winslow, Daniel P. Wood, James Wood, William B. Woodin—27.

NAY—Mr. *Jacob Hardenburgh.*

IN ASSEMBLY, *February* 8, 1872.

YEAS—Messrs. Frank Abbott, Thomas G. Alvord, Albert Badeau, George Baltz, Eugene D. Berri, Elijah E. Brown, Ira D. Brown, Peter Burns, Leonard Burritt, William W. Crandall, John N. Davidson, James B. Dykeman, *John A. Foley*, Daniel G. Fort, Thomas M. Fowler, Edward M. Goring, William Greenhalgh, Matthew Griffin, E. Kirk Hart, Albert L. Hayes, *James Healy*, Castle W. Herrick, Enoch Holdridge, Edmund W. Hollister, Nathaniel M. Houghton, Martin L. Hungerford, James W. Husted, Francis A. Hyatt, *John C. Jacobs*, Edmund Kingsland, Volney G. Knapp, Anson W. Knettles, William Lewis, jr., Cyrillo S. Lincoln, John W. Lippitt, George P. Lord, Peter Lott, George H. Mackay, John S. Mercy, Darius A. Moore, Charles B. Morton, Severn D. Moulton, William W. Niles, *David S. Paige*, Stephen Pell, Jerome Preston, L. Bradford Prince, Eleazer C. Rice, Parker W. Rose, Chauncey S. Sage, Andrew Shepardson, John Simson, Amos V. Smiley, George W. L. Smith, William Smyth, Gustavus Sniper, Henry Smith Speaker, Stephen Springsted, Robert H. Strahan, George M. Swain, David Tompkins, J. Lee Tucker, Horatio N. Twombly, Ambrose L Van Dusen, George West, William Whitbeck, Edward D. White, Allen A. Whitaker, Joseph Woodward, Oliver C. Wyman, Lucien T. Yeomans—71.

NAYS—Messrs. *Samuel W. Buell, Alfred Chamberlain, William W. Cook, Peter Couchman, James Dunphy, Nicholas Haughton, Augustus Hill, David B. Hill, William W. Moseley, James M. Oakley, Benjamin Ray, Dominick H. Roche, Milton M. Tompkins*—13.

[Before the adoption of the resolution there was a separate vote taken on the preamble. The judiciary committee of the Assembly had recommended that the clause which denounced the action of the Legislature of 1870 as "an unwarranted assumption of authority," should be stricken out. The clause was restored in the committee of the whole. A division of the question was then called, and the preamble was adopted—yeas 63, nays 19. Of the negative vote, Messrs. A. L. Hayes, Moulton, and Prince were Republicans, the others Democrats.]

Action of the Legislature of New Jersey, 1871, on the Fifteenth Amendment, after the Proclamation by Mr. Secretary Fish of its Ratification.

The joint resolution passed by the vote given below is as follows:

"That the Legislature of this State do hereby ratify the amendment to the Constitution of the United States, proposed at the third session of the Fortieth Congress by resolution of the Senate and House of Representatives of the United States of America in Congress assembled, to the several State Legislatures; said amendment being in the following words, to wit:

[The fifteenth amendment is here inserted]

IN HOUSE OF REPRESENTATIVES, *February* 8. 1871.

YEAS—Messrs. Thomas C. Alcott, John Auness, William H. Barton, Albert M. Bradshaw, Joseph H. Bruere, Albert P. Condit, James F. Fielder, Isaac L. Fisher, Rochus Heinisch, jr., Charles Hemingway, Theodore Horn, Josiah Hornblower, William A. House, Edward L. Joy, Farrand Kitchell, Richard S. Leaming, W. B. Lefevre, Stevenson Leslie, Isaac W. Nicholson, Nathaniel Niles, Benjamin H. Overheiser, Edward F. Roberts, Liscomb T. Robins, John S. Rulon, Albert L. Runyon, Joseph F. Sanxay, John R. Staats, Edward T. Thompson, Robert M. Torbet, *Caleb H. Valentine*, George Warrin, Charles Wilson, Henry W. Wilson, Nimrod Woolery—34.

NAYS—Messrs. *Ferdinand Blancke, Herman D. Busch, Michael Coogan, John W. Dickinson, James Doty, Charles C. Grosscup, John T. Haight, John Hitchner, Henry A. Hopper, William S. Horner, James G. Irwin, John Kugler, Lebbeus Martin, John J. Maxwell, John O'Brien, Austin H. Patterson, Abraham Perkins, Absalom Pursell, Augustus E. Sanderson, William Silverthorn, Peter Smith, Jacob G. Van Riper, Peter Voorhees, Joseph W Yates*—24.

IN SENATE, *February* 15, 1871.

YEAS—Messrs. Jesse Adams, Columbus Beach, Thomas Beesley, John C. Belden, Edward Bettle, Samuel Hopkins, Henry J. Irick, Levi D. Jarrard, James H. Nixon, John W. Taylor, John Torrey, jr. Henry A. Williams—12.

NAYS—Messrs. David H. Banghart, James A. Brinkerhoff, Calvin Corle, Henry S. Little, Noah D. Taylor, James T. Wiley, John Woolverton—7.

Approved February 21, 1871, by Hon. Theodore F. Randolph, Governor.

Constitutional Amendment in Ohio and Pennsylvania.

The proposed amendment to the constitution of Ohio—given in full in McPherson's History of Reconstruction, page 258—which would have stricken the word "white" from the suffrage clause, and also have disfranchised persons who bore arms in support of the rebellion or fled to avoid the draft or deserted the service in time of war and not subsequently honorably discharged, was negatived at the election of 1867—yeas 216,987, nays 255,340; not voting on amendment, 12,276; constitutional majority against it, 50,629.

In the fall of 1871 a question of calling a constitutional convention was submitted to popular vote, and resulted—yeas 266,608, nays 100,412. But the Legislature failed to pass a bill calling a convention.

IN PENNSYLVANIA a like question was submitted at the same time, and resulted—yeas 328,354, nays 70,205; and a convention will be elected on the second Tuesday of October, and meet on the second Tuesday of November next. It will consist of one hundred and thirty-three members. to be elected as follows:

Twenty-eight members to be elected in the State at large, each voter to vote for not more than fourteen candidates, and the twenty-eight highest in vote shall be declared elected. Ninety-nine delegates shall be apportioned to the different senatorial districts of the State;

* Reform Democrat.

three delegates to be elected for each senator therefrom; and in choosing all district delegates each voter shall be entitled to vote for not more than two of the members to be chosen from his district, and the three candidates highest in vote shall be declared elected, except in the county of Allegheny, forming the twenty-third senatorial district, where no voter shall vote for more than six candidates, and the nine highest in vote shall be elected; and in the counties of Luzerne, Monroe, and Pike, forming the thirteenth senatorial district, where no voter shall vote for more than four candidates, and the six highest in vote shall be elected; and six additional delegates shall be chosen from the city of Philadelphia, by a vote at large in said city, and in their election no voter shall vote for more than three candidates, and the six highest in vote shall be declared elected.

State Elections—1872.

In NEW HAMPSHIRE the result was (two towns wanting:) Governor, Straw, Republican, 38,702; Weston, Democrat, 36,361; Cooper, Labor Reformer, 352; Blackmer, Temperance, 441.

In CONNECTICUT the vote was: Governor, Jewell, 46,563; Hubbard, 44,562; Gillette, 1,549; Harrison, Labor Reform, 390; scattering, 25. Jewell over all, 28.

In RHODE ISLAND the vote was: Governor, Padelford, Republican, 9,463; Arnold, Democratic, 8,308.

The First Effort at Reconstruction.

Now that all the States have been restored to their relations to the Union, it may be interesting to reproduce the first bill reported in Congress on this subject. It was made in the House by the Committee on Territories, Messrs. James M. Ashley, (chairman,) F. C. Beaman, A. Scott Sloan, Owen Lovejoy, and G. F. Bailey uniting in its favor; and Messrs. J. A. Cravens, Aaron Harding, and George K. Shiel opposing it. It was reported in the House March 12, 1862. Its principal provisions are:

That the President be, and he is hereby, authorized and required to take possession of and to occupy the insurrectionary States named, and to institute, establish, and protect with the military and naval forces of the United States a temporary civil government, with such names and within such geographical boundaries as he may by proclamation designate; that said civil government shall be maintained and continued in each of the districts thus named and designated until such time as the loyal people residing therein shall form new State governments, republican in form, as prescribed by the Constitution of the United States, and apply for and obtain admission into the Union as States.

Section two vests the executive power in a Governor, the legislative power in a council of not less than seven nor more than ten, the judicial in a superior court consisting of three judges and such inferior courts as the council may establish; all the officers designated to be appointed by the President, by and with the advice and consent of the Senate.

Section three gives the legislative authority general legislative power, but prohibits the passing of any act establishing, protecting, or recognizing the existence of slavery; and no law to be valid that is disapproved by Congress; and prescribes the manner of organizing the Legislative Council—vacancies to be filled by the President.

SEC. 4. That the Governor and Legislative Council are hereby authorized to take possession of all abandoned, forfeited, or confiscated estates within the limits of said districts, in the name and on behalf of the President and the Congress of the United States, and to lease the realty thereof, on such terms and for such time, not to exceed five years, as the Governor and Legislative Council may by law prescribe: *Provided*, That all leases shall be to actual occupants, who are loyal, and have not been in rebellion against the Government of the United States: *And provided further*, That all leases shall be for limited quantities, not to exceed one hundred and sixty acres to any person, it being the intent and purpose of this act to establish justice and promote the peace, safety, and welfare of the inhabitants by securing all in the enjoyment of life, liberty, and the fruits of their own labor.

Section five makes it the duty of the Governor and Legislative Council to establish schools, provide for the attendance of children not less than three months in each year, and to fix the number of hours constituting a day's work for field hands and laborers.

SEC. 6. That all public lands in each of said districts, held by said recent States at the time of their act of secession, shall be seized, occupied, and held by the Governor of the districts in which they may be located, in the name of the President of the United States, until otherwise disposed of by Congress. That all public lands thus acquired and which may become vested in the United States by confiscation or forfeiture by the provisions of any law now in force, or which may hereafter be passed, shall be held for the use of the soldiers, sailors, and marines, regular and volunteer, who have been or may be called into the service of the United States to crush the existing rebellion, and who shall be honorably discharged at the close of the war, and the widows and minor children of such as may be killed in battle or die in the service, or die of wounds received, or by diseases contracted in the service, and for the purpose of compensating such loyal citizens of said recent States as may sustain damages or losses by reason of the said revolt, or by the provisions of this act, to be distributed and apportioned as Congress may hereafter provide.

Section 7 authorizes the superior court to hold terms, appoint a clerk, and establish rules of practice, and gives it the same general jurisdiction of causes as are cognizable by the circuit and district courts of the United States or the territorial courts, with right of appeal to the Supreme Court of the United States.

Section 8 provides that all loyal persons and all admitted by the council to the privileges of electors shall be qualified to serve as grand and petit jurors; provided that no person who has heretofore held office under the United States or any one of the States, or any lawyer or other person who has taken an oath to support the Constitution of the United States, or any professed minister of the Gospel in open rebellion against the national Government, or who has given aid and comfort to the enemies of the United States, shall act as juror, or be entitled to any privileges of election, or be eligible to any office.

Section 9 provides for the appointment and salary of a secretary, a marshal, and a district attorney, and for the salaries of the Governor, members of the council, and the judges.

Section 10 authorizes the President, by proclamation, to establish ports of entry and delivery, to appoint collectors and such other officers as are usual in such ports; such officers to have the same powers and discharge such duties as like officers in other ports of the United States, and prescribing their salaries.

Section 11 repeals any inconsistent legislation with the provisions of this act.

Same day—Mr. ASHLEY moved that the bill be recommitted to the Committee on Territories, and be printed.

Mr. PENDLETON moved that the bill be laid upon the table; which was agreed to—yeas 65, nays 56:

YEAS—Messrs. *Sydenham E. Ancona*, Joseph Bailey, *Charles J. Biddle*, Francis P. Blair, jr., Jacob B. Blair, *George H. Browne*, William G. Browne, Charles B. Calvert, Samuel L. Casey, Andrew J. Clements, *George T. Cobb*, Schuyler Colfax, *Erastus Corning*, *James A. Cravens*, John W. Crisfield, John J. Crittenden, Charles Delano, Alexander S. Diven, George W. Dunlap, W. McKee Dunn, *James E. English*, George P. Fisher, Bradley F. Granger, Henry Grider, John A. Gurley, *Edward Haight*, *Aaron Harding*, Richard A. Harrison, William Kellogg, John W. Killinger, *John Law*, *Jesse Lazear*, Cornelius L. L. Leary, *William E. Lehman*, Robert McKnight, Robert Mallory, *Henry May*, John W. Menzies, *James R. Morris*, John T. Nixon, *Warren P. Noble*, *John W. Noell*, *Elijah H. Norton*, *George H Pendleton*, *Nehemiah Perry*, Timothy G. Phelps, Albert G. Porter, Alexander H. Rice, *William A. Richardson*, *William P. Sheffield*, Samuel Shellabarger, *George K. Shiel*, *John B. Steele*, John L. N. Stratton, Benjamin F. Thomas, Francis Thomas, Charles R. Train, William H. Wadsworth, *Elijah Ward*, Edwin H. Webster, Killian V. Whaley, William A. Wheeler, *Chilton A. White*, Charles A. Wickliffe, *Benjamin Wood*—65.

NAYS—Cyrus Aldrich, Isaac N. Arnold, James M. Ashley, Stephen Baker, Portus Baxter, Fernando C. Beaman, John A. Bingham, Samuel S. Blair, Harrison G. Blake, James Buffinton, James H. Campbell, Jacob P. Chamberlain, Ambrose W. Clark, Frederick A. Conkling, Roscoe Conkling, William P. Cutler, William Morris Davis, R. Holland Duell, Sidney Edgerton, Thomas M. Edwards, Thomas D. Eliot, Samuel C. Fessenden, Richard Franchot, Augustus Frank, James T. Hale, Samuel Hooper, Valentine B. Horton, John Hutchins, George W. Julian, William D. Kelley, Francis W. Kellogg, William E. Lansing, Dwight Loomis, Owen Lovejoy, Edward McPherson, William Mitchell, James K. Moorhead, Anson P. Morrill, Justin S. Morrill, Frederick A. Pike, Theodore M. Pomeroy, John H. Rice, Albert G. Riddle, Edward H. Rollins, Aaron A. Sargent, Charles B. Sedgwick, A. Scott Sloan, Thaddeus Stevens, Rowland E. Trowbridge, Robert B. Van Valkenburgh, William Wall, Charles W. Walton, E. P. Walton, James F. Wilson, William Windom, Samuel T. Worcester—56.

Letter of President Grant to the Supplementary Civil Rights Meeting in Washington City.

EXECUTIVE MANSION,
WASHINGTON, D. C., *May* 9, 1872.

GENTLEMEN: I am in receipt of your invitation extended to me to attend a mass meeting to be held for the purpose of aiding in securing civil rights for the colored citizens of our country. I regret that a previous engagement will detain me at the Executive Mansion this evening, and that I shall not be able to participate with you in person in your efforts to further the cause in which you are laboring. I beg to assure you, however, that I sympathize most cordially in any effort to secure for all our people, of whatever race, nativity, or color, the exercise of those rights to which every citizen should be entitled.

I am, very respectfully,

U. S. GRANT.

XXII.

STATE PLATFORMS.*

1871.

CALIFORNIA.

Republican, June 28, 1871.

Resolved, That the Republicans of California, by their representatives in State convention assembled, avow their determination to maintain and perpetuate the principles of their National Republican party; that we recur with pride and satisfaction to the many practical and substantial triumphs of those principles achieved during the past ten years; in the coercion by force of the rebellious States into obedience to the Federal Constitution and laws; in maintaining through a long, severe, and bloody struggle the authority of the General Government against powerful armies; in front of English and French interference on

* Such only of the State platforms, and such portions of them, are given as seemed most important or interesting.

the flank and the Democratic party in the rear; in rooting out the Democratic institution of slavery and banishing it forever from the jurisdiction of the United States; in prohibiting any State from abridging the privileges of any citizen of the Republic; in providing irrepealable guarantees for the payment of the public debt incurred in suppressing the rebellion and securing the people of all the States against being taxed for the payment of the debt of the late rebel Confederacy; in declaring the civil and political equality of every citizen, and in establishing all these principles in the Federal Constitution by amendments thereto as the paramount law.

2. Indorses Ulysses S. Grant.

3. Declares that the present national administration, despite unparalleled domestic and foreign complications, has achieved a most gratifying success.

4. That the concentration of the landed property of the country in the possession and ownership of a few, to the exclusion of the many, is in contravention of the theory of the American Government, subversive of the rights, liberties, and happiness of the masses of the people, and if permitted would inevitably terminate in the speedy establishment of an odious aristocracy upon the ruins of our free institutions; and we are in favor of such legislation, both by the nation and the State, as shall secure a just and equal distribution of the public lands remaining to them respectively, to the actual settlers and proprietors in small quantities, at the lowest reasonable price, and for homestead purposes only.

5. That the safety and perpetuity of republican institutions depend mainly upon popular education and intelligence. We therefore approve and recommend a common school system that shall not only extend its benefits to all, but which shall be compulsory upon all, and we are inflexibly opposed to any application of the public school moneys with any reference to the distinctions in religious creeds.

6. Denounces legislative enactment having for its object the establishment of creed, regulation of mode of worship, or the enforcement of religious observances of any kind.

7. That the presence in our midst of large numbers of Chinese, who are incapable of assimilation with our races, ignorant of the nature and forms of our Government, and who manifest no disposition to acquire a knowledge of the same, or to conform to our own habits, manners, and customs, is a serious and continuing injury to the best interests of the State; that their employment, under the plea of cheap wages, is offensive to the exalted American idea of the dignity of labor, detrimental to the prosperity and happiness of our own laboring classes, and an evil that ought to be abated; that while we unsparingly reprobate and denounce all acts of violence, wheresoever and by whomsoever committed upon them, we are inflexibly opposed to their admission to citizenship, and demand of the Federal Government the adoption of such treaty regulations and legislation as shall discourage their further immigration to our shores.

8. Favors an amendment to the Constitution prohibiting subsidies in land or otherwise to railroads or other private corporations.

9. Demands immediate repeal of the five per cent. subsidy law.

10. That the scandalous abuse of power exhibited by a Democratic Legislature, in the creation of useless offices, boards, and commissions, and the inexpedient increase of salaries and fees for partisan purposes; its palpable and wanton violation of a plain provision of the Constitution by the infamous enactment commonly known as the lottery bill; its measureless subserviency to a corrupt lobby, evinced by numerous profligate grants of subsidies to railroad companies; the official sanction of the most pernicious measures, including the aforesaid lottery bill, by the present Democratic State executive, and in addition thereto, his official approval of a series of legislative enactments whereby railroad companies have been subsidized to the extent of $400,000,000, afford convincing proof of the apostacy of a Democratic administration to all the pledges upon the faith of which it was elevated to power, and that the affairs of the State cannot with safety be recommitted to its control.

11. Welcomes our newly enfranchised citizens to the rights of citizenship.

ILLINOIS.

Republican, September 20, 1871.

Resolved, That the party which preserved the Union from dismemberment, abolished slavery, and established the civil and political equality of all men before the law, is entitled to the thanks of patriots, the confidence of the nation, and the gratitude of mankind; and while the measures by which these noble results were rightfully accomplished must be sacredly maintained, the time has come when the enmities engendered by the war should yield to the friendships of peace.

2. That the continuance of the political disabilities imposed for participation in the rebellion longer than the safety of the rebellion requires, not only tends to perpetuate feelings of unkindness among the people, but is incompatible with that principle of political equality which lies at the basis of the Republican creed; and the members of the House of Representatives from this State deserve the thanks of its people for their unanimous support of the bill for the general removal of political disabilities, which passed that body at its recent session by a vote of three fourths of its members.

3. That as it will be necessary and desirable to obtain from duties on imports a large portion of the revenue needed to defray the expenses of the Government, to pay the interest on the national debt, and the principal as it matures, such duties should be so adjusted as not to prejudice but promote the interests of every section and branch of industry as far as may be possible.

4. That the large surplus remaining in the national Treasury after the payment of all the expenses of the Government, including the interest on its public debt, calls for a still further reduction of the public burdens, and that in effecting that reduction regard should be had to relief from that species of taxation which, while it adds but slightly to the revenue of the country, taxes heavily its labor and productive interests; and we heartily approve the bills repealing the duty on coal and salt which have already passed the House of Representatives.

5. That we refer with pride and admiration to the eminently wise, patriotic, honest, and economical administration of President Grant, and we confidently commend it to the approbation of the entire country.

6. That we congratulate the administration of the General Government on the reduction of taxes and the public debt at the same time—a result which could only have been accomplished by an honest and efficient collection and disbursement of the public revenues; that we indorse and approve the general policy of the Administration and of our State government in the conduct of public affairs, and that the Republican party, without any new departures, is equal to the correcting of existing abuses and the perfecting of needed reforms, and that its mission will not have ended until they are accomplished.

7. That the recent exposures of fraud in the government of the city of New York, unparalleled in the history of civilized communities, prove that it is unsafe to trust the Democratic party with the practical administration of public affairs, as it would be to follow their political principles, and the recent elections in California and Maine show that the American people are generally of this opinion.

Democratic, October 5, 1871.

1. Indorses Thomas Jefferson's principles, and declares that the Democratic party has always maintained them, and has no new principles to advocate.

2. Accuses General Grant of despotism, and protests against centralization of power in his hands.

3. Declares that the usurpations of the present Administration directly involve the destruction of all republican guarantees.

4. That the Democratic party of the State of Illinois regard the Constitution, with its amendments, as the supreme law of the Union, to be respected and obeyed in all its parts, and the political disabilities founded on race and color being now abolished, in the future as in the past to maintain at all times the constitutional right and franchises of all men, without regard to previous conditions.

5. That taxes should be levied solely for the support of the Government and the maintenance of its credit, and that the imposition of taxes having for their object transfer of capital from one class, section, or individual to another, without the consent of the owners, is unjust, delusive, impolitic, and opposed to all the principles of a republican Government.

6. That commerce, trade, and industry are founded upon the mutual exchange of services among men, and that whatever operates to cripple or obstruct such exchange can only be productive of loss to the whole community.

7. That the present tariff has destroyed the ship-building industry, and almost annihilated the foreign commercial marine of the United States; that it has prohibited the construction on our lakes and rivers of iron vessels with increased carrying capacity, in proportion to the tonnage and draught of water, with greater durability, and diminished outlay for repairs and insurance, all of which tend to materially cheapen the transportation of products; that while this tariff is unnecessarily increasing the profits of the iron producer, it is crippling the ship-building and ship-owning interests of the great lakes and rivers; so that as respects competition with our Canadian rivals those interests are placed by the General Government at a great disadvantage, and this in the face of the most abundant natural resources for ship-building and navigation.

8. That the same unwise policy is chargeable in a great degree to the heavy cost of railroad transportation; the cost of such transportation being always in proportion to the cost of iron; and that it is idle for the western farmer, notwithstanding his superior advantages of soil and climate, to expect to compete with agriculturists in other parts of the world when his products are conveyed to market over roads which cost seventy per cent. more than they cost elsewhere.

9. That our system of transportation should be readjusted and simplified, with a view to raising the necessary amount of revenue from the smallest number of articles, to the end that the cost of collection may be decreased and a fruitful source of corruption removed.

10. Declares the legislative, executive, and judicial departments coördinate, and their independence should be maintained.

11. Requires a speedy return to specie payments.

12. That any American citizen should be entitled to the enjoyment of all his rights under the Constitution as amended. We demand of Congress full amnesty for all past political offenses, and the restoration of all privileges withheld by the fourteenth amendment.

13. That the full weight of American assertion and influence should be given to the doctrine that the citizens and subjects of all civilized States have the right to choose in what country and under what government they will live, and we especially insist that all American citizens, whether native or naturalized, shall be promptly and efficiently protected by the national Government in every part of the world against the oppression and injustice of all Governments whatever.

14. That labor is the true source of all wealth, and the men of labor are not only the real authorities of the material well-being, but the best defenders of the honor and interests of the country. It is, therefore, no less the dictate of a wise policy than of sound prin-

ciples that the rights of labor be fully maintained; and every possible opportunity of individual improvements secured by laws to the workingmen of the country.

15. Demands State laws for the protection of coal miners.

16. That we view with alarm the profligate squandering of the public domain by the party now in power, and demand that hereafter the public lands be held for the benefit and use of actual settlers only.

17. That honor and duty alike require the honest payment of the public debt and the faithful performance of all public obligations, the more especially such obligations as have been entered into to preserve and maintain our national Union; but we do not admit that creditors more than other men are entitled to special favor in any such interpretation of laws as would confer on them the rights which were neither intended nor warranted by the acts of Congress under which the obligations or debt was created.

18. That it is the duty of citizens to arrest all wasteful expenditures; to alleviate the burdens of taxation by a wise distribution of the revenue as far as possible, the more especially those which bear upon production and labor, and to prevent mismanagement, fraud, and corruption in all branches of the Administration and the collection of its revenue. It is the duty of every branch of the Government to enforce and practice the most rigid economy in the conduct of public offices.

19. That we denounce the assumption of the war-making power by General Grant in the San Domingo question as a gross violation of the Constitution.

20. That all taxes or tariffs levied for protection constitute robbery; that experience has shown that revenue raised by a tariff is unequal in its nature, most burdensome in its character, and most productive of evasion and crime; therefore we declare, as a correct principle of democratic Government, that we are in favor of full and absolute free trade with all nations as soon as it can be legally reached by the United States.

21. That we call upon Congress to establish a separate department of the Government by law, which department shall be known as the Department of Labor, and its functions shall be the promotion of the material and social welfare of all classes of the producers of our country.

22. That we are hereby opposed to, and hereby denounce, any and all combinations or rings, Tammany or otherwise, for political or partisan purposes, whether Federal, State, county, or municipal, and desire the thorough abolition of the abuses of Government and State patronage.

IOWA.

Republican, August 17, 1871.

Resolved, That we refer with pride to the history of the Republican party, and congratulate the people of this country upon its successful career. It has given to the poor man a homestead; it has abolished slavery and established manhood suffrage; crushed treason; given us the Pacific railroad; settled the doctrine of the right of expatriation; maintained the honor, integrity, and credit of our nation. It has vindicated the Monroe doctrine by preventing foreign Powers from interfering with the Government on this continent, and to perpetuate its power is the only safe guarantee for peace and prosperity in the future.

2. Indorses President Grant's administration.

3. That a tariff for revenue is indispensable, and should be so adjusted as not to become prejudicial to the industrial interests of any class or section of the country, while securing to our home producers fair competition with foreign capital and labor.

4. That we are opposed to any system or plan of granting public lands to railroads, or other corporations, without ample provision being made for securing their speedy sale at moderate prices, and occupancy upon fair and liberal terms by any and all who desire to purchase and settle upon them.

5. Indorses the present State administration.

6. That we are in favor of such legislation as will protect the people from the oppression of monopolies controlled by and in the interest of corporations.

7. That while as Americans we feel in duty bound to preserve a just and equitable neutrality in the contest now waging in Europe, yet we cannot forget that in our late war the sympathies and material aid of the German States were freely given us, and we do not hesitate to declare our unqualified sympathy with the earnest efforts of the Germans to maintain and defend their national unity; and we condemn the course the Democratic party of the country has been and are now pursuing in support of a despotic imperial dynasty and a causeless war against a people deserving peace and aspiring to perfect liberty.

8. That the Republican party of Iowa welcomes to our shores all human beings of every nation, irrespective of race or color, voluntarily seeking a home in our midst, and that all the rights which we as citizens demand for ourselves we freely accord them.

9. That we are in favor of amending our naturalization laws by striking out the word "white" from the same wherever it occurs.

10. Favors removal of national capital to the Mississippi valley.

Democratic, August 17, 1871.

Resolved, That the present internal revenue system of the United States is unendurable in its oppressive exactions; that to impose burdens on one class of citizens, or upon one branch of industry, to build up another, and to support an army of officeholders to enforce their collection, is an abuse of the taxing power; and that we are in favor of the collection of taxes through State governments.

2. That we are opposed to the present unjust, unequal, and oppressive tariff system, and in favor of one which, while adapted to

the purposes of raising the necessary revenue to provide for the liquidation of our national debt and meet the expenditures of economical administration, will not oppress labor and build up monopolies.

3. That we are in favor of such disposition of our public lands as will secure their occupation by actual settlers and prevent their absorption by mammoth monopolies.

4. That we assert the right of the people by legislative enactment to regulate and control all moneyed corporations upon which extraordinary rights are conferred by charter.

5. That we are opposed to any attempt to abridge the most full and free enjoyment of civil and religious liberty.

6. Asks support for these principles.

KENTUCKY.

Republican, 1871.

Resolved, That a State convention shall be called for the purpose of making such amendments to the constitution of Kentucky as experience and events have shown to be necessary.

II. We are in favor of and most cordially invite immigration to our State. Kentucky needs immigration, that its vast agricultural, mineral, and manufacturing resources may be developed. To this end the people of Kentucky should give immigrants a hearty welcome, and by legislation and otherwise assure them that they will be secure in their lives, liberty, and property, free to express their political and religious opinions. We favor the largest individual liberty, secured by impartial laws efficiently enforced.

III. We arraign the so-called Democratic party of Kentucky because of its unjust and timid policy through the Legislature, composed almost exclusively of members of that party. It is culpable alike for its action and non-action:

1. It persistently refused to pass any efficient law for the suppression of that form of lawlessness known as Kukluxism, which notoriously prevailed in many parts of the State, intimidating and murdering peaceful citizens, defying the officers of the law, overawing the courts, and boldly invading the capital while the General Assembly was in session.

2. No man's life, liberty, or property is or can be secure without the right to complain and be heard before the public tribunals of the country; and yet the Kentucky Legislature stubbornly refused to pass a law giving equal rights in this regard before and in the courts to our colored fellow-citizens. We denounce the denial of this equal right before the law as unchristian, and unworthy the age in which we live.

3. It has largely increased the public debt and wasted the public money.

4. It has so shaped the legislation of the State as to turn the tide of immigration and capital from this to other States, and so pandered to the passions incident to the late civil war as to keep alive a spirit of sectionalism and place the people of Kentucky in an attitude of hostility to the inevitable results of the war.

5. It has unjustly discriminated against the colored population by exempting from sale for debt the homesteads of white persons only.

6. It failed to perform the high and solemn duty of a government in not making adequate provision for the education of all the children of the State.

7. The platform of the late Democratic convention promises no change of policy by that party.

IV. We trust that every portion of the State will ere long be traversed by railroads, thereby securing to the people of each locality easy and cheap communication with every part of the country. Enterprise and capital should, by liberal and prudent legislation, be invited to the accomplishment of works of internal improvement; and all legislation tending to make stronger and perpetuate existing railroad monopolies, absorbing the capital of the State and controlling its politics, or a denial to any portion of the State of equal railroad facilities with any other, should not be tolerated, because it is detrimental to the best interests of the State and unjust. And we condemn the Kentucky Legislature for its persistent refusal to adopt and act upon this principle.

V. Acquiescence in the thirteenth, fourteenth and fifteenth amendments to the Constitution of the United States, and their enforcement by equal, just, and impartial laws in all parts of the country, are essential to our peace and prosperity, and to the perpetuity of republican institutions. The attempt of the so-called Democracy of Kentucky to prevent the enforcement of the provisions of those amendments is revolutionary in character, hostile to the peace of the State and nation, and perilous to republican institutions.

VI. With charity for all; with malice toward none; with a firm determination to pursue the right, as God gives us to see the right, we are in favor of complete amnesty to all of our fellow-citizens of every State who are laboring under disabilities by reason of their participation in the late rebellion. We earnestly desire the restoration of friendly relations with the people of our sister States lately in arms against the national authority, and earnestly wish for them all the blessings and prosperity to be enjoyed under a republican form of government.

VII. The Federal and State Governments are parts of one system, alike necessary for the common prosperity, peace, and security, and ought to be regarded alike with a cordial, habitual, and immovable attachment. Respect for the authority of each, and acquiescence in the just constitutional measures of each, are duties required by the plainest considerations of national, State, and individual welfare. But the Constitution and the laws of the United States made in pursuance thereof, and all treaties made under the authority of the United States, are the supreme law of the land, anything in the constitution and laws of any State to the contrary notwithstanding.

VIII. It is the duty of every branch of the

Government to enforce and practice the most rigid economy, and no more revenue ought to be raised than is necessary to fulfill the obligations, maintain the honor, and defray the legitimate expenses of the Government, including the payment of pensions to our patriotic soldiers and sailors, their widows and children, and for the gradual but certain extinguishment, in good faith, of the debt created in the suppression of the rebellion.

IX. We are in favor of a further reduction of the tariff and internal revenue taxes, whenever it can be done consistently with the maintenance of the national credit. We are in favor of correcting every practical injustice, inequality, and irregularity in the present mode of raising revenue as experience may from time to time show to be necessary and proper. We are, however, opposed to the system of direct taxation which our opponents suggest but have not the courage to designate or explain.

X. The prospect of an early adjustment of our difficulties with Great Britain upon terms honorable to both countries; the increased vigor to be seen in the Treasury Department, whereby the revenues of the country have been greatly increased, the reduction of internal revenue and tariff taxes, the diminution of the national debt at the average rate of $8.000,000 per month during the administration of General Grant, the increased value of the national currency, having been brought twenty per cent. nearer a specie standard; the overthrow of corrupt rings which existed in the revenue system under the last Administration; the inauguration of a more humane and less expensive Indian policy, are all results for which the country owes a debt of gratitude to the present Federal Administration.

XI. That the Republican party in Kentucky condemn the action of the Legislature of the State in its refusal to charter the Cincinnati Southern railway.

XII. That we favor the construction, under properly regulated charters, of any and all railroads that may be proposed in this State, no matter where the capital for their construction may come from.

XIII. That whereas the Legislature of Kentucky has twice refused to charter the Cincinnati Southern railway; and whereas, after the second refusal, the trustees of the city of Cincinnati, for the construction of said railway, applied to the Congress of the United States to delegate to them its power to construct a post road from Cincinnati to Chattanooga; and whereas the House of Representatives of said Congress promptly delegated said power: Therefore,

Be it resolved, That we approve of the action of the said House of Representatives and of the said trustees in this particular, and express our desire to have the Congress of the United States pass a bill authorizing the Cincinnati trustees to build a railroad from that city to Chattanooga, if, within a reasonable time after the meeting of the next Legislature of Kentucky, said Legislature persists in its refusal to grant the charter asked for said railway.

Democratic, May 3, 1871.

Resolved, That wise statesmanship and true patriotism require universal and unqualified amnesty.

2. That the industries of the country demand the abolition of the present mode of raising the revenues, by which portions of the Republic are oppressed and robbed to enrich monopolies and certain sections, and the speedy adoption of a system by which the burdens of taxation will be equally and justly distributed, and the taxes actually paid may reach the Treasury.

3. That the preservation of liberty is possible only through the States; and we protest against every act by which the States are deprived of their just and constitutional powers, and State tribunals ousted of their proper and necessary jurisdiction; and we are ready to join in all lawful and just measures to reverse the tyrannical acts of the party in power, whereby it is sought to strip the States of all rights, and concentrate all the powers of the Government in a great centralized despotism.

4. We indorse the address recently issued by the Democratic members of Congress, and unite in condemning all acts by which unconstitutional and despotic powers are conferred upon the President, by which, with the use of the Army and Navy, the suspension of the writ of *habeas corpus*, the power to declare martial law, call out the militia, and invade the States, without the request of their Executives or Legislatures, and other undefined means, he can destroy the freedom of elections, the independence of the judiciary, and the sovereignty of the States.

5. Kentucky is unalterably opposed to every form of lawlessness, whether committed under the cover of unconstitutional enactments or organized bands, and we pledge ourselves, as occasion may arise, to use every legal means to prevent the one, and to have enacted such laws as experience may demonstrate to be necessary to put down and punish the other, and secure to every person ample protection of life, liberty, and property, under laws enacted by our own Legislature, and administered by our own courts.

MARYLAND.

Republican, September 13, 1871.

1. Praises the State ticket.

2. Declares for General Grant's renomination for the Presidency.

3 and 4. Eulogizes the national Administration and Congress.

5. Indorses Postmaster General Creswell.

6. That the Democratic party is at present without any definite views on the national situation; that the large part of it sullenly rejects the results of the war and cherishes the hope of one day overturning all the good that has been done, while a smaller part gives a late, unwilling, and untrustworthy adhesion to what they are forced to conclude they cannot help. Their leading papers are in violent debate as to the most vital principles. The recent conduct of their most influential par-

tisans, the Tammany Democracy of New York, shows that the large part of their adherents are not even true to the time-honored American principle of entire religious freedom, and this condition of things, added to the astounding extravagance and corruption recently exposed on the part of the Democratic government of New York, shows how unfit is this divided, and, to a great extent, corrupt organization to govern a country saved by loyal blood and preserved in peace by the great party of liberty and progress.

7. That we are heartily in favor of such a reform of the civil service as shall make appointments to public office dependent upon fitness and character, and allow removals for cause only.

8. That the Democratic administration in Maryland has failed to provide the people with a sufficient system of public education. It has squandered hundreds of thousands of dollars on a militia, for which it has now nothing to show but one crack regiment and thousands of useless guns and worthless uniforms. It has administered the oyster laws so as to spend a great deal of money, and uselessly to harass that large class who make their living by the oyster fisheries. It has, both at Annapolis and in the counties and city, spent largely more than the former Union government, and has less to show for it, with cheaper times to spend in; and it has now no policy except to try and flourish on the decaying prejudices of race and color.

9. That the Republican party of Maryland places education among the first duties of the State, and that the safety and success of popular government depend upon the general education of all classes of its citizens. That efficient measures should be at once adopted so that schools shall be established where those portions of our population recently enfranchised and heretofore deprived of all school advantages shall have full opportunities for education. That the repeal of the school law adopted by the Legislature of 1865, and the criminal neglect of the party in power in a majority of the counties of the State to properly expend the money so lavishly furnished by the people for the education of the children of the State, meet our severest condemnation. That the provisions of the act of 1865, which required the levy and collection of taxes for school purposes, and did not leave the education of the masses of the people to the mere caprice of aristocratic land-holders, ought to be reënacted.

10. Urges a full vote.

11. Announces that the Republican party earnestly desires to bury all the animosities of the past.

12 and 13. Concern the time of meeting and composition of State central committee.

MASSACHUSETTS.

Republican, September, 1871.

Whereas the Republican party needs no "new departure," but only a strict adherence to those principles that have preserved the Union, secured freedom and equality before the law to all classes, and diminished the burdens of the people by an honest and economical administration of the Government: Therefore,

Resolved, That the Republicans of Massachusetts renewedly give their adherence to the great principles that have guided the National Republican party, and pledge to it their undivided support in enforcing all the laws for the protection of life and liberty in every part of our land; in the honest payment of our national debt; in reducing taxation, and in such reform of the civil service as shall secure efficiency and honesty in every department of the Government.

2. That the present national Administration, by the large reduction of the national debt and interest upon the public bonds, so that the national credit has been restored and the burdens of taxation diminished; by its successful adjustment of the controversy with Great Britain, and by its vigorous and successful action in learning the political rights of the people, is entitled to our hearty commendation.

3. That the Republican party of Massachusetts has been and is the party of progress and reform; that its great mission has been to blot out all class distinction on American soil; that it knows no class to be favored, and will permit none to be oppressed, but regarding all citizens of the State as equals before the law, it seeks to secure for them the blessings of free education and protection in every field of honest industry, and the position of Massachusetts in its credit at home and abroad, and in its rank among the most forward States of the world, in all that makes a powerful and happy Commonwealth, is the best proof of the wisdom and success of the present and past Republican administration of the State government.

4. That the long-continued depression of American shipping interests should receive the immediate and careful consideration of Congress, and that such changes in our revenue and navigation laws as will tend to restore the business of ship-building and ship owning to a condition of healthful prosperity should be made without loss of time.

5. That the Republican party of Massachusetts is mindful of its obligations to the loyal women of America for their patriotic devotion to the cause of freedom; that we rejoice in the late action of State Legislatures in recognizing the fitness of women for public trust, and that in view of the great favor which the movement has received from many of the Republican party, the subject of suffrage for women is a question that deserves the most careful and respectful consideration.

6. Indorses Governor William Claflin.

7. Nominates Hon. William B. Washburn for Governor.

8. That the Republican party will do its best to elevate the condition of the wages of the receiving portion of its citizens by a full, searching inquiry into the facts bearing upon their condition, and by such legislation as that inquiry shall show to be for their advantage,

having respect to the judgment of the laborers of the Commonwealth themselves as to what measures shall be best adapted to their wants.

MICHIGAN.

Republican, February 23, 1871.

Resolved, That as the Republican party proved a good party in time of war, and with fidelity, constancy, and unshaken courage sustained the Government and the cause of civil liberty in the dark days of the rebellion, until peace and freedom were secured to the country, so it has proved a good party in time of peace, reconstructing rebellious States in the interest of freedom, maintaining inviolate the public faith, establishing equality of all men before the law, and administering the Government in such a manner as best to promote the general good.

2. Eulogizes Grant, especially as to reduction of taxation and of national debt.

3 and 4. Praise the candidate for the Supreme Court, and appeal to the people for support.

NEW HAMPSHIRE.

Republican.

Resolved, That in the fulfillment of its mission it is the duty of the Republican party to establish and enforce such a national system of education as shall place within reach and ultimately compel every subject of the Government, of sufficient capacity, to embrace and improve such opportunities for mental and moral culture as will qualify him to discharge with fidelity and wisdom the responsible duties of an American citizen.

2. That all laws which favor capital at the expense of labor, or offer bounty to accumulated wealth at the expense of productive industry, are inconsistent with the principles of democratic republicanism, and we hereby repudiate and denounce them as in direct conflict with the purposes and aims of the Republican party.

3. That as the success of any system of goverment depends almost wholly upon the character and ability of those who administer its affairs, it is preëminently important in a free republic that the selection of public officers should be determined by merit and qualifications; we are therefore in favor of rigidly applying the Jeffersonian tests of honesty and capacity to the choice and appointment of all officers in the civil service.

4. That we protest against the so-called revenue reform movement now being inaugurated by a few quasi Republicans, in concert with the great body of Democrats, because while we desire, in common with the great majority of the people, that all taxation shall be reduced so far and so fast as is consistent with the necessities of the Government, we still believe that necessary taxes should be imposed chiefly upon the rich rather than the poor, upon the luxuries of life rather than its necessaries, and that a duty upon such articles of foreign manufacture as come in direct competition with the products of our own industry is essential to the well being and permanent prosperity of the nation.

5. That the sympathies of the Republican party have ever been and still are with and for the laboring men of this country. Prompted by this sympathy, we struck the fetters from the slave, and threw open the public domain for the location of free homesteads for the workingman thereon. We have always favored all legislation calculated to advance the true interests of labor, and will continue so to do.

6. That the wealth of the nation should pay its debt, and hence we are opposed to abolishing the income tax, or taxes upon those luxuries that wealth only can afford, while we favor the reduction of all taxes upon the necessaries of life.

7. That the Republican party of New Hampshire looks with alarm upon the efforts made to squander the public lands in the interest of schemes backed by railroad speculators, lobbyists, and stock-gamblers, and is opposed to each and every one of them; and, while it opposes them, looks with favor upon any act that may give a homestead to each disabled soldier who periled his life to put down the slaveholders' rebellion, and save this nation to equality of labor, religious toleration, and liberty.

NEW JERSEY.

Republican, September 7, 1871.

1. Pledges the Republican party to faithfully complete its unfinished work.

2. That the fifteenth amendment to the Constitution, embodying the principles of the equality of all men before the law, is not only just in theory, but is ennobling in practice, and we will by all lawful means oppose any attempt to blot it from the grand record of our country's progress.

3. That the Republican party is now, as heretofore, pledged to economy in the expenditure of the public money; to good faith in the payment of the public debt; to the careful fostering of all branches of trade and industry; to wholesome laws, a pure and learned judiciary, and an upright administration of the Government, both State and national.

4. That by the unprecedented reduction of the national debt; by the large reduction of interest upon the public loans, and the restoration of the national credit in all the markets of the world; by the wise and happy adjustment of the late threatening controversy with Great Britain; by its honest, straightforward policy, and its high patriotic spirit, the national Administration is entitled to our warmest commendation and active support.

5. That we are heartily in favor of such a reform of the civil service as shall make appointments to public office dependent upon fitness and character, and allow removals for cause only.

6. Considers that national recognition should be accorded by the erection of Jersey City into

a port of entry, and the establishment there of an independent custom-house.

7. Approves liberal provision for education.

8. That the present system of special and private legislation is the source not only of unnecessary expenses to the State and the public, but also of legislative corruption, and this convention therefore declares itself in favor of the passage of a general law of incorporation, and of the abolition, as far as practicable, of all special and private legislation.

Democratic, September 13, 1871.

DEMOCRATIC—September 13, 1871:

1 and 2 refer to the State record of the party.

3. That we favor a prompt and complete amnesty of all persons for political offenses.

4. That we favor the raising of a revenue for the economical support of the Government and the payment of the principal and interest of the national debt, and so far as such revenue is raised from the tariff it is to be upon the principle of taxation upon luxuries and the abolishment of taxes upon the necessaries of life.

5. That the Democratic party recognize the laboring element of the country as the true source of national wealth and strength, between which and capital no antagonism can exist so long as the rights and dignity of labor are properly recognized; and there is no duty the party owes to the country or to itself superior to the full protection of the laboring interests.

6. That, denouncing all conspiracies against law and good order, North or South, we protest against the extraordinary grant of military power given by the late Congress to the President, and declare the same to be most dangerous in precedent and unnecessary in fact.

7. That the Democratic party in the present, as in the past, recognize the Constitution and the amendments thereto as the organic law of the country, and not as open political questions of the day.

8. We believe that the Government of the United States is, as it ought to be, a Government of limited powers; that these powers are described and enumerated in the Constitution of the United States, which Government is founded upon its adoption by the people, and creating direct relations between it and all its subjects. It is not a supreme, unlimited, imperial, consolidated Government, but it has its distinct and recognized sphere of action, already ample; the governments of the separate States have their distinct and recognized sphere of action; and it is to the last degree important to the preservation of local independence, to the universal diffusion of political vitality, to the prevention of military despotism, to the security of individual rights, and the perpetuity of our institutions, that these separate spheres of action should be kept forever distinct and inviolable.

9. That we regard the creation of commissions by the Legislature for the regulation and government of municipal corporations as hostile to the principles of self-government.

10. Recommends rigid enforcement of election law.

11. Indorses Governor Randolph's administration.

NEW YORK.

Republican, September 28, 1871.

1. Recites the various triumphs of President Grant's administration.

2. That we have seen with horror and grief the astounding revelations of fraud, corruption, and municipal criminality in the city of New York; we have seen an infamous cabal take possession of its treasury, apply its resources to their own profit, issue bonds without stint and without law for the payment of dishonest and exorbitant claims under the pretext of reform. This desperate ring of conspirators and plunderers, controlling a Democratic Legislature, has secured the passage of laws and ordinances giving them irresponsible power; they have destroyed the sacred rights of the franchise by repeated piracies upon the ballot box; the judiciary has been polluted, the right of speech and petition, and the freedom of the press and of public procession have been assailed, and by weakness and vacillation a piteous massacre has been encouraged and provoked. The name and credit of the first city in the Union have been dishonored at home and abroad. Rejoicing in every effort to prevent these crimes and punish their authors, we shall gladly welcome the aid of men of all parties in our labors to redeem the honor of New York city. We hold the Democratic party responsible at the bar of public opinion for these manifold and unparalleled crimes. That party gave these men power, influence, authority, and dignity, and has at all times supported and acted with them. They have sat in its councils, and controlled its policy. By the assistance and encouragement of the whole Democratic party the men who have made the government of New York city a reproach to the republic and republican institutions in every part of the world, have aimed, and do now aim to seize the State and national Government, and rule the State and the Republic as they now rule the city. In view of the crimes perpetrated by those having the control of the Democratic party in New York, we should regard the success of the party as a calamity almost as disastrous as would have been the triumph of the rebellion in its war against the Union; and having by harmony and earnest efforts crushed treason and secession, the Republican party enters this canvass resolved to achieve a triumph over misgovernment organized for corruption and fraud.

3. That we call upon Congress, as far as may be compatible with the national credit, to continue to reduce taxation, and as rapidly as possible remove the burdens from the national industry; that while our interest account, our pension rolls, and other obligations entailed by the rebellion shall remain, we are in favor of such a tariff as will yield the needed revenue with the least injury to the people, at the

same time affording protection to our own rather than to foreign manufactures.

4. That as the Government owes to the citizen every guarantee of fairness and legality in the performance of his duties at the polls, we cordially approve of the measures taken by Congress for the protection of the franchise, and are in favor of such a law for the registration of votes as will give to our elections freedom and purity.

5. That as honest and justly paid labor is the foundation of a nation's greatness and its protection the highest mission of the Government, we earnestly urge all wholesome legislation fostering relations and conditions in which all who labor may be properly rewarded for their toil, and encouraged in every effort toward their prosperity, education, and advancement.

6. That so long as the people of the several localities have the right by law to license the sale of intoxicating liquors, they also, by a majority of voters, should have the right to prohibit such sale

7. That the Republican party is the party of enterprise and progress, and declares for cheap transportation, and for bringing the breadstuffs and products of the West, with the least expense, to the homes and markets of the East; and, reprobating as we do the profligacy and extravagance which have characterized the Democratic management of our canals, we are in favor of low tolls, and of making the great avenues of trade as rapidly and nearly free as can be done without increasing the burden of taxation.

8. Congratulates the country on recent Republican successes.

9. Counsels harmony in the party and deprecates faction.

10. Eulogizes the ticket.

Democratic, October 4, 1871.

Resolved, That the Democracy of New York arraign before the people of the Union the Administration at Washington as false to its pledges and faithless to its constitutional obligation. It has prolonged the dissensions that follow civil war, kept alive sectional animosities, refused amnesty to submissive citizens, and denied peace to the restored States. It has set up privileged classes and initiated a system of exemptions from taxation and protection to moneyed interests, the tendency of which is to make the rich richer and the poor poorer. It has squandered on mammoth corporations the lands which were the pledged heritage of the settlers, and it now attempts to perpetuate its power by a recourse to the grossest corruptions, by the direct interference of Federal office-holders in popular elections, and by a resort to military force to repress the civil tribunals of the country, and to control popular assemblages and elections—acts and usurpations which all history shows are strides toward despotism, and which, if not arrested, must prove fatal to our republican institutions.

II. That we recognize the emancipation of the freedmen of the South and their enfranchisement and perfect equality before the law as the inevitable sequence of the civil war and of the overthrow of the rebellion against the Union, and we hold it to be the duty of all to sustain them in the enjoyment of their established rights, and to aid them in promoting their own welfare and the general prosperity of the country.

III. That we view with indignation the corruption and extravagance recently brought to light in the management of the municipal affairs of the city of New York, and denounce as unworthy our countenance or toleration all who are responsible therefor; we pledge our best efforts to prevent a repetition of such abuses, and will look with satisfaction upon the punishment of all upon whom guilt can be fixed. We appeal to the record and the facts to prove that the deplorable condition of affairs existing in New York was inaugurated and fastened upon the city by a system of irresponsible government, instituted by the Republican party, and continued by them through many years, under which the growth of extravagance, peculation, and fraud was inevitable; and we demand on the part of our next Legislature such further reforms in the city charter as shall eradicate the legislation through which such frauds were possible, and secure, among other things:

1. An early opportunity for the people of the city to choose new municipal officers.
2. On the part of the mayor more complete control, and consequently more complete responsibility, for the subordinate departments of the administration.
3. The liability of the mayor of New York, with all mayors of cities, to be removed by the Governor in the same manner as sheriffs of counties are now removed, upon proof before him of malfeasance in office or neglect of duty.
4. Elections in the spring of each year, so as to place in the hands of the people the power to make a complete change of the city government.
5. Publicity of accounts at all times, and facilities to the tax-payer to restrain and punish abuses, and to secure speedy trials of offenders in independent courts.

IV. That experience has shown the necessity of restraining and defining by constitutional enactment the power of towns, counties, and municipalities to create debt and to tax the property of citizens.

V. That while ready and determined to purge local administration of abuses, we must not lose sight of the duty of correcting the confessed and all-prevailing corruption in the Federal Government, Congress and the Executive, in consummating their scheme of centralization, openly disregarded their constitutional obligation and tampered with the judiciary, and so manipulate the system of expenditure, debt, and paper money as to demoralize public sentiment, to corrupt social and business life, as well as nearly all the channels of political administration; and the profligacies in the custom-house, the internal revenue boards, in the Army and Navy, and in the highest walks of office, as well as in municipalities, are the ripe fruits of this system; and we call the attention of the people to the fact that this corrupt power triumphed in and controlled the recent Republican convention at Syracuse.

VI. That as registry laws so far from preventing frauds in elections have proved to be shields under cover of which they can more easily be consummated, we demand that some other safeguards be provided against a fraudulent repetition of votes and a dishonest canvass of the ballots—crimes which are treason to representative government; and that we approve of the passage of the constitutional amendment now pending making bribery a ground of challenge to the elector, and denying the suffrage alike to him that receives and him that offers a corrupt inducement.

VII. Refers to the State record of the party.

VIII. That the freest exchange of commodities between this and every other country, as between various districts of our own land, is of the greatest benefit both to the buyers and the sellers; that Government should lay no tax on imports except for revenue purposes; that revenue to be justly levied should be moderate in amount and fairly based upon the value of the property taxed; that raw materials and unfinished articles cannot be especially taxed without an unjust burden being laid upon our domestic manufactures so as to prevent them from competing fairly with those of other countries; that our present tariff violates every principle of political economy: it is complicated in its provisions, requiring an enormous body of officials for its collection, and thus debauching our politics by throwing into party contests a large element of persons subservient to the selfish aggrandizement of the appointing power; it has driven our manufactures, though the most skillful in the world, from all foreign markets by enhancing the cost of the materials they use. Many of its duties are so high as to encourage smuggling, and so complicated as to entrap the honest importers. That in the present circumstances of the country an ample revenue for the payment of the interest and large installments of the principal of the debt, and for the ordinary expenses of the Government, can be had without levying any tariff whatever upon necessary articles, such as iron, coal, clothing, medicines, and all materials used in the mechanic arts.

IX. Eulogizes Governor Hoffman.

X. That now that apprehensions are expressed that the religious and civil equality of citizens is menaced, we renew the pledge of our fidelity to the great Democratic doctrine of equal and exact justice to all men, of whatever creed or nationality, and special favors to none.

OHIO.

Republican, June 21, 1871.

1. The Republican party of the United States may well challenge the admiration and confidence of the country for its patriotism, courage, and wisdom in preserving the Union of the States, for its justice, firmness, and magnanimity in establishing for all the people liberty and equality before the law, for its gratitude to and provision for the national defenders and pensioners, for honor and good faith toward the national creditors, and generally for the successful administration of public affairs in peace as well as in war.

2. We not only recognize the XIIIth, XIVth, and XVth amendments to the Constitution of the United States as accomplished facts, but also as just, wise, and valid articles of organic law, to be jealously defended and enforced as parts of the Constitution now, henceforth, and forever.

3. As it will be necessary and desirable to obtain from duties on imports a large proportion of the revenues needed to defray the expenses of the Government, to pay the interest on the national debt and the principal as it matures, such duties should be so adjusted as not to prejudice but promote the interests of every section and branch of industry, as far as may be possible.

4. The present Administration of the national Government has vindicated its right to the continued confidence of the people. Its success has been illustrated in the impartial execution of the law, in its faithfulness, honesty, and economy in the collection of the public revenues, and in the expenses of the Government, so that, while taxation has been reduced to the extent of $100,000,000 per year, the national debt has been paid to the amount of over $230,000,000, a reduction unparalleled in history. The Administration has been equally successful in the management of our foreign relations, and has achieved imperishable honor in the settlement of our differences with Great Britain upon terms creditable to both countries as embodied in the Treaty of Washington. The head of the Administration thus distinguished by success and statesmanship, is justly entitled to be regarded as a wise and careful civil magistrate, and his uniform deference to public sentiment shows him to be one whom the country may trust, having fully redeemed the pledge he made before entering upon the duties of Chief Magistrate, that he would have no policy of his own to enforce against the will of the people.

5. We repeat our condemnation of the policy of granting subsidies of public lands to corporations and monopolies, and having originated the policy of granting homesteads to actual settlers, we declare that the public domain should be kept for our laboring population.

6. We are in favor of the adoption of a thorough system of civil service reform, and we indorse heartily the action of President Grant in selecting commissioners under the action of the recent so-called civil service act.

7. We unite with our fellow-citizens in every portion of the Union in the hope that the enmities and resentments of the war may be soon ended, and that the day may soon come when, in every State, every citizen may be safe in life, person, property, and civil rights, and may have the equal protection of the laws, so that no man that was loyal to the Union dur-

ing the great struggle may for that reason be the victim of persecution, outrage, and assassination, and so that some encouragement may be offered for the removal in proper cases of political disabilities for participation in the rebellion.

8. Recommends the calling of a convention to amend the constitution of the State.

9. Indorses the administration of Governor R. B. Hayes.

***Democratic, June 1, 1871.**

1. That, denouncing the extraordinary means by which they were brought about, we recognize as accomplished facts the three amendments to the Constitution recently declared adopted, and consider the same as no longer political issues before the country.

2. We demand that the rule of strict construction, as proclaimed by the Democratic fathers, accepted by statesmen of all parties previous to the war, and embodied in the tenth amendment to the Constitution, be rigorously applied now to the Constitution as it is, including the three recent amendments above referred to, and insist that these amendments shall not be held to have, in any respect, altered or modified the original theory and character of the Federal Government, but only to have enlarged the powers delegated to it, and to that extent, and no more, to have abridged the reserved right of the States; and, that as thus construed, the Democratic party pledges itself to a full, faithful, and absolute execution and enforcement of the Constitution as it now is, so as to secure rights to all persons under it, without distinction of race, color, or condition.

3. That the absolute equality of each and every State within the Union is a fundamental principle of the Federal Government; that we shall always cherish and uphold the American system of State and local government for State and local purposes, and the General Government for general purposes only, and are unalterably opposed to all attempts at centralization or consolidation of power in the hands of the General Government, and more especially when such attempts are in the form of usurpation by any department of that Government.

4. That we adhere firmly to the principle of maintaining perfect independence between

---

*May 18, 1871, the Democratic convention of Montgomery county, Ohio, adopted the following platform:

Whereas the Democratic party of 1871 is made up of men who previous to and during the late war, as also for a time since, entertained totally different opinions and supported totally opposite measures as to the questions and issues of those times; and whereas it is reasonable to assume that these same men still entertain, to a large extent, their several opinions, and would, if in like circumstances, support again substantially the same measures; and whereas a rational toleration among men resolved to unite in a present common purpose does not require a surrender, in any particular, of former opinions, or any acknowledgment of error as to measures heretofore supported:

Resolved by the Democracy of Montgomery county, 1. That, agreeing to disagree in all respects as to the past, we cordially unite upon the living issues of the day, and hereby invite all men of the Republican party who believe now upon present issues as we believe, to coöperate fully and actively with us upon the basis of perfect equality with every member of the Democratic party.

2. That, waiving all differences of opinion as to the extraordinary means by which they were brought about, we accept the natural and legitimate results of the war so far as waged for its ostensible purpose to maintain the Union and the constitutional rights and powers of the Federal Government, including the three several amendments *de facto* to the Constitution recently declared adopted, as a settlement in fact of all the issues of the war, and acquiesce in the same as no longer issues before the country.

3. That thus burying out of sight all that is of the dead past, namely, the right of secession, slavery, inequality before the law, and political inequality; and further, now that reconstruction is complete, and representation within the Union restored to all the States, waiving all question as to the means by which it was accomplished, we demand that the vital and long-established rule of strict construction, as proclaimed by the Democratic fathers, accepted by the statesmen of all parties previous to the war, and embodied in the tenth amendment to the Constitution, be vigorously applied now to the Constitution as it is, including the three recent amendments above referred to, and insist that these amendments shall not be held to have in any respect altered or modified the original theory and character of the Federal Government as designed and taught by its founders, and repeatedly in early times, in later times, and at all times, affirmed by the Supreme Court of the United States; but only to have enlarged the powers delegated to it, and to that extent, and no more, to have abridged the reserved rights of the States; and that, as thus construed, according to these ancient and well-established rules, the Democratic party pledges itself to the full, faithful, and absolute execution and enforcement of the Constitution as it now is, so as to secure equal rights to all persons under it, without distinction of race, color, or condition.

4. That the absolute equality of each and every State within the Union is a fundamental principle of the Federal Government, and that no department of that Government has power to expel a State from the Union, or to deprive it, under any pretext whatever, of its equal rights therein, including especially the right of full and complete representation in Congress and in the electoral colleges.

5. That we will always cherish and uphold the American system of State and local self-government for State and local purposes, and a General Government for general purposes only; and are unalterably opposed to all attempts at centralization and consolidation of power in the hands of the General Government; and the more especially when such attempts are in the form of usurpation by any department of that Government. And further, that we adhere firmly to the principle of maintaining a perfect independence between the coördinate departments of that Government, the legislative, the executive, and the judicial, condemning all encroachments by one upon the functions of the others.

6. That outside of fundamental law all legislation is in its nature and purposes temporary, and subject to change, modification, or repeal at the will of a majority of the people, expressed through the law-making power, and that the pretense that any act of Congress, not executed and spent, or any legislative policy of a party, is an absolute finality, is totally inconsistent with the whole theory of republican government; and that it is the unquestionable right of the people, of themselves and through their Representatives, at each successive election, and in each successive Congress, to judge of what legislation is necessary and proper or appropriate to carry into execution or enforce the constitutional powers, rights, and duties of the Federal Government.

7. That as an instance of eminently appropriate legislation under the fourteenth amendment, in the name of wisdom, justice, and republican government, and to secure universal political rights and equality among both the white and the colored people of the United States, to the end that we may have peace at last, we call now, as well on behalf of

the coördinate departments of the Government, the legislative, executive, and judicial, condemning all encroachments by the one upon the functions of the other.

5. While the fundamental law as expressed in the Constitution is necessarily paramount until abrogated as prescribed by that instrument, all legislation is in its nature and purpose temporary, and subject to change, modification, or repeal, at the will of the majority of the people, as expressed through the law-making power, and that the pretense that any act of Congress, not executed or spent, or any legislative policy of party is an absolute finality, is totally inconsistent with the whole theory of government, and that it is the unquestionable right of the people of themselves, and through their Representatives at each successive election and in each successive Congress, to judge what legislation is necessary, proper, or appropriate to carry into execution or enforce the central powers, rights, and duties of the Federal Government.

6. That as an instance of the eminently appropriate legislation under the fourteenth amendment we demand now of Congress universal amnesty.

7. That while we denounce all riotous combinations and conspiracies against law or to disturb peace in the South or elsewhere, and demand of all good citizens their utmost influence to put all such down, we also denounce the act commonly called the bayonet bill, recently passed by Congress, and the more recent act commonly called the Ku Klux bill, extending by its terms to every State, and enacted for no other purpose than to complete the centralization of all power in the hands of the General Government and to establish a military despotism, and thus to perpetuate the present Administration, without regard to the will of the people, and as not only inconsistent with the whole theory and character of the Federal Government, and as revolutionary and dangerous in their character, but are in direct conflict with the spirit and letter of the Constitution, including the amendments which they pretend to enforce.

8. That holding still to the good old Democratic doctrine of annexation, or the acquisi-

---

the North as of the South, upon Congress for a universal amnesty.

8. That we are in favor of the payment of the public debt at the earliest practicable moment consistent with moderate taxation; and the more effectually to hasten the payment, we demand the strictest honesty and economy in every part of the administration of the Government.

9. That we are in favor of such revenue reform as will greatly simplify the manner of and reduce the number of officers engaged in collecting and disbursing revenue, and largely diminish the now enormous expense to the Government and annoyance and vexation to the people attending the same; and further, will make the burdens of taxation equal, uniform, and just, and no greater than the necessities of the Government, economically administered, shall require.

10. That we are in favor of a searching and adequate reform in the civil service of the Government so as to secure faithfulness, honesty, and efficiency in all its branches, and in every officer and appointee connected with it.

11. That we are in favor of a strictly revenue tariff, conformed to the theory and principles of all other just and wise tax laws.

12. That all taxation ought to be based on wealth instead of population; and that every person should be required to contribute to the support of the Government in proportion to the amount, and not with reference to the character, of his property.

13. That specie is the basis of all sound currency, and that true policy requires as speedy a return to that basis as is practicable without distress to the debtor class of the people.

14. That there is no necessary or irrepressible conflict between labor and capital; that without capital or consolidated wealth no country can flourish; that capital is entitled to the just and equal protection of the laws, and that all men, whether acting individually or in a corporate capacity, have the right, by fair and honest means, and not for the purposes of wrong or oppression, to so use their property as to increase and consolidate it to the utmost extent within their power. But, conceding all this, we declare our cordial sympathy and coöperation with the producers and workingmen of the country, who make and move all capital, and who only seek by just and necessary means to protect themselves against the oppressive exactions of capital, and to ameliorate their condition and dignify their calling.

15. That we are totally and resolutely opposed to the grant of any more of the public lands, the common property of the people of the States, to corporations for railroad or other purposes, holding that these lands ought to be devoted as homesteads to actual settlers, or sold in small quantities to individuals at a price so low as to induce speedy occupation and settlement.

16. That holding still to the good old Democratic doctrine of annexation or acquisition of territory, we are yet totally opposed to the scheme of President Grant to acquire San Domingo, as a "job," and by the means and for the purposes evidently intended, and accept the issue he has tendered in his late message submitting the subject to the decision of the people.

17. That the act commonly called the "bayonet bill," recently passed by Congress, amendatory to the act of May 31, 1870, and a supplement to the act of July 14, 1870; each and all intended and so contrived as to interfere with and practically subvert free popular elections in all the States, subjecting them to the absolute control, through the military power, whenever called forth, of the President and Commander-in-Chief, for the time being, of the land and naval forces of the United States; and the more recent act of Congress, commonly called the Ku Klux bill, extending by its terms to every State, intermeddling with the exclusively local concerns of every State, authorizing the President upon the existence of a condition of things to be ascertained and determined by himself, and in the exercise of his sole judgment, to suspend the writ of *habeas corpus* in time of peace, and to march the standing Army into any State and declare martial law therein at his own mere will and pleasure—thus subverting the entire civil power, legislative, executive, and judicial, of such State, destroying freedom of speech and of the press, and the peaceable assembling of the people, and subjecting every person therein to military arrest, trial, and execution—were enacted for no other purpose than to complete the centralization of all power in the hands of the General Government, establish a military despotism, and thus perpetuate the present Administration, without regard to the will of the people, and are not only utterly inconsistent with the whole theory and character of the Federal Government, and revolutionary and dangerous in their nature, but in direct conflict with the spirit and letter of the Constitution, including the amendments which they pretend to enforce.

18. That the Radical party of 1871, as now constituted, is not the Republican party of the period previous to the war, nor the so-called "Union party" during the war, and is in no respect entitled to beg the public confidence as such; that it is now only an "Administration" or "Grant party," dating back to March 4, 1869, and to be judged by its record since; and that upon that record, totally hostile to the doctrines and policies herein maintained, and wholly committed to the policies and doctrines herein denounced, it deserves the emphatic condemnation of the people.

tion of territory, we are yet totally opposed to the scheme of President Grant to acquire Santo Domingo, as a job, and by the means and for the purposes evidently intended.

9. That we are in favor of a strictly revenue tariff, conformed to the theory and principles of the other just and wise tax laws, and opposed to the protective theory, so called.

10. That the profligate corruption and wanton extravagance which pervade every department of our Federal Government, sacrifice the interests of labor, and aggrandize a handful of aristocrats, are a wicked deprivation of the people of their rightful heritage in public lands, which have been made gifts to railroad and other monopolists, paying more than twenty millions premium during the administration of President Grant in Government bonds, payable at par, maintenance at an annual cost to the people of nearly thirty millions, and an unconstitutional, oppressive, and extortionate system of banking, whereby money is made scarce and interest high, are abuses which call for wise and thorough remedies.

11. That we are in favor of strict economy; of a large reduction in expenditures of the Federal and State Governments; of the collection of internal revenue by the State authorities, thereby returning to honest labor myriads of tax-gatherers who afflict our land and eat up its substance; and of the speedy trial, conviction, and punishment of the thieves who have stolen the taxes paid by the people.

12. That while we reject repudiation we equally reject the proposition to pay the bondholders more than the contract with them demands; that if bondholders have rights so have tax-payers, and we insist upon justice being done to both; that the creditor is entitled to be paid in the same currency he loaned to the Government; that where he loaned greenbacks he should be paid in greenbacks, unless the contract otherwise provides, and where he loaned gold he should be paid in gold; that to guard against a too great expansion greenbacks should be made convertible into three per cent. bonds at the option of noteholders, said bonds to be redeemed in greenbacks on demand; that the true method of returning to specie payments is to make customs dues payable in legal-tender currency, whether paper money or gold; that such policy would secure uniform currency, stop gambling in gold, and thereby elevate the credit of the Government.

13. That with the watchword of reform we confidently go to the country; that we believe the interests of the great body of the people are the same; that, without regard to political associations, they are the friends of free government; that they are equally honest, brave, and patriotic; and we appeal to them as to our brothers and countrymen, to aid us to obtain relief from grievous abuses which wring and oppress every one except the wrong-doers and oppressors themselves.

14. Upon the State issues we resolve that we are in favor of calling a convention as provided for by article sixteen, section three of the State constitution.

PENNSYLVANIA.

Republican, May 17, 1871.

1. Demands a State convention.

2. They demand of Congress that the credit of the nation shall be faithfully maintained; home industry encouraged and protected; an adequate civil service system established for regulating appointments to office; taxes reduced to the lowest possible limit consistent with the steady but not too rapid extinction of the national debt; the honor of the Republic sustained at home and abroad; the rights of every man protected in all the States, and every man entitled thereto secured in the polling of one vote, and no more, at each election.

3. They declare their unalterable attachment to the principle of protection to home industry in the levying of tariff duties in accordance with the wise policy which has existed from the foundation of the Government to this time.

4. Commends the Republican national and State policy of retrenchment and reform.

5, 6, and 7. Relate to State matters.

8. Indorses Governor Geary.

9. Eulogizes President Grant's administration.

Democratic, May 24, 1871.

1. Favors revision and amendment of State constitution.

2. Rebukes the Republican party for refusal to modify provisions of the registry law relating to Philadelphia.

3. Eulogizes Democratic action upon apportionment bill and Philadelphia registry law.

4. That the force and bayonet bills recently enacted by Congress are gross attacks upon the reserved rights of the States, destructive of the elemental principles of civil liberty, intolerable to a free people, centralizing in tendency, and should be forthwith repealed.

5. That the language of Senator Carl Schurz, in his St. Louis speech, wherein he says: "I consider it one of the most pressing needs of our days that we should return to the sound practice of constitutional government. The safeguards of our common rights and liberties contained in the Constitution are too sacred and valuable a boon to be permanently jeopardized in providing for a passing emergency. It is time that the American people open their eyes to the dangerous character of this tendency, and that neither a great name nor an object appealing to our sympathies should be permitted to disguise it. As for me, I have seen the working of irresponsible power and personal government in other countries, and I may assure my constituents that while I am a citizen of this Republic I shall struggle to the last gasp against its introduction here," was but the utterance of well-known and frequently announced Democratic doctrine.

6. That the public debt is binding upon the nation, and must be paid; and that we are unalterably opposed to any and all movements

looking towards repudiation, direct or indirect; but, in justice to the laboring and producing classes, the rate of interest thereon should be reduced at the earliest practicable date.

7. That the Democratic party is opposed to the existing system of Federal taxation and finance, ruinous as it is in its effects upon the laboring, producing, mining, and manufacturing interests of the people, and the fruitful source of "hard times," personal indebtedness, and individual bankruptcy.

8. That labor and capital have no just cause of antagonism; that we deprecate strife between these two great forces, and earnestly seek to place the laborer and capitalist on such a platform as will enable both to amicably adjust their differences; and we are unalterably opposed to the importation of a servile race for the purpose of degrading the standard and lowering the position of the laboring men of the nation.

9. That we recognize the binding obligation of all the provisions of the Constitution of the United States as they now exist, and we deprecate the discussion of issues which have been settled in the manner and by the authority constitutionally appointed.

10. That we are for a Government rigorously frugal and simple, applying all the possible saving of the public revenue to the discharge of the national debt, and opposed to a multiplication of officers and salaries merely to make place for partisans and for increasing by every device the public debt.

11. That the continuance by a Republican Congress of the income tax, when the same is at least of doubtful constitutionality, and the necessity therefor has long since ceased to exist, is an exercise of a power oppressive to the people and a gross violation of their rights and interests.

12. That the present tariff is in many of its features oppressive, and should be revised, and that we herewith request our Representatives in Congress, when the tariff shall be the subject of readjustment, to see that the immense products of the State and its industries are properly cared for.

13. Demands equalization of bounties, in lands and money, for Pennsylvania soldiers and sailors.

14. Indorses the State nominees.

TEXAS.

***Democratic, August 15, 1871.**

Resolved, That the Democracy of Texas have an abiding confidence in the devotion of the national Democratic party to the correct principles of government, and we pledge ourselves to coöperate with it, as an integral part thereof, in its future efforts to restore the Government in its administration to the principles on which it was founded.

2. That we rely upon the honesty and capacity of the people for self-government.

3. That the Constitution, as formed by the free voice of the State, is the foundation of the powers of the Government.

4. That the powers of the General Government are restricted to the express grants of the Constitution, and all powers not granted are reserved to the States and the people thereof.

5. That the regulation of suffrage and elections belongs to the respective States, and any interference by the General Government, with intent to control either, is a gross usurpation of power; and the use of the military at elections, to overawe the people and prevent a full and fair expression of their political sentiments, is utterly subversive of free government, and should be restricted by all proper means until the evil is abolished and an honest and untrammeled ballot restored.

6. That abolition of slavery, as a result of the war, is accepted as a fixed fact, and it becomes our duty, by State legislation, to provide for the security and well being of all classes of men, native or foreign, white or black.

7. That the immigration of the white races from all quarters of the world should be encouraged, and there should be no unreasonable impediments or delay to naturalization and citizenship, the Democratic party having been uniformly in favor of a liberal policy towards persons of foreign birth who, in good faith seek a home among us.

8. That we will yield obedience to the Constitution and laws.

9. That we, the Democratic party of Texas, are in favor of a judicious, liberal, and uniform system of internal improvements.

10. Attacks at great length the State Republican administration.

VIRGINIA.

Republican, September 21, 1871.

1. The Republican party of Virginia in convention assembled reaffirm their devotion to the principles of the national Republican party of the United States, as enunciated in the Chicago platform at the last national convention. We are in favor of and support as national principles—

2. A tariff which, while securing the necessary revenue, shall give incidental protection to American industry.

3. A national banking system that shall give us safe, uniform currency, and absolute security to bill holders.

4. The policy of extending Government aid to the States in improving their rivers and harbors.

5. The absolute payment of all obligations of the Government, and a sufficient yearly reduction of the national debt to convince the world of our determination to ultimately extinguish it; while at the same time we carefully avoid burdening the people with onerous and unnecessary taxation.

6. That we heartily indorse the Administration of President Grant, and are unanimously in favor of his renomination.

* This platform was not adopted by a Convention, but was officially issued in the address of the Democratic State Committee of Texas.

WISCONSIN.

Republican, August 31, 1871.

Resolved, That we refer with pride to the history of the Republican party of the United States. By its early resistance to the encroachments of slavery; by its patriotic devotion to the cause of the Union during the late civil war; by its emancipation, at the proper time, of an oppressed people from bondage; by its signal overthrow of disloyalty and treason; by its justice, firmness, and magnanimity in guarding and securing the results of the war, and giving and assuring to all citizens liberty and equality before the law; by its grateful care and just provision for the nation's defenders; by its honor and good faith toward the nation's creditors; by its wise and liberal policy in granting homesteads to settlers, and in aiding the development of the western States and Territories; by its successful advocacy of humane principles of international law, not hitherto recognized by the civilized world; by its peaceful settlement of our controversies with Great Britain on terms honorable, advantageous, and tending to secure permanent peace and concord between the two nations; by its judicious direction of our financial system, whereby the nation was enabled to meet the emergencies of a great war, to furnish a sound and uniform currency, and to prevent the commercial depression, revolution, and disaster usually attendant upon civil strife; and generally, by its succesful administration of national affairs during ten eventful years, it has proved, on all occasions, its fidelity to the highest interests of the country. A party, whose career has thus been signalized at every step by great triumphs of human freedom and progress, needs not to depart from the path of honor and duty in which its victories have been won, and we believe that upon its continued ascendency and a steadfast adherence to its cardinal principles, the peace, prosperity, and honor of the country depend.

2. That we regard the recent amendments to the Constitution of the United States as just and wise articles of organic law, essential at the present time to secure constitutional liberty, and ever to be zealously upheld and enforced; that under the Constitution thus amended the Federal Government posseses, and ought to exercise, whenever and wherever necessary, sufficient power to protect every citizen under our flag in the free expression of his sentiments, the free exercise of the ballot, the full enjoyment of his property, and the absolute safety of his person.

3. That we rejoice in the recuperation of the southern States under the benign influence of free labor; that we urge upon those lately in rebellion not to retard the prosperity of the South by permitting lawlessness and violence therein. We entreat them to take a bold stand for law and order, to accept the results of the war, and to coöperate with us in efforts to advance the prosperity of the whole country; and we hope that the time may speedily come when persecution and outrage of loyal men shall wholly cease, and when political disabilities imposed for participation in rebellion may be removed without danger to the rights of those who have remained faithful to the Union.

4. That we believe that the prosperity of the country and the stability of its monetary system, as well as its credit and influence in the family of nations, depend upon the maintenance of the public faith. To that end we favor the continued reduction of the national debt, so steadily as to prevent depreciation of our bonds and currency, so gradually as not to burden too heavily the present industries of the country.

5. That in our judgment the most efficient and satisfactory means of raising the larger portion of revenue to meet the obligations of the Government is from duties on imports; that such duties should be so laid as, first, to make sure of the amount required; second, to fairly distribute the burdens of the nation upon all sections of the country, all classes of people; and third, so as never to burden one interest that another may thrive.

6. That we commend the policy of the Government in abolishing the most burdensome taxes of the internal revenue system; that we favor a further reduction as the exigencies of the country will permit.

7. Urges the early completion of the Fox and Wisconsin rivers improvement.

8. Asks Congress to renew the Lake St. Croix and Lake Superior railroad land grant.

9. That in view of the present rapid settlement of the country the residue of the public domain should be kept mainly for actual settlers. The homestead law should be so modified that when honorably discharged Union soldiers and sailors claim the benefits of the same the period of their service shall be deemed a part of the time of occupancy necessary to acquire title. Grants of land to aid in the building of railroads should be made only where necessary to open the country up to settlement, and under such restrictions as will facilitate the occupation of the public lands.

10. That we favor every practicable reform in the public service, State or National, in the direction of greater purity, simplicity, efficiency, and economy of administration.

11. Eulogizes the State administration.

12. Eulogizes the national Administration.

13. That we know no duty more urgent than to mature and enforce new safeguards of the purity of elections, and to effect a thorough reform of the civil service.

Democratic, August 23, 1871.

1. Attacks the State administration.

2. That the wise restrictions enacted in the tenth amendment to the national Constitution, reserving to the States respectively and to the people all powers not delegated to the United States, is one of the strongest safeguards of popular freedom; that the acts of Congress and of the Federal Administration in usurping powers not delegated by the Constitution, and the breaking down of the distinctions between the powers of State governments and

those of the General Government, are destructive to constitutional liberty, and threaten an overthrow of our existing form of local and Federal Government, and tend to the establishment of a permanent centralized despotism in Congress and the national Executive; and that we denounce as a vicious offshoot of the centralizing tendencies of the General Government the frequent attempts of the agents of the Federal Administration to interfere in local political affairs.

3. That we are in favor of a tariff for revenue; that under the pretext of raising a revenue within the past ten years the national Congress has established and continues that enormous robbery of the masses for the enrichment of the few known as the protection tariff system, which has swept our commerce from the seas and fettered and oppressed every agricultural pursuit, a system of which the conventions of the Republican party equivocally and haltingly speak in their platform, but which that party perpetuates in Congress, and from which the people may hope for no relief but by the restoration of Democratic rule.

4. That by corruption and profligacy the present Administration have squandered a large portion of the national domain and enormous sums from the national Treasury; that it is no answer to this complaint that they have reduced the proportions of the national debt, as a wise and economical use of the immense revenue, which is raised by an unprecedented tax, would have produced a much greater reduction of the debt, and should have been accomplished; but the Democratic party opposes oppressive taxation for the mere sake of a speedy payment of the debt, believing that by wisdom and justice in the adjustment of taxes and economy in expenditure the national debt may be paid with sufficient rapidity, with but a light burden upon the industry and resources of the people; and that we are opposed to all forms of national repudiation, either of the debt or the pensions and bounties of the soldiers.

5. That as the late amendments to the Constitution have been declared by the properly constituted authority to be a part of the fundamental law of the land, they are binding on the people, and that the Democratic party now, as in the past, know no higher law than the Constitution; that the time-honored principle of the strict construction of the Constitution, applied by its powers and accepted by the wisest statesmen and jurists of the country, should be observed in all legislation by Congress relative to the Constitution and its amendments; that the Democratic party is opposed to the withdrawal of civil or political rights from any class of the people, and that we demand the removal of all political disqualifications.

6. That the defalcations, embezzlements, and corruptions of the national Administration, and the prostitution of legislation to the demands of unscrupulous lobbyists and greedy monopolists, are a national scandal and disgrace, and the most dangerous blow to the public credit, and an intolerable outrage on the tax-payers of the country.

7. That, as the representatives of a Constitution-loving, law-abiding party, we deprecate and denounce every outbreak of lawlessness and violence, whether committed at the North or South, and that the acts of Congress which authorize the employment of the standing Army to garrison the places where elections are to be held, and to constitute a local police in the States, and which empowers the officers of the Federal Administration to interpose military force for the purpose of overawing political conventions of the people, are subversive of free government and a perpetual menace to public liberty.

8. That while the people of this country hope they may extend the blessings of our form of government over the entire continent, the course pursued by the national Administration in its efforts to annex San Domingo was an unjustifiable usurpation, and a wicked attempt to lay hold of the faith of this people in their high destiny for unworthy purposes of personal gain.

9. Favors the Fox and Wisconsin rivers improvement.

10. Asks for support of the people.

1872.

ALABAMA.

Republican, May 15, 1872.

1, 2, 3, 4, and 5. Indorse the administration of President Grant and favor his renomination; pledge support for the Republican nominee, eulogize President Grant, and favor Henry Wilson for Vice President.

6. That we request and enjoin upon our delegates to the Philadelphia convention that they represent to that honorable body the importance and justice of paying loyal citizens the claims now before the commissioners, and that they may hereafter be submitted under act of Congress passed May 3, 1871.

Democratic, June 22, 1872.

1. That in the opinion of this convention, under existing circumstances, the National Democratic convention ought not to make nominations in opposition to the nominations recently made at Cincinnati.

ARKANSAS.

***Republican, May 18, 1872.**

The resolutions adopted indorse President Grant's administration, and instruct for him for renomination; extend to Powell Clayton

* Press telegraphic report.

a hearty sympathy in the assaults which the enemies of the Republican party have made upon him in the United States Senate and elsewhere, and express unshaken confidence in his honesty, ability, patriotism, and fidelity to the great Republican party.

2. Declares that to him more than to any other man in the State are we indebted for the peace and tranquillity we now enjoy.

3. Indorses the administration of Governor Hadley, pledging him the confidence and support of the true Republicans of Arkansas in the execution of the laws and in carrying forward the great works of reform inaugurated by the Republican party.

4. Repudiates and denounces Brooks, Rice, and Hodges, who are attempting to disrupt the party of the State; denounces the action of Rice and the minority of the State central committee on the 6th of April as revolutionary and done for the purpose of accomplishing the disintegration of the Republican party, and indorses the course pursued by the majority of the State central committee as wise, patriotic, and just.

5. Declares to those Republicans who are following after the strange gods set up at Cincinnati, in the words of Horace Greeley during the late rebellion: "Erring brothers, depart in peace."

6. Republicans of the State who have been led astray by unscrupulous and designing demagogues are cordially invited to return to the Republican ranks.

Democratic, June 22, 1872.

1. Declares the necessity of union and harmony among the Opposition.

2. That the chairman of each Democratic Conservative county executive committee be requested to put into operation the amendment of the enforcement act of Congress in regard to the appointment of supervisors of registration in each voting precinct of their respective counties.

3. That the delegates appointed to the Baltimore convention, to meet July 9, be instructed to vote for the ratification of the nomination of Greeley and Brown as candidates for President and Vice President of the United States in the ensuing election.

4. That we indorse the Cincinnati platform of political principles, and the platform of principles adopted by the Reform Republican party in their convention of May 22, 1872, at Little Rock.

5. That it would be unwise and inexpedient for the Democratic party to nominate a State ticket at the ensuing election, and we declare against it.

6. That the State Democratic central executive committee be, and hereby is, authorized to act with the Reform committees of all Reform Republican organizations in this State opposed to the present Administration, in the conduct of the ensuing canvass. We pledge ourselves to oppose the election of all independent candidates for any of said offices, running against the regular nominees of the Liberal Republican convention.

Republican, (Other Wing,) May 23, 1872.

Whereas the ring which controls the State government has inflicted on the people the worst government ever tolerated by a people: they have robbed the people of the benefit of the ballot by fraudulent registration, ballot-box stuffing, &c., increased taxation and our State indebtedness to millions, without any corresponding benefit to the State; have prostituted the courts of the State until they have become the engines of oppression, &c.: Therefore be it resolved

1. That we are in favor of universal suffrage, universal amnesty, and honest men for office; in favor of honest elections, reduction of taxes, reform in the courts; opposed to the enormous appointing power of the Government; opposed to the corrupt management of the finances; in favor of civil as against military government, and unqualifiedly condemn the use of the military in times of peace to carry elections against the choice of a majority of the legal electors; oppose the repudiation of any honest debt; but equally determined to shield the State against all pretended debts imposed upon our people by fraudulent issues of loan and railroad bonds; reiterate relentless adherence to the republicanism that all men are entitled to equal civil and political equality, and favor the removal of all civil and political disabilities; and

Whereas a large number of persons indicted in the Federal courts in this State for a most flagrant violation of the election laws, and President Grant, upon the application and in the interests of such indicted criminals and their successors, suspended honest and efficient officers for no other reason than that they would vigorously enforce the law, and allowed and permitted such indicted criminals to designate the name of the marshal to select the jury by which they were to be tried and the attorney to prosecute them for such offenses, whereby the criminals were turned loose without punishment, and the law trampled under foot, and frauds and crime encouraged, and has seen fit to take sides with and support and sustain the corrupt State-house ring in their iniquities against the people; and

Whereas it is now evident that President Grant will receive the nomination for President by the convention of office-holders to be held in Philadelphia: Therefore, be it resolved

2. That we emphatically condemn the course of the President in his intermeddling with Arkansas affairs in the interest of crime and disorder, and decline to send delegates to the Philadelphia convention.

Whereas Horace Greeley and Gratz Brown are now before the American people as Republican candidates for President and Vice President, upon a platform which we heartily approve, and that they are men of unquestioned ability, integrity, and patriotism, and have for many years been the earnest and consistent advocates and champions of republicanism and universal freedom: Therefore be it resolved

3. That we cordially indorse the nomina-

tion of the said Horace Greeley and Gratz Brown, and the platform upon which they stand, and pledge ourselves to coöperate with the friends of civil government and reform throughout the land in securing their election.

CALIFORNIA.

Republican, April 25, 1872.

1. That we have a firm and abiding faith in the principles of the Republican party, and point with pride to its achievements, believing that the party which brought order out of chaos, saved and preserved the nation, is alone worthy of administering its affairs in the future.

2. That we fully and heartily indorse the wise, patriotic, just, and economical administration of U. S. Grant as President of the United States; and that our delegates to the national convention are hereby instructed to use all honorable means to secure his renomination, he being the unanimous choice of the Republican party of the State of California.

3. That the delegates from California to the national convention at Philadelphia be instructed to vote as a unit for the candidate for Vice President.

4. Indorses the administration of Governor Newton Booth.

Democratic, June 25, 1872.

1. That the best interests of the nation require a change in the administration of the Government, and all good citizens should disregard the prejudices and differences of the past, and unite in one grand effort to restore the Government to its original purity.

2. That we earnestly condemn and protest against the machinations, tyranny, extravagances, and corruptions of the administration of U. S. Grant, which, for lobbying schemes and building up monopolies, has no parallel in the history of our country.

3. That we fully recognize the patriotism and pure motives of the Liberal Reform Republicans, and trust that such action may be taken at the Baltimore convention as will result in the hearty coöperation of all parties opposed to the present Administration, and that we recommend to the consideration of the National Democratic convention the principles enunciated in the platform of the Cincinnati convention.

4 and 5. Pledge support to nominees of Baltimore convention and leave delegates uninstructed.

CONNECTICUT.

Republican, January 24, 1872.

1. We again express our cordial adherence to the doctrines and principles of the Republican party as manifested in our former statements and in the national platforms, and we reflect with increasing pride upon its wonderful work. It proved that a free Government, based on the will and affection of a free people, is the strongest known form of government. It suppressed a great rebellion, freed millions of laborers, established equal rights, perfected the national Constitution, and justified the Declaration of Independence. By its great reduction of the Army and Navy the party proved that it had neither desire nor expectation of war. Having incurred a great debt for the best reason a nation ever gave, it resolutely began an immediate reduction of that debt. Yet having cut down expenses it has been yearly cutting down taxation. Notwithstanding the marvelous sacrifices of men and money, the nation has steadily grown in wealth and population.

2. During the existing Administration the debt has been reduced nearly three hundred million dollars; peace and order have made great progress in the lately rebellious regions; a new policy toward the Indians has been adopted, marked by firmness, justice, and good faith; the rights of all, especially the poor and friendless of whatever race or where ever found, have been scrupulously protected; a self-respecting yet peaceable policy has been pursued toward all the world, and our controversy with Great Britain has been treated in a manner greatly creditable to both nations.

3. That we have undiminished confidence in the patriotism, integrity, and ability of President Grant, and for great and good work done in the country's behalf we heartily thank him and his Cabinet and the two Houses of Congress.

4. The future must be as honorable as the past to deserve and keep its lead of the world. The Republican party must be free to examine and criticise, and utterly without fear, favor, or partiality, in attacking all fraud, dishonor, and corruption, legislative, executive, or judicial, in the nation or State. We demand economy, industry, and honesty in our political affairs, and rejoice at the brightening prospect of a thorough reform of the civil service. For the President's efforts and pledges in this matter we tender him our cordial thanks, and therein we pledge him an enthusiastic, unwavering support.

5. In national affairs we urge, first, a large reduction of taxation; second, constant study and labor to bring about a resumption of specie payment, that the evil of a depreciated paper currency may be removed and the best possible measure of value furnished us; third, retaining a tariff sufficient to raise the needed revenue, we would have it carefully adjusted to favor American industry, working rather to interests widely extended than to merely local and limited pursuits; fourth, a perfected system of national banks, with abundant security to the bill-holder, and inflexible and peremptory laws for prompt redemption; fifth, the abolition of the franking privilege; sixth, that public lands shall no more be granted to corporations, but given in limited quantities to actual settlers.

6. Adverts to the State Republican record.

7. Commends the General Assembly for correcting election frauds.

8. Denounces lobby abuses.

9. That it is the duty of the State to be vigilant in the protection of the rights and interests of the people against the encroachment of power-

ful corporations, and especially in holding corporations strictly to the responsibilities and duties contemplated in their charters.

10. While recognizing the fundamental principles which have brought unparalleled success to our country, and believing that only a Republic should exist on this continent, we would urge upon our Representatives in Congress, to keep before them the great ideas of liberty and freedom which have been so identified with our great party of progress from its birth; and we would earnestly desire to extend all sympathy and aid, consistent with our ability, to other nations and peoples struggling to be free.

11. Indorses Governor Jewell's administration.

Democratic, February 6, 1872.

Resolved, That the Democrats of Connecticut regard emancipation, equality of civil rights, and enfranchisement as established facts now embodied in the Constitution, and deserving the support of good citizens of all parties.

2. That a true and lasting peace can come only from such profound reconciliation as enfranchisement has brought to the State of Missouri; nor can those governments be pure or great in which tax-payers have no active part. We therefore demand, with equal suffrage for all, a complete amnesty for all; that the intellect and experience of every State may be welcomed to active service for the common welfare.

3. That no form of taxation is just or wise which puts needless burdens upon the people. We demand a general reform of the tariff, so that those duties shall be removed which, in addition to the revenue yielded to the Treasury, involve an increase in the price of domestic products and consequent tax for the benefit of favored interests.

4. That the shameless abuse of Government patronage for the control of conventions and elections, whether in the interest of an individual, faction, or of a party, with its corruption and demoralization of political life, demands a thorough and genuine reform of the public. Those who would suppress investigation forget that they owe a higher duty to the country than to any party; we honor those Senators whose courageous course has compelled the disclosure of gross misdeeds, and they deserve the thanks and support of all good citizens.

5. That local self-government, with impartial suffrage, will guard the rights of all citizens more securely than any centralized authority. It is time to stop the growing encroachments of the executive power, the use of coercion or bribery to ratify a treaty, the packing of a Supreme Court to relieve rich corporations, the seating of members of Congress not elected by the people, the resort of unconstitutional laws to cure the Ku Klux disorder. We demand for the individual the largest liberty consistent with public order, for the State self-government, and for the nation a return to the methods of peace and the limitation of power.

6. That it is alike the duty of honest men of all parties to expose corruption, denounce the usurpation of power, and work for reforms necessary for the public welfare. The times demand the uprising of honest citizens to sweep from power men who prostitute their official positions to selfish interests.

7. That we repudiate with scorn the oft-repeated slander of our opponents, that the Democracy of Connecticut are in favor of repudiating any portion of the national debt, even so much as has been fastened on us by extravagance and fraud, and that we are for paying that debt to its last dollar.

8. That the Democratic party, remembering the example of their fathers in the expression of their sympathy for the struggling republics of South America, as well as the oppressed Greeks, and grateful for the aid which the founders of our own Republic received from the countrymen of La Fayette, Montgomery, Steuben, and Pulaski, feel impelled by these considerations, as well as by our obligations to our common humanity, to lift up our voices in behalf of the suffering Cubans, now desperately struggling for relief from their oppressors, who set at naught all the usages of civilized warfare in their savage butchery of captive men, women, and children.

9. That we are in favor of a liberal system of free schools, and protest against all interference by the General Government with institutions so purely local and concerning so deeply and tenderly the ties which bind them to our homes and to the State.

10. Eulogizes ex-Governor English.

11. Indorses R. D. Hubbard for Governor.

Labor Reform, January 3, 1872.

Whereas by the divine decree the condition of productive labor is made the condition of man and the only basis of all prosperity and wealth; and whereas the burdens of maintaining the Government in all its various departments rests upon those engaged in productive labor; and whereas the interests of the productive classes have long been practically held to be of secondary importance by the legislative powers, in contravention of the organic law of this State that all men when they form a social compact are equal in rights, and that no man or set of men are entitled to exclusive public emoluments or privileges from the community: Resolved,

1. That the two prominent political parties having taken their pledge to the wealth-producing classes, having persistently disregarded our interests, have thereby proved themselves to be unworthy of our support. It therefore becomes our duty in order to preserve and maintain the rights and interests of labor, and to prevent the disintegration and ruin of that social and political system established and reëstablished by the blood of martyred patriots, to form and maintain a political organization under the name of the Labor Reform party of Connecticut.

2. That we recognize the platform of the National Labor Reform congress, adopted in St. Louis in 1870, as the basis of our national

policy, the following being its cardinal principles: a national paper currency that shall be a full legal tender, based on the wealth of the nation and not on gold, and issued by the Government directly to the people at a low and uniform rate of interest; the convertibility and reconvertibility of the Government bonds into money, and the money into bonds at the option of the holder, at a rate of interest not above the average advance of the nation into wealth; that the public lands be held for actual settlers; the payment of the five-twenty bonds in lawful money; pledging our active coöperation in the use of all honorable means to secure the adoption of the principles set forth in the above resolution.

3. That we cordially approve the amendment to the national Constitution offered by Charles Sumner, of Massachusetts, rendering the President of the United States ineligible to reëlection.

4. That the rotten borough system of representation in this State is worse and more unequal than that of England before the passage of the reform bill of 1832, and we oppose and will endeavor to abolish this absurd outrage upon republican equality by using all the efforts in our power to secure a constitutional convention to revise the constitution and have representatives according to population and taxation.

5. Man's equal right to the soil cannot be rightfully abridged by law, because it is a right as necessary to the life of man as the right to the air we breathe.

6. That we call on our delegates to the national convention to adopt a national platform which shall look to legislation for the abolition of land monopoly.

7. That indictments under the common law for the purpose of preventing workingmen from protecting their interests by the same means that corporations and capitalists are allowed to protect theirs is an unwarrantable and partial exercise of judicial power worthy of the despotic ages.

8. That the interests of labor demand that a bureau of labor be established by the Legislature of the State for the purpose of collecting statistics relative to the condition of the workingmen as affected by the laws and customs of society, and that the workingmen should be fairly represented in doing the work of the bureau.

9. That the refusal of the Legislature to exempt fifty dollars of wages from foreign attachment is an act of wrong and injustice toward the employés while exempting from attachment a much larger amount of the property of the capitalist.

10. That the employers who purchase the labor of the workmen for a consideration do not for the same consideration purchase the votes of the laborers, and any attempt on the part of the employer to control the vote or the political action of the employé by coercion or intimidation, either directly or indirectly, is an innovation on the sacred rights of citizenship and a base attempt to corrupt the purity of the ballot-box, and should be punished by imprisonment in the penitentiary.

11. That any system that permits convict labor to come into competition with the labor of honest men is a grievance that should not be allowed.

12. That justice to workingmen and small property-holders demand that legal provision be made for a more equitable assessment of the taxable property of this State.

13. That the recent attempt of executive and legislative authorities of this State to legalize a higher rate of interest on money is a direct attempt to impose additional burdens on labor and perpetuate an oppressive system of robbery and public plunder.

14. That the law of this State which imposes $100 fine and six months' imprisonment for using any means to intimidate any workman with intent to cause such workman to leave his employer is a law arbitrary and *ex parte* in its provisions, and made wholly in the interest of the capitalist.

15. That the law of this State whereby a bargain made in a foreign country with a man, a married woman, or a minor over 17 years of age, to labor in this State for the purpose of paying the expense of their passage to this country is made a lien on the wages of the immigrant after his or her arrival in this State is an extraordinary exercise of legislative power, devised wholly in the interest of capital.

16. That all persons in official positions who use the money of the tax-payers, without the sanction of law, for any purpose, and especially for the purpose of lobbying in our Legislative Assemblies, are thieves and robbers, and should receive the penalties due to their crimes; and all who receive such money, knowing it to be stolen, are themselves partakers of the crime.

17. That labor has a right to its share of the profits of its producing; that all legislation for the incorporation of capital should tend to that end.

DELAWARE.

Republican, May 9, 1872.

1. That the delegates of the Republican party of Delaware in convention assembled, reviewing the condition of the nation since the overthrow of the rebellion, and especially during the three years of the administration of President Grant, feel highly gratified that we are able, heartily and consistently, to congratulate our fellow-citizens upon the unexampled prosperity of the country, and upon the encouraging prospects of the great party whose patriotism and valor saved the country from disruption, whose fidelity has enabled the nation to garner the fruits of its great triumph, and whose statesmanship has done so much to repair the disasters, material and moral, which a great war involves.

2. That this Administration has justified the confidence of the people who placed it in power; that it has been true to every pledge of its platform; has restored peace and harmony; has consummated a complete reconstruction, until every State now answers to the roll-call in Congress; has diminished the

public debt three hundred millions of dollars, with an annual decrease of the interest charge of twenty-two millions, and funded a large portion of the remainder at a lower rate, while at the same time it has reduced taxation to the amount of two hundred millions per annum; it has maintained peace with foreign Powers amid complications of the gravest character, and preserved the honor and dignity of the nation inviolate and inviolable; it has instituted an Indian policy, humane, Christian, and economical; it has checked Mormon insolence and aggression, and by a temperate and firm policy, placed it in process of ultimate and speedy extinction; it has instituted a practical reform in the civil service which is rapidly and surely eradicating the corruptions which have been the outgrowth of many years; and it has accomplished all these results in the face of a persecution and misrepresentation the most unjustifiable and malignant, with a steadiness of purpose and a self-sacrificing devotion to principle worthy the admiration and indorsement of the American people.

3 and 4. Indorse U. S. Grant, and S. Colfax.

5. While we view with satisfaction the general prosperity of the country, we are pained and mortified to realize that the State of Delaware, under the rule of a party which has been and still is in antagonism with the great national movement of the last decade, has not relatively participated in the general improvement and progress; but on the contrary has suffered in every material interest, and in her character and reputation as a Commonwealth of free and enlightened people.

6. That having foisted upon the people an enormous debt, necessitating heavy taxation, the ruling party has shown its utter incompetency to devise a system of revenue that shall meet the financial exigencies without oppressing the people and crippling our productive energies, and that relief from ruinous and reckless expenditures and intolerable taxation, demands the removal of this party from power, and its substitution by one pledged to retrenchment and to a revision of one system of taxation, and its adjustment in accordance with the principle of justice and equality.

7. That in the persistent opposition of their Representatives in Congress, their press and their legislators, to all measures looking to the improvement of our school system, this Bourbon party has committed itself thoroughly against popular education, and a reform in this direction that shall place the blessings of good schools within the reach of rich and poor alike can only come through the success of the Republican party, and to this reform we pledge the Republicans of Delaware.

8. That a wise political economy, as well as common justice and humanity, demands that legislation shall protect as far as practicable the poor and unfortunate, and that our present statutes for the collection of debts, under which the last dollar's worth of property may be seized and sold and the helpless victims left to abject penury and want, are unwise and inhuman, and that such a law should be enacted as will secure a liberal exemption of property from seizure and sale for debt.

9. That security to the public and honesty in officials demand that those intrusted with the people's money shall be required to render frequent, clean, and precise exhibits of all receipts and disbursements, to the end that those interested may ascertain at all times, and easily, what disposition is made of the funds committed to their custody; and that the determination manifested by our public servants to hide from the people the financial condition of our State and the counties, is a standing insult to their intelligence, and a sign of conscious incompetence or guilt on the part of those servants well calculated to arouse the fears and incite the vigilance of the people.

10. That the conferring of office upon men for mere party service who are devoid of integrity and capacity, as is constantly done in this State, is a reckless and dangerous perversion of the spirit of popular government, deserving the severest reprobation of every good citizen.

11. That as a practical people we believe that constitutions are made for man, and not man for constitutions and laws, and we owe no tribute of veneration to old institutions except in so far as the same may be adapted to present wants; and that we favor a policy adjusted in all things in harmony with the requirements of the times, and which tends to promote the moral and material advancement of the Commonwealth.

12. That we invite our fellow-citizens who favor an honest, progressive, and economical rule, to lay aside all mere partizan prejudices, and unite with us in rescuing our noble Commonwealth from the corrupt and incompetent hands into which she has fallen, and in placing her side by side with the first and foremost in the nation in character and prosperity, in civilization and patriotism.

13. That the principle of representation according to population lies at the basis of all popular Governments, and we recognize the inequality of representation in the representative branch of the Legislature of this State under the present system, and affirm our desire that this question shall be established on a fair and equal basis whenever in our power to do so.

14. That we affirm our continued devotion to the policy of "protection to American industry" as indispensable to the prosperity of the nation; that the whole history of the country demonstrates its benefits, and the ruinous effect of "free trade" upon all our national interests, and that the unexpected facility with which we have been enabled to surmount the enormous financial difficulties growing out of the war is largely due to the policy so wisely restored at the beginning of the struggle.

FLORIDA.

Republican, April 11, 1872.

1. Indorses President Grant's administration.

2. Urges the renomination of President Grant.

3. That the Congress of the United States be, and it is hereby, requested to enact such laws as may be necessary to secure to all the citizens of the United States, irrespective of color, every constitutional right.

4. Indorses acting Governor Day's administration.

5 and 6. Praise the Republican State executive committee and the Republican press.

Whereas the patriots of the island of Cuba have been struggling for a national existence for the last four years against a foreign and alien Power, and are attempting to establish for themselves a free government and to secure the blessings of free institutions for themselves and their posterity; and whereas the war waged by Spanish despotism against this feeble and struggling people has no parallel for its atrocity and inhumanity in the annals of modern warfare, and should in no manner be countenanced by civilized nations: Therefore, resolved,

7. That the Congress of the United States is hereby requested to adopt such legislation as may be necessary to enable the national Government to extend such aid to the patriots of Cuba as becomes a great and free Republic whose people so ardently sympathize with the struggles and hopes of the oppressed of all nations.

8. That our delegates to the national nominating convention be instructed to incorporate into the platform of the Republican party the sentiment as herein expressed.

9. That this Republican State convention of Florida demand as an act of justice that, with as little delay as possible, such appropriate laws shall be framed and adopted by Congress as shall forever secure and give to colored men in the United States the same rights and privileges, at all *times* and in all *places*, as are now possessed and enjoyed by their white brethren.

10. That our delegates to the national nominating convention be instructed to urge the adoption of this resolution by said convention.

GEORGIA.

Republican, May 8, 1872.

1. That the Republican party of Georgia, in convention assembled, hereby reiterates its former declarations in favor of liberty, union, and equal rights.

2. That a system of public schools, affording the means of education to all the children of the State, is demanded by justice, humanity, and sound policy.

3. That Congress having granted to this State the proceeds of a large quantity of the public lands as an endowment of a college or colleges for instruction in "such branches of learning as are related to agriculture and the mechanic arts, in order to promote the liberal and practical education of the industrial classes," the appropriation of that grant to the exclusive benefit of one portion of our people is at variance with the purposes of Congress, and we protest against the disposition which the Governor has made of that fund by bestowing it upon an institution from which colored persons are excluded, unless the State shall promptly make an equal endowment for the benefit of the excluded class.

4. That all political disabilities imposed by the Constitution for participation in the rebellion should be removed; and that the equal rights guaranteed by the Constitution to all citizens alike should be enforced by appropriate legislation.

5. That we indorse the administration of President Grant, and the interests of the whole country will be promoted by his reëlection. His vigorous efforts to protect the oppressed against disguised assassins; his reduction of the public debt, while at the same time lessening the taxes of the people; his wisdom, firmness, and statesmanship in the conduct of our foreign affairs; his recommendations of amnesty and civil service reform, and prompt execution of the power conferred by Congress to inaugurate this reform; his faithful collection of the revenues due the Government; his prompt prosecution of offenders who abuse official trusts; his watchful care over the interests of the whole people, and faithful and impartial administration of all the laws of the United States, entitle him to the gratitude and confidence of the people of this nation.

6. Favors renomination of President Grant.

Democratic, June 26, 1872.

1. That the Democratic party of Georgia stand upon the principles of the Democratic party of the Union, bringing into special prominence, as applicable to the present extraordinary condition of the country, the unchangeable doctrine that this is a union of States, and that the indestructibility of the States, of their rights, and of their equality with each other is an indispensable part of our political system.

2. That in the approaching election the Democratic party invites everybody to coöperate with them in a zealous determination to change the present usurping and corrupt Administration by placing in power men who are true to the principles of constitutional government and to a faithful and economical administration of public affairs.

3. Delegates to Baltimore convention uninstructed.

ILLINOIS.

Republican, May 22, 1872.

1. That the past acts of the Republican party are a better guarantee than the mere resolutions of the new party. The Republican party is the only one in the United States that while in power destroyed, or even tried to destroy, that infamous sum of all villainies, chattel slavery; the only party that questioned the dogma that "to the victors belong the spoils of the vanquished," and endeavored to introduce reforms in the civil service so that honesty, capacity, and faithful attention to official duties might be a better recommendation to office than partisan services, and whose Pres-

ident has proclaimed this new rule of action to the nation. It is the only party that introduced the eight-hour labor system in the public service. It is the only party that has made treaties with other Governments fully protecting our naturalized citizens from foreign claims of allegiance. It has shown unusual energy in guarding our frontier settlers from Indian raids, and the Indians from the frauds and plunder of Government agents. Under its patriotic, resolute, and statesman-like administration, a deeply-plotted and long-matured rebellion, that was declared by the enemies of our country, domestic and foreign, as unconquerable, has been effectually suppressed, and peace and union, law and order, in a great measure restored, with a magnanimity unparalleled in the history of nations. No one, for rebellion, perjury, or treason in the late conflict, has been deprived of even the right of suffrage, and few of the right to hold office; and, with charity for all and malice toward none, universal amnesty will be proclaimed as soon as it can be done consistently with the public safety.

2. That the national tax and the national debt have been reduced, the public revenue been faithfully collected, and defaulting officers promptly removed and prosecuted for their defalcations. The credit of the nation was never in a better condition, and the people have been furnished with a good national currency, that will soon be made better, and equal to gold and silver; and, above all, the humblest citizens have been defended in their constitutional rights at home and abroad.

3. That the principles of the Declaration of Independence, and of the recent amendments to the Constitution of the United States to secure the enjoyment of natural and civil liberty, adopted by the influence of the Republican party, will not execute or enforce themselves, and no party that does not cordially sympathize with those principles, or that is chiefly composed of men hostile to those principles and those amendments, is entitled to the confidence or support of patriots and freemen, or can be safely intrusted with the national Government.

4. That by the fundamental principles of the Republican party it is the right and duty of all its supporters to condemn every existing abuse in national, State, and municipal governments, and zealously advocate all needful reforms, as has been done with success from the time the party was first organized. No party that ever existed in the country can justly boast of so much independence of thought, speech, and action. It is this freedom that has drawn to it the enthusiastic support of so many intelligent, unbiased, and generous young men, and repelled so many sordid and disciplined office-hunters, who would make merchandise of their fellow men by reducing them to political slavery.

5. That all sovereignty emanates from the people, a portion of which they have delegated to the United States Government for national purposes, and to guard the people against oppression in and out of the United States; a still larger portion of which they have delegated to the State governments for local, domestic, and municipal purposes, and the residue of that sovereignty over natural rights and civil privileges they have expressly reserved for themselves, in bills of rights and restrictions against the encroachments of national, State, and municipal governments, and no sound Republican wishes to deprive the nation, the States or counties, cities, towns, villages, or individuals, of any of their legitimate constitutional rights; and all pretenses that the Republican party desires or intends to establish a consolidated government of unlimited powers are gratuitous slanders unworthy of the age.

6. That the Republican party is the party of progress and human rights and duties. We are for the equality of all before the law and the preservation of constitutional rights, and we disapprove of all unconstitutional legislation for the cure of any of the disorders of society, whether irreligious, intemperance, or any other evil. We oppose the surrender of individual freedom to those who ask that their prejudices, practices, or creed shall be the law of the land. We demand equal and just rights and duties for every human being, and the largest liberty consistent with the public good and the preservation of social order.

7. That the necessities of the Government require so large a tariff upon importation that the question of free trade is not one now before the American people. The only question left is how to so adjust the tariff that it will most promote the labor, industry, and general welfare of the country without being oppressive to any interests of society, and we know of no better way to dispose of this subject than that adopted by the Republican party in Congress, to learn wisdom by experience, reduce taxation as fast as possible, and remove unnecessary burdens upon the necessities of life.

8. That in adjusting the details of a system for raising a revenue to cover the necessary requirements of the Government, and meet its liabilities, care should be taken to so regulate the imports that they will press least upon the growing industries of the country, cheapen the necessaries of life, and afford to labor the fairest promise of permanent reward.

9. That we most heartily indorse the recommendations by President Grant of the adoption of proper measures by the national Government for the protection of immigrants, recognizing as we do in those natives of other countries who flock to our shores a most valuable addition to the population and wealth of our whole country.

10. That the gratitude of the nation is due to our soldiers and sailors, whose patriotism and valor saved the Union, and made our country in fact, as well as in word, a nation of freemen.

11. That the people of the United States owe U. S. Grant a great debt of gratitude for his patriotic devotion to the interests of the people in war and in peace; that we have unabated confidence in his integrity, patriotism, ability, prudence, and good judgment, and

hereby instruct our delegates to the Philadelphia convention to vote for and use all honorable means to secure his nomination as the Republican candidate for the Presidency of the United States.

Democratic, June 26, 1872.

1. That the platform of principles adopted by the Cincinnati convention, and the interpretation of the same enunciated in the letter of Horace Greeley, accepting the nomination of that convention for the office of President of the United States, afford a common ground upon which the liberal men of all political parties can consistently unite in opposition to personal government and its attendant official corruption.

2. Instructs delegates to vote in accordance with above.

Liberal Republican, June 26, 1872.

1. That we cordially approve and reaffirm the principles contained in the Cincinnati platform, and that in the success of these principles, and particularly in the thorough reformation of the civil service and the discontinuance of political patronage, whereby the taxes collected from the whole people are employed to overrule the will of the majority, we see the only solution of free government.

2. That in the administration of our State affairs every effort should be made to lighten taxation by the strictest economy in the expenses of the Government; that in the construction of our public buildings and in the management of our public institutions all extravagance should be avoided; that the officers of the Government should be held to a strict accountability in the discharge of their duties, and that all unnecessary and cumbersome legislation should be avoided.

3. That we can never forget the sacrifices made by the soldiers and sailors whose bravery saved the nation, and we deem it our duty to secure to them the full reward of their patriotism. We therefore declare ourselves in favor of the equalization of their bounty, and in favor of the most liberal recognition of their services in the public employments of the country, having regard only to their fitness for such employment and not to the rank they had in the military service.

4. That the cause of equal rights cannot be considered permanently established so long as any organized opposition thereto exists; therefore we hail with unfeigned satisfaction the evidence presented to us of the cessation and disappearance of such opposition in all parts of our common country.

5. Upon this declaration of principles we take our stand before the people of this State as the party of liberal reforms, of reconciliations, of peace, inviting all persons without regard to previous political associations to coöperate with us in the endeavor to insure the success of these principles, which, while just and true in themselves, are broad enough to include all the political necessities of the hour and the aspirations of every patriotic citizen.

6. A resolution placing colored soldiers on the same footing as white soldiers was also adopted.

INDIANA.

Republican, February 22, 1872.

Resolved, That in the future, as in the past, we will adhere to the principles of the Declaration of Independence, and firmly sustain the Constitution of the United States as the true basis of popular freedom; and will maintain the equal rights of all men before the law, and the authority of the national Government against all false theories of State rights.

2. That we therefore approve of the acts of Congress and of the Administration, which put the rights of all citizens under the protection of the national authority when they are assailed by hostile legislation or by the violence of armed associations, whether open or secret, and we demand the enforcement of the laws, that these rights may be securely and amply protected wherever and whenever invaded.

3. That we congratulate the country on the complete restoration of the Union; and now, as heretofore, the Republican party remembers with gratitude our brave soldiers and seamen, who imperiled their lives in the service of the country, and to whom as men who saved the nation in the hour of her peril we owe the highest honor, and we declare that our obligations to them shall never be forgotten; and we demand that the bounties and pensions now, or which may be provided for these brave defenders of the nation, shall be paid without cost to the recipients, and that the widows and orphans of the gallant dead, the wards of the nation, shall receive the nation's protecting care, and while we cheerfully assume all these burdens we cannot forget, and the American people can never forget, that to the Democratic party, South and North, we owe all the calamities of the late slaveholders' rebellion, and the debt now resting upon the industry of our State and nation.

4. That we indorse the action of Congress and of the Administration in maintaining the traditionary policy of the nation, of living in friendly relations with other Governments, yet avoiding entangling alliances with them, as evidenced in checking hostile expeditions from our shores, refusing to interfere in domestic revolutions, even where our sympathies are strongly enlisted, and agreeing to the arbitration of disputed claims, while demanding admission of the wrong done.

5. That we approve the action of Congress and of the present Administration in all their efforts to reduce expenditures in the several departments, and in the reduction of the tariff and internal taxes as rapidly as the exigencies of the Government will admit, while continuing to maintain the public credit by the sure and gradual payment of the debt of the nation, and by discharging the obligations due her soldiers, sailors, and pensioners.

6. That we favor all efforts looking to the development of the great industrial interests

of the State, and we request our Senators and Representatives in Congress to use their influence in any revision of the tariff to secure to the coal and iron interests of our State all the incidental protection consistent with a due regard to the principles of reducing the burden of taxation.

7. That the adherence of Congress and the Administration to the present financial policy, in spite of the hostility of political opponents, has been fully justified by the payments made on the public debt, and in the stability, security, and increased confidence it has given to all the business affairs of the country.

8. That the financial affairs of the State and nation should be conducted on the principles of economy, and to this end all useless offices should be abolished, fees and salaries limited to a fair compensation for the services rendered, and by prohibiting the allowance of all perquisites, and by avoiding all unnecessary appropriations and expenditures; and in this State we favor the abolition of the offices of agent of State and State printer.

9. That we are opposed to granting further donations of public lands to railroads or other corporations, and demand that the public domain be reserved for the use of actual settlers, the discharge of the obligations of the country to its brave defenders, and the purposes of general education.

10. That Congress ought to interfere for the protection of immigrants, to shield them from the unjust exactions levied upon them in the shape of capitation taxes, under the laws of New York and other sea-board States, the true policy of the country being to extend a cordial invitation to the citizens of other countries to cast their lot with us and share on terms of perfect equality the blessings which we enjoy.

11. That we approve the efforts being made for the vindication of honest government by the exposure, removal, and punishment of corrupt officials, whether of municipalities, State, or nation. We hail such exposures, undeterred by fears of party injury, as proof of the integrity of the party, and we spurn the attempts of the Opposition to turn these efforts of self-purification into proofs of party venality; and we demand of all public officers honesty, sobriety, and diligence in the discharge of their duties. And we announce our unrelenting hostility to all attempts by corporations, monopolies, or combinations to influence elections or the Legislature of the State by the use of corrupt means.

12. That as a general dissemination of knowledge and learning among the people is essential to the existence of a free republic, we hold the public free schools to be the safe guard of our liberties, and pledge ourselves to cherish and maintain them.

18. That we are in favor of such a revision of our criminal code as will secure the more speedy and effectual administration of justice, and such wise and judicious legislation as will enforce individual responsibility for all acts affecting public interests.

14. That the efforts now being made by the workingmen of the nation to improve their own condition and more completely to vindicate their independence of class subordination meet our cordial approbation; and for proof that the Republican party is the true friend of the laborer, we point to the fact that while opposing all attempts to array capital and labor against each other, as mutually destructive, it has been by the efforts of this party that labor was emancipated from the ownership of capital, free homesteads provided for settlers on the public domain, the hours of labor reduced, and complete equality of rights established before the law; and therefore we invite workingmen to seek whatever further advantage or melioration they may desire within the embrace of the party of liberty and equality.

15. That the joint resolution passed by the last General Assembly, proposing to amend the constitution so as to prohibit the Legislature from ever assuming or paying the canal debt, which was charged exclusively upon the Wabash and Erie canal under the legislation of 1846 and 1847, commonly called the Butler bill, ought to be adopted by the next General Assembly, and submitted to the people, to the end that it may be ratified and become a part of the constitution.

16. That we indorse the administration of Governor Conrad Baker, and applaud the firm, able, and courteous manner in which he has discharged the duties of his high office, and we greatly regret that he has not had the coöperation of a Republican Legislature, to carry out the various measures proposed for the reformation of abuses, the protection of the people against fraudulent canal claims, and the further development of the immense resources of the State.

17. That our Senators and Republican members of Congress deserve the approbation of their constituents for the firm, able, and energetic manner in which they have discharged their duties.

18. That the administration of General Grant has been consistent with the principles of the Republican party, and eminently just, wise, and humane, and such as fulfills his pledges, and deserves our cordial support; and, therefore, we instruct our delegates to the national convention to vote for the renomination of Grant and Colfax as our candidates for President and Vice President.

Democratic, June 12, 1872.

1. *Resolved by the Democracy of Indiana in convention assembled*, That the principles of the Cincinnati "Liberal Reform" convention, taken in connection with the propositions contained in Horace Greeley's letter, accepting the nomination of that convention, constitute a platform on which all the elements of opposition to the present corrupt administration of the Federal Government can stand, and which propositions are as follows:

All the political rights and franchises which have been acquired through the late bloody convulsions must and shall be guarantied, maintained, enjoyed, and respected everywhere.

All the political rights and franchises which have been lost through that convulsion should and must be promptly restored and reëstablished, so that there shall be henceforth no proscribed class and no disfranchised caste within the limits of our Union, whose long-estranged people shall reunite and fraternize upon the broad basis of universal amnesty and impartial suffrage.

That, subject to our solemn constitutional obligation to maintain the equal rights of all citizens, our policy shall aim to local self-government and not at centralization; that the civil authority should be supreme over the military; that the writ of *habeas corpus* should be jealously upheld as the safeguard of personal freedom; that the individual citizens should enjoy the largest liberty consistent with public order, and that there shall be no Federal supervision of the internal policy of the several States and municipalities, but that each shall be left free to enforce the rights and promote the well-being of its inhabitants by such means as the judgment of the people shall prescribe.

That there shall be a real, and not merely a simulated reform in the civil service of the Republic, to which end it is indispensable that the chief dispenser of its vast official patronage shall be shielded from the various temptations to use his power selfishly by a rule inexorably forbidding and precluding his reëlection.

2. That we regard it as unwise and imprudent to place two tickets in nomination for the offices of President and Vice-President as the representatives of these principles, as the division of its friends would insure the defeat of both; and it is, therefore, the fixed conviction of this convention that the Democratic convention to assemble in Baltimore in July should adopt the nominees of the "Liberal Republican" convention, instead of making other nominations for the Presidency and Vice Presidency of the United States.

3. Instructs delegates to act as a unit.

4. That all drainage and other laws by which the owners of property may be divested of their title by arbitrary assessments or summary process should be carefully guarded so as to protect the people from undue oppression, and their property from being taken without just compensation and due process of law, and that all laws contravening these principles should be promptly repealed or modified so as to conform thereto.

Whereas the Union soldiers and sailors, by their patriotism and courage in the great rebellion of 1861, preserved the life of the nation and made our public domain valuable: Therefore,

5. That we demand for each of the living who were honorably discharged, and for th widows and orphans of the dead, one hundred and sixty acres of the public lands not heretofore entered or given away by a Republican Congress to railroad corporations, to be theirs absolutely without requiring them to become actual settlers thereon.

6. That justice and equality demand that all soldiers who enlisted in the military service of the country during the war of the late rebellion, and who have been honorably discharged therefrom, shall have a bounty granted to them by Congress in proportion to the time they may have served, whether that time shall have been for three months or a longer period.

IOWA.

Republican, March 27, 1872.

1. Indorses the administration of U. S. Grant, and favors his renomination.

2. Favors James F. Wilson for the Vice Presidency.

Democratic, June 11, 1872.

1. That the principles enunciated at the late Cincinnati convention, taken in connection with the letter of Horace Greeley accepting the nomination of that convention, constitute a platform in which all the elements of opposition to the present corrupt administration of the Federal Government can stand.

2. Delegates to act as a unit.

Liberal Republican, April 23, 1872.

1. We, the Republicans of Iowa, believing that the present Administration and office-holders through the country have assumed unconstitutional authority, and are endeavoring to subvert the Republican party to their own personal interests for the retention of themselves, their relatives, and personal friends in office and war; the best interests of the country are on the eve of demanding a better Government, and sympathize with the liberal movement throughout the country for reform; hereby declare that we are opposed to the renomination of General U. S. Grant to the Presidency, and will in no event give him our cordial support; that we will support any one of the many good and able men of the party for the first place in the gift of the people, nominated upon a platform declaring in favor of honesty, economy, general amnesty, and a thorough general reform, and the one-term principle for the Presidency.

KANSAS.

Republican, February 21, 1872.

Whereas the Republicans of Kansas, in convention assembled for the purpose of electing delegates to unite with the delegates of other States, on June 5th ensuing, for the purpose of nominating the next President and Vice President of the United States, desire to give renewed and most emphatic expression to their confidence in the principles, their pride in the record, and their faith in the future of that national political organization which carried the country through the difficulties and preserved amid the disasters of one of the stormiest conflicts of all history, and which has addressed itself to the solution of those delicate and difficult problems which are the general legacy of all wars, and more especially of such a strife as ours, in such a manner as with such moral exceptions as would be inseparable from any policy of qualification, to secure to the country at large a degree of internal peace, organic unity, financial standing and credit, and general business prosperity, which are the wonder and admiration of all the nations of the earth; and believing, as this convention does, that this satisfactory condition of public affairs is largely attributable to the patent courage and wisdom of the man who was first the trusted commander-in-chief of the armies and then the honored President of the councils of the Republic, it is therefore

Resolved, That the delegates this day chosen to attend the Philadelphia National convention be, and are hereby, instructed to cast their votes for the patriotic President and citizen soldier, Ulysses S. Grant, who in the dark and disastrous days of the Republic displayed those qualities of courage, wisdom, and loyalty, unyielding and persistently, which inspired the friends of freedom with new energy and hope, filled and fired the gallant soldiers of the Union with the spirit to fight, and if need be to die in its defense, and which crowned our long conflict with the inestimable boon of a complete victory and permanent peace, and who, in the less dangerous but more difficult duties to which a grateful people called him, has proved himself an able, steady, and successful pilot of the ship of State, amid conflicting opinion and trying exigencies; the earnest advocate of all judicious attempts at political reform; the foremost friend of all oppressed and distressed people, of whatever condition or color, who are struggling for the inalienable rights of perfect equality before the law; the undaunted defender of our national claims and equities in the great parliament of the nations; whose administration, in short, has brought us a degree of prosperity at home and respect and dignity abroad which it would be suicidal to interrupt or interfere with until time has been given to complete and cement the work so well begun and so auspiciously prosecuted to the present time.

Democratic, June 11, 1872.

1. That the paramount duty of every citizen is devotion and obedience to the Constitution and laws of the Republic, made as they were with a design and purpose to perpetuate individual liberty to its utmost limit consistent with good government and public order.

2. That political organizations are useful and beneficial only when their purpose and action demonstrating love of country control their counsel and dictate their policy, but when lawless ambition, imbecility, corruption, and man-worship shall dominate in a political party, it is the duty of all citizens, without regard to previous political affiliations and forgetful of the past and buried differences, to join hands and hearts in the efforts to crush such party and to drive its leaders from power.

3. Believing as we do that the Chief Executive of the nation, and the nominee of the Republican party for reëlection, is utterly unfitted for the high position he holds; that his administration of the Government stands alone in the history of the nation for shameless ignorance, nepotism, and gift-taking; for reckless disregard of law; for forgetfulness of the ancient honor of the Republic; for utter want of that dignity and statesmanship which should characterize the executive government of the first Republic of the earth; that his continuance in power would be dangerous to the nation, would degrade the liberties of the people, and so believing, we are willing to join with all good citizens in the pending canvass in the effort to drive him from the place.

4. Instructs delegates to vote for Cincinnati platform and candidates.

Liberal Republican, April 10, 1872.

1. That we, the Liberal Republicans of Kansas, mindful of the early record of our State so closely interwoven with the history of the Republican party and struggle for national existence, and still steadfast, and true to vital principles which called that party into existence, would ever maintain as a part of our birthright the rightful sovereignty of union, emancipation, equality of civil rights, and enfranchisement, with a loyalty to the principle that is higher and stronger than loyalty to party or party leaders. Zealous and watchful of the fair fame of our young State, earnest and resolute now as in the struggle to save its soil from the encroachment of slave power, we call upon the people of Kansas to unite in an effort to put a stop to attempted absorption of the civil functions of the Government by the military, and encroachment of executive power, to inaugurate a thorough and genuine reform of the civil service that shall put a stop to the shameless abuse of official patronage for the control of conventions and elections, whether in the interests of individual faction or party; to effect modification of our revenue system so that no class or special interest of our country shall be encouraged at the expense of the rest; to secure the wisest system of taxation which shall place no needless burden on the people; to save the public lands of the nation to actual settlers under principles of homestead law; to establish general amnesty as the correct avenue of impartial suffrage; to extend our national sympathy to all people who are struggling to emulate our example of popular enfranchisement.

KENTUCKY.

Republican, March 13, 1872.

Resolved, That we reaffirm our adherence to the principles of the Republican party, pledging ourselves to maintain them as the truest safeguard of our liberties. We also reaffirm our adherence to the right of all American citizens according to the Constitution to exercise, without diminution or restriction, elective franchise in all elections, national, State, or municipal, and hereby express our condemnation of the acts of the Democracy in this State in contravention of this principle.

2. To the people of Kentucky and the nation we send our congratulations upon the fulfillment of the promises given by the Republican party in the national convention assembled in 1868, resulting in restoration to the Union of all the States, in giving equal rights to all men before the law, and surrounding us with prosperity at home and increased honor among all nations of the civilized world.

3. We recognize with pride the beneficial achievements of the present Administration in the management of the national affairs, in executing the wishes of the people as declared by law, in condemning and punishing corruption, and in relieving the industries of the country from the grievous burdens thrust upon them.

4. To an extent beyond our most sanguine expectations the Republican party has reduced the public debt, and at the same time appreciated to a high standard the national currency and securities of the Government.

5. We express undiminished confidence in the personal and official integrity and honor of President Grant; and we have witnessed with satisfaction the refutation and exposure of the falsehoods and calumnies directed against him.

6. Indorses President Grant for reëlection.

7. Favors General John M. Harlan for the Vice Presidency.

8. That it is the crowning glory of the Republican party that it has successfully maintained the doctrine that all citizens, without distinction as to race or color, are equal before the law, and alike entitled to places of trust.

Democratic, June 20, 1872.

1. That the administration of the Federal Government, with President Grant as its executive head, has persistently violated the Constitution and the purity of its administration, and the elective franchise, and unless arrested in its centralization, its doctrines and corrupt practices will subvert and destroy our liberties.

2. That the Democracy of the State of Kentucky now reaffirm the principles contained in the platforms adopted by former conventions of the party since and including the convention of the 1st day of May, 1866. These platforms contain substantially the theory and practice which, we believe, if carried out, will secure the protection of life, liberty, and property, and all the essential ends of a free government.

3. That while we adhere to the principles declared in said platforms, and while we are deeply impressed with the conviction that the peace, prosperity, freedom, and happiness of the people of the United States will be best served and promoted by a strict adherence to said principles in the administration of both State and Federal Governments, yet recognizing and appreciating the necessity of preventing, if possible, the continuance in power of the present corrupt Administration, while we do not precisely instruct our delegates to the national convention as to the course they shall pursue, we expect them, after consultation with the representatives of Democracy of the whole country, to take such action as will most likely insure perfect union to all the elements in opposition to the nominees of the Philadelphia convention, and that the Democrats of Kentucky unhesitatingly pledge themselves to give the ticket that may be presented to the country by the Baltimore convention their earnest and active support, not only because it will be the representative body of the whole party, but because in party organization it is ultimately to judge the line of policy which members of the party should pursue.

LOUISIANA.

Republican, (One Wing,) April 30, 1872.

1. That we recur to the platform of principles adopted by the National Union convention at Chicago, May 20, 1868, as the true principles on which our Government should be administered, and hereby reaffirm the same; and further, that we recognize those principles to have been fully and practically carried out by the present Administration.

2. Indorses President Grant.

3. Commends the management of the national finances.

4. Praises the management of the foreign relations of the Government.

5. That the laws passed by Congress, and the police and temporary regulations made necessary as the natural effects of the war, and the strict enforcement thereof by the Executive, for the supression of disorder and riot in the States when the State authorities were either unable or unwilling to do so, and the protection of Union citizens against the violence and outrages perpetrated by the Ku Klux organizations in the southern States, merit the warmest approval of all good and law-abiding citizens.

6. Recommends the renomination of President Grant.

7. That it is a matter of congratulation that the national Republican party in this State has united to expel from the party H. C. Warmoth, the corrupt chief Executive of the State, who has fraudulently manipulated the election laws, passed for good and proper purposes, to maintain himself and his minions in power, and in order to enable them to plunder the State treasury; and who has by revolutionary acts and by bribery, and by the unscrupulous use of power vested in him as commander-in-chief of the metropolitan police and militia, controlled the General Assembly so as to prevent him from being impeached for high crimes and misdemeanors; and who has refused to permit reform measures passed by the last Legislature to become laws by withholding his signature therefrom, among which acts are those guarding and restricting the registration and election laws, so as to prevent election

frauds, although the passage of such acts was recommended in his message to the General Assembly.

8. That this convention approves and adopts the principles of State reform contained in the resolutions passed at the National Republican convention of this State on the 9th of August, 1871, and enlarged on by the resolutions adopted by the State central executive committee of the party on the 7th of November, 1871, and which measures were reduced to the form of bills and introduced into the Legislature at its last session, but failed to pass on account of the opposition of the friends of Governor Warmoth, or failed to become laws on account of his withholding his signature. The following are some of those bills:

A bill to amend the registration law.

A bill to amend the election law.

A bill amending the printing law.

A bill amending the law in regard to assessing and collecting State and parish taxes, reducing the expenses thereof.

A bill providing for the general expenses of the State, and reducing the expenses of the State government to within $800,000, whereas it is now more than double this amount.

A bill repealing the constabulary law.

This convention, on behalf of the national Republican party of this State, pledges itself that the above and all similar State reforms meet with its earnest approval, and that this convention recommends that no candidate for State office shall be nominated by our party who is not, by his acts and antecedents, as well as by his pledges, fully committed to all such reforms.

9. That while steadfastly maintaining the integrity of the Republican platform and organization, yet, in the interest of reform and good government, in view of the present exigencies of our State, we welcome the coöperation of all honest men in securing the deliverance of our people from their present distresses, and to this end, as far as may be necessary, we are willing to concede such personal considerations to those of our fellow-citizens who may differ from us in political convictions as will not conflict with our obligations to our party, and as may be needful in compassing the common objects sought by the good people of the State.

10. That in the opinion of this convention, the only legal remedy left to prevent the repetition of the election frauds perpetrated under the direction and control of Governor Warmoth at the election of 1870, again at the election next November, (inasmuch as he has refused to sign the amended registration and election laws passed at the last session of the Legislature,) and which we feel confident he will repeat in favor of any party with which he may act—and we believe it will be the sole object of any party combining with him to obtain this service from him—will be the extension of the act of Congress of the 28th of February, 1871, so as to embrace all the parishes in this State; and we earnestly recommend Congress to so amend this act as to enable the people of this State, as citizens of the United States, fully and freely, and without restraint, to express their sentiments at the ballot-box.

11. That in pursuance of the recommendation of President Grant in his last annual message, and of the resolution to that effect passed by the Legislature of this State, we earnestly urge Congress to pass a bill of universal amnesty for all past political offenses.

12. That we, as the representatives of the Republican masses of Louisiana, in convention assembled, in behalf of ourselves and our constituents, invoke the national Congress to pass, prior to its adjournment, the supplemental "civil rights bill," a measure not only due for the protection of the rights of four millions of our fellow-citizens, but one that will contribute to the peace and harmony of the people of the whole country by eliminating from the political issues the question of race.

13. That we earnestly recommend Congress to pass a bill refunding the cotton tax collected on cotton since the war, as we deem such tax to have been unconstitutional, and the refunding the same would be an act of justice, and, at present, a great help to cotton-planters.

Republican, (Other Wing,) May 29, 1872.

1. That we declare the Republican party of Louisiana in full sympathy with the national Republican party; that we indorse the platform of principles laid down by the Chicago convention.

2. That we pledge ourselves and our party to the faithful execution of the constitutional and statutory provisions for the public education of all children without distinction.

3. That we insist upon the enforcement of the constitutional and legal guarantees of the civil and political rights of all men without distinction of race or color.

4. That a long train of evils must necessarily result from the effort being made by the Democratic party to obtain control of our State government through dissensions in the Republican party. Among them we may mention the repeal of the civil rights law, the establishment of qualified suffrage, the destruction of our common-school system, repudiation of the State debt and subjection of the colored elements to bitter political and commercial proscription, and an abundant evidence is to be found in the tone of the press and in speeches that the sole object of the Democrats and reformers is our political overthrow, and to this end they are subordinating the presidential and all other questions.

5. That, in order to save the State from Democratic rule, and to perpetuate free government, it is highly important that all Republican elements in the State should be united upon a ticket to be composed of true and tried Republicans, and to secure this end we recognize and tolerate existing differences of opinion upon national affairs.

6. That we contemn the action of the Federal officials of the State in attempting, through illegal and arbitrary exercise of power, to interfere with the right of the people to peaceably assemble, to overthrow our State govern-

ment, and through combination with our political enemies to overthrow the Republican party.

7. That we recognize in Governor Warmoth an officer who has combined with an efficient discharge of public duties an unimpeachable fidelity to the principle and the policy of the party by which he was elevated to his high position; that to him the Republican party largely owes whatever of credit may be its due for the faithful fulfilment of those obligations which it assumed toward the people of the State, by carrying out the principles of justice and equality which are the basis of its organization; that the public owe to him chiefly the preservation and maintenance of public order in spite of perils which were surmounted only by the exercise of extraordinary wisdom, courage, and discrimination; that with his powerful coöperation the State may hope for deliverance from many evils, the existence of which cannot be disputed, and the continuance of which would be disgraceful to the Republican party, and that he is our first choice for the office of Governor at the next election; that we present him as our candidate, and urge all other Republican organizations to indorse and support him.

8. That in our honorable fellow-citizen, Lieutenant Governor Pinchbeck, we have a bold, able, and manly leader in the Republican party—one who can be trusted in the future with its interests, as he has been in the past, and that we indorse him and declare him to be our first choice for Lieutenant Governor, and we present him as our candidate and urge all other Republican organizations to indorse and support him.

9. That all true Republicans are devoutly desirous of averting the dangers which beset their party, and of reuniting their party for a common purpose, &c.

Reform, June 7, 1872.

1. That in the opinion of this convention the attitude originally assumed by the Reform party of strict non-interference with Federal politics is the true and correct policy.

2. That the situation of our State at this time is such as to demand, in our opinion, the most earnest and exclusive attention of her people, and that while we appreciate the importance of a good Federal Government, and are anxious to see our national affairs properly administered, such are the peculiar difficulties by which, as a community, we are oppressed, and such the necessity for immediate relief, that it would be extremely unsafe to add to our embarrassments those necessarily entailed by an active participation in the national contest.

3. That in the judgment of this convention no permanent or enduring relief can be obtained without a cordial reconciliation between the two races inhabiting our territory, and for this reason, as well as for a sense of justice to the colored race, who are now entitled to all the privileges and immunities of American citizens, we accept as settled their civil and political status as now fixed by the constitution and laws both of the United States and of Louisiana.

4. That as one of the primal objects of this organization was the eradication of mere partisan differences, by which our people have been divided, and the inculcation of a broad, catholic spirit of toleration, by which means it was hoped and intended that the strength of our population should be concentrated for the redemption of the State, it is now declared to be the policy of this party to receive assistance from any source looking to the deliverance of our people from the dreadful oppression under which they labor, while at the same time it is distinctly understood that we will reject any unworthy proposition or corrupt coalition, and that the administration of our affairs for the future must be confided to men of known integrity and capacity.

MAINE.

Republican, June 13, 1872.

1. That the Republicans of Maine, assembled by delegates in State convention, reaffirm the declaration of principles made by the National Republican convention at Philadelphia, and point with pride to their past record, in war and in peace, as the best and only satisfactory evidence that any political organization can give of its ability and disposition to wisely and successfully deal with whatever questions may arise in the future.

2. That the Republicans of Maine most cordially and unitedly indorse the nomination of General Ulysses S. Grant as President, and Hon. Henry Wilson as Vice President, and pledge to the great soldier and patriot, and the eminent Senator and friend of the workingman, the electoral vote of Maine by a majority even greater than was given the Republican ticket in 1868.

3. That the thanks of the people of this State are due to Congress, and to our delegation in that body, through whose able and earnest advocacy the measure was secured, for the recent legislation to promote the interests of ship-building and revive commerce; and we accept what has been accomplished as an assurance that their efforts in this direction will continue until that great interest is placed upon an equitable basis.

4. That we reaffirm our faith in the principle of prohibition and its impartial enforcement, and we view with satisfaction the popular movement in favor of temperance reform recently inaugurated in this State.

Democratic, June 18, 1872.

1. That the principles enunciated by the late Cincinnati convention, taken in connection with the letter of Horace Greeley accepting the nomination, constitute a platform on which all elements in opposition to the present corrupt administration of the Federal Government can stand, and we hereby adopt as the platform of the Democracy of Maine the following propositions of Horace Greeley's letter:

(Here follow the nine propositions formally

stated in the letter referred to, for which see index.)

2. That we believe the great reform for which the patriotic men of all parties are now laboring can be best obtained by supporting as candidate for our next President Horace Greeley, and we recommend our delegates to vote for the Cincinnati candidates.

3. That we pledge to the nominee of this convention our united efforts, and shall hail his election as the commencement of a purer political era.

MASSACHUSETTS.

Republican, April 10, 1872.

Resolved, That we, the delegates of the Republican party of Massachusetts in convention assembled, congratulate our brethren of this Commonwealth on the national recognition of those great social and civil rights for the establishment of which the Republican party was organized, and for which it has contended earnestly through all the trials of peace and war.

2. That we see with profound satisfaction the progress of the American Republic on that path which leads to an honorable nationality, guided by the Republican party, which has enforced the doctrine of equality and right upon which our Government was founded, and given it additional guarantees in the national Constitution; has expunged oppression from the statute-book; has inspired the people with a high and holy purpose in a great war; has cherished the memory of patriotic service and sacrifice; has appealed to a prosperous and honorable people to remember their obligations; has required strictly republican forms of government in the States rescued from the rebellion; has recognized education as the corner-stone of our institutions; has shown its interest in workingmen by destroying slavery and affirming the right of every man to himself and to the legitimate fruits of his labor; has placed in our history a chapter of success and renown that wins the admiration of a civilized world, and we now enter upon a national campaign to support this great record against all opponents of national progress, peace, humanity, and prosperity.

3. That we congratulate the nation that in this great work, the highest civil service known among men, we have an Administration which has developed public opinion in the direction of honor, justice, and philosophy; an Administration which has brought with it peace and a wise adjustment of the violent political controversies which preceded it; which has established our national credit on firm foundations; which has sought, wisely and firmly, to enforce law against disorder and complete the work of reconstruction in the restored States; which seeks to enforce a generous and humane policy toward the Indian tribes; which has reformed the abuses, exposed corruption, punished offenders, and sought to improve and elevate the character of the civil service. And we, moved by an earnest appreciation of the fidelity and wise patriotism of President Grant, do most cordially recommend that he be renominated and reëlected.

4. Urges the nomination of Henry Wilson for the Vice Presidency.

MICHIGAN.

Republican, May 16, 1872.

1. That the unexampled prosperity of the country, the universal feeling of stability which encourages enterprise of all kinds, the steady diminution of the national debt, the large reduction of taxation, the enhancement of the public credit, the rapid extension of every right to every citizen, and the visible dissolution of the Democratic party, so long hostile to justice and equal rights, are the satisfactory proofs of national confidence in a Republican administration of the Government.

2. That in our judgment General Grant has been as faithful and patriotic in the Cabinet as he was in the field, and that, relying upon his honest heart and pure purpose, his renomination to the Presidency is earnestly desired by the great mass of the Republican party.

Democratic, July 2, 1872.

1. That we indorse the principles embodied in the Cincinnati platform.

2. That our delegates to Baltimore be directed to vote as a unit.

MINNESOTA.

Republican, May 8, 1872.

1. The Republican party of the United States had its origin in the necessities of the nation, and since it came into power has decreed and executed measures by which liberty has been preserved and the Union saved from dismemberment and overthrow. Since the close of the rebellion it has substantially accomplished the work of complete reconstruction, and freedom and equal rights have been secured to all our people by irrevocable guarantees. In this great work the Republican party has shown its wisdom and patriotism, and by its unswerving good faith toward the nation's creditors it has fully vindicated our national honor and integrity.

2. With such a record, unequaled by that of any other political party known to history, it can proudly challenge the confidence of the people, and we declare that the best interests of the country demand that the Republican party should continue to administer the Government.

3. We renew our expressions of confidence in the present administration of the General Government. Since it came into power the taxes upon the people have been reduced, and the public revenue faithfully collected and honestly applied, so that while the burden of taxation has been very materially diminished, both in the amount of principal and rate of interest, the Ku Klux disorders and violent persecution of loyal citizens in the South have been suppressed in a prompt and efficient manner, meeting the approval of every friend of justice. The liberal system of pensions

and bounties provided for our brave soldiers and sailors, and the homes founded and maintained for such as were disabled in the service of the country, are referred to with satisfaction and pride. The administration of President Grant, as illustrated by his philanthropic management of Indian affairs, by his efforts to reform the civil service and purify the same, and by his management of our foreign relations, has exhibited rare humanity, wisdom, courage, and dignity, which fully entitles it to the confidence and support of every patriot.

4. Instructs delegates to vote for Grant and Colfax.

Democratic, June 19, 1872.

1. That it is the sense of this convention that the platform adopted at Cincinnati, as accepted and explained by Horace Greeley in his letter of acceptance, expresses the true Democratic idea upon every living political issue of the day, and that we therefore heartily indorse the same and the candidates by that convention nominated.

2. Instructs delegates accordingly.

MISSISSIPPI.

Republican, May 1, 1872.

1. *Resolved*, That the Republican party of Mississippi, in State convention assembled, recognizes the fact that it has accomplished much, in spite of all opposition, toward the fulfillment of its unwavering purpose to establish and maintain order, to build up and make perfect its free public schools, and to secure freedom and equality of rights under the laws and institutions of republican government.

2. That reposing full confidence in the integrity and intelligence of the people of Mississippi, and in the ultimate triumph of the right, we renew our pledge to the people and the world to guard well the public Treasury and the public credit; to maintain our free-school system, obey and enforce the laws, administer impartial justice, contend for amnesty for all past political offenses, and transmit the inheritance of free government untarnished to our posterity.

3. Indorses President Grant.

4. Expresses confidence in Governor Powers.

5. That we invite all the people of our State, and especially all our young men, to unite with us in the effort to convince the Government and people of the Union that our State is redeemed from the power and influence of the ancient enemies of her peace, and is henceforth devoted to the permanent prosperity and glory of the whole Union.

Democratic, June 26, 1872.

1. That to defeat the Administration of President Grant and restore the Government to the paths of peace, freedom, honesty, and economy, we are prepared to lay down all prejudices upon the altar of our common country, and in obedience to the promptings of duty and patriotism, to clasp hands with the friends of constitutional liberty in the North across the bloody chasm made by war, and help to elevate to the Presidency and Vice Presidency of the United States Horace Greeley and B. Gratz Brown.

2. Instructs delegates accordingly.

MISSOURI.

Republican, February 22, 1872.

Resolved, That we congratulate the people of Missouri and the United States that the principles of the Republican party, as enunciated by the national convention of 1868, and which have determined the internal and foreign policy of our Government, have realized the blessings of peace and prosperity at home and vindicated the honor, stability, and power of the American Republic among the nations of the world, and we reaffirm our adherence to those principles.

2. That we heartily indorse the present national Administration in its conduct of national affairs, and point with patriotic pride to its great and lasting achievements. It has given to the country peace and prosperity; it has fulfilled its pledge that the will of the people should be the paramount law of its action; it has established the credit of the country on a firm financial basis by a steady adherence to the obligations of plighted faith, enhanced the value of public securities, and appreciated the national currency to the verge of a gold standard; it has reduced the public debt beyond all precedent, and at the same time relieved the industry of the country from vast burdens of taxation necessarily imposed upon the people for the preservation of the Republic. It has rebuked corruption and dishonesty wherever found to exist, and with firm, unsparing justice it has meted out punishment wherever the law has declared punishment to be due. It has corrected abuses and chronic evils inherited from the past. It has inaugurated and made zealous endeavors to secure a practical and efficient civil service reform; it has adopted a successful and humane Indian policy; it has executed with a firm hand the will of the people as expressed in the Constitution and laws of Congress; and, finally, it has negotiated a treaty with Great Britain, in settlement of the intricate and threatening complication, which is no less glorious as a vindication of the honor of the American flag than it is distinguished in establishing a great Christian principle of international law.

3. That, inasmuch as disorganizing elements of other States are now looking to Missouri for a confirmation of their hopes of division in our ranks, we take this occasion to proclaim to the representatives of the nation that the party in this State is now united, vigorous, and enthusiastic. There is no cause for schism, and there is no schism; and that it will poll the full Republican vote of the State for the nominees of the National Republican convention. That the present so-called Liberal Republican faction, if considered apart from the Democratic party—as it should not be—

is contemptible in numbers, too feeble to organize, and too cunning to expose its weakness by a separate organization—a mere clique of disaffected persons, seeking to perpetuate a division which is now utterly groundless, with the indorsement of a respectable minority of Republicans, and powerless to embarrass the party.

4. We declare our unswerving confidence in the integrity, patriotism, and zealous devotion to the public interests of the present Chief Magistrate of the nation. We pledge ourselves and the Republican party to abide by, support, and carry to victory the platform and candidates presented to the people by the national convention to be assembled at Philadelphia on the 5th of June next.

5. That in our opinion the true policy of the Government toward those lately in rebellion against its authority is general and universal amnesty; and to this end we indorse the recommendation of the President of the United States in his last annual message to Congress.

Democratic, June 12, 1872.

The Democratic party of Missouri cannot be unmindful of the fact that, prior to the last general election in this State, while tyranny, oppression, and plunder prevailed, the large majority of citizens were powerless to rid themselves of these terrible evils, or accomplish any political result; that large numbers of them were disfranchised, and by the wicked machinery of the registration laws, and their more wicked execution, and by unscrupulous and systematic frauds, the people were doomed to hopeless subjection to the corrupt rule of an unprincipled minority; and it was by this patriotism and sense of justice of the Liberal Republican party, in aid of the heroic struggles of the Democracy, that the State of Missouri has been redeemed, and all of her citizens stand forth to-day freemen once more. The same Radical party now in power in the nation, animated by the same spirit of hate and oppression, have for a long series of years of profound peace subjected the people of many of the States of this Union to a system of tyranny, spoliation, and plunder even more aggravated than that under which the people groaned and suffered in Missouri. By frauds the most gigantic, force most unlawful and oppressive, they now hold the reins of power and wield the machinery of government. They have established a military despotism in many of the States, and may, under the legislation of a subservient Congress, establish the same military rule in other portions of this country at the will of the President, who has required them to make him the candidate for reëlection. The Liberal Republican party of the country, impelled by the same sense of justice, offers, in coöperation with the Democracy, to reëstablish throughout the entire country the liberty of all citizens and their local self-government, to overthrow military rule, to establish justice, and to restore fraternal relations between the different sections of our entire country. The Democracy of Missouri declares that it is our duty to coöperate with them in this great national achievement, and we will earnestly discharge that duty. The Liberal Republicans have already placed their ticket in the field, pledged to carry out the great and controlling objects above referred to, and to the support of that ticket a large portion of both the Liberal Republican and Democratic parties of the country are already committed. It would be not only unwise, but in our solemn judgment a wicked trifling with the dearest interests of the people, should the Democracy place another ticket in the field for the Presidency and Vice Presidency, and thus insure the reëlection of Grant, the continued oppression and plunder of the people, and the destruction of liberty and constitutional government throughout the land: Therefore,

Resolved, That the delegates appointed to the convention to be held in Baltimore in July are instructed to vote as a unit against the nomination of any candidates for President and Vice President at the approaching election.

Liberal Republican, January 24, 1872.

Resolved, That we, the Liberal Republicans of Missouri, faithful now as we were in the dark days of civil war to the vital principles of true Republicanism, by no act or word will endanger rightful sovereignty of the Union, emancipation, equality of civil rights, or enfranchisement. To these established facts now imbedded in the Constitution we claim the loyalty of all good citizens.

2. That a true and lasting peace can come only from such profound reconciliation as enfranchisement has wrought in this State, nor can those Governments be true or just in which the tax-payers have no active part. We therefore demand, with equal suffrage for all, complete amnesty for all, that the intelligence and experience of every State may be welcomed to active service for the common welfare.

3. That no form of taxation is just or wise which puts needless burdens upon the people. We demand a genuine reform of the tariff, so that those duties shall be removed which, in addition to the revenue yielded to the Treasury, involve increase in the price of domestic products and a consequent tax for the benefit of favored interests.

4. That the shameless abuse of Government patronage for control of conventions and elections, whether in the interests of an individual, a faction, or a party, with the consequent corruption and demoralization of political life, demands a thorough and genuine reform of public service. Those who would suppress investigation forget that they owe a higher duty to the country than to any party. We honor those Senators whose courageous course has compelled the disclosure of grave misdeeds, and they deserve the thanks and the hearty support of all good citizens.

5. That local self-government, with impartial suffrage, will guard the rights of all citizens more securely than any centralized authority.

It is time to stop the growing encroachments of executive power, the use of coercion or bribery to ratify a treaty, the packing of a Supreme Court to relieve rich corporations, the seating of members of Congress not elected by the people, the bristling of bayonets about State conventions, the resort to unconstitutional laws to cure Ku Klux disorders, irreligion, or intemperance, and the surrender of individual freedom to those who ask that the pleasure, practice or creed, of some shall be the law of all. We demand for the individual the largest liberty consistent with public order, for the State self-government, and for the nation return to the methods of peace, and the constitutional limitations of power.

6. That true Republicanism makes it not the less our duty to expose corruption, denounce usurpation of power, and work for reforms necessary to the public welfare. The times demand an uprising of honest citizens to sweep from power the men who prostitute the name of an honored party to selfish interests. We therefore invite all Republicans who desire the reforms herein set forth to meet in national mass convention at the city of Cincinnati, on the first Wednesday of May next, at 12 m., there to take such action as their convictions of duty and the public exigencies may require.

NEBRASKA.

Republican, May 15, 1872.

1. Indorses the administration of President Grant.

2. That our delegates to the National Republican convention be, and are hereby, instructed to offer the following resolution, and to use all honorable means to secure its incorporation into the National Republican platform:

"That we are in favor of a sixteenth amendment to the Federal Constitution requiring United States Senators and all other civil officers of the Government, except heads and clerks of Departments, foreign ministers and consuls, with their attachés, and judges, attorneys, and clerks of Federal courts, to be elected by the people of the State, Territory, district, or county which they represent, or wherein they discharge their official duties, provision being made by law for the filling of vacancies by temporary appointment."

3. That we are in favor of the dedication of the public lands to actual setters under the homestead and preëmption laws, and for educational and school purposes.

4. Favors Grant and Colfax for renomination.

NEW HAMPSHIRE.

Republican, January 3, 1872.

Resolved, That the Republican party is still, as it ever has been, the party of freedom, improvement, retrenchment, and reform; that having, during its past short but eventful career, secured and established the right of every man to his own limbs and sinews and earnings, the equality of all men before the law, the inability of a State to enslave any portion of its people, and the duty of the Union to guarantee to every citizen the full enjoyment of his liberty and rights, until he forfeits them by crime, its mission henceforth is one of peaceful but active progress; to protect the weak and humble from violence and oppression; to extend the boundaries and diffuse the blessings of civilization; to promote universal education and the general diffusion of knowledge; to see that all laws are faithfully executed and justice impartially administered; to stimulate ingenuity to the discovery of new inventions for economizing labor, and thus enlarging production, the only real source of individual or national wealth; to encourage agriculture as well as manufactures, mining, and the mechanic arts, thereby bringing nearer together the producers of food and fabrics, and furnishing both with a home market, thus enhancing the gains of industry and the wages of labor by reducing the cost of transportation and diminishing the expense of exchanges between farmers and artisans; to retrench unnecessary expenditures, reduce taxation to the lowest point consistent with the maintenance of the national credit, abolish all unnecessary offices, rebuke venality and expose and punish corruption and robbery; to wrest power from the hands of mere politicians by trade, and confide it to those most worthy and best qualified to wield it, by electing and appointing to office only honest and faithful men; so, to administer every department of the Government, with the most rigid economy and the strictest fidelity, that its burdens may bear as lightly and its benefits be as generally diffused as possible, and thus make a happier and brighter future for the toiling masses, and contribute to the welfare, enlightenment, and happiness of the whole people.

2. That the success of the present national Administration in reducing the public debt, diminishing and equalizing taxation, administering every branch of public affairs with economy and efficiency, reforming and improving the civil service, enforcing the laws without fear or favor, protecting the nation's wards with paternal care against the cruel avarice of speculation and fraud, and maintaining friendly relations with foreign Powers, has been such as to command the approbation of the great majority of the American people, and justly entitle it to the confidence and commendation of every true Republican.

3. That while not unwilling to let the dead past bury its dead, we cannot forget, and the American people can never forget, that to the so called Democratic party and its leaders, South and North, we owe all the calamities of the late slaveholders' rebellion, and the burden of debt now resting upon the industry of our State and the nation.

4. That so long as a single soldier disabled in the war for the Union remains to be provided for, so long as one dollar of the national debt incurred in the prosecution of that war remains unpaid, so long as loving hands do not cease to garland with flowers the graves of our heroes fallen in defense of liberty and

country, so long should not the Government of that country be surrendered to the control of those who sought or would have permitted its destruction.

5. That the Republican party, while justly proud of its history, is not unmindful of its duties to the present, or of its obligations to the future. In its name, therefore, and in the name of the people of New Hampshire, we inscribe upon our banners honesty, economy, retrenchment, and reform—honesty in the public service, economy in the public expenditures, retrenchment of all unnecessary offices, and reform, moral, social, and political, everywhere.

6. That one of the primary objects of civil government being the protection of property, the wealth of the country should bear its full proportion of the expenses of the Government, and all taxation, to be just, must be equal.

7. That we call upon Congress to abolish the franking privilege, give the people the cheapest practicable postage, make no more grants of the public lands except as free homesteads to actual settlers, reduce the expenses of the Army and Navy, encourage every department of honest industry, secure to labor everywhere its just reward, and promote universal education.

8. That the Democratic party, in the course of its brief and accidental control of our State government, by its wanton expenditure of the public money, and consequent increase of the State debt; by its greed for office and recklessly partisan legislation; by its complete subserviency to demagogues, and the appointment of incapable and inefficient men to office, has shown itself to be signally unworthy of the confidence and support of the people; and that, particularly, the course of the leaders of that party, in attempting to gerrymander senatorial districts and ward lines, thus outraging the most sacred rights of the people, and in prolonging the session of the Legislature for weeks after the public business was completed, for no other purpose than to secure the offices of the State for its adherents by a resort to bribery, fraud, intimidation, and revolution, has merited the rebuke and should receive the condemnation of every honest man in New Hampshire.

9. Indorses President Grant for renomination.

10. Favors Ezekiel A. Straw for Governor.

11. Recommends Albert S. Twitchell for railroad commissioner.

NEW JERSEY.

Republican, May 23, 1872.

1. We recognize the great principles laid down in the immortal Declaration of Independence as the true foundation of Democratic government, and we hail with gladness every sincere effort toward making these principles a living reality on every inch of American soil.

2. The wisdom of the passage of the thirteenth, fourteenth, and fifteenth amendments to the Constitution having been fully demonstrated by their operation, we are opposed to any repeal or modification thereof.

3. We favor the removal of the disqualifications and restrictions imposed upon the late rebels, in the same measure as their spirit of loyalty will direct, and as may be consistent with the safety of the loyal people, and we approve the recent action of Congress in the passage of the amnesty bill as a wise step in that direction.

4. We are heartily in favor of such a reformation in the civil service that good character and ability shall be the chief recommendations to office, and not political service rendered or to be rendered; therefore we cordially indorse the appointment and labors of the civil service commission and the messages of President Grant thereon.

5. We desire the early and total repeal of the income tax and franking privilege.

6. While remembering we have a large national debt, which must be paid with accruing interest, we nevertheless desire that the burdens of taxation should be removed from the people as rapidly as the national faith will permit.

7. We take especial pride in commending the economy of the national Administration in all its branches, and with gratification we point to the fact that since the inauguration of President Grant the national debt has been reduced $328,000,000.

8. We are in favor of such legislation as will secure to all men equal and exact justice under the laws, without regard to color, creed, or race.

9. We earnestly invite all those who for any cause are temporarily alienated, and yet believe in Republican doctrines, to unite in mutual concessions with us, in preserving intact the ever-living principles of that great party that saved the nation, crushed rebellion, freed the slaves, enfranchised the bondmen, and brought peace and prosperity out of rebellion and discord.

10. We acknowledge our gratitude and deep obligation to the soldiers and sailors of the Republic who on land and sea fought the nation's battles against the armed hosts of the South; as they have proved their devotion and fealty in the past, when the life of our country was in danger, and as combinations are forming which may jeopardize the great results of the war, we call upon them again to give us their powerful aid and support in maintaining our Republican principles and the priceless legacies of the war against all and every combination whatsoever.

11. Indorses the administration of President Grant, and demands his renomination and that of Schuyler Colfax.

Democratic, June 26, 1872.

1. That the true interests of our country require the establishment of the principles, policy, and administrative experience of the Democratic party.

2. That we cordially invite the coöperation of all our fellow-citizens who are opposed to the pernicious principles and conduct of affairs of the present Administration, and who are in favor of the decentralization of Govern-

ment, the remission of local self-government to the several States, the relief from existing taxation by restricting the expenses of the collection and the enormous expenditures of the Government, the inviolability of personal freedom, and a return to those principles of government which distinguished the administrations of Jefferson, Madison and Jackson.

3. That local self-government is a right inherent to the people and essential to liberty. That in creating a central Government, with a gran d power for general purposes, the people did not surrender their right but reserved to themselves the control of home affairs; that any attempt on the part of Congress to interfere, under any pretext, with the full and free exercise of this right is an usurpation which the people ought not to tolerate, because its toleration leads to the destruction of the personal liberties and municipal privileges of the citizen, and the abandonment of all that renders free government valuable.

4. That so far as the Cincinnati platform agrees with the above principles it meets our approval.

5. That we do authorize and instruct our State executive committee to unite and coöperate with any other committee or organization in this State opposed to the present national Administration.

6. That we pledge ourselves to abide by and support the nominees of the Democratic national convention.

Liberal Republican, June 20, 1872.

1. Believing that the recent Liberal Republican convention at Cincinnati originated from a correct judgment of the public feeling and public need, and that it uttered the fit protest of an aroused people against a demoralized Administration, we do cordially approve and indorse the address and platform of principles enunciated by that convention, and adopt the same as the earnest sentiments of this convention.

2. We recognize in Horace Greeley, the presidential candidate for the Cincinnati convention, the living embodiment of those principles; and we adopt his letter accepting the nomination as a good enough platform for all patriotic men determined upon a thorough reform in the administration of the Federal Government.

3. We welcome B. Gratz Brown, the candidate for the Vice Presidency, as the fit associate of our illustrious leader—for years the champion of freedom—and among the first to demand amnesty.

4. We invite all our fellow-citizens, without regard to past political differences, to unite with us and make common cause for our common country, to overthrow a corrupt and disgraceful Administration and its sycophantic partisans, with the assurance that all who are with us are of us.

5. We hereby authorize and instruct our State executive committee to unite and coöperate upon equitable terms with any other committee or organization in this State seeking to accomplish the same end.

NEW YORK.

Republican, May 15, 1872.

The Republicans of New York, in convention assembled, declare their principles and adopt the following resolutions:

1. That all American citizens, whether native or foreign born, and without distinction of race, color, or religion. are entitled to the same civil and political rights, subject to the Constitution of the United States, and to equal and exact justice before the law.

2. That the acts relating to emancipation and enfranchisement—the thirteenth, fourteenth, and fifteenth amendments to the Constitution—shall remain inviolate.

3. That the obligations to pay the public debt, and every part thereof, in coin. shall in no manner and under no guise be impaired.

4. That while favoring a gradual reduction of the national debt, we are opposed to a hurried payment thereof, through oppressive taxation, thinking it clearly more wise and just to divide the burden with the vastly increased population of future years, when to the augmented wealth and multiplied numbers the debt will be less onerous.

5. That the civil service ought to be reformed; the income tax, submitted to as a measure of war, ought immediately to cease; the franking privilege and all the internal revenue taxes, save only the tax on tobacco and spirituous liquors, ought to be abolished.

6. That there should be a tariff for revenue so adjusted as to bear as equally as possible upon every kind of labor, property, and industry.

7. That it is the duty of the Federal Government to do all within its legitimate sphere to restore harmony, prosperity, and honest administration to the reconstructed States, while it should guard with jealous care against any tendency to usurp authority which belongs exclusively to the several States.

8. That the Government of the United States should by every honorable means seek to preserve peace with foreign nations, but that it should at all times and everywhere protect American citizens, extend its sympathy to all downtrodden and oppressed peoples who are struggling for liberty, and that in dealing with foreign Powers it should demand nothing which is not clearly right and should submit to no wrong.

9. That the heroism of the brave soldiers and sailors whose valor preserved the Republic will keep alive the deepest gratitude of the nation so long as patriotism shall last, and we denounce all attempts to reduce the hard-earned pay or pension now allowed them for their inestimable services; that whatever of temporary criticism may be made or of personal disaffection may exist, the honest people of the United States will not forget that the Union was preserved, the nation saved, and liberty secured by their stern and determined maintenance of the great principles of the Republican party.

10. That no disguises, no cunning play upon the jealousies of disappointed men, no false pretenses about a passive policy, will conceal from the true friends of the Union that a surrender of the Republican party at this time is a surrender of the principles for which patriots sacrificed their lives, and virtually throws away the chiefest fruits of an immortal victory.

11. That the cry about universal amnesty is calculated to deceive the people by concealment of the fact that those lately in rebellion are excluded by no Federal law from the same right to vote and to hold property which the most loyal citizens enjoy; and intelligent people will remark that so unwilling were Liberal Republicans to grant common justice to the freedmen of the South, that recently, by their own votes in the Senate, they combined with Democrats, who alone were not sufficient, and sacrificed the amnesty law which had passed the House, rather than give to the colored people the common civil rights secured by Mr. Sumner's bill, to which the Senator so consistently and honorably adhered.

12. That no patriot can fail to discover that politicians of the late seceded States and their northern sympathizers have not suddenly changed their principles, but only their policy; that there can be at this time but two equal, real parties in the political field—the same which were lately arrayed on the battle-field —each animated by the same principles and impelled by the same purposes as before. The success of the one will bring peace, order, and continued prosperity. The success of the other forebodes strife, distrust, and civil commotion.

13. That we earnestly invite all those who for any cause are temporarily alienated, and yet believe in Republican doctrines, to unite in mutual concessions and join heartily in resisting the revival of disunion sentiment which seeks an unnatural alliance for no good, but for the overthrow of those principles for the maintenance of which the great Republican party sprang into life at the call of the nation—a party whose patriotism is not less, whose mission is not ended, and whose victory shall be secured against all the combined enemies of the Union.

14. That considering its eminent success as conclusive proof of the wise administration of President Grant, there stands the fact that since his inauguration up to the first day of the present May $327,719,818 of the public debt has been paid; that the gold premium has become comparatively nominal; that the Government securities, which a little while ago would bring but sixty cents on the dollar, now sell at par in gold; that taxes amounting to more than $100,000,000 per annum have been already taken off; that peace reigns, and that general prosperity and rapid development in material wealth were never so great in our history.

15. Conclusively that with the eminent success of the present Administration, and the auspicious promises of the future, we deem it exceedingly unwise to change our able, tried, and safe Chief Magistrate, who has met the best expectations of the country, for an untried and uncertain ruler in his stead, and we unitedly advise the renomination of Ulysses S. Grant for the next President of the United States.

Democratic, May 15, 1872.

The Democratic party of the State of New York, assembled in regular convention to select delegates to a national convention, to be held at Baltimore to nominate candidates for President and Vice President, declare and resolve,

1. That we recognize the changes in the nature and constitution of the Government which have taken place, and, without reopening the questions of the past, are ready now to coöperate with those, whatever their previous party affiliations, who favor united and localized governments, who seek to restrain the exercise by Congress of absolute and general powers; to prevent its entering on general private legislation; to restrain the growth of vast corporations, and to work a permanent civil service reform.

2. That the recent declaration of political principles by the convention of Cincinnati is evidence of the progress of public opinion toward sound and wholesome views of government; that we believe all patriotic citizens may unite upon that platform for the purpose of restoring the honest administration of national affairs and enforcing the obligations of the Constitution; and our delegates to Baltimore are instructed to take the course best calculated to secure the triumph of these principles, and the selection of any candiates representing them who shall meet the approval of the Democracy in national convention assembled.

Colored People's, May 9, 1872.

1. That the duty of every colored American citizen lies within the lines of the Republican party, and that any departure therefrom must inevitably lead into the camp of the common enemy.

2. That we are greatly endeared to the Republican party, because in its ranks are to be found all that remains true to the ever-to-be-revered Liberty and Abolition parties, and because the Republican party, true to its baptismal vows, has, during the twelve years of its existence, not only suppressed the most cruel and wicked rebellion that ever cursed a land, and established the supremacy of republican institutions all over the country, but has forced traitors, great and small, wherever and whenever found, to bow in honorable submission to the majesty of the law; and not only because this great party has, through its Legislatures, Executives, and its judiciary, emancipated the American slave, and clothed him with citizenship and political rights, but because it also has and does guarantee and vouchsafe to him and his, despite the opposition and protest of the Democratic party and its allies, the recognition of their manhood

and a liberal share of the Federal patronage under its control.

3. That we indorse the administration of President Grant; that we regard it as being eminently wise, liberal, and statesmanlike; as fulfilling our expectations of what a Republican Executive ought to be.

4. That we will in the future, as we have in the past, support the regular Republican nominations, when made, both State and national.

5. That we recommend to the Republican State convention, to be held at Elmira on the 15th instant, the propriety of sending a representative colored man to the national convention at Philadelphia, as a delegate at large; and respectfully but earnestly appeal to that State convention to recognize the respectability and influence of the colored Republicans of the State of New York by naming as such delegate William F. Butler, of New York, our chosen representative.

NORTH CAROLINA.

Republican, April 17, 1872.

1. The platform and principles of the Republican party of North Carolina, as heretofore enunciated in its conventions, are hereby reaffirmed, and events have proved that their practical enforcement is essential to the welfare of the country and to the maintenance of the rights, interests, and liberties of the people.

2. Indorses the administration of President Grant, and delegates are instructed to vote for his renomination.

3. That the Republican party of North Carolina favors as rapid a diminution and as early an extinction of all internal revenue taxation as the exigencies of the Government will permit, for the reason that the details of its collection are necessarily offensive, and in many respects oppressive to the people.

4. That all internal revenue taxes on the distillation of fruits ought to be abolished.

5. That the Republican party of North Carolina recommend to the Congress of the United States the passage of a general amnesty bill, and the adoption of all necessary measures for the enforcement and protection of the civil and political rights of all classes of American citizens.

6. That in a free and representative Government we recognize the paramount obligation to provide efficiently for the general education of the people, and we favor such legislation as will accomplish that end; that we respectfully recommend and ask of the national Government such aid, by the provision of a public fund or the donation of public lands, to the purposes of establishing schools in the several States, as will secure to the masses of the people of all classes the benefits of a liberal education.

7. That we fully indorse the acts of Congress passed to secure equal rights and protection to the citizens of the United States in the several States; and we respectfully recommend a continuance of the present laws, and the adoption of such further legislation as will more certainly secure to the citizens full and practical enjoyment of all their rights, privileges, and liberties.

8. In the opinion of this convention the Democratic majority of the last Legislature, by consolidating into one act its numerous propositions to amend the State constitution, endeavored to force upon the people a forced issue and to coerce them into the adoption of obnoxious amendments, and insomuch as all these propositions must be submitted to the next Legislature for ratification before the same can be referred to the people: therefore, *Resolved*, 1. That the amendments proposed as a whole do not meet the approval of the Republican party, because their adoption would subvert essential principles of the existing constitution. 2. That Republicans can indorse a portion of said amendments, and the next General Assembly may adopt such of them as shall seem best for the general welfare.

9. Indorses administration of Governor Caldwell.

10. Pledges support to the ticket.

Democratic, May 1, 1872.

1. That the time has arrived when it becomes the duty of all patriots, without distinction of party, to unite in an honest effort to restore constitutional government, an equal and moderate system of taxation, economy in expenditures, honesty among the officials, and universal amnesty, and thus secure the permanent peace and prosperity of our common country.

2. That the present system of internal taxes on spirits and tobacco is unequal, vexatious, and tyrannical, ought forthwith to be abolished, and thus by its extinction relieve the country from the curse of a numerous horde of officers whose conspiracies and frauds demoralize the public mind, and who are harassing and plundering the people, and by their extortions fattening on the hard earnings of a helpless, impoverished, and oppressed people.

3. That the late Radical convention of this State by recommending J. C. Abbott to a seat in the Senate of the United States, though he did not receive one third of the votes cast, manifested an utter disregard of the rights of the people of the State, a contempt of the Constitution of the United States and a plain act of Congress made in pursuance thereof, and a preference for the laws of Great Britain, where the minority rule prevails and the rights of majorities are habitually disregarded.

4. That their indorsement of W. W. Holden, who was deposed from office for gross violations of the constitution and laws of the State, squandering its funds, and illegal arrests of its citizens, is well calculated to alarm our people with the dread that, in the event of the return to power of his associates, the State is again to be oppressed with military arrest, penitentiary and railroad swindles, and general waste, profligacy, fraud, and corruption.

5. That the general tendency, both at Washington and in our own State, of Radical action

is entirely in the interests of monopolists and the wealthy classes, and for the oppression of the masses of our countrymen, and that instead of such conduct it is the duty of the Government to aid, elevate, and dignify the laborer, to whose efforts mainly we must look for our prosperity.

6. That education and enlightened public virtue are indispensably essential in a government of and for the people, and we insist that a fair and just proportion of the public lands, or their proceeds, which belong in common to all the States of the Union, shall be given to them for the education of all classes of the people, without distinction of race or color, instead of being granted by Congress, as they have heretofore been, under the most corrupting influences and in vast quantities, to overpowering railroad corporations and other monopolies of accumulated wealth, so dangerous to the rights and liberty, the labor and welfare, of the people.

7. That while we accept and faithfully abide by the Constitution of the United States as it is, with all the amendments, including emancipation and equality before the law, thus conferring equal civil and political rights upon all who are citizens of this Federal Republic, we oppose and denounce that latitudinous construction which makes the discretion of Congress or the President superior to the Constitution, and under pretense of enforcing the laws destroys the most important provisions securing the personal liberty of the citizens, and dwarfs the States themselves into mere provinces or corporations, under the control of a central government, with no rights "reserved" to them, or the people, except such only as that central government may confer.

8. That we desire a real, and not merely a pretended civil-service reform, and that we believe the "one-term principle" for the Presidency would greatly tend to produce that desirable result.

9. That the patronage of the Government should not be brought in conflict with the freedom of elections, and that the elective franchise should be free and untrammeled.

10. That the amendments to the Constitution proposed by the last Legislature will, if adopted, tend materially to benefit the State, and we unhesitatingly recommend their support to all citizens without distinction of party.

11. That all secret political societies are dangerous in a free Government, engender violence, combinations against the peace of society, insecurity of person and property, and ought to be discountenanced by all good citizens.

OHIO.

Republican, March 26, 1872.

1. The Republican party of the United States had its origin in the necessities of the nation, and since it came into power has decreed and executed measures by which liberty has been preserved and the Union saved from dismemberment and overthrow. Amid the disorganization and confusion existing at the close of the rebellion, the Republican party, exercising its organizing and restoring power, has succeeded in the difficult task of complete reconstruction, and has established freedom and equality of rights for all the people of the Republic. In this quiet work the Republican party has shown its wisdom and patriotism, and by its unswerving good faith toward the national creditors it has vindicated the national integrity and honor. No other party known to the people has so grand a record, and no other party in the United States can so proudly challenge the continued confidence of the public; and we declare that the good of the country demands that the Republican party should continue to administer the Government.

2. We renew our expression of confidence in the present Administration of the General Government. Since it came into power the taxes upon the people have been reduced, and the public revenues have been carefully collected and honestly applied, so that while the burden of taxation has been lightened, the public debt has been diminished, both in the amount of principal and the rate of interest. The Administration deserves also the warmest approval of every friend of justice, order, and law, for the prompt and efficient manner in which it has suppressed the Ku Klux disorders and persecutions of loyal citizens in the South, a protection due from every good Government to its people. And we refer with great satisfaction and pride to the system of pensions and bounties provided for our brave soldiers and sailors, and the homes founded and maintained for such as were disabled in the service of their country. These manifestations of public gratitude and justice must command the approval of every patriot. We commend the policy of fairness and kindness toward the Indian tribes as shown by the wisdom and humanity of the President; and in his efforts to reform the civil service we recognize a laudable desire to promote its efficiency and purity; and in the management of our foreign relations, including important questions of international law involved in the Treaty of Washington, the Administration has shown rare wisdom, courage, and dignity, and has maintained the honor of the nation untarnished.

3. A large portion of the revenue necessary to defray the current expenses of the Government and to pay its liabilities must be derived from duties on imports. These duties should be levied with a view to equalize their burdens and benefits among the people, so as to promote, as far as possible, the interests of every section and branch of industry, and so that labor of every kind may have constant employment and just reward.

4. We are opposed to further grants of the public lands to corporations and monopolies, and demand that the national domain be set apart for homes for the people and for purposes of education.

5. As there can be no product of industry without a union of capital and labor, therefore we are in favor of such legislation as will

give all proper guarantees for the safety and prosperity of the one, and remunerative investment of the other.

6. Favors the renomination of President Grant, and proposes ex-Governor William Dennison for the Vice Presidency.

Democratic, June 27, 1872.

1. That the platform of principles adopted by the Cincinnati convention, together with the clear interpretation of the same enunciated in the letter of Horace Greeley accepting the nomination of that convention for the office of President of the United States, affords common ground on which liberal men of all political parties can consistently unite in opposition to the present Administration and its attendant official corruption.

2. Instructs delegates for Greeley and Brown.

Prohibition, February 23, 1872.

1. That we approve and affirm the platform of principles adopted by the National Prohibition party on the 22d day of February, 1872, and pledge to the candidates nominated by it our cordial support.

2. That it is the sentiment of this convention that in the progress of Christian civilization the time has come when a movement ought to be made by the leading Christian nations in favor of an international system of permanent arbitration; and we are therefore in favor of the United States Government making a proposition, at an early date, to the nations to coöperate in the movement.

OREGON.

Republican, March 21, 1872.

1. To the Constitution of the United States and all its amendments we pledge our unfaltering allegiance; to its authority a willing obedience; to its full and legal construction and enforcement our constant support.

2. That the success of the present national Administration in reducing the public debt, diminishing and equalizing taxation, administering every branch of public affairs with economy and efficiency, forming and improving the civil service, enforcing the laws without fear or favor, protecting the nation's wards with paternal care against the cruel avarice of speculation and fraud, and maintaining friendly relations with foreign Powers, has been such as to command the approbation of the great majority of the American people, and justly entitle it to the confidence and commendation of every true Republican.

3. We regard the payment of our national debt in full compliance with all legal obligations to our creditors everywhere, and in accordance with the true letter and spirit of its contracting, as no longer a question in issue; but, that we may be clearly understood, we denounce all forms and degrees of repudiation of that debt, as affirmed by the Democratic party and its sympathizers, as not only national calamities but positive crimes, and we will never consent to a suspicion of lack of honor or justice in its complete satisfaction.

4. We admit of no distinction between citizens, whether of native or foreign birth, and therefore we favor the granting of full amnesty to the people of those States lately in rebellion; and we here pledge the full and effective protection of our civil laws to all persons voluntarily coming to or residing in our land.

5. We favor the encouragement of railroads by the General Government of the United States, and hold that such disposition should be made of the public lands as shall secure the same to actual settlers only, in quantities not exceeding one hundred and sixty acres.

6. That we are in favor of a revenue for the support of the General Government by duties upon imports. Sound policy requires such adjustment of those duties on imports as to encourage the development of the industrial interests of the whole country, and we recommend that policy of national exchange which secures to the workingmen liberal wages, to agriculture remunerative prices, to mechanics and manufacturers an adequate reward for their skill, labor, and enterprise, and to the nation commercial prosperity and independence.

7. We believe that popular education is the sole true basis and hope of a free Government, and shall ever oppose any diversion of or interference with the common-school funds or lands in this State for any other than their legitimate purpose, and we condemn the act of favoritism by the last Legislature whereby $200,000, taken from the school fund, were granted to a corporation consisting mainly of Democratic leaders and party favorites, for the construction of a work which another corporation, entirely sound and responsible, offered to construct for $75,000 less; and that we are in favor of the passage by the Legislature of an efficient school law, such as will secure to all citizens of our State a good common-school education.

8. We find no terms sufficiently strong to express our disapproval of those acts of the last Legislature whereby the swamp lands belonging to this State have been taken from the needy settlers and given without limit or proper competition in price to the land-grabber and speculator, whereby the emoluments and salaries of State officers have been unconstitutionally increased, and the taxes increased thousands of dollars by the creation of new and unnecessary offices and salaries, for the purpose of providing for party favorites; and whereby the citizens of our metropolis have been deprived of and denied the right of controlling their police authority; and we equally condemn the administration of our State officers and laws as extravagant, reckless, illegal, and destructive, and rightly charge all these results as the acts of the Democratic party.

9. We are in favor of the United States giving to each honorably discharged soldier who served in the armies of the United States to put down the rebellion a warrant for a homestead of one hundred and sixty acres of public lands.

10. That we demand the repeal of the so-

called litigant act, which was devised to support pauper Democratic newspapers at public expense.

11. That the Republican party of this State are in favor of the General Government extending aid toward building a railroad from Portland, Oregon, to Salt Lake City, and from Jackson county to Humboldt; and we hereby pledge our party Representative to the same.

12. That the indiscriminate licensing of persons to sell spirituous liquors, without being placed under responsibilities for the abuse thereof, having been found by experience to promote the growth of crime and pauperism, and thereby seriously increase the rate of taxation, the Republican party recognize the right and duty of the law-making power to prevent and limit the evils and abuses of such sale, so far as concerns the public good and is consistent with individual liberty, by refusing to license others than law-abiding and responsible persons, who can furnish sufficient sureties for good conduct.

13. That the Republican party of Oregon is in favor of obtaining assistance from the General Government for the construction of a wagon-road from the city of Portland to the Dalles, recognizing this as a most important and necessary improvement for the State.

14. We affirm that the continuance in power of the Republican party is the only sure preservation of national peace and prosperity, and for reasons therefor we point to its brilliant record in the late civil war; to a complete nationality; to a united sisterhood of thirty-seven States; to our Territories rapidly warming into State life; to a nation freed from the taint of human slavery; to an elevated and enlarged citizenship; to our national standing at home and abroad; to the work of vigorous reform in all discovered abuses of authority or trust; to an unequaled foreign credit; to a successful and solid financial system, and the unparalleled peace and prosperity everywhere in our broad domain; and these are our pledges for the future.

Democratic, April 10, 1872.

1. That we, the Democratic party of the State of Oregon, are pledged to a strict construction of the Constitution; the restoration and preservation of the rights of the States to regulate their internal affairs, and especially the elective franchise, free from the control or interference of the General Government; the protection of individual rights in accordance with the fundamental laws of the land, including the rights to the writ of *habeas corpus*, trial by jury, and freedom from unreasonable searches and seizures.

2. That we are opposed to every species of corruption in all departments of the municipal, State, and national Governments.

3. That our motto is, no privileged classes and no privileged capital.

4. That we are in favor of a tariff to raise money only for the necessary expenses of the Federal Government, and not for the benefit of monopolists.

5. That we view with alarm the flagrant and open violations of the Constitution by the party now controlling the General Government, in the passage and enforcement of the reconstruction and Ku Klux laws, and the corruption and fraud which characterize their administration of every department of Government, and we pledge ourselves to use all lawful and peaceable means to secure a speedy correction of these outrages and usurpations.

6. That the freedom, welfare, and rights of the people are superior to the interests of incorporators, and should be protected against the exactions of oppressive monopolies.

7. Favors the appropriation of the fund arising from the sale of the swamp lands to purposes of internal improvement, and to aid common schools.

8. Favors development of local commercial facilities.

9. Indorses the administration of Governor Grover.

PENNSYLVANIA.

Republican, April 10, 1872.

Resolved, That we reaffirm our devotion to the principles of the Republican party, and our belief that the continued existence of that party is necessary to the maintenance and success of those principles. The grand and fundamental idea of the equality of all men in political rights is not professed by any other party, and can be sustained faithfully only by those who are sincerely committed to it.

2. That the adoption of the thirteenth, fourteenth, and fifteenth amendments to the Constitution of the United States has not been sufficiently acquiesced in by all to render certain and secure their permanent incorporation in that instrument, and hence the administration of the Government can safely be intrusted only to that party which is heartily and beyond question committed to them and the policy necessary to put them into successful operation.

3. That we are now more than ever called to sustain the policy of national protection to American industry. If the laborer is worthy of his hire, and a fair day's work entitles the worker to a fair day's pay, we must continue to throw the protecting arm of the Government around those who toil for their daily bread. The protective policy alone makes labor contented and capital secure. It renders employment certain, and pay ample and satisfactory, while free trade means that our laborers and mechanics must either work for lower wages or that our factories should be closed through foreign competition and the workingmen of the country deprived of employment.

4. That the public lands belong to the people, and should be reserved for the people. We therefore pronounce most decidedly against any further appropriation of the public lands in behalf of corporations or individuals. All lands not sold according to law should be open to preëmption and actual settlement.

5. That we demand a continued adherence to the policy hitherto pursued under Repub-

lican auspices in our State and in the nation of a steady and gradual reduction of the public debt. The interests of the people require that the most rigid economy should be practiced in the administration of both the national and State Governments, and that taxes should be reduced in both as rapidly as is consistent with the honorable maintenance of the public credit and the certain extinguishment of the public debt.

6. That we heartily approve of the act of General Grant in giving a trial to the plan of civil service reform. We demand that that plan, or any other that may be substituted in its place as better, shall have a fair and unembarrassed trial; that every effort shall be made to secure competent men for the public service, and that honesty and incorruptibility shall be deemed qualifications as essential as competency and intelligence.

7. That the Republican party has given full evidence during the past eleven years of its ability to administer the Government honestly, faithfully, and successfully. It has within that time maintained the honor of our national flag at home and abroad, preserved the Union from disruption, and restored it in its integrity, secured to all classes and conditions of men the rights given to them by their Maker, and having proclaimed liberty throughout all the land to all the inhabitants thereof, has given to that proclamation the full effect to which it was entitled, and we therefore in its name claim from the people a continuance of their confidence, and fearlessly challenge their scrutiny into its acts.

8. That we point with pride to the record of General Grant's administration of the national Government. Not only has the weight of internal taxation been almost wholly removed from the people's shoulders, but three hundred millions of the national debt have been paid off, a result never before attained by any other people under like circumstances, and for which we are indebted to the rigid honesty, strict economy, and sterling integrity which the President has brought to the administration of national affairs.

9. That we present his name for renomination to the Presidency, confident that the people will again rally to the support of the man who so nobly fought their battles, who, under the guidance of Providence, brought the nation safely through its struggle to maintain its existence, and who has since so successfully administered the affairs of the Government as to command general admiration at home and abroad.

10. That we will stand by the Government in the foreign policy so firmly marked out and adhered to by President Grant. The honor of the nation, we feel, is safe in his hands, and the flag under which he never suffered defeat will not be dishonored while he is kept in the front.

11. That we congratulate the people of Pennsylvania on the final accomplishment of the call for a convention to revise and amend the constitution of Pennsylvania, and we earnestly urge upon our friends to see that delegates are chosen in their respective districts committed to the policy of incorporating in that instrument a clear and decisive prohibition of special legislation.

12. That we hereby declare our opposition to every effort to withdraw from the sinking fund of the Commonwealth, by substitution, exchange, or otherwise, any of the bonds, securities, or moneys now pledged to it, and through it to the payment of the public debt, and our inflexible determination to preserve the same inviolably for the fulfilment of the common obligation.

13. Compliments Governor Geary.

14. That the oil-producing, mining, lumbering, and manufacturing interests of the State require protection from the efforts of dangerous combinations, and that such laws should be enacted by the General Assembly of the Commonwealth as will promote said interests, both in their development and the transportation of their products to market.

15. That we are earnestly in favor of the earliest possible removal of the duties on tea and coffee, and urge the prompt passage of the bill for that purpose, now before Congress.

16. Asks popular support for nominees for delegates to constitutional convention.

Democratic, May 30, 1872.

1. That the Democratic party, while in the future, as in the past, firmly upholding the Constitution of the United States as the foundation and limitation of the powers of the General Government and the safe shield of the liberties of the people, demands for the citizen the largest freedom consistent with public order, and for every State the right of self-government; that to uphold the former and protect the latter the Democracy of Pennsylvania can find no better platform upon which to stand than the great leading principles enunciated in the inaugural of President Jefferson and the farewell address of the immortal Jackson. Upon these two great State papers we plant ourselves and enter the contest of 1872.

2. That, abused as the public confidence has been by a long period of official mismanagement, waste, and fraud, this convention invites the coöperation of all citizens of the Commonwealth in the earnest effort which the great constituency it represents is about to make to remove from our State administration every taint of political corruption. The interest of every Pennsylvanian is directly and vitally concerned in the eradication of all unjust usages and practices by which individual fortunes may be created at public cost, and the attempt to do this can be made certainly successful by the union of upright and fair-minded men of all parties, and by sustaining candidates of unquestioned ability and unspotted reputation.

3. That this convention appeals to the people of Pennsylvania for the support of the candidate for Governor whom it has placed in nomination, because his election will secure at once a correction of existing wrongs and the

permanent future prosperity of the State. It asks for his support because he has been nominated not to subserve the views or promote the interests of any section or faction, but to meet the requirements of an urgent and common need; because he fully represents, and his life and character fairly illustrate, the true spirit and principles of popular government; because he has been an earnest, sincere, and efficient opponent of the fraudulent practices and false doctrines of the party that has held power through many long years of misrepresentation and misrule; because he stands pledged by the record of his whole life to administer his office, if elected, for the benefit, and only for the benefit, of the people; because he can be trusted to secure careful, economical, and responsible control of the agents and officials and the treasury of the Commonwealth; because he can be relied on to withstand unfounded and unjust demands to the prejudice of public rights, to oppose with vigor the encroachments of powerful corporations, and energetically resist the grant to aggregated capital of privileges which could be used to injure, hamper, and impede the efforts of individuals in the various enterprises and fields of labor which the State affords; and because his action in the past is proof that his official influence will be used hereafter to prevent the mischief of special legislation, and to destroy the possibility of procuring the enactment of any statute by the use of money or any other corrupt means.

4 and 5. Eulogize candidates for judge of supreme court, auditor general, Congressmen at large, and delegates to the constitutional convention.

6. That the grant by the Radical Legislature of this State of numerous charters creating such corporations as the South Improvement Company, Continental Improvement Company, and others of similar character, is unjust to the interests of trade, is dangerous to the rights and liberties of the people, and as such meets with our unqualified condemnation.

Labor Reform, May 7, 1872.

Adopted the Columbus platform, and then resolved:

1. Absolute purity of the elective franchise as the sacred birthright of every citizen, the only safeguard of liberty, and the security of justice and equal rights to all.

2. The repeal of all partial and unjust legislation, by which corrupt politicians, irresponsible commissioners, and gigantic monopolies have been able to disregard and defy the people and grow rich at their expense.

3. That the present system of assessments, patronage, speculation, and defalcation of public officers in this Commonwealth shall give place to one requiring honesty, capacity, and fidelity, as necessary qualifications for employment as public servants, giving them just compensation in salaries for work done, and requiring the payment of all fees into the public Treasury.

4. An equitable system of taxation, legislative encouragement of coöperative enterprises among the working people, and laws for the protection of the lives, limbs, and health of all employés on railroads, mines, factories, mills, &c., in Pennsylvania.

5. The question of the tariff and protection having been disposed of by the sixth resolution of the Columbus convention in a manner declared to be satisfactory by the earliest advocates of that policy, we deem it unnecessary for this convention to make any further declaration on the subject.

6. That we pronounce the existence of company stores, better known as the passbook or truck system, which prevails to such a great extent, against the workingmen, and that we demand by legal enactment the abolition of the same immediately.

SOUTH CAROLINA.

Republican, February 20, 1872.

Resolved by the Union Republican party of the State of South Carolina in convention assembled, That we indorse the administration of President U. S. Grant in its wise and successful policy, which has reduced the national debt, while lessening the public taxes, and at the same time preserved full faith with the public creditors.

2. That the profound gratitude of the Republicans of South Carolina is due to the Republican majority in the Forty-Second Congress for their enactment of the act to enforce the fourteenth amendment to the Constitution of the United States, and to President U. S. Grant for his prompt and timely enforcement of that act, whereby the armed bands organized and operated by the Democratic party for the suppression of free speech and a free ballot in South Carolina have been themselves suppressed.

3. That while we thus accord a merited indorsement to the man who in peace as in war has deserved the "well done" of the whole country, we respectfully but earnestly remonstrate against the great majority of the Federal appointments that have been made in this State during the past three years, whereby the Republican party of South Carolina has been wounded in the house of its friends; and we do here express our belief that such appointments of persons not in sympathy with the Republican party of the State or nation is due largely to the misrepresentations of Senator F. A. Sawyer.

4. That the national Republican party having declared in its platform of 1868 in favor of amnesty, we do hereby instruct our delegates to the National Republican convention to move and advocate the adoption of a clause in the national platform in favor of the rigid enforcement of universal civil rights for every American citizen on every inch of American soil, and their full and equal enjoyment of all public privileges.

Democratic, June 12, 1872.

1. That this convention recognizes the movement which was organized at Cincinnati

in May last as the only one in this crisis calculated to revive individual liberty and restore local self-government.

2. That this convention accepts the Cincinnati platform as broad, liberal, and just to all portions and classes and citizens of the Republic.

3. That the interest of the whole country requires that no separate and distinct Democratic nomination should be made by the Baltimore convention, and the delegates appointed by this body are hereby instructed to oppose such nominations.

TENNESSEE.

Republican, May 15, 1872.

The Republicans of Tennessee, in convention assembled, appeal to the records of the country in exemplification of their principles, namely:

1. The American Union and the suppression of armed rebellion, and the abolition of slavery to maintain it.

2. Civil rights and political privileges for all, with protection to persons and property, and the elective franchise, not only from vindictive action of the Government, but against organizations which seek their ends by violence and other unlawful methods.

3. For those who suffered in our several wars, and the widows and orphans, bounties, pensions, and the payment of just claims for property taken or destroyed by the national Army.

4. The public credit maintained against all attempts to impair it by reducing and, as far as possible, repealing all taxes which fall upon industry, by impartially collecting and honestly applying such as remain; by curtailing expenditures and abolishing unnecessary offices; thus rapidly diminishing the public debt, while the burdens of the people are constantly lightened and the business of the country undisturbed.

5. The rigid accountability of all officials, punishing swiftly and sternly the dishonest, removing the incompetent, and making efficiency and fidelity tests of fitness in preference to political opinions, partisan service, race, color, or nationality.

6. The national honor inviolate, either by unwarranted demands upon other Powers, or by unworthy concessions to them, by menaces to the weak, or by discourtesy from the proud.

7. The interests of labor by free schools, free homes, and an industrial policy, which has doubled the rate of wages and increased the annual production of the country fourfold.

8. Immigrants from all other lands invited and cordially welcomed to the enjoyment of equal rights and privileges with the nativeborn, themselves descended from parents who arrived as emigrants to our shores.

9. Eulogizes President Grant and indorses him for renomination.

10. Proposes Horace Maynard for Vice President.

Democratic, May 9, 1872.

1. Indorses the administration of Governor John C. Brown, and renominates him for Governor.

2. Refers to the formation of a State executive committee.

3. That we recognize, among other things, as cardinal points in our political faith, the following:

The preservation of our local State governments against Federal encroachment and centralization of power.

The equality of all men before the law, and an equal participation of all citizens in the rights and benefits of government.

The subordination of the military to the civil authority.

The inviolability of the right of *habeas corpus*.

The purification of the corrupt civil service of the Government.

A rigid economy in the expenditures of Government, and a faithful compliance with its obligations.

The preservation of the national honor at home and abroad.

The Union of the States, and all the guarantees of the Constitution respected.

And, for the purpose of securing the recognition and faithful application of these principles in the administration of our national Government, we are ready and willing to coöperate with all good citizens in the pending presidential contest, without regard to other and minor differences of creed or policy or past political names or associations.

4. That inasmuch as the convention of Liberal Republicans, held at Cincinnati on the first and succeeding days of the present month, has presented to the country the names of Horace Greeley, of New York, and Benjamin Gratz Brown, of Missouri, as candidates for President and Vice President of the United States, pledged to the maintenance and enforcement of the doctrines above enunciated, and have invited the coöperation of all patriotic citizens in their support, we deem it but the part of patriotic duty to declare that in the contest now well-nigh upon us the said nominees deserve the support of every patriot in the land, as against a ticket representing the principles, policy, and practices of the present Federal Administration. And while reaffirming our purpose and desire to preserve the integrity of the Democratic party, we do nevertheless declare in our behalf, and, as we are well satisfied, in behalf of the people we here represent, that in our opinion, with the lights before us, the presentation of candidates for the Presidency and Vice Presidency, in the approaching contest, by the Democratic party of the nation, would be unwise, unnecessary, and exceedingly dangerous to the welfare of the people at large.

5. Appoints twenty-two delegates to the National Democratic convention at Baltimore, "with special instructions to carry out the spirit of the foregoing declarations, believing as we do that the election of the ticket presented by the Liberal Republicans, with the

coöperation of the northern and southern people, would go far toward a healing of the nation."

6. Refers to nomination of electors.

TEXAS.

Republican, May 14, 1872.

1. We declare our full fellowship with the national Republican party of the United States, and our unqualified devotion to its principles and to its fortunes.

2. We declare that the grand and fundamental idea of the political equality of all men and their equal rights before the law is peculiarly Republican, and is not professed by any other party in this nation; that it is the mission of the Republican party to carry this idea into full practical effect, and therefore the Democratic party cannot safely be intrusted with the powers of Government, either national or local.

3. That there are but two political parties in the nation, the Republican and the Democratic; that the nomination of Horace Greeley for the Presidency of the United States was made in the interest of the Democratic party, and that the Republicans of Texas will follow no such lead, but will give their firm and zealous support to the nominees of the convention to assemble at Philadelphia on the 5th of June next.

4. Indorses the administration of President Grant and declares for his renomination.

5. Regards free education of all the children of Texas a sacred duty.

6. Declares emphatically for State internal improvements, but opposes State aid in bonds or money.

7. Indorses Governor E. J. Davis.

8. That we declare our unqualified condemnation of all corruption and peculation on the part of public officials; we will do all that in us lies to promote honest and wise legislation, to secure honest and just administration, and to guard with a jealous care all the interests of all the people.

9. That we will endeavor to give protection to our frontier by every means at our command, and we pledge ourselves to cut down every superfluous expense in the State government, and to reduce taxation to the very least amount compatible with efficient government.

Democratic, June 18, 1872.

1. That we have undiminished confidence in the time-honored principles of the Democracy as embodied in the platform of the Democratic State convention at Austin, January 25, 1871, hereto annexed and made part of this platform, and believe that the welfare and prosperity of the country will never be fully restored till those principles are in the ascendant; but we recognize as an alarming fact that the issues determined in the next presidential election not only concern matters of constitutional construction and expedience, but also involve the far greater and vital question whether we are hereafter to live under a government of law or a government of force.

2. That the present Administration has been subversive of constitutional government and free institutions throughout the country, and in the southern States has been a system of lawless spoliation and central tyranny; that its chief, by accepting gifts and bestowing offices in return, by appointing incompetent and unfit relations and personal adherents to positions of profit and trust, and by devoting to unbecoming pleasures and pursuits time that should be given to official duties, has been culpably reckless of the responsibilities and dignity of the high station, has set a bad example to the people, and has violated alike the obligation of good faith and the usages of common decency, and that, encouraged and aided by the party in power, he has attempted to usurp or control legislative and judicial functions, and thus establish a consolidated personal government, destructive of the rights of the States and the liberties of the people.

3. That in view of the threatening pretensions and great power of those now in authority we consider their expulsion from offices of honor or trust to be essential to the people and welfare of the country and to the preservation of constitutional government.

4. That we have seen with profound satisfaction that patriotic movement of the Liberal Republicans lately assembled in convention at Cincinnati, and we fully concur with them in believing that local self-government with impartial suffrage will guard the rights of all citizens more securely than any centralized power. The public welfare requires the supremacy of the civil over the military authority, and freedom of person under the protection of the *habeas corpus*. We demand for the individual the largest liberty consistent with public order, and for the State self government, and for the nation a return to the methods of peace and the constitutional limitation of power. The civil service of the Government has become a mere instrument of partisan tyranny and personal ambition, and an object of selfish greed, and is a scandal and reproach on free institutions, and broods a demoralization dangerous to the perpetuity of republican government. We therefore regard a thorough reform of the civil service as one of the most pressing necessities of the hour; that honesty, capacity, and fidelity constitute the only valid claims to the public employment; that the offices of the Government cease to be a matter of arbitrary favoritism and patronage, and again a post of honor. We demand Federal taxation which shall not necessarily interfere with the industry of the people, which shall provide the means necessary to pay the expenses of the Government, economically administered, pensions, the interest on the public debt, and a moderate reduction annually of the principal thereof.

5. That we recognize the movement of the Liberal Republicans in opposition to the present administration of the General Government in behalf of reform and constitutional

liberty, and we, the Democratic party of Texas, confiding in the wisdom, patriotism, and integrity of the great National Democratic party, to assemble in Baltimore, do hereby pledge ourselves to give a vigorous support to the policy to be enunciated by the Baltimore convention, and do battle for the restoration of civil government under whatever leadership it may direct.

6. That whoever may be the nominee of the Baltimore convention, this convention finds no reason therefrom for destroying, impairing, or even modifying the present organization of the Democratic party, which should maintain its organization vigorously for the purpose of putting down and removing the abuses under which our people labor from the tyrannical, dishonest, and unscrupulous State government of Texas.

7. That we are in opposition to all moneyed subsidies to private corporations by the State government, and regard the same as unsound in principle and dangerous in practice.

8. That it is the duty of the General Government to protect our citizens from the marauding bands of Mexicans and savages who are daily pillaging our country, murdering our citizens, and driving back the tide of civilization upon our western frontier.

9. That as the school fund sacredly set apart for the education of the children of this State has, under the political misrule of the last two years, been plundered by peculation, squandered, and perverted to political purposes, the Democratic party deem it fitting on this occasion to reaffirm the opinion that, agreeably to the policy the party have ever pursued, it is the duty of the State to establish common schools and furnish the means of a good common education to every child within our State.

UTAH.

Republican, May 16, 1872.

1. That the delegates be instructed to call the attention of the National Union Republican convention to a resolution of the Republican convention of 1860, denouncing polygamy, in truth, as "the twin relic of barbarism," and that we now hold the National Union Republican party accountable for the extirpation of the chief social and political evil of the age. This is the platform of Utah Republicans.

Democratic, June 15, 1872.

1. The equality of all men before the law, and the duty of government in its dealings with the people to mete out equal and exact justice to all, of whatever nativity, race, color, or persuasion, religious or political.

2. The maintenance of the Union, the Constitution inviolate, and for the individual the largest liberty consistent with public order.

3. Local self-government, with impartial suffrage, instead of centralized power to guard the rights of all citizens.

4. The supremacy of the civil over the military authority, and freedom of person under the protection of the *habeas corpus*.

5. The public credit sacredly maintained, and a speedy return to specie payment demanded alike by the highest considerations of commercial morality and honest government.

6. The civil service of the Government having become a mere instrument of partisan tyranny and personal ambition, and an object of selfish greed, a scandal and reproach upon free institutions, breeding a demoralization dangerous to the perpetuity of republican government, we therefore regard a thorough reform of the civil service as one of the most pressing necessities of the hour; that honesty, capacity, and fidelity should constitute the only valid claim to public employment; that the offices of the Government should cease to be a matter of arbitrary favoritism and patronage, and that public station should become again a post of honor.

VERMONT.

Republican, May 1, 1872.

1. That, first, we cordially approve and indorse the present national Administration and commend it as distinguished among the best of our history for ability, integrity, economy, and fidelity to principle.

2. Declares that the first preference of the State is for the nomination of Grant and Colfax.

3. We deeply regret the defection of Republicans from the regular organization. We believe that the objects of reform professed to be right by the Liberal Republican movement are mainly such as can be secured only in the Republican party, while the only practical result of the movement will be to strengthen the Democracy.

4. We deprecate the restoration of the Democratic party to power as endangering the equal laws which, against the opposition of that party, have recently been ingrafted upon our system, as preventing any further progress in the same direction, and as likely to lead to the allowance of unjust and excessive southern war claims against the Government, which would greatly increase taxation and severely impair the national credit.

5. We pledge ourselves anew in this, our first State convention for two years, to the great leading aims of the Republican party, namely, the most complete liberty and the most exact equality of right under the law for all men throughout the Republic; the promotion of the education, intelligence, and thrift of every class, and especially of the laboring class of our population; the most strict observance of the public faith both toward our creditors by the payment of the national debt and toward our veteran soldiers and sailors by a prompt and generous provision of pensions for them and their widows and orphans; the preservation of peace so far as consistent with national honor and safety; the cultivation of relations of confidence and good will with all, from the old nations of the East to the savage tribes of the West; faithfulness and economy

in the administration of the laws, and promptitude and thoroughness in the correction and reform of all abuses in any department of the public service.

VIRGINIA.

Republican, April 18, 1872.

The Republicans of Virginia in convention assembled, about to enter upon the canvass for the election of a President and Vice President of the United States, now formally announce their principles to the voters of this Commonwealth.

From 1865 to 1872 they have continually and unwaveringly held and proclaimed the same principles; and they hereby reiterate and reaffirm the resolutions of their State conventions held in 1866, 1867, 1868, 1869, 1870, and 1871.

These principles have been embodied in the thirteenth, fourteenth, and fifteenth amendments of the national Constitution, and in the civil rights act of April 9, 1866, the enforcement act of May 30, 1870, and the amended enforcement act of April 20, 1871; which principles in brief are:

1. That slavery shall never exist in this Union;

That all native and naturalized inhabitants of these States shall be citizens of the Union, entitled to absolutely equal rights, civil and political;

That the elective franchise and the right of office holding shall belong to all citizens of proper age, not guilty of crime, irrespective of race, color, or of any other proscriptive qualification.

2. That the laws of Congress passed for the enforcement of these rights should be diligently executed; and that if in practice these laws should be found inadequate for this purpose, other laws should be enacted by Congress effectual to that end.

3. That these constitutional amendments and the laws for their enforcement embody not only the just principles of equality and right, but those of true Christian toleration; and that we oppose all proscription for opinion's sake, and all endeavors to infuse a spirit of hatred and hostility in the minds of one class of citizens against another on political grounds.

4. That we challenge the world to produce financial results more successful than have been achieved by the national Administration. The national debt has been diminished $300,000,000, while taxation by the national Government has been largely and steadily reduced. Our credit has improved and strengthened at home and abroad; the perpetrators of fraud and embezzlement have been vigorously pursued and promptly punished; the revenues have been collected by officers held by the President to the most rigid accountability; all of which has produced the present satisfactory condition of the national Treasury.

5. That a well-conducted and faithfully administered system of free schools, in pursuance of the State constitution, whereby the children of the people shall be universally educated, is a cardinal policy of the Republican party, and necessary to the well-being of society; and as one means of securing an efficient management of the free schools of Virginia we favor the election of school trustees by the people in such manner that the minority as well as the majority may be represented in the school boards.

6. Indorses the State superintendent of public instruction.

7. That the so-called conservative party of this State, by its unjust laws and proscriptive spirit, by its attempts to hold the mass of the people in ignorance, by its pernicious financial legislation and its oppressive taxation, has forfeited all claim to the support of the people of Virginia; and has shown that a party is unfit to exist which, like it, is organized on the principle of political and social proscription, and held together by no common bond but that of hatred toward the national Government and its supporters.

8. That the wise provisions of the homestead clause in our State constitution have been ignored by the judiciary, or ruled upon in such a manner as to deny to our people its intended benefits.

Suffering debtors find no adequate relief upon appeal to the State courts or Legislature, but are compelled to see the little wreck of property left them by the war sacrificed under the sheriff's hammer at forced sale, and themselves and families left homeless beggars.

In view of these facts the Republican party of Virginia, as the author of the homestead clause and its advocate to the present time, believes the extension of the exemptions under the general bankrupt act so as to include the homestead exemptions under our State constitution to be the only means of relief now offered to our people, and they therefore ask Congress to pass the amendment to that effect offered in the Senate by Hon. J. F. Lewis, and hereby pledge themselves to the support of this measure.

9. That we extend a hearty welcome to immigration and capital from abroad, and advocate the development in every possible manner of the magnificent resources of forest, soil, water-power, and mineral wealth in which Virginia abounds.

10. That the national currency given the nation by the Republican party has proved a national blessing; that a protective tariff is the true policy for the South, tending as it does to produce that variety of employments which we so much need; and that State and national taxation should be reduced as rapidly as possible, consistently with a due regard to the public faith.

11. Indorses John F. Lewis for the Vice Presidency.

12. Urges the renomination of President Grant.

Democratic, June 27, 1872.

1. That we greet with lively satisfaction the movement of the Liberal Republicans at Cincinnati, and desire to express our sincere admiration of the moral heroism displayed by

them in subordinating party to patriotism, and pledge ourselves to meet their courageous and patriotic proffer of coöperation for the public deliverance in the same catholic and magnanimous spirit in which it is tendered.

2. That the delegates appointed by this convention to the Democratic convention at Baltimore should give a vigorous, persistent, and united support to the Greeley and Brown ticket, nominated at Cincinnati, as holding forth the fairest promise for allaying the passions of the war, reviving real peace within our borders, restoring integrity to the public service, establishing the States in their legitimate functions in the Federal system, preserving intact the great writ of liberty, and rescuing the Republic from the despotism of the sword.

WASHINGTON.

Republican, April 29, 1872.

1. That the Republicans of Washington Territory remain true to the principles and will hold fast to the organization of the Republican party.

2. That the administration of President Grant has been marked by prudence, wisdom, and success in managing our national finances and our foreign relations; in its policy with the Indians; in its suppression of disorder in the South; in its efforts to reform the civil service and the revenue department; and especially in its reducing taxation $80,000,000 yearly for the past three years, and yet at the same time reducing the national debt $100,000,000 yearly; and for all these reasons merits our warmest approval and has our most decided indorsement.

3. That the Constitution of the United States, with all its amendments, is entitled to our most cordial support, and that we will use our best energies to uphold its letter and spirit, and to render effective all laws made to enforce this supreme law of the land.

4. That the record of the Republican party by its emancipation of the slaves of the South; its extension of civil rights to all men; its maintenance of national honor; in paying the war debt, in securing pensions and homesteads to the Union soldiers, its giving of public lands to settlers, the economy which it has introduced into all branches of the public service, and its bringing fraud, peculation, and corruption to speedy justice, manifests its ability and integrity, and affords overwhelming reasons for its continuance in power.

5. That the encouragement given to railroads already running across the continent to the Pacific coast, and to the Northern Pacific railroad, has been the work of the Republican party, in order to bind together in one common prosperity the most distant sections of our beloved Union, and that we rejoice that our own Territory is now about to share in this prosperity, and that we hail with satisfaction the energy, skill, and enterprise displayed by the Northern Pacific railroad in our immediate vicinity, as well as east of the Rocky mountains, in hastening the time when the cars shall transport us directly from Puget sound to Lake Superior.

6. That we congratulate the Republican party on the success of its policy in bringing currency to a near equality of value with gold, and that we hail with pleasure the rapid approach of the time when any paper dollar can be at once exchanged for a dollar in gold or silver without the slightest discount or loss.

7. That while we recognize all the legitimate rights of each State within the limits of its own authority, we are proud to see how truly the Republican party has made of all the States and Territories one grand nation, whose glory it is to have given complete equality of rights to all men upon its soil, without distinction of race, of birth, or of origin.

8. That while the Democratic party has been a mere party of opposition without distinctive and vital principles, it does now, by its "new departure" and "passive policy," impliedly recognize the soundness of the principles of the Republican party and the impossibility of overthrowing them by an open and direct struggle.

9. That we favor a tariff for revenue, but so adjusted as to protect incidentally, though equally, every branch of American industry—agricultural, mechanical, mining, manufacturing, and commercial, as well as every section of our common country—North, South, East, West, and Central.

10. That we favor such legislation, national and territorial, as shall encourage the activity and security of labor, and yet protect the investment of capital so that both may work hand in hand together for the united progress of all our interests of every kind and degree.

11. Instructs delegates for U. S. Grant.

12. Indorses Congressman Garfielde.

WEST VIRGINIA.

Republican, May 23, 1872.

1. We favor a continued reduction of taxation, a gradual payment of the national debt, civil service reform as proposed by the President, and the restoration of harmony and good-will in the reconstructed States by an impartial execution of the laws; a jealous guarding of our national honor in our intercourse with foreign Powers, submitting to nothing wrong and demanding only what is right.

2. We declare that the recent amendments relating to emancipation, enfranchisement, and the sacred obligation of the national debt having been duly ratified and promulgated, are to be taken and held as part of the organic law of the land and forever remain inviolate.

3. No passive policy, no disguises, however cunningly assumed by malcontents, no false pretenses of disappointed men and self-constituted delegates, can alienate the adherents of the great Republican party, which, through the maintenance of its organization, has preserved the union of States and secured liberty, happiness, and prosperity throughout the land.

4 and 5. Indorse President Grant and instruct delegates to vote for Grant and Boreman.

6. That we denounce the effort of the so-called leaders of the Democratic party to make the adoption or rejection of the proposed constitution a partisan measure, inasmuch as it affects the vital interests of every citizen of the State.

Democratic, May 30, 1872.

1. We congratulate the people upon the faithful redemption of all the pledges upon which the Democratic party was placed in power in West Virginia.

2. We heartily indorse the Democratic State administration, and point to its honesty and efficiency as a full guarantee of our continued fidelity to the interests of the State and people.

3. That in the opinion of this convention the elements of opposition to the national Administration should be consolidated in the approaching presidential campaign without prejudice to the unity and perpetuity of the Democratic organization.

4. That with full confidence in the wisdom and patriotism of the National Democratic convention soon to assemble at Baltimore, we pledge the Democracy of West Virginia to abide its action or recommendation and to express their approval thereof at the polls.

5. We pledge to the nominees of this convention our earnest and active support.

6. We indorse the proposed new constitution of the State of West Virginia, and recommend its ratification by the people without distinction of party.

WISCONSIN.

Republican, March 13, 1872.

1. That we cordially indorse the platform of principles adopted by the last Republican nominating State convention, and to this avowal of policy we invite the earnest attention of the electors of the State.

2. That the continued confidence of the people of the country is due to the administration of President Grant, whose reduction of the public debt and consequent lessening of taxation, under whose recommendation we have reason to hope for further equalization of the tariff laws, whose judicious and patriotic foreign policy, whose respect for the will of the people, and whose efficient enforcement of the laws and pacific dealing with a part of the Union which was chaotic when he became President, have justified the highest expectations of the great party that designated him for his present high place, and of the voters of the country who clothed him with executive power.

3. Favors President Grant's renomination.

Democratic, June 13, 1872.

1. That the address and resolutions of the "Liberal Republican" convention, held at Cincinnati on the 1st of May, embody fundamental principles which the Democratic electors of the State of Wisconsin cordially indorse, and that they cheerfully acquiesce in the reference to the people of the several States of the political questions upon which that convention expressed no opinion; that the exposition and elucidation of the platform of the Cincinnati convention by Horace Greeley in his letter of acceptance of the nomination for President furnish a satisfactory assurance to the American people that he will, if elected, administer the Government upon the principles in that platform. Therefore, in devotion to principle, waiving our preference for men, and believing that the approval of the nominees of the Cincinnati convention is a sure mode of obtaining the triumph and ascendency of those principles, we approve the same, and recommend that our delegates to the Baltimore convention do ratify the action of the Cincinnati convention.

XXIII.

STATISTICAL TABLES.

A.—POPULATION AND ELECTIONS.

STATES.	1868. § Popular vote.		1868. § Electoral vote.		State elections.				Apportionment.		Elect'l College.		Population. ‡	
	Republican, Grant.	Democratic, Seymour.	Republican, Grant.	Democratic, Seymour.	1870. Republican.	1870. Democratic.	1871. Republican.	1871. Democratic.	Census of 1860.	Census of 1870.	Census of 1860.	Census of 1870.	Census of 1860.‡	Census of 1870.‡
Maine	70,426	42,396	7	-	54,040	44,534	58,757	48,126	5	5	7	7	628,279	626,915
N. H.......	38,191	31,224	5	-	*34,912	*25,023	†33,892	†34,699	3	3	5	5	326,073	318,300
Vt..........	44,167	12,045	5	-	33,367	12,058	-	-	3	3	5	5	315,098	330,551
Mass......	136,477	59,408	12	-	*79,549	*48,536	†75,129	†47,725	10	11	12	13	1,231,066	1,457,351
R. I........	12,993	6,548	4	-	10,493	6,295	8,822	5,249	2	2	4	4	174,620	217,353
Conn	50,641	47,600	6	-	43,285	44,128	47,473	47,370	4	4	6	6	460,147	537,454
N. Y.......	419,883	429,883	-	33	*366,436	*390,532	†387,119	†368,212	31	33	33	35	3,880,735	4,382,759
N. J.......	80,121	83,001	-	7	80,426	77,003	76,292	82,299	5	7	7	9	672,035	906,096
Penn......	342,280	313,382	26	-	*267,278	*267,393	283,999	269,509	24	27	26	29	2,906,215	3,521,791
Del.......	7,623	10,980	-	3	9,982	12,458	-	-	1	1	3	3	112,216	125,015
Md.........	30,438	62,357	-	7	76,595	57,727	58,824	73,959	5	6	7	8	687,049	780,894
Va..........	-	-	-	-	*101,291	*119,492	-	-	8	9	10	11	1,596,318	1,225,163
N. C........	96,226	84,090	9	-	83,427	87,648	†95,252	†87,007	7	8	9	10	992,622	1,071,361
S. C........	62,301	45,237	6	-	85,071	51,537	-	-	4	5	6	7	703,708	765,606
Ga..........	57,134	102,822	-	9	69,822	96,685	-	-	7	9	9	11	1,057,286	1,184,109
Ala.........	76,366	72,086	8	-	77,676	79,447	-	-	6	8	8	10	964,201	996,992
Miss........	-	-	-	-	*76,143	*38,133	-	-	5	6	7	8	791,305	827,922
La..........	33,263	80,225	-	7	65,647	41,170	-	-	5	6	7	8	708,002	726,915
Ohio.......	280,128	238,700	21	-	*221,715	*205,047	238,273	218,105	19	20	21	22	2,339,511	2,665,260
Ky..........	39,566	115,889	-	11	57,261	88,945	89,083	126,059	9	10	11	12	1,155,684	1,321,011
Tenn	56,757	26,311	10	-	41,500	78,979	-	-	8	10	10	12	1,109,801	1,258,520
Ind.........	176,552	166,980	13	-	157,501	160,059	-	-	11	13	13	15	1,350,428	1,680,637
Ill..........	250,293	199,143	16	-	*168,579	*144,923	137,191	116,171	14	19	16	21	1,711,951	2,539,891
Missouri.	85,671	59,788	11	-	63,336	104,374	-	-	9	13	11	15	1,182,012	1,721,295
Ark.........	22,152	19,078	5	-	-	-	-	-	3	4	5	6	435,450	484,471
Mich	128,550	97,069	8	-	*100,176	*83,391	93,269	74,740	6	9	8	11	749,113	1,184,059
Florida....	-	-	3	-	12,439	11,810	-	-	1	2	3	4	140,424	187,748
Texas......	-	-	-	-	*39,838	*39,055	-	-	4	6	6	8	604,215	818,579
Iowa	120,399	74,040	8	-	103,377	60,888	108,801	67,547	6	9	8	11	674,913	1,191,792
Wis.........	108,857	84,710	8	-	77,929	68,903	78,301	68,910	6	8	8	10	775,881	1,054,670
Cal.........	54,592	54,078	5	-	-	-	62,581	57,520	3	4	5	6	379,991	560,247
Minn......	43,542	28,072	4	-	36,739	29,395	46,425	31,437	2	3	4	5	172,023	439,706
Oregon ...	10,961	11,125	-	3	11,095	11,726	-	-	1	1	3	3	52,465	90,923
Kansas ...	31,049	14,019	3	-	40,666	20,496	-	-	1	3	3	5	107,206	364,399
W. Va.....	29,025	20,306	5	-	26,742	28,865	†27,638	†30,220	3	3	5	5	-	442,014
Nevada...	6,480	5,218	3	-	6,148	7,200	-	-	1	1	3	3	6,857	42,491
Neb.........	9,729	5,439	3	-	11,126	8,648	-	-	1	1	3	3	28,841	122,993
Total ...	3,012,833	2,703,249	214	80	-	-	-	-	243	292	317	366	31,183,744	38,113,253
Territ's ‖..	......	......	......	......	......	......	......	......	......	......	......	......	259,577	442,730
G'd total.	......	......	......	......	......	......	......	......	......	......	......	......	31,443,321	38,555,983

There was a question as to the right of Georgia to participate in the presidential election of 1868, and the result was announced as it would stand with Georgia voting and as it would stand with Georgia not voting. In Florida, the choice of electors was made by the Legislature.

*ELECTION OF 1870.—In New Hampshire, the Labor Reform vote was 7,369; Prohibition, 1,167. In Massachusetts, the Labor Reform and Prohibition vote was 21,946. In Ohio, the Temperance vote was 2,812. In Illinois, the Prohibition vote was 3,712. In Pennsylvania, the votes given to those Independent Republican candidates who were adopted by the Democrats are included in the Democratic column. In New York, the Labor Reform vote was 1,907; the Prohibition, 1,459. In Michigan, the Temperance vote was 2,710. The elections in Virginia, Mississippi, and Texas were held in 1869.

†ELECTION OF 1871.—In New Hampshire, the Labor Reform vote was 782; Temperance, 356. In Massachusetts, the Labor Reform vote was 6,848; Temperance, 6,598. In New York, the Temperance vote was 1,820. In North Carolina and West Virginia, the vote was on calling a State Constitutional Convention, and was not strictly a partisan contest.

§1860.—The popular vote for President was: Lincoln, Republican, 1,866,452; Douglas, Democrat, 1,375,157; Breckinridge, Democrat, 847,953; Bell, Union, 590,631; total vote, 4,680,193. In 1864, Lincoln, Republican, had 2,223,035; McClellan, Democrat, 1,811,754; total vote, 4,034,789. Total vote in 1868, 5,716,082. The electoral vote of 1860 stood: Lincoln, 180; Breckinridge, 72; Bell, 39; Douglas, 12. Of 1864: Lincoln, 212; McClellan, 21.

‖1870.—Arizona, 9,658; Colorado, 39,864; Dakota, 14,181; District of Columbia, 131,700; Idaho, 14,999; Montana, 20,595; New Mexico, 91,874; Utah, 86,786; Washington, 23,955; Wyoming, 9,118.

‡The representative ratio, under the census of 1860, was 126,823. The representative ratio, under the census of 1870, is 135,239, which is ascertained by taking the whole population of the States, 38,113,253, excluding therefrom 381,420, being the population of the four States of Delaware, Oregon, Nevada,

B.—WEALTH, LOCAL DEBT, AND TAXATION.*

in the several States and Territories, by census of 1850, 1860, *and* 1870.

(Compiled from advance sheets of census of 1870.)

STATES.	True value of real and personal estate.			State, county, town, and city taxation.		State, county, town, and city debt.
	1850.	1860.	1870.	1860.	1870.	1870.
Alabama	$228,204,332	$495,237,078	$201,855,841	$851,171	$2,982,932	$13,277,154
Arkansas	39,841,025	219,256,473	156,394,691	635,293	2,866,890	4,151,152
California	22,161,872	207,874,613	638,767,017	2,981,122	7,817,115	18,089,082
Connecticut	155,707,980	444,274,114	774,631,524	1,015,037	6,064,843	17,088,906
Delaware	21,062,556	46,242,181	97,180,833	(*a*) 205,891	418,092	526,125
Florida	22,862,270	73,101,500	44,163,655	159,112	496,166	2,185,838
Georgia	335,425,714	645,895,237	268,169,207	797,885	2,627,029	21,753,712
Illinois	156,265,006	871,860,282	2,121,680,579	6,121,766	21,825,008	42,191,869
Indiana	202,650,264	528,835,371	1,268,180,543	3,701,352	10,791,121	7,818,710
Iowa	23,714,638	247,338,265	717,644,750	2,378,400	9,055,614	8,043,133
Kansas	-	31,327,895	188,892,014	195,857	2,673,992	6,442,282
Kentucky	301,628,456	666,043,112	604,318,552	2,148,241	5,730,118	18,953,484
Louisiana	233,998,764	602,118,568	323,125,666	4,960,780	7,060,722	53,087,441
Maine	122,777,571	190,211,600	348,155,671	2,257,213	5,348,645	16,624,624
Maryland	219,217,364	376,919,944	643,748,976	2,158,895	6,632,842	29,032,577
Massachusetts	573,342,286	815,237,433	2,132,148,741	7,436,578	24,922,900	69,211,538
Michigan	59,787,255	257,163,983	719,208,118	1,766,694	5,412,957	6,725,231
Minnesota	-	52,294,413	228,909,590	666,007	2,648,372	2,788,797
Mississippi	228,951,130	607,324,911	209,197,345	954,806	3,736,432	2,594,415
Missouri	137,247,707	501,214,398	1,284,922,897	4,109,653	13,908,498	46,909,865
Nebraska	-	9,131,056	69,277,483	91,863	1,027,327	2,089,264
Nevada	-	-	31,134,012	-	820,308	1,986,093
New Hampshire	103,652,835	156,310,860	252,624,112	1,261,866	3,255,793	11,153,373
New Jersey	200,000,000	467,018,324	940,976,064	1,457,506	7,416,724	22,854,304
New York	1,080,309,216	1,843,338,517	6,500,841,264	15,363,422	48,550,308	159,808,234
North Carolina	226,800,472	358,739,399	260,757,244	1,044,732	2,352,809	32,474,036
Ohio	504,726,120	1,193,898,422	2,235,430,300	9,611,021	23,526,548	22,241,988
Oregon	5,063,474	28,930,637	51,558,932	199,056	580,956	218,486
Pennsylvania	722,486,120	1,416,501,818	3,808,340,112	8,729,736	24,531,397	89,027,131
Rhode Island	80,508,794	135,337,588	296,965,646	686,133	2,170,152	5,938,642
South Carolina	288,257,694	548,138,754	208,146,989	1,280,386	2,767,675	13,075,229
Tennessee	201,246,686	493,903,892	498,237,724	1,102,793	3,381,579	48,827,191
Texas	52,740,473	365,200,614	159,052,542	533,265	1,129,577	1,613,907
Vermont	92,205,049	122,477,170	235,349,553	908,080	2,135,919	3,594,700
Virginia	430,701,082	793,249,681	409,588,133	3,672,689	4,613,798	55,921,255
West Virginia	-	-	190,651,491	-	1,722,158	561,767
Wisconsin	42,056,595	273,671,668	702,307,329	2,330,011	5,387,970	5,903,532
Total	$7,115,000,800	$16,086,519,771	$29,822,535,140	$93,774,421	$278,391,286	$864,785,067
TERRITORIES.						
Arizona	-	-	$3,440,791	-	$31,323	$10,500
Colorado	-	-	20,243,303	-	362,197	681,158
Dakota	-	-	5,599,752	(*b*)	13,867	5,761
District of Columbia	$14,018,874	$41,084,945	126,873,618	$260,218	1,581,569	2,596,545
Idaho	-	-	6,552,681	-	174,711	222,621
Montana	-	-	15,184,522	-	198,527	278,719
New Mexico	5,174,471	20,813,768	31,349,793	29,790	61,014	7,560
Utah	986,083	5,596,118	16,159,995	65,006	167,255	-
Washington	-	5,601,466	13,562,164	57,311	163,992	88,827
Wyoming	-	-	7,016,748	-	34,471	
Total	$20,179,428	$73,096,297	$245,983,367	$412,325	$2,789,026	$3,891,691
Grand total	$7,135,780,228	$16,159,616,068	$30,068,518,507	$94,186,746	$281,180,312	$868,676,758

and Nebraska, which, having less population than the representative ratio, are, nevertheless, assigned one Representative each by law, and dividing the remainder by 279, being the whole number of Representatives originally determined upon, less those assigned to the four States above named. *By subsequent act, approved May* 29, 1872, *nine Representatives* additional to the original number of 283 were assigned, one to each of the following States: New Hampshire, Vermont, New York, Pennsylvania, Indiana, Tennessee, Louisiana, Alabama, and Florida.

The relative rank of the States, (according to population,) in the order given in table A, was, in 1860: 22, 27, 28, 7, 29, 24, 1, 21, 2, 32, 19, 5, 12, 18, 11, 13, 14, 17, 3, 9, 10, 6, 4, 8, 25, 16, 31, 23, 20, 15 26, 30, 34, 33, 0, 36, 35; and in 1870: 23, 31, 30, 7, 32, 25, 1, 17, 2, 34, 20, 10, 14, 22, 12, 16, 18, 21, 3, 8, 9, 6, 4, 5, 26, 13, 33, 19, 11, 15, 24, 28, 36, 29, 27, 37, 35.

* No valuation of the property of the General Government is attempted in the census of 1870.

(*a*) Returns of taxation at 1860 incomplete.

(*b*) No returns of taxation at 1860.

C.—AGRICULTURAL STATISTICS.*

Lands, productions, &c.	1870.	1860.	1850.
Farm lands, improved, acres	188,921,099	163,110,720	113,032,614
Farm lands, woodland, acres	159,310,177	244,101,818	180,528,000
Farm lands, other, unimproved, acres	59,503,765		
Farms, cash value of	$9,262,803,861	$6,645,045,007	$3,271,575,426
Farming implements and machinery, cash value	$336,878,429	$246,118,141	$151,587,638
Wages, including value of board, during the year	$310,286,285	-	-
Total (estimated) value of all farm productions, including betterments and additions to stock	$2,447,538,658	-	-
Orchard products	$47,335,189	$19,991,885	$7,723,186
Produce of market gardens	$20,719,229	$16,159,498	$5,280,030
Forest products	$36,808,277	-	-
Value of home manufactures	$23,423,332	$24,546,876	$27,493,644
Value of animals slaughtered or sold for slaughter	$398,956,376	$213,618,692	$111,703,142
Value of all live stock	$1,525,276,457	$1,089,329,915	$544,180,516
Horses, number of	7,145,370	6,249,174	4,336,719
Mules and asses, number of	1,125,415	1,151,148	559,331
Milch cows, number of	8,935,332	8,585,735	6,385,094
Working oxen, number of	1,319,271	2,254,911	1,700,744
Other cattle, number of	13,566,005	14,779,373	9,693,069
Sheep, number of	28,477,951	22,471,275	21,723,220
Swine, number of	25,134,569	33,512,867	30,354,213
Wheat, spring, bushels	112,549,733	173,104,924	100,485,944
Wheat, winter, bushels	175,195,893		
Rye, bushels	16,918,795	21,101,380	14,188,813
Indian corn, bushels	760,944,549	838,792,742	592,071,104
Oats, bushels	282,107,157	172,643,185	146,584,179
Barley, bushels	29,761,305	15,825,898	5,167,015
Buckwheat, bushels	9,821,721	17,571,818	8,956,912
Rice, pounds	73,635,021	187,167,032	215,313,497
Tobacco, pounds	262,735,341	434,209,461	199,752,655
Cotton, bales	3,011,996	5,387,052	2,469,093
Wool, pounds	100,102,387	60,264,913	52,516,959
Peas and beans, bushels	5,746,027	15,061,995	9,219,901
Potatoes, Irish, bushels	143,337,473	111,148,867	65,797,896
Potatoes, sweet, bushels	21,709,824	42,095,026	38,268,148
Wine, gallons	3,092,330	1,627,192	221,249
Butter, pounds	514,092,683	459,681,372	313,345,306
Cheese, pounds	53,492,153	103,663,927	105,535,893
Milk sold, gallons	235,500,599	-	-
Hay, tons	27,316,018	19,083,896	13,838,642
Seed, clover, bushels	639,657	956,188	468,978
Seed, grass, bushels	583,188	900,040	416,831
Hops, pounds	25,456,669	10,991,996	3,497,029
Hemp, tons	12,746	74,493	34,871
Flax, pounds	27,133,034	4,720,145	7,709,676
Flax-seed, bushels	1,730,444	566,867	562,312
Silk cocoons, pounds	3,937	11,944	10,843
Sugar, cane, hogsheads	87,043	230,982	247,577
Sugar, sorghum, hogsheads	24	-	-
Sugar, maple, pounds	28,443,645	40,120,205	34,253,436
Molasses, cane, gallons	6,593,323	14,963,996	12,700,896
Molasses, sorghum, gallons	16,050,089	6,749,123	
Molasses, maple, gallons	921,057	1,597,589	
Beeswax, pounds	631,129	1,322,787	14,853,790
Bees' honey, pounds	14,702,815	23,366,357	

F.—PUBLIC DEBT.

(Being a statement of outstanding principal of the public debt of the United States on the 1st of July of each year, from 1857 to 1872, inclusive; vide report Secretary Treasury, December 4, 1871, page 13, and public debt statement of same, July 1, 1872:)

Year	Amount	Year	Amount
1857	$28,699,831 85	1865	$2,680,647,869 74
1858	44,911,881 03	1866	2,773,236,173 69
1859	58,496,837 88	1867	2,678,126,103 87
1860	64,842,287 88	1868	2,611,687,851 19
1861	90,580,873 72	1869	2,588,452,213 94
1862	524,176,412 13	1870	2,480,672,427 81
1863	1,119,772,138 63	1871	2,353,211,332 32
1864	1,815,784,370 57	1872	2,253,251,328.78

Debt of each Administration.

The public debt at the close of each Administration was: Washington, (first term,) ending 1793, $80,352,634 04; (second term,) $82,064,479 33; John Adams, $83,038,050 80; Jefferson, (first term,) $82,312,150 50; (second term,) $57,023,192 09; Madison, (first term,) $55,962,827 57; (second term,) $123,491,965 16; Monroe, (first term,) $89,987,427 66; (second term,) $83,788,432 71; John Quincy Adams, $58,421,413 67; Jackson, (first term,) $7,001,698 83; (second term,) $3,308,124 07; Van Buren, $13,594,480 73; Tyler, $15,925,303 01; Polk, $63,061,858 69; Fillmore, $59,803,117 70; Pierce, $28,699,831 85; Buchanan, $90,580,873 72; Lincoln, $2,680,647,869 74; Johnson, $2,588,452,213 94.

* Compiled from advance sheets of the census.

G.—REVENUE REDUCTIONS.

Official estimates of the annual reduction in internal and customs revenues of the United States by legislation since the act of 1866.

INTERNAL REVENUE.*

Under what law.	*Amount.*
Act of July 13, 1866†	$65,000,000
Act of March 2, 1867‡	40,000,000
Act of February 3, 1868§	23,000,000
Act of March 31, 1868‖ } Act of July 20, 1868, }	45,000,000
Act of July 14, 1870¶	55,000,000
Act of June 6, 1872**	21,131,183

CUSTOMS.

Under what law.	*Amount.*
July 14, 1870	$30,000,000
May 1, 1872,†† } June 6, 1872,‡‡ }	31,215,409

J.—ELECTORAL COLLEGE.

Number of electoral votes under the census of 1860 and 1870.

New England and Middle States.	1860.	1870.	Western States.	1860.	1870.	Former slave States.	1860.	1870.	Pacific States.	1860.	1870.
Connecticut	6	6	Illinois	16	21	Alabama	8	10	California	5	6
Maine	7	7	Indiana	13	15	Arkansas	5	6	Nevada	3	3
Massachusetts	12	13	Iowa	8	11	Delaware	3	3	Oregon	3	3
New Hampshire	5	5	Kansas	3	5	Florida	3	4			
New Jersey	7	9	Michigan	8	11	Georgia	9	11			
New York	33	35	Minnesota	4	5	Kentucky	11	12			
Pennsylvania	26	29	Nebraska	3	3	Louisiana	7	8			
Rhode Island	4	4	Ohio	21	22	Maryland	7	8			
Vermont	5	5	Wisconsin	8	10	Mississippi	7	8			
						Missouri	11	15			
						North Carolina	9	10			
						South Carolina	6	7			
						Tennessee	10	12			
						Texas	6	8			
						Virginia	10	11			
						West Virginia	5	5			
Total	105	113	Total	84	103	Total	117	138	Total	11	12

E.—PUBLIC LANDS.§§

		Acres.
Total number of acres of public lands of United States, including those disposed of as well as those yet on hand		1,834,998,400.00
Quantity sold	161,766,426.46	
Entered under the homestead laws of 1860, 1864, and 1866	20,500,216.69	
Granted for military services	62,115,202.03	
Granted for agricultural colleges:		
Selected in place	1,461,157.64	
Located with scrip	6,175,431.35	
Approved under grants in aid of railroads	26,027,673.52	
Approved swamp selections, (given to the States)	48,775,990.05	
Quantity granted to the States and Territories for internal improvements	12,403,054.43	
Donations and grants for schools	67,983,922.00	
Donations and grants for universities	1,082,880.00	
Located with Indian scrip	732,165.21	
Located with floatscrip under act of March 17, 1862	15,296.24	
Estimated quantity granted for wagon-roads	3,857,213.00	
Quantity granted for ship-canal	1,450,000.00	
Salines	514,485.00	
Seats of government and public buildings	146,860.00	
Granted to individuals and companies	2,482,861.32	
Granted for deaf and dumb asylums	44,971.11	
Reserved for benefit of Indians	13,280,699.94	
Reserved for companies, individuals, and corporations	8,955,383.75	
Confirmed private land claims	18,696,947.62	
Total disposed of		458,468,837.36
Remaining unsold and unappropriated June 30, 1871		1,376,529,562.64

*The number of articles on the schedule has been reduced from two hundred and eighty-six, under act of March 3, 1865, to fifty-five under act of July 14, 1870.

† Reduction effected chiefly by repeal of extra duty of twenty per cent. imposed on manufactures by section five, act of March 3, 1865, and by additions to free list.

‡ By raising exemption on income from $600 to $1,000, establishing uniform rate of five per cent. instead of differential rates of five and ten per cent., increasing exemptions, and, in some cases, reducing rate of tax.

§ Mainly by repeal of duty on raw cotton.

‖ By repeal on all manufactures then taxable except gas, enumerated in section ninety-four, act of June 30, 1864.

¶ By repeal of tax on gross receipts, sales other than sales paid by stamps, and sales of tobacco, spirits, and wines, legacies, successions, articles in schedule A, passports, and special taxes, except those relating to spirits, tobacco, and fermented liquors, by raising income exemption from $1,000 to $2,000, and reducing the rate from five to two and a half per cent.

** By reductions on tobacco $6,854,000, gas $2,800,000, stamps $10,977,183, and banks $500,000.

†† Repeals duty on tea and coffee—a reduction of $15,893,846 67.

‡‡ Reduction on dutiable imports $11,975,848 34, and additions to free list $3,345,713 99.

§§ Compiled from the report of the Secretary of the Interior, 1871.

Distributed in the various States and Territories as follows:

	Acres.		Acres.		Acres
Missouri	102,817.15	**Minnesota**	32,328,510.57	**Montana Territory**	86,768,100.09
Alabama	5,810,171.92	Oregon	50,887,411.45	Arizona Territory	68,855,730.00
Mississippi	4,577,674.95	Kansas	39,627,793.49	Idaho Territory	52,103,783.04
Louisiana	6,292,932.78	Nevada	67,049,529.93	Wyoming Territory,	59,163,834.49
Michigan	3,130,994.82	Nebraska	37,988,601.53	Indian Territory	44,154,240.00
Arkansas	10,444,740.85	Washington Ter'y,	40,976,976.60	Alaska Territory.	369,529,600.00
Florida	17,262,459.76	New Mexico Ter'y,	70,677,735.84		
Iowa	1,084,486.64	Utah Territory	48,659,916.27		
Wisconsin	7,713,376.47	Dakota Territory	90,567,020.47	Total	1,376,529,562.64
California	98,388,435.22	Colorado Territory,	62,382,773.26		

The Commissioner of the General Land Office, January 9, 1872, estimates the quantity of land embraced in the limits of all the railroad grants, after deducting 8,740,264.55 acres lands reverted and lapsed, at 207,460,031.77 acres, and estimates the quantity they will receive from such grants, after deducting 6,314,005.45 acres reverted and lapsed, at 172,739,430.80 acres.

I.—VOTES ON GENERAL TARIFF ACTS.

(1842 *to* 1870,)

by States, in the House of Representatives, on their passage.

STATES.	1842.		1846.		1857.		Mar. 2, 1861.		Aug. 5, 1861.		Dec. 24, 1861.		July 14, 1862.		June 30, 1864.		Mar. 3, 1865.		July 28, 1866.		July 14, 1870.		June 6, 1872.
	Yea.	Nay.	Yea.	Nay.	Yea.	Nay.	Yea.	Nay.	Yea.	Nay.	Yea.	Nay.	Yea.	Nay.	Yea.	Nay.	Yea.	Nay.	Yea.	Nay.	Yea.	Nay.	
New England States:																							No test vote taken. Bill finally passed without division.
Maine	4	2	5	1	6	...	3	...	5	...	6	...	6	...	3	...	3	...	3	...	4	...	
New Hampshire	...	4	3	1	2	1	2	...	...	1	1	...	2	...	2	1	2	1	3	...	2	...	
Vermont	4	...	...	2	...	3	3	...	3	...	3	...	2	...	3	...	3	...	3	...	3	...	
Massachusetts	10	1	...	9	9	...	9	...	8	...	9	...	7	...	8	...	7	...	10	...	8	...	
Connecticut	6	...	1	4	...	4	4	...	1	2	1	...	1	1	1	...	2	1	2	...	3	...	
Rhode Island	2	...	...	2	1	1	2	...	1	1	...	1	1	...	1	...	2	...	2	...	...	...	
Middle States:																							
New York	23	8	15	14	15	10	18	6	25	2	20	1	13	4	14	2	10	12	16	5	16	10	
New Jersey	6	...	...	6	2	1	4	...	3	1	1	...	...	3	1	1	...	4	1	3	2	2	
Pennsylvania	20	...	2	23	3	15	22	...	14	6	9	1	13	5	15	...	19	1	19	2	19	4	
Delaware	1	...	...	...	...	1	...	1	...	1	...	...	...	...	1	...	1	...	...	...	...	...	
Maryland	4	2	1	1	4	1	...	2	...	3	3	1	...	3	1	...	2	...	1	4	...	3	
West Virginia	...	...	...	...	...	...	...	...	...	...	...	...	...	...	...	...	2	...	3	...	2	...	
Western and northwestern States:																							
Ohio	8	6	11	8	5	15	13	...	10	10	8	6	7	5	4	9	3	9	15	3	13	2	
Indiana	3	3	5	2	3	8	5	3	2	5	5	5	5	2	2	4	2	4	...	7	5	3	
Illinois	1	2	5	...	3	4	3	3	2	3	3	4	3	3	3	3	4	5	...	12	11	2	
Michigan	1	...	3	...	1	3	3	...	4	...	2	...	2	...	4	...	3	1	4	...	5	...	
Wisconsin	...	...	...	...	1	...	1	1	1	...	...	1	1	...	2	2	3	2	2	...	5	1	
Minnesota	...	...	...	...	...	...	2	...	...	2	1	1	2	...	1	...	1	...	1	1	2	...	
Iowa	...	...	...	...	1	...	...	...	1	...	...	...	1	...	6	...	5	...	2	3	5	...	
Missouri	...	2	5	...	...	3	...	5	1	2	1	1	1	1	5	...	6	1	2	3	8	...	
Kansas	...	...	...	...	...	...	1	...	...	...	...	...	...	...	1	...	1	...	1	...	1	...	
Nebraska	...	...	...	...	...	...	...	...	...	...	...	...	...	...	...	...	...	...	...	...	1	...	
Southern and southwestern States:																							
Virginia	3	17	13	1	13	...	...	8	1	1	3	...	...	1	...	...	...	...	...	...	5	1	
North Carolina	...	10	7	3	6	...	1	6	...	...	...	...	...	...	...	...	...	...	...	...	1	...	
South Carolina	...	5	7	...	4	...	...	...	...	...	...	...	...	...	...	...	...	...	...	...	1	...	
Georgia	1	7	5	2	4	...	...	...	...	...	...	...	...	...	...	...	...	...	...	...	...	...	
Alabama	...	4	7	...	7	...	...	...	...	...	...	...	...	...	...	...	...	...	...	...	1	4	
Mississippi	...	3	4	1	4	...	...	...	...	...	...	...	...	...	...	...	...	...	...	...	4	...	
Florida	...	...	1	...	1	...	...	...	...	...	...	...	...	...	...	...	...	...	...	...	1	...	
Louisiana	2	1	3	1	4	...	...	...	...	...	...	...	...	...	...	...	...	...	...	...	2	...	
Texas	...	...	2	...	2	...	...	...	...	...	...	...	...	...	...	...	...	...	...	...	3	1	
Arkansas	...	1	...	...	1	...	...	...	...	...	...	...	...	...	...	...	...	...	...	...	3	...	
Kentucky	4	8	4	6	7	2	4	1	...	7	...	6	...	5	...	4	...	2	1	6	5	1	
Tennessee	...	13	5	6	7	...	2	6	...	...	1	...	...	2	...	...	...	...	...	...	8	...	
Pacific States:																							
California	...	...	...	...	2	...	...	1	...	...	...	...	2	...	3	...	3	...	1	...	2	1	
Oregon	...	...	...	...	...	...	...	...	...	...	...	1	...	1	...	...	1	...	2	...	...	...	
Nevada	...	...	...	...	...	...	...	...	...	...	...	...	...	...	...	...	...	...	1	...	1	...	
Total	103	99	114	93	118	72	102	43	82	48	76	29	69	36	81	26	85	43	95	49	152	35	

The above table, excepting the last column, is from Mr. Edward Young's "Special Report on the Customs-Tariff Legislation of the United States," 1872.

K.—REVENUES OF THE GOVERNMENT

*For each fiscal year (ending June 30) from each source since 1859.**

	1860.	1861.	1862.	1863.	1864.	1865.
Customs	$53,187,511 87	$39,582,125 64	$49,056,397 62	$69,059,642 40	$102.316,152 99	$84,928,260 60
Internal revenue	-	-	-	37,640,787 95	109,741.134 10	209.464.215 25
Direct taxes	-	-	1,795.331 73	1,485.103 61	475.648 96	1,200,573 03
Public lands	1,778.557 71	870.658 54	152.203 77	167,617 17	588,333 29	996,553 31
Misc. sources	1,088,530 25	1,023.515 31	915,327 97	3,741,794 38	30,291,701 86	25,441,556 00
Totals	$56,054,599 83	$41,476,299 49	$51,919,261 09	$112,094,945 51	$243,412,971 20	$322,031,158 19
	1866.	**1867.**	**1868.**	**1869.**	**1870.**	**1871.**
Customs	$179,046.651 58	$176,417,810 88	$164,464,599 56	$180,048.426 63	$194.538,374 44	$206,270,408 05
Internal revenue	309.226.813 42	266,027.537 43	191,087,589 41	158,356,460 86	184,899,756 49	143,098,153 63
Direct taxes	1,974,754 12	4,200,233 70	1,788.145 85	765,685 16	229.102 88	580,355 37
Public lands	665.031 03	1,163,575 76	1,348,715 41	4,020,344 34	3.350.481 76	2,388,616 68
Misc. sources	29.036,314 23	15,037,522 15	17,745,403 59	13,997,338 65	12.912,118 30	22,093,541 21
Totals	$519.949,564 38	$462.846,679 92	$376,434,453 82	$357,188,255 64	$395,959,833 87	$374,431,104 94

Receipts since the formation of the Government, from March 4, 1789, to June 30, 1871: customs, $2,981,260,790 71; internal revenue, $1,631,820,461 33; direct taxes, $27,239,-672 42; public lands, $191,713,472 08; miscellaneous sources, $220,467,039 79—being $5,052,501,436 33.

[The Secretary of the Treasury reports, February, 1871, the aggregate proceeds of sales of abandoned and captured property covered into the Treasury as $26,709.268, ($19.204,211 being proceeds of cotton.) Of this there had been expended in purchase of products of insurrectionary States, $2,465,833; returned to claimants under awards of United States Court of Claims, $1.556.247; expenses of collection and disposition of such property, $75,000; leaving a balance of $22,612,188 in the Treasury.]

EXPENDITURES OF THE GOVERNMENT

For each fiscal year (ending June 30) since 1859.†

	1860.	1861.	1862.	1863.	1864.	1865.
Civil list	$6.148,655 41	$6,156,199 25	$5.939,009 29	$6,350.618 78	$8.059,177 23	$10.833,944 87
For'n intercourse	1,163,207 15	1,142,973 41	1,339.710 35	1.231,413 06	1.290,691 92	1.260,818 08
Navy Departm'nt	11.514.649 83	12.387,156 52	42,640.353 09	63.261,235 31	85.704,963 74	122,617.434 07
War Department	16,472,202 72	23.001,530 67	389,173.562 29	603.314.411 82	690.391 048 66	1,030.690,400 06
Pensions	1.100,802 32	1.034,599 73	852,170 47	1,078,513 36	4.985,473 90	16.347.621 34
Indians	2,991,121 54	2,865,481 17	2,327,948 37	3,152.032 70	2.629,975 97	5.059,360 71
Miscellaneous	20,666,115 74	16,028.115 03	14,107,142 95	15,616.350 53	18,222,347 72	30,894,620 15
Total	$60,056,754 71	$62,616,055 78	$456.379,896 81	$694,004,575 56	$811.283.679 14	$1,217.704.199 28
Int. on pub. debt	$3,144,120 94	$4,034,157 30	$13,190,344 84	$24,729,700 62	$53,685,421 69	$77,395,090 30
	1866.	**1867.**	**1868.**	**1869.**	**1870.**	**1871.**
Civil list	$12,287.828 55	$15.585,489 55	$11.950.156 58	$12.443.712 07	$19,031.283 56	$18,760,779 46
For'n intercourse	1.3[illegible]8.388 18	1.548,589 26	1.441.344 05	8,365 416 77	1.490,776 25	1.604,373 87
Navy Departm'nt	43.363 654 17	31,034.011 04	25.775.502 72	20,000.757 97	21,780,2[illegible]9 87	19,431.027 21
War Department	286.776.456 13	95.224,415 63	123.2[illegible]6.648 62	78.501,990 61	57.655.675 40	35.799 991 82
Pensions	15.615,287 75	20.936,551 71	23.782.386 78	28.476.621 78	28.340.202 17	34.443.894 88
Indians	3.349,015 93	4.642,531 77	4.100,682 32	7.042.923 06	3.407 938 15	7,426,997 44
Miscellaneous	27,705,666 96	33.976,144 91	39,618,367 04	35,664,932 69	32.715.401 75	40.116,762 90
Total	$390,436,297 67	$202.947,732 87	$229,915 088 11	$190,496.354 95	$164.421.507 15	$157.583,827 58
Int. on pub. debt	$133,070,513 39	$143,781,591 91	$140,424,045 71	$130,694.242 80	$129,235,498 00	$125,576,565 93

Expenditures since the formation of the Government, from March 4, 1789, to June 30,

---

* Premiums received on sales of gold are excluded from this table, and premiums paid in purchase of bonds are excluded from the table of expenditures. The former aggregated in the above twelve years $166,589,922 60; the latter, $46,278,907 43.

† In elucidation of the expenditures, the following data, taken from the official reports for the respective years, are appended:

Civil List.—The largest items in expenditures (cents omitted) under this head are: 1860—Congress, $2,619,520; executive, $1.826.804; judiciary, $1,181,667. 1861—Congress, $2.819,930; executive, $1,882,357; judiciary, $958,464. 1862—Congress, $2.516,852; executive, $1,953,410; judiciary, $958,464. 1863—Congress, $2,252,510; executive, $2,515,853; judiciary, $1,088,460. 1864—Congress, $2,937,192; executive, $3,433,031;

1871: civil list, $262,594,207 97; foreign intercourse, $101,417,652 81; Navy, $835,651,337 37; War, $3,962,688,814 43; pensions, $255,597,051 20; Indians, $180,043,570 77;

---

judiciary, $1,159,479. 1865—Congress, $3,585,171; executive. $4,993,328; judiciary $1,627,349. 1866—Congress, $4,034,533; executive, $5,921,050; judiciary, $1,627,349. 1867—Congress, $3,251,611; executive, $9,603,101; judiciary, $2,022,778. 1868—Congress, $3,609,135; executive, $6,757,402; judiciary, $723,378. 1869—Congress, $3,041,938; executive, $6 098,818; judiciary, $2,357,661. 1870—Congress, $6,218,221; executive, $9,297,053; judiciary, $2,610,342. 1871—Congress, $5,004,820; executive, $9,412,418; judiciary, $3,320,918.

Foreign Intercourse.—Leading items, (cents omitted:) 1860—Diplomatic salaries, $276,527; consuls salaries, $252,304; relief of American seamen, $212,023; British boundary commission, $150,000. 1861—Diplomatic, $2 5,340; consuls, $255,133; American seamen, $198,231; boundary commission, $110 000. 1862—Diplomatic, $326,950; consuls, $352,829; American seamen, $166,233; treaty awards, $146,387. 1863—Diplomatic, $305,982; consuls, $412,331; contingent expenses, $111,188; American seamen, $146,590. 1864—Diplomatic, $303,141; consuls, $390,480; contingent expenses, $108,288; American seamen, $153,196. 1865—Diplomatic, $295,378; consuls, $406,381; contingent expenses, $136,722; American seamen, $125,476. 1866—Diplomatic, $320,226; consuls, $361,976; contingent expenses, $108,239; American seamen, $120,161; treaty awards, $89,872. 1867—Diplomatic $318,035; consuls, $393,608; contingent expenses, $193,953; American seamen, $69,669; Paris exposition, $163,903; Scheldt dues, $111,168. 1868—Diplomatic, $291,300; consuls, $362,646; contingent expenses, $147,923; American seamen, $82,425; Paris exposition, $38,305; Brazil mail, $150,000. 1869—Diplomatic, $312,390; consuls, $405,671; contingent expenses, $3,521; American seamen, $58,147; Scheldt dues, $111,168; diplomatic dispatches per Atlantic cable, $60,000; purchase of Alaska, $7,200,000. 1870—Diplomatic, $473,745; consuls, $471,744; consulate expenses, &c., $124,721; contingent and miscellaneous, $229,558; American seamen, $54,171; Scheldt dues, $55,584. 1871—Diplomatic, $467,731; consuls, $414,329; consulate expenses, &c., $91,187; contingent and miscellaneous, $165,228; American seamen, $40,257; Scheldt dues, $66,584; Hudson Bay and Puget Sound Agricultural Company, $325,000.

Navy Department.—Leading items (cents omitted) from 1862 to the present time: 1862—Pay and subsistence, $11,246,091; increase, repairs, &c., $13,009,393; ordnance, &c., $5,148,294; temporary increase of Navy, $3,000,000; new vessels, $4,914,228. [Four powerful squadrons were blockading the entire Atlantic and Gulf coasts. The Navy had grown since March, 1861, from 47 vessels to 427 vessels, with an aggregate of 240,028 tons and 1,577 guns.] 1863—Pay of Navy, $12,495,516; Construction and Repair, $32,272,253; Ordnance, &c., $6,515,590; Provisions and Clothing, $4,143,764; Equipment and Recruiting, $3,071,395; Yards and Docks, &c., $3,434,929. [Blockade of 3,549 miles of coast, much of it double shore, and 5,615 miles of inland navigation patrolled by over 100 vessels. The Navy during this year comprised 588 vessels of 467,967 aggregate tonnage, and 4,443 guns.] 1864—Pay of Navy, $20,099,760; Provisions and Clothing, $5,316,805; prize-money, $2,229,872; Construction and Repair, $30,649,300; Steam Machinery, $9,101,998; Equipment and Recruiting, $7,185 171; Ordnance, $7,179,302; Yards and Docks, $2,405,328. [Number of vessels, 671; tons, 510,396; guns, 4,610.] 1865—Pay of Navy, $27,500,997; prize-money, $5,740,909; Provisions and Clothing, $10,588,882; Construction and Repairs, $34,411,258; Ordnance, $7,199,135; Equipment and Recruiting, $15,475,440; Yards and Docks, $4,046,706; Steam Engineering, $14,464,997. [This, the maximum year, there were 51,500 men in the naval service, besides 16,880 in the navy yards.] 1866—*Items:* Secretary's bureau, $10,831,260; Marine corps, $1,492,617; Yards and Docks, $4,777,868; Equipment and Recruiting, $5,103,661; Navigation, $351,061; Ordnance, $3,494,216; Construction and Repair, $8,675,216; Steam Engineering, $6,154,888; Provisions and Clothing, $2,244,775; Medicine and Surgery, $95,708; relief of sundry individuals, $102,841. [Navy reduced to 278 vessels, armed with 2,351 guns, 115 of which vessels, carrying 1,029 guns, being in commission and on active duty. In naval and Coast Survey service, 13,600 men.] 1867—Secretary's bureau, $10,545,843; Marine corps, $1,440,993; Yards and Docks, $3,828,198; Equipment and Recruiting, $3,577,311; Navigation, $551,981; Ordnance, $1,921,788; Construction and Repair, $4,545,509; Steam Engineering, $2,940,665; Provisions and Clothing, $1,440,642; medicine, &c., $88,099; relief of sundry individuals, $152,976. [238 vessels and 1,869 guns in Navy; in use, 103 vessels and 898 guns; of which 56 vessels and 507 guns for squadron service, the balance being apprentice ships, receiving ships, special and lake service, attached to Naval Academy, and tugs, coal-barges, &c., at yards and stations. In naval and Coast Survey service, 11,900 men. From close of rebellion to November 22, 1867, there had been sold 420 Navy vessels for the aggregate sum of $9,663,396.] 1868—Secretary's bureau, $8,949,477; Marine corps, $1,493,192; Yards and Docks, $2,389,780; Equipment and Recruiting, $2,492,754; Navigation, $553,355; Ordnance, $1,272,140; Construction and Repair, $2,123,191; Steam Engineering, $4,796,492; Provisions and Clothing, $1,527,781; medicine, &c., $134,605; reliefs, $42,732. [206 vessels, 1,743 guns. Of these, 81 vessels, 693 guns, in use; 42 vessels, carrying 411 guns, being in squadron service.] 1869—Pay of Navy, $8,525,952; Marine corps, $1,191,297; miscellaneous, $145,624; Yards and Docks, $1,267,557; Equipment and Recruiting, $1,588,901; Navigation, $670,687; Ordnance, $476,391; Construction and Repair, $3,338,548; Steam Engineering, $2,004,495; Provisions and Clothing, $551,312; medicine, &c., $209,825; relief of sundry individuals, $30,162. [March 9, 1869, 203 vessels, (151 wooden and 52 iron-clad,) 183,442 tons, 1,366 guns; 43 vessels, including store-ships, 40,052 tons, 356 guns, attached to fleets or returning therefrom, 6 mounting 36 guns in special service, 6 employed as receiving ships. Of the above 43 vessels not more than 18 were in condition for real service, some condemned as unseaworthy, and almost all required considerable repairs. Most of them steamers, without adequate sail-power. Since March 1, 80 vessels of every class repaired or altered or put in process of repairs; 46 vessels, with 426 guns, attached to fleets at close of year; torpedo corps established; seamen limited to 8,000; employed in the navy-yards March 1, 4,788 men; December 1, 12,092.] 1870—Navy pay and contingent, $6,502,676; Marine corps, $1,018,486; Yards and Docks, $2,388,645; Equipment and Recruiting, $2,228,339; Navigation, $493,765; Ordnance, $639,598; Construction and Repair, $5,333,069; Steam Engineering, $1,209,013; Provisions and Clothing, $1,570,607; medicine, &c., $389,813; reliefs, $15,213. [Navy consists of 181 vessels of 1,309 guns—52 being monitors, 99 steamers or sailing vessels with auxiliary steam power, and 30 sailing vessels; 45 of these vessels, mounting 465 guns, are attached to the fleets, 4 others, with 7 guns, in special service, and 10 others, with 143 guns, ready for sea.] 1871—Navy pay and contingent, $7,200,763; Marine corps, $838,791; Yards and Docks, $2,037,542; Equipment and Recruiting, $1,462,625; Navigation, $404,922; Ordnance, $574,331; Construction and Repair, $4,233,590; Steam Engineering, $1,082,864; Provisions and Clothing, $1,286,715; medicine, &c., $235,301; salvage, $15,000; reliefs, $58,578. [Navy comprises 179 vessels and 1,390 guns, exclusive of howitzers and small carronades; 29 are sailing ships, the remainder side-wheel steamers or sailing vessels with auxiliary screws; 53, with 601 guns in service, and 6 others nearly ready for sea.]

War Department.—Leading items, (cents omitted,) from commencement of rebellion: 1862—Pay Army proper, $13,329,477; transportation volunteers and regulars, $46,942,407; clothing for Army, $56,724,952; cavalry horses, $13,748,297; quartermaster's department, $42,875,758; arms, &c., $27,499,238; pay and subsistence volunteers and militia, $175,918,867; armories, ordnance, fortifications, gun-boats on western rivers, &c., $13,300,344. [In the ten military departments, 775,336 officers and privates. Before the year closed 90,000 men were in 151 general hospitals. There had been issued 1,926 field and siege cannon; 1,206 fortification cannon; 7,294 gun-carriages, caissons, mortar-beds, traveling forges and battery miscellaneous, $554,624,993 78—being $7,275,021,980 43. In payment of interest on public debt $1,172,404,352 10 had been expended.

[The foregoing figures are taken from the tabular statement contained on pages 18 and

---

wagons; 1,276,686 small-arms; 987,291 sets equipments and accouterments; 213,991,127 rounds of ammunition for artillery and small-arms; and 3,571 miles of land and submarine Army telegraph lines constructed.] 1863—Pay Army proper, $5,179,196; volunteers' pay, $201,270,432; subsistence volunteers and regulars, $69,151,724; quartermaster's department, $239,005,029; arms, ordnance, &c., $42,746,114; organizing volunteers, and bounty, $19,724,091; medical department, $11,896,796; forts, &c., $4,300,236. [Purchased and made 1,577 field, siege, and sea-coast cannon, with carriages, caissons, &c.; 1,082,841 muskets and rifles; 282,389 carbines and pistols, 1,251,995 cannon balls and shells, 48,719,862 pounds of lead and lead bullets; 1,435,046 cartridges for artillery, 259,022,216 cartridges for small-arms, 347,276,400 percussion caps, 3,925,369 friction primers, 5,764,768 pounds of gunpowder, 919,676 sets of accouterments for men, 94,639 sets equipments for cavalry horses, 3,281 sets artillery harness, each set for two horses. There were 182 general hospitals, with 84,472 beds, eleven per cent. of the Army sick and 2¼ per cent. wounded; 1,755 miles of land and submarine Army telegraph lines constructed, and 250,000 square miles of once rebel territory reconquered. From January 1 to November 1, 1863, 83,242 volunteers were recruited, most of them for three years. At the latter date the draft had brought into service 50,000 men.] 1864—Pay of regulars, $4,360,213; pay of volunteers, $204,047,917; subsistence of volunteers and regulars, $95,230,415; quartermaster's department, $309,078,752; arms and ordnance, $35,228,748; forts and arsenals, $5,732,639; medical department, $11,044,288; bounties, $12,258,847; collecting and drilling volunteers, $5,688,180; draft and substitute fund, $5,302,641. [There were supplied 1,141 pieces of ordnance, 1,896 artillery carriages and caissons, 455,910 small-arms, 502,044 sets accoutrements and harness, 1,913,753 prosectiles for cannon, 7,624,685 pounds bullets and lead, 464,549 rounds of artillery ammunition, 152,067 jets of horse equipments, 112,087,553 cartridges for small-arms, 7,544,044 pounds gunpowder; 1,000 miles military railroads in operation; 3,000 miles military telegraph lines constructed this year; 500 horses and mules per day destroyed and 500 supplied; 190 general hospitals with 120,520 beds; sick and wounded less than sixteen per cent. of the whole Army; 489,826 recruits and 136,300 furloughed veterans forwarded to the field, against 131,814 troops mustered out and discharged. February 1, call for 500,000 volunteers; March 14, call for 200,000.] 1865—Pay department, $351,573,554; Surgeon General, $19,584,634; Commissary General, $147,035,231; Provost Marshal General, $10,676,267; quartermaster's department, $446,585,474; ordnance department, $46,774,854; engineers' department, $6,183,587. [May 1, national military force, 1,000,516 men. During June, July, and August, $270,000,000 paid to 800,000 disbanded volunteers who had been mustered out, the reduction to continue until Army reduced to 50,000 men.] 1866—Pay department, $205,934,240; commissary department, $7,430,606; quartermaster's department, $49,856,986; ordnance department, $9,932,402; engineers, $2,651,903; Provost Marshal General, $6,779,114; Secretary's office, (Army expenditures,) $3,594,375. [By June 30, 1866, 1,010,670 volunteers had been paid and mustered out since the close of the rebellion, and by November 1, 1,023,021; leaving in service 11,043 volunteers, white and colored. To the Army proper and Military Academy, $10,431,004 were disbursed, and to volunteers, $248,943,313. A fleet of 590 ocean transports in service July 1, 1865, at daily expense of $82,400, was reduced before June 30, 1866, to fifty-three vessels, costing $3,000 per diem. Of 262 vessels employed in inland transportation, at an expense of $3,193,533, none remained in service June 30. The military roads operated during the war at total expenditure of $45,422,719, to the extent of 2,630½ miles, (with 433 engines and 6,605 cars,) had all been transferred to loyal local companies or Boards of Public Works. The military telegraph, 15,389 miles, constructed and operated at a cost of $3,787,037, discontinued and material sold. Of 64,438 patients in hospitals at beginning of the year, but ninety-seven remained under treatment at its close. Among the sales of material, &c., this year were: 207,000 horses and mules for $15,269,075; 4,400 barracks, hospitals, and buildings, $447,873; damaged clothing, $902,770; river transports, steamers, barges, &c., $1,152,895; railroad equipments, cash sales, $3,466,739; credit sales, $7,442,073.] 1867—Pay department, $30,700,776; commissary department, $10,331,174; quartermaster's department, $35,438,367; ordnance department, $4,690,677; engineer department, $3,233,414; Inspector General, $105,658; Adjutant General, $1,495,788; Secretary's office, (Army expenditures,) $8,514,008; relief of sundry individuals and miscellaneous, $756,466. [The habit of indulging at every headquarters ambulances and mounted orderlies broken up. Bureaus of rebel archives and of exchange of prisoners, &c., transferred to Adjutant General's office; large numbers of Government clerks and officers discharged. Great quantities surplus and useless quartermaster's stores sold and issued to destitute; unserviceable animals sold for $268,572; 1,000 temporary buildings, $112,000; 16,086 horses and mules purchased. The $1,000,000 sheltering fund for troops on the plains expended.] 1868—Pay department, $57,347,589; commissary department, $7,254,195; quartermaster's department, $28,953,113; ordnance department, $1,702,959; engineer department, $5,334,897; Inspector General, $174,368; Adjutant General, $6,741,777; Surgeon General, $1,028,146; Secretary's office, (Army expenditures,) $14,308,659; reliefs and miscellaneous, $400,941. [Strength of Army, 48,081; further reductions contemplated. In national cemeteries 316,233 remains of soldiers have been collected to this time, at a total cost of $2,700,000. Disbursed for reconstruction purposes, $2,261,415; additional bounties, $23,649,157—total to this time being $54,000,000.] 1869—Pay department, $17,919,175; commissary department, $7,916,795; quartermaster's department, $20,436,304; ordnance department, $1,259,683; engineer department, $4,457,802; Inspector General, (Military Academy,) $127,880; Adjutant General, $459,819; Surgeon General, $373,584; refunding to States expenses incurred in raising volunteers, $2,315,823; reimbursing several States for military expenses, $523,628; support of Bureau of Refugees, Freedmen, &c., $2,508,431; Oregon and Washington volunteers in 1856 and 1857, $34,846; suppressing Indian hostilities in Minnesota in 1862, $106,845; Colorado for militia in 1864, $55,238; bounties under act July 28, 1866, $19,729,350; horses and other property lost in military service, $232,364; Secretary's office, (Army expenditures,) $36,852; relief of sundry individuals, $7,561. [Army maximum 52,234 enlisted men—34,822 actual service—distributed in twelve departments and three districts, each under command of a general officer, the departments being formed into four military divisions, commanded by the four generals next in rank to the General of the Army. Number of civilians hired by quartermaster's department reduced since February, 1869, from 10,000 persons to 4,000.] 1870—Pay department, $6,146,981; commissary department, $3,483,668; quartermaster's department, $12,746,330; ordnance department, $778,490; forts and fortifications, $1,287,167; improvement rivers and harbors, $4,834,277; Military Academy, $178,956; medical department, $173,294; Freedmen Bureau, $463,210; National Asylum for Disabled Volunteers, $296,287; bounties, $10,656,300; reimbursing States for raising volunteers, $2,379,246; horses, &c., lost in service, $228,836; Army contingencies, $257,404; Washington and Oregon volunteers in 1855 and 1856, $42,131; payments under relief acts, $110,887; capture of Jefferson Davis, $1,611; bronze statue of General Scott, $15,000. [Army consists of 34,870 enlisted men and 2,488 officers, stationed in 42 States and Territories, at 203 organized military posts. In the 73 national cemeteries 333,000 soldiers lie buried. One million six hundred thousand dollars' worth of supplies furnished to Indians on the upper Missouri and in the Indian territory. Storm signal corps organized and at work. More than 1,340,000 stands of arms of obsolete pattern and unfit for use have been sold since close of war. Since commencement of this fiscal year sales of surplus arms and ordnance to citizens of the United States to the amount of $5,600,000.] 1871—Pay department, $6,571,159; commissary department,

19 of the Report on Finances for 1871, the amount of the civil list and of the foreign intercourse being separated from the other miscellaneous items and stated for the respective years as found in reports for those years.]

NOTE.—The above figures do not represent the operations of the Post Office Department, the expenses of which are paid from its own receipts, and the deficiency only is a charge upon the Treasury. From a letter of Postmaster General Creswell (Mis. Doc., Senate, No.

$4,361,725; quartermaster department, $20,892,572; forts, &c., $556,788; rivers and harbors, $3,668,060; Military Academy, $94,367; medical department, $756,586; Freedmen's Bureau, $1,449,694; capture of Jefferson Davis, $80,783; National Asylum for Disabled Volunteers, $801,088; bounties, $17,106,504; reimbursing States for raising volunteers, $1,291,303; expenditures under reconstruction acts, $381,384; horses, &c., lost, $201,072; Washington and Oregon volunteers in 1855 and 1856, $41,908; Army contingencies, $255,446; payments under relief acts, $91,747. [Army comprises 30,000 enlisted men. Up to this date, during the fiscal year, there has been paid into the Treasury, as realized from the sale of arms and from other sources, $21,766,403. Pay of soldiers reduced from $16 to $13 per month. Large quantities of supplies forwarded from the Army depots to the relief of the Chicago and Wisconsin sufferers. Sales of military clothing, &c., $1,875,728.]

PENSIONS, (cents omitted:) 1860—Military, $956,828; naval, $135,898; relief of sundry individuals, $135,304; Army pensioners, 10,345; Navy pensioners, 939. [Up to this time the total amount paid for pensions since the organization of this Government was $88,813,898.] 1861—Military, $876,493; Navy, $161,401; Army pensioners, 9,752; Navy pensioners, 957. 1862—Military, $731,693; Navy, $118,388; Army pensioners, 9,233; Navy pensioners, 996. 1863—Military, $908,232; Navy, $167,597; Army pensioners, 13,659; Navy pensioners, 1,132. 1864—Military, $4,799,669; Navy, $167,443; Army pensioners, 49,630; Navy pensioners, 1,505. 1865—Military, $9,130,165; Navy, $152,443; Army pensioners, 84,130; Navy pensioners, 1,856. 1866—Military, $12,905,847; Navy, $2,699,504; Army pensioners, 124,509; Navy pensioners, 2,213. 1867—Military, $19,016,263; Navy, $1,920,288; Army pensioners, 153,093; Navy pensioners, 2,381. 1868—Military, $23,433,651; Navy, $358,735; Army pensioners, 167,025; Navy pensioners, 2,618. 1869—Military, $27,968,361; Navy, $508,260; Army pensioners, 185,125; Navy pensioners, 2,838. 1870—Military, $27,332,220; Navy, $448,590; Army pensioners, 195,739; Navy pensioners, 2,947. [Investigation and revision of pension-rolls resulted in reduction of expenditure in face of increase of pension-list.] 1871—Military, $32,495,996; Navy, $581,387; Army pensioners, 204,445; Navy pensioners, 3,050. [The increase over last year in amount is chiefly accounted for by operation of law of July 8, 1870, making pensions payable quarterly, under which the whole amount of pensions accruing between March 4, 1870, and June 4, 1871, fifteen months, became due and payable during the fiscal year.]

INDIANS.—The expenditures in the main are for money, goods, and provisions. 1860—Peace generally prevailed. 1861—Southern tribes in rebellion; Indians generally perturbed. 1862—Loyal refugee Indians by thousands fed and collected in Kansas; loyal Indians in arms; policy recently adopted of confining Indians to reservations, and as they become accustomed to the idea of individual property, allotting to them lands in severalty; massacre of whites in Minnesota. 1863—Actual hostilities in some localities; largely increased number of refugees subsisted by the Government. 1864—Large additional expense in returning portion of refugees to their old homes, supplying and subsisting them. 1865—Several treaties made. 1866—Numerous treaties made and violated by Indians, whose numbers in the United States are estimated at 300,000 in 200 tribes, in charge of 14 superintendents and some 70 agents. 1867—Peace treaties with several previously hostile tribes; considerable subsistence furnished; hostilities in some quarters continue. 1868—At peace with most of the tribes, but an Indian war impending; several treaties made; the question of transferring the Indian Bureau to the War Department agitated. 1869—The war policy ends and the peace policy commences; the Indians are supplied with means for engaging in agricultural and mechanical pursuits, and for their education and moral training; the $2,000,000 appropriated in 1868 by act of Congress for peace commission in process of disbursement. 1870—Quiet generally prevails; Red Cloud, Spotted Tail, and other chiefs visit Washington. 1871—Good order and peace generally maintained; various commissions at work; including Alaska, 350,000 Indians in the United States.

MISCELLANEOUS.—Leading items, (cents omitted:) 1860—Light-House establishment, $973,539; refunding excess of deposits for unascertained duties, $814,826; collecting customs revenue, $3,324,4[illegible]0; deficiencies in revenue of Post Office Department, $8,196,009; court-houses, post offices, &c., $119,307; expenses of eighth census, $42,000; surveys of public lands, $587,659. 1861—Light-House, $896,332; refunding excess of deposits, &c., $764,575; collecting customs, $2,834,764; deficiency in Post Office, $4,064,234; court-houses, &c., $445,310; eighth census, $911,614; surveys of public lands, $313,989. 1862—Light-House, $664,175; refunding excess of deposits, $1,642,940; collecting customs, $3,284,724; deficiency in Post Office, $2,932,596; court-houses, $22,454; eighth census, $557,386; surveys of public lands, $264,370. 1863—Light-House, $873,085; refunding excess of deposits, $2,262,770; revenue-cutter service, $68,749; collecting customs, $3,238,936; deficiency in Post Office, $249,313; court-houses, $83,740; eighth census, $129,977; surveys of public lands, $185,600; commissions to effect national loan, $1,782,456. 1864—Light-House, $930,761; refunding excess of deposits, $2,597,891; revenue-cutter service, $377,666; collecting customs, $4,146,584; court-houses, &c., $39,842; eighth census, $59,950; surveys of public lands, $192,103; national loan commissions, $2,040,127. 1865—Light-House, $875,825; refunding excess of deposits, $2,283,313; revenue-cutter service, $393,187; collecting customs, $5,437,490; court-houses, &c., $68,758; eighth census, $28,979; surveys of public lands, $62,780; national loan commissions, $6,588,641; purchase of gold coin, $5,072,900. [The expenses of collecting the internal revenue taxes from September 1, 1862, when the internal revenue act took effect, to June 30, 1865, were $6,133,114.] 1866—Light-House, $1,378,858; refunding excess of deposits, $2,920,171; revenue-cutters, $743,182; collecting customs, $5,356,457; assessing and collecting internal revenue, $5,800,752; court-houses, &c., $87,225; eighth census, $8,210; surveys of public lands, $145,241; national loan commissions, $2,909,036. 1867—Light-House, $2,194,651; refunding excess of deposits, $2,472,928; revenue-cutter service, $128,357; collecting customs, $5,738,971; assessing and collecting internal revenue, $7,892,050; deficiency in Post Office, $2,550,000; court-houses, &c., $628,365; eighth census, $16,435; surveys of public lands, $729,898; national loan commissions, $1,786,568. 1868—Light-House, $2,613,738; refunding excess of deposits, $2,279,377; collecting customs, $7,615,675; assessing and collecting internal revenue, $8,730,357; court-houses, &c., $733,397; eighth census, $26,701; surveys of public lands, $2,017,822; mail service, $4,053,191; expenses of United States courts, $1,768,358. 1869—Light-House, $1,926,635; refunding excess of deposits, $2,293,950; revenue-cutter service, $1,204,841; collecting customs, $5,376,738; assessing and collecting internal revenue, $7,200,114; deficiency in Post Office, $2,524,604; surveys of public lands, $429,000; national loan commissions, $1,851,313. 1870—Light-House, $2,598,300; refunding excess of deposits, $1,835,375; revenue-cutter service, $1,138,393; collecting customs, $6,237,137; assessing and collecting internal revenue, $7,234,531; deficiency in Post Office, $2,762,500; court-houses, &c., $1,293,230; eighth and ninth censuses, $24,464; surveys of public lands, $641,497. 1871—Light-House, $2,712,638; refunding excess of deposits, $1,787,266; revenue-cutter service, $1,251,934; collecting customs, $6,550,672; assessing and collecting internal revenue, $7,075,137; deficiency in Post Office, $3,700,000; court-houses, &c., $1,523,879; eighth and ninth censuses, $1,955,111; surveys of public lands, $554,940.

134, second session Forty-Second Congress) the following figures are compiled, (cents omitted:)

	1868.	1869.	1870.	1871.
Ordinary postal revenues	$16,292,600	$18,344,510	$19,772,220	$20,037,045
Total expenditures	22,730,592	23,698,131	23,998,837	24,390,104
Deficiency paid from Treasury	$6,437,992	$5,353,621	$4,226,617	$4,353,059

Comparing the postal revenues, expenditures, and deficiency of 1868 with 1871, the percentage of increase in revenue is 23; the percentage of increase in expenditures is $7\frac{3}{10}$; and the percentage of decrease in deficiency is 32½.

GOLD FLUCTUATIONS.*

Period.	Highest.									Lowest.								
	1862	1863	1864	1865	1866	1867	1868	1869	1870	1862	1863	1864	1865	1866	1867	1868	1869	1870
First quarter	105	172½	169¾	234½	144⅝	140½	144	136¾	123⅛	101⅛	134	151	148⅛	125	132	133¼	130⅛	110¼
Second quarter	109½	159	251	160	167¾	141⅞	141¾	144¾	115⅝	101½	140½	166	128⅝	125	132⅝	137¾	131⅜	110⅞
Third quarter	124	145	285	146½	155⅝	146⅜	150	162½	122¾	109	122½	185	138	143¼	138⅛	140¼	130¾	111⅛
Fourth quarter	137	156¾	260	149	154⅜	145⅝	140½	131¾	114¼	122	140⅜	189	144	131¼	133	132⅝	119½	110

Mean annual average (computed from the highest and lowest *monthly* quotations) during the above period: 1862, 113⅞; 1863, 146⅛; 1864, 203¾; 1865, 158¼; 1866, 141½; 1867, 138⅝; 1868, 139¾; 1869, 134⅞; 1870, 114⅞.

D.—MANUFACTURES.†

Total value, gross production, at the censuses of 1850, 1860, *and* 1870.

States, &c.	1870.‡	1860.	1850.	States, &c.	1870.‡	1860.	1850.
Alabama	$13,220,655	$10,538,566	$4,528,876	Missouri	$206,687,354	$41,782,731	$24,324,418
Arizona	185,410	-	-	Montana	2,494,511	-	-
Arkansas	7,699,676	2,880,576	537,908	Nebraska	5,892,512	607,328	-
California	73,116,756	68,253,328	12,862,522	Nevada	15,870,539	-	-
Colorado	2,797,820	-	-	N. Hampshire	71,678,013	37,586,453	23,164,503
Connecticut	160,974,574	81,924,555	47,114,585	New Jersey	169,969,895	76,306,104	39,851,256
Dakota,	178,570	-	-	New Mexico	1,489,868	1,249,123	249,010
Delaware	18,343,818	9,892,902	4,649,296	New York	787,776,218	378,870,939	237,597,249
Dist. of Col'a	9,294,489	5,412,102	2,690,258	N. Carolina	20,701,532	16,678,698	9,111,050
Florida	4,707,903	2,447,969	668,335	Ohio	280,969,151	121,691,148	62,692,279
Georgia	32,994,267	16,925,564	7,082,075	Oregon	6,901,412	2,976,761	2,236,640
Idaho	1,047,624	-	-	Pennsylvania	715,545,302	290,121,188	155,044,910
Illinois	209,392,657	57,580,886	6,534,272	Rhode Island	110,469,650	40,711,296	22,117,688
Indiana	109,120,684	42,803,469	8,725,423	S. Carolina	13,438,226	8,615,195	7,045,477
Iowa	46,782,497	13,971,325	3,551,783	Tennessee	38,587,953	17,987,225	9,725,608
Kansas	11,798,353	4,357,408	-	Texas	15,369,731	6,577,202	1,168,538
Kentucky	54,149,043	37,931,240	21,710,212	Utah	2,351,011	900,153	291,220
Louisiana	45,737,346	15,587,473	6,779,417	Vermont	31,976,899	14,637,807	8,570,920
Maine	79,822,005	38,193,254	24,661,057	Virginia	33,496,077	50,652,124	29,602,507
Maryland	75,924,104	41,735,157	33,043,892	West Virginia	24,169,051		
Massachus'ts	551,805,067	255,545,922	157,743,994	Washington	3,045,802	1,406,921	-
Michigan	118,776,853	32,658,356	11,169,002	Wisconsin	78,606,308	27,849,467	9,293,068
Minnesota	23,541,325	3,373,172	58,300	Wyoming	765,424	-	-
Mississippi	11,263,102	6,590,687	2,912,068				
Aggregate§	-	-	-	-	$4,305,932,032	$1,885,861,676	$1,019,106,616

* Showing the variations in value of United States currency.

† These returns are official, of date June 10, 1872, but are subject to revision and change.

‡ The census of 1870 does not include the products of mines and fisheries under the head of manufactures, as had previously been the case. In 1860 the products of mines and fisheries amounted to about ninety million dollars.

§ Increase: 1860 over 1850, 85 per cent.; 1870 over 1860, 128 per cent.; 1870 over 1850, 323 per cent.

H.—CUSTOMS SCHEDULE,

Showing the changes made therein by the acts of May 1 and June 6, 1872. (See General Notes at foot of page.)

Articles enumerated.	Acts of 1870.	Act of 1872.
Absinthe	pf. gal. $2.	pf. gal $2.
Acetates; pyroligneate of ammonia	℔. 70 c.	℔ 25 c.
of baryta	℔ 40 c.	℔ 25 c.
of copper	....	℔ 10 c.
of iron, strontia, or zinc	℔ 50 c.	℔ 25 c.
of lead, (sugar of lead)	℔ 20 c.	℔ 5 & 10 c.
of magnesia and soda	℔ 50 c.	℔ 50 & 25 c.
of lime	25 p. ct.	25 p. ct.
of potash	℔ 75 c.	℔ 25 c.
Acids, acetic, acetous, and pyrol., 1864:		
spec. grav.* above 1.040	℔ 80 c.	℔ 30 c.
not above 1.040*	℔ 25 c.	℔ 5 c.
benzoic	10 p. ct.	10 p. ct.
boracic	℔ 5c.	free.
chromic	15 p. ct.	15 p. ct.
citric	℔ 10 c.	℔ 10 c.
gallic	℔ $1 50.	℔ $1.
nitric, (yellow and white)	10 p. ct.	10 p. ct.
sulphuric, (oil of vitriol)†	℔ 1 c.	free.
tannic	℔ $2.	℔ $1.
tartaric	℔ 20 c.	℔ 15 c.
for med. use and art's n. o. p	10 p. ct.	10 p. ct.
Acorn coffee, & other subs. for coffee, exc. chic	℔ 3 c.	℔ 3 c.
Alabaster and spar ornaments	30 p. ct.	30 p. ct.
Albata, unmanuf'td or in sheets	35 p. ct.	10 p. ct.
Alcohol, amylic, (fusel oil)	pf. gal. $2.	pf. gal. $2.
Ale, beer, and porter, in bottles	gal. 35 c.	gal. 35 c.
otherwise	gal. 20 c.	gal. 20 c.
Alkaline silicates	℔ ½ c.	℔ ½ c.
Almonds	℔ 6 c.	℔ 6 c.
shelled	℔ 10 c.	℔ 10 c.
paste	50 p. ct.	50 p. ct.
Alum, (pat. sub., sulph. and cake)	100 ℔s 60 c.	100 ℔s 60 c.
Alumina, sulphate of	100 ℔s 60 c.	100 ℔s 60 c.
Amber beads	50 p. ct.	free.
Ammonia, refined, sulph. and carb	20 p. ct.	20 p. ct.
muriate of, and sal	10 p. ct.	10 p. ct.
Anchovies, pres. in oil, or otherwise	50 p. ct.	50 p. ct.
Animals living‡	20 p. ct.	20 p. ct.

GENERAL NOTES.—1. The column for 1870 is condensed from Young's Custom-House Statistics and Heyl's Rates of Duties, &c.; that of 1872 is made up direct from the law, with the coöperation of the office of the Commissioner of Customs. 2. Goods in bonded warehouse may be withdrawn under present tariff. 3. A drawback is allowed on exported fire-arms, scales, balances, shovels, spades, axes, hatchets, hammers, plows, cultivators, mowing-machines, and reapers with stocks or handles of American wood, where the imported raw material predominates. 4. Materials for ship-building, imported in bond, are free under certain conditions. 5. Materials for repairing American vessels in foreign trade, free. 6. Several articles of mixed composition are marked the same in 1872 as in 1870 column, because it is impossible to judge whether or not the ten per cent. reduction applies to them. That will be determined in each case by the material predominating. 7. R. means reduction. 8. N. o. p. means not otherwise provided for.

* Specific gravity changed to 1.047. (1872.)

† Fuming per pound, 1 cent. (1872.)

‡ Exempt from duty: teams of animals, including harness and tackle, actually owned by immigrants to the United States and in actual use for purposes of such immigration; all animals brought into the United States temporarily and for a period not exceeding six months, for the purposes of exhibition or competition. (Act of July 1870.)

Articles enumerated.	Acts of 1870.	Act of 1872.
Anodyne, (Hoffman's)	℔ 50c.	℔ 50 c.
Antimony, crude, or regulus of	10 p. ct.	}
Aquafortis	10 p. ct.	} free.
Argols, refined, (cream tartar)	℔ 10 c.	}
Arrack	pf. gal. $2.	pf. gal $2.
Arms, fire, n. o. p	35 p. ct.	} 10 p. ct. R.
side, n. o. p., (see swords, &c.)	35 p. ct.	}
Arrow-root	30 p. ct.	30 p. ct.
Articles worn by men, wom, or ch., of what'v'r mat., n. o. p. made by hand	35 p. ct.	35 p. ct.
Asbestos, manufactured,	25 p. ct.	25 p. ct.
Asphaltum	25 p. ct.	25 p. ct.
Assafœtida	20 p. ct.	20 p. ct.
Asses' skins	30 p. ct.	free.
Bacon	℔ 2 c.	℔ 2 c.
Bagatelle balls, ivory or bone	50 p. ct.	10 p. ct. R.
Balsam copaiva	℔ 20 c.	free.
medicinal, n. o. p	30 p. ct.	30 p. ct.
Peruvian	℔ 50 c.	} free.
Tolu	℔ 30 c.	}
Bananas	10 p. ct.	10 p. ct.
Bark, all medicinal, n. o. p.	20 p. ct.	free.
Barley	bush. 15 c.	bush. 15 c.
pearl or hulled	℔ 1 c.	℔ 1 c.
Barytes	℔ ⅛ c.	℔ ⅛ c.
nitrate of	20 p. ct.	20 p. ct.
sulphate of, crude or refined	℔ ⅛ c.	℔ ⅛ c.
Baskets, and other articles of grass, osier, palm-leaf, &c., n. o. p	35 p. ct.	35 p. ct.
Bay-rum water, dist'd f'm the leaf	gal. $1 50.	gal. $1.
Beads and bead ornaments	50 p. ct.	50 per ct.
Beans, tonqua	20 p. ct.	} free.
vanilla	℔ $3.	}
Beef	℔ 1 c.	℔ 1 c.
Beeswax	20 p. ct.	20 p. ct.
Benzoates	30 p. ct.	30 p. ct.
Berries, n. o. p	10 p. ct.	10 p. ct.
Bezoar stones	10 p. ct.	free.
Birds	20 p. ct.*	20 p. ct.*
Bituminous substances, crude, n. o. p.	20 p. ct.	20 p. ct.
Blacking, of all descript's	30 p. ct.	30 p. ct.
Black lead, (plumbago)	ton $10.	free.
Bladders, manufactures of	30 p. ct.	30 p. ct.
Bone black and ivory drop	25 p. ct.	}
Bone dice, draught, chessmen, chess balls, and bagatelle balls	50 p. ct.	} 10 p. ct. R.
manufactures of, n. o. p	35 p. ct.	}
Bonnets, hats, &c., of straw, chip, &c	40 p. ct.	}
Books, blank	25 p. ct.	}
Books, printed, bound or not, periodicals, &c	25 p. ct.	25 p. ct.
Borate of lime	℔ 5 c.	}
Borax, crude or tincal	℔ 5 c.	} free.
refined	℔ 10 c.	}
Boxes, of paper, and other fancy	35 p. ct.	} 10 p. ct. R.
Braids, and other tr'm'gs of grass, straw, &c	30 p. ct.	}
Brandy, (1870, and other spirit from grain, &c	pf. gal. $2.	pf. gal, $2.
Brass, (copper not component of chief value, 1869,) bars or pigs	15 p. ct.	}
old, fit for remanuf. only	15 p. ct.	} 10 p. ct. R.
manufactures of, n. o. p	35 p. ct.	}
Brazil paste	10 p. ct.	free.

* Free under decision of the United States Supreme Court.

Articles enumerated.	Acts of 1870.	Act of 1872.
Bricks, fire	20 p. ct.	20 p. ct.
Brimstone, rolls or ref'd	ton $10.	ton $10.
Bristles	℔ 15 c.	℔ 15 c.
Britannia ware	35 p. ct.	
Bronze, and all m. of n. o. p.	35 p. ct.	10 p.ct. R.
if copper chief value, 1869.	45 p. ct.	
liquor	10 p. ct.	10 p. ct.
metal in leaf	10 p. ct.	10 p.ct. R.
powder	20 p. ct.	
Brooms, of all kinds	35 p. ct.	35 p. ct.
Brushes, of all kinds	40 p. ct.	40 p. ct.
Bulbous roots	30 p. ct.	30 p. ct.
Burgundy pitch	20 p. ct.	free.
Burning fluid	gal. 50 c.	gal. 50 c.
Burrstones, manufact'd or bound up into millstones	20 p. ct.	20 p. ct.
Butter	℔ 4 c.	℔ 4 c.
Buttons and button-molds.	30 p. ct.	30 p. ct.
Cabinets of coins, medals, antiquities	℔ 3 c.	℔ 3 c.
Cables, Manilla, untarred	℔ 2½ c.	℔ 2½ c.
all other, untarred	℔ 3½ c.	℔ 3½ c.
Cachous, aromatic	50 p. ct.	50 p. ct.
Calomel	30 p. ct.	30 p. ct.
Cameos, set in gold or other metal	20 p. ct.	25 p. ct.
not set	10 p. ct.	10 p. ct.
Camphor, crude	℔ 30 c.	free.
refined	℔ 40 c.	℔ 5 c.
Candles and tapers, adamantine	℔ 5 c.	℔ 5 c.
paraffine	℔ 8 c.	℔ 8 c.
spermaceti	℔ 8 c.	℔ 8 c.
stearine	℔ 5 c.	℔ 5 c.
wax, pure, mixed	℔ 8 c.	℔ 8 c.
tallow	℔ 2½ c.	℔ 2½ c.
all other, n. o. p.	℔ 2½ c.	℔ 2½ c.
Candy, not colored	℔ 10 c.	℔ 10 c.
Canes for walking, finished or not.	35 p. ct.	free.*
Canvas, for sails†	30 p. ct.	10 p. ct. R.
Capers	35 p. ct.	35 p. ct.
Caps, made on frames of any material worn, &c., n. o. p	35 p. ct.	35 p. ct.
of fur	35 p. ct.	35 p. ct.
of silk. (See man'fac's of cotton, wool, &c.)	60 p. ct.	60 p. ct.
Card-cases	35 p. ct.	35 p. ct.
Carbolic liquid	3 rates.	10 p. ct.
Cards, play, cost'g not over 25 cents per pack	pack, 25 c.	
over 25 cents per pack	pack, 35 c.	
Carpets, n. o. p.	40 p. ct.	
Aubusson, Axminster, Med'n, or whole, value less than $1 25 p. yard	50 p. ct.	
Brussels, (Jacq'd m,) value less than $1 25 p. yard	sq. yd. 44 c. and 35 p. ct.	
Saxony, Wilton, and Tournay, (1864, by Jacq'd m,) value over $1 25 per yard	sq. yd. 70 c. and 35 p. ct.	10 p.ct. R.
pat't vel't, Tournay vel't, tapestry velvet, value over $1 25 per yard	sq. yd. 40 c. and 35 p. ct.	
Brussels, printed on warp, &c	sq. yd. 50 c.	
tapestry, on warp, &c	sq. yd. 28 c. and 35 p. ct.	
treble ingrain, three-ply, worsted chain Venetian.	sq. yd. 17 c. and 35 p. ct.	
yarn, Venetian, two-ply, ingrain	sq. yd., 12c. & 35 p. c.	
of cotton	40 p. ct.	
of flax	40 p. ct.	40 p. ct.
of hemp or jute	sq. yd., 8c.	sq. yd., 8c.
of wool, also mix'd, n. o. p.	40 p. ct.	10 p. ct. R.

* Canes, finished, thirty-five per cent.
† If other than cotton, thirty per cent. (1872.)

Articles enumerated.	Acts of 1870.	Act of 1872.
Carpets, druggets, bockings, p'd, col'd, or otherwise	sq. yd., 25c.	10 p. ct. R.
[Hassocks, rugs, screens, mats, &c., pay duty as carpeting, similarly.]		
Carriages, and parts of.	35 p. ct.	35 p. ct.
Casks, barrels, &c., n. o. p.	35 p. ct.	30 p. ct.
Cassia	℔ 10c.	℔ 10c.
buds and ground	℔ 20c.	℔ 20c.
Cassia vera	℔ 10c.	℔ 10c.
Castor beans, bush. of 50 ℔s.	bush. 60c.	bush. 60c.
Catsup	40 p. ct.	40 p. ct.
Cement, Roman	20 p. ct.	20 p. ct.
Chalk, billiard	50 p. ct.	50 p. ct.
French and red	20 p. ct.	20 p. ct.
white	ton, $10	ton $10.
all n. o. p.	25 p. ct.	25 p. ct.
Charts and maps	25 p. ct.	25 p. ct.
Cheese	℔ 4c.	℔ 4c.
Chessmen, chess balls, bone or ivory	50 p. ct.	10 p. ct. R.
Chiccory, root	℔ 4c.	℔ 1c.
ground, burnt, or prep'rd	℔ 5c.	℔ 1c.
Chinaware, plain	45 p. ct.	45 p. ct,
ornamental	50 p. ct.	50 p. ct.
Chloroform	℔ $1.	℔ $1
Chocolate	℔ 7c.	℔ 5c.
Chronometers, box, ships, or parts	10 p. ct.	10 p. ct.
Cinnamon	℔ 20c.	℔ 20c.
Clapboards, pine	20 & 35 p. ct.	1,000, $2.
spruce	20 & 35 p. ct.	1,000, $1.50.
Clay, pipe and fire, unwr. or prepared	ton $5.	10 p. ct. R.
Cliff stone	ton $10.	ton $10.
Clocks, and parts thereof	35 p. ct.	35 p. ct.
Cloth, water proof, n. o. p.	45 p. ct.	
Clothing, ready-m., and w'g app., ev. desc., wholly or in part wool, worst'd, hair, alpaca goat, &c., (except knit goods)	℔ 50c. and 40 p. ct.	10 p.ct.R.
ready-m. silk, or if s. shall be mat'l of chief val	60 p. ct.	
all other, n. o. p	35 p. ct.	
Cloves	℔ 5c.	℔ 5c.
Clove stems	℔ 3c.	℔ 3c.
Coach furniture	35 p. ct.	*
Coal, bituminous and shale.	ton $1.25.	ton 75c.
all other, n. o. p	ton 40c.	ton 40c.
culm of, and coke	25 p. ct.	ton† 40c.
Cobalt, and oxide of	20 p. ct.	20 p. ct.
ores	10 p. ct.	free.
Cocoa	℔ 2c.	
prepared or manuf'd	℔ 5c.	℔ 2c.
leaves and shells	℔ 1c.	
nuts	10 p. ct.	free.
Coffee	℔ 3c.	
sub. for, excluding chic'ry	℔ 3c.	℔ 3c.
Coins, copper	45 p. ct.	45 p. ct.
Coir	ton $15.	free.
yarn	℔ 1½c.	
Collodion, fluid	℔ $1	℔ $1
Cologne water, and other perf. of wh. alco. f'ms prin. ingred't	gal. $3 and 50 p. ct.	gal. $3 and 50 p. ct.
Colors, analine	℔ 50c. and 35 p. ct.	℔ 50c. and 35 p. ct.
barytes, comb's with ac'd or water	℔ 3c.	℔ 3c.
Berlin blue	25 p. ct.	25 p. ct.
blanc fixé	℔ 3c.	℔ 3c.
carmine lake, dry or liq'd.	35 p. ct.	35 p. ct.
Chinese blue	25 p. ct.	25 p. ct.
chrome yel., ch'te of lead	25 p. ct.	25 p. ct.
Dutch pink	25 p. ct.	25 p. ct.
enameled white	℔ 3c.	℔ 3c.
Frankfort black	25 p. ct.	25 p. ct.
Fr'ch green, dry or moist.	30 p. ct.	30 p. ct.
Indian red	25 p. ct.	25 p. ct.
ivory black	25 p. ct.	25 p. ct.
mineral blue, dry or moist	30 p. ct.	30 p. ct.

* According to material of which composed.
† "Slack coal or culm." Coke not changed.

Articles enumerated.	Acts of 1870.	Act of 1872.
Colors, green, dry or moist.	30 p. ct.	30 p. ct.
painters, n. o. p.	25 p. ct.	25 p. ct.
Paris green, dry or moist.	30 p. ct.	30 p. ct.
white, dry...	℔ 1c.	℔ 1c.
ground in oil	℔ 1½c.	℔ 1½c.
Pr'n blue, dry or moist...	30 p. ct.	30 p. ct.
rose pink	25 p. ct.	25 p. ct.
satin white	℔ 3c.	℔ 3c.
Sp'sh brown, dry or in oil.	25 p. ct.	25 p. ct.
ultramarine	℔ 6c.	℔ 6c.
umber	100 ℔s 50c.	100 ℔s 50c.
Vandyke brown	20 p. ct.	20 p. ct.
Venetian red, dry or in oil	25 p. ct.	25 p. ct.
vermillion, dry or in oil...	25 p. ct.	25 p. ct.
wash blue	25 p. ct.	25 p. ct.
water colors, moist, used in man. p'r-h'ng'gs, &c.	25 p. ct.	25 p. ct.
n. o. p.	35 p. ct.	35 p. ct.
wood-lake, dry or in oil...	25 p. ct.	25 p. ct.
Coloring for brandy, (containing no spirits)	50 p. ct.	50 p. ct.
Combs of all kinds, for the hair	35 p. ct.	10 p. ct. R.
Comfits, preserved in sugar, brandy or molasses, n. o. p.	35 p. ct.	35 p. ct.
Compositions of glass or paste, set	30 p. ct.	30 p. ct.
Composition, scagliola, and other tops for tables, &c.	35 p. ct.	35 p. ct.
Compounds or preparations of which distilled sp'ts are comp't part of chief value	same as spirits.	same as spirits.
Confectionery, col'd, value 30c or less per ℔	℔ 15c.	℔ 15c.
above 30c. 1 ℔., or by box, &c	50 p. ct.	50 p. ct.
Copper ore	℔, fine, 3c.	℔, fine, 3c.
old, fit for remanuf'e only	℔ 4c.	
pigs, bars, ingots, or plates	℔ 5c.	
braziers' sheets,	45 p. ct.	
other sheets	45 p. ct.	
bolts, nails, spikes, rods...	45 p. ct.	
bottoms, (still bottoms)...	45 p. ct.	
manf't's, n. o. p. of cop. or in wh. cop. is com't p't of ch'f val	45 p. ct.	10 p.ct.R.
regulus, and black or coarse	℔ 4c.	
sheathing, 48 in. long, 14 in. wide, weight 14 to 34 ozs., pr. sq. ft	45 p. ct.	
sulphate of	℔ 5c.	℔ 5c.
Copperas	℔ ½c.	℔ ½c.
Coral, cut or manufact'd...	30 p. ct.	30 p. ct.
Cordage, Manila, untarred.	℔ 2½c.	℔ 2½c.
all other untarred	℔ 3½c.	℔ 3½c.
all tarred	℔ 3c.	℔ 3c.
Cordials	gal. $2.	gal. $2.
Corks	50 p. ct.	30 p. ct.
Cork bark, manufactured...	50 p. ct.	30 p. ct.
Corn, Indian or maize	bush. 10c.	bush. 10c.
meal of	10 p. ct.	10 p. ct.
Corsets, at $6 pr. doz. or less.	doz. $2.	doz. $2.
over $6 per doz.	35 p. ct.	35 p. ct.
Corset, crin., &c., wire, (see steel)	℔ 9c. and 10 p. ct.	℔ 9c. and 10 p. ct.
Cosmetics	50 p. ct.	50 p. ct.
Cotton, on spools, not over 100 yards	doz. 6c. and 30 p. ct.	
over 100 yards	each add'tl 100 yds, doz. 6c. & 35 p. ct.	
thread, &c., unwound, value 40c. pr. ℔. or less.	℔ 10c. and 20 p. ct.	10 p.ct.R.
ditto, val. 40 to 60c. pr. ℔.	℔ 20c. and 20 p. ct.	
ditto, value over 60c., not over 80c	℔ 30c. and 20 p. ct.	
ditto, value over 80c.	℔ 40c. and 20 p. ct.	

Articles enumerated.	Acts of 1870. Unbleached. Cts.	Bleached. Cts.	Col'd, printed, painted, or stained. Cts.	Act of 1872.
Cotton—				
tissues, (ex. of jeans, &c., see next page,) weighing over 5 oz. pr. square y'd not over 100 threads per square inch, warp and filling (Square yard.)	5	5½	5½ & 10 p. c	
ditto, finer and lighter over 100, not over 140	5	5½	5½ & 20 p. c	
ditto, over 140, not over 200 threads	5	5½	5½ & 20 p. c	
ditto, over 200 threads.	5	5½	5½ & 20 p. c	
jeans, denims, drillings, bed tickings, ginghams, plaids, cottonades, pant stuffs, &c., weighing over 5 ounces per square yard, and not exceeding in value 16 cents per square yard, not over one hundred threads per square inch, warp and filling	6	6½	6½ & 10 p. c	
over 100, not over 140 per sq. in., warp and filling	6	6½	6½ & 15 p. c	10 p.ct.R.
over 140, not over 200 per sq. in., warp and filling	6	6½	6½ & 15 p. c	
over 200 threads per sq. in., warp and f'g	7	7½	7½ & 15 p. c	
goods not included in foregoing schedules	35 p. ct.			
value 7 cents or less	℔ 2 c.			
over 10 cents per sq. yd.	℔ 3 c.			
bobbinet	35 p. ct.			
braids	35 p. ct.			
caps, hose, &c	35 p. ct.			
carpets and carpetings	40 p. ct.			
cords, gimps, &c	35 p. ct.			
drawers, shirts	35 p. ct.			
embroidered, &c	35 p. ct.			
hat bodies	35 p. ct.			
lace, insertings, &c	35 p. ct.			
lace, colored	35 p. ct.			
velvets.	35 p. ct.			
manufactures n. o. p.	35 p. ct.			
Court-plaster	35 p. ct.			35 p. ct.
Cowhage or cowitch-down	20 p. ct.			free.
Crayons of all kinds	30 p. ct.			30 p. ct.
Cream of tartar	℔ 10 c.			℔ 10 c.
Crockery ware, white, glazed, &c	40 p. ct.			40 p. ct.
Crocus colcottra	25 p. ct.			25 p. ct.
Cubebs	℔ 10 c.			free.
Currants, Zante, and other	℔ 2½ c.			℔ 1 c.
Cutlery of all kinds n. o. p.	35 p. ct.			10 p. ct. R.
Dandelion root, raw or prepared	℔ 3 c.			℔ 3 c.
Dates, green, ripe, or dried	℔ 2 c.			℔ 1 c.
Dentifrices	50 p. ct.			50 p. ct.
Diamonds, glaziers', set or not	10 p. ct.			free.
other, not set	10 p. ct.			10 p. ct.
set	25 p. ct.			25 p. ct.
Dice, ivory or bone	50 p. ct.			10 p. ct. R.
Dolls of all kinds	35 p. ct.			35 p. ct.
Downs for beds or bedding	30 p. ct.			free.
Draughts, ivory or bone...	50 p. ct.			
Druggets	sq. yd. 25 c. & 35 p. ct.			10 p.ct. R.
Drugs, medicine, &c., crude, n. o. p.	20 p. ct.			20 p. ct.

Articles enumerated.	Acts of 1870.	Act of 1872.
Dutch and bronze metal in leaf	10 p. ct.	10 p. ct. R.
Dye-woods, decoctions of	10 p. ct.	10 p. ct.
Dyes for the hair	50 p. ct.	50 p. ct.
Earthenware, brown or common	25 p. ct.	25 p. ct.
glazed, edged, &c	40 p. ct.	40 p. ct.
Embroideries, gold, silver, &c	35 p. ct.	35 p. ct.
Emery, manufactured, ground, &c	lb 1 c.	lb 2 c.
ore	free.	ton $6.
Engravings, bound or unbound	25 p. ct.	25 p. ct.
Envelopes, paper	35 p. ct.	10 p. ct. R.
Ergot	lb 20 c.	free.
Essences, or essential oils, n. o. p.	50 p. ct.	50 p. ct.
Ethers of all kinds and prep's. fl'd	lb $1.	lb $1.
Ethers, fruit, essences or oils, &c	lb $2 50.	lb $2 50.
Explosive substances, val. not over 20 cts. per lb	lb 6 c. and 20 p. ct.	lb 6 c. and 20 p. ct.
value over 20 cents per lb.	lb 10 c. and 20 p. ct.	lb 10 c. and 20 p. ct.
Extracts, perfumes, &c., hair, mouth, or skin	50 p. ct.	50 p. ct.
Extracts, ethereal, fluid	lb $1.	lb $1.
of annatto	20 p. ct.	free.
of dye-woods, n. o. p.	10 p. ct.	10 p. ct.
of indigo	10 p. ct.	10 p. ct.
of logwood	10 p. ct.	10 p. ct.
of madder, (garancine)	10 p. ct.	free.
of opium	100 p. ct.	100 p. ct.
of safflower	20 p. ct.	free.
Eyelets of every description	mille 6 c.	10 p. ct. R.
Fans, all, n. o. p.	35 p. ct.	35 p. ct.
palm-leaf	each 1 c.	free.
Feather beds	20 p. ct.	20 p. ct.
Feathers, artificial, n. o. p.	50 p. ct.	50 p. ct.
for beds or bedding	30 p. ct.	free.
ostrich, vulture, crude	25 p. ct.	25 p. ct.
ostrich, vulture, dressed	50 p. ct.	50 p. ct.
Feldspar	20 p. ct.	20 p. ct.
Fig blue	25 p. ct.	25 p. ct.
Figs	lb 5 c.	lb 2½ c.
Filberts	lb 3 c.	lb 3 c.
Files, &c., not over 10 inches long	lb 10 c. and 30 p. ct.	10 p. ct. R.
over 10 inches long	lb 6 c. and 30 p. ct.	
Finishing powder	20 p. ct.	
Fire-crackers, box of forty packs	box $1.	box $1.
Fire-screens, all kinds	35 p. ct.	35 p. ct.
Firewood	20 p. ct.	free.
Fish, all foreign caught, not in barrels and n. o. p.	lb ½ c.	lb ½ c.
all, in oil, n. o. p.	30 p. ct.	30 p. ct.
all pickled, in barrels, except herrings, mackerel, and salmon	bbl. $1 50.	bbl. $1 50.
glue, (isinglass)	30 p. ct.	free.
skins, raw	20 p. ct.	
Flats, for ornamenting hats, &c	30 p. ct.	30 p. ct.
Flax* straw	ton $5.	ton $5.
tow of	ton $10.	ton $10.
not hackled or dressed	ton $20.	ton $20.
hackled or dressed	ton $40.	ton $40.
manufactures of, n. o. p.	40 p. ct.	40 p. ct.
ditto, value 30 c. or less per sq. yd.	35 p. ct.	35 p. ct.
ditto, value above 30 cents, &c	40 p. ct.	40 p. ct.
yarns, &c., v. 24 cents or less per lb	30 p. ct.	30 p. ct.
ditto, &c., value above 24 cents per lb	35 p. ct.	35 p. ct.
thread, or linen thread, &c	40 p. ct.	40 p. ct.
Flints	10 p. ct.	free.
Floor cloth, of whatever material, n. o. p.	(See Oil-	Cloth.)

*See Jute.

Articles enumerated.	Acts of 1870.	Act of 1872.
Flour, of sago	lb 1½ c.	free.
Flowers, all medicinal, n. o. p.*	20 p. ct.	
artificial and ornamental	50 p. ct.	50 p. ct.
Frames or sticks for umbrellas	35 p. ct.	35 p. ct.
for looking-glasses	30 p. ct.	30 p. ct.
Fruit, green, ripe, or dried, n. o. p.	10 p. ct.	10 p. ct.
juice, and fruits preserved in	25 p. ct.	25 p. ct.
pres'v'd otherwise, n. o. p.	35 p. ct.	35 p. ct.
Fulminates, or fulminating powder	30 p. ct.	30 p. ct.
Fullers' earth	ton $3.	10 p. ct. R.
Furniture, rough	35 p. ct.	30 p. ct.
finished	35 p. ct.	35 p. ct.
Furniture springs, wire spiral	lb 2 c. and 15 p. ct.	10 p. ct. R.
Fur, all manufactures of	35 p. ct.	35 p. ct.
Furs, hatters', not on the skin	20 p. ct.	20 p. ct.
on the skin, dressed	20 p. ct.	20 p. ct.
Game, fish and poultry	35 p. ct.	35 p. ct.
Gas retorts	25 p. ct.	25 p. ct.
Gelatine and all similar preparations	35 p. ct.	35 p. ct.
Gems, not set	10 p. ct.	10 p. ct.
set	25 p. ct.	25 p. ct.
German silver, unmanufactured	35 p. ct.	10 p. ct. R.
manufactures of	40 p. ct.	
Gilt and plated ware	35 p. ct.	
Ginger, essence	50 p. ct.	35 p. ct.
Ginger, ground	lb 5 c.	lb 3 c.
preserved or pickled	50 p. ct.	35 p. ct.
root, (dried or green)	lb 2 c.	free.
Glass, man'fac's of, n. o. p.	40 p. ct.	10 p. ct. R.
plain, molded, and pressed	35 p. ct.	
cut, engraved, col'd, &c	40 p. ct.	
bottles or jars with preserves	40 p. ct.	
crystals for watches	40 p. ct.	
plates or disks, unwrought	10 p. ct.	
porcelain or Bohemian glass	40 p. ct.	

	R'gh plates, fluted, &c.	Unp. cyl., cr., & com. w.	Pol., cyl., & crown	Cast or pol., not silv'd.	Cast or polished, silvered, &c.
	Cts.	Cts.	Cts.	Cts.	Cts.
window,† not above 10 by 15 inches	¾	1½	2½	3	4
above 10 by 15, not above 16 by 24	1	2	4	5	6
above 16 by 24, not above 24 by 30	1½	2½	6	8	10
above 24 by 30, not above 24 by 60, (1862)	2	3	20	25	35
above 24 by 60 inches	-	-	40	50	60

Articles enumerated.	Acts of 1870.	Act of 1872.
Gloves, kid or leather, all	50 p. ct.	50 p. ct.
Glue	20 p. ct.	20 p. ct.
Glycerine	30 p. ct.	30 p. ct.
Gold, articles of, n. o. p.	40 p. ct.	10 p. ct. R.‡
leaf, (pack'e of 500 leaves)	P'k'e $1 50.	10 p. ct. R.
and silver epaulets, &c	35 p. ct.	25 p. ct.
size	20 p. ct.	free.
Goldbeaters' skins	10 p. ct.	free.
Grapes	20 p. ct.	20 p. ct.
Grass cloth	30 p. ct.	30 p. ct.
manufactures, n. o. p.	35 p. ct.	35 p. ct.

* Flowers, leaves, plants, roots, barks, and seeds for medicinal purposes in a crude state, not otherwise provided, free, 1872.

†The rates upon window-glass—rough plate, fluted, rolled, unpolished cylinder, crown, and common window; polished cylinder and crown; cast or polished, not silvered; and cast or polished, silvered or looking-glass frames; are the same as required by act of June 30, 1864, as above, less ten per cent. by act of June, 1872.

‡ If not jewelry or articles of ornament.

Articles enumerated.	Acts of 1870.	Act of 1872.
Grease, all not specified	10 p. ct.	10 p. ct.
Grindstones, rough or unfi'd	ton $1 50.	ton $1 50.
finished	ton $2.	ton $2.
Gums, sub. or burnt starch	10 p. ct.	10 p. ct.
Gunny-bags and cloth, value not over 10 cts. per sq. yd	℔ 3 c.	} 40 p. ct.*
bleached and cleaned, v. over 10 cts. per sq. yd	℔ 4 c.	}
Gunpowder, valued at 20 cents or less per pound	℔ 6 c. and 20 p. ct.	℔ 6 c. and 20 p. ct.
valued at above 20 c. p. lb	℔ 10 c. and 20 p. ct.	℔ 10 c. and 20 p. ct.
Gun-wads, sporting, of all descriptions	35 p. ct.	} 10 p.ct. R.
Gutta-percha, manufac'd	40 p. ct.	}
Hair, all kinds, cleaned but not manufactured	10 p. ct.	}
curled, for matt's & beds	20 p. ct.	} free.
goats, unm'd, (not Ang'a)	(See Wool.)	}
hogs	℔ 1 c.	}
human, uncl'd, not d'wn	30 p. ct.†	30 p. ct.
cleaned or prepared	30 p. ct.	30 p. ct.
all manufac's of, n. o. p.	40 p. ct.	40 p. ct.
bonnets, hats, and hoods	40 p. ct.	}
bracelets, bd's, ch'ns, &c.	35 p. ct.	}
braids, plaits, flats, laces, &c., and all manufactures of, n. o. p	30 p. ct.	} ‡
Hair-cloth, (hair seating, 1870,) 18 in. wide or over	sq. yd. 40 c.	}
less than 18 inches wide	sq. yd. 30 c.	}
crinoline cloth	30 p. ct.	}
Hair dyes, oils, perfumeries, &c	50 p. ct.	50 p. ct.
pencils	35 p. ct.	35 p. ct.
pins, of iron wire	50 p. ct.	10 p. ct. R.
Hams	℔ 2 c.	℔ 2 c.
Harness furniture, n. o. p	35 p. ct.	35 p. ct.
Hassocks, mats, &c., n. o. p.	45 p. ct.	45 p. ct.
Hats, of straw, or other mat., not otherwise provided	40 p. ct.	10 p. ct. R.
of fur	35 p. ct.	35 p. ct.
of silk	60 p. ct.	60 p. ct.
of wool, value not exceeding 40 cents per pound	℔ 20 c. and 35 p. ct.	}
above 40 cents, not exceeding 60 c. per lb	℔ 30 c. and 35 p. ct.	}
above 60 cents, not exceeding 80 c. per lb	℔ 40 c. and 35 p. ct.	} 10 p.ct.R.
above 80 c. per pound	℔ 50 c. and 35 p. ct.	}
Hatters' plush, silk and cotton, (cotton chief mat'l)	25 p. ct.	}
Hemp, Manila, and other like substances	ton $25.	ton $25.
Indian	20 p. ct.	free.
sunn	ton $15.	ton $15.
tow of, (codilla)	ton $10.	ton $10.
yarn of, untarred	℔ 5 c.	℔ 5 c.
manufactures, n. o. p., (see Linen)	30 p. ct.	30 p. ct.
Herrings, pickled or salted	bbls. $1.	bbls. $1,
Hides, raw, &c., skins, all kinds	10 p. ct.	free.
Hollow ware, glazed or tinned	℔ 3½ c.	℔ 3½ c.
Honey	gal. 20 c.	gal. 20 c.
Hops	℔ 5 c.	℔ 5 c.
Horn, manufact's of, n. o. p.	35 p; ct.	10 p. ct. R.
Household furnit'e, n. o. p.	35 p. ct.	35 p. ct.
Hubs, for wheels, &c.	20 p. ct.	20 p. ct.
India-rubber, manufactures of, mixed	50 p. ct.	}
braces, &c., n. o. p	35 p. ct.	} 10 p.ct.R.
articles wholly of, n. o. p.	20 p. ct.	}
Indigo, carmined	20 p. ct.	20 p. ct.
Ink, printers', ink powder	35 p. ct.	35 p. ct.
Instruments, musical, of all kinds	30 p. ct.	30 p. ct.
philosophical	40 p. ct.	10 p. ct. R.

*See Jute. †Resolution January 10, 1871.

‡Doubtful whether the 10 per cent. reduction applies to these. If not, then same rates by acts of 1872 as before.

Articles enumerated.	Acts of 1870.	Act of 1872.
Insulators, except glass	....	25 p. ct.
Iodine, resublimed	℔ 75 c.	℔ 75 c.
salts of	15 p. ct.	15 p. ct.
Iron, Moisic	....	ton $15.
old scrap, cast	ton $6.	}
wrought	ton $8.	}
pig	ton $7.	}
bars, rolled or ham'd, includ'g flats, various sizes	℔ 1 c.	}
ditto, other sizes	℔ 1½ c.	}
other descriptions, ditto, not otherwise provided	℔ 1¼ c.	}
bars, r. r., n. ab. 6 in. h	100 ℔s 70 c.	}
band, hoop, &c., cer. size	℔ 1¼ c.	}
ditto, certain other size	℔ 1½ c.	}
ditto, other size	℔ 1¾ c.	}
boiler, and other plate	ton $25.	}
not less 3-16 in. thick	℔ 1½ c.	}
rods, n'l or spike, s. r. or h	℔ 1½ c.	}
sheet, smooth or pol'd, all	℔ 3 c.	}
galvanized or coated	℔ 2½ c.	} 10 p.ct.R.
other, of certain size	℔ 1¼ c.	}
certain other size	℔ 1½ c,	}
other size	℔ 1¾ c.	}
squares, m'k'd on one s'de	℔ 3 c. and 30 p. ct.	}
all other, of iron or st'l	℔ 6 c. and 30 p. ct.	}
anchors, and p'ts thereof	℔ 2¼ c.	}
andirons, cast	℔ 1½ c.	}
anvils	℔ 2½ c.	}
axles, or parts thereof	℔ 2½ c.	}
blacksmiths' ham'ers, &c.	℔ 2½ c.	}
bolts, wrought	℔ 2½ c.	}
butts, cast	℔ 2½ c.	}
castings, n. o. p.	30 p. ct.	}
cables or chains, or p'ts of	℔ 2½ c.	}
chains, &c., of wire, &c., one size	℔ 2½ c,	} Same rat's as m'l of w. com'd (See Iron Wire.) paid 1870.
ditto, another size	℔ 2½ c.	}
ditto, another size	℔ 3 c.	}
ditto, another size	35 per ct.	}
hatters' irons	℔ 1½ c.	}
hinges, cast	℔ 2½ c.	}
wrought	℔ 2½ c.	}
hollow ware, gl'zd or tin'd	℔ 3½ c.	}
malleable, in castings	℔ 2½ c.	}
mill-irons and cranks	℔ 2 c.	}
nails and spikes, cut	℔ 1½ c.	}
board n'ls, wr'ght, (spikes and rivets)	℔ 2½ c.	}
nails, horseshoe	℔ 5 c.	}
nuts, &c., w., r'dy p'nch'd	℔ 2 c.	}
pipe, c'st, for st'm, gas, &c.	℔ 1½ c.	}
railroad chairs, wrought	℔ 2 c.	}
sad-irons	℔ 1½ c.	}
screws, bed	℔ 2½ c.	}
wood-screws, over 2 inches	℔ 8 c.	}
under 2 inches	℔ 11 c.	}
wash'd, plat'd, all other	35 p. ct.	}
stoves and st'e-plates, c'st	℔ 1½ c.	} 10 p.ct.R.
tailors' irons	℔ 1½ c.	}
tacks, &c., not exceeding 16 oz. per mille	mille 2½ c.	}
exceeding 16 oz. p. mille	℔ 3 c.	}
taggers' iron	30 per ct.	}
tire, for locomotives	℔ 3 c.	}
tubes, flues, &c., wrought	℔ 3½ c.	}
vessels, cast iron, n. o. p.	℔ 1½ c.	}
wire, bright, &c., one size	℔ 2 c. and 15 p. ct.	}
another size	℔ 3½ c. and 15 p. ct.	}
another size	℔ 4 c. and 15 p. ct.	}
cover'd, cott'n, silk, &c., (additional)	℔ 5 c.	}
wrought, for ships, loco's w'ght 25 pounds or more	℔ 2 c.	}
all manufact's of, n. o. p.	35 p. ct.	10 p. ct. R.*
liquor	10 p. ct.	10 p. ct.
sulphate of	℔ ½ c.	℔ ½ c.
Isinglass, (see Fish Glue)	30 p. ct.	free.
Istle, or Tampico fiber	℔ 1 c.	free.
Italian cloth, w'le or p't w'l, &c., v. n. ex. 20 c. p. s. y	sq. yd. 6 c. & 35 p. ct.	} 10 p.ct. R.

*Excepting cotton machinery.

Articles enumerated.	Acts of 1870.	Act of 1872.
Italian cloth, value above 20 cts. per sq're yard..	sq. yd. 8 c. & 40 p. ct.	
all weighing 4 ounces or over, per square yard	℔ 50 c. and 35 p. ct.	
Ivory, all manufac's, n. o. p.	35 p. ct.	10 p.ct.R.
Japan'd coach and harness furn. and h'dw'e, n. o. p.	35 p. ct.	
leather of all kinds	35 p. ct.	
ware, n. o. p.	40 p. ct.	
Jellies, of all kinds	50 p. ct.	50 p. ct.
Jet and man'fac's of, &c.	35 p. ct.	35 p. ct.
Jewelry, imitations, and all other	25 p. ct.	25 p. ct.
Juice, lemon and lime	10 p. ct.	10 p. ct.
other fruit	25 p. ct.	25 p. ct.
Jute,* unmanufactured	ton, $15.	ton, $15.
butts	ton, $6.	free.
all manufactures, n. o. p.	30 p. ct.	30 p. ct.
wool. fab., w. or p. jute, 30c. or less	35 p. ct.	35 p. ct.
over 30 cts. p. sq. yd.	40 p. ct.	40 p. ct.
yarns of	25 p. ct.	25 p. ct.
Kaoline	ton, $5.	10 p. ct. R.
Kermes, mineral	10 p. ct.	10 p. ct.
Kirschwasser	pf. gal. $2.	pf. gal. $2.
Laces and insertings, th'd	30 p. ct.	30 p. ct.
Lampblack	20 p. ct.	20 p. ct.
Lard	℔ 2 c.	℔ 2 c.
Lastings	10 p. ct.	10 p. ct.
Laths	20 p. ct.	1,000 15 c.
Lead, ore, and dross	℔ 1½ c.	℔ 1½ c.
old scrap, fit for rem. only	℔ 1½ c.	
bars or pigs	℔ 2 c.	
pipes	℔ 2¾ c.	10 p. ct. R.
shot	℔ 2¾ c.	
sheets	℔ 2¾ c.	
pencils, in wood	gross 50 c., and 30 p. c.	gross 50 c., and 30 p. c.
not in wood	gross, $1.	gross $1.
nitrate of	℔ 3 c.	℔ 3 c.
sugar of	℔ 20 c.	℔ 20 c.
manufactures of, n. o. p.	35 p. ct.	10 p. ct. R.
white and red, dry or	℔ 3 c.	℔ 3 c.
Leather, japanned, patent, or enameled	35 p. ct.	20 p. ct.
tanned, all, n. o. p.	25 p. ct.	20 p. ct.
sole and bend	35 p. ct.	15 p. ct.
calfskin, upper	30 p. ct.	25 p. ct.
all manufactures, n. o. p.	35 p. ct.	10 p. ct. R.
Leaves, n. o. p.	20 p. ct.	free.
Lemons	20 p. ct.	20 p. ct.
Licorice, juice	℔ 5 c.	10 p.ct.R.
paste and in rolls	℔ 10 c.	
Lime	10 p. ct.	10 p. ct.
white	℔ 3 c.	℔ 3 c.
chloride of, (bleaching powder)	100 ℔s 30 c.	100 ℔s. 30 c.
Limes	10 p. ct.	10 p. ct.
Linen, &c., v. 30c. or less p. sq. yd	30 p. ct.	30 p. ct.
over 30c. p. sq. yard	35 p. ct.	35 p. ct.
another class, 30c. or less	35 p. ct.	35 p. ct.
the same, ov. 30c. p. s. y.	40 p. ct.	40 p. ct.
yarns, carp't, one class	30 p. ct.	30 p. ct.
another class	35 p. ct.	35 p. ct.
Liqueurs	pf. gal $2.	pf. gal. $2.
Litharge, dry or in oil	℔ 3c.	℔ 3 c.
Lumber, saw'd boards, &c., heml'k, &c	20 p. ct.	1,000 ft. $1.
pl'd, &c., for each side	35 p. ct.	1,000 ft. ad'l 50 c.
p. one side, tong'd and grooved	35 p. ct.	1,000 ft. ad'l

*"On all burlaps, and like manufactures of flax, jute, or hemp, or of which flax, jute, or hemp shall be the component material of chief value, excepting such as may be suitable for bagging for cotton, thirty per cent. *ad valorem;* on all oil-cloth foundations or floor-cloth canvas, made of flax, jute, or hemp, or of which flax, jute, or hemp shall be the component material of chief value, forty per cent. *ad valorem;* on all bags, cotton bags and bagging, and all other like manufactures, not herein otherwise provided for, except bagging for cotton, composed wholly or in part of flax, hemp, jute, gunny-cloth, gunny-bags, or other material, forty per cent. *ad valorem.*"—(Act, June, 1872.)

Articles enumerated.	Acts of 1870.	Act of 1872.
Lumber, p. two sides, tong'd and grooved	35 p. ct.	$1. 1,000 ft. ad'l $1 50.
sawed, n. o. p.	20 p. ct.	1,000 ft. $2.
Macaroni	35 p. ct.	free.
Mace	℔ 25 c.	℔ 25 c.
Machinery, steam towage and steam plows	35 p. ct.	free for 2 years.
Mackerel	bbl. $2.	bbl. $2.
Magnesia, carbonate of	℔ 6 c.	℔ 6 c.
calcined	℔ 12 c.	℔ 12 c.
Malt	20 p. ct.	20 p. ct.
Manganese	10 p. ct.	free.
Mangoes	10 p. ct.	10 p. ct.
Maps, (see charts and maps.)		
Marble, various kinds, in block, &c., (unmanufactured)	cub. ft. $1, & 25 p. ct.	cub. ft. $1, & 25 p. ct.
veined, and all other, n. o. p.	cub. f. 50 c., & 20 p. ct.	cub. f. 50c., & 20 p. ct.
all sawed, dressed, polis'd slabs not ab. 2 in. thick	sq. ft. 25 c., & 30 p. ct.	sq. f. 25 c., & 30 p. ct.
ditto, more than 2 in. in thickness	ea. ad'tl in. p. s. ft. 10c.	each ad'l in p. s. f. 10c.
ditto, exceeding 6 inches	as marble in block.	as marble in block.
all other manf's, n. o. p.	50 p. ct.	50 p. ct.
Marrow	10 p. ct.	free.
Mats, cocoa-nut	30 p. ct.	30 p. ct.
Matting, grass, &c.	30 p. ct.	30 p. ct.
cocoa, or coir	25 p. ct.	25 p. ct.
Matting, &c., not exclusively vegetable	45 p. ct.	45 p. ct.
Meats, prepared	35 p. ct.	35 p. ct.
Medicinal barks, &c., n. o. p.	20 p. ct.	free.
preparations, n. o. p.	40 p. ct.	40 p. ct.
preparations, patent	50 p. ct.	50 p. ct.
Melada, concentrated	℔ 1¼ c.	℔ 1¼ c.
Mercurial preparations, n. o. p.	20 p. ct.	20 p. ct.
Metal, Bessemer, &c., process	as steel.	
manufactures of, n. o. p.	35 p. ct.	
silver-plated	35 p. ct.	10 p.ct. R.
Metals, unmanufactured, n. o. p.	20 p. ct.	
Milk, pres'v'd or con'd	20 p. ct.	20 p. ct.
Mineral and bitu's subs., crude, n. o. p.	20 p. ct.	20 p. ct.
Mineral or med. water, per quart	ea. 3 c., & 25 p. ct.	free.*
otherwise than in bot'ls	30 p. ct.	
Molasses	gal. 5 c.	gal. 5 c.
concentrated	℔ 1¼ c.	℔ 1¼ c.
Morocco skins	25 p. ct.	10 p. ct.
Morphia, and all salts of	oz. $1.	oz. $1.
Mosaics, real and imitation, not set	10 p. ct.	10 p. ct.
set in metal	25 p. ct.	25 p. ct.
Moss, for beds or mat's	20 p. ct.	free.
Mungo	℔ 12c.	℔ 12 c.
Murexide	25 p. ct.	free.
Music, printed with lines	20 p. ct.	20 p. ct.
Musical instruments	30 p. ct.	30 p. ct.
Muskets	35 p. ct.	10 p. ct. R.
Mustard, ground, in bulk	℔ 12 c.	℔ 10 c.
inclosed in glass or tin	℔ 16 c.	℔ 14 c.
Natron	as carbonates of soda.	as carbonates of soda.
Needles, sewing, darning, knitting	25 p. ct.	25 p. ct.
for knitting or sew. mach.	mille $1, & 35 p. ct.	mille $1, & 35 p. ct.
Nickel	℔ 30 c.	10 p.ct.R.
oxide, and alloy of	℔ 20 c.	
Nitric ether, spirits of	℔ 50 c.	℔ 50 c.
Nutmegs	℔ 20 c.	℔ 20 c.
Nuts, all, n. o. p.	℔ 2 c.	℔ 2 c.
Oatmeal	10 p. ct.	℔ ½ c.

*"All not artificial."

Articles enumerated.	Acts of 1870.	Act of 1872.
Oats	bush. 10 c.	bush. 10 c.
Ochres, or ochery earths, dry	100 ℔s. 50 c.	100 ℔s 50 c.
ground in oil	100 ℔s. $1 50	100 ℔s $1 50.
Oil-cloth, (floor,) v. 50c., or less p. s. yd	35 p. ct.	
ditto, ov. 50c. pr. sq. yd	45 p. ct.	10 p. c. R.
all other, (except silk.)	45 p. ct.	
silk	60 p. ct.	
Oils, all animal, n. o. p	20 p. ct.	20 p. ct.
all essential, n. o. p	50 p. ct.	50 p. ct.
all expressed, n. o. p	20 p. ct.	20 p. ct.
almonds, essential	℔ $1 50.	
expressed or fixed	℔ 10 c.	
amber, essential, crude	℔ 10 c.	free.
rectified	℔ 20 c.	
anise, or anise-seed, ess'l.	℔ 50 c.	
all fruit ethers, &c., n. o. p	℔ $2 50.	℔ $2 50.
bay leaves, essential	℔ $17 50.	℔ $17 50.
bay or laurel, (fixed)	℔ 20 c.	℔ 20 c.
bay-rum essence	oz. $2.	oz. 50 c.
behen, (cenne)	gal. 30 c.	gal. 30 c.
bergamot, essential	℔ $1.	
cajeput, essential	℔ 25 c.	free.
caraway, essential	℔ 50 c.	
cassia, essential	℔ $1.	
castor	gal. $1.	gal. $1.
cinnamon, essential	℔ $2.	
citronella	℔ 50 c.	free.
civet	30 p. ct.	
cloves	℔ $2.	℔ $2.
coal, crude	gal. 15 c.	gal. 15 c.
refined (See Oil Illum.)		
cognac, or œnanthic ether	oz. $4.	oz. $4.
cotton-seed	gal. 30 c.	gal. 30 c.
croton	℔ $1.	℔ $1.
cubebs	℔ $1.	℔ $1.
fennel	℔ 50 c.	free.
fish, n. o. p	20 p. ct.	20 p. ct.
flax-seed	gal. 30 c.	gal. 30 c.
hemp-seed	gal. 23 c.	gal. 23 c.
illuminating naphtha, &c.	gal. 40 c.	gal. 40 c.
juniper	℔ 25 c.	free.
laurel	℔ 20 c.	℔ 20 c.
lemons, essential	℔ 50 c.	℔ 50 c.
linseed	gal. 30 c.	gal. 30 c.
mace	℔ 50 c.	free.
mustard, not salad	gal. 25 c.	gal. 25 c.
neat's-foot	20 p. ct.	20 p. ct.
olive, in fl'ks or bot'ls, sal.,	gal. $1.	gal. $1.
not sal., not in flasks or bottles	gal. 25 c.	gal. 25 c.
orange, essential	℔ 50 c.	℔ 50 c.
origanum, or red thyme, essential	℔ 25 c.	
white thyme	℔ 30 c.	free.
roses, or otto	oz. $1 50.	
petroleum, crude	gal. 20 c.	gal. 20 c.
rape-seed	gal. 23 c.	gal. 23 c.
rum, essential	oz. $2.	oz. 50 c.
salad, all	gal. $1.	gal. $1.
seal	20 p. ct.	20 p. ct.
sesame seed	gal. 30 c.	free.
spermaceti	20 p. ct.	20 p. ct.
valerian	℔ $1 50.	free.
whale	20 p. ct.	20 p. ct.
Olives	30 p. ct.	free.
Opium	℔ $1.	℔ $1.
smk'g, & all prep's, n. o. p	℔ $6.	℔ $6.
Oranges	20 p. ct.	20 p. ct.
Orpiment, (sul. of arsenic	20 p. ct.	free.
Osier or willow, p. for b. m. use	30 p. ct.	30 p. ct.
Paddy	℔ 1½ c.	℔ 1½ c.
Paintings, n. o. p	10 p. ct.	10 p. ct.
Paintings, on glass or glasses	40 p. ct.	40 p. ct.
Paints, all n. o. p	25 p. ct.	25 p. ct.
Pamphlets	25 p. ct.	25 p. ct.
Paper, all n. o. p.	35 p. ct.	
manufactures of, &c	35 p. ct.	10 p. ct. R.
hangings, &c	35 p. ct.	
Paper, printing, sized	35 p. ct.	25 p. ct.
p'g uns., bk. & newsp. exc	20 p. ct.	20 p. ct.
sheathing	10 p. ct.	10 p. ct. R.
stock	20 p. ct.	free.
Papers, illustrated	25 p. ct.	25 p. ct.
Papier-maché, manuf's of	35 p. ct.	10 p. ct. R.

Articles enumerated.	Acts of 1870.	Act of 1872.
Paraffine	℔ 10 c.	℔ 10 c.
Parchment	30 p. ct,	10 p. ct. R.
Parian ware, plain, white, not decorated	45 p. ct.	45 p. ct.
gilded, or decorated	50 p. ct.	50 p. ct.
Patent size, (mordant, 1846)	20 p. ct.	20 p. ct.
Paving stones	10 p. ct.	10 p. ct.
Paving tiles	20 p. ct.	20 p. ct.
Peanuts, or ground beans	℔ 1 c.	℔ 1 c.
shelled	℔ 1½ c.	℔ 1½ c.
Pearls, not set	10 p. ct.	10 p. ct.
Pearls, set	25 p. ct.	25 p. ct.
Pebbles, for spectacles	40 p. ct.	free.
Pencils, slate	40 p. ct.	40 p. ct.
Penholders or parts thereof,	35 p. ct.	35 p. ct.
Penknives, jack-knives, and pocket	50 p. ct.	
Pens, metallic, (other than gold or silver)	gross 10 c. & 25 p. ct.	10 p.ct. R.
Pen-tips	35 p. ct.	
Pepper, n. o. p	℔ 5 c.	℔ 5 c.
all ground	℔ 10 c.	℔ 10 c.
Percussion caps	40 p. ct.	40 p. ct.
Perfumeries, all n. o. p	50 p. ct.	50 p. ct.
of which alc. p. ing'dt	gal. $3 and 50 p. ct.	gal. $3 and 50 p. ct.
Periodicals	25 p. ct.	25 p. ct.
Pewter, manufactures of	35 p. ct.	35 p. ct.
old, fit for remanf. only	℔ 2 c.	free.
Philosophical apparatus, one class	40 p. ct.	40 p. ct.
another class	15 p. ct.	15 p. ct.
Pickets and palings	20 p. ct.	20 p. ct.
Pickles, all n. o. p	35 p. ct,	35 p. ct.
Pimento	℔ 5 c.	℔ 5 c.
ground	℔ 10 c.	℔ 10 c.
Pineapples	20 p. ct.	20 p. ct.
Pins, solid head or other	35 p. ct.	10 p. ct. R.
Pipes & pipe bowls, n. o. p.	gross $1 50 & 75 p. ct.	gross $1 50 & 75 p. ct.
Pipe cases, stems, tips, &c	75 p. ct.	75 p. ct.
Pipes, clay, com. or white	35 p. ct.	35 p. ct.
Pitch	20 p. ct.	20 p. ct.
Plaits & plait'gs for bonnets.	30 p. ct.	10 p. ct. R.
Plantains	10 p. ct.	10 p. ct.
Plants, medicinal, n. o. p	20 p. ct.	free.
all n. o. p	30 p. ct.	30 p. ct.
Plaster of Paris, ground (sulph. lime)	20 p. ct.	20 p. ct.
calcined	20 p. ct.	20 p. ct.
Plated ware of all kinds copper not c. v.	35 p. ct.	
Plates engraved, of steel, &c., n. o. p	25 p. ct.	10 p.ct. R.
copper	45 p. ct.	
Platina, articles of, n. o. p.	40 p. ct.	
Plumbago, (see Black Lead)	ton $10.	free.
Plums, (dried)	℔ 2½ c.	℔ 2½ c.
Pocket-books of all kinds	35 p. ct.	10 p. ct. R.
Polishing powder, all	25 p. ct.	25 p. ct.
Pomades	50 p. ct.	50 p. ct.
Porcelain, plain, white not decorated	45 p. ct.	45 p. ct.
gilded, ornamented, &c	50 p. ct.	50 p. ct.
Pork	℔ 1 c.	℔ 1 c.
Potash, acetate of	℔ 75 c.	℔ 75 c.
bichromate of	℔ 3 c.	℔ 3 c.
chlorate of	℔ 6 c.	℔ 3 c.
chromate of	℔ 3 c.	℔ 3 c.
hydriodate of	℔ 75 c.	℔ 75 c.
iodate and iodide of	℔ 75 c.	℔ 75 c.
nit. of, crude, (See saltpeter)	℔ 2½ c.	℔ 2½ c.
refined	℔ 3 c.	℔ 3 c.
prussiate of, red	℔ 10 c.	℔ 10 c.
yellow	℔ 5 c.	℔ 5 c.
Potatoes	bush. 25 c.	bush 15 c.
Poultry, prep'd in cans, &c.	35 p. ct.	35 p. ct.
Printed matter, n. o. p	25 p. ct.	25 p. ct.
Prunes	℔ 2½ c.	℔ 1 ct.
Pulp, dried	20 p. ct.	20 p. ct.
Putty	℔ 1½ c.	℔ 1½ c.
Quicksilver	15 p. ct.	10 p. ct. R.
Quills	30 p. ct.	free.
Quinine, sul. & all salts of.	45 p. ct.	20 p. ct.
Rags, all, of what material, not otherwise provided,	10 p. ct.	free.
woolen	℔ 12 c.	10 p. ct. R.

Articles enumerated.	Acts of 1870.	Act of 1872.
Raisins, all n. o. p.	℔ 5 c.	℔ 2½ c.
Rasps, not over 10 inches in length	℔ 10 c. and 30 p. ct.	}
exceeding 10 inches	℔ 6 c. and 30 p. ct.	} 10 p.ct. R.
Ratafia	pf. gal. $2.	pf. gal $2.
Rattans and reeds, wholly or p. man'd	25 p. ct.	25 p. ct.
Red precipitate	20 p. ct.	20 p. ct.
Resins, gum, n. o. p.	20 p. ct.	20 p. ct.
Rice, cleaned	℔ 2½ c.	℔ 2½ c.
not cleaned	℔ 2 c.	℔ 2 c.
Rifles	35 p. ct.	10 p. ct. R.
Roofing-slates	35 p. ct.	35 p. ct.
tiles	20 p. ct.	20 p. ct.
Roots, bulbous, all n. o. p.	30 p. ct.	30 p. ct.
Rubies, not set	10 p. ct.	10 p. ct.
set	25 p. ct.	25 p. ct.
Rum	gal. $2.	gal. $2.
Russia sheetings, flax or hemp	35 p. ct.	35 p. ct.
Rye	bush. 15 c.	bush. 15 c.
flour	10 p. ct.	10 p. ct.
Saddlery, all n. o. p.	35 p. ct.	10 p. ct. R.
Saffron cake	10 p. ct.	} free.
Sago and sago flour	℔ 1½ c.	}
Sail-duck	30 p. ct.	10 p. ct. R.
Saleratus	℔ 1½ c.	℔ 1½ c.
Salmon, pickled	bbl. $3.	bbl. $3.
preserved	30 p. ct.	30 p. ct.
Salt,* in bulk	100 lbs. 18 c.	100 lbs. 8 c.
in sacks, barrels, &c	100 lbs. 24 c.	100 lbs. 12 c.
Salpeter, crude	℔ 2½ c.	℔ 1 c.
partially refined	℔ 2 c.	℔ 2 c.
refined	℔ 3 c.	℔ 2 c.
Salts, Epsom, (sul. of mag.)	℔ 1 c.	℔ 1 c.
glauber	℔ ½ c.	℔ ½ c.
Rochelle	℔ 15 c.	℔ 5 c.
and prep's of, n. o. p.	20 p. ct.	20 p. ct.
of tin	30 p. ct.	30 p. ct.
Santonine	℔ $5.	℔ $3.
Sardines, preserved in oil, &c	50 p. ct.	50 p. ct.
Sauces of all kinds, n. o. p.	35 p. ct.	35 p. ct.
Sausage, Bologna	30 p. ct.	free.
Saws, cross-cut	lin. feet 10 cents.	}
mill pit and drag, not over 9 inches wide	lin. feet 12½ cents.	}
over 9 inches	lin. feet 20 cents.	}
hand, not over 24 in. long	doz. 75 c. & 30 p. ct.	} 10 p.ct. R.
over 24 inches long	doz. $1 and 30 p. ct.	}
back, not over 10 in. long	doz. 75 c. & 30 p. ct.	}
Saws, back, over 10 inches long	doz. $1 and 30 p. ct.	}
Scagliola tops for tables, &c.	35 p. ct.	35 p. ct.
Screws, other than iron, n. o. p.	35 p. ct.	35 p. ct.
Sealing-wax	35 p. ct.	35 p. ct.
Sea-weed, used for beds or mattresses	20 p. ct.	free.
Seeds, agricultural, n. o. p.	30 p. ct.	20 p. ct.
anise	℔ 5 c.	}
star	℔ 10 c.	} free.
canary	bush. $1.	}
castor	bush 60 c.	bush. 60 c.
flax	bush 20 c.	bush. 20 c.
flower, n. o. p.	30 p. ct.	20 p. ct.
garden, n. o. p.	30 p. ct.	20 p. ct.
hemp	℔ ½ c.	℔ ½ c.
horticultural, n. o. p.	30 p. ct.	20 p. ct.
linseed	bush. 20 c.	bush. 20 c.
medicinal, n. o. p.	20 p. ct.	} free.
mustard	℔ 3 c.	}
oil, like hemp and rape	℔ ½ c.	℔ ½ c.
rape	℔ ½ c.	℔ ½ c.
sesame	10 p. ct.	free.
Seines	℔ 6½ c.	℔ 6½ c.
Shaddocks	10 p. ct.	10 p. ct.
Shale, (ton 28 bushels of 80 pounds)	ton $1 25.	ton $1 25.
Shell, boxes, and other m's	35 p. ct.	35 p. ct.
Shingles	35 p. ct.	1,000, 35 c.
Shrubs, n. o. p.	30 p. ct.	20 p. ct.
Silicate of soda, or other alk. sil	℔ ½ c.	℔ ½ c.
Silk, in the gum, not bey'd singles, &c	35 p. ct.	35 p. ct.
twist, of silk, or silk and mohair	40 p. ct.	40 p. ct.
floss	35 p. ct.	35 p. ct.
for sewing, in the g'm and purified	40 p. ct.	40 p. ct.
spun, for fill'g in sk'ns, &c.	35 p. ct.	35 p. ct.
aprons, bonnets, braid	60 p. ct.	60 p. ct.
button-cloth. (See Las'gs) buttons, &c.	50 p. ct.	50 p. ct.
ch'm'tt's, &c., to webbing	60 p. ct.	60 p. ct.
all other man. of, n. o. p.	50 p. ct.	50 p. ct.
Silver, manuf's of, n. o. p.	40 p. ct.	}
leaf, (package of 500 l'ves).	pack. 75 c.	} 10 p. ct. R.
Silver-pl'd me'l, in sh's, &c.	35 p. ct.	}
Sirup of sugar-cane juice	℔ 1½ c.	℔ 1⅓ c.
Sisal grass, unmanufact'd	ton $15.	ton $15.
manufactures	30 p. ct.	30 p. ct.
Skates, costing 20 cents or less per pair	8 c.	}
above 20 cents per pair	35 p. ct.	} 10 p.ct.R.
Skin, bone, ivory, &c., all manufactures of	35 p. ct.	}
Skins, raw, n. o. p.	10 p. ct.	free.
tanned and dres'd, n. o. p.	25 p. ct.	10 p. ct. R.
dried, salted, or pickled	10 p. ct.	free.
Angora, unm., wool on	30 p. ct.	30 p. ct.
asses	30 p. ct.	free.
sheep, raw or unman., &c.	30 p. ct.	free.
calf, tanned	30 p. ct.	10 p. ct. R.
Slate, chimney pieces, &c., n. o. p.	40 p. ct.	40 p. ct.
Slates	40 p. ct.	40 p. ct.
Smalts	20 p. ct.	20 p. ct.
Soap stocks and stuffs	10 p. ct.	free.
fancy, perfumed, &c., all toilet and shaving soap	℔ 10 c. and 25 p. ct.	℔ 10 c. and 25 p. ct.
all other, n. o. p.	℔ 1 c. and 30 p. ct.	℔ 1 c. and 30 p. ct.
Soda, ash	℔ ½ c.	℔ ¼ c.
bicarbonate of	℔ 1½ c.	℔ 1½ c.
carbonates of, all n. o. p.	20 p. ct.	20 p. ct.
caustic	℔ 1½ c.	℔ 1½ c.
hyposulphate of	20 p. ct.	20 p. ct.
sal, or brinal	℔ ½ c.	℔ ¼ c.
Sparterre, for m'k'g hats, &	30 p. ct.	free.
Spelter, in blocks or pigs	℔ 1½ c.	}
in sheets	℔ 2¼ c.	} 10 p. ct. R.
manufactures of	35 p. ct.	}
Spices, all, n. o. p.	℔ 20 c.	℔ 20 c.
if ground or prepared	℔ 30 c.	℔ 30 c.
Spirits, dis'd from grain, &c.	pf. gal. $2.	pf. gal. $2.
Spirituous liquors, n. o. p.	gal. 50 c. & 100 p. ct.	gal 50 c. & 100 p. ct.
beverages, &c., n. o. p.	gal. $2.	gal. $2.
Sponges	20 p. ct.	20 p. ct.
Spunk	10 p. ct.	10 p. ct.
Starch, burnt, (see Gum, Substitute)	10 p. ct.	10 p. ct.
Starch, of potatoes or corn	℔ 1 c. and 20 p. ct.	℔ 1 c. and 20 p. ct.
of rice or any other mat'l	℔ 3 c. and 20 p. ct.	℔ 3 c. and 20 p. ct.
Statuary, n. o. p.	10 p. ct.	10 p. ct.
Staves for pipes, hhds, &c.	10 p. ct.	10 p. ct.
other	20 p. ct.	20 p. ct.
Steel, ingots, v. 7 c. or less per pound	℔ 2¼ c.	}
above 7 c. not ab. 11 cents	℔ 3 c.	}
valued at above 11 cents per pound	℔ 3½ c. and 10 p. ct.	} 10p.ct.R*
in any other form, n. o. p.	30 p. ct.	}
wire, one class	℔ 2¼ c.	}

* Salt used in curing fish, *free*.

* Except steel rope, strand or chain made of steel wire, which is now subject to pay the same rate of duty that was levied by acts of 1870 upon the steel wire of which said rope or strand or chain is made.

Articles enumerated.	Acts of 1870.	Act of 1872.
Steel, wire, another class...	℔ 3 c.	
another class,	℔ 3½ c. and 10 p. ct.	
another class	℔ 2½ c. and 20 p. ct.	
another class	℔ 3 c. and 20 p. ct.	
crinoline, corset, &c	℔ 9 c. and 10 p. ct.	10 p.ct.R*
all n. o. p	30 p. ct.	
railway bars	℔ 1¼ c.	
part steel	℔ 1 c.	
squares.	℔ 6 c. and 30 p. ct.	
manufactures of, n. o. p...	45 p. ct.	
Stereotype-plates	25 p. ct.	10 p. ct. R.
Stone for building, except marble	ton $1 50.	ton $1 50.
Stones, precious, not set...	10 p. ct.	10 p. ct.
set...	25 p. ct.	25 p. ct.
Stoneware, above cap. of 10 gallons..,	20 p. ct.	20 p. ct,
common and plain	25 p. ct.	25 p. ct.
all other, gilt, &c	40 p. ct.	40 p. ct.
Straw, manufac's of, n. o. p.	35 p. ct.	10 p. ct. R.
Strings, of gut, for musicians, &c	30 p. ct.	free.
Strychnine, and its salts	oz. $1 50.	oz. $1.
Sugar, all not ab. No. 7 Dutch standard	℔ 1¾ c.	℔ 1¾ c.
do. ab. No, 7, not ab. No. 10	℔ 2c.	℔ 2 c.
do. a. No. 10, n. a. No. 13	℔ 2¼ c.	℔ 2¼ c.
do. a. No. 13, n. a. No. 16	℔ 2¾ c.	℔ 2¾ c.
do. a. No. 16, n. a. No. 20	℔ 3¼ c.	℔ 3¼ c.
do. above No. 20	℔ 4 c.	℔ 4 c.
all refined loaf, &c	℔ 4 c.	℔ 4 c.
do. v. less than 30 c. per lb.	℔ 15 c.	℔ 15 c.
do. v. above 30 cents, &c.	50 p. ct.	50 p. ct.
Sulphur flour	ton $20 and 15 p. ct.	ton $20 and 15 p. ct.
Sumac	10 p. ct.	10 p. ct.
Sweetmeats, jars of, &c., n. o. p.	35 p. ct.	35 p. ct.
Sword-blades	35 p. ct.	10 p.ct. R.
Swords	45 p. ct.	
Tallow	℔ 1 c.	℔ 1 c.
Tannin	℔ $2.	℔ $2.
Tar	20 p. ct.	20 p. ct.
Tartar emetics or tartrate of antimony	℔ 15 c.	℔ 15 c.
Teas of all kinds	℔ 15 c,	
Teasels	10 p. ct.	free.
Teeth, manufactured	20 p. ct.	
Terra alba	20 p. ct.	
Terne tin and tagger tin...	25 p. ct.	15 p. ct.
Tica, crude	20 p. ct.	free.
Tiles, encaustic	35 p. ct.	35 p. ct.
Timber, hewn or sawed	20 p. ct.	c. ft. 1c.
squared, &c., n. o. p	20 p. ct.	c. ft. 1 c.
used in building wharves	20 p. ct.	c. ft. 1 c.
Tin, in bars, blocks, or pigs	15 p. ct.	free.
manufactures of, n. o. p...	35 p. ct.	10 p. ct. R.
in plates or sheets	25 p. ct.	15 p. ct.
foil	30 p. ct.	10 p. ct. R.
Tin plates, gal'zed, c'd, &c..	℔ 2½ c.	℔ 2 c.
muriate and oxide of	30 p. ct.	30 p. ct.
Tobacco, leaf, unmanufactured, not stemmed	℔ 35 c.	℔ 35 c.
stemmed	℔ 50 c.	℔ 50 c.
do int. rev. tax	℔ 32 c.	℔ 32 c.
smoking, refuse, &c	℔ 50 c.	℔ 50 c.
do. internal rev. tax	℔ 16 c.	℔ 16 c.
stems	℔ 15 c.	℔ 15 c.
chewing, &c	℔ 50 c.	℔ 50 c.
do., internal rev. tax	℔ 32 c.	℔ 32 c.
unmanufactured, n. o. p...	30 p. ct.	30 p. ct.
cigars and cheroots	℔ $2 50 and 25 p. ct.	℔ $2 50 and 25 p. ct.
do., int. rev. tax	mille $5.	mille $5.
cigarettes, wt. ov. 3lb. per thousand	lb $2 50 and 25 p. ct.	lb $2 50 & 25 p. ct.
do. internal rev. tax	mille $5.	mille $5.

*Except steel rope, strand or chain made of steel wire, which is now subject to pay the same rate of duty that was levied by acts of 1870 upon the steel wire of which said rope or strand or chain is made.

Articles enumerated.	Acts of 1870.	Act of 1872.
Tobacco, not ov'r 3lb. per M	lb $2 50 and 25 p. ct.	lb $2 50 & 25 p. ct.
do. internal rev. tax..	mille $1 50.	mille $1 50.
snuff of tobacco or subst..	lb 50 c.	lb 50 c.
ditto, internal rev. tax	lb 32 c.	lb 32 c.
snuff flour, unprepared	lb 50 c.	lb 50 c.
Tooth-washes, pastes, &c	50 p. ct.	50 p. ct.
Toys, wooden and other, for children	50 p. ct.	50 p. ct.
Trees, fruit, shade, lawn, &c., n. o. p	30 p. ct.	20 p. ct.
Turpentine, spirits of	gal. 30 c.	gal. 30 c.
Tutenag, (teutenegue,) in blocks, &c	lb 1½ c.	
in sheets	lb 2¼ c.	
manufacture of	35 p. ct.	
Type-metal	25 p. ct.	10 p.ct.R.
Types, new	25 p. ct.	
Umbrellas, parasols, &c., cotton	50 p. ct.	
sticks, crude	35 p. ct.	free.
not silk, &c	50 p. ct.	45 p. ct.
silk, &c	60 p. ct.	60 p. ct.
Varnish valued at $1 50 or less per gallon	gal. 50 c. & 20 p. ct.	gal. 50 c. & 20 p. ct.
valued at above $1 50 p. g.	gal. 50 c. & 25 p. ct.	gal. 50 c. & 25 p. ct.
Vegetable substances for beds, &c	20 p. ct.	free.
unmanufactured, n. o. p..	ton $5 and 10 p. ct.	ton $5 and 10 p. ct.
for cordage, unmanufactured, n. o. p	ton $15.	ton $15.
Vegetables, n. o. p	10 p. ct.	10 p. ct.
prepared	35 p. ct.	35 p. ct.
Vellum	30 p. ct.	30 p. ct.
Vermicelli	35 p. ct.	free.
Vermuth	pf. gal. $2.	same as wines.
Vinegar	gal. 10 c.	gal. 10 c.
acetous or concentrated...	see Acetic Acid.	see Acetic Acid.
Vitriol, blue, or Roman, (sul. cop.)	lb 5 c.	lb 4 c.
green, (sulphate of iron)..	lb ½ c.	lb ½ c.
white, (sulphate of zinc)..	20 p. ct.	20 p. ct.
Wafers	35 p. ct.	free.
Walnuts, all kinds	lb 3 c.	lb 3c.
Waste, flocks, or shoddy of wool	lb 12 c.	10 p.ct.R.
all, n. o. p	20 p. ct.	
Watches, gold and silver, &c	25 p. ct.	25 p. ct.
Watch cases, movements, &c	25 p. ct.	25 p. ct.
materials	25 p. ct.	25 p. ct.
jewels	10 p. ct.	10 p. ct.
Whalebone, for. fisheries...	20 p. ct.	free.
all man. of, n. o. p	35 p. ct.	35 p. ct.*
Wheat	bush. 20 c.	bush. 20c.
Whiting, dry	lb 1 c.	lb. 1 c.
ground in oil	lb 2 c.	lb. 2 c.
Wines, v. not ov. 40 cts. p. g.	gal. 25 c.	gal. 25 c.
v. over 40 c. not ov. $1 p. g.	gal. 60 c.	gal. 60 c.
value over $1 per gallon...	gal. $1 and 25 p. ct.	gal $1 and 25 p. ct.
Champ., &c., one class	doz. $1 50.	doz. $1 50.
another class	doz. $3.	doz. $3.
another class	doz. $6.	doz. $6.
another class	gal. $2.	gal. $2.
Wine bottles, extra	each 3 c.	10 p. ct. R.
Wood, unman'd, n. o. p	20 p. ct.	see timber.
manufactures of	35 p. ct.	35 p. ct.
boards, planks, &c	20 p. ct.	see lumber.
Wool, Class I, cl'th'g w. unw'sh'd, v. 32c. or less per lb	lb 10 c. and 11 p. ct.	
v. exceed'g 32c. per lb	lb 12 c. and 10 p. ct.	
Class II, comb'g wools, val. 32c. or less per lb..	lb 10 c. and 11 p. ct.	10 p.ct.R.
v. exc'd'g 32c. per lb	lb 12 c. and 10 p. ct.	

*If whalebone is construed to be "bone," then this duty is subject to the 10 per cent. reduction.

Articles enumerated.	Acts of 1870.	Act of 1872.
Wool, Class III, carpet w'ls, val. 12c. or less per lb..	lb 3 c.	
value exc'd'g 12c. per lb..	lb 6 c.	
of Class I, washed...........	double d'ty	
of all classes, scoured......	double d'ty	
Woolen rags.....................	lb 12 c.	
Woolen and worsted yarns, not exc'd'g 40c. per lb...	lb 20 c. and 35 p. ct.	
ditto, over 40 cents, not exceeding 60c. per lb....	lb 30 c. and 35 p. ct.	
Woolen, ditto, over 60c. and not over 80c. per lb.......	lb 40 c. and 35 p. ct.	
ditto, above 80c. per lb.....	lb 50 c. and 35 p. ct.	
Woolen balmorals, &c., one class..............................	lb 20 c. and 35 p. ct.	
another class....................	lb 30 c. and 35 p. ct.	
another class....................	lb 40 c. and 35 p. ct.	
another class....................	lb 50 c. and 35 p. ct.	
another class....................	lb 50 c. and 35 p. ct.	
balmoral skirts & sk'rt'g, and other goods not knit	lb 50 c. and 40 p. ct.	
belts, endless, for pr't'g machines, &c.................	lb 20 c. and 35 p. ct.	10 p.ct.R.
belt'gs, bind'gs, braid, &c.	lb 50 c. and 50 p. ct.	
blanketing for pr'g. ma...	lb 20 c. and 35 p. ct.	
cloth, n. o. p..................	lb 50 c. and 35 p. ct.	
hats................................	see bal'm's.	
hat bodies........................	see man'f's of wool, n. o. p.	
hosiery (knit goods)........	see bal's, &c	
listings...........................	lb 50 c. and 35 p. ct.	
shawls.............................	lb 50 c. and 35 p. ct.	
women and children's g'ds &c., one class...............	sq. yd. 6 c. & 35 p. ct.	
ditto, another class..........	sq. yd. 8 c. & 40 p. ct.	
ditto, another class..........	sq. yd. 50 c. & 35 p. ct.	
manufactures of, n. o. p.	lb 50 c. and 35 p. ct.	
ditto, v, not over 40 cts....	lb 20 c. and 35 p. ct.	
ditto, another class..........	lb 30 c. and 35 p. ct.	
ditto, another class..........	lb 40 c. and 35 p. ct.	
ditto, another class..........	lb 50 c. and 35 p. ct.	
Yams................................	10 p. ct.	free.
Yellow metal or sheathing metal............................	lb 3 c.	10 p. ct. R.
Zaffre..............................	20 p. ct.	free.
Zinc, in blocks or pigs........	lb 1½ c.	
in sheets..........................	lb 2¼ c.	
oxide of, dry or gr'd in oil..............................	lb 1¾ c.	10 p.ct.R.
manufacturers n. o. p......	35 p. ct.	

Articles enumerated.	Acts of 1870.	Act of 1872.
Unenumerated art's,*crude	10 p. ct.	10 p. ct.
worked..............................	20 p. ct.	20 p. ct.
Goods, wares, merch. (ex. raw cotton and silk, r'ld f. t. cocoon, 1865,) produced in countries b'y'd the Cape of Good Hope, when imported from places this side the Cape, in addt'n to duties on such art's when imported direct from the place or places of their production............	10 p. ct.	10 p. ct.
Upon the reimportation of articles, once exported, of the growth, product, or manufacture of the United States, upon which no internal tax has been assessed or paid, or upon which such tax has been paid and refunded by allowance or drawback, there shall be paid a duty equal to........................	internal revenue tax.	internal revenue tax.

*In addition to the articles above named, the following are also *enumerated* in the FREE list of 1872:

SPECIFIC—Charcoal, (formerly) 40 cents per ton; chlorate of lime, 30 cents per 100 lbs; mustard seed, 3 cents per lb; Brazil nuts, 2 cents per lb; oil of thyme, 25 cents per lb; quick-grass root, $5 per ton.

AD VALOREM—(*Formerly*) 50 per cent.: Ambergris; dried flowers, &c.; oils of anthos or rosemary, cedrat, chamomile, jessamine, juglandium, and lavender; 40 per cent.: balm of Gilead, Brazil pebbles, salacine, sugar of milk; 35 per cent.: bamboos, horn strips, indio or Malacca joints, josstick, magnets, sauerkraut, tamarinds; 30 per cent.: bed feathers and downs, cat-gut strings, hop roots, (for cultivation,) sugar-cane seeds, forest tree seeds, storax; 25 per cent.: books, (20 years old,) leather, (old scrap); 20 per cent.: aluminium, angelica root, annatto, &c., (extracts of,) aniline, birds, (stuffed,) black salts, black tares, chamomile flowers, china root, cinchona, colcotha, contrayerva, cow or vaccine virus, curling stones or quoits, curry powder, cyanite, dried bugs, dried blood, elecampane root, farina, galanga or galangal, gentian root, gut for whips, &c., guts, (salted,) hellebore root, hones, &c., lithographic stones, loadstones, marsh mallows, matico leaf, meerschaum, (crude or raw,) mica, (and waste,) poppy oils, oil cake, osmium, oxidizing paste, palladium, pellitory root, polypodium, pulu, railroad ties, rennets, saffron, &c., (and extracts of,) salep, sassafras, (bark and root,) shark skins, stavesacre, talc, tin, (grain,) uranium, wax, (bay or myrtle, Brazil or Chinese,) yeast cakes; 10 per cent.: agates, (unmanufactured,) almond shells, balsam, (Canada,) bladders, (crude,) diamonds, (rough,) fossils, garancine, grease, (soap stock,) madder, &c., (and extract of,) orange flowers, St. John's beans, snails, spunk, straw, (unmanufactured,) succinic acid.

FORMER DUTIES NOT DETERMINED.—Phanglein, root flour, sausage skins, chia seeds, oxide of strontia, Venice turpentine.

The following on the free list of 1870 are again placed on the free list for 1872: Amber gum, iridium, jalap, logs and ship timber, musk, (crude,) nux vomica, persis, Peruvian bark, rattan and reeds, (unmanufactured,) tripoli.

INTERNAL REVENUE SCHEDULE,*

Showing the changes made therein by the act of June, 1872.

Articles and occupations taxed.	Act of 1870.	Act of 1872.
Spirits distilled from grapes, per gallon.....	$0 50	$0 70
Spirits distilled from apples and peaches, per gallon.....	50	70
Spirits distilled from materials other than grapes, apples, and peaches, per gallon...........	50	70
Distilleries, aggregate capacity for mashing and fermenting 20 bushels of grain, or less, or 60 gallons of molasses or less, in 24 hrs. per day..........	2 00	
Distilleries of capacity exceeding 20 bush. of grain or 60 gallons of molasses in 24 hours for every 20 bushels of grain in 60 gallons of molasses in addition, per day................	2 00	
Distillers distilling 100 barrels or less peryear, (special tax)........	400 00	R'p'ld
Distillers of brandy from appl's, grapes, and peaches, exclusively, annual product less than 150 bbls. (and $4 per bbl. of 40 proof gallons on all over 100 barrels)..............	50 00	
Distillers distilling over 100 bbls. per year, for every barrel over 100 barrels.....	4 00	
Rectifiers, (special tax)........	200 00	200 00
Rectifiers of any quantity of distilled spirits exceeding 200 barrels per year, for every bbl. over 200 barrels	50	Rep'ld.

Articles and occupations taxed.	Act of 1870.	Act of 1872.
Wine made in imitation of champagne, and liquors produced by being rectified, or mixed with distilled spirits to be sold as wine or a substitute therefor, in bottles containing more than 1 pint and not more than 1 quart, per dozen	$6 00	p. qt. 20 c.
Wine made in imitation of champagne, and liquors produced by being rectified, or mixed with distilled spirits, in bottles containing not more than 1 pint, and at the same rate for any quantity, however put up, per doz....	3 00	p. pt. 10 c.
Dealers, retail liquor, (special tax).......	25 00	$25 00
Dealers, wholesale liquor, annual sales not over $25,000, (special tax)...	100 00	100 00
Dealers in liquor, annual sales (including other merchandise) ov. $25,000, for all sales of liquors over such $25,000...	1 p. ct.	Rep'ld.
Manufacturers of stills, (special tax)........	$50 00	$50 00
Stills or worms, manufactured, each...............	20 00	20 00
Stamps, distillery warehouse, each...	25	10
Stamps for rectified spirits, each.........	25	10
Stamps, wholesale liquor dealers, each.	25	10
Stamps for distilled spirits intended for export..........	....	25

Articles and occupations taxed.	Act of 1870.	Act of 1872.
Tobacco.		
Cigars and cheroots, of all descriptions, whether of domestic manufacture or imported, per 1,000	$5 00	$5 00
Cigarettes, domestic or imported, weighing not over 3 lbs. per 1,000, per 1,000.	1 50	1 50
Cigarettes, domestic or imported, weighing over 3 pounds per 1,000, per M....	5 00	5 00
Manufacturers of cigars, annual sales not over $5,000, (special tax)..	10 00	10 00†
Manufacturers of cigars, annual sales over $5,000, for every $1,000 over $5,000............	2 00	Rep'ld †
Snuff of all descriptions, domestic or imported, and snuff-flour sold for use, per pound.....	32	32
Tobacco, chewing, fine-cut, plug, or twist; smoking, with a portion of the stem removed before, during, or after the process of manufacturing; twisted by hand or reduced from leaf into a condition to be consumed or otherwise prepared, &c.; all other manufactured kinds not otherwise herein provided for, domestic or imported, per pound...........	32	20
Tobacco, smoking, exclusively of stems		

After Oct. 1, 1872, stamps of two cents on bank checks, (sight or demand,) drafts or orders, under Schedule B.

All stamps now taxable on proprietary medicines, &c., (Schedule C not having been interfered with,) four per cent.

* These comparative Schedules were compiled with the assistance of the Commissioner's office.

† All manufacturers of cigars must pay special tax of $10.

Articles and occupations taxed.	Act of 1870.	Act of 1872.
or of leaf, all stems in; fine-cut shorts and refuse scraps and sweepings of tobacco, domestic or imported, per pound......	$0 16	$0 20
Stamps for tobacco or snuff intended for export, each	25	10
Dealers in leaf tobacco, annual sales not over $10,000, (special tax ...	25 00	25 00
Dealers in leaf tobacco, annual sales over $10,000 for every $1,000 over $10,000....	2 00	Rep'ld.
Dealers (retail) in leaf tobacco, annual sales not over $1,000, (special tax)........	....	500 00
Dealers (retail) in leaf tobacco, annual sales over $1,000, for every $1 over $1,000............	....	50
Dealers in manufactured tobacco, annual sales over $100 and not over $1,000, (special tax)........	$5 00	$5 00*
Dealers in manufactured tobacco, annual sales over $1.000, for every $1,000 over $1,000............	2 00	Rep'ld *

Articles and occupations taxed.	Act of 1870.	Act of 1872.
Peddlers,† 1st class, (special tax)	....	$50 00
2d class, (special tax).	....	25 00
3d class, (special tax)......	....	15 00
4th class, (special tax).......	....	10 00
Manufacturers of tobacco, (special tax,).	$10 00	10 00
Manufacturers of tobacco, the penal sum of whose bond exceeds $5,000, for every $1 000 over $5,000............	2 00	Rep'ld.‡
Fermented liquors.		
Fermented liquors, per barrel...........	1 00	1 00
Brewers, annual manufacture less than 500 bbls., (special tax.).	50 00	50 00
Brewers, annual manufacture not less than 500 bbls., (special tax.)............	100 00	100 00
Dealers, (wholesale,) in malt liquors.........	....	50 00
Dealers, (retail.) in malt liq'rs.	....	20 00
Banks and Bankers.		
Bank deposits, per month.....	1-24 of 1 p. ct.	1-24 of 1 p. ct.
Bank deposits, savings, &c., having no capital stock per 6 months.	¼ of 1 p. ct.	¼ of 1 p. ct.

Articles and occupations taxed.	Act of 1870.	Act of 1872.
Bank capital, per month.....	1-24 of 1 p. ct.	1-24 of 1 p. ct.
Bank circulation, per m'th	1-12 of 1 p. ct.	1-12 of 1 p. ct.
Bank circulation, exceeding 90 p. ct. of capital, in addition, per month..........	1-6 of 1 p. ct.	1-6 of 1 p. ct.
Banks, on am't of notes of any person, State bank, or State banking association, used for circulation, and paid out.......	10 p. ct.	10 p. ct.
Gas.		
Gas, one class...	10 c.	Rep'ld.
another class.	15 c.	
another class.	20 c.	
another class.	25 c.	
Income.		
Income exceeding $2,000.......	2½ p. ct.	All tax on incomes expired by limitation with the assessment on incomes for the Calendar year, ending Dec. 31, 1871.
Bank, divid'ds, &c..................	2½ p. ct.	
Canal, divid'ds, &c	2½ p. ct.	
Insurance, dividends, &c.....	2½ p. ct.	
R. R. Co's, dividends, &c.....	2½ p. ct.	
Turnpike Co's, divid's, &c.....	2½ p. ct.	

XXIV.

NATIONAL CONVENTIONS.

REPUBLICAN NATIONAL CONVENTION.

Philadelphia, June 5-6, 1872.

For President, ULYSSES S. GRANT, of Illinois; Vice President, HENRY WILSON, of Massachusetts.

President GRANT was nominated on the first ballot, receiving 752 votes, the entire vote of every State and Territory in the Union.

Senator WILSON was nominated on the first ballot, which stood: HENRY WILSON, 364½; SCHUYLER COLFAX, of Indiana, 321½; JOHN F. LEWIS, of Virginia, 22; EDMUND J. DAVIS, of Texas, 16; HORACE MAYNARD, of Tennessee, 26; JOSEPH R. HAWLEY, of Connecticut, 1; E. F. NOYES, 1. Made unanimous.

The Platform.

The Republican party of the United States, assembled in national convention in the city of Philadelphia on the 5th and 6th days of June, 1872, again declares its faith, appeals to its history, and announces its position upon the questions before the country:

1. During eleven years of supremacy it has accepted with grand courage the solemn duties

* All dealers in manufactured tobacco must pay special tax of $5. No tax of $2 per thousand on sales, as formerly.

† Any person who sells, or offers to sell and deliver manufactured tobacco, snuff, or cigars, traveling from place to place, in the town or through the country, is regarded as a peddler of tobacco.

‡ $20,000 is the maximum bond, but it is in the discretion of the Commissioner to increase it.

of the time. It suppressed a gigantic rebellion, emancipated four millions of slaves, decreed the equal citizenship of all, and established universal suffrage. Exhibiting unparalleled magnanimity, it criminally punished no man for political offenses, and warmly welcomed all who proved loyalty by obeying the laws and dealing justly with their neighbors. It has steadily decreased with firm hand the resultant disorders of a great war, and initiated a wise and humane policy toward the Indians. The Pacific railroad and similar vast enterprises have been generously aided and successfully conducted, the public lands freely given to actual settlers, immigration protected and encouraged, and a full acknowledgment of the naturalized citizen's rights secured from European Powers. A uniform national currency has been provided, repudiation frowned down, the national credit sustained under the most extraordinary burdens, and new bonds negotiated at lower rates. The revenues have been carefully collected and honestly applied. Despite annual large reductions of the rates of taxation, the public debt has been reduced during General Grant's Presidency at the rate of a hundred millions a year, great financial crises have been avoided, and peace and plenty prevail throughout the land. Menacing foreign difficulties have been peacefully and honorably composed, and the honor and power of the nation kept in high respect throughout the world. This glorious record of the past is the party's best pledge for the future. We believe the people will not intrust the Government to any party or combination of men composed chiefly of those who have resisted every step of this beneficent progress.

2. The recent amendments to the national Constitution should be cordially sustained because they are right, not merely tolerated because they are law, and should be carried out according to their spirit by appropriate legislation, the enforcement of which can safely be intrusted only to the party that secured those amendments.

3. Complete liberty and exact equality in the enjoyment of all civil, political, and public rights should be established and effectually maintained throughout the Union by efficient and appropriate State and Federal legislation. Neither the law nor its administration should admit any discrimination in respect of citizens by reason of race, creed, color, or previous condition of servitude.

4. The national Government should seek to maintain honorable peace with all nations, protecting its citizens everywhere and sympathizing with all peoples who strive for greater liberty.

5. Any system of the civil service under which the subordinate positions of the Government are considered rewards for mere party zeal is fatally demoralizing, and we therefore favor a reform of the system by laws which shall abolish the evils of patronage and make honesty, efficiency, and fidelity the essential qualifications for public positions, without practically creating a life tenure of office.

6. We are opposed to further grants of the public lands to corporations and monopolies, and demand that the national domain be set apart for free homes for the people.

7. The annual revenue, after paying current expenditures, pensions, and the interest on the public debt, should furnish a moderate balance for the reduction of the principal, and that revenue, except so much as may be derived from a tax upon tobacco and liquors, should be raised by duties upon importations, the details of which should be so adjusted as to aid in securing remunerative wages to labor, and promote the industries, prosperity, and growth of the whole country.

8. We hold in undying honor the soldiers and sailors whose valor saved the Union. Their pensions are a sacred debt of the nation, and the widows and orphans of those who died for their country are entitled to the care of a generous and grateful people. We favor such additional legislation as will extend the bounty of the Government to all our soldiers and sailors who were honorably discharged, and who in the line of duty became disabled, without regard to the length of service or the cause of such discharge.

9. The doctrine of Great Britain and other European Powers concerning allegiance—"once a subject always a subject"—having at last through the efforts of the Republican party been abandoned, and the American idea of the individual's right to transfer allegiance having been accepted by European nations, it is the duty of our Government to guard with jealous care the rights of adopted citizens against the assumption of unauthorized claims by their former Governments, and we urge continued careful encouragement and protection of voluntary immigration.

10. The franking privilege ought to be abolished, and the way prepared for a speedy reduction in the rates of postage.

11. Among the questions which press for attention is that which concerns the relations of capital and labor, and the Republican party recognizes the duty of so shaping legislation as to secure full protection and the amplest field for capital, and for labor, the creator of capital, the largest opportunities and a just share of the mutual profits of these two great servants of civilization.

12. We hold that Congress and the President have only fulfilled an imperative duty in their measures for the suppression of violent and treasonable organizations in certain lately rebellious regions, and for the protection of the ballot-box; and therefore they are entitled to the thanks of the nation.

13. We denounce repudiation of the public debt, in any form or disguise, as a national crime. We witness with pride the reduction of the principal of the debt, and of the rates of interest upon the balance, and confidently expect that our excellent national currency will be perfected by a speedy resumption of specie payment.

14. The Republican party is mindful of its obligations to the loyal women of America for their noble devotion to the cause of freedom.

Their admission to wider fields of usefulness is viewed with satisfaction; and the honest demand of any class of citizens for additional rights should be treated with respectful consideration.

15. We heartily approve the action of Congress in extending amnesty to those lately in rebellion, and rejoice in the growth of peace and fraternal feeling throughout the land.

16. The Republican party proposes to respect the rights reserved by the people to themselves as carefully as the powers delegated by them to the State and to the Federal Government. It disapproves of the resort to unconstitutional laws for the purpose of removing evils, by interference with rights not surrendered by the people to either the State or national Government.

17. It is the duty of the General Government to adopt such measures as may tend to encourage and restore American commerce and ship-building.

18. We believe that the modest patriotism, the earnest purpose, the sound judgment, the practical wisdom, the incorruptible integrity, and the illustrious services of Ulysses S. Grant have commended him to the heart of the American people, and with him at our head we start to day upon a new march to victory.

19. Henry Wilson, nominated for the Vice Presidency, known to the whole land from the early days of the great struggle for liberty as an indefatigable laborer in all campaigns, an incorruptible legislator and representative man of American institutions, is worthy to associate with our great leader and share the honors which we pledge our best efforts to bestow upon them.

President Grant's Acceptance.

EXECUTIVE MANSION,
WASHINGTON, D. C., *June* 10, 1872.

HON. THOMAS SETTLE, *President National Republican Convention;* PAUL STROBACH, ELISHA BAXTER, C. A. SARGENT, *and others, Vice Presidents:*

GENTLEMEN: Your letter of this date, advising me of the action of the convention held in Philadelphia, Pennsylvania, on the 5th and 6th of this month, and of my unanimous nomination for the Presidency by it, is received.

I accept the nomination, and through you return my heartfelt thanks to your constituents for this mark of their confidence and support.

If elected in November, and protected by a kind Providence in health and strength to perform the duties of the high trust conferred, I promise the same zeal and devotion to the good of the whole people for the future of my official life as shown in the past.

Past experience may guide me in avoiding mistakes inevitable with novices in all professions and in all occupations.

When relieved from the responsibilities of my present trust by the election of a successor, whether it be at the end of this term or the next, I hope to leave to him, as Executive, a country at peace within its own borders, at peace with outside nations, with a credit at home and abroad, and without embarrassing questions to threaten its future prosperity.

With the expression of a desire to see a speedy healing of all bitterness of feeling between sections, parties, or races of citizens, and the time when the title of *citizen* carries with it all the protection and privileges to the humblest that it does to the most exalted, I subscribe myself, very respectfully, your obedient servant, U. S. GRANT.

Senator Wilson's Acceptance.

WASHINGTON, *June* 14, 1872.

HON. THOMAS SETTLE *and others, President and Vice Presidents of the National Republican Convention, held at Philadelphia on the 5th and 6th of the present month:*

GENTLEMEN: Your note of the 10th instant, conveying to me the action of the convention in placing my name in nomination for the office of Vice President of the United States, is before me. I need not give you the assurance of my grateful appreciation of the high honor conferred upon me by this action of the fifth national convention of the Republican party.

Sixteen years ago, in the same city, was held the first meeting of the men who, amid the darkness and doubts of that hour of slave-holding ascendency and aggression, had assembled in national convention to confer with each other upon the exigencies into which that fearful domination had brought their country. After full conference, the highest point of resolve they could reach, the most they dared to recommend, was the avowed purpose to prohibit the existence of slavery in the Territories. Last week the same party met by its representatives from thirty-seven States and ten Territories, at the same great center of wealth, intelligence, and power, to review the past, take note of the present, and indicate its line of action for the future.

As typical facts, headlands of the nation's recent history, there sat on its platform, taking prominent and honorable part in its proceedings, admitted on terms of perfect equality to the leading hotels of the city, not only the colored representatives of the race which were, ten years before, in abject slavery, but one of the oldest and most prominent of the once despised abolitionists, to whom was accorded, as to no other, the warmest demonstrations of popular regard and esteem—an ovation, not to him alone, but to the cause he had so ably and for so many years represented, and to the men and women, living and dead, who had toiled through long years of obloquy and self-sacrifice for the glorious fruitions of that hour. It hardly needed the brilliant summary of its platform to set forth its illustrious achievements. The very presence of those men was alone significant of the victories already achieved, the progress already made, and the great distance which the nation had traveled between the years 1856 and 1872.

But grand as has been its record, the Republican party rests not on its past alone. It looks to the future, and grapples with its problems of duty and of danger. It proposes as objects of its immediate accomplishment "complete liberty and exact equality" for all; the enforcement of "the recent amendments to the national Constitution;" reform in the "civil service;" the "national domain to be set apart for homes to the people;" the adjustment of duties on imports so as to secure "remunerative wages to labor;" the extension of bounty to all soldiers and sailors "who in the line of duty became disabled;" the continual and careful encouragement and protection of voluntary immigration, and the guarding "with jealous care the rights of adopted citizens;" the abolition of the franking privilege and "the speedy reduction of the rates of postage;" the reduction of the national debt and the rates of interest and "the resumption of specie payments;" the encouragement of American commerce and of ship-building; the suppression of violence and "the protection of the ballot-box." It also placed on record the opinions and purposes of the party in favor of amnesty, against all forms of repudiation, and indorsed the humane and peaceful policy of the Administration in regard to the Indians.

But while clearly defining and distinctly announcing the policy of the Republican party on these questions of practical legislation and administration, the convention did not ignore the great social problems which are pressing their claims for solution, and which demand the most careful study and wise consideration. Foremost stands the labor question. Concerning "the relations of capital and labor" the Republican party accepts the duty of "so shaping legislation as to secure the full protection and the amplest field for capital, and for labor, the creator of capital, the largest opportunities, and a just share of the mutual profits of those two great servants of civilization."

To woman, too, and her great demands, it extends the hand of grateful recognition, and proffers its most respectful inquiry. It recognizes her noble devotion to country and freedom, welcomes her admission to "wider fields of usefulness," and commends her demands for "additional rights" to the calm and careful consideration of the nation.

To guard well what has already been secured, to work out faithfully and wisely what is now in hand, and to consider the questions which are looming up to view but a little way before us, the Republican party is to-day what it was in the gloomy years of slavery, rebellion, and reconstruction, a natural necessity.

It appeals, therefore, for support to the patriotic and liberty loving, to the just and humane, to all who would dignify labor, to all who would educate, elevate, and lighten the burdens of the sons and daughters of toil. With its great record, the work still to be done under the lead of the great soldier whose historic renown and whose successful Administration for the last three years begat such popular confidence, the Republican party may confidently, in the language of the convention you represent, "start upon a new march to victory."

Having accepted thirty-six years ago the distinguishing doctrines of the Republican party of to-day; having, during years of that period, for their advancement, subordinated all other issues, acting in and coöperating with political organizations with whose leading doctrines I sometimes had neither sympathy nor belief; having labored incessantly for many years to found and build up the Republican party, and having, during its existence, taken an humble part in its grand work, I gratefully accept the nomination thus tendered, and shall endeavor, if it shall be ratified by the people, faithfully to perform the duties it imposes.

Respectfully, yours,

HENRY WILSON.

NATIONAL LIBERAL REPUBLICAN CONVENTION.

Cincinnati, May 1-3, 1872.

[Met pursuant to a call of the Liberal Republican State convention of Missouri.]

For President, HORACE GREELEY, of New York;. Vice President, BENJAMIN GRATZ BROWN, of Missouri.

Ballot for President—1st, Adams 205, Trumbull 110, Davis 92½, Greeley 147, Brown 95; 2d, Greeley 239, Adams 243, Trumbull 148, Davis 81, Brown 2, Chase 1; 3d, Greeley 258, Trumbull 156, Adams 264, Davis 44, Brown 2; 4th, Adams 279, Greeley 251, Trumbull 141, Davis 51, Brown 2; 5th, Adams 309, Greeley 258, Trumbull 91, Davis 30, Brown 2, Chase 24; 6th, Adams 187, Greeley 482.

Ballot for Vice President—1st, Brown 237, Trumbull, 158, Julian 134½, Walker 84½, Tipton 8, Cox 25, Clay 34, Scovel 12; 2d, Brown 435, Julian 175, Walker 75, Tipton 8, Palmer 8. Declared unanimous.

Address to the People of the United States.

The Administration now in power has rendered itself guilty of wanton disregard of the laws of the land, and of usurping powers not granted by the Constitution; it has acted as if the laws had binding force only for those who are governed, and not for those who govern. It has thus struck a blow at the fundamental principles of constitutional government and the liberties of the citizen.

The President of the United States has openly used the powers and opportunities of his high office for the promotion of personal ends.

He has kept notoriously corrupt and unworthy men in places of power and responsibility, to the detriment of the public interest.

He has used the public service of the Government as a machinery of corruption and personal influence, and has interfered with tyrannical arrogance in the political affairs of States and municipalities.

He has rewarded with influential and lucrative offices men who had acquired his favor by valuable presents, thus stimulating the demoralization of our political life by his conspicuous example.

He has shown himself deplorably unequal to the task imposed upon him by the necessities of the country, and culpably careless of the responsibilities of his high office.

The partisans of the Administration, assuming to be the Republican party and controlling its organization, have attempted to justify such wrongs and palliate such abuses to the end of maintaining partisan ascendency.

They have stood in the way of necessary investigations and indispensable reforms, pretending that no serious fault could be found with the present administration of public affairs, thus seeking to blind the eyes of the people.

They have kept alive the passions and resentments of the late civil war, to use them for their own advantage; they have resorted to arbitrary measures in direct conflict with the organic law, instead of appealing to the better instincts and latent patriotism of the southern people by restoring to them these rights, the enjoyment of which is indispensable to a successful administration of their local affairs, and would tend to revive a patriotic and hopeful national feeling.

They have degraded themselves and the name of their party, once justly entitled to the confidence of the nation, by a base sycophancy to the dispenser of executive power and patronage, unworthy of republican freemen; they have sought to silence the voice of just criticism, and stifle the moral sense of the people, and to subjugate public opinion by tyrannical party discipline.

They are striving to maintain themselves in authority for selfish ends by an unscrupulous use of the power which rightfully belongs to the people, and should be employed only in the service of the country.

Believing that an organization thus led and controlled can no longer be of service to the best interests of the Republic, we have resolved to make an independent appeal to the sober judgment, conscience, and patriotism of the American people.

Resolutions.

We, the Liberal Republicans of the United States in national convention assembled at Cincinnati, proclaim the following principles as essential to just government:

1. We recognize the equality of all men before the law, and hold that it is the duty of Government, in its dealings with the people, to mete out equal and exact justice to all, of whatever nativity, race, color, or persuasion, religious or political.

2. We pledge ourselves to maintain the Union of these States, emancipation, and enfranchisement, and to oppose any reopening of the questions settled by the thirteenth, fourteenth, and fifteenth amendments of the Constitution.

3. We demand the immediate and absolute removal of all disabilities imposed on account of the rebellion, which was finally subdued seven years ago, believing that universal amnesty will result in complete pacification in all sections of the country.

4. Local self-government, with impartial suffrage, will guard the rights of all citizens more securely than any centralized power. The public welfare requires the supremacy of the civil over the military authority, and the freedom of person under the protection of the *habeas corpus*. We demand for the individual the largest liberty consistent with public order, for the State self government, and for the nation a return to the methods of peace and the constitutional limitations of power.

5. The civil service of the Government has become a mere instrument of partisan tyranny and personal ambition, and an object of selfish greed. It is a scandal and reproach upon free institutions, and breeds a demoralization dangerous to the perpetuity of republican government. We therefore regard a thorough reform of the civil service as one of the most pressing necessities of the hour; that honesty, capacity, and fidelity constitute the only valid claims to public employment; that the offices of the Government cease to be a matter of arbitrary favoritism and patronage, and that public station shall become again a post of honor. To this end it is imperatively required that no President shall be a candidate for reëlection.

6. We demand a system of Federal taxation which shall not unnecessarily interfere with the industry of the people, and which shall provide the means necessary to pay the expenses of the Government, economically administered, the pensions, the interest on the public debt, and a moderate reduction annually of the principal thereof; and recognizing that there are in our midst honest but irreconcilable differences of opinion with regard to the respective systems of protection and free trade, we remit the discussion of the subject to the people in their congressional districts and the decision of Congress thereon, wholly free from executive interference or dictation.

7. The public credit must be sacredly maintained, and we denounce repudiation in every form and guise.

8. A speedy return to specie payments is demanded alike by the highest considerations of commercial morality and honest government.

9. We remember with gratitude the heroism and sacrifices of the soldiers and sailors of the Republic, and no act of ours shall ever detract from their justly earned fame or the full rewards of their patriotism.

10. We are opposed to all further grants of lands to railroads or other corporations. The public domain should be held sacred to actual settlers.

11. We hold that is the duty of the Government in its intercourse with foreign nations to cultivate the friendships of peace by treating with all on fair and equal terms, regarding it alike dishonorable either to demand what is not right or submit to what is wrong.

12. For the promotion and success of these vital principles and the support of the candidates nominated by this convention we invite

and cordially welcome the coöperation of all patriotic citizens, without regard to previous political affiliations.

Mr. Greeley's Acceptance.

NEW YORK, *May* 20, 1872.

GENTLEMEN: I have chosen not to acknowledge your letter of the 3d instant until I could learn how the work of your convention was received in all parts of our great country, and judge whether that work was approved and ratified by the mass of our fellow-citizens. Their response has from day to day reached me through telegrams, letters, and the comments of journalists independent of official patronage and indifferent to the smiles or frowns of power. The number and character of these unconstrained, unpurchased, unsolicited utterances satisfy me that the movement which found expression at Cincinnati has received the stamp of public approval, and been hailed by a majority of our countrymen as the harbinger of a better day for the Republic.

I do not misinterpret this approval as especially complimentary to myself, nor even to the chivalrous and justly esteemed gentleman with whose name I thank your convention for associating mine. I receive and welcome it as a spontaneous and deserved tribute to that admirable platform of principles wherein your convention so tersely, so lucidly, so forcibly, set forth the convictions which impelled and the purposes which guided its course—a platform which, casting behind it the wreck and rubbish of worn-out contentions and by-gone feuds, embodies in fit and few words the needs and aspirations of to-day. Though thousands stand ready to condemn your every act, hardly a syllable of criticism or cavil has been aimed at your platform, of which the substance may be fairly epitomized as follows:

I. All the political rights and franchises which have been acquired through our late bloody convulsion must and shall be guarantied, maintained, enjoyed, respected evermore.

II. All the political rights and franchises which have been lost through that convulsion should and must be promptly restored and reëstablished, so that there shall be henceforth no proscribed class and no disfranchised caste within the limits of our Union, whose long-estranged people shall reunite and fraternize upon the broad basis of universal amnesty with impartial suffrage.

III. That, subject to our solemn constitutional obligation to maintain the equal rights of all citizens, our policy should aim at local self government, and not at centralization; that the civil authority should be supreme over the military; that the writ of *habeas corpus* should be jealously upheld as the safeguard of personal freedom; that the individual citizen should enjoy the largest liberty consistent with public order; and that there shall be no Federal subversion of the internal polity of the several States and municipalities, but that each shall be left free to enforce the rights and promote the well-being of its inhabitants by such means as the judgment of its own people shall prescribe.

IV. There shall be a real and not merely a simulated reform in the civil service of the Republic; to which end it is indispensable that the chief dispenser of its vast official patronage shall be shielded from the main temptation to use his power selfishly by a rule inexorably forbidding and precluding his reëlection.

V. That the raising of revenue, whether by tariff or otherwise, shall be recognized and treated as the people's immediate business, to be shaped and directed by them through their Representatives in Congress, whose action thereon the President must neither overrule by his veto, attempt to dictate, nor presume to punish, by bestowing office only on those who agree with him or withdrawing it from those who do not.

VI. That the public lands must be sacredly reserved for occupation and acquisition by cultivators, and not recklessly squandered on the projectors of railroads for which our people have no present need, and the premature construction of which is annually plunging us into deeper and deeper abysses of foreign indebtedness.

VII. That the achievement of these grand purposes of universal beneficence is expected and sought at the hands of all who approve them, irrespective of past affiliations.

VIII. That the public faith must at all hazards be maintained, and the national credit preserved.

IX. That the patriotic devotedness and inestimable services of our fellow-citizens, who, as soldiers or sailors, upheld the flag and maintained the unity of the Republic, shall ever be gratefully remembered and honorably requited.

These propositions, so ably and forcibly presented in the platform of your convention, have already fixed the attention and commanded the assent of a large majority of our countrymen, who joyfully adopt them, as I do, as the bases of a true, beneficent, national reconstruction—of a new departure from jealousies, strifes, and hates, which have no longer adequate motive or even plausible pretext, into an atmosphere of peace, fraternity, and mutual good-will. In vain do the drill-sergeants of decaying organizations flourish menacingly their truncheons and angrily insist that the files shall be closed and straightened; in vain do the whippers-in of parties, once vital because rooted in the vital needs of the hour, protest against straying and bolting, denounce men nowise their inferiors as traitors and renegades, and threaten them with infamy and ruin. I am confident that the American people have already made your cause their own, fully resolved that their brave hearts and strong arms shall bear it on to triumph. In this faith, and with the distinct understanding that if elected I shall be the President not of a party, but of the whole people, I accept your nomination, in the confident trust that the masses of our countrymen, North and South, are eager to clasp hands across the bloody chasm which has too long divided them, forgetting that they have been enemies in the joyful consciousness that they are and must henceforth remain brethren.

Yours, gratefully, HORACE GREELEY.

Gov. Brown's Acceptance.

EXECUTIVE OFFICE,
JEFFERSON CITY, *May* 31, 1872.

GENTLEMEN: Your letter advising me of the action of the Liberal Republican convention at Cincinnati has been received, and I return through you my acknowledgment of the honor which has been conferred upon me. I accept the nomination as a candidate for Vice President, and indorse most cordially the resolutions setting forth the principles on which this appeal is made to the whole people of the United States.

A century is closing upon our experience of republican government, and while that lapse of time has witnessed great expansion of our free institutions, yet it has not been without illustration also of grave dangers to the stability of such system. Of those successfully encountered it is needless to speak; of those which remain to menace us the most threatening are provided against, as I firmly believe, in the wise and pacific measures proposed by your platform.

It has come to be the practice of those elevated to positions of national authority to regard the public service not as a public trust, but only as means to retain power. This results in substituting a mere party organization for the Government itself, constitutes a con trol amenable to no laws or moralities, impairs all independent thought, enables the few to rule the many, and makes personal alle giance the road to favor. It requires little fore cast to perceive that this will wreck our liberties unless there be interposed a timely reform of administration, from its highest to its lowest station, which shall not only forbid those abuses but likewise take away the incentive to their practice. Wearied with contentions that are carried on in avarice of spoils, the country demands repose, resents the effort of officials to dragoon it again into partisan hostilities, and will zealously sustain any movement promising a sure deliverance.

Of the perils which have been connected with the war it is safe to say that only those are now to be feared which come of an abuse of victory into permanent estrangement. The Union is fortified by more power than ever before, and it remains as an imperative duty to cement our nationality by a perfect reconciliation. At the North a widespread sympathy is aroused in behalf of those States of the South which long after the termination of resistance to rightful Federal authority are still plundered under the guise of loyalty, and tyrannized over in the name of freedom. Along with this feeling is present, too, the recognition that in complete amnesty alone can be found hope of any return to constitutional government as of old, or any development of a more enduring unity and broader national life in the future. Amnesty, however, to be efficacious must be real, not nominal; genuine, not evasive. It must carry along with it equal rights as well as equal protection to all; for removal of disabilities as to some, with enforcement as to others, leaves room for suspicion that pardon is measured by political gain. Especially will such proffered clemency be futile in presence of renewed attempt at prolonging a suspension of the *habeas corpus*, in persistent resort to martial rather than civil law, in upholding those agencies used to alienate races where concord is most essential, and in preparing another elaborate campaign on a basis of dead issues and arbitrary interventions. All will rightly credit such conduct as but a mockery of amnesty, and demand an Administration which can give better warrant of honesty in the great work of reconstruction and reform.

In the array of sectional interests a republic so widespread as ours is never entirely safe from serious conflicts. These become still more dangerous when complicated with questions of taxation where unequal burdens are believed to be imposed on one part at the expense of another part. It was a bold as well as admirable policy, in the interest of present as well as future tranquillity, to withdraw the decision of industrial and revenue matters from the virtual arbitration of an Electoral College, chosen with a single animating purpose of party ascendency, and refer them for a more direct popular expression to each congressional district. Instead of being muzzled by some evasive declaration, the country is thereby invited to its frankest utterance, and sections which would revolt at being denied a voice, out of deference to other success, would be content to acquiesce in a general judgment honestly elicited. If local government be, as it undoubtedly is, the most vital principle of our institutions, much advance will be made toward reëstablishing it by enabling the people to pass upon questions so nearly affecting their well-being dispassionately, through their local representation. The precipitancy which would force a controlling declaration on tax or tariff through a presidential candidacy is only a disguised form of centralization involving hazardous reaches of executive influence. Conclusions will be much more impartially determined, and with less disturbance to trade and finance, by appealing to the most truthful and diversified local expression. Industrial issues can be thus likewise emancipated from the power of great monopolies, each canvass made to determine its own specific instruction, and each Representative held to fidelity toward his immediate constituents.

These are the most prominent features of that general concert of action which proposes to replace the present Administration by one more in sympathy with the aspirations of the masses of our countrymen. Of course such concert cannot be attained by thrusting every minor or past difference into the foreground, and it will be for the people, therefore, to determine whether these objects are of such magnitude and present urgency as to justify them in deferring other adjustments until the country shall be first restored to a free suffrage, uninfluenced by official dictation, and ours becomes in fact a free republic, released from apprehension of a central domination.

Without referring in detail to the various other propositions embraced in the resolutions of the convention, but seeing how they all contemplate a restoration of power to the people, peace to the nation, purity to the Government; that they condemn the attempt to establish an ascendency of military over civil rule, and affirm with explicitness the maintenance of equal freedom to all citizens, irrespective of race, previous condition, or pending disabilities, I have only to pledge again my sincere coöperation.

I have the honor to remain, very respectfully, yours,

B. GRATZ BROWN.

NATIONAL DEMOCRATIC CONVENTION.

Baltimore, July 9-10, 1872.

For President, HORACE GREELEY, of New York; Vice President, BENJAMIN GRATZ BROWN, of Missouri.

Mr. GREELEY was nominated on the first ballot, receiving 686 votes, the remainder being: for JAMES A. BAYARD, of Delaware, 15; JEREMIAH S. BLACK, of Pennsylvania, 21; WILLIAM S. GROESBECK, of Ohio, 2; blank, 8

Mr. BROWN was nominated on the first ballot, which stood: BENJAMIN GRATZ BROWN, 713; JOHN W. STEVENSON, of Kentucky, 6; blank, 13.

The Platform.

We, the Democratic electors of the United States in convention assembled, do present the following principles, already adopted at Cincinnati, as essential to just government:

1. We recognize the equality of all men before the law, and hold that it is the duty of Government in its dealings with the people to mete out equal and exact justice to all, of whatever, nativity, race, color, or persuasion, religious or political.

2. We pledge ourselves to maintain the union of these States, emancipation, and enfranchisement, and to oppose any reopening of the questions settled by the thirteenth, fourteenth, and fifteenth amendments to the Constitution.

3. We demand the immediate and absolute removal of all disabilities imposed on account of the rebellion, which was finally subdued seven years ago, believing that universal amnesty will result in complete pacification in all sections of the country.

4. Local self-government, with impartial suffrage, will guard the rights of all citizens more securely than any centralized power. The public welfare requires the supremacy of the civil over the military authority, and freedom of person under the protection of the *habeas corpus*. We demand for the individual the largest liberty consistent with public order; for the State self-government, and for the nation a return to the methods of peace and the constitutional limitations of power.

5. The civil service of the Government has become a mere instrument of partisan tyranny and personal ambition and an object of selfish greed. It is a scandal and reproach upon free institutions and breeds a demoralization dangerous to the perpetuity of republican government. We therefore regard a thorough reform of the civil service as one of the most pressing necessities of the hour; that honesty, capacity, and fidelity constitute the only valid claim to public employment; that the offices of the Government cease to be a matter of arbitrary favoritism and patronage, and that public station become again a post of honor. To this end it is imperatively required that no President shall be a candidate for reëlection.

6. We demand a system of Federal taxation which shall not unnecessarily interfere with the industry of the people, and which shall provide the means necessary to pay the expenses of the Government, economically administered, the pensions, the interest on the public debt, and a moderate reduction annually of the principal thereof; and recognizing that there are in our midst honest but irreconcilable differences of opinion with regard to the respective systems of protection and free trade, we remit the discussion of the subject to the people in their congressional districts, and to the decision of the Congress thereon, wholly free from executive interference or dictation.

7. The public credit must be sacredly maintained, and we denounce repudiation in every form and guise.

8. A speedy return to specie payment is demanded alike by the highest considerations of commercial morality and honest government.

9. We remember with gratitude the heroism and sacrifices of the soldiers and sailors of the Republic, and no act of ours shall ever detract from their justly earned fame for the full reward of their patriotism.

10. We are opposed to all further grants of lands to railroads or other corporations. The public domain should be held sacred to actual settlers.

11. We hold that it is the duty of the Government in its intercourse with foreign nations to cultivate the friendships of peace, by treating with all on fair and equal terms, regarding it alike dishonorable either to demand what is not right or to submit to what is wrong.

12. For the promotion and success of these vital principles, and the support of the candidates nominated by this convention, we invite and cordially welcome the coöperation of all patriotic citizens, without regard to previous political affiliations.

NATIONAL LABOR REFORM CONVENTION.

Columbus, February 21-22, 1872.

For President, DAVID DAVIS, of Illinois; Vice President, JOEL PARKER, of New Jersey.

Ballot for President, (informal.)—John W. Geary, 55; Horace F. Day, 59; David Davis,

42; Wendell Phillips, 13; John M. Palmer, 8; Joel Parker, 7. First, (formal)—David Davis, 88; Wendell Phillips, 52; John W. Geary, 45; Horace F. Day, 8; Joel Parker, 7; George W. Julian, 1. Second—Davis, 93; Day, 59; Phillips, 12; Gratz Brown, 14; Horace Greeley, 11; Parker, 7; Julian, 5. Third—The names of Phillips, Greeley, Julian, and Brown being withdrawn, Davis received the nomination.

The Platform.

We hold that all political power is inherent in the people, and free government founded on their authority and established for their benefit; that all citizens are equal in political rights, entitled to the largest religious and political liberty compatible with the good order of society, as also the use and enjoyment of the fruits of their labor and talents; and no man or set of men is entitled to exclusive separable endowments and privileges, or immunities from the Government, but in consideration of public services; and any laws destructive of these fundamental principles are without moral binding force, and should be repealed. And believing that all the evils resulting from unjust legislation now affecting the industrial classes can be removed by the adoption of the principle contained in the following declaration: Therefore,

Resolved, That it is the duty of the Government to establish a just standard of distribution of capital and labor by providing a purely national circulating medium, based on the faith and resources of the nation, issued directly to the people without the intervention of any system of banking corporations, which money shall be legal tender in the payment of all debts, public and private, and interchangeable at the option of the holder for Government bonds bearing a rate of interest not to exceed 3-65 per cent., subject to future legislation by Congress.

2. That the national debt should be paid in good faith, according to the original contract, at the earliest option of the Government, without mortgaging the property of the people or the future exigencies of labor to enrich a few capitalists at home and abroad.

3. That justice demands that the burdens of Government should be so adjusted as to bear equally on all classes, and that the exemption from taxation of Government bonds bearing extravagant rates of interest is a violation of all just principles of revenue laws.

4. That the public lands of the United States belong to the people and should not be sold to individuals nor granted to corporations, but should be held as a sacred trust for the benefit of the people, and should be granted to landless settlers only, in amounts not exceeding one hundred and sixty acres of land.

5. That Congress should modify the tariff so as to admit free such articles of common use as we can neither produce nor grow, and lay duties for revenue mainly upon articles of luxury and upon such articles of manufacture as will, we having the raw materials, assist in further developing the resources of the country.

6. That the presence in our country of Chinese laborers, imported by capitalists in large numbers for servile use, is an evil, entailing want and its attendant train of misery and crime on all classes of the American people, and should be prohibited by legislation.

7. That we ask for the enactment of a law by which all mechanics and day-laborers employed by or on behalf of the Government, whether directly or indirectly, through persons, firms, or corporations, contracting with the State, shall conform to the reduced standard of eight hours a day, recently adopted by Congress for national employés, and also for an amendment to the acts of incorporation for cities and towns by which all laborers and mechanics employed at their expense shall conform to the same number of hours.

8. That the enlightened spirit of the age demands the abolition of the system of contract labor in our prisons and other reformatory institutions.

9. That the protection of life, liberty, and property are the three cardinal principles of Government, and the first two are more sacred than the latter; therefore money needed for prosecuting wars should, as it is required, be assessed and collected from the wealthy of the country, and not entailed as a burden on posterity.

10. That it is the duty of the Government to exercise its power over railroads and telegraph corporations, that they shall not in any case be privileged to exact such rates of freight, transportation, or charges, by whatever name, as may bear unduly or unequally upon the producer or consumer.

11. That there should be such a reform in the civil service of the national Government as will remove it beyond all partisan influence, and place it in the charge and under the direction of intelligent and competent business men.

12. That as both history and experience teaches us that power ever seeks to perpetuate itself by every and all means, and that its prolonged possession in the hands of one person is always dangerous to the interests of a free people, and believing that the spirit of our organic laws and the stability and safety of our free institutions are best obeyed on the one hand, and secured on the other, by a regular constitutional change in the chief of the country at each election: therefore, we are in favor of limiting the occupancy of the presidential chair to one term.

13. That we are in favor of granting general amnesty and restoring the Union at once on the basis of equality of rights and privileges to all, the impartial administration of justice being the only true bond of union to bind the States together and restore the Government of the people.

14. That we demand the subjection of the military to the civil authorities, and the confinement of its operations to national purposes alone.

15. That we deem it expedient for Congress to supervise the patent laws, so as to give labor more fully the benefit of its own ideas and inventions.

16. That fitness, and not political or personal considerations, should be the only recommendation to public office, either appointive or elective, and any and all laws looking to the establishment of this principle are heartily approved.

Judge Davis's Response.

WASHINGTON, *February* 22, 1872.

E. M. CHAMBERLAIN, *President of the National Labor Reform Convention:*

SIR: Be pleased to thank the convention for the unexpected honor which they have conferred upon me. The Chief Magistracy of the Republic should neither be sought nor declined by any American citizen.

DAVID DAVIS.

Judge Davis's Declination.

BLOOMINGTON, *June* 24, 1872.

Hon. E. M. CHAMBERLAIN, *President of the Columbus Convention, Boston, Massachusetts:*

DEAR SIR: The national convention of Labor Reformers, on the 22d of February last, honored me with the nomination as their candidate for the Presidency. Having regarded that movement as the initiation of a policy and purpose to unite various political elements in compact opposition, I consented to the use of my name before the Cincinnati convention, where a distinguished citizen of New York was nominated. Under these circumstances I deem it proper to retire absolutely from the presidential contest, and thus leave the friends who were generous enough to offer their voluntary support free to obey their convictions of duty unfettered by any supposed obligation. Sympathizing earnestly with all just and proper measures by which the condition of labor may be elevated and improved, I am, with great respect, your fellow-citizen, DAVID DAVIS.

Governor Parker's Declination.

FREEHOLD, N. J., *June* 28, 1872.

EDWIN M. CHAMBERLAIN, *President Columbus Convention, Boston, Massachusetts:*

SIR: Your letter, informing me that the convention of the Labor Reform party, which met at Columbus on the 22d day of February last, placed me in nomination for the office of Vice President of the United States, has been received. I feel honored by the preference thus expressed by the representatives of a large and influential body of my fellow-citizens. I am in favor of all legal and just measures that tend to improve the condition of the workingmen. I have always been a member of the Democratic party. For nearly thirty-five years I have shared its triumphs and defeats, adhering to its fortunes because I considered its success essential to good government and to the elevation of the laboring classes. Having been placed in an important public position as the nominee of that party, I am bound in honor, as well as by inclination, to stand by its organization and abide by the decision of its national convention. To be the candidate of one party while supporting the nominees of another, although the two may agree substantially in principle, would be inconsistent, and I therefore respectfully decline the nomination tendered me by the convention you represent.

JOEL PARKER.

The convention has been called to meet again July 30, 1872.

NATIONAL COLORED CONVENTION.

New Orleans, April 10-14, 1872.

[Met under call of the "southern States convention of colored men," issued from Columbia, South Carolina, October 18, 1871.]

The Platform.

Regretting the necessity which has called into existence a colored convention, and deeply sensible of the responsibilities which have been intrusted to our consideration, we hereby acknowledge our gratitude for past triumphs in behalf of equal rights, and respectfully submit our peculiar grievances to the immediate attention of the American people in the following platform and resolutions:

1. We thank God, the friends of universal liberty in this and other lands, the bravery of colored soldiers, and the loyalty of the colored people for our emancipation, our citizenship, and our enfranchisement.

2. Owing our political emancipation in this country to Republican legislation, to which all other parties and political shades of opinion were unjustly and bitterly opposed, we would be blind to our prospects and false to our best interests did we identify ourselves with any other organization; and as all roads out of the Republican party lead into the Democratic camp, we pledge our unswerving devotion to support the nominees of the Philadelphia convention.

3. We sincerely and gratefully indorse the administration of President U. S. Grant in maintaining our liberties, in protecting us in our privileges, in punishing our enemies; in the dawn of recognition of the claims of men without regard to color, by appointing us to important official positions at home and abroad; in the assurances that he has given to defend our rights, and that while we in our gratefulness acknowledge and appreciate his efforts in behalf of equal rights, we are not unmindful of his glory as a soldier and his exalted virtues as a statesman.

4. Our thanks are due and are hereby tendered to President Grant for overriding the precedents of prejudice in the better recognition of the services of men without regard to color in some parts of the country, and we earnestly pray that colored Republicans of States where there are no Federal positions given to colored men may no longer be ignored, but that they may be stimulated by some recognition of Federal patronage.

5. It would be an ingratitude, loathed by men and abhorred by God, did we not acknowledge our overwhelming indebtedness to the services

of the Hon. Charles Sumner, who stood for a long time alone in the Senate of the United States the Gibraltar of our cause and the north star of our hopes; who forfeited caste in the estimation of a large portion of his countrymen by his unswerving devotion to equal rights; who has been maligned for his fidelity to principles; who has been stricken down by an assassin for advocating liberty throughout all the land and unto all the inhabitants thereof, and in whose giant body, rising as it were almost out of the grave to marshal the hosts of impartial justice with his mighty ideas, going to the farthest part of the land, and finding a responsive echo in the triumph of liberty over slavery, we have an assurance of this good, great, and beloved patriot that he will be as faithful to the Republican party in the future as he has been unfaltering in the past.

6. Having been by solemn legislation of the American Congress raised to the dignity of citizenship, we appeal to law-abiding people of the States, and especially of those who in the days of the fugitive slave law exhorted obedience to statutes however offensive, to protect and defend us in the enjoyment of our just rights and privileges upon all conveyances which are common carriers, at all resorts of public amusements, where tastes are cultivated and manhood is quickened, and in all places of public character or corporate associations which owe their existence to the legislation of the nation or States; against the spirit of slavery, which attempts to degrade our standard of intelligence and virtue by forcing our refined ladies and gentlemen into smoking-cars amid obscenity and vulgarity; which humiliates our pride by denying us first-class accommodations on steamboats, and compelling us to eat and sleep with servants, for which we are charged the same as those who have the best accommodations; and which closes the doors of hotels against famishing colored persons, however wealthy, intelligent, or respectable they may be, while all such public places and conveyances welcome and entertain all white persons, whatever may be their character, who may apply. Now, in view of this disgraceful inconsistency, this affectation or prejudice, this rebellion against the laws of God, humanity, and the nation, we appeal to the justice of the American people to protect us in our civil rights in public places and upon public conveyances, which are readily accorded, and very justly, to the most degraded specimens of our white fellow citizens.

7. That wherever Republicans have betrayed colored constituencies, we recommend that better men be elected to succeed them, and especially do we pledge ourselves to elect successors in Congress, wherever we have the power, to every Republican who voted against or dodged the supplementary civil rights bill recently introduced into the United States Senate by Hon. Charles Sumner; and also successors to those who shall not show a satisfactory record on the civil rights bill now in the United States House of Representatives.

8. That while men professing strong radical sentiments, and elected to Congress by overwhelming majorities of colored voters, were found voting against the supplementary civil rights bill in the Senate of the United States, we honor that manly exhibition of devotion to the principles of the Republican party which influenced the Hon. Schuyler Colfax, Vice President of the United States, to honor the cause of justice by recording his casting vote as President of the Senate in favor of equality before the law as indicated in the supplementary civil rights bill as it passed the Senate by virtue of the aforesaid casting vote.

9. That we, in the name of the colored men of the United States, repudiate any sympathy or connection whatever with the late Labor Reform convention, lately held at Columbus, Ohio, and also the convention of Liberal Republicans called for the 1st of May, 1872, at Cincinnati.

ADDENDUM.

Mr. Greeley's Second Letter of Acceptance.

NEW YORK, *July* 18, 1872.

Hon. JAMES R. DOOLITTLE, *chairman of the National Democratic Convention, and Messrs.* F. W. SYKES, JOHN C. MACCABE, *and others, committee:*

GENTLEMEN: Upon mature deliberation, it seems fit that I should give to your letter of the 10th instant some further and fuller response than the hasty, unpremeditated words in which I acknowledged and accepted your nomination at our meeting on the 12th.

That your convention saw fit to accord its highest honor to one who had been prominently and pointedly opposed to your party in the earnest and sometimes angry controversies of the last forty years, is essentially noteworthy. That many of you originally preferred that the Liberal Republicans should present another candidate for President, and would more readily have united with us in the support of Adams or Trumbull, Davis or Brown, is well known. I owe my adoption at Baltimore wholly to the fact that I had already been nominated at Cincinnati, and that a concentration of forces upon any new ticket had been proved impracticable. Gratified as I am at your concurrence in the Cincinnati nominations, certain as I am that you would not have thus concurred had you not deemed me upright and capable, I find nothing in the circumstance calculated to inflame vanity or nourish self-conceit.

But that your convention saw fit, in adopting the Cincinnati ticket, to reaffirm the Cincinnati platform, is to me a source of the profoundest satisfaction. That body was constrained to take this important step by no party necessity, real or supposed. It might have accepted the candidates of the Liberal Republicans upon grounds entirely its own, or it might have presented them (as the first Whig national convention did Harrison and Tyler) without adopting any platform whatever. That it chose to plant itself deliberately, by a vote nearly unanimous, upon the fullest and clearest enunciation of principles which are at once incontestably Republican and emphatically Democratic, gives trustworthy assurance that a new and more auspicious era is dawning upon our long distracted country.

Some of the best years and best efforts of my life were devoted to a struggle against chattel slavery—a struggle none the less earnest or arduous because respect for constitutional obligations constrained me to act for the most part on the defensive—in resistance to the diffusion rather than in direct efforts for the extinction of human bondage. Throughout most of those years my vision was uncheered, my exertions were rarely animated, by even so much as a hope that I should live to see my country peopled by freemen alone. The affirmance by your convention of the Cincinnati platform is a most conclusive proof that not merely is slavery abolished, but that its spirit is extinct; that, despite the protests of a respectable but isolated few, there remains among us no party and no formidable interest which regrets the overthrow or desires the reëstablishment of human bondage, whether in letter or in spirit. I am thereby justified in my hope and trust that the first century of American independence will not close before the grand elemental truths on which its rightfulness was based by Jefferson and the continental Congress of '76 will no longer be regarded as "glittering generalities," but will have become the universally accepted and honored foundations of our political fabric.

I demand the prompt application of those principles to our existing condition. Having done what I could for the complete emancipation of blacks, I now insist on the full enfranchisement of all my white countrymen. Let none say that the ban has just been removed from all but a few hundred elderly gentlemen to whom eligibility to office can be of little consequence. My view contemplates not the hundreds proscribed, but the millions who are denied the right to be ruled and represented by the men of their unfettered choice. Proscription were absurd if these did not wish to elect the very men whom they are forbidden to choose.

I have a profound regard for the people of that New England wherein I was born, in whose common schools I was taught. I rank no other people above them in intelligence, capacity, and moral worth. But while they do many things well, and some admirably, there is one thing which I am sure they can not wisely or safely undertake, and that is the selection, for States remote from and unlike their own, of the persons by whom those States shall be represented in Congress. If they *could* do this to good purpose, then republican institutions were unfit, and aristocracy the only true political system.

Yet what have we recently witnessed? Zebulon B. Vance, the unquestioned choice of a large majority of the present Legislature of North Carolina—a majority backed by a majority of the people who voted at its election—refused the seat in the Federal Senate to which he was fairly chosen, and the Legislature thus constrained to choose another in his stead or leave the State unrepresented for years. The votes of New England thus deprived North Carolina of the Senator of her choice, and compelled her to send another in his stead—another who, in our late contest, was, like Vance, a rebel, and a fighting rebel, but who had not served in Congress before the war as Vance had, though the latter remained faithful to the Union till after the close of his term. I protest against the disfranchisement of a State—presumptively, of a number of States—on grounds so narrow and technical as this. The fact that the same Senate which refused Vance his seat proceeded to remove his disabilities after that seat had been filled by another, only serves to place in stronger light the indignity to North Carolina and the arbitrary, capricious tyranny which dictated it. I thank you, gentlemen, that my name is so conspicuously associated with yours in a determined effort to render amnesty complete and universal, in spirit as well as in letter. Even defeat in such a cause would leave no sting, while triumph would rank with those victories which no blood reddens and which evoke no tears but those of gratitude and joy.

Gentlemen, your platform, which is also mine, assures me that Democracy is not henceforth to stand for one thing and Republicanism for another, but that those terms are to mean in politics, as they always have meant in the dictionary, substantially one and the same thing—namely, Equal Rights, regardless of creed, or clime, or color. I hail this as a genuine New Departure from outworn feuds and meaningless contentions in the direction of Progress and Reform. Whether I shall be found worthy to bear the standard of the great Liberal movement which the American people have inaugurated is to be determined not by words but by deeds. With me, if I steadily advance; over me, if I falter, its grand array moves on to achieve for our country her glorious, beneficent destiny.

I remain, gentlemen, yours,

HORACE GREELEY.

INDEX TO HAND-BOOK OF 1872.

OMISSION.

www.ingramcontent.com/pod-product-compliance
Lightning Source LLC
LaVergne TN
LVHW050525100826
845148LV00002B/441

* 9 7 8 1 4 2 5 5 1 9 9 6 4 *